David Laidler's Contributions to Economics

David Laidler's Contributions to Economics

Edited by

Robert Leeson

palgrave
macmillan

First published 2010 by
PALGRAVE MACMILLAN

Palgrave Macmillan in the UK is an imprint of Macmillan Publishers Limited, registered in England, company number 785998, of Houndmills, Basingstoke, Hampshire RG21 6XS.

Palgrave Macmillan in the US is a division of St Martin's Press LLC, 175 Fifth Avenue, New York, NY 10010.

Palgrave Macmillan is the global academic imprint of the above companies and has companies and representatives throughout the world.

ISBN: 978–0–230–01898–3 hardback

This book is printed on paper suitable for recycling and made from fully managed and sustained forest sources. Logging, pulping and manufacturing processes are expected to conform to the environmental regulations of the country of origin.

A catalogue record for this book is available from the British Library.

Library of Congress Cataloging-in-Publication Data

David Laidler's contributions to economics / edited by Robert Leeson.
p. cm.
Includes bibliographical references and index.
Summary: "This book provides a collection of essays by leading economists in honour of David Laidler's contributions to the field of macroeconomics, with important essays on central banking, monetary policy implementation, inflation targeting, monetary theory, monetary framework debates, and the mathematical theory of banking"—Provided by publisher.
ISBN 978–0–230–01898–3 (hardback)
1. Macroeconomics. 2. Monetary policy. 3. Laidler, David E. W. I. Leeson, Robert.

HB172.5.D377 2010
339.092—dc22 2009044075

10 9 8 7 6 5 4 3 2 1
19 18 17 16 15 14 13 12 11 10

Printed and bound in Great Britain by
CPI Antony Rowe, Chippenham and Eastbourne

Contents

List of Charts, Figures and Tables

Charts

Figures

Tables

Preface

On 18–20 August 2006, a group of economists and policy makers from North America, Europe, and Australia gathered at the University of Western Ontario (U.W.O.) to reflect on and to celebrate David Laidler's contributions to economics. A small Festschrift conference had initially been planned, but the numbers grew as news of the conference spread: such is the esteem in which David is held. The conference was sponsored by the Economic Policy Research Institute, the Department of Economics, and the Faculty of Social Science at U.W.O. Paul Davenport (President of U.W.O.), and Brian Timney (Dean of Social Science, U.W.O.) opened the conference; we thank them for this and for their support and encouragement. Thanks are also due to Al Slivinski, Chair of the U.W.O. Department of Economics, for his valuable help, and to Chantal Collins and Leslie Kostal for their excellent administrative assistance.

The conference had many inspiring and enlightening moments. One highlight that must be singled out was the presentation by David's former teacher Milton Friedman, of one of his final academic papers. (See http://economics.uwo.ca/centres/epri/LaidlerFestschrift/LaidlerFestschriftProgram.html for this videoed talk and John Taylor's response.) All the Festschrift participants were deeply saddened at the news of Professor Friedman's death, which came a few weeks after this event.

These chapters were written by monetary economists, historians of economic thought, central bankers, think tank directors, a political scientist, and others. The breadth and scope of the papers reflect the range of David's intellectual contributions and achievements, as well as the impact he has had on so many people in so many areas. During the conference there were also many opportunities to reflect on David's generosity towards his colleagues and correspondents. As these essays were about to be published, David was chosen as the 2009 Distinguished Fellow of the History of Economics Society.

To David, his wife Antje and daughter Nicole, from David's students and colleagues, this volume is an expression of gratitude for their patience and generosity and for David's contributions to our careers and to our discipline.

James Davies and Robert Leeson
May 2009

Foreword

Otmar Issing

David Laidler's oeuvre comprises publications of rigorous theory as well as those which show that he is a master of the "rhetoric" in economics. He is an expert in the field of history of economic thought and at the same time has done research at the frontier on current issues. He has been a successful teacher in economics with world-wide experience as well as an advisor, directly and indirectly, to central banks. What a rare combination!

It is not my objective to present a laudatio of his work. Instead, I would like to concentrate on my personal experience with David's contribution to economics which covers the field of academia as well as the world of central banking. For me as a young professor, but still a student of monetary economics, David's various publications greatly helped me to better understand the debate in the heyday of the controversy on the monetarist revolution. In the list of recommended reading in my textbook *Introduction to Monetary Theory* (14th ed., 2007) his publications still rank high. This is especially true for his book *The Demand for Money: Theories, Evidence, and Problems*, undoubtedly a classic in this field. I think the title of this book neatly summarizes his approach: bring theory and empirical evidence together, but never forget about the problems which remain in spite of all progress in research.

Another good example in this respect is his preeminent work on the quantity theory of money. His book *The Golden Age of the Quantity Theory* is a masterpiece on the development of theory and an important contribution to the history of economic thought. And the title of his article "The Quantity Theory is Always and Everywhere Controversial – Why?" inherently indicates a general problem in economics: Even such an empirically well-founded theory continues to be controversially discussed.

My academic background turned out to be essential in my (unexpected) later life as a central banker. Economic theory has to guide you through the uncertainties with which policymakers are confronted. For instance, the Lucas critique particularly needs to be respected in times of regime shifts such as German unification or even to a greater extent when a new currency is introduced. David's work on money in all its aspects clearly is among those guideposts. Again I will just quote a title chosen by David in various contributions which asks "to take money seriously". I wished that there were no longer such a need nowadays for this reminder.

David, thanks for your outstanding contributions to our discipline and personally for all that I have been able to learn from you.

Axel Leijonhufvud

David Laidler's teaching career stretches back to the early 1960s, to a time when Keynesian economics (of a sort) was still in its heyday. Macroeconomics and monetary theory have gone through a number of metamorphoses since that time. Later in that decade Keynesianism began to wane as monetarism gained adherents and influence. However, monetarism soon mutated into a New Classical form which proved to have no staying power. Its demise put Real Business Cycle theory in the forefront. More recently, monetary theory and policy is making a comeback by returning to the pre-Keynesian ideas of Wicksell in (needless to say) technically modernized form.

If you have lived through all these shifts in the worldviews of economists (and I have), you come to particularly value those rare colleagues who, while keeping abreast of developments, make up their own minds and chart a course of their own. These are the people whose writings you ponder over and whose judgments you take seriously. Always generous in acknowledging what he has learned from others, David has nonetheless been one of these intellectual independents throughout his long career.

In the nature of the case, the independent stance is not always popular. Bringing the outlandish message that "inflation is always and everywhere a monetary phenomenon" did not meet with general acclaim in Britain in the early 1970s. But as a monetarist he was a bit of a deviationist as well, stressing the role of the interest rate in the money demand function and being rather too open-minded about reverse causation. Later, after due consideration, he let the Rational Expectation bandwagon pass him by.

If David has kept his distance vis-à-vis Dynamic Stochastic General Equilibrium economics it is because he has thought more deeply than anyone else about the fundamental role that money and monetary institutions perform in actual economies and, therefore, what is missed by relying on Walrasian constructions that have no room for them. This work of Laidler's involves no formal modeling or statistical inference, but it is his most subtle theoretical contribution and I wish it were more widely known.

It is natural that someone, who has participated for decades in a field undergoing so many changes, would come to reflect on its development, and the history of monetary economics has become his main preoccupation in recent years. History also calls for the exercise of judgment rather than for cleverness at deduction and the balance of a man's talents is apt to shift towards the former with age. David is now the unchallenged champion of the history of our field and this work of his mature years displays the admirable characteristics one fondly remembers from countless conferences over the years – it is clear, forceful, balanced, measured.

Most people who take money very seriously do so in order to get more of it. Some forty years of "taking money seriously" has not earned David Laidler great wealth. But it has earned him the respect and affection of the extraordinary group of contributors who pay him homage in this volume – and of a great many students and other friends besides.

Contributors

Michael Bordo is Professor in the Department of Economics, Rutgers University

Filippo Cesarano is Head of the Historical Research Office, Bank of Italy

James B. Davies is Professor in the Department of Economics, University of Western Ontario

Robert W. Dimand is Professor in the Department of Economics, Brock University

Michel De Vroey is Professor in the Department of Economics, Université catholique de Louvain, Belgium

Charles Freedman is Scholar in Residence, Economics Department, Carleton University

Milton Friedman was Senior Fellow, Hoover Institution, and the recipient of the 1976 Nobel Prize for Economic Science

Charles Goodhart is Emeritus Professor of Banking and Finance, London School of Economics

Otmar Issing is an Honorary Professor at University of Frankfurt and was formerly a member of the Executive Board of the European Central Bank

David Laidler is Professor Emeritus at the University of Western Ontario

Robert Leeson is Adjunct Professor of Economics, University of Notre Dame Australia

Axel Leijonhufvud is Professor in the Department of Economics University of California Los Angeles

J. Clark Leith is Professor Emeritus in the Department of Economics, University of Western Ontario

Perry Mehrling is Professor in the Department of Economics, Barnard College

Donald D. E. Moggridge is Professor in the Department of Economics, University of Toronto

Angela Redish is Professor in the Department of Economics, University of British Columbia

William B. P. Robson is President and Chief Executive Officer, C. D. Howe Institute

Nick Rowe is Professor in the Department of Economics, Carleton University

John B. Taylor is the Mary and Robert Raymond Professor of Economics, Stanford University, and Bowen H. and Janice Arthur McCoy Senior Fellow, Hoover Institution

Warren J. Samuels is Professor Emeritus the Department of Economics, Michigan State University

Roger J. Sandilands is Professor in the Department of Economics, University of Strathclyde

Anna J. Schwartz is an Economists at the National Bureau of Economic Research

Neil T. Skaggs is Professor in the Department of Economics, Illinois State University

Hans-Michael Trautwein is Professor in the Department of Economics, University of Oldenburg

Robert Young is Professor in the Department of Political Science and Canada Research Chair in Multilevel Governance, University of Western Ontario

1
Interview with David Laidler

Filippo Cesarano, Charles Freedman, Charles Goodhart, Robert Leeson, William Robson, Nick Rowe, Roger Sandilands and Robert Young

Pre-University: 1938–56

RL: Where and when were you born?

DL: 12 August 1938, North Shields.

RL: Can you tell us a little about your family and childhood?

DL: Father a fishmonger and fryer in Whitley Bay – born 1899, left school at 11, gassed at Arras at 18, was therefore at home throughout World War II, which was unusual. Mother born 1904, left school at 13, thereafter a shop assistant until marriage in 1929 (i.e., an unremarkable but insecure lower middle-class couple).

Only child, and bearer of considerable parental ambitions, to be fulfilled through education, which of course was to lead to qualifications, a good job, steady income and no other deviations from my family's norms. I suspect that many of the first-generation-to-go-to-university kids that I've taught here in recent years will give their parents the same kind of surprises that I gave mine – which can be summarized in my mother's complaint that I 'picked up funny ideas' along the way. A private school was a manifestation of their social ambitions for me, and must have stretched the budget at times, though we were certainly not poor.

House damaged three times by bombing during war (once seriously), with me in it on each occasion (under stairs or under steel-topped kitchen table – no back garden for a proper shelter). This was unusual for the town, which wasn't attacked all that often. I just lived on an unlucky block I think. But people did die, though I wasn't scratched. The experience impressed on me early and deeply the role that luck, good and bad, can play in determining the turns a life can take. I wonder nowadays whether perhaps this experience is one of the roots of my inability to swallow the view that all will be well with society if you simply let people make their own choices and take the consequences.

As a teenager, I worked in the shops during school holidays and sometimes on Saturdays too. The fryer was interesting, since many of the customers were working class – miners, shipyard workers, etc., and during the summer included lots of Glaswegian holidaymakers who were too poor to afford Blackpool. We sold cod and chips for a shilling – cheap even by the standards of the 1950s. I learned that we really were not quite as far removed socially from these folk as my mother liked to pretend – a salutary lesson that stuck.

RL: Can you tell us a little about your schooling: for example, did you wear that distinctive King's School uniform in those days?

DL: It wasn't the King's School (which I think is nowadays a public school, in the English sense of the word 'public') then – just Tynemouth School, a private day school for boys aged 8–18. (It had an elementary school for 4–8 year olds, which I also attended.) The uniform was red cap with badge, red and blue striped tie, and optional navy blazer with badge, grey flannels. Nothing out of the ordinary (i.e., straw hats or striped blazers) – all grammar schools had variations on this kind of uniform.

I always did well academically at school, but I resolutely resisted its efforts to socialize me to middle-class ways, and ended up with a pretty large chip on my shoulder by the time I left. I had a few excellent teachers (English and History in particular) but some were snobs, who made my life uncomfortable when they could, for example, on the rugby field (games were compulsory). I didn't make my own life easier by figuring out quite early that I was smarter than them, and making sure that they were aware that I knew this.

University: LSE 1956–59

RL: You chose Economics because you didn't fancy studying French or English literature (your other two A level subjects)?

DL: My third A level subject was History, not Economics, though there was a special paper in Economic History. I didn't fancy any of these, because they all seemed likely to lead to a career in school teaching. With no science but O level Maths, a social science degree was the only available alternative, and Economics the only social science I had heard of. I thought it would be like Economic History.

RL: Which subjects (and with whom) did you take in your first and second years?

DL: It was a two-year part 1 – large-scale lectures (LSE old theatre) in economics from Andrew Ozga (micro theory), Kurt Klappholz (macro theory), Arnold Plant, Frank Paish, Roy Allen (various applied economics topics including descriptive statistics). Other lectures from Michael Oakeshott (political thought), W. A. Robson (local government), Eleanora Carus-Wilson and Jack Fisher (economic history), and we also had lectures in government and political history (I forget from whom). I took logic and scientific method as an optional subject (John Wisdom and Karl Popper in a class of about eight) and also 'elements of social structure' (Norman

Birnbaum). I believe that I failed this last paper – I certainly deserved to, for I didn't learn a thing. Classes – which, if I remember properly, had maybe eight to a dozen students, and where the real teaching was done – I took from, among others, Ed Mishan, Chris Archibald, Bob Gould (economics) and Leonard Schapiro (politics).

RL: Which subjects (and with whom) did you take in your third year?

DL: Part 2 papers were in economic theory, applied economics, public finance and history of economic thought, plus a three-hour essay. Teaching was mainly in seminars – theory and applied economics with Chris Archibald and Jack Wiseman, history of thought with Klappholz and Corry (this was the three books event you ask about below – we really did work through them chapter by chapter), and there were lots of short lecture series – Bill Phillips on macro, Kelvin Lancaster on demand theory, etc. There were also longer lecture courses – Robbins on theory (I didn't learn a thing) and Corry on history of thought – a 'Moses to Marshall' (his phrase) survey. Finally, there was Robbins' informal Friday afternoon session where he talked about anything that came into his head – much better than his theory course, which I'm sure had nevertheless been meticulously prepared.

RL: Bernard Corry taught a history of economic thought course that consisted of just Smith's *The Wealth of Nations*, Ricardo's *Principles* and Marshall's *Principles*?

DL: Yes, along with Klappholz (see above) – the seminars, by the way, were held in the Graham Wallas Room, which was hung at that time with Dürer woodcuts (*Life of the Virgin*, formerly the property of William Morris, or so the label said). I'd never seen anything remotely like that before – my idea of art was 'When did you last see your father?' and 'The boyhood of Raleigh' – that's probably where my interest in visual art started.

RL: You got to know a lot of people who would later become colleagues. Which ones stand out and why?

DL: Archibald, Lipsey and Corry among my teachers (though I don't think I ever took a formal class from Lipsey) – Corry was my third-year tutor, Mishan in my first year, and Bob Gould, later the tutor of Mick Jagger and George Morton, in my second. These people, along with Klappholz and Wiseman, were unbelievably enthusiastic about the subject, and turned me into an economist. Among my fellow students, I particularly remember Sam Hollander – immensely erudite, and such a genuinely nice person.

RL: What did you make of Karl Popper? How did he influence you?

DL: I was entranced by him, and for a while I was determined to study methodology. That ambition didn't last, but I caught the empiricism bug from him, and that did last. He had no political influence on me at the time – I remained resolutely left wing (at least in my own eyes) till quite a few years later. See below on learning from those you disagree with.

RL: Kurt Klappholz was famous for a lecture he gave on 'the blessing of hunger' (a talk about his time in Auschwitz). Do you recall much about that?

DL: I recall the very moving talk he gave about his time in Auschwitz and his walk to (I think) Buchenwald. I found it hard to grasp that a human being whom I knew and liked so much could have been treated so appallingly and even harder to understand that he was one of the lucky ones. Remember that this was the 1950s, so it was as if, today, we were discussing something that happened in the early 1990s and which most of those around us had either ignored or even encouraged – see below on true believers and social conservatives. I didn't know what to say to him for weeks afterwards.

RL: You got to know Don Patinkin at that time?

DL: No – though I attended his public lectures, which I didn't understand, and I later got a heavy dose of the Archibald–Lipsey critique of the real balance effect. I got to know Don at UWO, where he had a big influence on my approach to the history of thought.

RL: Did you talk to Bill Phillips much?

DL: I attended his short course, and I'm sure I must have asked lots of questions, but I don't recall seeing much of him informally. When later he gave a paper at Chicago, he recognized me and knew exactly who I was. The regulars in the bar whom I still remember were Corry, Archibald and Lipsey, and that's where I socialized with my teachers.

MA: University of Syracuse 1959–60

RL: You obtained an MA from the University of Syracuse (just south of Lake Ontario). Was this your first overseas trip? Why Syracuse? What do you recall of that year: the courses you took, the professors who taught you, people you met?

DL: Yes, apart from one hitchhike to Italy and back. The opportunity to go to the US was too good not to have a try at, and Syracuse let me in with a little financial support, unlike any other place – my first had not been forecast! Theory with Theo Suranyi-Unger (later I discovered he had allegedly been a fascist sympathizer but I didn't see any signs of that, and he was a friend of Frank Knight. He did have some odd collectivist ideas about 'group utility', though). He also supervised my brief thesis on methodology. Trade with Carl Bye (who died during the term), intro to math econ with the department chair, called (I think) Archibald McIsaac (who also died during the term) and then Joe Berliner, as well as intro to statistics, with a business instructor whose name I've forgotten. The basic technical instruction was long overdue, and it did me no harm to repeat a lot of price theory. The thesis enabled me to learn (a) that there seemed to be no future for me in methodology, and (b) that the idea of testing theories was altogether more complicated than I had thought – how on earth do you 'refute' perfect competition? When I left, I bought my first car from another graduate student – in politics, I think – Robert Scheer, who later became a prominent radical journalist. It was a Citroen 2cv, and I once had Alvin Hansen and Milton Friedman together in its back seat!

RL: Were you obliged to wear a beanie (under threat of being dunked in a sink by the Goon Squad)?

DL: No beanie, but I went to all the home games of the 1959–60 season. It wasn't very exciting, because Syracuse won them all so easily that year.

RL: Did you appreciate American football? (Syracuse won its only national championship in 1960.)

DL: Not really – it seemed altogether too mechanized and disciplined – almost military. And all the university's profits from the championship were spent on further development of athletics. The importance attached to athletics disturbed academic standards too – some teaching assistant (TAs) really did come under serious pressure to raise grades, and if they resisted, mysterious misprints nevertheless were rumoured to have occurred in the offices of various Deans.

PhD: University of Chicago 1960–61, 1962–63

RL: At Chicago you took price theory with Milton Friedman, public finance with Arnold Harberger, agricultural economics with Gale Johnson, monetary economics with Harry Johnson, history of banking theory with Earl Hamilton. Any others?

DL: Bayesian statistics in the Business School – it was Harry Roberts' course, but was taught by a visitor – I think he was called John Smith, but I'm no longer sure. He was certainly a fine teacher.

RL: In summer 1961 you worked for Harry Johnson on the Commission on Money and Credit (CMC) papers and for Anna Schwartz on the Monetary History, which after 13 years was close to being finished? Did you move to New York for the summer? What did you work on? What did you learn? Did these experiences attract you towards monetary economics?

DL: Yes in the summer of 1961 I lived in New York (we lived in Queens with my first wife's family). Mainly I drew versions of the charts that then went to the draughtsman, Mr Forman, to be copied for printing, and spent a lot of time interpolating and adding up series to become what were the final versions of the basic money supply series that ended up in the *History*, and later the *Statistics*. The arithmetic was all done on mechanical calculators and adding machines. I learned to be careful above all – having to repeat tasks was no fun – and to check everything, but I also learned how data could indeed tell a story. There is nothing like hand-drawing a time series chart to establish familiarity with the facts that need explaining. I read and abstracted the CMC papers – all of them I think, in mimeo form – for Harry in the evenings, and mailed him the results. I was disappointed than none of this turned up in his *AER* survey, though much later I detected traces of my efforts (I think) in some of his Porter Commission work.

RL: Arnold Harberger supervised your thesis on Income Tax Incentives for Owner Occupied Housing? What was your conclusion?

DL: Yes – but Margaret Reid, Martin Bailey and Dick Muth also played their far from trivial parts. The main results were that the failure to tax imputed rent created a very large welfare loss, and did much to undermine the apparent progressivity of the income tax. I also discovered that agents seemed systematically to respond to the incentive in deciding how much housing to consume – this was the part of the work that took most of the time and ingenuity (those mechanical calculators again!). The latter finding surprised me, because very few people actually understood how the subsidy worked at that time (including one or two professors to whom I had to explain it) so it was a fantastic example of 'as if' on the hoof.

Assistant Lecturer: LSE 1961–62

RL: You had a year (1961–62) as an assistant lecturer at the LSE. How did that come about? What did you teach? Did you attend the M2T seminars? Any other memories?

DL: After 5 years of continuous study and exams, I was tired. National Service in the UK had been abolished, so I could interrupt my studies without having to go into the army for two years, and someone passing through Chicago (Chris Archibald?), or maybe it was Harry, suggested I apply. I was pretty much accepted by my erstwhile teachers as one of the crowd and did indeed attend the M2T seminar, where I found the ratio of talking about testing to actually doing so uncomfortably high – apart from Lipsey and Brechling on trade credit. I think the seminar was running out of steam by 1961–62. Teaching was mainly backup classes to Lipsey's intro course, more exciting than you might think, because his lectures were the basis of what became his great 1963 *Positive Economics* text. I would have more memories had I gone to fewer parties, and most of those that I do have, though precious, are best left unpublished (Birgit Nilsson as Isolde, though, and the Solti–Zeffirelli *Don Giovanni* come to mind).

RL: Can't we tempt you to share some of these party stories?

DL: No – memories become even more unreliable than usual when filtered through hangovers, there are libel laws for the living, and the dead might come back to haunt me with their own versions of events!

RL: What was the reaction from Archibald and others when Friedman and Stigler refused to be engaged, testing-wise, over monopolistic competition?

DL: Archibald was in parts upset, angry and contemptuous. You must understand that Chicago people, or at least Friedman's circle, were widely regarded at that time as ideologically motivated lunatics whose work was on no account to be taken at face value, but rather studied with a view to exposing the right-wing agenda that was undoubtedly buried just beneath its surface. The young LSE people were not quite immune to this opinion, so though the 'methodology of positive economics' fitted in rather well with their own Popper-influenced views and they made us read it, it was also regarded as a piece of propaganda on behalf of perfect competition in particular and therefore American capitalism in general. I suspect that Chris thought that the Chicago response to his paper provided confirmation of some of those suspicions. Someone – my memory tells me it was Chris, but it could have been just about anyone in the M2T crowd – told me around that time that the real purpose of the *Theory of the Consumption Function* was to launch an attack on income redistribution policies (because if the consumption function is a straight line through the origin, redistributing income downwards doesn't increase aggregate demand). This was most likely said in a bar rather than a classroom, but it does illustrate the way even serious scholars reacted to Milton in those days.

Assistant Professor: Berkeley 1963–66

RL: How did you stumble on the error in Friedman's 1959 *JPE* essay?

DL: Beats me – I just read it carefully I suppose, and there were two errors. One concerned the cyclical properties of permanent and transitory income and the integral of the latter, and the second concerned the secular correlation between velocity and interest rates which Milton had missed – the latter insight surely came from looking at the data closely, as befitted a recent Research Assistant to Anna Schwartz. Milton was very gracious about what I did with the first of these, but less so about my work on the second.

RL: What else did you do research-wise at Berkeley?

DL: My *Oxford Economic Papers* essay on IS-LM dynamics when you have distributed lag relations (I was an early discover of the 'overshooting' effects these can generate) was mainly written there, so was the first draft of my Thomas Tooke paper. And I wrote a paper on empirical work on the demand for money, based on my lecture notes, which ended up as an outline of my little book on the topic. I also did a confused piece with Bernard Corry on the Phillips curve, which was followed up later with a never published empirical piece mainly done at Essex. This work led me to believe quite early that the real action in that area would lie in introducing expectations into the Phillips curve and using the same kind of analysis that I was applying to permanent income in the consumption and demand for money functions in the IS-LM paper. But I put that to one side when I made the sudden move to Essex, and by the time I got reorganized, there was the Phelps paper!!! Ah well, I might not have cracked the problem, I suppose.

RL: What did you teach?

DL: Introductory statistics, intermediate macro, introductory economics for non-majors – using the Alchian and Allen *University Economics* text – micro theory for MA students, and graduate money – not all in the same year of course.

RL: Who influenced you at that time?

DL: Tom Mayer was visiting, and a great influence. Also Lipsey and Corry passed through for a year each, and I had some contact with Karl Brunner at UCLA too.

RL: What did you learn from Hyman Minsky?

DL: I talked to Hy almost daily until he left, but what he had to say didn't really sink in till much later. It was pretty difficult, in the mid-1960s, to believe that US capitalism was on the verge of another collapse in its financial system.

RL: What other memories do you have of Berkeley and California?

DL: Getting divorced finally, meeting and marrying my second (still current) wife, and spending lots of pleasant evenings at the Pic. (espresso bar on Telegraph), Steppenwolf and Albatross (real bars on San Pablo). It was a relaxed and tolerant time, at least until the campus troubles started in 1964, but once again, most of the best memories should not be published – Schwartzkopf, Seefried and Grist in *Rosenkavalier*, though, Gobbi in *Nabucco* and *Gianni Schicchi*, Tebaldi and Tucker in *Andrea Chénier*, Evelyn Lear in *Lulu*, Vickers and Nilsson in *Fidelio*, etc. – San Francisco had great opera.

RL: You taught a history of economic thought course at Stanford when Paul Baran unexpectedly died? Did you interact much with the Stanford faculty?

DL: Hardly at all – I just went to teach the class and came home. The only one I remember was Moe Abramovitz. Most of the Berkeley–Stanford connections were in pure theory, and I wasn't part of that crowd – my problem, I just wasn't interested.

RL: You left because you were in danger of being drafted to Vietnam?

DL: Yes, Green Card holders were eligible, and suddenly I was in real and imminent danger – my deferment (granted because I was a university teacher) was lifted, I passed the pre-induction medical and, while all this was going on, the University either couldn't or (as I think more likely) wouldn't help. Since they were drafting 30,000 a month at that time, and the usual lag between medical and receipt of an induction notice was

10–14 days, I left very quickly. It's just as well all this came to a head in July and not the middle of term.

Lecturer: Essex 1966–69

RL: Who was at Essex? What did you teach? What were you working on?

DL: The professors were Archibald, Lipsey and Clower – Brechling was a reader but mainly on leave – visitors included Edmond Malinvaud, Herschel Grossman, Carl Christ, Michio Morishima, Al Marty, Ed Feige, Art Goldberger. Lecturers included Michael Parkin, Balwanth Reddy, Joe Ostroy, Jim Richmond, Paddy Geary, and a slew of undergraduates (John Whalley, Roy Bailey, Louis Christophides among them) who ended up academics – not to mention the grad. students, including some Canadians – Bill Scarth, Les and Roberta Robb, Ken Grant, John Evans. It was an amazingly exciting place. My main output there was the first edition of *The Demand for Money*, as well as finishing the things that I had brought from Berkeley in first draft form. I also did some work on Pesek-Saving inspired questions about money as net wealth and related issues that was published in 1969 (*JMCB* and *Canadian Journal*) just after I had moved to Manchester, as well as starting work on a demand for money in the UK piece with Michael, which eventually appeared in the *Manchester School*. I really can't remember what I taught, but I spent a lot of time in the classroom – micro and macro theory, I'm pretty sure, lectures on what they called 'The State in Economic Life' (i.e., public finance and then some) and maybe six lectures on history of thought in a 'selected topics' series.

Professor: Manchester 1969–75

RL: You and Michael Parkin formed an SSRC-funded money research group (with George Zis, Malcolm Gray, Mike Burns and Michael Sumner). Was the department as split as was rumoured in those days?

DL: Michael came a year later than me, in 1970, to replace Alan Prest, and our research group was supposed to deal with 'Inflation, its Causes, Consequences and Cures'. The department of economics – there were separate departments of econometrics and agricultural economics – was a very unhappy place, split along more than one fault line, but at least united in its unhappiness that I had been appointed by a university committee on which such departmental representation as there was had been outvoted – if I'd known that at the time, I would probably have stayed away. But once I was there, I needed support – hence Michael, appointed essentially by the same people as had appointed me, but with my hearty support – more departmental unity in misery was created by this. Apart from George Zis, the others all had Essex connections and were appointed by us.

RL: You became pessimistic about Britain in the mid-'70s?

DL: There was a lot to be pessimistic about! But a lot of my problems stemmed from closer to home. I had some personal financial problems caused by the fact that my house, bought new in 1969, had been built on a bad site and was falling down (literally, it was demolished eventually). I had to hire engineers and a lawyer. The case against the builder was eventually settled in spring 1975 – in my favour – but not before costing me a great deal, not all of which was recoverable. Also, by 1975, some of the people responsible for bringing myself and Michael to Manchester had long since decided that we had been more trouble than we were worth, so there was not much support for us within the University. Time to move on, even though my wife and I loved the city, and it wasn't too far from Newcastle, where my parents expected and got regular family visits. Emigration seemed wiser than moving around in the UK, especially in the eyes of my wife. Above all, I wanted to restore the family finances while remaining a full-time academic, and that looked impossible in the UK!

CG: Could you tell us your experience with your review article 'Inflation' for the *Economic Journal*, including how you came to be picked to do this? What did this experience tell you about British economics, economic journals, etc?

DL: The Royal Economic Society originally commissioned this article – one of a series of surveys of applied economics – from Dick Lipsey, I think, but for some reason he couldn't do it. He suggested as a replacement for himself Michael Parkin, with whom he'd written a paper on the effectiveness of wage–price controls, and Michael in turn suggested me as a co-author. Though we were a natural choice for this task, given our SSRC programme, I strongly suspect that, when they took us on, the RES and the editors of the *Economic Journal* neither knew who we were nor what we were likely to write. They were probably hoping for an article that would debunk the monetarist ideas that were beginning to creep into Britain in the early 1970s, and reaffirm the then mainstream view. This view had inflation a cost-push consequence of competition for income shares that could be cured by increasing the aggregate amount of income available and then keeping it growing faster than aspirations. The policy that followed from this view was to increase aggregate demand, impose direct controls on money wages and prices, and adopt a flexible exchange rate if that was needed to avoid the balance of payments problems that had interfered with Reginald Maudling's first experiment along these lines a decade earlier. That's what the Heath–Barber policies were all about (and the Nixon–Burns policies in the US, too, for a while) and they had a lot of support among the economics establishment. The idea that the great inflation was mainly the consequence of policymakers trying to exploit an inflation–unemployment trade-off is, by the way, largely an *ex post* myth, constructed by people who have not made a serious study of the economic thought of the time.

Anyway, the central message of our paper was that the above-mentioned conventional wisdom was wrong and that a monetarist interpretation of inflation, based on the role of monetary expansion and the expectations augmented Phillips curve fitted the facts rather well. The editors did not like the paper's early drafts at all. At one point, they suggested that the section on the Quantity Theory of Money be deleted altogether as not relevant to a paper on the applied economics of inflation, and they were continuously and highly sensitive to some of our criticisms of the opinions of some rather prominent people concerning inflation. (Interested readers may check the article – the names survived, even if the comments were toned down a bit.) After much going back and forth, during the course of which I seriously thought about withdrawing the paper and submitting it to the *JPE* – Michael rightly talked me out of this – a version that was pronounced by Brian Reddaway, the *EJ*'s editor, to be 'not as bad as we first feared' appeared in December 1975. By then its authors were both in Canada. I now very much regret that my copies of the correspondence with the editors about this paper were discarded when I moved, but I dare say that the *EJ* files will contain some of it.

Visitor: Brown 1973

RL: Why Brown? Who was there?

DL: The Herschel Grossman connection – Michael Parkin and I replaced Jerry Stein while he was on leave, one term each. Brown had tried hard to hire Michael a little earlier, and maybe they were still at it then. We had to take a leave from Manchester that year so that our salaries could be used to keep junior temporary people (I think Mick Gray and George Zis) employed for another year. There was no other funding available at the University.

UK: Policy advising

NR: Very soon after you left the UK, Margaret Thatcher became prime minister and began some serious changes in economic policy. Did you feel tempted to return to the UK, and participate more closely in setting economic policy? (Is that story true about Sir Keith Joseph flying into London Ontario on a secret mission?)

DL: I had talked to Keith Joseph a few times while still in the UK, and, indeed, in 1975 there was a small pre-emigration dinner for Harry Johnson, Michael Parkin and myself, organized by Bob Nobay on behalf of the Money Study Group, which Joseph attended. He did indeed visit me in

London Ontario (on a side trip from New York, I think) while still in opposition, to sound me out about returning should there be a change of government. (I think he was a little surprised to find himself in the final hometown of some of the Tolpuddle Martyrs.) Soon after that, and earlier than expected, there was an election, which Mrs Thatcher won, and he phoned me with a job offer. Of course, I was tempted, and I even talked to Jim Melvin (chair at UWO) about the prospects of taking an extended leave. However, my wife refused to contemplate a return to the UK for any length of time, so that put a quick end to negotiations.

I don't regret this outcome – I would have been an unhappy bureaucrat, and in particular I don't think I could have tolerated being on the inside during the confrontation with the miners. Of course, that industry had to be shrunk radically, but, frequently forgotten nowadays, mining communities had taken it for granted that, after their misery during the Depression and their efforts in wartime and in the immediate post-war years, they had earned an implicit guarantee of future security from the rest of the country. So the confrontation was a tragedy in which a promise that could not be kept, but which nevertheless had been a promise, was broken. Viewed from the distance of Canada at least, the government seemed unnecessarily callous in its handling of the affair – I don't know whether I could have stood up to the personal stress that being part of all this would have created.

RS: Did Joseph offer you the job as the government's chief economist?

DL: The offer was by telephone. I don't remember how specific he was about the position, and I'm sure he must have uttered the usual caveats too – but I was certainly left with the impression that a very senior job was there for me if I wanted it.

RS: Did you have an input into the UK Expenditure Review process at that time?

DL: No – I was supposed to visit the Chancellor of the Exchequer, Sir Geoffrey Howe during a visit to London arranged by Brian Griffiths, but I collapsed from exhaustion the day before the appointment, ended up in hospital and had to come back to Canada as soon as I was strong enough to travel. That was the extent of it.

RS: Your 1980 evidence to the Treasury and Civil Service Committee was entitled 'Notes on Gradualism'. What do you recall about that Committee?

DL: I remember that I didn't enjoy it nearly as much as the 1974 Expenditure Committee, where I think I did much better as a witness, too. My recollection is that the 1980 invitation asked witnesses who had done empirical work to use its results to discuss the output and unemployment costs of the government's efforts at getting inflation down. I had a little model (see Laidler and O'Shea, *Economica,* 1977 for a version of it). It wasn't a forecasting framework but a product of my efforts to produce macro models that were simple enough to take into an undergraduate classroom and be analysed, but which also had some empirical content, but I suspected that if I didn't find out what it had to say about the matter, someone else might, so I played the Committee's game – being very careful (or so I thought) to tell them all the reasons why I thought the results the model produced probably seriously underestimated the costs in question. But some Committee members – I remember Jeremy Bray being particularly aggressive – seemed intent on casting me as an over-optimistic supporter of what was a very tough policy, and didn't seem very interested in nuanced argument. My recollection is that if you look at the views that the Committee's report ended up attributing to me, these were a good deal more simplistic and hardhearted than my opinions as they appear in the minutes. I was stuck between a rock and a hard place though: I thought that policy was too harsh, but I also feared that any moves to pull back even a little might end up in a complete reversal – cf. Heath, Barber, and the short life of Selsdon man. I honestly believed (as I still do) that there was no alternative to fiscal and monetary restraint in dealing with the situation, so once the government had started out on that path, the policy had to be seen through. Closely related, I was completely unprepared for the sheer amount of animosity that permeated the British debate at that time.

The deeper moral I drew from this episode was that, to be really effective in giving policy advice or writing policy commentary, you need to be living in and with the economy you are discussing, and with the local political debate, too. That way, you maximize your chances of having a proper feel for the economic situation, about which official statistics can often be quite misleading, and of being able to frame what you have to say about it in language that will enable the message to be understood even by those who disagree with you. I've pretty much confined my policy commentary to Canada since 1980, often trying to fend off the influence of badly informed advice offered by visiting experts, for which there is a sometimes dangerously unhealthy appetite among people who really ought to know better.

RY: What did Mrs Thatcher get right and what did she get wrong?

DL: On the plus side, getting inflation under control and the fiscal balance too (though with extreme clumsiness – maybe I could have helped there?). It is interesting that in this instance, it was the absence of central bank independence that enabled the politicians to act quickly against inflation! Straightening out the labour market, and particularly the laws on secondary picketing, was also a big plus – but see above on the coal industry. Also – recovering some of the Danegeld that Heath and co. had offered up as the price of a late entry to Europe. On the negative side, the poll tax was a truly harebrained idea, and shifting towards the EMS when money growth targeting was obviously not working was not much better. A 'trust us while we try everything else' muddle (cf. Canada in the 1980s) would at least have avoided a crisis later on, but since the EMS crisis played its part in scaring the electorate off the Euro, there was, I suppose, a silver lining.

Professor: UWO 1975

NR: Can you tell us how the intellectual climate evolved at UWO Economics Department during your 30 years there? Who did you learn the most from? Tell us about your one (brief) foray into university administration, as Chair of Economics at UWO. You stayed at UWO far longer than at any other university. Why?

DL: From the outset, Western was (and remained) a department that took its standards from the international community – it wasn't interested in just being the 'best in Canada'. This was a more distinctive attribute then among Canadian departments than it is now, and it made us the object of a certain amount of suspicion, particularly within the University, where, in my view, many people who should have known better never really appreciated how good we became. This attitude hampered the department's progress.

The department also had the reputation, which still sticks in some quarters, of being interested only in 'theory'. That's a hard case to make when serious applied work here goes back to Reuber and Bodkin on inflation–unemployment trade-offs and Wonnacott on free trade in the early 1960s, but it does get made nevertheless, and at times when academic work is supposed to be 'relevant', particularly to the business community, it has played a role in undermining the department's access to resources and support.

All in all, the current department is not too different from the one I joined – full of very bright and productive young people, but very thin in experienced senior members, who are therefore seriously overburdened with administration. It's smaller than it was though, and narrower in its interests as a result. I very much regret the virtual disappearance of economic history and the history of thought. (No I didn't bring it here – Ron Bodkin taught it long before me.)

I've had many marvellous colleagues at Western – you could easily put together a top 10 department staffed solely with people who have passed through, and though I'm well aware that if a department doesn't lose a few people to other and better places, then it probably isn't ambitious enough in its hiring, I still think that the above-mentioned refusal in some quarters in the university to believe that anything or anyone already located at Western really could be that good, and the misperception that the department's work lacks practical relevance as compared with that of some other units, contributed to many of the losses. It won't surprise you to learn that, given my interests, the colleague I miss most is Peter Howitt – a genuinely original economist who always goes where his own thinking takes him, regardless of current intellectual fashions, and he shares his ideas, too.

As to being chair, I took my turn, and in my three years – it was supposed to be seven – I presided over a dozen or more promotion and tenure cases, not all of them easy, I hired maybe 15 people a year (including visitors and temporary appointees of course) and dealt successfully with two really bad and enormously time- and energy-consuming disciplinary cases involving graduate students. There was sometimes acute controversy, particularly over hiring, and I'm sure I was not right about every decision, but all of this came out pretty well overall, and I left the department better than I found it. It was an extremely taxing time, though, and I didn't enjoy it. Nor do I regret resigning in protest against the Dean's behaviour in a matter that, to my mind, went to the heart of my responsibility to defend the department's standards of student evaluation. I still think I was right to make a stand, and that I deserved more support than I got. It would have been easier for me had I quit immediately the decision to do so was made, rather than hanging on for a year so that a successor could be chosen in an orderly fashion. I paid a very high personal price for that stupidity.

I stayed at Western because, as it happened, it offered me more intellectual space to get on with the work I wanted to do than any of the available alternatives in Canada. I ran into problems with administrators shortly after I ceased to be department chair, however, about the conditions of appointment that had been offered to me to keep me at Western in the face of a tempting outside offer, and these left me with little in the way of loyalty towards the University.

RY: What is wrong with university administrators?

DL: They've become professionals and detached from the academic values that I have cherished since the very beginning of my career. Providing a university system for 20 or 30 per cent of the cohort is not like providing it for 3 or 5 per cent, of course, and old academics like me are always exaggerating the virtues of the old days. Even so, early in my career, I was at Clark Kerr's Berkeley, where I got a glimpse of the future, not just as exhibited in the way in which the administration avoided dealing with my problems with the draft, but also more generally in the overall managerial style that provoked the University's serious problems with its students. I hated what I saw then, and I count myself lucky that the future that Kerr was trying to create took quite a long time to catch up with me again. But it did, and there don't seem to be any successors to the 1960s generation among the current crop of students to do anything about it. That's a pity.

Canada: Policy advising

RY: Was the Macdonald Commission structured properly?

DL: It's the only royal commission I've ever been associated with, so I have no standards of comparison. That being said, I think the structure worked well. Ideas provided by discipline-based academics really did filter up through the research programme to provide a basis for the interdisciplinary analysis of the economic legal and political aspects of the issues that the Commission addressed, and I'd be willing to argue the case that the Commission's success owed a great deal to this intellectual foundation. But note that the Commissioners' work was firmly based on the output of distinct disciplines that they and their senior staff brought together for specific purposes.

WR: Your work on Canadian policy issues has covered a wide range of subjects – money and inflation, exchange rates, measurement of economic well-being, national unity, and much else – and involved many institutions – the Macdonald Commission, advisory groups, the C.D. Howe Institute. Which of these have you found most and least engaging or rewarding, and why?

DL: Honestly, I've enjoyed it all, because I have always been able to write and say just what I think in every case, and I've never expected to win every battle or convince every colleague – even though I've been known to try pretty hard. On the odd occasion where I've found myself fundamentally out of sympathy with the position being taken by an institution or organization I've been associated with, I have just walked away – I did that with the Fraser Institute when I thought they were becoming too supportive of the South African government. I've always tried to make such academic expertise as I have available to anyone who is interested in it, while avoiding a level of commitment that might put me in the position of having to defend publicly policies or ideas that I don't believe in. That's why I've never joined a political party since I left the Whitley Bay Young Conservatives (which I had joined at my mother's behest) in 1956. In the UK, I talked to Keith Joseph about monetary policy, to be sure, but I also talked to Robert Carr – no Thatcherite – and Michael English too – an influential Labour backbencher.

WR: Your year as special adviser at the Bank of Canada presented a unique opportunity to test your ideas in the policymaking cockpit. Did you come out of that experience with any advice for academics who find themselves in that position, or for central bankers who want to make good use of outside expertise?

DL: Not really – you take what you have to a position like that and hope that it's useful, and the central bankers surely knew much better than me what they wanted. My practical advice to others going into that position has been to have a project of your own to fill in the times when no one seems to want to talk to you, but to make sure it's the kind of thing you can put down when you suddenly find yourself asked to contribute to more in-house discussions than is decent in the time available.

CF: How do you compare the willingness of government and central bank in Canada to consider policy advice from academics relative to England?

DL: It's difficult to disentangle the effects of the passage of time from those of change of country. Some time in the 1960s – I don't remember whether it was during my year at LSE or my time at Essex – I was at an early (maybe the very first) joint academic–Bank of England seminar, organized (I think) by Alec Cairncross. I vividly recall a senior Bank of England official (Michael Thornton, I think) remarking that there was no point in the Bank making data available to academics on a regular basis since they would be bound to misunderstand the information. And later, after the 1969 Hove conference to mark the 10th anniversary of the Radcliffe Report, some innocuous remarks by Kit McMahon about how even the Bank itself sometimes had difficulty in understanding what was going on in the economy, were leaked to the *Guardian* (coincidentally to Frances Cairncross), and this led to questions in Parliament!

But things slowly got better – The Money Study Group, which evolved from that Hove conference, helped a lot, and the Brunner–Meltzer conferences at Konstanz always had central bankers and academics in attendance. In the UK, personalities mattered, too. Charles Goodhart, for example, managed to keep one foot in academia even when he was inside the Bank, and he was clearly reading, listening and contributing to the academic discussion. But the Bank of Canada was more open even then, despite the fact that the Coyne affair was not that far in the past. There was no one at the Bank of England quite like George Freeman (who used to go to Konstanz, it should be remembered), always willing to listen, and to be very direct in disagreeing, too.

CF: Looking back, how do you feel about the year that you spent at the Bank of Canada as special adviser? Do you feel that you had an impact on policy and/or ways of thinking about policy?

DL: It was one of the most productive and enjoyable years of my career. It would have been nice if some of the work I helped with could have established a useful role for monetary aggregates in the day-to-day conduct of policy, but it didn't, and even negative results have their uses, after all. But I still think that these results reflect the institutional changes of the 1990s, working against the background of a rather stable macroeconomic environment. Central banks that don't keep an eye on monetary aggregates neglect them at their peril.

As to my impact on policy, if any, it's hard to say. Gordon Thiessen was so skilled at creating a consensus that it was usually impossible to figure out just who had influenced what aspect of any decision at the end of the day. I'd like to think that I contributed to keeping policy discussions focused on the medium term during the crises of late 1998, that I helped clarify some of the potential virtues of fixed-decision dates, and that my warnings that people were likely to take very seriously the proposals then being made to abandon the Canadian dollar, so the Bank had better pay attention too, were useful. But if I hadn't been at the Bank, I find it hard to believe that any policy outcome would have been different.

CF: Your C.D. Howe pamphlet on governance at the Bank of Canada played a role in the establishment of the Manley Subcommittee. What are your views about that?

DL: I thought the Manley Report itself was an excellent document, so I'm quite proud of having helped to provoke it (and to have been the teacher of some of the professional staff who helped the Committee to write it, too). I wrote the pamphlet because I was alarmed at the extent to which public criticisms of monetary policy were becoming politicized, and personalized too, in the form of attacks on the Governor. Under Harry Johnson's influence, I had been a sometimes attentive spectator of the Coyne affair while a student at Chicago, and I began to fear that the Bank's independence from day-to-day politics (at the beginning of the 1990s it seemed to me to be one of the few federal institutions that had any integrity left) was again under threat. Though none of my specific proposals was adopted, subsequent changes that diffused decision making within the Bank to an informal governing council, led to the opening of regional offices, and saw the Bank increase its efforts to communicate regularly to the public at large the reasons for its policy decisions, addressed the problems I had raised. How much of that was a response to my critique, and how much a series of changes that would have come about in any event, I haven't the faintest idea.

CF: More generally, your C.D. Howe publications have been very policy-orientated. Has this work influenced your more academic work in any significant way?

DL: Indirectly – the main causation has run in the other direction of course, but the fact that I often found Thornton, Bagehot, Marshall, Hawtrey, Keynes et al. more useful sources of policy ideas than many of my contemporaries gave me the confidence I needed to persevere with my academic work in the history of economic thought. The similarities between the LTCM crisis of 1998 and the Baring crisis of 1890, for example, are uncanny. Between them, my two books *The Golden Age of the Quantity Theory* and *Fabricating the Keynesian Revolution* (the latter finished off while I was at the Bank) took more than ten years to write, and I didn't undertake them merely for the fun of it. Analysis doesn't necessarily cease to be policy-relevant just because it was created a long time ago, and ideas need to be kept alive even when they are temporarily out of fashion.

CF: How do we get more academic economists to involve themselves in policy work?

DL: There is no problem on average in the worldwide profession that I can see, but there is in Canada. Here it would help if American journals were more willing to publish, and American authors to cite, papers that deal with Canadian policy problems. They publish and cite lots of applied work on US problems, which is one reason why so many young Canadians whose applied research has potential policy applications use US data sets. They have careers to make, and the profession operates by certain standards. These are set in the US because that's where most of the best work is done, but the profession there nevertheless can be remarkably parochial. I haven't done a formal study of the matter, but, to give one example, my impression is that the currently very active US discussion of inflation targeting neglects the Canadian experience and the local literature it has generated to a quite scandalous extent.

General

NR: Looking back over your career as an economist: What was your biggest regret? What was (with hindsight) your biggest mistake? What was your most important success? Which of your publications are you most proud of? Which of your writings is most deserving of more attention than it received?

DL: It's not really a regret, but I sometimes wonder how my career would have turned out if I had been able to stay longer in the US and find my place in the profession there. Going to Essex didn't cut me right off, of course – far from it – and it was a wonderful academic environment, but that move out of the US was forced on me. I didn't choose it, and it was horribly disruptive of my ability to keep in touch and keep up for two or three years, a long time at that stage of a career. Nothing that I actually published while at Essex – even *The Demand for Money* – had been started there from scratch. To judge from publication dates, I didn't begin anything new much before 1968. And of course I was soon to get sucked into UK policy debates about inflation, so my career ended up on a rather different path than it would have followed in the US. As I said, I don't regret any of this, but I do wonder what other directions I might have gone off in.

My biggest mistake was becoming department chair at Western.

Probably *The Demand for Money* was my biggest success. Many people over the years have told me how it helped them with macro-core and even money field exams and their equivalents, and I sometimes let myself think that it has had more influence than a simple citation count would suggest. But it is my two books on the history of monetary economics that give me the most satisfaction. My reasons for coming to Canada, for remaining an academic, for staying at Western, etc., were many and various, but always among them was the desire to find the time and the intellectual space to try to fill the gap in the literature created by the absence of a systematic history of the development of macroeconomics from Mill and Bagehot down to the *General Theory*. I first formed that ambition – essentially to pick up the story where Fetter had left it – when I was at Manchester, and I finally fulfilled it 25 years later. If the end product leaves things to be desired, I have no one to blame but myself for that, because I had the chance to do my best, and it is a very lucky academic who can say such a thing.

As to your last question, economics has made a dreadful mistake in downgrading the study and teaching of its own history, so it is my writings on that history, including those two books, for which I'd like a wider readership.

NR: Do you enjoy teaching? Do you have any particular philosophy of teaching?

DL: I did enjoy teaching very much indeed, but I don't think I'd dignify my approach with so grand a phrase as 'philosophy of teaching'.

I always tried to be professional, which to me meant preparing properly, both in the sense of thinking through what was to be done in the course as a whole and how it might relate to what my colleagues were doing, and then getting an outline and reading list out on time, and also in the sense of taking an hour or so before each class to organize my mind about what I wanted to cover that day and how I was going to do it. I also always used written examinations and papers for evaluation, never multiple-choice tests, and I always did my own marking. If what students write is read carefully, it gives invaluable feedback about what the teacher has done well or badly – there is always going to be a significant proportion of the latter, no matter how hard you try – and this helps immensely with preparations for the next time around.

More generally, I am strongly committed to the individual discipline as the foundation for all good academic work, and hence as the foundation for the curriculum, too. I don't have much faith in the 'interdisciplinary approach' to undergraduate education (and to much else) that is all the rage nowadays. If you want good interdisciplinary research or teaching on specific issues of current importance, and you often do, then you need a team of people who understand their own disciplines inside out and respect each other's expertise too, not a bunch of half-trained generalists – see my comments on the Macdonald Commission. In economics, students must learn how to do theoretical and empirical analysis before they start criticizing the limitations of the subject in whatever current state they find it. Of course it always has had many limitations, and will continue to do so, but a properly trained economist will see these from the inside of the subject, not from the outside, and will therefore have at least half a chance of being able to do something about them.

FC: Why is history of economic thought important?

DL: The answer is complicated, and I discussed it in some detail in the paper I wrote for Charles Goodhart's *Festschrift*. But to summarize: (a) economics has attracted some remarkable intellects over its history, and it's simply arrogant to think that today's students have nothing to gain from encountering them at first hand; (b) the subject also has a very long history of forgetting good ideas, and this has sometimes done great harm – see, for example, macroeconomic policy in the 1960s and 1970s; but most important of all, (c) economics is about rational choices and their coordination; people can't make such choices without making predictions about their outcomes, and to do that they need an understanding of how the economic system works. The history of economic thought teaches us about how diverse that understanding has usually been, and also about how it has evolved. We can't understand the processes that have generated our subject's empirical basis if we don't appreciate the ways in which economic ideas have affected behaviour in the past, and the ways in which the outcome of the behaviour in question has in turn caused economic ideas to be revised. This fact, unfortunately for the history of economic thought, makes the sub-discipline extremely subversive of currently fashionable ideas about how to do economics. It tells us that, although it may be analytically attractive to postulate that the agents in our typical model use that same model to form expectations about the consequences of their choices, it also relies on a hypothesis that is grossly inconsistent with all the evidence we have about how economic models have in fact evolved and been deployed in the past.

RL: What is the future of the past?

DL: Or as Bernard Corry once famously asked: Should economists abandon HOPE? As a regular but not-very-well-informed reader of the *New York Review of Books* I've noticed that the idea that history in general came to an end sometime during the second Reagan administration hasn't had a very long life, even in the US. The idea that the only way to do economics is to postulate a 'true model' of the economy about which all agents can agree and whose deployment will enable the 'market' to coordinate their choices come what may, and that all other approaches have now been rendered obsolete and unworthy of attention, seems to me to be a closely related postulate, based on a similar (maybe, at some deeper level, the same) naïve and insular view of the way societies work. If that's true, then this idea, which is the main factor that has undermined the status of the history of thought within the discipline, has little chance of surviving in the long run. But a lot of people have major investments in economic analysis that relies on it, and, having rid their departments of a field that shows up the narrowness and historical shallowness of their approach – very useful though it often may be – they can't be expected to welcome the history of economic thought back with open arms. So it will take time, and in the meanwhile, we'll just have to hang on as best we can.

CG: Did you make any contribution to the debate on the appropriate policies in response to the oil price shocks in the 1970s?

DL: I recall being at one meeting called by the Treasury immediately after the first shock. I think I suggested that either the OPEC countries would find a way of spending their extra incomes or they would have to lend out the resulting savings, so that the international monetary system was likely to survive. I think I also noted that the price increase implied a substantial windfall to the UK in the shape of an increase in the present value of North Sea reserves. Whether anyone took any notice or not, I haven't the faintest idea. Otherwise, when asked, I argued as did some others – notably Michael Parkin – that oil price increases were rather lumpy events that were nevertheless largely endogenous to an ongoing inflationary process whose root causes were monetary.

CG: Since, I presume, you are an ardent floater: why do you think that real exchange rates have been so variable and volatile since floating? What do you blame for that?

DL: I'm uneasy about being classified an ardent floater, as if that were a free-standing policy preference. Rather, I'm a strong advocate, for political reasons, of the idea that monetary policy is sufficiently important that those who conduct it need to be accountable to those affected by it – see *How Shall We Govern the Governor?* In the world as it is, it is only feasible to arrange for such accountability through the institutions of the nation state. This seems to me to imply that (a) separate national currencies are highly desirable, and that (b) the domestic politics of monetary policy are likely to be easier to manage if its goals are for domestic variables, and this means that the exchange rate should not be among them. Though it's not quite the same issue, and though I'm an outsider who may be missing something, it's considerations like this that make me still rather uneasy about the future of the Euro. A common currency is more than just a limiting case of a fixed exchange rate, of course, but I really do wonder whether European institutions are well enough developed to manage the politics of monetary policy, and particularly its interaction with fiscal policy, within the Euro system.

As to exchange rate volatility, asset prices today are affected by all the news that arrives about what is going to happen on every day into the future, and this gives uncoordinated improvisation in national monetary policies with no long-term anchors, such as we had in the '70s and '80s, a lot of scope to cause volatility. This, though, is an *ex post* rationalization, and I haven't done any systematic testing of it. Furthermore, I was as surprised as anyone else about the degree of volatility in those years. I don't think that the greater stability we have seen in the 1990s is unrelated to the international spread of inflation targeting, however.

Also, as Canadians are very aware, there is such a thing as a real exchange rate, and its equilibrium value does move quite a lot in some cases. One of the curiosities of the modern exchange rate literature (which is changing now) is that for quite a while, it was taken for granted that PPP was the right long-run model for nominal exchange rates among advanced countries, but that you really needed to pay careful attention to international commodity prices when dealing with North–South exchange rate issues. Well some advanced countries are major commodity producers.

CG: Tell us about your relationships with Harry Johnson and the Money Study Group.

DL: Harry's is a long and complicated story, and to get all of it people should consult Don Moggridge's forthcoming biography. Even my small part in it is too complicated to spell out in full here, for it began in the mid-1950s and went on until his death.

Though I don't recall meeting him in person then, I knew about Harry from the people who taught me as an undergraduate – the brouhaha over James Meade's successor was heard all the way down into the undergraduate programme at LSE – and he was my first adviser at Chicago. The support he gave me as a graduate student put me permanently and deeply in his debt, and he also published my first two papers on the demand for money in the *JPE*, and that got my career off to a flying start. He was instrumental in getting me the offer from Manchester (I think) and in persuading me to accept it (I'm sure) – though he was not as forthcoming as he might have been about what he was getting me into! And, of course, Michael Parkin and I took over his LSE graduate macro course, first when he went on leave, and then after his stroke. I also led the SSRC visiting team that assessed his application for what became the LSE-Geneva programme of research in international monetary economics, so I had the immense pleasure of administering an oral grilling to my mentor – I think his sense of humour was as much tickled by this anomalous event as was mine. But there was a serious side to this visit too. Harry was not universally popular at the LSE, and our visiting team spent at least as much – maybe more – time on trying to convince some of his colleagues that his work was worth supporting as they did on trying to persuade us to fund it – a bizarre reversal of the usual roles on such occasions. And finally, my move to Western was partly in response to Harry's advice too.

As to the MSG, it grew out of the 1969 Hove conference on the Radcliffe Report which worked so well that Harry in particular thought it was worth repeating. I think that the conference held at Sheffield the next year was probably already being planned by George Clayton, Jack Gilbert and Bob Sedgwick before the MSG was actually founded, but Harry was certainly involved in getting Milton Friedman to come to it, while Alan Peters of Shell, who helped finance it, was also his contact.

The group's main activities at first were one-day seminars held at LSE, occasionally formal like the 1971 *Inflation in Britain* conference, but mostly informal afternoon workshops held, if my memory is right, about twice a term. The idea was to organize such events and, in particular, to pay the fares to London of interested people working in what were still at that time rather isolated provincial departments (particularly for junior staff) so that they could be in regular contact with what was going on in the area. We also produced what was, at the time, a useful and rather widely used book of undergraduate readings on British monetary economics. More elaborate conferences such as the one at Bournemouth in 1972 and weekends at Merton College, Oxford were initially thought of as one-off affairs, but in due course the Oxford gatherings became annual events. The group soon obtained modest financial support from the SSRC too, mainly to support its LSE workshops, as did its imitators in Trade and Econometrics. (It's also worth noting that the Canadian Macro Study Group is one of the MSG's indirect descendants.)

Harry knew how to raise money and get people to come to conferences, and he understood as no one else did before or since, how the state of play in the monetary field stood worldwide, and how it was evolving. He also had contacts all over the place, so, through the MSG, people had links to Brunner and Meltzer's Konstanz Seminar, and to Pascal Salin and Emile Claassen at Paris Dauphine too, among others. It's hard to appreciate how much difference all this made to the professional atmosphere in UK economics at that time if you weren't there. To call it a very exciting time in which to have been around is platitudinous, but it was.

Let me also note that much of the heavy lifting in getting the MSG going and helping it flourish was done by Bob Nobay, who deserves a huge amount of credit for his input – any historian interested in the evolution of monetary economics in the UK at that time should interview him about his role, and get his perspective on how the thing evolved.

RL: Johnson became interested in the sociology of economic knowledge: dissecting the nature of influence etc. Why do you think Milton Friedman and George Stigler were successful in this regard and Left Keynesians (Joan Robinson in particular) were not?

DL: I'm very tempted to say that it was because they were right about most things while Joan and her acolytes were wrong – but that would be too simple. The basic failing of the Left Keynesians in the UK was to be too sure of their own importance. They routinely patronized those of us who disagreed with them when they weren't being downright rude. Joan was extremely and publicly nasty to me at the 1972 BAAS meetings over a period of days, Nicky Kaldor's performance at the MSG Bournemouth conference was a disgrace, and Roy Harrod's was not much better at Sheffield. These people, and others like them, forgot what I think was also one of Harry's maxims: that debates in economics are not conducted so that people can convince their opponents and impress their supporters, but so that competing points of view can be exhibited to younger spectators whose minds are not yet made up. Logic and well-marshalled evidence always trump sarcasm and personal abuse in that kind of encounter. Or, to put it another way, Milton, George and co. did their homework more carefully and treated their audiences with more respect than did Joan et al. That doesn't mean that they couldn't be tough – even ruthless – with opponents, because they could, or that they always deserved to win their encounters on the logical and empirical merits of their case, because sometimes they didn't. But they were always well prepared and serious, and in the long run that counted for everything.

RL: You said at the *Festschrift* conference: 'listen to and argue with those you disagree with'. This is close to one of Milton Friedman's dictums: 'understand your opponent's arguments better than they do themselves'. Was this something you learnt at Chicago? Can you provide some examples of the merits of this approach?

DL: No – I first learned it at high school from my English teacher Eric Milne and my history teacher Colin Gray, who were both experts at forcing me to deal with objections and counter-arguments to anything I believed. I was too young to go to university after my first (pretty successful) go at A levels, so I stayed on for a further year to do them (and S levels) again. I essentially had a year of private tuition from these two, who exposed me to open-minded dissenters such as Shaw and Russell – a biographer later labelled the latter a 'passionate skeptic' though I think it might have been his own phrase – and they taught me how to recognize what was then called 'cant' (we now call it 'spin') when I saw it, and also to be highly suspicious of the 'true believers' who purveyed it, particularly those who appealed to the emotions. I'm a great devotee of Mill too – I think it was Leonard Schapiro who made sure we read *On Liberty* when I was a second-year undergraduate.

Earlier at school, I had got into trouble in a compulsory 'religious studies' class for comparing Billy Graham's speaking style to Adolf Hitler's – one of my more successful efforts, as I then thought, at showing a teacher which of us was the smarter. Later I heard and saw the same techniques put to work at first hand by Oswald Mosley at the Odeon, Notting Hill Gate in 1959. And later still, one of my practices when bringing up my daughter was to watch TV evangelists with her, while discussing the ways in which camera angles, lighting and sound, not to mention the pitch of the voice, were used to distract attention from the claptrap that they were talking. Yes, I know that I see related techniques put to work all the time in the opera house, but it's usually in a good cause there – think Mozart, Verdi, Jancáček and Britten, rather than Wagner (whom I nevertheless can't resist) – and my passion for opera is probably some kind of displaced religious instinct anyway (a good direction in which to displace it in my opinion).

To get back to the point, my encounter with Popper also taught me rather early that much can be learned even from true believers, and my choice of Chicago was much influenced by the chance it offered to be challenged by Friedman, whose policy ideas disturbed me deeply at the time, but whose willingness to put the analysis that underlay them to the test of logic and evidence seemed (and still does) so utterly admirable. So that's where the Chicago link you correctly notice came from.

I'm not sure if it's a merit of this approach or not, but applying it as best I could over the years it has left me, at this late stage in my career, (a) convinced of the basic soundness of neoclassical economics as a basis for policy analysis (notwithstanding the true believer streak that is so deeply embedded among the RE clearing markets crowd and has made those segments of the profession that they dominate so inhospitable to the history of economic thought), and (b) terrified of the totalitarian impulses implicit in social conservatism, particularly the religiously motivated sort, and therefore (c) acutely uncomfortable both within economics, but even more so in contemporary North American society, where a thoroughly unholy alliance exists between the socially conservative right and exponents of market mechanisms. Why won't social democrats believe that demand curves slope down, supply curves up (usually) and that these facts have implications for the way in which their policy proposals are likely to work out? And why won't so many of those who share my views on the virtues of market mechanisms recognize that the ethical arguments for freedom of choice among a wide range of alternative goals apply well beyond the bounds of the marketplace?

David Laidler's Publications (as of February 2007)

Books and Monographs

The Demand for Money - Theories and Evidence, Scranton, PA, International Textbook Company, 1969; 2nd edition, New York, NY, T.Y. Crowell, 1977. 3rd edition (*The Demand for Money, Theories, Evidence and Problems*) New York, Harper Row, 1985. 4th Edition, New York, Harper-Collins, 1993. (Spanish translation 1972, French translation 1975, Italian translation 1976, Spanish translation of 2nd edition 1981, Japanese translation of 3rd edition 1989, Chinese Translation of 3rd Edition, Shanghai 1990.)

Introduction to Microeconomics, Oxford, Philip Allan Publishers, Ltd., 1974; New York, Basic Books, 1975. 2nd Edition, Oxford, Philip Allan Publishers, Ltd., New York, Halstead Press, 1981, 3rd edition (with Saul Estrin) Hemel Hempstead, Philip Allan Publishers Ltd. 1989. 4th edition, with (Saul Estrin) Hemel Hempstead, Harvester Wheatsheaf, 1994. (Spanish translation of 1st edition, 1979, Polish translation of 3rd Edition, 1992, Italian translation of 3rd Edition, 1992, Spanish translation of 3rd edition, 1992, Bulgarian translation of 3rd Edition, 1992, Spanish translation of 4th edition, 1995.)

Essays on Money and Inflation, Manchester, Manchester University Press, Chicago, University Chicago Press, 1975. (Republished, Aldershot, Gregg Revivals, 1993.)

Monetarist Perspectives, Oxford, Philip Allan Publishers, Ltd.; Cambridge, MA, Harvard University Press,1982. (Japanese Translation 1987.)

Taking Money Seriously, Hemel Hempstead, Philip Allan Publishers, Ltd.; Cambridge, MA, MIT Press, 1990.

The Golden Age of the Quantity Theory – the Development of Neoclassical Monetary Economics: 1870-1914, Hemel Hempstead, Philip Allan Publishers Ltd.; Princeton, NJ, Princeton University Press, 1991. (Japanese translation, 2000, republished, Pearson Education Print on Demand Edition, Harlow, UK., 2002)

How Shall We Govern the Governor? A Critique of the Governance of the Bank of Canada, Toronto, C.D. Howe Institute, 1991.

Two Nations One Money? Canada's Monetary System Following a Quebec Secession, Toronto, C.D. Howe Institute 1991 (with W.B.P. Robson, et al.).

The Great Canadian Disinflation: The Economics and Politics of Monetary Policy in Canada 1988-1993, Toronto, C.D. Howe Institute 1993 (with W.B.P. Robson).

Money and Macroeconomics: The Selected Essays of David Laidler, Cheltenham, UK and Lyme, USA, Edward Elgar (Economists of the Twentieth Century Series), 1997.

Fabricating the Keynesian Revolution: Studies of the Inter-war Literature on Money, the Cycle, and Unemployment, Cambridge, UK, and New York, Cambridge University Press, 1999.

Two Percent Target: Canadian Monetary Policy Since 1991, Toronto, C. D. Howe Institute, 2004 (with W. B. P. Robson).

Macroeconomics in Retrospect: The Selected Essays of David Laidler Cheltenham UK, Lyme USA, Edward Elgar 2004 (Economists of the Twentieth Century Series).

Books, Reports, etc. Edited

Readings in British Monetary Economics (with H.G. Johnson et al.), London, Oxford University Press, 1972.

Labour Markets and Inflation (with David Purdy), Manchester, Manchester University Press; Toronto, University of Toronto Press, 1974.

Report on the Role of Primary non-Labour Incomes in the Inflationary Process in the United Kingdom, Brussels, EEC Commission, 1976. (Dutch translation, 1978.)

Approaches to Economic Well-Being Vol. 26 of Research Studies prepared for the Royal Commission on the Economic Union and Development Prospects for Canada (The Macdonald Commission) Toronto, University of Toronto Press, 1985.

Responses to Economic Change Vol. 27 of Research Studies prepared for the Royal Commission on the Economic Union and Development Prospects for Canada (The Macdonald Commission) Toronto, University of Toronto Press, 1986.

Understanding Velocity - New Approaches and Their Policy Relevance, Special Issue of *Journal of Policy Modeling* 12(2) Summer, 1990.

Where We Go from Here – Inflation Control and Monetary Policy in Canada (with an introductory essay) Toronto, C.D. Howe Institute, 1997.

The Foundations of Monetary Economics 3 Vols. (a collection of readings, with an introductory essay) Cheltenham, UK and Northampton, MA., Edward Elgar, 1999.

Renovating the Ivory Tower: Canadian Universities and the Knowledge Economy (with an introductory essay) Toronto, C. D. Howe Institute, 2002.

Prospects for Canada: Progress and Challenges 20 Years after the Macdonald Commission (with Rapporteur's Commentary) Toronto, C. D. Howe Institute, 2005 (with W. B. P. Robson).

ARTICLES AND NOTES IN LEARNED JOURNALS AND THEIR REFEREED SUPPLEMENTS:

"Some Evidence on the Demand for Money." *Journal of Political Economy* February 1966, 55–68.

"The Rate of Interest and the Demand for Money – Some Empirical Evidence." *Journal of Political Economy* December 1966, 543–555.

"The Phillips Relation: A Theoretical Explanation." *Economica* May 1967, 189–197 (with B.A. Corry).

"The Permanent Income Concept in a Macroeconomic Model." *Oxford Economic Papers* March 1968, 11–23.

"The Phillips Relation – a Reply." *Economica* 1968, 184 (with B.A. Corry).

"The Definition of Money – Theoretical and Empirical Problems." *Journal of Money, Credit and Banking* August 1969, 508–525.

"The Case for Raising the Price of Gold a Comment." *Journal of Money, Credit and Banking* August 1969, 675–678.

"Money, Wealth and Time Preference in a Stationary Economy." *Canadian Journal of Economics* November 1969, 526–535.

"The Demand for Money in the U.K. 1956–1967, Preliminary Estimates." *The Manchester School* September 1970 (with J.M. Parkin), 187–208.

"The Demand for Money in the U.K. 1956-1967 – a Reply." *The Manchester School* June 1971, 125-129 (with J.M. Parkin).

"On Wicksell's Theory of Price Level Dynamics." *The Manchester School* June 1972, 125–143.

"Expectations, Adjustment and the Dynamic Response of Income to Policy Changes." *Journal of Money, Credit and Banking* February 1973, 157–172.

"Simultaneous Fluctuations in Prices and Output – a Business Cycle Approach." *Economica* February 1973, 60–72.
"Monetarist Policy Prescriptions and their Background." *The Manchester School* March 1973, 59–71.
"Price and Output Fluctuations in an Open Economy – Abstract." *Nebraska Journal of Economics* Autumn 1973.
"The Influence of Money on Real Income and Inflation – a Simple Model with Some Empirical Tests for the United States 1953–1972." *The Manchester School* December 1973, 367–395.
"Information, Money and the Macroeconomics of Inflation." *The Swedish Journal of Economics* Vol. 76, 1974, 26–42. (German translation by Klaus Hennings, Kieler Vortrage 81, J.C.B. Mohr, Tubingen, 1975.)
"The 1974 Report of the President's Council of Economic Advisors: The Control of Inflation and the Future of the International Monetary System." *American Economic Review* September 1974, 535–543.
"Inflation – a Survey." *Economic Journal* December 1975, 741–809 (with J.M. Parkin).
"Expectations and the Phillips Trade-Off: A Commentary." *Scottish Journal of Political Economy* February 1976, 55–72.
"Mayer on Monetarism – Comments from a British Point of View." *Kredit und Kapital*, No. 1, 1976, 56–68.
"Comment on Myhrman." *Scandinavian Journal of Economics* 1976.
"Inflation: Alternative Explanations and Policies – Tests on Data Drawn from Six Countries," in Brunner, K. and A.H. Meltzer (eds.), *Institutions, Policies and Economic Performance, Carnegie-Rochester Conference Series on Public Policy*, Vol. 4, North-Holland, 1976, 251–306.
"Inflation in Britain – a Monetarist Perspective." *American Economic Review* September 1976, 485–500.
"Expectations and the Behaviour of Prices and Output Under Flexible Exchange Rates." *Economica* November 1977, 327–336.
"Inflation – Alternative Explanations and Policies – a Reply to Rasche." *Journal of Monetary Economics* November 1977, 479–481.
"Money and Money Income – an Essay on the Transmission Mechanism." *Journal of Monetary Economics* April 1978, 151-191.
"I Costi dell'Inflazione Anticipata." *Rivista Internazionale Di Scienze Sociale* April-June 1978, 215–230. (Revised version of "The Welfare Costs of Inflation in Neo-Classical Theory – Some Unsettled Questions," translated by M.F. Ambrosanio.)
"Comment on Frenkel," in Brunner, K. and A.H. Meltzer (eds.), *Public Policies in Open Economies*, Carnegie-Rochester Conference Series, Vol. 9, Amsterdam, North Holland, 1978, 141–144 (with R.S. Boyer).
"Inflation in Britain – Reply to Fane." *American Economic Review* September 1978, 726–729.
"Recent Macroeconomic Policy Proposals of the Joint Economic Committee on the U.S. Congress: A Critique." *Journal of Monetary Economics* July 1979, 397–412.
"Concerning Currency Unions." *Zeitschrift fur Wirtschafts-und Sozialwissenschaften* 99, No. 1/2 1979, 147-162.
"An Empirical Model of an Open Economy Under Fixed Exchange Rates – The United Kingdom 1954–1970." *Economica* NS 47, May 1980, 141–158 (with P. O'Shea).
"Simmel's Philosophy of Money – a Review Article for Economists." *Journal of Economic Literature* March 1980, 97–105 (with N. Rowe).
"The Demand for Money in the United States Yet Again," in Brunner, K. and A.H. Meltzer (eds.), *The State of Macroeconomics*, Carnegie-Rochester Conference Series on Public Policy, Vol. 12, Amsterdam, North Holland, 1980, 219–272.
"Monetarism – an Interpretation and an Assessment." *Economic Journal* 91, March 1981, 1–21.
"Inflation and Unemployment in an Open Economy – a Monetarist View." *Canadian Public Policy* 7, April 1981, Supplement 179–188.

"Has Monetarism Failed – Introduction." *Canadian Public Policy* 7, April 1981, Supplement, 215–217.
"Adam Smith as a Monetary Economist." *Canadian Journal of Economics* 14, May 1981, 185–201.
"Some Policy Implication of the Monetary Approach to Balance of Payments and Exchange Rate Analysis." *Oxford Economic Papers*, July 1981 (Special issue on 'The Money Supply and the Exchange Rate'), 70–84.
"Friedman and Schwartz on Monetary Trends – a Review Article." *Journal of International Money and Finance* 1, 1982, 293–305.
"Jevons on Money." *The Manchester School*, December 1982, 326–353.
"John Hicks' *Money, Interest and Wages: Collected Essays in Economic Theory* Vol. II – a Review Essay." *Journal of Money, Credit and Banking*, August 1983, 385–389.
"A Small Macro Model of the Post-War United States." *The Manchester School*, December 1983, 317-340 (with Brian Bentley).
"Misconceptions about the Real Bills Doctrine – a Comment on Sargent and Wallace." *Journal of Political Economy*, February 1984, 149–155.
"The Buffer Stock Notion in Monetary Economics" (The 1983 Harry Johnson Lecture), *Conference Papers*, Supplement to the *Economic Journal*, 1984, 17–34.
"Harry Johnson as a Macroeconomist." *Journal of Political Economy*, August 1984, 592–615.
"Monetary Policy in Britain - Successes and Shortcomings." *Oxford Review of Economic Policy*, Spring 1985, 35–43.
"Expectations and Adjustment in the Monetary Sector Revisited, a Comment," in Brunner K. and A.H. Meltzer (eds.), *Understanding Monetary Regimes, Carnegie-Rochester Conference Series on Public Policy*, Vol. 22, Amsterdam, North Holland, 1985, 243–254.
"Comment on Money Demand Predictability." *Journal of Money, Credit and Banking*, 17 November 1985, Part 2, 647–654.
"Money in Crisis - a Review Essay." *Journal of Monetary Economics*, 17, 1986, 305–313.
"What Do We Really Know about Monetary Policy?" (The 40th Joseph Fisher Lecture in Commerce) *Australian Economic Papers*, June 1986, 1–16.
"Wicksell and Fisher on the 'Backing' of Money and the Quantity Theory: A Comment on the Debate between Smith and Michener," in K. Brunner and A.H. Meltzer (eds.) *Empirical Studies of Velocity, Real Exchange Rates Unemployment and Productivity, Carnegie Rochester Conference Series on Public Policy*, Vol. 27, Amsterdam, North Holland, 1987, 325–337.
"Some Macroeconomic Consequences of Price Stickiness." *Manchester School*, March 1988, 37–54.
"British Monetary Orthodoxy in the 1870s." *Oxford Economic Papers*, March 1988, 74–109.
"Are Perceptions of Inflation Rational? Some Evidence from Sweden" (with L. Jonung), *American Economic Review*, December 1988, 1080–1087.
"Presidential Address – Taking Money Seriously," *Canadian Journal of Economics*, November 1988, 687–713.
"What Remains of the Case for Flexible Exchange Rates," *Pakistan Development Review*, 24 Winter 1988 (Papers and Proceedings), 1147–1159.
"Comment on 'Development Policy in a Multiprovincial Economy'," *Pakistan Development Review*, 24 Winter 1988 (Paper and Proceedings), 419–420.
"Dow and Saville's Critique of Monetary Policy – a Review Essay." *Journal of Economic Literature*, 27 September 1989, 1147–1159.
"Understanding Velocity: New Approaches and Their Policy Relevance - Introduction," in D. Laidler (ed) *Understanding Velocity*...Special Issue of *Journal of Policy Modeling* 12(2) Summer, 1990 141–164.
"Hicks and the Classics." *Journal of Monetary Economics*, 25, June 1990, 481–489.
"Money as a Metaphorical Garment before the Great War – a Comment on Patinkin and Steiger." *Scandinavian Journal of Economics*, 1990, 92(4), 613–615.

"What Was New about Liquidity Preference Theory?" *Greek Economic Review*, Autumn 1990, 12 Supplement, 9–37.
"Karl Brunner's Monetary Economics – an Appreciation." *Journal of Money, Credit and Banking*, November 1991, 633–658.
"The Quantity Theory is Always and Everywhere Controversial – Why?." *Economic Record*, December, 1991, 289–306.
"Monetarism – the Unfinished Business," *Cyprus Journal of Economics* 5, December 1992, 60–74.
"Hawtrey, Harvard, and the Origins of the Chicago Tradition," *Journal of Political Economy* 101, December 1993, 1068–1103.
"Robertson in the 1920s," *European Journal of the History of Economic Thought* 2 (Spring) 1995, 151–174.
"Monetarism circa 1970: A View from 1994," *Kredit und Kapital*, 1995, 28, 323–345.
"Comment," on "Irving Fisher, J.M. Keynes, and the Transition to Modern Macroeconomics," by R.W. Dimand in Cottrell, A.F. and Lawlor, M.S. (eds.), *New Perspectives on Keynes*, Supplement to *History of Political Economy*, 1995, 267–271.
"Notes on the Microfoundations of Monetary Economics," *Economic Journal*, 107, July 1997, 1213–1223.
"More on Hawtrey, Harvard and Chicago" and "Hawtrey, Harvard and Chicago – a Final Comment." *Journal of Economic Studies* 25, 1998 4–16, 24–28.
"Perspectives on Modern Macroeconomic Theory and its History: an Interview with David Laidler." *Review of Political Economy* 10, No.1, 1998, 27–56 (with Christof Ruehl).
"Monetary Explanations of the Weimar Republic's Hyper-inflation: Some Neglected Contributions in the Contemporary German Literature." *Journal of Money, Credit and Banking*, 30 November 1998, 816–831 (with G. Stadler).
"Canada's Exchange Rate Options" in The W. Irwin Gillespie Round Table on Public Policy, *Canadian Public Policy* 25, September 1999, 324–332 (revised and abbreviated version of AThe Exchange Rate Regime and Canada's Monetary Order' Bank of Canada Working Paper 99–7).
"Phillips in Retrospect." *Research in the History of Economic Thought and Methodology: A Research Annual 20-A* 2002, pp. 223–235.
"Skidelsky's Keynes: A Review Essay." *European Journal of the History of Economic Thought* 9 (Spring) 2002, 97–110.
"Rules, Discretion and Financial Crises in Classical and Neoclassical Monetary Economics." *Economic Issues*, 7 (Part 2), September 2002, 11–34.
"An Early Harvard *Memorandum* on Anti-Depression Policies: An Introductory Note." *History of Political Economy* 34 (2) Fall 2002, 515–532 (with Roger J. Sandilands).
(ed.) "Memorandum Prepared by L. B. Currie, P. T. Ellsworth, and H. D. White (Cambridge, Mass., January 1932)" *History of Political Economy* 34, (2) Fall, 2002, 533–552 (with Roger J Sandilands).
"Review of *Making Money: An Insider's Perspective on Finance, Politics and Canada's Central Bank* by John Crow." *Canadian Journal of Economics* 36, No.3, August 2003, 758–764.
"Meltzer's *History of the Federal Reserve*." *Journal of Economic Literature* 41, No. 4, December 2003, 1256–1271.
"Two Views of the Lender of Last Resort – Thornton and Bagehot." *Cahiers d'economie politique* No.45, 2003, 61–78.
"Monetary Policy after Bubbles Burst: The Zero Lower Bound, the Liquidity Trap and the Credit Deadlock." *Canadian Public Policy*, 30(3), September 2004, 333–340.
"What Was Lost with IS-LM," in M. de Vroey and K.D. Hoover (eds.)*The IS-LM Model: Its Rise, Fall and Strange Persistence* (Annual Supplement to *History of Political Economy*, 36, 2004, 25–57 (with Roger Backhouse).
"Inflation Targeting versus International Monetary Integration: A Canadian Perspective." *Structural Change and Economic Dynamics* 16, 2005, 35–64.

"Canada's Monetary Choices in North America and their Dubious Parallels with Britain's in Europe." *Current Politics and Economics of Europe*, 17(1), 2006 (Special Issue on Britain and Canada and Their Large Neighbouring Monetary Unions, Part 1) 71–98.
"Woodford and Wicksell on *Interest and Prices:* the Place of the Pure Credit Economy in the Theory of Monetary Policy." *Journal of the History of Economic Thought,* 28 (2) June 2006, 151–159.

Articles and Notes in Edited Volumes, Bank Reviews, Other Periodicals and Pamphlets

"Income Tax Incentives for Owner-Occupied Housing," in Harberger, A.C. and M.J. Bailey (eds.), *The Taxation of Income from Capital,* Washington, D.C., The Brookings Institution, 1969.
"Recent Developments in Monetary Theory – a Comment," in Croome, D.R. and H.G. Johnson (eds.), *Money in Britain* 1959-1969, Oxford University Press, 1970.
"The Influence of Money on Economic Activity: A Survey of Some Current Problems," in G. Clayton, Gilbert, J.S. and Sedgwick, R. (eds.), *Monetary Theory and Monetary Policy in the 1970s,* Oxford University Press, 1971.
"The Phillips Curve, Expectations, and Incomes Policy," in Johnson, H.G. and A.R. Nobay (eds.), *The Current Inflation,* Macmillan, 1971.
"Monetarism, Stabilization Policy and the Exchange Rate," *The Bankers' Magazine,* September 1971.
Memorial to the Prime Minister, with "The Economic Radicals" (H.G. Johnson, et al.), 1972.
"Thomas Tooke on Monetary Reform," in M.Peston and B.A. Corry (eds.), *Essays in Honour of Lord Robbins,* Weidenfelt and Nicholson, London, 1972.
The Basis of Monetarism, Audio Learning, London, 1973 (with J.M. Parkin).
"The Current Inflation – Explanations and Policies," *National Westminster Bank Quarterly Review,* November 1972 and in Robinson, J. (ed.), After Keynes, Blackwell, Oxford, 1973.
"Income and the Demand for Housing: Some Evidence for Great Britain," in J.M. Parkin (ed.), *Essays in Modern Economics, Proceedings of 1972 AUTE Conference,* Longman's, 1973 (with I.C.R. Byatt and A. Holmans).
"The Economy Mismanaged," *The Banker,* October 1973.
Dear Prime Minister, with 'The Economic Radicals' (H.G. Johnson, et. al.), 1974.
"A Policy for the New Government," *The Banker,* March 1974.
"Money, Financial Markets and Economic Activity, Introduction," and "Discussion Paper," in Johnson, H.G. and A.R. Nobay (eds.), *Issues in Monetary Economics,* Oxford University Press, 1974 (with J.M. Parkin).
"Inflation and Its Control: A Monetarist Analysis," in Grant, B.M. and G.K. Shaw (eds.), *Issues in Economic Policy,* Oxford, Philip Allan Publishers, Ltd., 1975. Second edition, 1979.
"The Crisis: When and Why Did It Start," in Lord Robbins et al., *Inflation, Causes and Cures,* Institute of Economic Affairs, 1975.
"Unemployment and Inflation, a British Commentary," in M. Friedman, *Unemployment and Inflation,* Institute of Economic Affairs, 1975.
"Discussion of 'A Dynamic Analysis of the Quantity Theory'," in Parkin, J.M. and A.R. Nobay (eds.), *Current Problems in Economics Proceedings of the 1974 AUTE Conference,* Cambridge, Cambridge University Press, 1975.
"Inflation, Excess Demand and Expectations in Fixed Exchange Rate Open Economies," in Parkin, J.M. and G. Zis (eds.), *Inflation in the World Economy,* Manchester, Manchester University Press, 1976 (with R.G. Cross).
"International Aspects of Inflation: A Survey," in Claassen, E. and P. Salin (eds.), *Proceedings of the 1974 Dauphine Conference,* Amsterdam, North Holland, 1976 (with A.R. Nobay).
"A Monetarist Analysis of Simultaneous Fluctuations in Prices and Output," in H. Frisch (ed.), *Inflation in Small Countries,* Proceedings of the 1974 Vienna Conference, Berlin, Springer Verlag, 1976.

"Money Creation and the Revenue of the Monetary Authority," in Artis, M. and A.R. Nobay (eds.), *Essays in Economic Analysis, Proceedings of the 1975 AUTE Conference*, Cambridge, Cambridge University Press, 1976.
"Comment on Boyer," in Artis, M. and A.R. Nobay (eds.), *Essays in Economic Analysis, Proceedings of the 1975 AUTE Conference*, Cambridge, Cambridge University Press, 1976.
"Lord Kahn on Monetarism" (letter), *Lloyds Bank Review*, April 1976.
"The Debate on Monetarism" (letter), *Lloyds Bank Review*, October 1976.
"Comment on Sjaastad," in Parkin, J.M. and G. Zis (eds.), *Inflation in the World Economy*, Manchester, Manchester University Press, 1976.
"Inflation and the Market for Owner-Occupied Housing," in D. Laidler (ed.), *Report on the Role of Primary non-Labour Incomes in the Inflationary Process in the United Kingdom*, EEC Commission, Brussels, 1976. (Dutch translation 1978).
"Anti-Inflation Policy: An Alternative to Wage and Price Controls," in J.L. Carr et al., *The Illusion of Wage and Price Control*, Vancouver, British Columbia, The Fraser Institute, 1976.
"Unwinding the Wage and Price Controls," in M. Walker (ed.), *Which Way Ahead?* The Vancouver, British Columbia, Fraser Institute, 1977 (with J.M. Parkin).
"Comments on RBA 76," in *Conference on Applied Economic Research*, Sydney, Reserve Bank of Australia, 1977.
"The Welfare Costs of Inflation in Neoclassical Theory – Some Unsettled Questions," in E. Lundberg (ed.), *Inflation Theory and Anti-Inflation Policy*, London, Macmillan, 1978.
"A Monetarist Viewpoint," in M. Posner (ed.), *Demand Management*, London, Heinemann, NIESR, 1978.
"How to Maintain Stability – a Monetarist View," *The Banker*, April 1978.
"Difficulties with European Monetary Union," in Fratianni, M. and T. Peeters (eds.), *One Money for Europe*, London, Macmillan, 1978.
"Abba P. Lerner," in *International Encyclopedia of the Social Sciences*, Vol. 18 (Biographical Supplement), New York, Macmillan and the Free Press, 1979.
"Recent Canadian Monetary Policy – a Critique," in R. Wirick and D. Purvis (eds.), *Issues in Canadian Public Policy* (II), Kingston, Queen's University (with P.W. Howitt), 1979.
"The Monetary Approach to Exchange Rate Analysis – a Discussion Paper," in L. Meyer (ed.), *Stabilization Policies: Lessons from the 1970s and Implications for the 1980s*, St. Louis, Federal Reserve Bank of St. Louis, Washington University, 1980.
"Comments," in Griffiths, B. and G.E. Wood (eds.), *Monetary Targets*, London, Macmillan, 1981.
"Comments," in D. Crane (ed.), *Beyond the Monetarists*, Ottawa, Canadian Institute for Public Policy, 1981.
"Entrepreneurship and Labour Mobility," in *Growth and Entrepreneurship*, Paris, I.C.C, 1981.
"Tips and Monetarism," *Canadian Taxation*, Summer 1981.
"Botched Monetarism," *Journal of Economic Affairs*, January 1982.
"Politica Monetaria e Rientro dall'Inflazione: Alcune Considerazione," in Spinelli, F. and G. Tullio (eds.), *Contributi al dibattito sull politica monetario e fiscale in Italia*, Milano, Angeli, 1982 (with and translated into Italian by F. Spinelli). English version: "The Role of Money in Controlling Inflation--an Elementary Exposition," in Spinelli, F. and G. Tullio (eds.), *Monetary Policy, Fiscal Policy and Economic Activity*, Gower, 1983.
"The Case for Flexible Exchange Rates in 1980," in Summer, M.T. and G. Zis (eds.), *European Monetary Union: Progress and Prospects*, London, Macmillan, 1982.
"A Small Macro Model of an Open Economy – the Case of Canada," in Claassen, E. and P. Salin (eds.), *Recent Issues in the Theory of Flexible Exchange Rates*, Amsterdam, North Holland, 1982 (with B. Bentley, D. Johnson, and S.T. Johnson).
"Roundtable: Comments," in Federal Reserve Bank of San Francisco *Interest Rate Deregulation and Monetary Policy*, 1983.

"Did Macroeconomics Need the Rational Expectations Revolution?," in Mason, G. (ed.), *Macroeconomics: Theory, Policy and Evidence*, Winnipeg, Institute for Social and Economic Research, University of Manitoba, 1983.

"What Could Reasonably Have Been Expected from Monetarism: An Overview," in The Fraser Institute, *Challenging Complacency*, Focus No. 6, Vancouver, B.C., 1983.

"Rapporteur's Remarks," in Conklin, D.W. and T.J. Courchene (eds.), Deficits: How Big and How Bad?, *Ontario Economic Council Conference Volume*, Toronto, Ontario, 1983.

"Comments on G.H. Moore's Paper," in *Price Level Measurement, Statistics Canada Conference Proceedings*, Ottawa, Ontario, November 1983.

"Comment on R. Gordon's Paper," in *Monetary Targeting and Velocity, Federal Reserve Bank of San Francisco Conference Proceedings*, San Francisco, California, December 1983.

"Comments" (on Beckerman) in A.C. Harberger (ed.), *World Economic Growth*, San Francisco, Institute for Contemporary Studies, 1984.

"Monetary Policy in an Open Economy," *The Economic Review*, March 1985.

"The Monetary Approach and the International Monetary System," in *Champions of Freedom, The Ludwig von Mises Lecture Series*, Vol. 11: *The International Economic Order* Hillsdale Michigan, Hillsdale College Press, 1985.

"Economic Ideas and Social Issues," in D. Laidler (ed.) *Approaches to Economic Well-Being* Vol 26 of Research Studies for the Royal Commission on the Economic Union and Development Prospects for Canada (The Macdonald Commission) Toronto, University of Toronto Press, 1985.

"International Monetary Economics in Theory and Practice," in J. Sargent (ed.) *Post-war Macroeconomic Developments* Vol. 20 of Research Studies for the Royal Commission on the Economic Union and Development Prospects for Canada (The Macdonald Commission) Toronto, University of Toronto Press, 1986.

"Summary Comments on the Symposium," in J. Sargent (ed.) *Foreign Macroeconomic Experience in a Symposium* Vol. 24 of Research Studies for the Royal Commission on the Economic Union and Development Prospects for Canada (The Macdonald Commission) Toronto, University of Toronto Press 1986 (with D.D. Purvis).

"The New Classical Contribution to Macroeconomics," *Banca Nazionale del Lavoro Quarterly Review* 156, March 1986.

"International Monetary Institutions and Deficits," in J. Buchanan, C.K. Rowley, and R.D. Tollison (eds.) *Deficits*, Oxford, Basil Blackwell, 1986.

"The Political Control of Inflation," *Economic Affairs*, February/March 1987.

"Buffer Stock Money and the Transmission Mechanism," *FRB of Atlanta Review*, March/April 1987. (Revised and extended version entitled 'Notes on the Idea of Buffer-Stock Money', in S. Honkapohja and A. Suvanto (eds.) *Raha, Inflaatio, ja Talouspolitiikka* Helsinki (1988).)

"The Bullionist Controversy," in Eatwell, J., M. Milgate and P. Newman (eds.), *The New Palgrave*, London, Macmillan 1987 (reprinted in *The New Palgrave Money*, and in the *New Palgrave Dictionary of Money and Finance*, 1992).

"Henry Thornton," in Eatwell, J., M. Milgate and P. Newman (eds.) *The New Palgrave*, London, Macmillan 1987.

"Walter Boyd," in Eatwell, J., M. Milgate, and P. Newman (eds.) *The New Palgrave*, London, Macmillan 1987.

"Radcliffe, the Quantity Theory and Monetarism," in Cobham, D., R. Harrington and G. Zis (eds.) *Money, Trade and Payments – Essays in Honour of Dennis Coppock*, Manchester, Manchester University Press, 1989.

"The Context of S.C. Tsiang's Monetary Economics," in M. Kohn (ed.), *Finance Constraints and the Theory of Money*, Boston, Academic Press 1989.

"Rapporteur's Remarks," in D. Purvis (ed.) *The Medium Term Macroeconomic Outlook*, Kingston, John Deutsch Centre, Queen's University, 1989.

"Comment on Capie and Wood," in M. Bordo (ed.) *Essays in Honour of Anna J. Schwartz*, Chicago, University of Chicago Press, 1989.

"Monetary Policy," in T. Kierans (ed) *Getting it Right (1990 Policy Review)* Toronto C.D. Howe Institute, 1990.
"The Zero Inflation Target – an Overview of the Economic Issues," in R.G. Lipsey (ed.) *Zero Inflation* Toronto C.D. Howe Institute, 1990.
Mainly Money: The Cause of Canadian Inflation, Toronto, C.D. Howe Institute 1990 (with W.B.P. Robson), pp. 15.
"The Legacy of the Monetarist Controversy" (The 1990 Homer Jones Lecture) FRB of St. Louis *Quarterly Review*, 72(2), March/April (1990), 49–64.
"Alfred Marshall and the Development of Monetary Economics," in J. Whitaker (ed.) *Centenary Essays on Alfred Marshall*, Cambridge, Cambridge University Press, for the Royal Economic Society, 1990 (republished first paperback edition 2005).
The Fix is Out: A Defense of the Floating Canadian Dollar, Toronto, C.D. Howe Institute 1990, (with W.B.P. Robson), pp. 14.
Money after Meech, Toronto, C.D. Howe Institute, 1990, pp. 12.
"Rapporteur's Remarks," in R.C. York (ed), *Taking Aim, the Debate on Zero Inflation* Toronto, C.D. Howe Institute, 1991.
"Comment," in R. Boadway, T.J. Courchene and D.D. Purvis (eds.), *Economic Dimensions of Constitutional Change*, Kingston, John Deutsch Institute, 1991.
"Contributions to Discussion ...," in R. Simeon and M. Janigan (eds.), *Toolkits and Building Blocks: Constructing a New Canada*, Toronto, C.D. Howe Institute, 1991.
Money Talks – So Let's Listen, Toronto, C.D. Howe Institute, 1991, pp. 16 (with W.B.P. Robson).
One Market One Money?, Toronto, C.D. Howe Institute, 1991, pp. 8, also in *Policy Implications of Trade and Currency Zones*, Federal Reserve Bank of Kansas City, 1991.
A Rough Re-entry, Toronto, C.D. Howe Institute, 1991, pp. 7 (with W.B.P. Robson).
"The Austrians and the Stockholm School: Two Failures in the Development of Modern Macroeconomics?," "Comments on Myhrman," "Comments on Hansson," "Contribution to Round Table Discussion on the Stockholm School," all in L. Jonung (ed) *The Stockholm School of Economics Revisited*, Cambridge, Cambridge University Press, 1991.
"Qualms about Inflation Targets," in M.F.J. Prachowny and D.D. Purvis (eds.), *The February 1991 Federal Budget*, Kingston, Ontario, The John Deutsch Institute, 1991.
Wage and Price Stickiness in Macroeconomics – an Historical Perspective (The 13th Henry Thornton Lecture) City University Business School, 20th November, 1991, reprinted in Capie, F. and Wood, G. F. (eds.), *Monetary Economics in the 1990s: The Henry Thornton Lectures, Numbers 9–17*, London, Macmillan, 1996.
"Notes on the Case for Flexible Exchange Rates," in M. Thomas Paul (ed.) *International Monetary, Banking and Trade Systems and Economic Development*, Pune, National Institute of Bank Management, 1992.
"Deflation," "Fiat Money," "Free Banking Theory," "Overissue of Currency," and "Unit of Account," all in J. Eatwell, M. Milgate, and P. Newman (eds.), *The New Palgrave Dictionary of Money and Finance*, London, Macmillan, 1992.
"The Cycle Before New-Classical Economics," in M.T. Belongia and M.R. Garfinkel (eds.), *The Business Cycle: Theories and Evidence*, Boston, Kluwer Academic Publishers, 1992.
"Issues in Contemporary Macroeconomics," in Vercelli, A. and Dimitri, N. (eds.), *Macroeconomics: A Survey of Research Strategies*, Oxford, The Clarendon Press, 1993.
"Was Wicksell a Quantity Theorist?" in Barkai, H., Fischer, S. and Liviatan, N. (eds.), *Monetary Theory and Thought, Essays in Honour of Don Patinkin*, London, Macmillan, 1993.
"Price Stability and the Monetary Order," in Shigehara, K. (ed.), *Price Stabilization in the* 1990s, London, Macmillan, 1993.
Re-entry in Progress, Toronto, C.D. Howe Institute, 1993, pp. 14 (with W.B.P. Robson).
"Commentary" (on Assessing Applied Econometric Research by Carl F. Christ) in Belongia, M.T. (ed.), *Dimensions of Monetary Policy, Essays in Honor of Anatol B. Balbach FRB of St. Louis Review*, March-April, 1993.
"Inflation in the 1990s," *The Global Asset Manager* (Summer 1993), 38–40.

"Monetarism, Microfoundations and the Theory of Monetary Policy," in Frowen, S.F. (ed.) *Monetary Theory and Monetary Policy: New Tracks for the 1990s*, New York, St. Martin's Press, 1993.

The One to Three Percent Solution: Canadian Monetary Policy Under the New Regime, Toronto, C.D. Howe Institute 1994, pp. 12 (with W.B.P. Robson).

The Courage to Act: Fixing Canada's Budget and Social Policy Deficits, Toronto: C.D. Howe Institute, 1994, pp. 28 (with T.E. Kierans, W.B.P. Robson, *et al.*).

"Conference Summary and Wrap Up," in *Bell Canada Papers on Economic Policy 2 1994 Stabilization, Growth, and Distribution: Linkages to the Knowledge Era*, 411–432.

"Hayek on Neutral Money and the Cycle," in M. Colonna and H. Hagemann (eds.), *Money and Business Cycles--The Economics of F.A. Hayek, Vol. 1.* Aldershot, Edward Elgar, 1994.

"Hicks' Later Monetary Thought," in H. Hagemann and O.E. Hamouda (eds.) *The Legacy of Hicks: His Contributions to Economic Analysis.* London, Routledge, 1995.

"Why Do Agents Hold Money – and Why Does It Matter?" in Kevin Hoover and Steven M. Sheffrin (eds.), *Monetarism and the Methodology of Economics, Essays in Honour of Thomas Mayer.* Aldershot, Edward Elgar, 1995.

"Endogenous Buffer-stock Money," in *Credit and Interest Rate Spreads in the Transmission Mechanism*, Bank of Canada, Ottawa, 1995 (with W.B.P. Robson).

Don't Break the Bank: The Role of Monetary Policy in Deficit Reduction. Toronto, C.D. Howe Institute, 1995 pp. 20 with W.B.P. Robson.

Too Much Noise: The Debate on Foreign Exchange Rate Variability and Policies to Control It. Toronto, C.D. Howe Institute 1995, pp. 31 (with M. Chandler).

Devils in the Details: Improving the Tactics of Recent Canadian Monetary Policy. Toronto, C.D. Howe Institute, 1996, pp. 20 (with K. Boessenkool and W.B.P. Robson).

More Money Than is Good for Us: Why the Bank of Canada Should Tighten Monetary Policy. Toronto, C.D. Howe Institute 1997, pp. 16 (with K. Boessenkool and W.B.P. Robson).

"Monetary Policy" and "Brunner, Karl" in Glasner, D. (ed.), *Encyclopedia of Business Cycles.* Garland, 1997.

"A Fiscal-Monetary Mix-up," in Cohen, A. J., Hagemann, H. and Smithin J. (eds.), *Money, Financial Institutions and Macroeconomics.* Boston, Kluwer, 1997.

"The Emergence of the Phillips Curve as a Policy Menu," in Eaton, B.C. and Harris, R. J. (eds.), *Essays in Trade, Technology and Economics in Honour of Richard G. Lipsey*, Cheltenham, UK, Edward Elgar, 1997.

"Inflation Control and Monetary Policy Rules," in Kuroda, I. (ed.), *Towards More Effective Monetary Policy,* London Macmillan, 1997.

Walking the Tightrope; Canada's Financial System between a "Yes" Vote and Quebec Secession: Toronto, C.D.Howe Institute, 1998, pp. 24 (with W.B.P.Robson), repr. In D. Cameron (ed.) *The Referendum Papers: Essays on Secession and National Unity* Toronto, Univ. of Toronto Press, 1999.

Birth of a New Currency: The Policy Outlook after Monetary Union in Europe: Toronto, C.D. Howe Institute 1998 (with F. Poschmann).

"The Wicksell Connection, the Quantity Theory and Keynes," in Streissler E.W. (ed.) *Studien zur Entwicklung der Oekonomischen Theorie XVIII, Knut Wicksell als Oekonom* Berlin, Dunker & Humblot, 1998; revised version "Variations on a Two Interest Rate Theme," in P. Howitt, E. de Antoni, and A. Leijonhufvud (eds.) *Money, Markets and Method-Essays in Honour of Robert W. Clower,* Cheltenham, Edward Elgar, (Spanish translation of revised version "Tres Variaciones del Modelo de Doble Tasa de Interes," *Banco Central del Uruguay Revista de Economia V (Mayo)* 1998).

"Notes on Inflation Targeting," in S. Daniel, P.Arestis, and J. Grahl, (eds.) *Money and Macroeconomic Policy: Essays in Honour of Bernard Corry and Maurice Peston, Vol. 1.* Cheltenham, UK, Edward Elgar, 1999.

"Passive Money, Active Money, and Monetary Policy," *Bank of Canada Review* Summer 1999 (abbreviated version of "The Quantity of Money and Monetary Policy" Bank of Canada *Working Paper* 99–5).

What Do the Fixers Want to Fix? The Debate about Canada's Exchange Rate Regime Toronto C.D.Howe Institute, 1999, pp. 17.
Leaving Well Enough Alone: Canada's Monetary Order in a Changing International Environment Toronto, C.D. Howe Institute, 2000, pp. 26 (with Finn Poschmann).
Highlights of the Bullionist Controversy, Research Report No. 13, Stockholm School of Economics, Institute for Research in Economic History, 2000, pp. 41.
"David Laidler (b.1938)" in R. Backhouse and R. Middleton (eds.) *Exemplary Economists: Vol. 1, North America* Cheltenham, Edward Elgar, 2000 (repr. from *Money and Macroeconomics:The Selected Essays of David Laidler* Cheltenham, Edward Elgar (1997).
"EMU as a Monetary Order" in M. Bordo and L. Jonung *Lessons for EMU from the History of Monetary Unions IEA Readings 50,* London, Institute of Economic Affairs, 2000.
Picking up the Beat: Why the Bank of Canada Should Move to a Fixed Schedule for Monetary Policy Announcements (Backgrounder) Toronto, C. D. Howe Institute, 2000, pp. 6.
It's Time to Ignore Core Inflation (Backgrounder) Toronto, C. D. Howe Institute, 2000, pp.8 (with Shay Aba).
"Discussion 3" in *Money, Monetary Policy and Transmission Mechanisms: Proceedings of a conference held by the Bank of Canada* Ottawa, Bank of Canada, 2000.
The Canadian Dollar: Still a Commodity Currency (Backgrounder) Toronto, C. D, Howe Institute, 2001, pp. 15, (with Shay Aba).
"Comment" (on a paper by R. E. Lucas Jr.) In A Leijonhufvud (ed.) *Monetary Theory as a Basis for Monetary Policy,* Houndmills, UK., Palgrave, in association with the International Economic Association, 2001.
"The Transmission Mechanism with Endogenous Money" in P. Arestis, M. Desai, and S. Dow (eds.) *Money, Macroeconomics and Method - Essays in Honour of Victoria Chick,* London, Routledge, 2002.
Productivity and the Dollar: Commodities and the Exchange Rate Connection (Commentary No. 158) Toronto, C. D. Howe Institute, 2002, pp. 15 (with Shay Aba).
No Small Change: The Awkward Economics and Politics of North American Monetary Integration (Commentary No. 167) Toronto, C. D. Howe Institute 2002, pp. 30 (with W. B. P. Robson).
"Discussant" (of Roger Middleton) Struggling with the Impossible: Sterling, the Balance of Payments and British Economic Policy, 1949–1972 in A. Arnon and W. Young (eds.) *The Open Economy Macromodel: Past, Present and Future,* Boston, Kluwer Academic Publishers, 2002.
No Excuse for Inaction: Inflation, Special Factors and the Case for Raising Interest Rates (Backgrounder No. 71). Toronto, C. D. Howe Institute, 2003, pp.8 (with W. B. P. Robson).
"Quantity Theory of Money" in H. Vane and B. Snowden (eds.) *An Encyclopedia of Macroeconomics,* Cheltenham, Edward Elgar 2003.
"The Role of the History of Economic Thought in Modern Monetary Economics" in P. Mizen (ed.) *Monetary History, Exchange Rates and Financial Markets: Essays in Honour of Charles Goodhart, Volume Two* Cheltenham, Edward Elgar 2003.
The Price Level, Relative Prices and Economic Stability: Aspects of the Inter-war Debate, BIS Working Papers No 136 Basel, September 2003.
Sticking to its Knitting: Why the Bank of Canada Should Focus on Inflation Control, not Financial Stability (Commentary No. 196) Toronto, C. D. Howe Institute, 2004, pp. 18 (Revised version in Spanish ALa estabilidad finaciera como un objectivo de la politica monetaria: una vision esceptica' in *clm economia, Revista Economica Castilla- la Mancha* 3, 2003. 13–36.)
"From Bimetallism to Monetarism: The Shifting Political Affiliation of the Quantity Theory" and "Roundtable Discussion" in I. Barens, V. Caspari and B. Schefold (eds.) *Political Events and Economic Ideas* Cheltenham, Edward Elgar, 2004.
"Monetary Policy without Money: Hamlet without the Ghost," in Bank of Canada *Macroeconomics, Monetary Policy, and Financial Stability: a Festschrift in Honour of Charles Freedman,* Bank of Canada, 2004.

"Incentives Facing Canadian Universities: some Possible Consequences," in Charles Beach, Robin Boadway and Marvin McInnis (eds.) *Higher Education in Canada,* Kingston, Ont. The John Deutsch Institute 2005.

"Towards a Macroprudential Framework – Comment," in Frank Milne and Edwin H. Neave (eds.) *Current Directions in Financial Regulation,* Kingston, Ont. The John Deutsch Institute, 2005.

"Redirecting Rae – Some Proposals for Post-secondary Education in Ontario," Backgrounder #92, Toronto, C. D. Howe Institute, October 2005, pp. 9.

"Free Banking and the Bank of Canada," in *Bank of Canada Review* Winter 2005–2006, 15–24.

"Commentary: Future Trends in Inflation Targeting, comments on Murray," in *Inflation Targeting: Problems and Opportunities: Proceedings of a Conference co-sponsored by the New York Association for Business Economics and the Canadian Consulate General in New York,* Ottawa, Bank of Canada, February 2006.

Three Lectures on Monetary Theory and Policy: Speaking Notes and Background Papers, Working Paper 128, Oesterreiches Nationalbank, Vienna June 2006.

"NAMU and the Neoliberals," *Literary Review of Canada,* June 2006.

"Keynes and the Birth of Modern Macroeconomics" B. Bateman and R. E. Backhouse (eds.) *The Cambridge Companion to Keynes,* Cambridge, Cambridge University Press, 2006.

"Monetary Cooperation in the North American Economy" in J. M. Curtis and A. Sydor (eds.) *NAFTA'10,* Ottawa, Minister of Public Works and Government Services Canada, 2006.

Grasping the Nettles: Clearing the Path to Financial Services Reform in Canada (Commentary No. 238), Toronto, C.D. Howe Institute, 2006, pp. 23.

Evidence to Parliamentary and Congressional Committees

"A Brief Note on Fiscal Policy, Inflation and the Balance of Payments," and Transcript of Oral Evidence in *Ninth Report from the Expenditure Committee, Public Expenditure, Inflation and the Balance of Payments,* London, HMSO, 1975.

"The Finance of Government Expenditure and the Control of the Money Supply," and Transcript of Oral Evidence in *First Report from the Expenditure Committee, 1975-76: The Financing of Public Expenditure,* Vol. II, London, HMSO, 1975.

"Statement," in *Recent Monetary Developments and Future Economic Performance, Hearing Before the Subcommittee on Domestic Monetary Policy of the Committee on Banking, Finance and Urban Affairs, House of Representatives 95th Congress,* Washington, D.C., U.S. Government Printing Office, 1977.

"A Note on Recent Proposals for European Monetary Union," House of Commons Expenditure Committee, London, HMSO, 1979.

"Notes on Monetary Policy, Inflation and the Behaviour of Interest Rates," and Transcript of Oral Evidence in *Minutes of Proceedings and Evidence of the Standing Committee on Finance, Trade and Economic Affairs, First Session of the Forty-First Parliament,* November 27, 1979. House of Commons, Ottawa.

"Notes on Gradualism" and Transcript of Oral Evidence in *Third Report from the Treasury and Civil Service Committee Session 1980-81 Monetary Policy,* Vol. 2, London, HMSO, February 24, 1981.

"Prepared Statement" and "The Case for Gradualism," and Transcript of Oral Evidence in *Monetarism in the United States and the United Kingdom – Hearing Before the Joint Economic Committee of the United States Ninety-Seventh Congress,* U.S. Government Printing Office, Washington, D.C., 1982.

Transcript of Oral Evidence in *Minutes of Proceedings... Thursday May 11, 1989 (Respecting... Annual Report 1988 of the Bank of Canada),* House of Commons, Standing Committee on Finance, Second Session of the 34th Parliament, Ottawa, Supply and Services, 1989.

Transcript of Oral Evidence in *Minutes of Proceedings of the Sub-committee on the Bank of Canada of the Standing Committee on Finance,* December 9, 1991, Third Session of the 34th Parliament, Ottawa, Supply and Services, 1991.
Transcript of Oral Evidence in *Journal des debats* de la Commission d'étude des questions afférentes à l'accession du Québec à la Souveraineté No. 26, 6 Février 1992, Quebec National Assembly.
Transcript of Oral Evidence in *Minutes of Proceedings and Evidence of the Standing Committee on Finance,* issue #59 (Wednesday, October 19, 1994), (*Respecting... Study on the Budgetary Policy* First Session of the 35th Parliament, Ottawa, Public Works and Government Services Canada, 1994.
Transcript of Oral Evidence in *Minutes of Proceedings and Evidence of the Standing Committee on Finance* Issue #96 (Monday, December 5, 1994) (*Respecting... Study on the Budgetary Policy*) First Session of the 35th Parliament, Ottawa, Public Works and Government Services Canada, 1999.

Miscellaneous

Two Recorded Discussions for Audio Learning Ltd., "Monetarism," with J.M. Parkin and "Inequality," with A.B. Atkinson, 1972.
Occasional Articles in the *Guardian, The Manchester Evening News, Financial Post, Toronto Star, Small Business, Globe and Mail, Neu Zürcher Zeitung.*
"Alexander Pope on the Inconvenience of Barter," back cover, *Journal of Political Economy,* August 1977.
"George Bernard Shaw on Rent and Bilateral Monopoly," back cover, *Journal of Political Economy,* December 1978.
"Talking with David Laidler," in Parkin, M. and Bade, R., *Economics: Canada in the Global Environment,* (2nd ed.), Addison Wesley, 1994.
"Interview with David Laidler," in Snowden, B., Vane, H., and Wynarczyk, P., *A Modern Guide to Macroeconomics,* Edward Elgar, 1996.
"We Were All Keynesians Then," back cover, *Journal of Political Economy,* October 1996.
"Foreword" to *The Thiessen Lectures: Lectures delivered by Gordon G. Thiessen, Governor of the Bank of Canada 1994–2001* Ottawa, Bank of Canada, 2001, i–iv.
"Foreword" to Pepper G. T. and Oliver M. J. *Monetarism under Thatcher: Lessons for the Future* Cheltenham UK, Edward Elgar, 2001, x–xiii.

Book Reviews

Canadian Journal of Economics, Economica, Economic Journal, Econometrica, Journal of Economic History, Journal of Economic Literature, Journal of International Economics, Journal of Money, Credit and Banking, Journal of Political Economy, The Manchester School, Financial Times, Times Literary Supplement, Wall Street Journal, European Journal of the History of Economic Thought, History of Political Economy, Economic Record.

Forthcoming Publications and Articles under Consideration

"Chicago Monetary Traditions," *Elgar Companion to the Chicago School.*
"The Lender of Last Resort: Trendy or Passe?" *Proceedings of National Bank of Poland Conference* (forthcoming).
"Keynesian Revolution," in *The New Palgrave,* 2nd *ed.*
"Monetary Policy and its Theoretical Foundations."
"Milton Friedman and the Evolution of Monetary Economics."
"Axel Leijonhufvud" and the Quest for the Microfoundations of Macroeconomics: Some Reflections.

Unpublished Work

"Some Reflections on the Testing of Economic Theories," 1961.
"The Permanent Income Hypothesis and the Demand for Money – a Note," 1964.
"The Demand for Money," Committee on Econometrics and Mathematical Economics, Institute of Business and Economic Research, University of California at Berkeley. Working Paper No. 56, December 1964.
"The Results and Implications of Recent Empirical Work on the Aggregate Demand for Money Function in the United States," 1966.
"The Phillips Relationship – Some Empirical Evidence," 1968 (with B.A. Corry).
"Stocks, Flows, and the Real Balance Effect – a Note," 1969.
"Wealth Effects, Substitution Effects and Interest Payments in the Analysis of Monetary Disequilibrium," 1969.
"A Note on the Role of Money in Keynesian and Friedmanian Models," 1969.
"A Keynesian View of the Relationship Between Accumulation, Money and the Money Wage Rate – Comment," 1969.
"Monetarism and Anti-Monetarism – a Comment," 1970.
"Wicksell's Cumulative Process – a Pedagogic Note," 1970 (with J.M. Parkin).
"Price Level Dynamics in a Hicks-Hansen Framework – Some Analytic Results," 1971.
"Monetarist Models of Inflation in Closed and Open Economies," 1972.
"Notes on Housing," 1972.
Lecture Notes on Macroeconomics (Term 1 of a 2 term course.) M.Sc. (Econ.), (L.S.E.) and M.A. (Manchester), 1972.
"Money and Inflation – the Monetarist View of the Transmission Process," 1974.
"Draft Chapter on Inflation and Output Fluctuations," 1975.
"The Exchange Rate Regime and the Conduct of Anti-Inflation Policy," 1976.
"Comment on Mussa," 1977.
"Notes on the Use of Optimal Control Theory in the Design of Macroeconomic Policy" (Memorandum Submitted to the Committee of Inquiry on Policy Optimization), 1978.
"Notes on the Role of the Output Gap and its Rate of Change in an Equilibrium Aggregate Supply Curve Formulation of the Inflation Equation," 1978.
"Notes for Introductory Remarks on the The Efficiency of National Anti-Inflation Policies," September 1979.
"Notes on Anti-Inflation Policy in an Open Economy."
"Mrs. Thatcher's Economic Policies – What Monetarist Experiment?," 1981.
"Text of Lecture" (On Macroeconomics and Financial Markets), given at Anahuac University, Mexico, D.F. Mexico, 1981.
"Notes on the Role of Gold in the International Monetary System," 1982.
"Assertions About Monetary Policy," Paper for Discussion by the E.A.P. of the Minister of Finance, 1983.
"Setting the Agenda – Keynote Address," for Macdonald Commission Seminar, 1983.
"Notes on Peru's Monetary Planning Framework," 1985.
"The Debt and the Deficit in Canada – Notes for a Panel Discussion," *Proceedings of McGill Conference on Debt and Deficits.*
"Comment on Sjaastad," *Proceedings of McGill Conference on Debt and Deficits.*
"Canada's Price Stability Experiment," paper presented at the 1992 Conference of the Association for Canadian Studies in Australia and New Zealand (with W.B.P. Robson) 1992.
"Notes on Pierre Fortin's Diversified Strategy for Deficit Control," for House of Commons Standing Committee on Finance, 1994.
"American Macroeconomics Between World War I and The Depression," Centre for Economic Studies, University of Munich, Working Paper 113, 1996.
"The Quantity of Money and Monetary Policy," Bank of Canada Working Paper 99–5, April 1999.

"The Exchange Rate Regime and Canada's Monetary Order," Bank of Canada Working Paper 99–7, March 1999.
"What Economists Know about Canada's Exchange Rate," Political Economy Research Group, University of Western Ontario, 1999.
"Getting on with Economics" (Acceptance Speech for the Hellmuth Prize Ceremony, University of Western Ontario, 1999).
"Introductory Remarks for the Finance Committee's Budget 2000 Economic Roundtable," University of Western Ontario 1999.
"Notes on the 2001 Budget, Prepared for Consideration by the House of Commons Standing Committee on Finance," University of Western Ontario, 2000.
"Notes for the Standing Committee on Finance," University of Western Ontario, 2001.
"Further Notes for the Standing Committee on Finance," University of Western Ontario, 2001.
"The Monetary Order and Canada's Prosperity" (Submission to the House of Commons Standing Committee on Finance) University of Western Ontario, 2002.
"Canada's Universities: Policies for the Next Decade" (report prepared for HRDC) 2004.
"The Precarious Place of Money in Mainstream Macroeconomics," 2004.

2
David Laidler's Contributions

Charles Goodhart and J. Clark Leith

Charles Goodhart

This has been a great conference, for which we need to thank the main organizers, James Davies and Robert Leeson. Tonight let me welcome you, David, into the ranks of us emeritus professors. I had always loosely translated 'emeritus' as being without much (continuing) merit, but that is far from the case in your instance.

One of the great advantages of being a historically rather than a mathematically based economist is that, like wine, you mature with age. Indeed, in your case the number and even the quality of your publications and your age seem to be positively correlated. On this trend, when you become a centenarian you will be simultaneously the most published economist in the world, just pipping Mike Bordo for the title. But perhaps like the US Current Account Deficit, this may be an unsustainable trend. I would, however, be prepared to bet which trend will reverse soonest. As you will soon discover in retirement, you do much the same work as before. The only difference is that you do not get paid for it.

Before coming to this conference I had the pleasure of reading a small selection of your recent papers. Both the quality and quantity of your work continue as strong as ever. You are the doyen historian of macro/monetary thought. Long may that continue.

But your current written work and your manifold abilities are as well, or better, known to your many friends and colleagues here as to me, since you chose to live amongst them in North America when you came over here to Ontario in 1975. My one comparative advantage is that I knew David early on, perhaps earlier than almost anyone else here, when he was a young economist in the UK, at Essex and then Manchester, though he had already left LSE by the time that I arrived there. He always had the qualities of scholarship, excellent clear writing, sage wisdom and balanced judgement (most of the time) that he shows even more clearly today. But to those qualities he then added the enthusiasm of a revolutionary. He wanted to overturn the conventional, bastard Keynesian analysis of cost-push inflation, then dominant in the UK, with the fresh new doctrine of monetarism, absorbed at Chicago, to some large extent from Harry Johnson, a large figure in every sense of the word in the pantheon of great Canadian economists.

Anyway, one of David's best known earlier studies, alongside his early (1969) textbook on *The Demand for Money*, was his survey article on inflation, co-authored with Mike Parkin, published in the *Economic Journal* in 1975, but largely written several years before. In this paper he bearded the Keynesian establishment in their central lair and fortress at the Cambridge faculty of Economics. Not surprisingly perhaps, this paper caused its young authors all kinds of trouble and strife, and ended up being more about labour markets and a frontal assault on cost-push theories than about the transmission mechanisms of monetary policy.

Those years were not good ones for academic economics in the UK. In several, far too many, universities Marxist economists got such a strong foothold that the faculties became virtually divided in two. That was part of the background to David's decision to leave the UK for a more attractive location, here. In fact a lot of UK residents were getting equally fed up with the Socialist status quo. We could not all emigrate, but we could at least vote for a quite revolutionary alternative in Mrs T. I have often wondered whether you might have played a significant role in advising the Thatcher government if you had stayed on in Britain. In practice we were pretty well served by Terry Burns, Alan Budd and Alan Walters (who is, alas, now seriously suffering with Parkinson's), but we might have done even better with you on board too.

But enough of the past, though it is perhaps becoming my comparative advantage. I was asked to consider your role in the global context, beyond your Canadian, and North American, domicile. This is fortunately easy enough. You have increasingly carved out a major role as the premier historian of economic thought in the monetary/macro field, ranging all the way from the early 19th century to today. If future generations want to know the interrelationships between the various monetary schools of thought, it is to Laidler that they will turn first and foremost. David, we salute you.

J. Clark Leith

David Laidler came to the University of Western Ontario in the midst of the era of Pierre Trudeau, the Canadian prime minister who pointedly asked for a one-handed economist, not one who would always add 'on the other hand'. And when David came to Western, that is what we got – a one-handed economist.

The UWO Economics Department in the early 1970s had a small core of senior people – Ron Wonnacot, Tom Courchene and Jim Melvin. Grant Reuber was Dean, and I was Chairman. Our most pressing need was to recruit senior people. We filled the gap by bringing in distinguished scholars for lengthy visits. Harry Johnson and Don Patinkin were among the regular fixtures.

Our horizon was the world beyond London Ontario and Canada. Workshop visitors from the world beyond would typically spend several days. Some that I recall from that era were Jagdish Bhagwati, Dick Caves, Bob Clower, Al Harberger, Egon Sohmen and, to give this anglophone community a glimpse of the new reality in Quebec, we had Jacques Parizeau. Each one, in his own way, forced us to think outside our own little box, which was why we wanted them to come.

Another prominent workshop visitor in that mould was David Laidler, then a promising young professor at Manchester. Our courtship of David (and his wife Antje) started on that first visit in the spring of 1973 and then continued over many months until his arrival at Western in 1975.

David's appointment at Western proved to be a superb match. His razor-sharp mind, and knowledge of the literature in all its dimensions (not just the latest fad in North America), interacted well with rising younger faculty such as Peter Howitt, and promising graduate students such as Roger Farmer, Tiff Macklem, Angela Reddish and Nick Rowe, as well as Michael Parkin whom we were able to recruit that same year. He also proved decisive in helping to recruit bright new faculty such as John Whalley.

Throughout his career at Western, David's firm commitment to scholarship helped both the Department and the University fix high academic standards as the institutional norm. The University celebrated his achievements in research with the award of its Hellmuth Prize, while nationally he was inducted as a Fellow of the Royal Society of Canada. Within the discipline of Economics David served as President of the Canadian Economics Association, and won the CEA's Purvis Prize (jointly with Bill Robson) for significant work on Canadian economic policy.

David was not content to confine his attention to the ivory tower. His energy and enthusiasm, as well as his pocketbook, contributed significantly to the musical and visual arts scenes both in London Ontario and in Toronto.

David became an important contributor to the Canadian policy debates. This was recognized most recently by the award of the Donner Prize to David, together with Bill Robson, for the best book of the year on Canadian public policy.

Pierre Trudeau's quest for guidance by a one-handed economist has been more than fulfilled. Today, long after Trudeau has passed from the scene, David continues to provide important insight both to the discipline of economics and to public policy in his adopted country.

3
David Laidler on Monetarism

Michael Bordo and Anna J. Schwartz

Introduction

David Laidler has always been a monetarist and was an important player in the debates marking the rise and fall of that doctrine. The literature on the demand for money was the focus of his primary contribution. He did pioneering work on the long-run demand for money function in the mid-1960s. In the four editions of his *The Demand for Money* from 1969 until 1993 he acted as the major-domo of the literature. Indeed his work was at the heart of the discussions over the long-run and short-run demand for money function, the stability of money demand, the missing money conundrum, the buffer stock approach, and the resurrection of long-run money demand. He also worked energetically in the 1960s, '70s and '80s on the key monetarist theoretical issues of the transmission mechanism of monetary policy, the shortcomings of the IS-LM model, the short-run and long-run Phillips curve, and the monetary approach to the balance of payments.

In addition to his work in monetary and macro theory and the econometric evidence, Laidler had important insights in monetary policy. His views evolved from strong advocacy of Friedman's 1960 constant growth rate rule (CGR) in the 1960s, to advocacy of monetary targeting and the case for gradualism in the 1970s; in the '80s, he supported the case for constrained discretion, in the '90s, the case for central bank independence and inflation targeting, and today, supports the case for putting M back into monetary policy. In the rest of the essay we review David Laidler's work on each of the above topics.

The Demand For Money and the Quantity Theory of Money

Much of David Laidler's early work was based on Milton Friedman's modern quantity theory of money (MQT) (Friedman, 1956). According to the MQT, nominal income and the price level were determined by the interaction of money supply and money demand. Money supply was assumed to be determined by the exogenous forces of the monetary standard, monetary authority actions, and the banking system. Money demand – the community's desired holdings of real cash balances – was posited a stable function of a limited number of important economic variables including a scale variable (permanent real income or wealth), several rates of return including the yields on securities (both long and short run), the own return on money and the return from goods and services (the expected rate of inflation). Given a stable demand function, changes in nominal income are determined by changes in the quantity of money. In the short run, in the face of nominal rigidities, change in money impacts real output, in the long run changes in money are fully reflected in changes in the price level.

Friedman viewed money as a durable good yielding a flow of services over time. According to Laidler (1982) Friedman's approach differed markedly from the prevailing Keynesian view which emphasized the motives for holding money. Friedman changed the question from "why money is held" to "given that money is held," "what are its empirical determinants."[1] This led to an enormous body of research beginning with Friedman (1959) estimating the parameters of a stable money demand function.

Laidler's research in the 1960s was at the heart of this investigation (Laidler, 1966*a*, 1966*b*). He extended Friedman's original money demand function which found a stable long-run relationship between real cash balances and permanent income,[2] and Latané's work (1954) which found an inverse relationship between money balances and the long-term interest rate to produce a stable long-run relationship for seven decades between real money balances, permanent income and both short-term and long-term interest rates for the US.[3] Laidler also was involved in the controversy over the short-run demand for money function which raged in the 1960s and '70s. Friedman's money demand function was postulated as a long-run equilibrium relationship in which agents' desired holdings of real cash balances equaled their actual holdings. Chow (1966) and others introduced a variant concept of short-run money demand according to which it may be costly for agents to adjust their desired money holdings to changes in the money stock or to changes in the arguments of money demand. Chow's specification involved adding a lagged real balance term to the long-run money demand function. By so doing, one could estimate the speed of adjustment between the short run and long run.

The short-run version of the demand for money function was used by many advanced country central banks as a key component in their monetary policy strategies beginning in the early 1970s. However, as early as 1973 Goldfeld presented evidence showing instability in the short-run money demand function used by the Fed. This finding as well as others by him – for example, "The Case of the Missing Money" (1976) surveyed in Laidler (1980) – was used to make the case against the monetarist approach to targeting monetary aggregates. Laidler in a number of publications (Laidler, 1980, 1982, 1984) emphasized that the problems with money demand were largely problems with the short-run adjustment mechanism.[4]

Laidler (1984, 1990*b*) posited an alternative approach to modeling short-run money demand based on the precautionary motive for holding money. He argued that in the short run agents could be viewed as being off their long-run demand curves and cash balances could be viewed as a buffer stock which agents held while the price level and the other arguments of money demand adjust. Evidence by Hendry and others (1991), who used cointegration techniques to isolate long-run equilibrium relationships between real balances and real income and interest rates, and an error correction technique to ascertain the temporal adjustment speeds of these variables, provided support for his view.

The Transmission Mechanism on the Links Between Money and Nominal Income

David Laidler studied transmission mechanisms to learn why changes in the quantity of money were mirrored in changes in nominal income, and to determine how the change in nominal income was divided between change in the price level and change in real income. How did the behavior of firms and households respond to changes in the quantity of money? Laidler's views at the time, in the 1970s and '80s, were allied to those of Brunner and Meltzer, Friedman, and Phelps rather than to the views of those identified with Keynesian perspectives. He was a consistent critic of models, including multiequation econometric models current at various points in time.

Laidler (1978, 1982) reported on work on the transmission mechanism in terms of one variation or another on the IS-LM model. The model was concerned with the determination of aggregate demand.

Laidler observed that the proposition that the structure of the economy is independent of the policy adopted has been challenged, but the proposition is a basic premise of research on the transmission mechanism.

Laidler turned to the discussion of money, first omitting quantitative significance of its effects. Firms and households hold various assets, one of which is money whose services yield diminishing marginal utility or product. In an economy initially in asset equilibrium, an increase in the quantity of money disequilibrates the structure of asset holding because the implicit yield on money declines. Substitution from money to other assets takes place, driving down their rates of return. Some rates of return are observable, others are implicit, such as rates of return on consumer durables.

Laidler then described the generally accepted version of the first stage of the transmission process. A general fall in rates of return is an increase in the present value of the income stream yielded by existing assets and thus a rise in their market values relative to the supply price of newly produced assets. This disequilibrium elicits an increase in output of durables, both consumer and producer. In addition, the price of current consumption in terms of future consumption foregone falls, so expenditure on non-durables may also increase. In an IS-LM model, the effects on whatever the category of expenditure are amplified by a multiplier process that is partially offset by subsequent interest rate responses.

There is disagreement about the quantitative significance of the expenditure effects of the transmission process. In the 1950s and 1960s, the interest sensitivity of investment as the key to the transmission mechanism was a generally accepted view that has since receded, although some British economists in 1980 still regarded it as the critical link.

Large-scale econometric models have frequently omitted monetary variables from expenditure functions with the exception of firms' investment decisions, narrowing the channels they investigate. They discover only weak links between money and economic activity.

Laidler (1982, 115–117) summarized studies using different statistical methodologies on the money-income relationship, concluding that a clear-cut correlation is easier to find for the US than for Canada or Britain, but an IS-LM type of transmission mechanism is as hard to pin down for the US as for others. He commented on studies of the importance of monetary factors in influencing business investment in fixed plant and equipment that show investment responds to interest variations. These studies have flaws, according to critics.

Laidler ended his commentary on various approaches to linking money or interest rates to expenditure in different countries in the three decades since the 1950s by listing three shortcomings of the IS-LM model: (i) It does not deal adequately with the division of nominal income between real income and prices; (ii) It ignores linkages between the government budget and the behavior of the money supply; (iii) It is a model of a closed economy. These shortcomings cast doubt about the evidence that he had thus far considered about the transmission mechanism.

Continuing his discussion of the IS-LM model, Laidler added that it holds the price level constant, and determines the level of real income. In adapting it to the determination of nominal income, a common practice has been to replace real variables with nominal ones, on the assumption that the way in which variations in the quantity of money affect nominal income is independent of the breakdown of changes in nominal income between changes in prices and changes in real income.

In fact, however, how much nominal income will change in response to a given change in the quantity of money depends upon how much of that change occurs in real income and how much in the price level. This implies that the mechanisms that determine the interaction of prices and output must be an integral part of the transmission mechanism which links the quantity of money to nominal income (Laidler, 1982, 150). A more fundamental reason for regarding price and output interaction as part of the transmission mechanism arises from analysis of the rational expectations hypothesis, discussed by Laidler at a later point.

The expectations augmented Phillips curve has become the centerpiece of models dealing with price and output interaction. In the literature there are two alternative accounts. One interprets the relationship in equilibrium terms, the other in disequilibrium terms. Laidler finds the idea of a transmission mechanism hard to square with the equilibrium interpretation of the curve, originally proposed by Irving Fisher in 1926, and adopted by Lucas, Sargent, and Barro, in Laidler's description, as the neo-Austrian approach to macroeconomics. If market clearing prices were always determined by the intersection of aggregate demand and aggregate supply curves, it would be impossible for discrepancies between demand and supply prices to occur and portfolio disequilibria underlying the aggregate demand side would not arise. The transmission mechanism would be that of Walrasian general equilibrium economics. Therefore, some degree of price stickiness is required to prevent markets clearing and to set a disequilibrium transmission mechanism to work. Laidler adds that it cannot be claimed that this interpretation has well-established micro foundations, but it has the advantage of treating prices as being set by firms rather than by markets dominated by specialist price setters (Laidler, 1988).

Each firm in the economy forms an expectation of the price it must charge to maintain constant its real level of sales. Suppose each firm sets its actual price above or below that level depending on whether it wants to contract or increase its level of sales. For the economy as a whole some level of output and sales exists at which the number of firms that want to expand just equals the number that want to contract. At that output level the general price level index resulting from the individual firms' price-setting behavior will equal an index of prices they expected would keep their sales constant. If output and sales exceed this level, there will be a preponderance of firms wanting to contract, so the actual price level will be above the expected price level.

An increase in the quantity of money leads to an increase in demand for goods and services at any price level. The increased demand, amplified by a multiplier process, leads to a higher level of real output and real sales. The number of firms wanting to contract increases. They face quantity disequilibria. As these firms revise upward the prices they set for their individual products, the price level will rise relative to its expected level.

An alternative description of this process is the response to a higher than equilibrium quantity of money. It causes attempts to substitute other assets and current consumption for money. This behavior by households increases firm sales. If output does not immediately increase, inventories decline, firm holdings of money and trade credit rise. The firm increases prices as an integral part of its response to the asset disequilibrium.

Laidler (1975*b*) reviewed research on interaction of money wages and unemployment, early research treating the supply of labor and employment as a positive function of the difference between actual and expected level of money wages. Expected money wages depend on expectations about the price level and labor productivity, all unemployment on this approach being of the voluntary search type. Phelps' (1968) original account of money wage unemployment interaction has firms forming expectations about the level of money wages that will maintain constant employment, setting wages above or below that level depending on whether they want to expand or contract their labor force. A natural level of search unemployment emerges in which there is equality between expected and actual wages on both sides of the market. In Phelps' early work (1968), unemployment varies as a result of voluntary quits. In his later work, this is no longer the case, as money wages are tied down by long-term contracts (Phelps and Taylor, 1977).

In Mussa's research (1976), the number of employees and man hours worked per employee are variables, chosen by the firm along with wages, rather than responses by the supply of labor to wages set by the firm. Laidler found this approach a complement to the contracts literature as a basis for generating wage and price rigidity to permit deviations of unemployment from the natural level to be interpreted as involuntary. That condition would arise from rational behavior, not in the face of arbitrary wage rigidity, but in the face of a failure of wages to fall fast enough to keep the labor market cleared, when adjustment costs and other factors make it rational for agents to set wages by contract for extended periods (Laidler, 1975*b*, 1978, 1990*b*).

Laidler (1975*a*, 1975*b*) then proceeded to replace the constant expected price level implicit in the IS-LM model with inflationary expectations as proximate determinants of the behavior of prices. He traced the consequences of an increase in the monetary expansion rate occurring when the economy is initially in a full equilibrium situation. He first attributed the formation of expectations of inflation to observation of the time path of actual inflation and extrapolating from it in such a way as to ensure that, if a constant inflation rate persists over time, the expected inflation rate will come into equality with it.

If an increase in the rate of expansion of the money supply exceeds that necessary to validate anticipated inflation, it will lead to a build-up of real money balances whose implicit rate of return will begin to fall relative to that on other assets. A process of substitution into other assets and into current consumption will be set in motion, with interest rates, both observable and unobservable, falling. The increase in current production that ensues will set in motion a multiplier process.

As production and employment increase, firms tend to raise their prices, and money wages rise to levels in excess of the values these variables were initially expected to take. This involves an increase in the actual inflation rate relative to the expected rate. In time, the actual inflation rate influences the expected rate, so the latter also begins to rise. Two interrelated effects on variables involved in the transmission mechanism follow. One is upward pressure on the rates of interest that assets denominated in nominal terms bear; the other is an increase in the opportunity cost of holding money. This accentuates the portfolio disequilibrium which sets going the first stage of the transmission mechanism. It also accelerates further the inflation rate through its effect on price-setting behavior. The process is stable and the new equilibrium to which the economy will eventually move and the path by which it is reached can be described, as Laidler does.

At the new equilibrium, like the initial one, the economy will operate with output not at its natural level. The expected rate of inflation will be higher, so the quantity of real balances held by the public will be smaller. If money is not super-neutral, that is, the natural output level is not independent of the inflation rate, real rates might be either higher or lower. In either event, a higher and more rapidly rising volume of nominal expenditure would be accompanied by higher nominal interest rates. During the transition to lower real balances, the rate of inflation must exceed the rate of monetary expansion and might follow a cyclical path. If nominal interest rates at first fall but end up higher than initially, they must on average rise during the transition.

Laidler (1975*a*) defended the propositions of the economy's new equilibrium as supported by empirical evidence. The assumption that the principal determinant of the expected inflation rate is the actual inflation rate has been challenged by the rational expectations approach. It argues that rational economic agents will not make systematic errors. They will act as if they form their expectations about the inflation rate by using the forecast that would be yielded by a correct model of the economy in which they are operating and as if they expected every other agent in the economy to form his or her expectations the same way.

The approach downplays the point that gathering and processing information is costly; and many agents might not find it worthwhile to compute the optimal forecast of the inflation rate. Agents are not automatically endowed with knowledge of the economy's structure, so learning about it must be an ongoing process. If agents are bound by long-term contracts, they will be unable to act on new information; however, it affects their view of the future. To act upon the expectation of the inflation rate and anticipate the behavior of the inflation rate is not easy.

Laidler added that under rational anticipations, any change in the monetary expansion rate, unaccompanied by an appropriate step change in the level of the money supply, will lead to an instantaneously explosive inflation or deflation unless the money market is cleared by an instantaneous and unforeseen step change in the price level before those anticipations become effective. Otherwise, as soon as it is known that the rate of monetary expansion is about to change, agents must recognize, not only that the long-run equilibrium has increased, but also that, in the absence of a step fall in the money supply, the economy must move to the higher price level associated with an increased velocity of circulation. The latter change, if it is foreseen, involves a step jump in the price level and hence an infinite rate of inflation for an instant. Rational agents would flee from money and generate an explosion in the price level. This problem turns up only in an extreme form of rational expectations.

Laidler (1982, 134–135) proposed a looser version of the hypothesis that would recognize that agents' knowledge of the way in which the economy works is imperfect, that data on the behavior of particular variables is expensive to generate and process, and that changed expectations do not lead immediately to changes in activity. The looser form would insist that in order to generate a more accurate forecast of the behavior of inflation than could be had simply by extrapolating from past data on that variable, and to do so at a cost which makes the exercise efficient. For some agents at least, it is possible to use extraneous information on the money supply and to act upon that forecast.

If the rate of monetary expansion increased and this led some firms to expect an increase in the inflation rate, they would increase prices of their output at a more rapid pace, without any intervening chain of asset disequilibrium or output change being necessary to prompt such behavior. The transmission mechanism operating through portfolio disequilibrium and output changes would never be called into play, and monetary policy would have no short-run real effects. These propositions follow from the extreme form of rational expectations Even if only some agents act upon rational expectations, their activities imply the existence of yet another channel whereby monetary changes affect nominal income and expenditure, one which operates directly through expectations and their influence on price behavior.

The rational expectations hypothesis is destructive for the analysis of the transmission mechanism as operating through the chain of asset disequilibrium and output changes. This is an important implication of the work of Sargent and Wallace and of Lucas.

Rational expectations makes it possible for variations in the quantity of money to directly affect nominal income, specifically prices, without generating evidence that expenditure decisions are sensitive to variations in interest rates or any other relative prices. Such linkages come into play and are observable when the consequences of monetary change are not fully anticipated by agents.

The division of nominal income between the price level and real income in terms of the expectations augmented Phillips curve

Monetarists attribute most of the variations in nominal income due to variations in the quantity of money to fall primarily on prices rather than real income. The Phillips curve in its augmented form, Friedman (1970, 221) stated, provided "the missing equation" in the monetarist model of inflation. The British view in 1970 of the determination of the price level was that exogenous factors accounted for it, and monetary policies, if they affected nominal income, would change real income (Laidler, 1982, 127–129). Monetarists argued that inflation, relative to expectations, would be low in recessions and high in good times. The coefficient on expected inflation would be equal to unity and an error learning process would lead to the formation of expectations. Any constant actual inflation would come to be fully anticipated.

Laidler (1975*a*) concluded that it is generally accepted that inflation varies with the level of aggregate demand, and that there has been a swing to the monetarist view that in the long run there is no significant inflation-output trade-off. He found substantial disagreement on the question of how long it takes for the economy to converge to the long-run solution. He believes monetarists are now willing to agree that exogenous variables affect the behavior of the price level temporarily, while monetary factors determine long-term trends and Keynesians are now willing to agree that monetary factors determine long-run price trends, but still stress the short-run importance of exogenous variables.

Laidler sees rapprochement between monetarists and Keynesians on the empirical properties of the Phillips curve but not on its theoretical basis. On the one hand, a view on inflation–unemployment interaction expressed by Phelps and Friedman stressed that disequilibrium in the labor market might affect real wages instead of nominal wages, and what might be critical to nominal wages would be what was happening to the general price level. On the other hand, there is a view of the augmented Phillips curve as an aggregate supply curve, an interpretation which Irving Fisher had adopted earlier.

Laidler (1982, 6) noted that the aggregate supply view of the Phillips curve raises issues that are not considered in the traditional monetarist subject matter. If the Phillips curve is an aggregate supply curve, that amounts to saying fluctuations in output and unemployment are voluntary choices of individuals who make expectational errors about prices in markets which are continually clearing. Deviations of output and employment from the levels they would attain were expectations correct, Laidler agrees is a serious problem but he rejects Willem Buiter's (1980) representation of this theory of unemployment as "The Macroeconomics of Dr. Pangloss" (Laidler, 1982, 17). In the aggregate supply curve approach, unemployment occurs not because markets fail to bring together all willing buyers and sellers in mutually satisfactory trades, but because markets and other institutions fail to provide enough information to generate accurate expectations on which trades are based. This makes the Rational Expectations Hypothesis an obvious complement to the aggregate supply curve interpretation of the Phillips curve. Agents have an incentive to use all available information in forming expectations to avoid making systematic errors.

Laidler says if individuals then make only random errors, and yet markets clear, two questions arise. One is why a predominant number of agents in the economy are in error in one direction, so that aggregate output and employment deviate from their natural rates. Another is why do fluctuations in output and employment observed in an actual economy display a pattern of serial correlation characterizing the business cycle?

An answer to the questions has been provided by Robert Lucas, Thomas Sargent and associates. The answer is a theory of the business cycle that derives from the Austrian business cycle theory of the interwar period proposed by Hayek and von Mises, based on the idea that all market phenomena are the outcome of voluntary choices of maximizing individuals. Lucas et al. have gone further than their Austrian predecessors by postulating that output, employment and prices fluctuate as a result of voluntary choice in markets that always clear. Laidler (1982, 76) admires the theory but denies its basic assumption that all markets always clear, in particular markets for many components of final output and, above all, the labor market. For the neo-Austrians, all unemployment is voluntary. For other macroeconomists, some unemployment is involuntary (Laidler, 1990*a*).

Laidler argues that the non-clearing market approach to the analysis of inflation–unemployment interaction does not conflict with the notion of rational expectations if the concept is interpreted as influences on expectations other than quantity signals, such as observations on the past behavior of the money supply as providing information on the way to set prices, or in an open economy, prices ruling elsewhere, or variations in exchange rates.

What the non-clearing approach needs to explain, however, is why there is not immediate adjustment of prices to a market-clearing level in response to output signals in a conventional transmission mechanism between money and aggregate demand. The reason for the tendency to under-react to quantity signals, Laidler states, is the time it takes for agents to determine whether a shock that gave rise to the signal is transitory or persistent. In addition, the existence of contracts prevents variation of wages and prices, and lengthens the response to quantity signals.

The debate on whether markets always clear or do not, according to Laidler, is not another round in the controversy between monetarists and their opponents. Agreement was much closer between them by 1980, when he was writing, than earlier on the stability of the demand for money function and about the empirics of output–inflation interaction. What still divides the two camps, as it did in the 1960s, is opinion on the proper conduct of macroeconomic policy, about which discussion by Laidler is introduced after consideration of monetarism and the open economy (Laidler, 1982, 34–35).

The Monetary Approach to the Balance of Payments and Exchange Rate Analysis

Monetarism became important outside the US, not least in Britain, in alliance with the monetary approach to the balance of payments, whose advocates postulated the existence of a stable demand for money function as an empirical hypothesis, transforming the approach from an accounting framework into a body of substantive theory. Initially, advocates anchored the real income argument of the function by assuming full employment, but soon replaced this assumption with an expectations augmented Phillips curve analysis of price–output interaction. The monetary approach provided the means whereby monetarist hypotheses were made relevant to economies other than that of the US, which, under the Bretton Woods system approximated a closed economy.

Until 1971 in any country other than the US, the arguments of a stable demand for money function were beyond the direct control of the domestic authorities, so money supply was an endogenous variable that had to adjust to the demand for money. This means that in the UK in the 1950s and 1960s, causation ran from nominal income to money, rather than the reverse. This did not embarrass monetarists, provided they attributed most of the changes in nominal income over that period to causes originating abroad. Although the augmented Phillips curve teaches that there is no stable long-run inverse trade-off between inflation and unemployment, in post-war UK the data displayed such a relationship down to 1967.

The monetary approach provided two reasons for the UK experience. One was that in a fixed exchange rate system, prices of tradable goods sold domestically, in the long run were determined on world markets. The domestic price level, therefore, in the long run behaved in line with prices in the world at large. Expectations by agents would incorporate this behavior. World prices were relatively stable until the late 1960s, and so were inflation expectations. Because the expectations term in the augmented Phillips curve equation will be an exogenous constant or time trend, the data will exhibit a stable and persistent inflation–unemployment trade-off.

Laidler reported two opposing views on UK stop–go in the 1950s and 1960s and subsequent deterioration of the economy's performance. Keynesians assumed that under the Bretton Woods system, the UK's high marginal propensity to import, in conditions promoting high capital utilization, produced a low and acceptable inflation rate but balance of payments pressure forced a policy reversal. The monetarist opposing view on stop–go was that high rates of domestic credit expansion that accompanied high levels of demand, under fixed exchange rates, resulted in balance of payments problems as an alternative to inflationary pressure (Laidler, 1981, 1985).

The Keynesian solution was that depreciation of the currency that adopting flexible exchange rates would permit, would offset balance of payments effects of a high propensity to import, so that the economy could operate at a higher level of capacity to achieve rapid growth without the constraint of the balance of payments. What undermined this promising strategy in their view was exogenous shocks and trade union activism in the 1970s.

Monetarists, on the other hand, regarded the deterioration of the UK economy in the 1970s as the predictable inflationary outcome of expansionary policies under exchange rate flexibility that raised aggregate demand with no influence on the growth of real income. A domestic inflation problem replaced a balance of payments problem.

The monetary approach to the balance of payments was relevant not only to Britain's performance but also to the international spread of inflation, as the repercussions on the world of US monetary expansion in the 1960s culminated in the breakdown of the Bretton Woods system (Cross and Laidler, 1976). Laidler adds that the analysis of the monetary approach performs less well applied to the international monetary system since exchange rates floated in the early 1970s. Although the data support the analysis of the behavior of exchange rates as consistent with efficient asset markets, evidence does not support the postulate of the monetary approach that the equilibrium value of the exchange rate between any two currencies mirrors purchasing power parity. The data under flexible exchange rates show systematic and persistent deviations from purchasing power parity. It nevertheless underlies the behavior of long period averages of data. A generally accepted explanation of these patterns is not yet at hand (Laidler, 1981).

Monetary Policy

David Laidler was a long-time advocate for Milton Friedman's (1960) constant growth of money supply rule. Based on the evidence of a stable money demand function Friedman and Laidler argued that if the monetary authorities were to set the growth rate of some monetary aggregate (preferably M2) equal to the long-run growth rate of the real economy adjusted for any secular trend in velocity, then long-run price stability could be maintained (Laidler, 1973). Like Friedman he was opposed to fine tuning – using monetary policy to stabilize short-run movements in real output. He also favored using the monetary base rather than short-term interest rates as the monetary policy instrument. The rapid run-up of inflation in the UK in the 1970s from low single digits to close to 30% Laidler attributed to excessive money growth to finance fiscal deficits (Laidler, 1976). His solution to high inflation in the UK and US in the 1970s was to follow a policy of gradualism – gradually lowering (by 1–2% per year) the rate of money growth towards the long-run growth of the economy. He argued that since it took over a decade to build up inflation it would take the same amount of time to return to price stability (Laidler, 1982).

Over the next decade Laidler changed his views significantly. Based on the evidence of instability in money demand, especially of the long-run money demand function reflecting institutional change, he lost his faith in monetary rules and became an advocate of "constrained discretion."

"It is a defensible position that a policy regime which permits the monetary authority to use discretion in the sense of their best judgement, in influencing money growth in pursuit of a precisely defined inflation target might be preferable to having it tied down by a rule for its behavior" (Laidler, 1997*b*, 80).

He also became an advocate for the current set of policy arrangements – inflation targeting and central bank independence – on the grounds that they would deliver both policy transparency and credibility (Laidler, 1997*a*).

Laidler attributed the failure of the monetarist experiment in the early '80s to a number of factors. First, he downplayed the importance of shifts in the demand for money function in the 1970s and '80s. These, he argued, reflected both financial innovation (which could have been adjusted to) and changes in regulations which, in turn, were a consequence of the buildup of inflation before the monetarist experiment (Laidler, 1997*a*).

A more important problem was the way in which the Bank of Canada and other central banks hit their monetary aggregate targets. Rather than follow the monetarist prescription of using the monetary base to hit their money growth targets, which Laidler calls "active money," central banks followed "passive money." They used their estimates of the short-run demand for money function (based on the Goldfeld specification) to solve for the short-term interest rate needed to hit their stated money target. This made money supply endogenous and responsive to whatever shocks would drive the demand for bank credit (Laidler, 1999). Finally, he criticized the original monetarist approach to inflation, which focused on the influence of expected inflation on money demand (Laidler, 1997*b*). According to that view the costs of expected inflation were trivial, and hence could be easily dealt with by a gradualist policy. This approach ignores money's role as unit of account and medium of exchange and the distortions inflation imposes on the payments and accounting systems (Laidler, 1997*b*, 2003).

Despite his later criticism of the early monetarist approach to policy rules, he continued throughout his career to emphasize the basic monetarist principle that inflation is a monetary phenomenon. Moreover, now that monetary policy is being conducted in most advanced countries without the explicit use of any monetary aggregates, Laidler warns that conducting monetary policy without money is like having "Hamlet without the Ghost" – that monetary aggregates convey information about the transmission mechanism that is crucial to the effective conduct of policy (Laidler, 2003).

Conclusion

David Laidler has been a major player in the development of the monetarist tradition. As the monetarist approach lost influence on policymakers he kept defending the importance of many of its principles. As monetary theory evolved during the past four decades he kept up with the changing models but did not change his philosophy. He also has made us aware that many of the original monetarist ideas – especially the long-run neutrality of money, and the importance of rules – have now been absorbed into the mainstream. His research on money demand and his development into the rapporteur par excellence of the rise and fall of the demand for money and of the monetarist approach to monetary policy guarantees him a place in the pantheon of that field.

Notes

1. Later Laidler (1997*a*) departed from the durable view approach. He argued that it "abstracts from its social function as a medium of exchange and a unit of account."
2. Meltzer (1963) using wealth instead of permanent income obtained similar results.
3. A large number of studies surveyed in various editions of Laidler's *Demand for Money* found powerful evidence on the long-run stability of money demand. This evidence, as well as the case made by Friedman and others, including Laidler for the UK (1976) of the role of monetary expansion in explaining the great inflation of the late 1960s and 1970s, led to the adoption of monetary aggregate targeting in the US and many countries (to be discussed below).
4. Although work by Bordo and Jonung (1981, 1987, 1990), discussed by Laidler, found extensive long-run evidence that institutional changes also shifted the long-run money demand function.

Discussion

Nick Rowe

There is no point in my trying to find Is to dot and Ts to cross in Michael Bordo's and Anna Schwartz's excellent chapter. I would fail miserably. Instead, I plan to complement their chapter by trying to provide some context.

Reading through this thorough and careful survey of David Laidler's contribution to monetarism, I kept asking myself "What is it that monetarists have in common, and distinguishes them from non-monetarists?" This survey of David's writings shows that monetarists are certainly not a monolithic group. In particular, David's repeated emphasis on disequilibrium processes, his belief that the assumption of continuous market-clearing and a Walrasian auctioneer are not adequate to understand short-run fluctuations in a monetary exchange economy, separates him from many monetarists, and seems to give him more common ground with Keynesians.

I came to the conclusion that what monetarists have in common, and what distinguishes them from non-monetarists, is not so much a set of shared beliefs about macroeconomic theory; rather it is a set of shared beliefs about macroeconomic policy. This is not to say that policy recommendations are unrelated to theory, but it is to say that differences in theoretical belief do not always create differences in policy recommendations, and that it is in their policy recommendations that monetarists differ most starkly from non-monetarists.

How did monetarists' policy recommendations differ from those of non-monetarists? The most important difference lies in the "assignment question": which policy instruments are assigned to which targets? For the non-monetarist consensus of 30 and 40 years ago: fiscal policy was assigned the primary macroeconomic target of controlling aggregate demand to keep output at its full-employment level; monetary policy was assigned a secondary role of keeping interest rates and/or the exchange rate at a level needed to achieve the target composition of demand between consumption and investment, or between net exports and domestic absorption; and the job of keeping inflation under control was assigned to various instruments like price–wage controls or industrial and labour market policy.

The monetarist assignment was almost the exact opposite to the old non-monetarist consensus: monetary policy was assigned the primary macroeconomic target of keeping inflation low and stable; fiscal policy was assigned a secondary role of determining the composition of demand between public and private expenditure, and between present and future expenditure; and the job of keeping unemployment low was assigned to various instruments, which might also be termed industrial and labour market policy.

Seen as a disagreement about which instruments to assign to which targets, the differences between monetarists and non-monetarists look very big indeed, and much bigger than the differences within the monetarist camp. It is also easier to understand how the debate over monetarism could sometimes be so sharp. Current debates over monetary policy, like whether to target an inflation rate of 0% or 3%, or whether to target the price level instead of inflation, have much less at stake, and seem almost trivial in comparison.

It is easy to forget that Canada, the US, and the UK, all tried price–wage controls in the 1970s to control inflation. And it is hard to remember the last time an increase in government expenditure was justified (as it so commonly used to be) for its role as a stimulus to aggregate demand, output, and employment. That shows just how far the monetarists' answer to the assignment question has become the new orthodoxy. And just because it is the new orthodoxy, it is all too easy to remember monetarists merely as the group that advocated the k% rule for the money supply growth rate. They lost that battle for a particular instrument rule; but we need to remember that they won the war of the assignment of instruments to targets.

And what was David Laidler's contribution to monetarism, seen in this light? In a nutshell, David's most important contribution to monetarism was to show that it was possible to take disequilibrium seriously, to reject the Walrasian model of continuous market-clearing, and still be a monetarist. He placed the monetarist answer to the assignment question on a much broader, and more robust, theoretical base. It needed that broader base.

References

Bordo, Michael D. and Lars Jonung (1981). "The Long-Run Behavior of the Income Velocity of Money in Five Advanced Countries, 1879–1975: An Institutional Approach." *Economic Inquiry* 19 (January), 96–116.

Bordo, Michael D. and Lars Jonung (1987). *The Long-Run Behavior of the Income Velocity of Circulation: The Institutional Evidence.* New York; Cambridge University Press.

Bordo, Michael D. and Lars Jonung (1990). "The Long-Run Behavior of Velocity: The Institutional Approach Revisited." *Journal of Policy Modeling* 12 (Summer), 165–197.

Buiter, Willem H. (1980). "The Macroeconomics of Dr. Pangloss A Critical Survey of the New Classical Macroeconomics." *Economic Journal* 90 (March), 34–50.
Chow, Gregory (1966). "On the Long-Run and Short-Run Demand for Money." *Journal of Political Economy* 74 (April), 111–131.
Cross, Rodney and David Laidler (1976). "Inflation, Excess Demand and Expectations in Fixed Exchange Rate Open Economies: Some Preliminary Empirical Results." In M. Parkin and G. Zis (eds.), *Inflation in the World Economy*. Manchester: Manchester University Press, pp. 221–258.
Friedman, Milton (1956). "The Quantity Theory of Money, a Restatement." In Milton Friedman (ed), *Studies in the Quantity Theory of Money*. Chicago: University of Chicago Press, pp. 3–21.
Friedman, Milton (1959). "The Demand for Money – Some Theoretical and Empirical Results." *Journal of Political Economy* 67 (June), 327–351.
Friedman, Milton (1960). *A Program for Monetary Stability*. New York: Fordham University Press.
Friedman, Milton (1970). "A Theoretical Framework for Monetary Analysis." *Journal of Political Economy* 78(2), 193–238.
Goldfeld, Stephen M. (1973). "The Demand for Money Revisited." *Brookings Papers on Economic Activity* 3, 537–633.
Goldfeld, Stephen M. (1976). "The Case of the Missing Money." *Brookings Papers on Economic Activity* 3, 683–730.
Hendry, David and Neil Ericsson (1991). "Modeling the Demand for Narrow Money in the United Kingdom and The United States." *European Economic Review* 35 (May), 833–883.
Laidler, David (1966*a*). "Some Evidence on the Demand for Money." *Journal of Political Economy* 74 (February), 55–68.
Laidler, David (1966*b*). "The Rate of Interest and the Demand for Money – Some Empirical Evidence." *Journal of Political Economy* 74 (December), 545–555.
Laidler, David (1969 and later editions). *The Demand for Money-Theories and Evidence*. New york: Harper and Row.
Laidler, David (1971). "The Influence of Money on Economic Activity: A Survey of Some Current Problems." In Clayton, G., Gilbert, J.C., and Sedgwick, R. (eds.), *Monetary Theory and Practice in the 1970s*. Oxford University Press, pp. 75–135.
Laidler, David (1973). "Monetarist Policy Prescriptions and Their Background." *Manchester School* XLI(1) (March), 59–71.
Laidler, David (1975*a*). *Essays on Money and Inflation*. Manchester: Manchester University Press.
Laidler, David (1975*b*). "Simultaneous Fluctuations in Prices and Output: A Business Cycle Approach." In David Laidler , ed., *Essays on Money and Inflation*. Manchester: University of Manchester Press, pp. 120–133.
Laidler, David (1976). "Inflation in Britain: A Monetarist Perspective." *American Economic Review* 66, No. 4 (September), 485–500.
Laidler, David (1978). "Money and Money Income: An Essay on the 'Transmission Mechanism'." *Journal of Monetary Economics* 4(2), 151–191.
Laidler, David (1980). "The Demand for Money in the United States-Yet Again." In Brunner, K. and Meltzer, A. H. (eds.), *The State of Macro-Economics*. Carnegie-Rochester Conference Series on Public Policy V. 12. North-Holland, pp. 219–271.
Laidler, David (1981). "Some Policy Implications of the Monetary Approach to the Balance of Payments and Exchange Rate Analysis." *Oxford Economic Papers* 33 Supplement (October), 70–84.
Laidler, David (1982). *Monetarist Perspectives*. Cambridge, MA: Harvard University Press, pp. 3–4.
Laidler, David (1984). "The Buffer Stock Notion in Monetary Economics." Conference Proceedings, Supplement to the *Economic Journal* 94 (March), 17–34.

Laidler, David (1985). "The 'Monetary Approach' and the International Monetary System." In *Champions of Freedom*, Vol. 11. Hillsdale, Michigan: Hillsdale College Press, pp. 1–18.
Laidler, David (1988). "Some Macroeconomic Implications of Price Stickiness." The *Manchester School* 56 (1), 37–54.
Laidler, David (1990*a*). "The New Classical Contribution to Macroeconomics." In David Laidler, ed., *Taking Money Seriously*. Cambridge: MIT Press, pp. 56–78.
Laidler, David (1990*b*). *Taking Money Seriously*. Cambridge, MA: MIT Press.
Laidler, David (1997*a*). "Price Stability and the Monetary Order." In David Laidler, ed., *Money and Macroeconomics*. London: Edward Elgar, pp. 327–351.
Laidler, David (1997*b*). "Inflation Control and Monetary Policy Rules." In Iwao Kuroda, ed., *Towards More Effective Monetary Policy*. New York: St. Martin's Press.
Laidler, David (1999). "Passive Money, Active Money and Monetary Policy." *Bank of Canada Review*, Summer, 15–25.
Laidler, David (2003). "Monetary Policy without Money; Hamlet without the Ghost." Charles Freedman's Festschrift, Bank of Canada, June.
Latané, Henry A. (1954). "Cash Balances and the Interest Rate: A Pragmatic Approach." *Review of Economics and Statistics* 36 (November), 456–460.
Meltzer, Allan (1963). "The Demand For Money: The Evidence from the Times Series." *Journal of Political Economy* 71 (June), 219–241.
Mussa, Michael (1976). "Output and Employment in a Dynamic Model of Aggregate Supply." London School of Economics Mimeo.
Phelps, Edward S. (1968). "Money Wage Dynamics and Labor Market Equilibrium," *Journal of Political Economy* 76(4) Pt. II, 678–711.
Phelps, Edward S. and John B. Taylor (1977). "Stabilizing Powers of Monetary Policy Under Rational Expectations." *Journal of Political Economy* 85(1), 613–690.

4

David Laidler's Contributions to the History of Monetary Economics

Robert W. Dimand

Introduction

Throughout his distinguished and productive career as a monetary (and monetarist) economist, David Laidler has paid close attention to the history of monetary economics, because of both the intrinsic pleasure and satisfaction from such an intellectual pursuit and his deep conviction that an economist is a better economist for having historical perspective on the current state of the discipline and for knowing more than the latest crop of fashionable journal articles. As he remarked in praise of an eminent contemporary,

> I intend it as a compliment to say that I do not regard Charles Goodhart as a modern macroeconomist... Charles's economics has been informed by a deep understanding of the history of monetary institutions and policy, and of the economic ideas that have underlain that history. It might appear paradoxical that this very characteristic of his intellectual equipment, which to many would seem to have suited him only for a life in the ivory tower, has also made him an important and effective policy advisor. But, as I hope to show, an approach of the type that Charles has always taken to economics is as productive and practical as it is unfashionable. (Laidler, 2003*b*, 12)

But historians of economic thought should not listen complacently to this call for modern macroeconomists to learn some history, for Laidler (1982*b*, 326) also laments 'the fact that Historians of Economic Thought habitually neglect Monetary Economics, and particularly the development of quantitative methods therein, when they write their textbooks'.

The leading North American graduate programs in economics, including that at the University of Chicago as it now exists, do not usually inspire historical awareness and insight in the theorists and empirical economists they produce. In the 1930s, when George Stigler was writing his dissertation there on the formative period of production and distribution theories, Frank Knight and Jacob Viner put the University of Chicago at the cutting edge of history of economic thought, and the 1960s was the last period when the history of economic thought still flourished there. When David was a student, PhD students were required to take a course in either economic history or the history of thought unless they took the field examination, which David did, as well as attending Earl Hamilton's course on the history of banking theory. The requirement was abolished some years later. Stigler himself supported abolition of the history of thought requirement for students, despite his own research interest, on libertarian grounds of increasing choice. David's dissertation, completed in 1964, was not on a historical topic, but on 'Income tax incentives for owner-occupied housing', a topic for which funding was available. Soon afterwards, he turned to empirical study of the demand for money, leading to his first two articles, both in the *Journal of Political Economy* in 1966 (the first in print when he was still only 27 years old), and to his first book, published in 1969 and reaching its fourth edition in 1993. In the 1960s, Milton Friedman and his Chicago students argued emphatically that the demand for money is a stable function of a few variables (and so provides a more reliable basis for policy than the Keynesian spending multiplier), that it is insensitive to the nominal interest rate (so that fiscal policy is crowded out, but monetary policy affects aggregate demand), and (not in the same paper) that it is sensitive to the nominal interest rate (so that even anticipated inflation has real costs by reducing demand for real money balances, and so the socially optimal nominal interest rate is zero for satiation with real balances of fiat money). As an undergraduate at the London School of Economics, he had (like his classmate Samuel Hollander) studied with Lionel Robbins, both a great historian of classical economics and a sound money man whose House of Lords speeches were collected under the title *Against Inflation*, and also with Bernard Corry. Most significantly for his future career, at the University of Chicago David came in close contact with the outstanding example of a first-rank monetary theorist undertaking serious historical research as the underpinning for his theorizing: he was one of the research assistants for Milton Friedman's and Anna Jacobson Schwartz's *Monetary History of the United States* (1963).

The profound and lasting impression left by this formative experience can be seen in David's review article of their subsequent volume on *Monetary Trends* and in his forthcoming introduction to a collection of Friedman's macroeconomic articles (Laidler, 1982*c* and forthcoming). David emerged from his immersion in the empirical evidence supporting Friedman's restatement of the quantity theory of money (dubbed 'monetarism' by Karl Brunner and, independently, by Nicholas Kaldor, who, unlike Brunner, intended the name as a term of abuse) with a lasting commitment to the quantity theory views that inflation is always and everywhere a monetary phenomenon, that is a costly, avoidable scourge, that monetary shocks drive short-run real fluctuations (so that the Great Depression of the 1930s followed from the Great Contraction of the US money supply) but are neutral in the longer run, and that the money supply is a key variable, not just one of many imperfectly substitutable financial assets, a set of views that he has consistently defended against Keynesian, New Classical, and neo-Wicksellian challenges. David's admiration for Friedman is by no means narrow or sectarian, as he has also drawn inspiration from Karl Brunner and Alan Meltzer, quantity theorists who have on occasion differed sharply with Friedman (see Brunner and

Meltzer in Gordon, 1974; Brunner and Meltzer, 1993; Laidler, 1991*b* on Brunner; Laidler, 2003*d* on Meltzer), and, like Harry Johnson, he has been skeptical about the continuity and uniqueness of the Chicago oral tradition of monetary theory (Laidler, 1993*a*, 1998). In particular, he has been interested in the history of these ideas: how they originated and evolved, in what contexts, and (the title of Laidler, 1991*e*), 'The Quantity Theory is Always and Everywhere Controversial – Why?' (on which question, see also Blaug et al., 1995).

David Laidler first taught the history of economic thought in 1964 when, as an assistant professor at Berkeley he taught a graduate course at Stanford after Paul Baran's sudden death (Laidler, 2004*b*, ix). Almost without exception, David Laidler's contributions to the history of economic thought have dealt with monetary economics. Although his policy writings pay due attention to open-economy considerations, his historical work emphasizes the history of monetary theory considered as a field distinct from international monetary economics, so that his volumes on the history of monetary theory from 1870 to the Keynesian Revolution (Laidler, 1991*a*, 1999*b*) neatly complement June Flanders's history of international monetary economics from 1870 to 1960 (Flanders, 1989). Both Laidler and Flanders take the British monetary orthodoxy of the 1870s, where Fetter (1965) ends, as the starting point for their stories. As Laidler (1982*b*, 327n2) acknowledged, 'The *locus classicus* for an account of the evolution of English monetary economics down to the 1870s is, of course, Frank Fetter (1965)'. Similarly, Laidler (2000) stated, 'As I hope is made clear from the frequency of references to the works in question', his study of the bullionist controversy 'owes a considerable debt to the classic studies of this controversy by Jacob Viner (1937, Chs. III and IV) and Frank W. Fetter (1965, Chs. I–IV)'. Laidler (2004*b*, xi) recalled that

> Fetter forced me to see Tooke's work in an altogether broader context, and made me self-conscious about the fact that the History of Economic Thought is not just a matter of who said what when, but also of how economic ideas evolve over time as they interact with institutions and events, both affecting the behaviour of the economy and being affected by it. It showed me an approach to history that was concerned not so much with the lives and times of the economists, as with the biographies of the ideas that they shared and debated. It took another 20 years for this lesson to have its full consequences for my work, but my own two monographs on the history of macroeconomics ... were the outcome of a self-conscious effort to tell the next seventy years of the story that Fetter had started.

Although David Laidler has assembled lecture notes for a full-year course covering the history of theories of production, distribution, and exchange as well as money, his only opportunity to teach the whole course was at the University of Toronto when Samuel Hollander was on sabbatical. The University of Western Ontario requires courses to be self-contained and last only one semester, so there Laidler divided his material between topics in "real" and monetary economics, and usually taught only the latter (2004*b*, x). David's only publication in the history of economic thought outside the history of monetary economics has been the entry on Abba Lerner in the *Biographical Supplement* to the *International Encyclopedia of the Social Sciences* (Laidler, 1979), his only contribution to that encyclopedia and a surprising topic since he cannot have felt much sympathy for Lerner's Keynesianism, functional finance, or incomes policy, and Lerner's neo-classical writings were in the non-monetary theory of international trade. David took over the assignment for the Lerner article upon the death of Harry Johnson, whose interests covered real as well as monetary international economics. He had gotten to know and like Abba Lerner while he was a Manchester colleague of Shirley Lerner, Abba's sister-in-law.

Bullionists, Central Bankers and the Real Bills Fallacy

Long interested in the bullionist controversy that raged among British monetarist theorists while the gold convertibility of Bank of England notes was suspended from 1797 to 1821, David Laidler likes to note that the suspension was sparked by a run on the Bank of England branch in his hometown of Newcastle-upon-Tyne (otherwise famed for its excellent beer) as rumors arrived exaggerating a minor French landing in distant Wales. Rather than a conventional journal article, his publications on the controversy began with three *New Palgrave* entries (1987*a*, 1987*b*, 1987*c*) and included a lecture at the Stockholm School of Economics published as a research report by the Swedish Institute for Research in Economic History (2000), but he became so identified with the topic that he was invited to give the Henry Thornton Lecture at London's City University (1991*d*) and to address a Paris conference on the bicentenary of Thornton's *Paper Credit* (Laidler, 2003*a*). Laidler (2000, 3) observed that 'in 1797, monetary economics, at least as it existed in the English language, lacked both a theory of flexible exchange rates and a theory of central banking under either a commodity standard or flexible rates' because, since Britain had been de facto on a gold standard since 1717, there was no experience with a fluctuating gold value of Bank of England notes (or, equivalently, a fluctuating price of gold bullion in bank notes) and English writers were apparently unaware of Swedish contributions (notably by Pehr Niclas Christiernin of the University of Uppsala) during the Seven Years War of 1756 to 1763 (see Eagly, 1971). In 1801, Walter Boyd, disgruntled at his firm's failure after the government passed it over as a loan contractor (and the subject of Laidler, 1987*a*), began the bullionist controversy by arguing that rising prices and falling exchanges resulted from the over-issue of Bank of England notes, which had been carried out to buy newly issued government debt and would not have been possible if the Bank was still required to convert its notes into gold upon demand. Henry Thornton's 1802 refutation of the real bills doctrine and David Ricardo's argument that the high price of bullion demonstrated the depreciation of banknotes due to over-issue were the highpoints of the controversy. The directors of the Bank of England defended themselves by claiming that as long as the Bank only discounted real bills (promissory notes generated by genuine commercial transactions, notes that would be self-liquidating in due course) they were only accommodating the needs of trade and therefore could not be artificially pushing up prices. Thornton and Ricardo had no difficulty in showing that this spurious defense rested on implicitly assuming prices fixed whatever the real needs of trade, the nominal needs of trade would expand as the Bank of England discounted more bills of exchange for its banknotes and pushed up prices. Furthermore, depending on how many transactions between merchants were involved in bringing goods to market, any number of real bills could be created with the same goods as security. David criticized the directors of the Bank of England for taking Adam Smith's real bills doctrine, as developed for a small open economy with strict gold convertibility, and assuming it applied with a flexible exchange rate, but he also felt that Thornton's critique of Smith did not give Smith the benefit of that crucial difference in context. Thomas Attwood and the Birmingham School were more willing to countenance inflation and inconvertibility than the bullionists (so that a few later commentators hailed them as proto-Keynesians), but, just as Samuel Johnson reporting parliamentary debates in the days before Hansard took care that 'the Whig dogs' did not have the best of it, the quantity theoretic opponents of the real bills doctrine came out best, not least in David's reckoning: 'Of course there were always, as there are nowadays, inflationary cranks who were unconcerned about price stability. In Tooke's day the Birmingham school sometimes took this position' (Laidler, 1984*a*, 151n2).

David Laidler's first contribution to the history of monetary economics was 'Thomas Tooke on Monetary Reform' (1972*a*), published in a *Festschrift* for his teacher Lionel Robbins but already drafted by 1966. Laidler (2004*b*, x) explains the origins of his paper:

> In 1965 and 1966 [before the 1967 sterling devaluation], questions about whether the UK was suffering from a "fundamental" or merely a "temporary" disequilibrium in its balance of payments, and what ought to be done about it, were raised even in the faculty coffee room at Berkeley, mainly by a series of visitors from the UK. These issues seemed to be related to the Currency School—Banking School controversy that I had studied as a student. This had dealt, among other questions, with the proper response of the Bank of England to gold outflows. It seemed odd to me that the Currency School, who had recommended enforced deflation in all such circumstances, were still regarded as the heroes of that debate, even though contemporary conventional wisdom was that temporary imbalances should be ridden out, fundamental ones met with devaluation, and deflation avoided at all costs. I began to wonder whether the Banking School had been quite as benighted as I had been led to believe. A few weeks in the library with the writings of Tooke soon revealed that the answer to this question was not straightforward.

Note particularly how he turned to the history of thought for perspective on a current, policy-relevant theoretical question, and how at the same time the contemporary issue in policy and theory suggested a new way of looking at a historical controversy.

Laidler (1972*a*) found it strange that the historical literature tended to agree with the Currency School's defense of Sir Robert Peel's Bank Charter Act of 1844, since the resulting bank structure failed to mitigate the recurrent financial crises, and the rules established in the Act had to be suspended to deal with subsequent crises. He argued that 'the recommendations of Thomas Tooke, the leading member of the Banking School, were based on greater insight into the manner in which the monetary system worked prior to 1844, and were very much what a modern economist might suggest within the constrain of the policy goals ruling in the nineteenth century' (1972*b*, 168). The Bank Act of 1844 implemented the Currency School rule that, apart from a fixed fiduciary issue, the note issue should vary exactly in proportion to the specie reserve of the Bank of England's note issue department, which was separated from the department handling the Bank's deposit business. While sharing the Currency School's insistence on the goal of maintaining gold convertibility of notes, Tooke and the Banking School wanted the Bank to hold a specie reserve large enough to ride out temporary balance of payments deficits from real shocks (such as a harvest failure) without having to contract the note issue. David found that Tooke overlooked the role of Bank of England liabilities as a reserve base for other components of the circulating medium, but that his Currency School opponents erred in considering only the Bank of England note issue, rather than all Bank of England liabilities including deposits. Following Fetter, David concluded that, while there were some elements of the real bills doctrine in Tooke's writings, Tooke had not embraced the real bills fallacy. As Laidler (1988) showed, the British monetary orthodoxy of the 1870s, exemplified by Walter Bagehot's *Lombard Street* (1873), combined elements of both the Currency and Banking Schools. Central bankers following Bagehot's principle would neither vary the note issue in strict proportion to the specie reserve, nor rely on a large specie reserve to ride out gold outflows caused by real shocks, but would instead vary the discount rate to halt the gold flows.

Both sides in the bullionist and Currency School–Banking School controversies invoked Adam Smith. David Laidler (2004*b*, xiv)

> read Smith's work for myself in the late 1970s, under the influence of my own earlier essay on Thomas Tooke and of the then widely-used small-open-economy-fixed-exchange-rate model associated with what was then called the monetary approach to the balance of payments... and it seemed to be of much higher quality than was commonly thought. One might challenge the reasonableness of assuming that a gold-standard economy has its price level determined for it in the world market for gold, but, once that assumption is made, certain results follow, and my effort to bolster Smith's reputation as a monetary economist [Laidler, 1981] hinged upon this point, just as had much of my earlier effort on behalf of Thomas Tooke.

At about the same time (and with one reference to David's then-forthcoming article, with regard to how Scotland's experience shaped Smith's analysis), Thomas Humphrey also offered a rehabilitation of Smith's monetary economics in a 1980 piece on 'Adam Smith and the Monetary Approach to the Balance of Payments' published by the Federal Reserve Bank of Richmond (reprinted in Humphrey, 1986, 180–187). Humphrey also stressed Smith's assumption of a small open economy under the gold standard taking its price level as given by the world market. For Humphrey, this explained why Smith did not include in *The Wealth of Nations* a discussion of David Hume's 1752 specie-flow mechanism of international adjustment, which stressed relative price effects: if mercantilist bounties on exports and tariffs on imports produced a trade surplus and gold inflow, the increased domestic money supply and reduced foreign money supply would raise domestic prices relative to foreign prices, eliminating the trade surplus. Humphrey read Smith as a precursor of the monetary approach to the balance of payments, with arbitrage establishing purchasing power parity, so that the gold inflow created an excess supply of money, which increased spending on imports and on exportable goods, re-establishing international payments equilibrium without changes in the terms of trade. Laidler (1981) was concerned with another implication of Smith's assumption: Smith's statement of the real bills doctrine was rendered innocuous by strict gold convertibility of banknotes and by the exogeneity to a small open economy of a price level set in the world market for gold. In those circumstances (but not more generally), any excessive issue of banknotes would alter the composition of the circulating medium between paper and gold, but could not affect prices. Smith's real bills doctrine was still fallacious over the distinction between real and fictitious bills, a distinction that vanished once it is recalled that the same goods can change hands many times on the way to market, generating "real" bills of exchange each time, but it was not, under Smith's assumptions about convertibility and the gold standard, unsound about prices.

Leading on from his study of Smith on the real bills doctrine (which followed from his rehabilitation of Tooke's reputation), Laidler (1984*a*, 149) objected to an attempted rehabilitation of the real bills doctrine by Thomas Sargent and Neil Wallace because '(1) the conclusions on whose basis they seek to rehabilitate the real-bills doctrine would have been anathema to its proponents; (2) what they refer to as the real-bills doctrine is not the real-bills doctrine; and (3) their interpretation of Adam Smith's analysis of the social productivity of banking is quite misconceived'. Laidler (1994*a*, 150) insisted that Smith, Robert Torrens, and the other 'eighteenth- and nineteenth-century advocates of the doctrine regarded the maintenance of price-level stability as a vital principle of social organization and would not have entertained a defense of their doctrine that showed that it failed to ensure such stability'. Smith disapproved of fluctuating, and particularly rising, prices because he noted the existence of long-term nominal contracts and did not assume that people had perfect foresight. For Sargent and Wallace (1982, 1212), the real bills doctrine 'asserts that unrestricted intermediation either by private banks or by a central bank has beneficial economic effects and should be promoted by public policy'. Laidler (2003*b*, 15) protested that

> They thereby appropriated a well-established label for the quite different hypothesis that if bank money is always issued by way of discount of good

> quality short-term commercial paper issued to finance inventories and goods in process, variations in its quantity can impart neither inflationary nor deflationary impulses to the economy. Since this latter hypothesis has been associated with the policies of the Reichsbank during the Weimar hyperinflation and the Federal Reserve system during the great contraction of 1929–33, among other episodes, the semantic confusion thus introduced has not been a minor matter for anyone trying to teach a little history to students who are simultaneously being "well trained" in modern monetary theory.

It will be recalled that during the German hyperinflation, when Keynes (1923) calculated that Germany's real money supply M/P had fallen by 92 per cent because of the soaring opportunity cost of holding real money balances, Reichsbank President Rudolf Havenstein lamented that the Reichsbank had not been able to print money fast enough to keep up with the rise in prices and the needs of trade, but promised that the situation would be remedied by the installation of thirty-eight new high-speed printing presses. Misplaced faith in the real bills doctrine by the Reichsbank and by German economists thus contributed to the decay of the Weimar Republic. Together with George W. Stadler, a graduate student who was a native speaker of German, David argued that neglected contributions by a small (but eminent) minority of German-speaking economists (Ladislaus von Bortkiewicz, L. Albert Hahn, and Ludwig von Mises) did reject the real bills fallacy and use the quantity theory of money to provide a monetary explanation of the hyperinflation while it was happening, although Mises later moved away from the quantity theory because of his growing disapproval of aggregate concepts such as the price level (Laidler and Stadler, 1998). Unnoticed by Laidler and Stadler, Thomas Humphrey had drawn attention in articles in 1978, 1979, and 1980 (reprinted in Humphrey, 1986, 207–208, 215, 225) to Walter Eucken, Fritz Machlup, and especially Ludwig von Mises as contemporary German-speaking economists who understood that exchange rate movements during the German hyperinflation reflected expected inflation and expected future growth of the money supply. Laidler and Stadler (1998) made extensive use of primary sources in German, whereas Humphrey relied on an existing translation of two Mises papers from 1919 and 1923 and on Ellis (1934). Ellis appears only once in Laidler and Stadler (1998), who remark in their introduction that 'the work we discuss here is not kindly treated in the later literature of the interwar years. Howard Ellis (1934) does discuss it in his survey of *German Monetary Theory*, albeit briefly and somewhat disparagingly' (cf. Ellis, 1934, 217, 280, 294). An endnote to that paragraph reports that in 1982 Gerald Merkin had discussed Bortkiewicz's contribution, but not Hahn or Mises, and a later endnote points out that Merkin, while translating the same three passages from Bortkiewicz, had stressed in his discussion what Bortkiewicz wrote about loss of confidence in the currency rather than his statement that the loss of confidence was due to expectations of future increases in the quantity of money.

Laidler and Stadler (1998) reflects David's longtime concern with the recurring contest between the quantity theory of money and the real bills doctrine, his conviction that mistaken monetary theory can have disastrous policy consequences, and his attention to the underappreciated contributions of past quantity theorists. As Laidler (2004*b*, xv) remarks, the article 'also demonstrates the extent to which developments outside of the English language literature are still neglected'. Laidler and Stadler (1998) exemplifies the characteristic strengths of Laidler's approach to the history of economic thought: careful attention to primary sources, insightful elucidation of the theoretical content of these primary sources, and a strong sense of historical context. The handling of secondary sources is more problematic: missing Humphrey's articles and giving only passing and unsympathetic mention to Ellis and Merkin obscures the nature of the article's original contribution, which lies in the exploration of untapped primary sources and the focusing of attention on the German and Austrian quantity theorists of the early 1920s, not in the discovery that Mises took a monetary approach to the balance of payments during the German hyperinflation (since that was known from Ellis and from Bettina Bien Greaves's translation of Mises's 1919 and 1923 essays). Another problem is that L. Albert Hahn is represented only by what he wrote in 1924, with no mention of Hahn (1920), the book that made him famous (or at least notorious), and which Hahn (1949) claimed had anticipated everything that was wrong or exaggerated in Keynes's *General Theory*. Without giving a reference, Laidler and Stadler mention in their first endnote that Hahn had gone 'beyond Schumpeter in presenting an optimistic (almost inflationist) view' of the power of bank credit expansion to promote real expansion, but make no mention of this anywhere else in their paper. Hahn's 1924 insight that the rise in velocity of circulation was due to the expectation of a continuing fall in the purchasing power of money is reported without contrasting it with his 1920 book, which contributed to an intellectual atmosphere conducive to inflationary policy, or with his later deflationist stand during the Depression.

The Giants of the Golden Age: Jevons and Marshall to Wicksell and Fisher

David Laidler took the 'British Monetary Orthodoxy of the 1870s', exemplified by Walter Bagehot's principle of central banking, William Stanley Jevons's empirical studies, and Alfred Marshall's first work on monetary theory, as the beginning of the Golden Age of the Quantity Theory, a golden age spanned by a single career and even by a single book because it lasted from Marshall's 1871 drafting of his manuscript on money to its final publication as part of his *Money, Credit and Commerce* in 1923.

As Professor of Economics at the University of Manchester from 1969 to 1975 (and as a member of the editorial board of *The Manchester School* from 1970 to 1975), David Laidler organized the History of Economic Thought conference held at the University of Manchester in 1971 to commemorate the centenary of the publication of Jevons's *Theory of Political Economy*, the foundation work of marginal utility economics published while Jevons was a Manchester professor. Although the conference resulted in a 1972 *Manchester School* issue celebrating Jevons, and although David published his first journal article on the history of economic thought (on Wicksell's price-level dynamics) in *The Manchester School* that year, he did not present a paper at the conference he organized. His *Manchester School* article about Jevons on money was written ten years after the conference, and published in 1982.

Laidler (1982*b*) noted that while Jevons's marginal utility analysis was abstract, deduced from *a priori* assumptions, and presented (in Marshall's view, excessively) as a revolutionary break with the classical political economy of Ricardo and Mill, Jevons's monetary was empirically grounded, made no mention of marginal utility, and was portrayed as an exposition of prevailing orthodoxy. To Laidler's observation that Jevons did not see the relevance of his marginal utility analysis to Jevons's monetary economics, one may add that Jevons (like Edgeworth 40 years later) wrote articles on the Brownian motion of particles with no suspicion of the relevance of Brownian motion to financial markets. Jevons was a quantity theorist, invoking the supply of money and its velocity to explain the general price level, and changes in transaction technology to explain changes in the velocity of circulation of money, but without as yet any notion of a money demand function or even the cash balance approach of Walras, Marshall, and Pigou. The quantity theory of money is an evolving tradition of thought for Laidler, not a single cut and dried model, and money demand functions, stable or not, emerged later than Jevons, let alone Hume or Thornton. Jevons wrote that the values of gold and silver ultimately depended on their cost of production, but Laidler (1982*b*, 334) argued that the word 'ultimately' allowed Jevons to still qualify as a quantity theorist who believed that the quantity of money explained 'temporary' effects on the price level lasting 'ten or fifteen years', while the cost of producing precious metals controlled the growth of the monetary base and the level of prices to which the quantity of money would ultimately have to conform.

While admiring Jevons's use of index numbers, Laidler (1982*b*, 348n22) felt that Jevons's 1868 paper 'On the Condition of the Coinage' went into 'excruciating detail...One or two pages of this chapter had been left uncut since 1884 in the copy of the *Investigations*...which I used in preparing this essay, and remain so. Nevertheless, as my colleague Michael Parkin has pointed out to me, one should resist the temptation to denigrate Jevons's insistence that his monetary reform proposals be based on a rigorous scrutiny of relevant empirical evidence'. David held that Jevons's proposal for an international money and his proposal for a tabular standard of value for indexed contracts had no technical flaws, 'but it is hard to resist the conclusion that Jevons both underestimated the difficulties of getting the public accustomed to such a unit of account, and overestimated the advantages that might accrue from it in a period of such relative monetary stability as the 1870s' (1982*b*, 349). Yet Jevons had more influence as a monetary economist than might be supposed, for David notes that Irving Fisher acknowledged Jevons's tabular standard as an influence on his own compensated dollar plan (a price-level rule for monetary policy) and also credited Jevons when discussing influences on velocity of circulation, and that Wesley Mitchell of the National Bureau for Economic Research (NBER) cited Jevons on index numbers of the value of gold and on seasonality, crediting Jevons with 'the first powerful impetus to statistical work in economic theory'. Laidler (1982*b*, 340) also insisted that there was much more to Jevons's analysis of the trade cycle than the notorious sunspots: 'when judged against the standards of his contemporaries, Jevons's account of the causative mechanisms underlying the cycle appears much more thorough than it does when judged by standards established by a further century of research in the area', a significant warning against ahistorical judgments. While certainly not placing Jevons on the level of Hume, Thornton, Bagehot, Marshall, Wicksell, or Fisher, Laidler (1982*b*) made a convincing case for taking Jevons seriously as an empirical monetary economist and reformer in the quantity theory tradition. Later books by Margaret Schabas, Sandra Peart, and Harro Maas take Jevons very seriously as an empirical, applied economist, including his monetary and cycle analysis, but when David published his article, Jevons was discussed almost exclusively as an abstract theorist of marginal utility analysis (with some exceptions, notably the articles by Keynes and Robbins on the 1936 centenary of Jevons's birth).

The three heroes portrayed on the cover of *The Golden Age of the Quantity Theory* are Alfred Marshall, Knut Wicksell, and Irving Fisher. Laidler (1990*a*), published in a volume marking the centenary of Marshall's *Principles of Economics*, made the same case for Marshall that Laidler (1981, 1982*b*) had made for Smith and Jevons: that he was an economist justly famous for his contribution to the theory of value, distribution, and production, whose monetary economics was nonetheless underrated and insufficiently known (as Laidler, 1972*a* claimed for Tooke), and in particular that their monetary economics held up well when considered in light of modern quantity-theoretic orthodoxy. Given that David then cites Keynes's well-known emphasis in his memorial article on Marshall and in his edition of Marshall's *Official Papers* on the pivotal role of Marshall's lectures and his evidence to official inquiries in the development of the Cambridge cash-balance approach to the quantity theory, the case for the high quality of Marshall's monetary economics may seem easier to make persuasively than the case for its neglect.

However, as David points out, there is an obstacle to bringing Marshall on money to the attention of modern readers. Thornton, Ricardo, and Keynes in his *Tract on Monetary Reform* (1923) wrote about inflation and real fluctuations in a world of flexible exchange rates, and so 'can command an interested audience among modern monetary economists not otherwise interested in the history of their discipline', whereas Marshall's *Official Papers* (1926) were responses to current policy issues during a quarter-century of secularly falling prices associated with the spread of the gold standard, hardly the world of today. In an encyclopedia entry on the quantity theory of money, Laidler (2002*d*) acknowledged Keynes's *Tract* as 'arguably the most distinguished work ever to deploy the Cambridge version of the quantity theory', going beyond the Cambridge cash balance version of the equation of exchange to analyze inflation as a method of taxation (of real money balance and government debt), the social loss from inflation-induced reduction of real money balances and from the interference of unanticipated inflation with price signals and with social cohesion, and covered interest arbitrage (equating the spread between spot and forward exchange rates to the difference between nominal interest rates in two currencies), contributions that also won the *Tract* praise from Milton Friedman and Thomas Sargent. Since Laidler (1995*a*, 1999*b*) has also been impressed with the treatment of money demand in Keynes's *Treatise on Money* (1930) and with the monetary analysis of Dennis Robertson's *Banking Policy and the Price Level* (1926), a work based on discussions with Keynes so significant that Robertson stated he could not tell which ideas in the book were his and which Keynes's, it is worth keeping in mind that the Cambridge Marshallian stream of pre-*General Theory* monetary analysis (often designated pre-Keynesian or non-Keynesian) includes a substantial contribution from Keynes himself (see also Humphrey, 1986, 38–48, and Dimand, 1988, chapter 1, on the *Tract*).

Marshall shares the dust jacket of *The Golden Age of the Quantity Theory* with two younger contemporaries of his, Knut Wicksell and Irving Fisher, the other central figures in Laidler's account of neoclassical monetary economics (with less central roles for Léon Walras on desired cash balances and Francis Ysidro Edgeworth on index numbers and on the mathematical theory of banking). For each of these two giants, David's story is a tale of two interest rates. With due acknowledgement to earlier brief statements by John Stuart Mill and Alfred Marshall, Irving Fisher's *Appreciation and Interest* (1896, in Fisher, 1997, vol. 1) equated the difference between interest rates in any two standards (gold and silver, paper money and commodities, two national currencies) to the expected rate of appreciation or depreciation of one standard in terms of the other. Expected inflation as the difference between nominal and real interest is one particular form of this Fisher relation, uncovered interest parity between national currencies is another. Laidler (1991*a*, 44) notes that, unknown to Fisher, Thornton made a similar observation in a parliamentary speech in defense of the Bullion Report in 1811 (reprinted in Hayek's 1939 edition of Thornton's *Paper Credit*), but not in *Paper Credit* in 1802 or the Bullion Report itself in 1810. The context of Fisher's contribution led Laidler (1999*a*) to reflect on the changing political uses of the quantity theory. *Appreciation and Interest* was published at the time of bimetallist William Jennings Bryan's first presidential campaign, after nearly a quarter-century of declining price levels under the gold standard (a decline about to be reversed by gold discoveries in the Klondike and elsewhere and by the cyanide process that greatly increased the extraction of gold from low-grade South African ores). Bimetallists such as the best-selling pamphleteer William 'Coin' Harvey argued that increasing the money supply by monetizing silver as well as gold would raise the price level (as the quantity theory of money predicted), and that rising prices would produce lasting real economic benefits, easing the burden of farm mortgages and other debts. Hard-money defenders of the gold standard, such as James Laurence Laughlin of the University of Chicago, rallied to the classical cost of production theory of the value of gold and rejected the quantity theory. In the 1890s, unlike later times, the quantity theory was upheld by inflationist populists and opposed by conservatives at the University of Chicago. Fisher attempted to restore the respectability of the quantity theory proposition that an increase in the quantity of money will ultimately cause prices to change in the same proportion by separating it from any claims about permanent real effects. If changes in the price level were expected, those expectations would be incorporated in nominal interest rates. Rising prices, if correctly anticipated, would not favor debtors over creditors: nominal interest rates would be higher, real interest the same as if inflation was lower. Fisher and his younger colleague Harry Gunnison Brown argued in *The Purchasing Power of Money* (1911, chapter IV, in Fisher, 1997, vol. 4) that changes in the quantity of money drove fluctuations in real economic activity in 'transition periods' of up to ten years, while inflationary expectations and nominal interest adjusted, but affected only prices in equilibrium. Such an insistence on the short-run non-neutrality and long-run neutrality of money goes back to David Hume in 1752 and Henry Thornton in 1802 (see Humphrey, 1986), but Fisher pursued the analysis further, with greater formality of analysis and systematic empirical investigation. For instance, Fisher used a distributed lag of past price-level changes as a proxy for expected inflation (a version of adaptive expectations), correlating it with nominal interest in his *Theory of Interest* (1930, in Fisher, 1997, vol. 9) and with unemployment in an article reprinted long after his death as 'Lost and Found: I Discovered the Phillips Curve' (1926). Even Fisher deviated on occasion from the quantity theory path, allowing his enthusiasm for 100 reserve requirements (to separate the medium of exchange function of bank money from risky financial intermediation) to carry him to praise for the Federal Reserve increase in reserve requirements, intended to mop up excess reserves and make the money supply easier to control, that contributed to the 1937 recession (because risk-averse banks really wanted to hold excess reserves and so contracted their lending to maintain them in face of higher reserve requirements). David's (and Don Patinkin's) greatest reservation about Fisher's quantity theory credentials concerned Fisher's compensated dollar plan from 1911 onward, which, without mention of the quantity of money or open market operations, proposed to maintain a price-level target by varying the gold weight of the dollar (or, inversely, the dollar price of gold). Targeting the price level (or nowadays its rate of change) rather than having a rule for the growth rate of the quantity of money no longer looks so clearly to be a flaw, given the 'Goodhart's law' problem that targeting a particular monetary aggregate changes its relationship to other monetary aggregates and to nominal income. Periodic resetting of the dollar price of gold was a more serious problem, exposing the compensated dollar to speculative attacks. Finally, in 1935 Fisher resolved that problem in his book *100% Money*, advocating open market operations to change the quantity of money to maintain a price-level target, but by then he had lost his audience. In 1913, with Fisher's advice, Senator Robert L. Owen (Fisher's ally in an earlier attempt to create a national Department of Health) managed to insert a mandatory price-level target in the Senate version of the Owen-Glass Bill creating the Federal Reserve System (see Dimand, 2003*b*), but it was removed by the House of Representatives, a lost opportunity that has been widely overlooked in the literature (see Mehrling, 2002; Laidler, 2003*d*; Meltzer, 2003).

Knut Wicksell has long fascinated, and to some degree perplexed, David Laidler (1972*b*, 1987*d*, 1993*b*, 1999*a*, 2006*b*), because Wicksell was one of the greatest quantity theorists – if he was a quantity theorist at all (see also Humphrey, 1997). The two interest rates stressed by Wicksell were the market rate of interest, set by the banking system, and the natural rate, the rate at which investment would equal saving at potential output, or at which actual investment would equal planned investment, or at which prices would be constant (ambiguities that occupied the next generation of the Stockholm school). As long as the natural rate of interest exceeded the market rate, entrepreneurs could profit by borrowing and investing, and cumulative inflation would occur, an approach followed by Keynes in *A Treatise on Money* (1930). In the pure credit economy of Wicksell's *Interest and Prices* (1898, chapter 9) or the cashless economy of Michael Woodford's neo-Wicksellian book of the same name (2003), payments are made with bank money or other forms of credit, and the quantity of cash and non-interest-bearing bank reserves is zero. Motivated by decades of financial innovation reducing reserve requirements and the payments role of cash, Woodford's title is a deliberate move back to Wicksell from Patinkin's *Money, Interest and Prices* (1965), a title that itself referred to Wicksell. Laidler (e.g., 1987*d*, 1993*b*) has consistently argued that the quantity of money played a larger role in Wicksell's analysis than later commentators often suggest, that the pure credit economy was only a limiting case of a thought experiment, and Wicksell was indeed a quantity theorist (as Wicksell himself claimed). Laidler (2006*b*, 151–152) accepts that changes in the stylized facts mean that

> the mean in which central bankers have always thought about these things – interest rate control – has become the right way for academics to approach them too. ... Even so, modern monetary systems have not yet evolved into Wicksellian pure credit economies. ... Woodford presents the modern approach to the theory of monetary policy as superceding an older one, which did indeed focus on the interaction of the supply and demand for money, whereas Wicksell, from whom Woodford's analysis draws inspiration, intended his model of the pure credit economy to supplement rather than replace such an approach.

Laidler (2006*b*, 155) insists than an analysis based on a pure credit economy ignores the continuing role of a major reserve currency such as the US dollar as an international means of payment, unit of account, standard of deferred payment, and store of value. For Woodford, money is a friction. For David, money is a medium for society to reduce frictions such as illiquidity and search and transactions costs, and the history of monetary theory sheds light on such issues. (In the later connection, it is worthy of note that Woodford came to the History of Economics Society annual meeting in Toronto in 2004 to respond to David and other commentators (Laidler, 2006*b*; Woodford, 2006), and that Laidler, 2003*b* singles out a paper by Woodford for 'a balanced and carefully nuanced account of the evolution of macroeconomics in the 20th century, written from the viewpoint of a modern practitioner'.)

Keynes, Chicago, and the Interwar Era

In an interview conducted in 1995, David Laidler told Christof Rühl that the working title for David's *Fabricating the Keynesian Revolution* (1999*b*) was '*The Synthetic*

Revolution. The word "synthetic" is ambiguous. It first of all suggests that the Keynesian revolution was largely a matter of synthesizing earlier ideas into a manageable framework, which I think is true; and it also suggests that the notion that there had been a great revolution in 1936, in the senses that a previous orthodoxy was destroyed, was a manufactured idea. So those two senses of synthetic capture the ambiguity of my attitude to Keynes's accomplishments' (Laidler and Rühl, 1998). Historians of economic thought will recognize the first half of this statement as Joseph Schumpeter's view of Adam Smith's *Wealth of Nations*: that many (by no means all) of the individual ideas in the work can be traced back to David Hume, or Richard Cantillon, or A. R. J. Turgot, or other 18th-century writers, but it was Smith, and not any of his predecessors, who succeeded in synthesizing these ideas and constructing a tractable framework for political economy. To Salim Rashid, this implied that the credit for Smithian political economy should be parceled out among the originators of the individual components of the framework, but where Rashid saw what would by later standards be plagiarism, Schumpeter (1954) understood the importance of the process of synthesis. *The General Theory*, like *The Wealth of Nations*, is a triumph of synthesis. Given David's praise for Keynes's *Tract on Monetary Reform* (1923), his recognition of the contribution to liquidity preference theory in Keynes's *Treatise on Money* (1930), and Keynes's very active participation in the creation of Robertson's *Banking Policy and the Price Level* (1926), it should also be noted that Keynes had no small role in the creation of the earlier ideas that he was synthesizing. As to creating a manageable, and therefore useful, framework, note that the first appearance of a small, simultaneous-equations formulation of Keynes's theory was as a four-equation model in a December 1933 lecture by Keynes, and that the first two published versions of models equivalent to the IS-LM framework were by David Champernowne and W. Brian Reddaway, who had attended that lecture (Dimand, 2007).

I have argued elsewhere (Dimand, 1988) that the synthesis in Keynes's *General Theory* had four building blocks: (1) the goods market equilibrium condition, with the level of income, along with the interest rate, bringing saving and investment into equality, with the multiplier as a corollary; (2) the money market equilibrium condition, with money demand (liquidity preference) a function of income and the interest rate; (3) the volatility of private investment, driven by shifting long-period expectations about a fundamentally uncertain future; and (4) the analysis of why the labor market does not always clear (including Chapter 19 on why flexibility of money wage rates may not clear the labor market), so that the synthesis yields a theory of the role of aggregate demand in determining the level of employment and real output in a monetary economy, not just of prices and nominal income.

Don Patinkin (1982) claimed that (1), income as the key variable equating saving to desired investment, was Keynes's 'central message' to the discipline. Sir Ralph Hawtrey saw (2), a money demand function with income and interest as arguments, as the crucial innovation: before *The General Theory*, Hawtrey's theory had aggregate demand affecting real output and he even made a series of contributions to the multiplier analysis, but because he viewed money demand as interest-inelastic, he thought that only monetary policy could be used to smooth the trade cycle, while fiscal policy would be crowded out. As Laidler (1990*c*) emphasizes, the liquidity preference function of *The General Theory* elaborated earlier concepts in Keynes's *Treatise on Money*, which had been developed considerably further by John Hicks in 1935, and there had been many discussions of the motives for holding money. In his *Theory of Interest* (1930, 216, in Fisher, 1997, vol. 9), Irving Fisher had stated the marginal opportunity cost of holding real money balances. Nonetheless, Keynes (1936) was the first to write money function explicitly as a function of a small number of variables: income and interest, given the state of long-period expectations. Don Patinkin (1981) argued, at length and to Friedman's annoyance, that Milton Friedman's money demand function was Keynesian in origin.

Post Keynesians emphasize (3), fundamental uncertainty about the future, but Laidler, like other monetarists, rejects this view of volatile private investment as the source of economic instability, requiring activist stabilization policy. To the contrary, Laidler, like Friedman and Schwartz (1963), finds the source of instability in mistaken public policies, such as those of the Federal Reserve from 1929 to 1933:

> the Depression provided no evidence that mechanism inherent in a monetary economy required that it subjected to continuous and rather large-scale government interventions. Such an economy was reliably self-regulating so long as monetary policy-makers refrained from creating chronic excess demands or supplies of money. In either circumstance, Say's Law might be violated – along the lines that Mill had hinted at in 1844, it might be noted – as friction-prone markets tried to eliminate the excesses in question, but there was no reason to follow Keynes in arguing that, in a monetary economy, the intertemporal co-ordination mechanism was chronically prone to failure. (Laidler, 2006*a*, 55)

James Tobin (1993) stressed (4), particularly the importance of Keynes's Chapter 19 on why the failure of the labor market to clear was not just due to the nominal stickiness emphasized by New Keynesian economists and denied by New Classical economists. As Laidler (1991*b*, 2) remarked in his Henry Thornton Lecture, 'If the criterion is the treatment of money wage and price flexibility, then the New-classical economics is new, but it is surely not Classical; and the New-Keynesian economics is neither new nor distinctively Keynesian'. Concerns about nominal stickiness and slow adjustment led Ricardo to endorse restoration of gold convertibility of sterling at a depreciated parity and Jean-Baptiste Say to advocate public works spending to provide employment during transition periods. The idea that downward stickiness of a particular price (such as the money wage) can lead to an excess supply in a particular market long predates Maynard Keynes. While economists and policymakers had long been conscious of the fact of unemployment (the *Encyclopaedia Britannica* first devoted an article to the topic in the 1911 edition), and monetary and cycle theorists had been motivated to analyze fluctuations in prices and nominal income because they believed that real fluctuations would follow (with, e.g., Fisher, 1926 presenting empirical evidence that this was so), there was no theory of employment with a role for aggregate demand before Keynes (1936).

The prevailing view of unemployment before *The General Theory* is not, I think, made sufficiently clear in *Fabricating the Keynesian Revolution* (Laidler, 1999*b*). Subtitled *Studies of the Inter-war Literature on Money, the Cycle, and Unemployment*, it carefully covers interwar writings *by monetary economists* on these subjects, but is thinner in its coverage of what other economists wrote about cycles and, especially, unemployment. With regard to the cycle, the bibliography lists nothing by Ragnar Frisch, and by Jan Tinbergen only a review of a book by Harrod. In Chapter 7 'British Discussions of Unemployment', Laidler (1999*b*) reports that Pigou (1933) attributed high unemployment to real wages being too high, conducting his analysis largely in real terms and with regard to the labor market alone, and that the 1909 first edition of Beveridge (1930) viewed unemployment as a frictional 'problem of industry', with the creation of labor exchanges as the appropriate remedy. However, Beveridge's approach was no mere pre-World War I relic. He published a much expanded *Unemployment: A Problem of Industry* in 1930, followed the next year by a shorter popular volume of *Causes and Cures of Unemployment* first presented as six talks over the BBC, and he responded to *The General Theory* with a long article on 'The Analysis of Unemployment' in three issues of *Economica* in 1936 and 1937 (reprinted in Dimand, 2002, vol. 8), arguing that existing British unemployment could be fully explained as frictional, structural, or seasonal, with no need for a macroeconomic theory of unemployment bringing in deficiency of aggregate demand. While Pigou was careful to dissociate himself from the policy implications of his *Theory of Unemployment* (as he later insisted that his analysis of the real balance effect was an abstract theoretical exercise with no policy significance), Edwin Cannan, in his 1932 Royal Economic Society presidential address (reprinted in Dimand, 2002, vol. 8), did emphatically draw the conclusion that wage cutting was the remedy for unemployment, which, like excess supply in any other market, indicated nothing other than that the price was too high in that market. Jacques Rueff, summarized for British readers by Sir Josiah Stamp, attributed interwar British unemployment to the dole, rather than aggregate supply and demand (Dimand, 1988, 2003*a*). Keynes owed much to Wicksell, Robertson, Hawtrey, Kahn, and others, but he did not simply summarize what all were saying. In particular, his analysis of why the labor market does not always clear, and his insistence that what became known as macroeconomics is the aggregate theory of output and employment, was distinctive.

David also spoke of the Keynesian revolution as a synthetic or fabricated revolution in a second sense, arguing that the revolutionary break in the evolution of the discipline had been, like the early reports of Mark Twain's death, much exaggerated. In this connection, Laidler (1999*b*) referred to the writings of Harry Johnson, especially Johnson's 1971 Ely Lecture 'The Keynesian Revolution and the Monetarist Counter-Revolution' (in Johnson and Johnson, 1978, 183–202). For Keynesianism or monetarism to succeed in capturing the rising generation of economists, they had to overstate their novelty by renaming familiar concepts, offer an apparently better analysis of an important problem (unemployment or inflation) not well handled by existing orthodoxy, use techniques just advanced enough to be difficult for established economists to master but accessible to young theorists, and provide a supply of publishable topics to investigate. In his Ely Lecture, Johnson (quoted by Laidler, 2003*b*, 16) wrote that 'The Keynesian Revolution derived a large part of its intellectual appeal from the deliberate caricaturing and denigration of honest and humble scholars, whose only real crime was that they happened to exist and stand in the way of the success of the revolution. The counter-revolution had to endow these scholars, or at least their intellectual successors, with a wisdom vastly superior to what their opponents had credited them with. *Obiter dicta* and an oral tradition are at least a semi-legitimate scholarly means to this polemical end'. Laidler (1984*b*), in his memorial article on Harry Johnson as a macroeconomist, remarked that these polemical tactics for a successful revolution were seen by some as characteristic not only of Keynesianism and monetarism, but also of Johnson's monetary approach to the balance of payments and exchange rates (notwithstanding Laidler's stalwart upholding of the substance of the monetary approach). Johnson, like Patinkin (1981), argued that Chicago monetarism had more in common with Keynesian macroeconomics, and owed less to a unique Chicago oral tradition of monetary theory, than Friedman claimed. Laidler (1993*a*, 1998) agreed, and also drew attention to quantity theorists outside Chicago, particularly Allyn Young, Lauchlin Currie, and Ralph Hawtrey at Harvard (where Hawtrey was a visiting professor in 1928–29, taking Young's place when Young moved to LSE). David's heresy about the immaculate conception of Chicago monetarism, uttered by a loyal Friedmanite quantity theorist, greatly distressed George Tavlas (1997, 1998*a*, 1998*b*). Laidler (2003*b*) perceived the same rhetorical strategy, including rhetorical misuse of the history of economic thought, in the rise of New Classical economics as in the Keynesian revolution, the monetarist counter-revolution, and the monetary approach to the balance of payments.

The Present in Light of the Past

According to David Laidler, 'since Adam Smith at least, economists have been arguing the question of whether a decentralized market economy can coordinate the choices of individuals who are pursuing their own self-interest. That seems to me to be a very interesting question to discuss; and Lucas and Sargent and Wallace invited us to settle it by *a priori* assumption and they come close to telling us we weren't doing economics if we don't swallow that assumption whole. And that's incredible I think' (Laidler and Rühl, 1998). Representative agent models dispose of the macroeconomic coordination problem by assuming that the economy behaves as if it consisted only of a number of identical agents (which eliminates not only coordination problems, but also exchange). Overlapping generations (OLG) models posit two representative agents, one young and one old, and rigorously derive the demand for fiat money from the assumption that there is no other way to hold wealth. David disapproves of modern macroeconomists (whether New Classical, or others following similar methodology) who assume away questions that have long interested economists. Laidler (2003*b*) is skeptical of economists who posit that all agents in their models believe in the same 'true' model as the modeler:

> If we treat the History of Economic Thought with any degree of seriousness, however, three truths become apparent, and one conjecture becomes plausible: first, in the real world, it is economists, not agents in general, who specialise in creating models of the economy; second, at no time in the past have economists ever provided a single model with an undisputed claim to embody the truth; third, the models that they have provided have always evolved continuously in the face of logical and empirical criticism; and, finally, it seems unlikely that the future is going to differ from the past in any of these respects.

Laidler (2003*b*, 21) stresses that 'It was narrative history [in Friedman and Schwartz 1963], rather than state-of-the-art theory and econometrics, that so profoundly changed the views of economists in the 1960s and 1970s: strong testimony to the importance then attached to the analysis of the interaction of economic ideas with events as a means of bringing empirical evidence to bear on the assessment of economic theories'. The prevailing ideas mattered for understanding how the Great Contraction of the early 1930s or the Great Inflation of the 1970s came about.

Citing such rhetorical misuses of history as Sargent and Wallace on the real bills doctrine and Sargent's claim (contrary to the evidence) that Paul Samuelson and Robert Solow advocated deliberately moving up the Phillips curve to reduce unemployment at the cost of higher inflation, Laidler (2003*b*, 25) eloquently objects that

> There is surely something amiss about the History of Economic Thought being used as a rhetorical weapon, in support of the intellectual credentials of their own work, by the same leading figures who denigrate the field's importance. The skills that would enable their intended audience to assess such arguments on their merits are, increasingly, not being taught. All this, when the substantive theoretical ideas that are defended by these means themselves imply that a knowledge of the economics of the past is critical to disciplining the empirical application and further development of those very ideas.

Like Blaug (2001) and Weintraub (1989), Laidler feels that knowledge of the history of economic thought and training in how to read past economists would prevent such rhetorical missteps, provide perspective on what questions to study and on what can be learned from past events and ideas, and train better economists. Modern macroeconomic theorists worry that if they were to study history of thought, people would think that they were not really mathematicians, unaware that mathematicians tend to be interested in the history of their discipline (see Bourbaki, 1960). David Laidler is an inspiring example of a monetary theorist and empirical monetary economist of the highest ability whose work in monetary economics has benefited greatly from the fact that he is also an adept and fully professional historian of monetary economics. Indeed, he has achieved a notable accolade to his professionalism as a historian of economic thought: when such self-consciously modern macroeconomic theorists as Olivier Blanchard (2000) and J. Bradford De Long (2000) had occasion, upon the turn of the millennium, to ruminate on the history of monetary economics and macroeconomics, they treated him as they would treat any clearly competent professional writing on such topics: they ignored everything that he has written.

Writings in the History of Economic Thought by David E. W. Laidler

(An asterisk indicates that an article is reprinted in Laidler 2004*b*.)

(1972*a**) "Thomas Tooke on Monetary Reform," in Maurice Peston and Bernard Corry, eds., *Essays in Honour of Lionel Robbins*, London: Weidenfeld and Nicolson, pp. 168–186, reprinted in Laidler, *Essays on Money and Inflation*, Chicago: University of Chicago Press, and Manchester, UK: Manchester University Press, 1975.

(1972*b*) "On Wicksell's Theory of Price Level Dynamics," *Manchester School* 40 (June), 125–144, reprinted in Laidler, *Essays on Money and Inflation*, Chicago: University of Chicago Press, and Manchester, UK: Manchester University Press.

(1979) "Abba P. Lerner," *International Encyclopedia of the Social Sciences*, Vol. 18 (*Biographical Supplement*), New York: Macmillan and the Free Press.

(with Nicholas Rowe) (1980), "George Simmel's *Philosophy of Money*: A Review Article for Economists," *Journal of Economic Literature* 18:1 (March), 97–105.

(1981*) "Adam Smith as a Monetary Economist," *Canadian Journal of Economics* 14:2 (May), 185–200.

(1982*a*) "On Say's Law, Money and the Business Cycle," Chapter 3 of Laidler, *Monetarist Perspectives*, Oxford, UK: Philip Allan, and Cambridge, MA: Harvard University Press.

(1982*b*) "Jevons on Money," *Manchester School* 50 (December), 326–353.

(1982*c*) "Friedman and Schwartz on Monetary Trends – a Review Article," *Journal of International Money and Finance* 1, 293–305.

(1983) "*Money, Interest and Wages, Collected Essays on Economic Theory,* Vol. II by Sir John Hicks – a Review Essay," *Journal of Money, Credit and Banking* 15, 385–389.

(1984*a*) "Misconceptions about the Real Bills Doctrine – a Comment on Sargent and Wallace," *Journal of Political Economy* 92:1 (February), 149–155.

(1984*b*) "Harry Johnson as a Macroeconomist," *Journal of Political Economy* 92:4 (August), 592–615.

(1987*a*) "Boyd, Walter (1754–1837)," in John Eatwell, Murray Milgate, and Peter Newman, eds., *The New Palgrave: A Dictionary of Economics*, London: Macmillan.

(1987*b*) "Bullionist Controversy," in John Eatwell, Murray Milgate, and Peter Newman, eds., *The New Palgrave: A Dictionary of Economics*, London: Macmillan, reprinted in Eatwell, Milgate, and Newman, eds., *The New Palgrave Money*, New York: Norton, 1989, as revised in Eatwell, Milgate, and Newman, eds., *The New Palgrave Dictionary of Money and Finance*, London: Macmillan, 1992, I, 255–261.

(1987*c*) "Thornton, Henry (1760–1815)," in John Eatwell, Murray Milgate, and Peter Newman, eds., *The New Palgrave: A Dictionary of Economics*, London: Macmillan.

(1987*d*) "Wicksell and Fisher on the 'Backing' of Money and the Quantity Theory: A Comment on the Debate between Smith and Michener," in Karl Brunner and A. H.

Meltzer, eds., *Empirical Studies of Velocity, Real Exchange Rates, Unemployment and Productivity, Carnegie-Rochester Conference Series on Public Policy* 27, Amsterdam: North Holland, pp. 325–337.

(1988) "British Monetary Orthodoxy in the 1870s," *Oxford Economic Papers* 40 (March), 74–109, revised as Chapter 2 of Laidler (1991*a*).

(1989*) "Radcliffe, the Quantity Theory, and Monetarism," in D. Cobham, R. Harrington, and G. Zis, eds., *Money, Trade and Payments: Essays in Honour of D. J. Coppock*, Manchester, UK: Manchester University Press, pp. 17–37.

(1990*a**) "Alfred Marshall and the Development of Monetary Economics," in John K. Whitaker, ed., *Centenary Essays on Alfred Marshall*, Cambridge, UK: Cambridge University Press, pp. 44–78.

(1990*b**) "The Legacy of the Monetarist Controversy," *Federal Reserve Bank of St. Louis Quarterly Review* (March/April), 49–64.

(1990*c**) "What was New about Liquidity Preference Theory?" *Greek Economic Review* 12 (Autumn), Supplement, 9–37 (NB: misdated as 1980 in Laidler, 2004*b*, pp. v, viii.)

(1991*a*) *The Golden Age of the Quantity Theory – the Development of Neoclassical Monetary Economics: 1870–1914*. Hemel Hampstead, UK: Philip Allan, and Princeton, NJ: Princeton University Press.

(1991*b*) "Money, Credit and Banking Lecture: Karl Brunner's Monetary Economics – an Appreciation," *Journal of Money, Credit and Banking* 23:4, 633–658.

(1991*c**) "The Austrians and the Stockholm School: Two Failures in the History of Modern Macroeconomics?" in Lars Jonung, ed., *The Stockholm School of Economics Revisited*, Cambridge, UK: Cambridge University Press (incorporated in Laidler, 1999, Chapters 2 and 3).

(1991*d**) "Wage and Price Stickiness in Macroeconomics: An Historical Perspective," The Thirteenth Henry Thornton Lecture, City University, London, 20 November.

(1991*e*) "The Quantity Theory is Always and Everywhere Controversial – Why?" *Economic Record* 67:199 (December), 289–306.

(1993*a**) "Hawtrey, Harvard, and the Origins of the Chicago Tradition," *Journal of Political Economy* 101(6), 1068–1103.

(1993*b*) "Was Wicksell a Quantity Theorist?" in Haim Barkai, Stanley Fischer, and N. Liviatan, eds., *Monetary Theory and Thought, Essays in Honour of Don Patinkin*, London: Macmillan.

(1994*a**) "Hicks's Later Monetary Thought," in Harald Hagemann and Omar Hamouda, eds., *The Legacy of Hicks*, London and New York: Routledge, pp. 163–173 (a revised version of Laidler, "Hicks and the Classics," *Journal of Monetary Economics* 25, June 1990).

(1994*b*) "Hayek on Neutral Money and the Cycle," in Marina Colonna and Harald Hagemann, eds., *The Economics of F. A. Hayek*, Vol. 1: *Money and Business Cycles*, Aldershot, UK, and Brookfield, VT: Edward Elgar Publishing (incorporated in Laidler 1999*b*, Chapter 2).

(1995*a*) "Robertson in the 1920s," *European Journal of the History of Economic Thought* 2:1 (Spring), 151–174 (incorporated in Laidler, 1999*b*, Chapter 4).

(1995*b**) "Some Aspects of Monetarism circa 1970: A View from 1994," *Kredit und Kapital* 3, 323–344.

(1995*c*) "Comment" on "Irving Fisher, J. M. Keynes, and the Transition to Modern Macroeconomics" by R. W. Dimand, in A. F. Cottrell and Michael S. Lawlor, eds., *New Perspectives on Keynes*, Supplement to *History of Political Economy*, Durham, NC: Duke University Press, pp. 267–271.

(1997*) "The Emergence of the Phillips Curve as a Policy Menu," in B. Curtis Eaton and Richard G. Harris, eds., *Trade, Technology and Economics: Essays in Honour of Richard G. Lipsey*, Cheltenham, UK, and Northampton, MA: Edward Elgar Publishing, pp. 88–106 (expanded version in Laidler, 2004*b*).

(1998*) "More on Hawtrey, Harvard, and Chicago," *Journal of Economic Studies* 25:1, 4–16, and "Hawtrey, Harvard and Chicago – a Final Comment," 22–24 responding to George S. Tavlas 1998*a*, 17–21 (only pp. 4 to 16 are reprinted in Laidler, 2004*b*.)

(with George W. Stadler) (1998*) "Monetary Explanations of the Weimar Republic's Hyperinflation: Some Neglected Contributions in Contemporary German Literature," *Journal of Money, Credit and Banking* 30 (November) (expanded version in Laidler, 2004*b*).
(with Christof Rühl) (1998) "Perspectives on Modern Macroeconomic Theory and its History: an Interview with David Laidler," *Review of Political Economy* 10:1, 27–56.
(1999*a**) "Variations on a Two-Interest-Rate Theme," in Peter Howitt, Elisabeta de Antoni and Axel Leijonhufvud, eds., *Money, Markets and Method: Essays in Honour of Robert W. Clower*, Cheltenham, UK, and Northampton, MA: Edward Elgar Publishing, pp. 121–139.
(1999*b*) *Fabricating the Keynesian Revolution: Studies of the Inter-War Literature on Money, the Cycle, and Unemployment*. Cambridge, UK: Cambridge University Press.
(2000) *Highlights of the Bullionist Controversy*. Stockholm: Institute for Research in Economic History, Stockholm School of Economics, Research Report #13.
(2002*a*) "Skidelsky's Keynes: a review essay," *European Journal of the History of Economic Thought* 9:1 (Spring), 97–110 (review article on Skidelsky (1983–2000)).
(2002*b**) "Rules, Discretion and Financial Crises in Classical and Neoclassical Monetary Economics," *Economic Issues* 7(2), 11–33.
(2002*c*) "Phillips in Retrospect," *Research in History of Economic Thought and Methodology* 20-A, 223–235.
(2002*d*) "Quantity Theory of Money," in Brian Snowdon and Howard Vance, eds., *An Encyclopaedia of Macroeconomics*, Cheltenham, UK: Edward Elgar Publishing.
(with Roger Sandilands) (2002) "An Early Harvard Memorandum on Anti-Depression Policies: An Introductory Note," *History of Political Economy* 34:3 (Fall), 515–532, followed by "Memorandum Prepared by L. B. Currie, P. T. Ellsworth, and H. D. White (Cambridge, MA, January 1932)," edited by David Laidler and Roger Sandilands, pp. 533–552.
(2003*a**) "Two Views of the Lender of Last Resort: Thornton and Bagehot," *Cahiers d'economie politique* 45 (Autumn), 61–78.
(2003*b**) "The Role of the History of Economic Thought in Modern Macroeconomics," in Paul Mizen, ed., *Monetary History, Exchange Rates and Financial Markets: Essays in Honour of Charles Goodhart, Volume Two*, Cheltenham, UK, and Northampton, MA: Edward Elgar Publishing, pp. 12–29.
(2003*c*) "The Price Level, Relative Prices, and Economic Stability: Aspects of the Inter-War Debate," presented to conference on "Monetary Stability, Financial Stability, and the Business Cycle" at the Bank for International Settlements, Basel, Switzerland, March 28.
(2003*d*) "Meltzer's *History of the Federal Reserve*," *Journal of Economic Literature* 41:4 (December), 1256–1271.
(2004*a**) "From Bimetallism to Monetarism: The Shifting Political Affiliation of the Quantity Theory," in Ingo Barens, Volker Caspari, and Bertram Schefold, eds., *Political Events and Economic Ideas*, Cheltenham, UK, and Northampton, MA: Edward Elgar Publishing, pp. 9–36.
(2004*b*) *Macroeconomics in Retrospect: The Selected Essays of David Laidler*. Cheltenham, UK, and Northampton, MA: Edward Elgar Publishing.
(with Roger E. Backhouse) (2004) "What Was Lost with IS-LM?" in Michel De Vroey and Kevin D. Hoover, eds., *The IS-LM Model: Its Rise, Fall, and Strange Persistence*, Annual Supplement of *History of Political Economy* Vol. 36, Durham, NC: Duke University Press, pp. 25–56.
(2006*a*) "Keynes and the Birth of Modern Macroeconomics," in Roger E. Backhouse and Bradley W. Bateman, eds., *The Cambridge Companion to Keynes*, Cambridge, UK: Cambridge University Press, pp. 39–57.
(2006*b*) "Woodford and Wicksell on *Interest and Prices*: The Place of the Pure Credit Economy in the Theory of Monetary Policy," *Journal of the History of Economic Thought* 28:2 (June), 151–159.

(Forthcoming) "Milton Friedman and the Evolution of Macroeconomics," introductory essay for Milton Friedman's collected writings on macroeconomic topics.

References

Bagehot, Walter (1873). *Lombard Street: A Description of the Money Market*, reprinted ed. F. C. Genovese, Homewood, IL: Richard Irwin, 1962.

Beveridge, William H. (1930). *Unemployment, a Problem of Industry, 1909 and 1930*. London: Longmans, Green.

Blanchard, Olivier (2000). "What Do We Know about Macroeconomics that Fisher and Wicksell Did Not?" *Quarterly Journal of Economics* 115 (November), 1375–1409.

Blaug, Mark (2001). "No History of Ideas, Please, We're Economists." *Journal of Economic Perspectives* 15:1 (Winter), 145–164.

Blaug, Mark, Walter Eltis, Denis O'Brien, Don Patinkin, Robert Skidelsky, and Geoffrey E. Wood (1995). *The Quantity Theory of Money from Locke to Keynes and Friedman*. Aldershot, UK, and Brookfield, VT: Edward Elgar Publishing.

Bourbaki, N. (1960). *Elements d'histoire des mathématiques*. Paris : Hermann; translated by John Meldrun, *Elements of the History of Mathematics*. Berlin and New York: Springer Verlag, 1994.

Brunner, Karl and Allan Meltzer (1993). *Money and the Economy*. Cambridge, UK: Cambridge University Press for the Raffaele Mattioli Foundation.

Capie, Forrest and Geoffrey E. Wood, eds. (1989). *Monetary Economics in the 1980s: The Henry Thornton Lectures, Numbers 1–8*. London: Macmillan in association with the City University Centre for Banking and International Finance.

De Long, J. Bradford (2000). "The Triumph of Monetarism?" *Journal of Economic Perspectives* 14:1 (Winter), 83–94.

Dimand, Robert W. (1988). *The Origins of the Keynesian Revolution*. Aldershot, UK: Edward Elgar Publishing, and Stanford, CA: Stanford University Press.

Dimand, Robert W., ed. (2002). *The Origins of Macroeconomics*, 10 volumes. London and New York: Routledge.

Dimand, Robert W. (2003*a*). "Interwar Monetary and Business Cycle Theory: Macroeconomics before Keynes." *Research in the History of Economic Thought and Methodology* 21-A, 121–148.

Dimand, Robert W. (2003*b*). "Competing Visions for the US Monetary System, 1907–1913: The Quest for an Elastic Currency and the Rejection of Fisher's Compensated Dollar Rule for Price stability." *Cahiers d'Economic Politique* 45, 101–121.

Dimand, Robert W. (2007). "Keynes, IS-LM, and the Marshallian Tradition." *History of Political Economy* 39 (Spring), 81–95.

Eagly, Robert V. (1971). *The Swedish Bullionist Controversy*. Philadelphia: American Philosophical Society.

Ellis, Howard (1934). *German Monetary Theory 1905–1933*. Cambridge, MA: Harvard University Press.

Fetter, Frank W. (1965). *The Development of British Monetary Orthodoxy 1797–1875*. Cambridge, MA: Harvard University Press.

Fisher, Irving (1926). "A Statistical Relation between Unemployment and Price Changes." *International Labour Review* 13:6 (June), 785–792, reprinted in Fisher (1997), Vol. 8, and as "Lost and Found: I Discovered the Phillips Curve – Irving Fisher," *Journal of Political Economy* 81:2 (1973), 496–502.

Fisher, Irving (1997). *The Works of Irving Fisher*, 14 volumes, edited by William J. Barber assisted by Robert W. Dimand and Kevin Foster, consulting editor James Tobin. London: Pickering & Chatto.

Flanders, M. June (1989). *International Monetary Economics 1870–1960: Between the Classical and the New Classical*. Cambridge, UK: Cambridge University Press.

Friedman, Milton and Anna J. Schwartz (1963). *A Monetary History of the United States, 1867–1960.* Princeton, NJ: Princeton University Press for the National Bureau of Economic Research.
Gordon, Robert J., ed. (1974). *Milton Friedman's Monetary Framework: A Debate with His Critics.* Chicago: University of Chicago Press.
Hahn, L. Albert (1920). *Volkswirthschaftliche Theorie des Bankkredits.* Tübingen: J. C. B. Mohr (Paul Siebeck), 3rd ed. 1930.
Hahn, L. Albert (1949). *The Economics of Illusion.* New York: Squier Publishing, distributed by the New York Institute of Finance.
Humphrey, Thomas M. (1986). *Essays on Inflation*, 5th ed. Richmond, VA: Federal Reserve Bank of Richmond.
Humphrey, Thomas M. (1997). "Fisher and Wicksell on the Quantity Theory." *Federal Reserve Bank of Richmond Economic Quarterly* 83 (Fall), 71–90.
Johnson, Elizabeth S. and Harry G. Johnson (1978). *The Shadow of Keynes.* Chicago: University of Chicago Press.
Keynes, John Maynard (1923). *A Tract on Monetary Reform.* London: Macmillan.
Keynes, John Maynard (1930). *A Treatise on Money*, 2 volumes. London: Macmillan.
Keynes, John Maynard (1936). *The General Theory of Employment, Interest and Money.* London: Macmillan.
Marshall, Alfred (1923). *Money, Credit and Commerce.* London: Macmillan.
Marshall, Alfred (1926). *Official Papers*, ed. J. M. Keynes. London: Macmillan.
Mehrling, Perry (2002). "Economists and the Fed: Beginnings." *Journal of Economic Perspectives* 16:1 (Winter), 207–218.
Meltzer, Allan H. (2003). *A History of the Federal Reserve*, Volume 1: *1913–1951.* Chicago: University of Chicago Press.
Patinkin, Don (1965). *Money, Interest and Prices*, 2nd ed. New York: Harper & Row.
Patinkin, Don (1981). *Essays on and in the Chicago Tradition.* Durham, NC: Duke University Press.
Patinkin, Don (1982). *Anticipations of the General Theory? And Other Essays on Keynes.* Chicago: University of Chicago Press.
Pigou, A. C. (1933). *The Theory of Unemployment.* London: Macmillan. Reprinted New York: Augustus M. Kelley, 1968.
Robertson, Dennis H. (1926). *Banking Policy and the Price Level.* London: P. S. King.
Sargent, Thomas J. and Neil Wallace (1982). "The Real-Bills Doctrine versus the Quantity Theory: A Reconsideration." *Journal of Political Economy* 90:6 (December), 1212–1236.
Schumpeter, Joseph A. (1954). *History of Economic Analysis.* New York: Oxford University Press.
Snowdon, Brian and Howard Vane (2005). *Modern Macroeconomics.* Cheltenham, UK, and Northampton, MA: Edward Elgar Publishing.
Tavlas, George S. (1997). "Chicago, Harvard, and the Doctrinal Foundations of Monetary Economics." *Journal of Political Economy* 105:1 (February), 153–177.
Tavlas, George S. (1998*a*). "More on the Chicago Tradition." *Journal of Economic Studies* 25:1, 17–21.
Tavlas, George S. (1998*b*). "Retrospectives: Was the Monetarist Tradition Invented?" *Journal of Economic Perspectives* 12:4 (Fall), 211–222, with comment by David Laidler, "The Chicago Monetarist Tradition," 13:1 (Winter), 240–241, and response by Tavlas, 241–242.
Thornton, Henry (1802). *An Enquiry into the Nature and Effects of the Paper Credit of Great Britain*, edited with an introduction by Friedrich A. Hayek, London: George Allen & Unwin, 1939.
Tobin, James (1993). "Price Flexibility and Output Stability: An Old Keynesian View." *Journal of Economic Perspectives* 7:1 (Winter), 45–65.
Viner, Jacob (1937). *Studies in the Theory of International Trade.* New York: Harper and Brothers.

Weintraub, E. Roy (1989). "Methodology Doesn't Matter, but the History of Thought Might." *Scandinavian Journal of Economics* 91:2 (90th Anniversary Symposium: Whither Macroeconomics?), 477–493.
Wicksell, Knut (1898). *Interest and Prices*, translated by Richard F. Kahn, London: Macmillan for the Royal Economic Society, 1936.
Woodford, Michael (2003). *Interest and Prices: Foundations of a Theory of Monetary Policy.* Princeton, NJ: Princeton University Press.
Woodford, Michael (2006). "Comments on the Symposium on *Interest and Prices*." *Journal of the History of Economic Thought* 28:2 (June), 187–198.

5
Laidler's Monetarism

Perry Mehrling

> From the point of view of the non-academic observer whose main concern was the conduct of economic policy, Monetarism involved first a theory of inflation, second a theory of the cycle, and third, as a corollary of these, a recommendation for the conduct of monetary policy. Specifically, inflation was said to be explicable in terms of the rate of growth of the money supply, and the cycle, or more precisely its turning points, in terms of changes in that rate of growth.
>
> (Laidler, 2004 [1990], 395)

To understand Laidler's work as a whole, we need to put ourselves in his shoes, and imagine what it was like to enter the profession during the years of Keynesian hegemony, when all of macroeconomics was supposed to be summarized by the simple two-curve IS-LM model, itself presumed to be an aggregative version of the Walrasian general equilibrium model, and when econometric estimation of multiple-equation versions of this simple model was seen as the epitome of empirical work in the field. With modern economic theory to guide their thinking, and modern computers to help them tie theory to the data, it seemed to many economists entirely possible that the business cycle could be conquered by science.

As an undergraduate at the London School of Economics (LSE), Laidler's first exposure to monetary theory came during the years when the famous Radcliffe Committee *Report on the Working of the Monetary System* (1959) was being prepared. The principal author of the *Report* was R. S. Sayers, a professor at the LSE and a man whose understanding of money stemmed from historical and institutional study of Bank of England operations since 1890 (Sayers, 1936). Laidler remembers: "Debates about the effectiveness of monetary policy certainly penetrated the undergraduate teaching" (Ruhl and Laidler, 1998, 28).[1] These debates, in a sense, have been the theme of Laidler's work ever since.

In his money and macro classes the young Laidler learned the standard stuff, which basically meant Patinkin plus the Phillips curve. But on Friday afternoons, in the seminar of Lionel Robbins, he read the classics of nineteenth-century monetary economics, including the classic debate between the Currency School and the Banking School. Here we find the origins of Laidler's subsequent two-track intellectual career, always with one foot in the Monetary Walrasianism that was the orthodoxy of his time, and the other one in the history of monetary thought. The dialectical tension between these two tracks would provide the energy for a long and productive intellectual career.

That dialectical tension was methodological (mathematico-statistical versus historico-institutional) but also substantive. Since Monetary Walrasianism emphasized the Currency School line, Laidler used his historical studies to explore the missing Banking School side of the debate: Smith, Thornton and Bagehot, Tooke, Hawtrey, the Radcliffe Report, and the late work of Sir John Hicks (Laidler, 2004, chs. 1, 3, 4, 10, 14, 15 [1981, 2003, 1972, 1993, 1989, 1994]). To the outside world, the two tracks of Laidler's intellectual career could easily look like two successive careers—econometrics when young, history when old—but this is to misunderstand the man.[2] The history of thought side took longer to mature, but it was very much a part of Laidler's internal dialogue from the very beginning.

Just so, when young Laidler continued on for graduate study at the University of Chicago, the two-track pattern continued, with exposure to Milton Friedman's version of Monetary Walrasian orthodoxy on the one hand balanced by Earl Hamilton's course on the history of banking theory on the other hand. These were the years when Friedman was hard at work (with Anna Schwartz) on his *Monetary History of the United States, 1867–1960* (1963) and Laidler's research assistance for that project exposed him to a way of doing empirical work that would sustain him through the first stage of his subsequent academic career. Although his dissertation (with Harberger) was in public finance, his first professional publications were all in money.

Starting his academic career at Berkeley, Laidler produced in quick succession two impressive empirical papers on money demand that were quickly published (1966, 1997, ch. 1 [1966]). And at the same time he produced a draft of his first paper in the history of monetary thought, an appreciation of Thomas Tooke that was eventually published as "Thomas Tooke on Monetary Reform" (1972). What did he like about Tooke? It is Tooke's empiricism that comes in for highest praise. Although not perhaps the "painstaking piece of econometric research" (68) that the standards of modern science would require, Tooke's understanding of how the banking system actually worked (specifically the flux and reflux of the note issue) was clearly superior to that of his intellectual opponents, who nevertheless managed to prevail in subsequent legislation (Peel's Act), as well as subsequent academic opinion.

For the young Laidler, even if for no one else, these two lines of research were intimately connected. Tooke and the other founders of British monetary orthodoxy (see Fetter, 1965) had distilled their wisdom largely from historical and institutional study because that was the best scientific method available to them. Econometrics appealed to the young Laidler for its promise of engaging even more deeply with the data; it seemed to him just a more modern and scientific way of doing historical and institutional study. In time he would come to question his youthful faith in the promise of econometrics, and develop greater appreciation for the less technical but more direct engagement of an earlier intellectual style. But at the beginning of his career econometrics seemed to be a way of testing how well theory fit the facts, and as such a force for improvement of theory.

But Tooke was not just an exemplary scientist, he was also the leader of the Banking School. Reading Tooke made Laidler aware of the positive contributions of the Banking School approach to monetary matters, by contrast to the stream of American monetarism that, starting with Irving Fisher and continuing through Milton Friedman, developed the Currency School line. For the Banking School, the gold standard already provided the necessary long-run discipline for the monetary system, and that institutional fact allowed them to focus their attention more on how best to manage the elasticity inherent in credit. Their policy answer, the real bills doctrine, was plainly unsatisfactory but in other respects their analysis was clearly superior. The challenge for Laidler was to understand how the balance of discipline and elasticity that Tooke had sought for his own time could be achieved under very different modern conditions, to wit a system of apparently fiat national currencies without any inherent nominal anchor. The modern dominance of Currency School thinking reflected understandable concern about the problem of discipline in such a system, but missed the important dimension of elasticity. Laidler's early engagement with Tooke's work thus marks the beginning of Laidler's doubts about the exogenous money model shared by Friedman and his critics.

Indeed, some hint of these emerging doubts can be seen even in Laidler's own painstaking econometric research. In the very first of his 1966 empirical papers, he is already testing his own non-Friedmanian theory of money demand: "This hypothesis states that transitory income and negative transitory consumption are *added* to money balances, so that their *level* at any time will depend upon all past levels of these transitory components" (1966, 56). Here is the origin of Laidler's later embrace of what he would call the "buffer stock" approach to monetary economics (Laidler, 1997, ch. 13 [1984]).

In 1966, however, these were only doubts, not convictions. Like his mentor Milton Friedman, Laidler more or less accepted the theoretical framework of Monetary Walrasianism that had been developed by the Keynesians Patinkin, Tobin, and Modigliani, and like Friedman he determined to fight the monetarist battle on empirical grounds. The battle was not about laissez-faire, since both sides agreed that money needed managing, but rather about the efficacy of monetary control for short-term business cycle stabilization (the Keynesian view), as opposed to long-term price level stabilization (the monetarist view). Thus did Laidler find his initial ecological niche as an empirical researcher focusing on the *Demand for Money* (Laidler, 1969).

That first book can be read as an attempt to answer the challenge of the Radcliffe Report. Whereas the central message of the Report had been the instability of money demand, narrowly conceived, and the consequent challenge of central bank policy, Laidler took the central message of Friedman's monetarism to be essentially the opposite. As a theoretical matter the demand for money seemed to be a problem quite amenable to applied price theory, and as an empirical matter it seemed to be a stable function well described by a small number of parameters (Friedman, 1956, 1959). To Laidler, Friedman's project thus seemed very much in line with the stream of neoclassical monetary economics that had been building on the foundations of British monetary orthodoxy ever since 1870 (as Keynes also). Possibly the Radcliffe Report was correct to emphasize the challenge of modern monetary management, but possibly also the tools of modern monetary economics could rise to that challenge.

In the British environment where Laidler moved after his initial Berkeley appointment (to Essex, then Manchester) the Radcliffe Report was interpreted not as a challenge but rather as a decisive repudiation of monetary orthodoxy. Fiscal policy, not monetary policy, was the main tool for economic stabilization and sociological explanations of wage inflation were all the rage. In this context, Laidler's ambition to revive monetary explanations of inflation earned him the label of monetarist, a label he decided to accept and thereafter wore proudly (Laidler, 1975). In the US context, by contrast, Laidler's gradualist "Manchester monetarism" might have placed him among the monetary Keynesians, such as Tobin and Modigliani, even though Laidler was never as convinced as the Keynesians of the potential for short-term fine-tuning using monetary policy.[3]

Upon reflection, neither classification captures the man very accurately. From a larger historical perspective, Laidler's monetarism was simply a modern version of the nineteenth-century quantity theory of money that provided the broad framework within which both Currency School and Banking School advocates argued their case. At the start of his career, Laidler seems to have understood Monetary Walrasianism (specifically the IS-LM model) as a similarly overarching framework within which similarly important argument could take place.

But, as I have said, a seed of doubt had been planted by Tooke, and soon enough that seed would be nourished by the work of Brunner and Meltzer (1971). As early as 1973, in a paper titled "Information, Money and the Macroeconomics of Inflation," Laidler is explicitly moving away from Friedman and toward Brunner and Meltzer.[4] Here we see his first explicit embrace of the "buffer stock" view of money demand, by contrast to Friedman's money-as-a-durable-consumer-good view. Equally important, we see his embrace of disequilibrium, by contrast to the Walrasian equilibrium approach adopted by both Friedman and his Keynesian interlocutors.

Laidler himself presents this intellectual shift as a consequence of his Popperian empiricist commitments—the data revealed to him the inadequacy of existing theories, suggested the source of that inadequacy, and hence proposed a line for fruitful future theoretical development. But there is more to it than that. Brunner and Meltzer provided for Laidler a line more continuous with Tooke and the classic nineteenth-century literature than anything offered by modern Monetary Walrasians of any stripe. Brunner and Meltzer's discussion of the supply of money (not just demand) and the process of credit expansion (not just the eventual equilibrium position) provided Laidler with a modern analytical framework within which the classic questions could be discussed. In 1973, his doubts became convictions.

The consequence of this intellectual shift was that, as Milton Friedman's monetarism rose in prominence during the 1970s, Laidler found himself increasingly in opposition not only to the Keynesian fine-tuners, but also to his own monetarist mentors and colleagues. On the surface, the problem was that empirically the demand for money did not show the degree of stability required to support Friedman's strong policy advocacy of a constant money supply growth rule. "[T]he case for governing monetary policy by long-run rules is impossible to sustain in the face of careful consideration of the influence of institutional change on the behavior over time of the demand for money function" (Laidler, 1982, 35). Similarly, "the belief...that the demand for money in the aggregate economy can be modeled in the long and short runs 'as if' money was a consumer durable good, is fallacious" (Laidler, 1982, 42).[5]

But these theoretical and empirical problems with money demand were in fact only symptoms of a deeper problem that came more and more to the forefront as the New Classical Macroeconomics of Robert Lucas and his colleagues took center stage. Laidler's own "Manchester monetarism" had in fact never assumed market clearing (nor had the Keynesian IS-LM model that he had used to express it) while Friedman's monetarism had explicitly drawn such a connection. Says Friedman (1968, 8): "the 'natural rate of unemployment' is the level that would be ground out by the Walrasian system of general equilibrium equations." This asserted connection between monetarism and Walrasianism proved to be unsupportable, as Frank Hahn (among others) has pointed out, but Friedman's *metaphorical* Walrasianism nevertheless played a crucial role in preparing the ground for the more thoroughgoing *analytical* Walrasianism of the New Classicals.[6] Quite apart from its evident lack of empirical grounding, the New Classical assumption of continuous market clearing left no room for money even in theory. As Laidler would say, "Money does in the world what markets do in our theories."[7]

The rise of New Classical Macroeconomics thus was not Monetarism Mark II (as James Tobin termed it) but rather the very antithesis of what Laidler always understood monetarism to be about. In the American historical context, monetarism had risen up as a corrective to the extreme anti-quantity theory views of the arch-conservative J. Laurence Laughlin, who had at the beginning of the century used his platform at the University of Chicago to promote an extreme version of the real bills doctrine.[8] How ironic then, that Milton Friedman's Chicago School monetarism should have paved the way for a restatement of much the same discredited idea in the paper of Sargent and Wallace, "The Real Bills Doctrine and the Quantity Theory: A Reconsideration" (1982). Just as Laughlin had misappropriated Tooke in the monetary debate leading up to the founding of the Federal Reserve System (Mehrling, 2002), so now were the New Classicals misinterpreting Tooke's message for the modern age, and Laidler felt compelled to respond (Laidler, 1984). But the problem was not just a misreading of Tooke. The problem, Laidler decided, was with Walrasianism itself.

Thus Laidler found himself keeping company increasingly with the critics of the Walrasian turn in macroeconomics, not just Brunner and Meltzer, but also Axel Leijonhufvud and Charles Goodhart, Robert Clower and Peter Howitt, the late work of Hicks, as well as post-Keynesians such as Hyman Minsky, Victoria Chick, and Paul Davidson. Laidler's monetarism was always about understanding the world, and if the economics profession was set on embracing a theoretical construct that abstracted from this monetary reality, so much the worse for the economics profession. Like his hero Tooke, Laidler would continue *Taking Money Seriously* (1990) even as his intellectual opponents prevailed in subsequent legislation and in the court of academic opinion, at least in the United States.[9]

Non-Walrasian monetary theory was what needed doing, but Laidler himself lacked the analytical tools to push that agenda very far. He turned instead to the analytical insights already available in the history of economic thought, insights he had been mining himself ever since reading Henry Thornton with Lionel Robbins as an undergraduate. Laidler's new insistence on history of economics as a way of *doing* economics put him in good company with Jacob Viner, Frank Fetter, and Don Patinkin. Although he engaged with and supported others who worked on the history of economics, he never viewed such work as comprising a subfield of economics, and that perhaps explains his occasional lack of attention to the secondary literature (noted by Dimand). Laidler reads old economics in order to gain insights for today. By watching how economists adapted to changing circumstances, he hopes to derive clues and inspiration about how we can do the same for our own modern changing circumstances.

A monetarist among Keynesians in his early career, Laidler's opposition to temporary orthodoxy was born of neither ideological anti-state conviction, nor starry-eyed faith in unfettered markets. Instead, his disequilibrium monetarism was an alternative road branching out from origins in the pre-World War I development of neoclassical monetary economics (Laidler, 1991) and the interwar literature on money, the cycle and unemployment (Laidler, 1999). For the post-World War II period it turned out to be a road not taken by the profession at large, at least not yet. Laidler's metaphorical non-Walrasianism can be understood as preparing the ground for a more thoroughgoing analytical non-Walrasianism yet to come.

Notes

1. See also Laidler's biographical essay "Economics as a way of life—a personal memoir" in Laidler (1997).
2. Unfortunately, the publication of Laidler's selected essays in two separate volumes, one *Money and Macroeconomics* (1997) and the other *Macroeconomics in Retrospect* (2004), tends to suggest this misinterpretation.
3. The harsh review of Laidler (1969) by Hyman Minsky (1972) suggests how Laidler's monetarism was viewed from the perspective of one of the few American radical Keynesians, albeit a friend and colleague from Berkeley days.
4. Laidler has written that he considers this paper to have been his best (Laidler 1997, 115). Be that as it may, it certainly represents a key turning point in his own intellectual development.
5. It would be an interesting exercise in the history of economic thought to investigate how Laidler's changing views are reflected, or not, in the four editions of his textbook *The Demand for Money* (1969, 1977, 1985, 1993).

6. Much the same could be said about the role of the metaphorical Walrasianism of the Keynesian IS-LM model.
7. Laidler Festschrift, August 19, 2006. This verbal quotation is just a more compact version of what Laidler has often expressed in print. For example, "money is a social institution which is a substitute for, and not a complement to, the Walrasian market, so that conventional general equilibrium theory and monetary economics do not mix" (1997, xxii).
8. The book of Lloyd Mints (1945) is the *locus classicus* of the old Chicago School reaction to Laughlin, and a common thread linking the old Chicago School of Simons and Knight to the new Chicago School of Friedman and Stigler. This link is the grain of truth in Friedman's otherwise overstated claim to have been continuing an oral tradition at Chicago.
9. Here a full appreciation of Laidler would require treatment of his extensive work as an advisor to the Bank of Canada, as well as Laidler's many other policy interventions.

References

Brunner, Karl and A. H. Meltzer. (1971). "The Uses of Money: Money in the Theory of an Exchange Economy." *American Economic Review* 61(:5), 784–805.

Fetter, Frank W. (1965). *The Development of British Monetary Orthodoxy*. Cambridge, MA: Harvard University Press.

Friedman, Milton. (1956). "The Quantity Theory of Money: a Restatement." In M. Friedman, ed., *Studies in the Quantity Theory of Money*. Chicago: Chicago University Press, 3–21.

Friedman, Milton. (1959). "The Demand for Money: Some Theoretical and Empirical Results." *Journal of Political Economy* 67 (June), 327–351.

Friedman, M. and Anna Jacobson Schwartz. (1963). *A Monetary History of the United States, 1867–1960*. Princeton, NJ: Princeton University Press.

Friedman, Milton. (1968). "The Role of Monetary Policy." *American Economic Review* 58:1, 1–17.

Laidler, David E. W. (1966). "Some Evidence on the Demand for Money." *Journal of Political Economy* 74 (February), 55–68.

Laidler, David E. W. (1969). *The Demand for Money: Theories and Evidence*. Scranton, Pennsylvania: International Textbook Company.

Laidler, David E. W. (1972). "Thomas Tooke on Monetary Reform." In *Macroeconomics in Retrospect, the Selected Essays of David Laidler*. Cheltenham, UK: Edward Elgar, pp. 57–76.

Laidler, David E. W. (1973). "Information, Money and the Macro-economics of Inflation." In *Essays on Money and Inflation*. Chicago: University of Chicago Press, pp. 1–18.

Laidler, David E. W. (1975). *Essays on Money and Inflation*. Chicago: University of Chicago Press.

Laidler, David E. W. (1982). *Monetarist Perspectives*. Cambridge, MA: Harvard University Press.

Laidler, David E. W. (1984). "Misconceptions about the Real Bills Doctrine—A Comment on Sargent and Wallace." *Journal of Political Economy* 92 (February), 149–155.

Laidler, David E. W. (1990). *Taking Money Seriously, and Other Essays*. Cambridge, MA: MIT Press.

Laidler, David E. W. (1991). *The Golden Age of the Quantity Theory: The Development of Neoclassical Monetary Economics 1870-1914*. Princeton: Princeton University Press.

Laidler, David E. W. (1997). *Money and Macroeconomics: The Selected Essays of David Laidler*. Cheltenham, UK: Edward Elgar.

Laidler, David E. W. (1999). *Fabricating the Keynesian Revolution, Studies of the Interwar Literature on Money, the Cycle, and Unemployment*. Cambridge: Cambridge University Press.

Laidler, David E. W. (2004). *Macroeconomics in Retrospect, the Selected Essays of David Laidler*. Cheltenham, UK: Edward Elgar.

Mehrling, Perry. (2002). "Economists and the Fed: Beginnings." *Journal of Economic Perspectives* 16:4 (Fall), 207–218.
Minsky, Hyman. (1972). Review of Laidler's *Demand for Money. Econometrica* 40:4 (July), 778–779.
Mints, Lloyd W. (1945). *A History of Banking Theory in Great Britain and the United States.* Chicago: Chicago University Press.
Ruhl, Christof and David Laidler. (1998). "Perspectives on Macroeconomic Theory and Its History: An Interview with David Laidler." *Review of Political Economy* 10:1, 27–56.
Sargent, T. J. and Neil Wallace. (1982). "The Real-bills Doctrine and the Quantity Theory: A Reconsideration." *Journal of Political Economy* 90 No. 6 (December): 1212–36
Sayers, Richard Sidney. (1936). *Bank of England Operations, 1890-1914.* London: P.S. King and Son.

6
What is Good Government? David Laidler's Views

Robert Young with David Laidler

Preface

In the course of a distinguished career as an economist, David Laidler has thought a lot about public policy, monetary and otherwise, and as a historian of economic thought he is quite familiar with those of his predecessors whose work on political economy led them to contemplate the political authorities more than most contemporary economists are inclined to do. But David, as far as I know, has never written about government per se, even though it is reasonable to think that his general views about this might colour his writing, just as they have doubtless been influenced in turn by his analyses of economics and policy. On this occasion, it seems appropriate that someone should fill this gap.

On the other hand, discerning what he thinks about government, and especially the characteristics of a 'good' government, would be difficult. The proper approach would be to sift through all of his writing, and induce his views about what are the desirable and undesirable features of government. I have rejected this approach for three reasons. First, it is too much work. Second, one might need to know a very great deal about economics to understand the shadings that Laidler reflects back upon the state. Finally, there are dimensions of government that David has not covered in his work, even indirectly, and his views about these would remain unknown. So my approach was more straightforward. I took an existing framework, and lured David into talking about it. We meandered for a morning through the various criteria according to which people judge whether a government is a good one. David had not read in advance the material containing these criteria. But he had much to say spontaneously. It's clear that he has thought a lot about government. And here are his views, edited, and indicated by DL.[1]

Introduction

Identifying whether a government is 'good' is a daunting task. Among the several difficulties involved is the fact that observers cannot look at any government in and of itself. We must operate at levels of generality that are both higher and lower. On the one hand, we are interested in general criteria of quality that transcend any particular government. On the other hand, we can evaluate a particular government only by investigating indicators of its performance or its quality (measures of its level of public support, for example, or of its transparency). Hence, analysts can disagree about the general criteria to be applied to governments; that is, about their relevance and relative priority. Second, we can disagree about indicators; that is, about their adequacy as measures and about whether the government scores well on any one indicator. Given this, we may predict that there will be little agreement in assessing the goodness of any government.

An example will help. Take the government of Paul Martin, recently in power in Ottawa. We can assess it using different criteria: let's use efficiency and honesty (including transparency). It is not obvious which of these is most important. Observers have different values, and they will disagree. As for indicators, how would we assess whether this government is honest and transparent? One measure is that it established the Gomery Commission to investigate irregularities in spending within the sponsorship programme. The use of such independent bodies to investigate malfeasance is an indicator of transparency. The Martin government also changed audit and accountability mechanisms within the bureaucracy in order to make corruption more difficult. This must count as a positive on the honesty/transparency front. On the other hand, legislation to protect whistleblowers – those who report maladministration – was introduced late, and it was relatively weak. Hence the record is mixed.

Another problem concerns comparison. Unless one is ruthlessly absolutist, the really interesting question is not whether a government is good but whether it is better than some comparator. Was the Martin government more efficient than the Chrétien government? Is the Canadian government more transparent than the British government? This is perhaps what analysts should be focusing on – relative quality – but we rarely attempt to compare whole governments, because of lack of resources or interest (Nye, 1997, 101).

In contrast to this point, though, and in contradiction with the view that we are most concerned with general criteria of goodness, is the fact that analysts sometimes deploy criteria that are jurisdiction-specific. In Quebec, for example, large majorities of citizens and political scientists believe that provincial governments should preserve and promote the Québécois language and culture, and indicators of this activity are closely watched. Similarly, federal governments in Canada are often evaluated by their success in maintaining 'national unity', at least in Canada-outside-of-Quebec. Recently, a sample of historians was asked to rank Canadian prime ministers on a scale of 0–10, where 0 was 'utter failure' and 10 was 'greatness'. No precise directions about criteria were given to the historians, but the researchers observed that '[f]or most, national unity, confronting and overcoming Canada's geographic and linguistic divisions, was the decisive factor in determining a prime minister's ranking' (Hillmer and Granatstein, 1997, 36). Analogously, in the United States and France, observers might judge governments according to their handling of racial and class cleavages rather than geographic and linguistic differences.

With respect to general criteria, not only may analysts disagree about their relative importance, but there are trade-offs. At one level, this is an obvious point. Is it more important that governments 'enact good policies' or that they 'maintain public support'? An example concerns once more the ratings of Canadian prime ministers. In their expanded work, Granatstein and Hillmer placed a lot of stress on pure survival: longevity, or keeping power, was an important criterion of evaluation (1999, 1, 7). The clear winner in this study, overall, was Mackenzie King. In a very similar study, the Institute for Research on Public Policy placed a lot of stress on social policy and foreign policy: the clear winner here, overall, was Lester Pearson (Schwanen, 2003). In the latter study, respondents were also asked to classify the leaders as 'transactional', or 'transformational', and these choices were closely associated with the final ranking: transformational leaders were more highly rated. But transformational leaders such as Pearson and Mulroney who introduce great changes are unlikely to maintain power for a very long time, as did the quintessentially transactional Mackenzie King. There are other trade-offs too. At times of rising inflation, 'enacting good policies' might mean tightening monetary policy. This, however, could cause unemployment to rise and popularity to decline. Meeting the 'good policy' criterion therefore contradicts the 'maintaining public support' criterion. Trade-offs can also be deeper than this. One criterion of goodness is that governments 'help people become better human beings'. This can obviously contradict a criterion of 'responsiveness to public opinion'. Governments aiming to change citizens into different and better selves, or to lead people to create new selves for themselves, can hardly be expected to be responsive to the views about the relevant policies that are held by the public's current selves. *Ex post* the policies would correspond with public opinion, but not *ex ante*.

These are some of the preliminary considerations and difficulties involved in deciding whether any government is a good one. In turning now to the criteria of 'good government', we find a large number of them. Even though the ones considered here are not exhaustive, they are numerous enough to require some categorization. This I have done in a straightforward fashion.

Categories of Good Government

How Are Governments Regarded?

This is the simple criterion of public opinion – is the government popular? In modern democracies, this is measured by polls or other indicators of the mood of the whole public; in less democratic systems, the relevant public may appear more restricted, but this is not necessarily so. As Cicero advised rulers, '[i]t is your part to have your eyes open for the security and benefit of all, with a ready courage, and a mind intent on all parts of the Commonwealth. Wisely consider in all your orders, decrees and acts how much you owe to the opinion of so many men, and to their judgments and esteem of you' (T.R., 1668, 88).

Popular approval is the 'good' government criterion. The converse indicator of 'bad' government is probably whether they are feared. Machiavelli made a (partial) living explaining to the Prince how to achieve the blend of these two attitudes that was most conducive to political success (1981). And a recent work analysed dictators as combining measures to generate loyalty on the one hand and fear on the other (Wintrobe, 1998).

Of course other attitudes towards government are possible – respect, awe, contempt, and so on. But popularity, or 'public support', is a summary measure of the goodness of a government in all its characteristics and activities. It represents a forced choice – approve or not – and this is the choice, crude though it is, that must be expressed at the ballot box.

Between elections, we could distrust the popularity criterion. We are also aware that public opinion can be manipulated and swayed by marginal events. Norpoth, for example, found that in Great Britain the Falklands War was worth 5 to 6 per cent to the Conservative Party in the following year's general election (1987, 956–957). The long-term answer to this problem is political competition, but such systemic concerns are beyond our purview here because we are interested in individual governments. And public support is a major criterion of the quality of governments.

DL: 'Popularity? Sure, and we can all go to the Nuremburg rally together.' No, really, one doesn't want to sound elitist here, but there are real problems. I'd want to put it together with other characteristics, and the relationship there is not additive, but multiplicative. Bad governments or awful ones can be nationalistic and popular, or economically illiterate and popular. Popularity just multiplies the damage they can do.

What Do Governments Do?

This set of criteria involves judgements about the adequacy of government activity. It comprises four main subcategories.

The first of these follows closely from the preceding one. It is whether governments are responsive to public opinion. Do their policies reflect the wishes of the citizenry? As several American presidents have declared, '*Vox populi, vox Dei*'. Here, the operative principle is not simply that the good government is a popular one, but that it does what the public desires. As the government of Tony Blair showed until recently, public support and responsiveness can be quite distinct in practice. True, there can be difficulties in assessing what the public wants, and in taking public desires seriously when citizens have little information about policy and especially the constraints upon it.[2] Another problem is that the public can be divided on issues. As Eric Nordlinger (1981) correctly noted, this allows governments to exercise policy autonomy. Despite all of this, there is an abiding sense that good governments do what citizens want them to do: they are responsive.

DL: Here is the same problem. And again the relationship is multiplicative. Governments can do some real damage in following ill-informed public preferences. 'The real question it seems to me is "can the public get rid of a government it doesn't like?"' Here is where Karl Popper is so important in his stress on the mechanisms through which bad government can be thrown out.

A second criterion here is that good governments keep promises. While it has a sound basis in democratic theory, for it means that the citizenry can pass judgement on political leaders and their governments prospectively as well as retrospectively, in Canadian politics this principle has emerged as something of a practical touchstone of good government. Commitment to a policy platform was a strong element in the Reform Party. It was also embodied in the 'Red Book' of the federal Liberal Party under Jean Chrétien and, more famously, in the 'Common Sense Revolution' platform of the Harris Tories in Ontario.[3] In Quebec, a perennial effort of militants within the Parti québécois is to enshrine within the party's platform a commitment to hold a referendum and accede to sovereignty as soon as possible after winning office, and the interplay of this crucial platform plank with public opinion often places the leadership in a difficult position. So the stress on this criterion is not universal, but it is widespread. A mark of good government is keeping promises, even when meeting the commitment means making bad policy (as in the Harper government's cuts to the GST, for example).

DL: 'On balance, yes – if I voted for them!' It's a plus.

A similarly narrow criterion is whether governments redistribute resources. Inequality is a fundamental attribute of most economic systems, and many people judge governments according to whether the poor and less fortunate are assured the necessities of life. Governments can be evaluated according to how they treat the weakest and most vulnerable members of society (a phrase often attributed to Mahatma Gandhi). For many, this is an overriding criterion.

DL: 'That's important'. The optimal redistribution is to what some call the deserving poor; that is, the sick, accident victims, the unlucky, and so on. Of course the danger lies in the need to use measures of income and wealth, and so the definition of the needy becomes endogenous to the taxation and redistribution systems. It's impossible to draw a clear-cut line between those in real trouble and those who have been negligent, short-sighted, feckless, and so on. My own preference is not to try too hard to do so, even at the risk of creating moral hazard. We should err on the side of generosity, accompanied if necessary by a few bad incentives, rather than having no social security, as some advocate. 'We can't have people starve to death because of their own previous fecklessness'. This is a better argument, I think, than the one from fear – that the mob must be bribed in order to keep it from confiscating wealth.

I didn't like how the Thatcher government's efforts to make families responsible for their own children by reducing aid to the latter as individuals put some young people on the street to beg, trade drugs, and so on, rather than face abuse at 'home'. But almost automatic council flats for single mothers had some unwelcome incentive effects too! There is no straight answer to these trade-offs – trial and error and a willingness to change programmes that are having unexpected effects is the best we can do.

Within this category of evaluative criteria, however, the most commonly used and probably the most important one concerns the policies that governments enact. Good governments are those which deliver good policies (or desirable inactions on some policy fronts). In this view, the multifarious policy activities of government can be described, analysed, and evaluated, and governments labelled as more or less good in consequence. This is probably the most widespread modern criterion in democratic states. Its use reflects the large scope of contemporary governments, and the huge effects that policy can have on other things that citizens care about, such as economic growth. In the case of developing countries, for example, Osborne (2004) argues that bad policy rather than endowments, culture, or terms-of-trade shocks is the source of a lot of poor economic performance. Of course the problem here is that observers will disagree about whether policy X in field Y was a good one, and they will also be unlikely to agree about the relative importance of policy fields. It may be necessary to rank policy fields. Hobbes, for instance, argued that the most fundamental task of governments is to ensure the physical security of their citizens. Other policy activities are therefore lesser priorities. Finally, evaluators will also need to consider the trade-offs that bedevil politicians: for example, is it better to increase growth at the cost of environmental degradation? But this is still a widely used criterion of what is a good government.

DL: 'Well, naturally, we're all in favour of good policies'. The most important surely is international peace and stability. That's the big one. Then, economically, it's security of property and the rule of law – all the nightwatchman-state type of activities. Here I rely on the functions that Smith wrote about in the Glasgow Lectures (Smith, 1956) – justice, police, revenue, and arms. These are critical. Then there are issues of distributional justice. The very need to tax to provide the most basic public services inevitably raises issues of distribution: it's no coincidence that Ricardo's book was called *Principles of Political Economy & Taxation* (see Ricardo, 1963).

What really bothers me about some modern economists is that they don't appreciate these connections. We need to view government as a necessary condition for an economy to function rather than as something that keeps getting in the way. Take the supply of public goods. It seems to me that Coase was wrong to argue that private mechanisms can substitute for institutions. The private sector might supply public goods, but only by evolving institutions that basically take the form of those that we think of as government. Take money, which is fundamental to economic life, because security of property depends, among other things, on monetary stability. Holding money is essentially holding a generalized claim on property. So stable monetary and financial institutions are essential to the stability and security of property rights, and are basic to the working of the market economy. As I have been known to argue, the invisible hand 'has financial and monetary fingers' (Laidler, 2006, 22).[4] The really basic point here is that there are limitations of economic models based on individual maximization coordinated by the 'market'. For some purposes, like models of international trade, this simplification is all well and good. But this approach does not work for modelling money. The monetary system requires institutions and collective institutions that are what we usually mean by 'the state'.

Adam Smith's *Moral Sentiments* is thought by many to be more important to Smith than the *Wealth of Nations*, because it deals with sympathy and the impartial spectator. *The Wealth* then seems to be dealing with how society works in the wide world beyond the rather limited range of interpersonal sympathy. Providence has provided natural laws that, properly understood and applied, will ensure that self-interest continues to promote the public good where the impartial spectator does not guide our dealings with others. Now, in the monetary realm there is a conflict between the cartelists and the spontaneous-order people, with the former arguing for a fundamental government role in the creation and management of the system, and the latter claiming that market structures will arise to handle matters spontaneously. But even when a monetary system evolves spontaneously, there are certain monopolistic elements involved, and this means that collective institutions must sort out these problems. Of course, the state needs a little supervision.

How Do Governments Do Things?

This is a large category. Perhaps surprisingly, many observers are more preoccupied with means and methods rather than government characteristics and goals. Here, there are five main subcategories.

The first is honesty. This is an important criterion of a good government. It is primordial for analysts of government in systems where corruption is widespread (Sabetti, 2000, part 3). And it is widely measured. The PRS Group, for example, computes an index of political risk in which corruption is weighted more heavily than bureaucratic quality (PRS Group, 2005, S-19). Transparency International also measures political corruption.[5] This criterion reverberates in contemporary Canadian and Quebec politics, where there is a clear desire for *'un gouvernement propre'*, even though the historical record shows a rather tolerant attitude towards political scandals involving patronage and pork-barrelling (Morton, 2005).

DL: Yes, this is a fundamental consideration. But I should add 'usually'. Remember that Roosevelt got the USA into World War II by stealth. The problem is that the public is rationally ignorant, and so we can't write Machiavelli off entirely. In the end, honesty is a populist virtue, and therefore should be regarded with some suspicion.

A closely related criterion is accountability. This is a rather amorphous concept, but it essentially asks whether citizens have the information to be able to hold governments responsible for what they do. This requires transparency, so that the public (and the press) can know what decisions were taken, by whom and – though this is more questionable – with what effect. So, first, governments must not refuse to provide such information. Second, they should not attempt to obscure their responsibility by burying decision-making in committees, or intergovernmental negotiations, or other devices to create opacity. This criterion is very important among those who look at 'governance' as a process rather than a set of policy results (Bovaird and Löffler, 2002, 20). In practice, holding governments accountable can require vast quantities of information and very close attention to detail, as was shown in the British investigations of the decision to participate in the invasion of Iraq (Blick, Byrne, and Weir, 2005, 408–416). But these are the hard cases. In general, the criterion is widely used as a measure of the adequacy of the method of governing, and therefore of the quality of government.

DL: Once more, yes, but with caution. It's fine, as long as it doesn't involve being accountable to people in church basements, and having them recall members. I remember the havoc wreaked on the British Labour Party by the activists in the Militant Tendency movement when Michael Foot was leader. It was a disaster. In the end, I don't favour direct democracy. It's fine when people have the time and the analytic capacity to oversee and judge their representatives, but usually they do not, and so I am cautious. I believe in representative democracy.

A third subcriterion is whether governments govern effectively. Do they achieve their goals? This generally boils down to an assessment of competence, but again the emphasis is on the process rather than the substance of policy. Naturally, this is an important issue that goes to the heart of good governance. Can governments identify problems, formulate means to address them, and implement policies that do actually solve or ameliorate the problems? (For a much more fine-grained set of indicators along these lines, see Barrett and Greene, 1999.) Many analysts cleave to this criterion. For Robert Kaplan, in a typically hard-nosed analysis, effectiveness is arguably more important than whether a government is democratic: 'Russia may be failing in part because it is a democracy and China may be succeeding in part because it is not' (1997, 58). This emphasis may be far more widespread than is assumed by analysts in advanced industrial democracies.

DL: Yes, of course, especially for fundamental things like civil order, justice and so on.

The next issue here is efficiency. This has to do with the cost incurred in providing some good or service, with lower cost per unit of output indicating greater efficiency. Less narrowly, the marginal social cost of policies should be equal to their marginal social benefits. In a sense, governments cannot be efficient if they are not effective, because it is senseless to measure and compare inputs with outputs if the outcomes of government activity do not advance its goals. In any case, efficiency matters because resources are scarce, and waste reduces the benefits that governments can deliver. There are many, many sources of government inefficiency, which have been ruthlessly explored most recently by scholars working in the Public Choice school: for a useful survey, see le Grand (1991).

> DL: 'Who could be against efficiency?'

The final subcriterion here is equality; that is, the extent to which governments treat classes of citizens equally. This is not simply a matter of redistribution, for such policies concern only one dimension of fairness. Instead, the issue here is procedural fairness – non-discrimination in the provision of publicly supplied goods and services, and also in matters of regulation and justice. For many citizens, and particularly for minorities, this is an exceedingly important criterion of good government (Hopkinson, 2001, 3).

> DL: Yes, this is important 'in law and in opportunity'. I would argue for equality before the law and equality of opportunity rather than equality of outcome. Here I tend to side with John Stuart Mill. He made a useful and fundamental distinction between the right of inheritance (which is not absolute) and the right of bequest (which is absolute). So, one has a right to dispose of property, but not to inherit it.

What Characteristics Do Governments Have?

Sometimes governments are evaluated according to their nature, rather than what they do and how they do it. The first measure here is simple longevity. Given the constant threat of overthrow or defeat, this characteristic indicates that the government has been successful, *grosso modo*, rather like the approval rating sums up all other criteria of assessment. This is a minimalist criterion, but it is not uninteresting, especially when extended from 'government' to 'regime'; hence, one can refer to the success of the Japanese Imperial Family, the Communist Party of China, or the Liberal Party of Canada. It is clear that no good can be done when one does not possess power, an observation that has justified much evil in power's pursuit. In any case, long rule is certainly what Machiavelli's Prince sought, and it was also a core counsel of Cicero: 'whoever undertakes the protection of many, ought first to provide for his own safety... [and] he should begin to govern by securing his own life and power' (T.R., 1668, 58–59)

> DL: 'I'm in favour of stable institutional frameworks, because people then learn to make them work.' The same is not true of incumbents. Think of the long-lasting prime ministers, like Lord Liverpool and Walpole. Neither of them did anything much. On the other hand, some of the really good ones were those who got in and got out, like Disraeli and Gladstone. They

were long-serving, but not in any one ministry. And didn't Sir Robert Peel manage quite a lot in a short time – the Bank Charter Act and the repeal of the Corn Laws?

A more common criterion of good government is that it be representative. The government should reflect the nature or composition of the population. In Iraq under Saddam Hussein, for example, the dominance in government and the military of the Sunni minority was deeply resented by the Kurds and the Shia Arabs. In democracies, there is a widespread sense that governments, especially but not exclusively legislatures, should reflect the composition of the electorate, by ethnicity, region, gender, and so on. Although there is a purely symbolic element in demands for such 'ascriptive representation' (Pitkin, 1967), the underlying assumption is that from an appropriately composed government will flow better policies and conduct. On the ideological front, the notion that parties should be represented fairly in legislatures (and cabinets) underpins support for systems of proportional representation. And appropriate representation can include subgovernments and regions as well as classes of individuals (Violini, 2002).

DL: 'It really doesn't matter who they are as long as you can throw them out'. No, seriously, I don't see what difference it makes. Representatives act on our behalf, and 'I don't see why an Italian Catholic can't represent me in Ottawa'. As for quotas, such as having one-half of party nominees be women, I'm not much in favour of this. Now there are nuances – remember, I had a significant role in drafting the section of the Macdonald Report that made the case for addressing perceived inequalities through affirmative action. What I like about such measures is that they can lead to changes in information and/or to a shift to a new equilibrium that renders the measures themselves redundant.

The final characteristic that is often taken as a standard of good government is democracy. Many analysts go beyond the elementary criteria that governments should reflect the public, be responsive to the popular will, and be accountable to the public, and proceed to require that governments (or regimes) exhibit some or all of the following characteristics: free assembly and the right to form associations and parties, competitive elections, a secret and universal ballot, a free press, representative institutions, an independent judiciary, a written constitution, and a full set of human and political rights. The assumption may seem to be that this *form* of government will *perform* well; that is, be accountable, responsive, and produce good policies. Yet this is not at all obvious. In many non-democratic states, as noted by Kaplan (1997), governments perform well, while many democracies fail to deliver. More generally, there are defects associated with democracy such that these governments may tend to falter on other criteria of good government. Caselli and Morelli (2004), for example, show that elective office can tend to attract 'low quality' citizens who have few comparable alternatives, and that such outcomes may be stable. Niskanen (1997) demonstrates that democracies are not optimally efficient because of transfers made to the winning coalition, while Downs got the same result long ago by showing that citizens are rationally ignorant about politics and policies (1957, 148). Like many more recent observers, Fenwick argued after the Great War that slow moving democracies were disadvantaged compared with autocracies, in part 'because of [their] choice of leaders who are either mediocre in ability or reluctant to put forward policies which may bring them into disfavor with current public opinion' (1920, 585). So the criterion of democracy may well contradict other criteria of good government. And its continuing favour, perhaps supremacy, among those who evaluate governments does not result because it performs optimally, but rather because the liberty protected by free democratic competition and constitutionalism prevents really bad governments, oppressive tyrannies, and dictatorships (Young, 1991). It takes only a modicum of familiarity with such governments to make analysts opt for democracy (see, for recent examples, Decalo, 1985).

DL: Yes, 'this is all part of being able to get rid of them and also of keeping the people well enough informed to do so'. About written constitutions, though, I'm not so sure. Less formal mechanisms might be adequate.

What Higher Purpose Do Governments Serve?

This is a surprising result of our survey – to find a deep and wide current of thought that locates politics and government within a larger sphere, a set of transcendent considerations, and that judges governments according to whether they promote some non-political end. In some of these views, other criteria are completely irrelevant. What governments do, what they are like, what people think of them: such questions matter little in and of themselves. They take on import only insofar as they are material to the advancement of other ends, which are taken to be the higher purpose of government.

The discussion of democracy as a criterion approaches this position. We value democratic government (or liberal democratic government) because it provides a sphere of liberty – 'negative freedom' – within which citizens have the autonomy to realize their own ends. At least this is a classic liberal defence of democratic government.

DL: 'That sounds good'.

We can also value governments because they enable people to lead a better life. Hence the goals of government, even as seen by a mundane practitioner, can include increasing the citizenry's income, knowledge, social mobility, and national pride (Hartle, 1973, 255–259).

DL: 'Just hold it. The sphere of negative freedom is perfectly appropriate, but the idea that governments should promote the purity of the nation and so on makes my flesh creep'.

A third strand of this thinking is that governments should help citizens to become better, to develop their capabilities and, in particular, to become better citizens. In Milner's terminology, governments should provide the means for citizens to increase their civic literacy (2002, part III).

DL: Well this is fine. Supplying libraries and education and so on just falls into the category of supplying public goods or goods that yield very large positive externalities that private markets have problems in internalizing through spontaneous institutional evolution. And if they do, they evolve collective arrangements that some of us think are what we mean when we refer to the institutions of government.

The real question is how to implement them. The last thing we want to end up with is the Saudi educational system. My own sense is that democratic competition will produce an appropriate supply, when it's supplemented with some modicum of private-sector competition. (Incidentally, when we think of public subsidies to the arts, I do tend to recall that Smith in *Moral Sentiments* had quite a bit to say about 'public magnificence'.) Of course there will be problems. But we need, in some respects, to remember Scott Gordon's distinction between problems that get solved and problems that get coped with. We shall just have to cope.

A final purpose involving individuals is to make people not merely better citizens, but better human beings. This is arguably one strong theme in Plato's *Republic*, though it is tempered by the need to keep politics within its rightful sphere (Schall, 1978, 104–108). No such restraint marks one modern argument for governments to remake human beings, whose author lamented that 'what is missing is the sense that governmental agencies are responsible for trying to improve the qualities of persons' (Lane, 1994).[6] But such goals are strongly disputed, of course, by those who argue that governments should restrict themselves to promoting conditions for people to realize their own, self-defined 'good life'.

DL: 'Oh crap, that's what many churches try to do'. Why shouldn't governments do it too? Because it presupposes moral superiority and a monopoly of goodness.

Of course, there have been two transcendent purposes that have most often been used to judge governments through the ages. The first is religion. When this purpose dominates, then politics should work to align citizens with correct religious principles, and governments should rule according to the sacred precepts. Imam Khomeini, for example, stressed that an Islamic state was a state ruled by law, first and foremost. But a ruler was needed, and '[t]he qualifications essential for the ruler derive directly from the nature and form of Islamic government. In addition to general qualifications like intelligence and administrative ability, there are two other essential qualifications: knowledge of the law and justice.... The ruler must surpass all others in knowledge' (Khomeini, n.d., 31–32). As for the law, it is designed to establish 'a just society that will morally and spiritually nourish refined human beings' (Khomeini, 47), but strong leadership is also necessary: 'the affairs of the state and religion are too exquisite to be delegated to those incapable of comprehending the real meaning of the *Quran* or the *hadith*, even if they enjoy majority support' (Milani, 1994, 159). These views are not confined to Islam, of course. As a prominent French cleric wrote just 50 years ago '[t]he object of the State is to protect the innocent and to repress evil. A government which is unfaithful to that mission ceases to be a "minister of God," and we shall see that the Revelation of John does not hesitate to qualify it as a tool of the "Dragon," that is, of Satan' (Héring, 1954, 15).

DL: Good grief. Here we see Popper's 'spell of Plato'. In *The Open Society*, Popper surely could have used Khomeini as a perfect example of what is dangerous.

There are other transcendent purposes that involve the attainment of some collective objective – the socialist revolution, or environmental sustainability. But the strongest such objective historically has been national self-determination. Nationalism has been powerfully associated with government in the modern age for over two centuries. The nation, on some readings, is the entity that legitimizes government, and governments have been judged according to whether they advance the national cause or not.

DL: Well, the environment is an objective problem. We shouldn't confuse it with the means of dealing with it. It amazes me sometimes how good economics seems to end at the oil patch. As for nationalism, it all depends on what the national collective cause is. What is required is keeping in place institutions that permit collective decisions. On the softwood lumber case – the dispute between Canada and the United States – the US Department of Commerce wants to determine the disposition of property rights in British Columbia. This to me is offensive, because this power was not delegated by Canadians to an elected government in another country. The pursuit of national interests is vigorous in the USA today. We see the systematic abrogation of treaties and the extraterritorial reach of Americans, as in the recent extradition of some British bankers for offences against American law that were not even committed in America.

Then there is the increase in US military power and its deployment throughout the world. What about the argument that America best embodies democracy and the rights and freedoms that I've celebrated above? Well, what counts is the method of spreading these values. It is essential to win the argument intellectually, even against closed societies and groups like the Islamists. So the approach in Afghanistan is all right, but not in Iraq. In Afghanistan, al-Qaeda was being allowed to mount attacks from there on other places, but I don't believe Iraq was involved in such activities. In any case, in these conflicts it is the intellectual argument that must be won, however long and hard the process. And on the home front, concerning the national interest, governments must leave room for scepticism, even though it's uncomfortable.

Discussion

My main purpose here has been to compile a checklist of the ways that people evaluate governments; that is, of the criteria that are deployed to assess the goodness of a government. It may well be that the discussion has erred on the side of comprehensiveness at the expense of usefulness. But the approach has been empirical. I have sought to cover the criteria that people actually bring to bear in judging governments. Even among political scientists, there is a huge diversity, and I have little doubt that in a sample of 100 or so, at least one would place the highest priority on each of the criteria discussed above.

Now empiricism is fine. But the end of a dry analysis begs the question of which criterion is the most important, and so I must advance my own opinion about this. To cut right to the quick, my view is that in democracies the very first criterion is the most important. What counts is how the citizenry regards the government; that is, how popular it is. From this gross summary measure, much follows, including the capacity of governments to win elections and continue to act.

There are two caveats to this conclusion. First, the rest of the public must not support a government that oppresses me; that is, there must be a system of protections for minorities. How this works in more authoritarian regimes is not evident, and so the most important criterion there is the non-democratic character of the government, which renders it 'bad'. I would still argue, however, that popularity is an important indicator in non-democracies.

The second caveat concerns the fact that ignorance about government is rational for members of the general public. Most people pay little attention to governments, even though they may have strong feelings about them. Certainly, few do any original work to investigate what they do, how they do it, what are their characteristics, and what purposes they serve; instead they take cues on these matters from closer observers such as the media and experts, and this information is distilled into a view of government – to support it or not. This means that it is incumbent on expert analysts to be very careful in evaluating governments and deciding whether or not they are good. They have a responsibility towards their fellow citizens. It is also their duty to be clear about the criteria they use in such judgements.

But this is a general conclusion: last word to David.

DL: Although I have not written explicitly about government, I do get explicit about some of the issues we've discussed in works on the governance of the Bank of Canada (Laidler, 1991), and in my introductory essay to my Macdonald Commission volumes on economic ideas and social issues (Laidler, 1985).

Otherwise my overall approach starts from a mixture of economics in the classical tradition (Smith, Ricardo, Mill) and Karl Popper. From the first I get the ideas that markets need the support of property rights and that the real world consists of nation states rather than a single entity. Hence, there must exist the 'nightwatchman state' at a minimum, which consumes real resources and hence implies the necessity for taxation, too. Thus government is ever-present in economics – or should be – and distributional issues come in at the beginning since taxation needs to be imposed according to some principles. Moreover, once you have government, you can't expect it to toe any line of its own accord, so all the other issues we might want to discuss – public goods, externalities, stabilization policy, the possibility of and limits to the welfare state – are all on the table. These raise questions the society copes with, rather than solves. Political economy (as it used to be called) provides many of the tools to be used in coping, as shown by the very titles of the works of the classical economists.

And from Popper comes a stress on asking the right questions – not what kind of people are best fitted to rule, but rather how do we organize government, with special concern about how can we get rid of the particular people running it if we don't like it? Indeed, as a first approximation, the answer 'no one more than any other' to the first question forces one on to the second.

Notes

1. The framework laid out here was developed in a paper titled 'How Do We Know What is a "Good" Government?' which was presented to the colloquium *Bilan des réalisations du gouvernement de Jean Charest* organized by the political science department at l'Université Laval in December 2005. I thank Andrew Quinlan for research assistance, Kelly McCarthy for help, the Canada Research Chair in Multilevel Governance for financial support, participants at the colloquium for valuable comments, and my colleague Charles Jones for a detailed and thoughtful critique.

   David Laidler contributed comments on each criterion on 19 July 2006. There are some direct quotations here, but most material is paraphrased. He later edited the results, providing some written comments that were incorporated into the paper.
2. Alcuin, who originated the term, actually wrote '[a]nd those people should not be listened to who keep saying the voice of the people is the voice of God [*Vox populi, vox Dei*], since the riotousness of the crowd is always very close to madness'.
3. It was not uncommon in that province, after the nastier effects of the government's rather radical policies had been sensed, to hear the expression 'Well, at least Mike Harris did what he said he would'.
4. At the *Festschrift* conference, Warren Samuels pointed out – correctly in Laidler's view – that the concept of 'secure property rights' is something of a simplification, because there is always a struggle to change and redefine the precise meaning of property rights.
5. In 2004, Canada stood 12th among 146 countries in being free of corruption (Transparency International, 2005).
6. Here we might note Rousseau's warning that perfectibility suits 'the children of Utopia, but it is worthless for the children of Adam' (quoted in Austin, 2001, note 3).

References

Austin, Dennis (2001). "Good Governance?" *The Round Table* 361, 497–505.

Barrett, Katherine and Richard Greene (1999). "Grading the States: A Management Report Card." *Governing* 12, 17–90.

Blick, Andrew, Iain Byrne, and Stuart Weir (2005). "Democratic Audit: Good Governance, Human Rights, War Against Terror." *Parliamentary Affairs* 58, 408–423.

Bovaird, Tony and Elke Löffler (2002). "Moving from Excellence Models of Local Service Delivery to Benchmarking 'Good Local Governance'." *International Review of Administrative Sciences* 68, 9–24.

Caselli, Francesco and Massimo Morelli (2004). "Bad Politicians." *Journal of Public Economics* 88, 759–782.

Decalo, Samuel (1985). "African Personal Dictatorships." *The Journal of Modern African Studies* 23, 209–237.

Downs, Anthony (1957). "An Economic Theory of Political Action in a Democracy." *The Journal of Political Economy* 65, 135–150.

Fenwick, Charles G. (1920). "Democracy and Efficient Government – Lessons of the War." *The American Political Science Review* 14, 565–586.

Granatstein, J. L. and Norman Hillmer (1999). *Prime Ministers: Ranking Canada's Leaders.* Toronto: Harper Collins.

Grand, Julianle (1991). "The Theory of Government Failure." *British Journal of Political Science* 21, 423–442.

Hartle, Douglas G. (1973). "A Proposed System of Program and Policy Evaluation." *Canadian Public Administration* 16, 243–266.

Héring, D. D. Jean (1954). *A Good and a Bad Government According to the New Testament.* Springfield, IL: Charles C. Thomas.

Hillmer, Norman and J. L. Granatstein (1997). "Historians Rank the Best and Worst: Canadian Prime Ministers." *Maclean's* 110, 34–39.

Hopkinson, Nicholas (2001). *Parliamentary Democracy: Is There a Perfect Model?* Aldershot, England: Ashgate.

Kaplan, Robert D. (1997). "Was Democracy Just a Moment?" *The Atlantic Monthly* 280, 55–80.

Khomeini, Imam (n.d.). *Islamic Government.* Tehran: The Institute for Compilation and Publication of Imam Khomeini's Works.

Laidler, David (1985). "Economic Ideas and Social Issues: An Overview." In Laidler, D., Research Coordinator, *Approaches to Economic Well-Being.* Collected Research Studies, Royal Commission on the Economic Union and Development Prospects for Canada, Vol. 26. Toronto: University of Toronto Press, pp. 1–47.

Laidler, David (1991). *How Shall We Govern the Governor: A Critique of the Governance of the Bank of Canada*, Canada Round Studies, no. 1. Toronto: C.D. Howe Institute.

Laidler, David (2006). "NAMU and the Neoliberals." Review of Eric Helleiner, *Towards North American Monetary* Union?, Literary *Review of Canada* 14:5 (June), 22–23.

Lane, Robert E. (1994). "Quality of Life and Quality of Persons: A New Role for Government?" *Political Theory* 22, 219–252.

Macdonald Commission (1985). Canada, Royal Commission on the Economic Union and Development Prospects for Canada, *Report.* Ottawa: Minister of Supply and Services Canada.

Machiavelli, Niccolò (1981). *The Prince*, Translated with an Introduction by George Bull. Harmondsworth: Penguin.

Milani, Mohsen M. (1994). The Making of Iran's Islamic Revolution: From Monarchy to Islamic Republic. Boulder: Westview Press.

Mill, John Stuart (1963). *Collected Works of John Stuart Mill.* Toronto: University of Toronto Press.

Milner, Henry (2002). *Civic Literacy: How Informed Citizens Make Democracy Work*. Hanover, NH: University Press of New England for Tufts University.
Morton, Desmond (2005). "Reflecting on Gomery: Political Scandals and the Canadian Memory." *Policy Options* 26, 14–21.
Niskanen, William A. (1997). "Autocratic, Democratic, and Optimal Government." *Economic Inquiry* 35, 464–479.
Nordlinger, Eric A. (1981). *On the Autonomy of the Democratic State*. Cambridge, MA: Harvard University Press.
Norpoth, Helmut (1987). "Guns and Butter and Government Popularity in Britain." *The American Political Science Review* 81, 949–959.
Nye Jr., Joseph S. (1997). "In Government We Don't Trust." *Foreign Policy* 108, 99–111.
Oakeshott, Michael (1962). *Rationalism in Politics and Other Essays*. London: Methuen.
Osborne, Evan (2004). "Measuring Bad Governance." *Cato Journal* 23, 403–422.
Pitkin, Hanna Fenichel (1967). *The Concept of Representation*. Berkeley: University of California Press.
Popper, Karl (1962). *The Open Society and Its Enemies*, 4th ed. rev. London: Routledge & Kegan Paul.
Plato (1985). *The Republic*, Translated by Richard W. Sterling and William C. Scott. New York; London: W.W. Norton & Company.
The PRS Group Inc (2005). *International Country Risk Guide*, vol. 26. East Syracuse, NY: The PRS Group Inc.
Ricardo, David (1963). *The Principles of Political Economy & Taxation*, intro. by William Fellner. Homewood, IL: R.D. Irwin.
Sabetti, Filippo (2000). *The Search for Good Government: Understanding the Paradox of Italian Democracy*. Montreal; Kingston: McGill-Queen's University Press.
Schall, James V. (1978). "The Best Form of Government: A Perspective on the Continuity of Political Theory." *The Review of Politics* 40, 97–123.
Schwanen, Daniel (2003). "Ranking Prime Ministers of the Last 50 Years: The Numbers Speak." *Policy Options* 24, 18–20.
Smith, Adam (1956). *Lectures on Justice, Police, Revenues and Arms*, delivered in the University of Glasgow by Adam Smith, reported by a student in 1763, edited with an introduction and notes by Edwin Cannon. New York: Kelley and Millman.
Smith, Adam (1976). *The Theory of Moral Sentiments*, eds., D.D. Raphael and A.L. Macfie. Oxford: Clarendon.
Smith, Adam (1968). *An Inquiry into the Nature and Causes of the Wealth of Nations*, ed., M. Blaug. Homewood, IL: R.D. Irwin.
T.R. (1668). Esq., *Cicero's Prince: The Reasons and Counsels for Settlement and Good Government of a Kingdom, Collected out of Cicero's Works*. London: Printed for S. Mearne.
Transparency International (2005). www.transparencyinternational.org.
Violini, Lorenza (2002). "A la recherche d'une bonne gouvernance." *The European Union Review* 7, 33–53.
Wintrobe, Ronald (1998). *The Political Economy of Dictatorship*. Cambridge, UK: Cambridge University Press.
Young, Robert (1991). "Tectonic Policies and Political Competition." In R. Wintrobe, A. Breton, P. Salmon and G. Galeotti, eds., *The Competitive State*. Dordrecht: Kluwer Academic Press, pp. 129–145.

Discussion

James B. Davies

Bob Young has provided us with more than a discussion of David Laidler's views on what constitutes good government. He has also given us a window into his own views, and provides us with a glimpse of the contrast in approaches to good government taken by two eminent representatives of the study of politics and economics.

Economists, as is well known, like to simplify. Since at least the time of Adam Smith they have started out by looking at the simplest possible world and have noted that it requires, as Laidler points out, only a 'nightwatchman' that protects against external enemies, maintains law and order, and enforces contracts. They then analyse phenomena such as externalities, public goods, and imperfect competition that may mean further government action is required for the achievement of efficiency. Finally, they also think about the redistributive impacts of taxes and public spending, although they agree that what one wants to do on this front depends both on value judgements and the trade-off between equality and efficiency. If they recommend measures to reduce inequality, the norm is that they must make clear they are doing this in their capacity as citizens rather than scientists. Laidler's comments on Young's analysis make it evident that he subscribes to a clear-headed and sophisticated version of this paradigm. While his views should not be construed as merely those of a 'typical economist', note that he recoils with horror at criteria for good government that lie outside this paradigm, such as making people better or raising the purity of the nation.

Bob Young's objective in the analysis to which David Laidler reacts is to provide a comprehensive list of the possible criteria for good government. This is an interesting enterprise. At the end of the essay Young tells us which of the criteria he thinks is most important, so we get not only a 'helicopter tour' of possible criteria for good government, but an indication of Young's own views. The criterion he identifies as most important is how the citizenry regards the government, that is, how popular it is. He adds two important caveats: minorities must be protected, and experts need to be careful in advising the public, which has a degree of rational ignorance about government. While this conclusion follows from deep consideration of what is required for good government, I would guess that other eminent political philosophers might choose another criterion as the most important. I would be curious to know how the level of consensus among them would compare with the degree of consensus among economists. For the latter, there is an agreed set of minimally necessary functions of government, and while as one considers adding further public functions there is diminishing agreement, there is at least consensus about what is needed to make a valid case for such activity. My guess is that this implies more consensus than one would find among political philosophers, but I must confess this is no more than a guess.

I think a common response to the question 'What is good government?' among social scientists would be, 'That requires value judgements, so there can be as many responses as there are people'. In other words, the question is normative, so it does not admit a scientific answer. Somehow this doesn't seem satisfactory. Is there any way we can do better, perhaps by making what appears to be a highly normative topic more positive? To answer this question I suggest looking at results from a perhaps unexpected quarter, the theory of repeated games.[1]

In the one-shot prisoners' dilemma, as all social scientists know, the prisoners rationally decide to confess despite the fact that they would both be better off if they did not. This is paradigmatic of many political and social situations, where we could all be better off with coordinated and cooperative action, but where institutions are lacking to enable this. Uncoordinated decision-making leads to a non-cooperative and inferior outcome. One of the interesting findings of game theory is that this miserable outcome can be avoided, even without institutions that allow bargaining and agreements, if the prisoners' dilemma is repeated a sufficient number of times. (This is the famous 'folk theorem' identified by Aumann (1981). See also Friedman, 1986, p. 103.) Then the players can mutually enforce cooperation by threatening to punish their opponent if the opponent does not behave cooperatively. Contests and simulations have confirmed the efficacy of punishment strategies in maintaining cooperation in repeated games. (See, for example, Axelrod, 1984 and Chess, 1988.)

We can think of the repeated prisoners' dilemma as a useful metaphor for much of social and political life. Cooperative behaviour is to be supported by punishment strategies. But when a large number of people are involved, there is a problem of coordinating punishments. It seems possible and plausible to me that the origin of statements like 'Bob has behaved badly' or simply 'John is bad' is that the speaker has detected non-cooperative play by John and wants to signal to the other players that they need to coordinate in punishing him. As the 20th century taught us abundantly, once people are convinced that a person or group is 'bad' they will often support surprisingly severe punishment of the perceived culprits. Announcing that somebody has behaved badly is potentially a powerful call for action.

A simple theory of government follows. Spontaneous punishment is ineffective compared with what can be applied by an efficient state, with its laws, police, courts, and jails. The state can be seen as an institution that has evolved to apply the punishments that are needed to sustain cooperation in repeated games. But the leaders of the state, in turn, need to be disciplined, and it must be possible to punish them if they do not perform their function properly. Thus, as Laidler says more than once in this chapter, the important question is whether the public can get rid of a bad government. This is the Popperian concern. If one looks at the state as a device for sustaining cooperative play in society it is absolutely central. Also note that in this view it becomes clear that a positive interpretation can be given to statements such as 'the government is good' or 'the government has behaved badly'. Saying a government is good may simply mean that the behaviour that would trigger its punishment in the equilibrium of the game we are playing has not been observed. Saying that a government is bad may just mean that such behaviour *has* been observed. If so, these statements lose most of their normative appearance.

Of course, governments do not merely attempt to enforce cooperative behaviour. They also must manage conflict.[2] This brings us to distributional issues, an area where economists have established important analytical results (such as the second theorem of welfare economics), but also an area where they are often shy to deliberate. Some reticence in recommending particular forms and degrees of redistribution is characteristic of mainstream economists. Laidler is a little unusual in advocating redistribution quite strongly here. He feels that governments should err on the side of helping the poor too much rather than too little. The danger of providing help to someone who doesn't deserve it is less significant than that of withholding help where it is genuinely needed. I couldn't agree more with the sentiment, but I do so as a citizen rather than a social scientist. I think it is clear that Laidler intends his statements to be regarded in that same light.

The problem with statements about the desirable redistributive role of government is that they may not win unanimous assent in the way that statements about enforcing cooperation can. Statements about desired redistribution inevitably depend on one's own position in the income distribution, and that of one's family and friends. We are altruistic beasts, but, as evolutionary theory has taught us, our altruism has some bounds. Nature condones more altruism towards a child than towards a cousin, and more towards a brother than to a great aunt. It is all summed up in Hamilton's kin selection rule (see, e.g., Ridley, 1996). It is to be expected that those whose 'weighted average relative'[3] has income below the average will favour redistribution from the rich to the poor, and that those who are not in this position won't be interested. Since the majority of people have income below the mean (the median is below the average in all real-world income distributions), it is to be expected that voters will opt for some degree of redistribution in modern democracies.

Does the fact that people will generally differ on the kind and degree of redistribution that they would like mean that we can say nothing unambiguous about the redistributive activities of a good government? I think that is too pessimistic. In a democracy we may expect, for familiar reasons, that the degree of redistribution from rich to poor will tend to correspond with the desires of the median voter. Suppose that my government is implementing this 'median voter redistribution', but that I and my family are of such high income and are so secure that I would prefer zero redistribution. Will I announce 'the government is bad'? If the purpose of such language, as I have argued, is to call for punishment, there would be no point in my making this statement. Median voter redistribution is a fact of life in the society I live in. There is no point, from my viewpoint, in punishing a government that implements this degree of redistribution. (A replacement government would behave in the same way.) On the other hand, if my government imposed more redistribution than desired by the median voter I might well announce 'this is not a good government', since that could, for example, help to hasten an election after which the problem would be corrected. The argument can be extended, and we see that if the government deviates from median voter redistribution a majority of voters will agree in saying the government is bad, despite the fact that they have different personally favoured degrees of redistribution. This is not quite unanimity, but it *is* something. If we know that citizens favour median voter redistribution in this way, it is reasonable to say that implementing such redistribution is a necessary characteristic of good government in the society concerned.

The above is a bare sketch, but I hope it is enough to persuade at least some that statements about what is good government do not have to merely reflect personal value judgements. I would argue that if we apply this analysis to the positions presented by Young and Laidler we see that they are less a reflection of personal values than might be supposed. Young argues that a good government is one that is well regarded by its people. Laidler warns that a government may be popular despite being bent on terrible things. Oversimplifying, Young's position is that a government is good if its citizens *say* that it is good. (This is subject to two caveats noted earlier.) Laidler's position seems to be that it is good if it is doing the things that its citizens would desire if fully informed, rational, and well intentioned. The latter 'ifs' are similar to Young's caveats, which reduces the gap between the positions. In the end, I would expect, Young and Laidler would agree that a central test of good government is whether properly informed, intelligent, and humane citizens would approve of their government's performance. To me this is not an arbitrary position, but a recognition that when people say a government is good, what they mean is that it is not time to implement the punishments citizens use to discipline governments in the great repeated game of social and political interaction.

Notes

1. See Binmore (1998) for a formal and extremely interesting analysis that inspired the following remarks.
2. An important point made by Laidler is that governments cannot avoid the conflict inherent in redistribution, since they must levy taxes in order to fund even the minimally necessary functions of government. Taxes and public spending inescapably have redistributive effects.
3. In calculating the characteristics of the 'weighted average relative' one should not forget to include oneself, with a weight of 1, and to include both living relatives and those as yet unborn using weights from Hamilton's rule.

References

Aumann, Robert J. (1981). "Survey of Repeated Games." In Aumann et al., eds., *Essays in Game Theory*. Mannheim: Bibliographisches Institut, pp. 11–42.
Axelrod, Robert (1984). *The Evolution of Cooperation*. New York: Basic Books.
Binmore, Ken (1998). *Game Theory and the Social Contract Volume 2, Just Playing*. Cambridge, MA: MIT Press.
Chess, David M. (1988). "Simulating the Evolution of Behavior; the Iterated Prisoners' Dilemma Problem." *Complex Systems* 2, 663–670.
Friedman, James W. (1986). *Game Theory with Applications to Economics*. Oxford: Oxford University Press.
Ridley, Mark 1996. *Evolution*, 2nd ed. Cambridge, MA: Blackwell Science.

7

Trade-offs in Monetary Policy

Milton Friedman

Phillips Curve

In 1958, A. W. Phillips came up with an empirical negative relation between the rate of inflation and the level of unemployment, quickly christened the Phillips curve (Phillips, 1958). Phillips himself did not present the curve as a policy tool, but less than two years later Paul Samuelson and Robert Solow published a celebrated article in the *American Economic Review* (1960) in which they did. Given the long period for which the Phillips curve appeared to hold in Britain, Samuelson and Solow concluded that it could be treated as a long-run structural equation which provided the missing equation that the then conventional Keynesian system needed. They treated it as a menu from which the monetary authorities could choose. By tolerating higher inflation they could experience lower average unemployment and vice versa.

Friedman/Phelps

In 1966 and 1967, E. S. Phelps and I criticized that approach, arguing that the Phillips curve was a short-term relation (Friedman, 1966, 1968; Phelps, 1967). In the long run, there was a natural rate of unemployment which could be combined with any level of inflation. The long-run Phillips curve was vertical. Inflation was a monetary phenomenon, not a real phenomenon.

The great inflation of the 1970s, labelled stagflation because both inflation and unemployment rose together, was a dramatic confirmation of the natural rate of unemployment view. That view became conventional wisdom in the monetary policy community.

The Taylor Curve

In 1979, John Taylor published an article that was to launch a fresh line of research. Its main objective was to estimate a simple general equilibrium model of the US economy incorporating rational expectations (Taylor, 1979). Taylor then sought to use his model to judge and develop monetary policy.

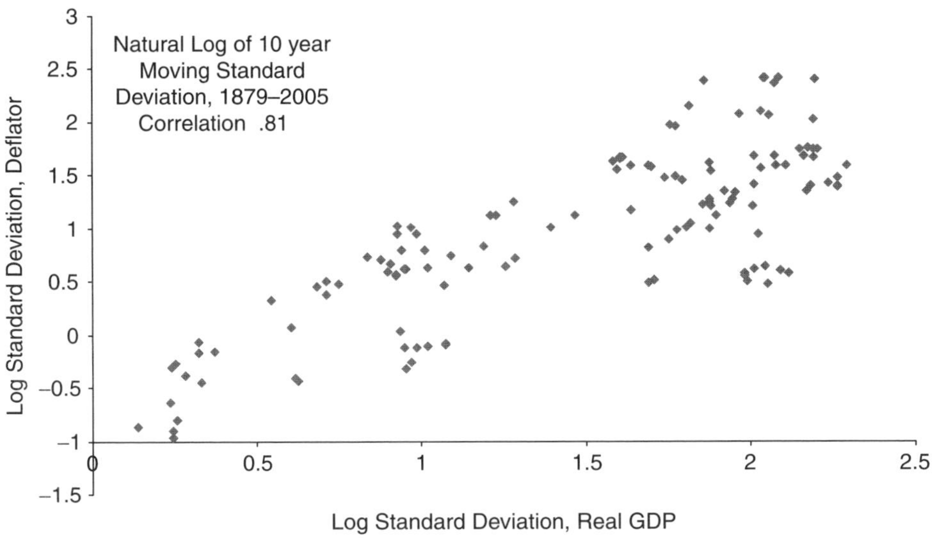

Chart 7.1 Variability of inflation vs variability of real income

He concluded, 'There is no long-run tradeoff between the level of output and the level of inflation in the model – the Phillips curve is vertical in the long run. However, there is a long-run tradeoff between fluctuations in output and fluctuations in inflation. In other words, there is a "second order" Phillips curve which is not vertical in the long run' (Taylor, 1979, 1280).

This comparison of the Taylor curve trade-off with the Phillips curve trade-off is not valid. The Phillips curve was based on empirical evidence, which was interpreted as reflecting a cause–effect relation: an increase in inflation will lead to a decline in unemployment.

The counterpart of the Phillips curve in terms of variability of inflation and output would be an analysis of the observed relation between the two as in the accompanying Chart 7.1 based on annual data for the United States from 1879 to 2005. Clearly, the observed correlation between the variance of unemployment and the variance of inflation is generally positive, not negative. There is no sign of the kind of trade-off offered by the Phillips curve.

The trade-off in the Taylor curve is not an inference from experience. It is an implication of a policy choice. The central bank is assumed to have two objectives: an inflation target and an output target. It seeks to minimize a loss function that is a weighted average of two terms: one based on deviations from the inflation target, one based on deviations from the output target. A zero weight on the output term reduces the bank's objective to inflation alone. Similarly, a zero weight on the inflation term reduces the bank's objective to output alone. As the weight varies between these two extremes the bank's objective shifts. Corresponding to each weight there is a policy rule that is optimal for the Taylor economic model. This policy rule will, in turn, imply for that model a variance of inflation and a variance of output. Understandably, the greater the weight on inflation, the lower the implied variance of inflation, and the higher the implied variance of output. Increase the weight for output and the implied inflation variance goes up, the implied output variance goes down. Plot these points on a chart and they generate an efficiency frontier showing a trade-off, but only for optimum monetary policy. Moreover, that curve will be different for every assumed economic model and at its best is based on a rough approximation of the way in which the economy works. Three or four estimated equations are crucial for the Taylor economic model but the economy as a whole is determined by millions of equations. At most, we could hope to get a rough picture of it.

The Taylor Rule

The instrument used by the Federal Reserve to control monetary policy is the federal funds rate – the overnight rate charged by banks to one another. The Open Market Committee of the Fed. specifies a target federal funds rate, and uses open market and other operations to keep the market rate equal to the target rate. Taylor accepts this set-up and develops a Taylor rule for the target rate. The rule gives the target rate as the algebraic sum of three terms: (1) estimated long-run equilibrium real federal funds rate at the levels of inflation and output chosen by the Fed.; (2) the deviation of inflation from its target rate multiplied by a coefficient; (3) the deviation of output from its target rate multiplied by a coefficient. The coefficients of the final two terms are, in turn, the product of two numbers: (1) the reaction of the target rate to the deviation of inflation or output from the target; (2) the fractional importance attributed to each of the objectives.

The rule thus embodies the idea of a policy trade-off. Give 100 per cent of the weight to preventing inflation and the recommended real interest rate will be affected only by inflation deviations and will not react to output deviations. Similarly, give 100 per cent of the weight to the output term and the recommended real interest rate will react only to output deviations. Fractional weights will lead to intermediate results.

I believe that it is a mistake to treat the Fed. as having two separate and independent objectives. The Fed. exists to define a monetary system. In my opinion, it has one and only one function: to keep the price level steady. The price level and inflation are monetary phenomena. They are defined by what happens to the quantity of money relative to output. Output is a real magnitude, not a monetary magnitude. Treating the Fed. as having two separate objectives is an open invitation to engage in fine-tuning, something that has almost always proved a mistaken practice.

My own preference for an instrument has always been a nominal monetary aggregate. Taylor estimates in his article the effect of a policy of a constant percentage increase in the quantity of money. He finds it 'interesting that this simple rule gives an output variance [for his economic model] considerably below the actual U.S. performance' (1979, 1282). I do not find that surprising at all. If, as I believe to be the case, inappropriate fluctuations in the quantity of money produce inappropriate fluctuations in output, keeping money growth constant would eliminate such inappropriate fluctuations in output.

On this interpretation, the Taylor rule is an attempt to specify the federal funds rate that will come closest to achieving the theoretically appropriate rate of monetary growth to achieve a constant price level or a constant rate of inflation. On these lines, the inclusion of the deviations in output from a target rate is not justified by a secondary objective of the Fed. It is rather to be justified by the inadequacy of inflationary deviations alone to generate the appropriate fluctuations in money. Suppose the federal funds target rate is equal to a Taylor rule that gives 100 per cent weight to inflation deviations. That may not be the right rate to achieve the desired inflation target because other variables, such as output or monetary growth, are not at their equilibrium levels. On this view, additional terms in the Taylor rule would reflect variables relevant to choosing the right target funds rate to achieve the desired inflation target.

Monetary Variability

I add two charts to bring out the role of monetary variability – the one item that central banks can control. I have used M2 as the monetary aggregate, though it may be that the base or some intermediate total would be a better instrument.

Chart 7.2 is a scatter diagram of the variability of M2 and the variability of real GDP – total output. The measure of variability is the log of a moving standard deviation of successive ten-year periods. There is clearly a strong positive correlation extending over the whole of the period.

Chart 7.3 shows the same data as time series. It brings out the sharp break between the period up to the end of the 1970s and the rest of the period.

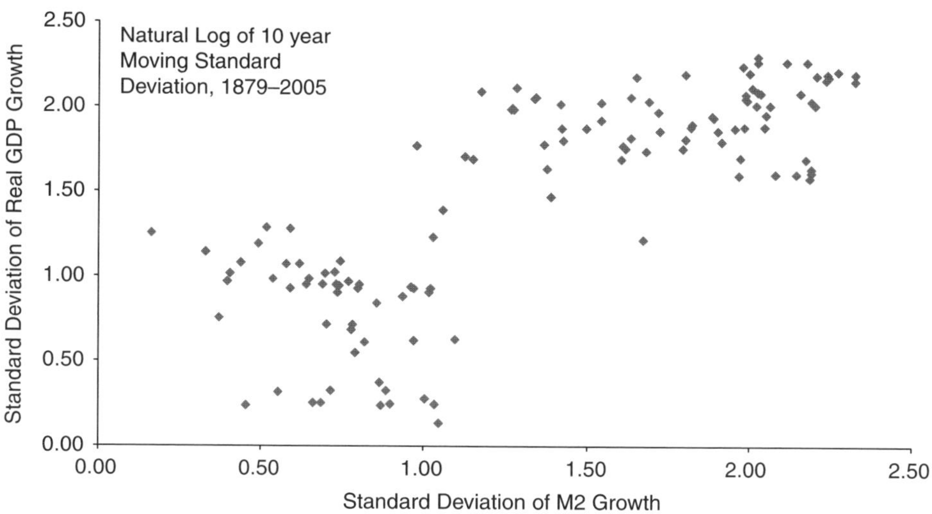

Chart 7.2 Variability of monetary growth and variability of output growth Correlation = .79

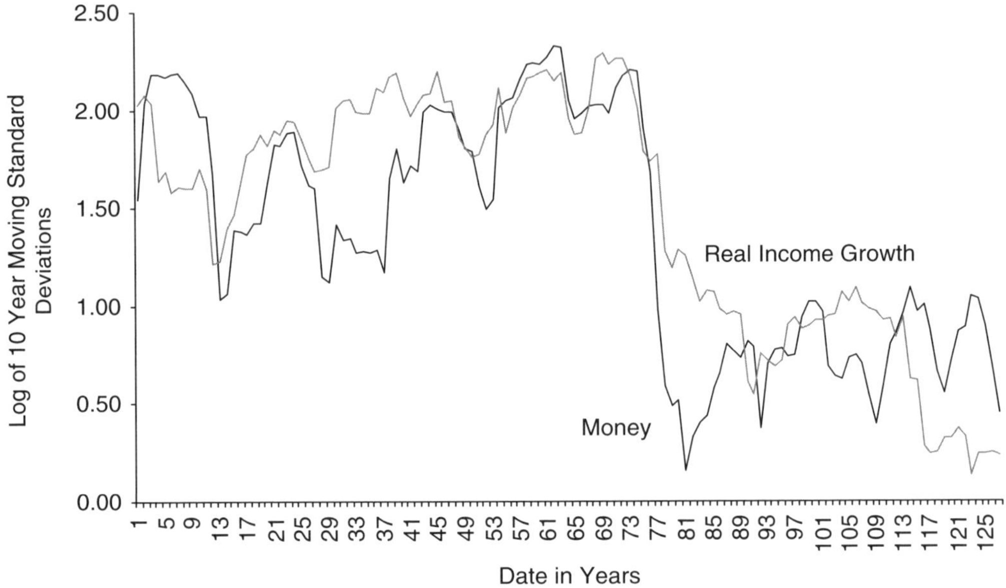

Chart 7.3 Standard Deviation of money growth and real output growth

The collapse of the variability of output is clearly an effect of the collapse of monetary variability. In my opinion, the same results could have been obtained at any earlier time and can continue to be achieved in the future. What is involved is not a trade-off but direct cause–effect.

References

Friedman, Milton (1966). "Comments on 'The Case against the Case against the Guideposts' by Robert M. Solow." In George P. Shultz and Robert Z. Aliber, eds., *Guidelines, Informal Controls, and the Market Place*. Chicago: University of Chicago Press, pp. 55–61.

Friedman, Milton (1968). "The Role of Monetary Policy." *American Economic Review* 58:1, 1–17.

Phelps, Edmund S. (1967). "Phillips Curves, Expectations of Inflation and Optimal Employment over Time." *Economica NS* 34:3, 254–281.

Phillips, A. W. H. (1958). "The Relation between Unemployment and the Rate of Change of Money Wage Rates in the United Kingdom, 1861–1957." *Economica NS* 25:2, 283–299.

Samuelson, Paul A., and Robert M. Solow (1960). "Analytical Aspects of Anti-Inflation Policy." *American Economic Review* 50:2, 177–194.

Taylor, John B. (1979). "Estimation and Control of a Macroeconomic Model with Rational Expectations." *Econometrica* 47:5, 1267–1286.

Discussion[1]

John B. Taylor

I greatly enjoyed reading Milton Friedman's paper and I appreciate the opportunity to offer some comments on it for David Laidler's *Festschrift* conference. The paper's assessment of recent research on monetary policy trade-offs and rules, as well as the comparison with earlier work, raises important questions and suggests interesting new lines of research. The charts on money growth, inflation, and output variability convincingly document the recent improvement in macroeconomic performance and also demonstrate the role of monetary policy in achieving this improvement. The paper should be required reading for today's students of monetary policy, and, indeed, I required it of my students in my monetary theory course that I taught this past spring at Stanford.

Let me focus on some of the key points the paper makes about trade-offs and policy rules.

Milton argues that the trade-off between the variability of inflation and output, which I first estimated in my 1979 paper – the so-called 'Taylor curve' – is not strictly analogous to a Phillips curve because the two curves relate to the data in different ways. I agree that they are conceptually different. One has to transform the estimated regression coefficients from an econometric model to compute the variability trade-off, while one can obtain the Phillips curve directly from the estimated regression coefficients. You can see the Phillips curve – or more accurately the shifts in a Phillips curve – in scatter plots of the data, while you do not see the Taylor curve in scatter plots of the data. One therefore relies on a specific model, or a theory, in the case of the variability trade-off, while one does not in the case of the Phillips curve trade-off.[2]

I would argue, however, that using theory and a model to compute the variability trade-off has some advantages. That it is based on theory is one reason why the variability trade-off has a greater chance of being stable over time, and why it is more useful for policy than the original Phillips curve. To the extent that the theory is accurate, including the use of rational expectations, the variability curve is less susceptible to the Lucas critique. Milton rightly cautions that the variability curve 'will be different for every assumed economic model and at its best is based on a rough approximation of the way in which the economy works', and that 'Three or four estimated equations are crucial for the Taylor economic model but the economy as a whole is determined by millions of equations'. While I agree, I also note that all our theories are approximations; moreover, other researchers with different models (different approximations) have computed these variability curves, and, in my view, they appear to be robust to modelling differences to be useful as a framework for policy analysis.

Another difference between these two curves is that the variability curve is an efficiency frontier. It does not predict that the observed points will only be on the curve, but rather that points should also be above and to the right of the curve. Points closer to the curve represent better policy – more efficient policy. The scatter diagram in Chart 7.1 of Milton's paper illustrates this in my view. It shows that the variability of both inflation and output has come down over time. They represent better – more efficient – monetary policy. That the scatter of inflation and output variability observations is positive sloping rather than negative sloping does not therefore represent a contradiction to the variability curve. If policy were on this trade-off, then there would be a negative correlation in the data. But if policy was in the inefficient area, which I believe it was in earlier years, there could be a positive correlation.

Milton raises another caveat about the trade-off curve, namely that 'Treating the Fed. as having two separate objectives is an open invitation to engage in fine-tuning, something that has almost always proved mistaken practice'. I agree that there is a potential danger, but I stress that the practical message in the trade-off is that one can go too far in trying to keep inflation within a very narrow band. This would require that the central bank move the instruments of policy around too much and would likely increase output variability.

Using the trade-off, as I originally calculated it, I showed that a fixed money growth rule – a Friedman rule – would have led to better performance than actual policy in the post-World War II period up until the time I published that paper. This was an important finding in my view, and I am glad that Milton brings attention to it in his paper. I stressed this point in the final lines of my 1979 paper, while also stating that a money growth rule which responded to economic developments could do even better. Since then I have found that policy rules in terms of interest rates – so called 'Taylor rules' – have worked better as practical guidelines for central banks, and Milton mentions one interesting reason for this which deserves careful study: 'The Taylor rule is an attempt to specify the federal funds rate that will come closest to achieving the theoretically appropriate rate of monetary growth to achieve a constant price level or a constant rate of inflation.'

Another issue raised in Milton Friedman's paper is the relationship between the weight on output in the objective function used to derive the Taylor curve and the weight on output in the Taylor rule. In general, a zero weight on output in the objective function does not imply a zero weight on output in the Taylor rule. The reason is that output is a factor in determining inflation; it even leads inflation according to statistical tests. So an interest rate reaction to output (as well as to inflation) can help stabilize inflation. Even if you had a zero weight on output in the objective function, therefore, it would be optimal to put some weight on output in the Taylor rule.

Finally, let me mention a connection between David Laidler's research and the work on money growth and interest rate policy rules that we are discussing here. I first got to know David Laidler by attending many monetary policy conferences with him in the late 1970s and 1980s, and I came to respect him greatly for his skills, knowledge, and judgement as a monetary economist. In writing my policy rule paper (Taylor, 1993), I was motivated in part by a concern that practical work on policy rules was being abandoned, stating in the paper that 'Even those who have advocated the use of policy rules in the past seem to have concluded that discretion is the only answer', and I was thinking of David Laidler when I wrote that sentence. Indeed, in my paper, I quoted a remark that David had recently made at a Bank of Japan conference which we both attended: 'We are left, then, with relying on discretionary policy in order to maintain price stability' (Laidler, 1993). That remark made an impression on me.

Since the quote was from a then unpublished piece, I sent a copy of a draft of my paper to David, enquired whether the quote was still accurate, and asked for his comments on my paper. He wrote back, half in jest, 'I'm never one to pass up the chance of being quoted in a paper that's likely to be as widely read as yours', but then added on a more serious note that 'former supporters of the money growth rule and variations on it, such as myself, could, with your rather broader and more helpful use of the term "rule" be thought of as still supporting it' (Laidler, 1992).

It is a real honour for me both to discuss Milton Friedman's paper on policy trade-offs and rules, and to participate in this conference in honour of David Laidler.

1. This is a written version of informal remarks presented by video from San Francisco at the conference in honour of David Laidler, which was held in Canada on 18 August 2006. I thank Milton Friedman, David Laidler, and Robert Leeson for comments on an earlier draft.
2. I note, however, that Phillips may have had a model in mind when he originally estimated his curve, though Milton and Ned Phelps later showed that popular policy interpretations (developed later) of the estimated curve had some serious problems. David Laidler (2002) discusses this possibility in his review of Robert Leeson's (2000) collection of Phillips' papers, which contains additional useful references. For a detailed historical review of how the estimated Phillips curve came to be viewed as a policy trade-off see Laidler (1997).

References

Friedman, Milton (2006). "Tradeoffs in Monetary Policy." Paper prepared for David Laidler's Festschrift.

Laidler, David (1992). Letter to John B. Taylor, 22 December 1992.

Laidler, David (1993). "Price Stability and the Monetary Order." In Kumihari Shigehara, ed., *Price Stabilization in the 1990s*. London: Macmillan.

Laidler, David (1997). "The Emergence of the Phillips Curve as a Policy Menu." In B. Curtis Eaton and R.G Harris, eds., *Trade Technology and Economics: Essays in Honour of Richard G. Lipsey*. Cheltenham, UK and Brrokfield, US: Edward Elgar pp. 88–106.

Laidler, David (2002). "Phillips in Retrospect." In W.J. Samuels and J.E. Biddle, eds., *Research in the History of Economic Thought and Methodology*. Amsterdam: JAI Press, pp. 223–235.

Leeson, Robert, ed. (2000). *A. W. H. Phillips Collected Works in Contemporary Perspective*. Cambridge, U.K.: Cambridge University Press.

Taylor, John B. (1979). "Estimation and Control of a Macroeconomic Model with Rational Expectations." *Econometrica* 47:5 (September), 1267–1286.

Taylor, John B. (1993). "Discretion versus Policy Rules in Practice." *Carnegie-Rochester Conference Series on Public Policy*, pp. 195–214, North Holland.

Discussion

David Laidler

I

To contribute to my own *Festschrift* is perhaps a little unusual, but is amply justified, even required, by the role that Milton Friedman has played in my career. I first encountered his work in 1957 when, as a second-year undergraduate at the LSE, my tutor E. J. Mishan had me read 'The Quantity Theory of Money – a

Restatement' as an antidote to the very orthodox IS-LM macroeconomics to which I was then being exposed. I'm bound to say that I didn't understand a word of it. I did a little better the following year with *A Theory of the Consumption Function,* even though I was warned by another teacher, who had better remain nameless, of the heretical implications of a straight-line-through-the-origin relationship for the then sacrosanct macroeconomic case for income redistribution – Milton's work was already an object of considerable political suspicion in the 1950s! Above all, however, it was 'The Methodology of Positive Economics', read just after I had completed Karl Popper's course in scientific method, that really caught my imagination.

There were many reasons why, in 1960, I ended up a graduate student at Chicago, including an offer of financial support which arrived at more or less the same time as Yale's refusal of admission, but the prospect of studying with Milton was high among them. Nor was I disappointed: his course in price theory, not to mention the B that he gave me in the first quarter – it still smarts – taught me to take my economics more seriously than I had previously thought possible – in more ways than one; and my summer 1961 work with his co-author Anna Schwartz (whose own contribution to this *Festschrift* is also a source of particular pleasure) on the *Monetary History of the United States* gave me a respect for data and the role of narrative history in their interpretation that I have tried to live up to ever since. All of this now seems a long time ago, and I am deeply moved to be the recipient of an essay written by a man who has been a constant source of help, encouragement, and criticism throughout my professional life.

Milton has written a paper on the theory of monetary policy, an area in which my own work could not have been done without the foundations he was already laying even before I was a student, and I am delighted that so distinguished a colleague as John Taylor is commenting on it. John was one of the very few members of the generation that came on the scene after Milton who did not let the theoretical attractions of clearing markets and rational expectations blind him to the existence of real-world frictions which, even if theory could not explain them, demanded to be taken into account if monetary economics was to retain its empirical relevance. The importance of his work for the post-monetarist development of the theory of monetary policy needs no advertisement from me, and I am flattered indeed to be the object of his attention today.

II

So what is there to be said about Milton's comments on the work of his most important successor on the trade-offs between real and nominal variables that monetary policymakers might or might not face as they go about their business? First, surely, that he is right about the part played by the old Phillips curve in the theory of monetary policy as it developed in the 1960s. The role then assigned to the trade-off between the rates of inflation and unemployment was indeed different to that which John's work now assigns to the trade-off between their variability. Though I think that Milton attributes too much to Samuelson and

Solow (1960) here, when the real culprits were Grant Reuber (1962, 1964), Dick Lipsey (1965) and Harry Johnson (1968), there is no doubt that mainstream macroeconomics did come to treat the Phillips curve as a structural relationship that provided a constraint, subject to which policymakers could maximize a social utility function.[1] The Taylor trade-off, on the other hand, is recognized to exist only when the economy is subjected to a particular kind of stabilizing policy, and Milton's charts provide more than enough evidence that policy of a different sort not only can reverse its slope, but all too often has done so.

Even so, let me suggest that there is a little more to be said about the comparison between these two trade-offs than Milton's argument might initially lead one to think. Ever since the Phillips curve was discredited by the painful experience of the 1970s and 1980s, we have tended to forget something rather important about that relationship: namely, that it was clearly visible in the pre-World War I British data that Phillips (1958) analysed, and in the post-World War II data against which he then tested it.[2] If it was not a structural relationship, and Phillips, be it noted, made no clear claims that it was, then it must still have been implicit in the macroeconomic systems ruling in those periods as some sort of reduced form. Nor, with the benefit of hindsight illuminated by four decades of work on the role of policy-regime-induced expectations in economic life, is it hard to form conjectures about what features of the two systems were particularly important here. In both episodes, British monetary policy rested on a credible overriding commitment to a fixed exchange rate for sterling against a stable international money, gold before World War I, and the US dollar after World War II. It is plausible that the workings of these regimes gave rise to a stable expected inflation rate around which variations in actual inflation were then correlated (positively) with output and (inversely) with unemployment.[3]

In short, though its exponents did not present it as such in the 1960s, the Phillips trade-off was, like the Taylor trade-off, a relationship generated by an economy operating under a particular monetary policy regime, and likely to disappear when that regime changed. The two differ, however, in that no policy regime that tries to exploit the Phillips trade-off in its original static form can preserve its existence, while this is not true of the Taylor trade-off.[4] This analytic contrast between the two reveals features of the problems facing monetary policymakers that Milton's (nevertheless accurate) contrast between the roles that they have played in the theory of monetary policy at different stages of its development tends to obscure.

After Friedman (1968) and Phelps (1967), if one was willing to set aside results about possible non-super-neutralities that were available in the then thriving money and growth literature, one could argue that policymakers should not try to exploit a static Phillips relation because the economy's structure made it impossible to do so. One can't say that about the Taylor relation, so if a case against trying to trade off variability in output and employment against variability in inflation is to be made, it has rested on the undesirability, not on the impossibility, of doing so. There does, indeed, exist a class of policy regimes within which the trick apparently can be worked, and that is why Friedman and Taylor, who agree about so much, can still find room to debate this issue. Their disagreements can, I suspect, be directly traced to the different policy implications that Friedman (1968) and Taylor's early co-author Phelps (1967) drew from their co-discovery of the expectations-augmented Phillips curve. For Friedman, that relationship made an analytic case against directing monetary policy in any way towards real variables, while for Phelps, as the title of his paper made quite clear, it revealed that a trade-off, widely believed to be static, was in fact intrinsically dynamic and, in that form, remained exploitable for policy purposes.

III

Present-day discussions of the theory and practice of monetary policy are often marred by an unfortunate ambiguity in their use of the phrase *policy rule*, which it would be helpful to clear up at this point. This phrase can refer first of all to a legally, even constitutionally, binding constraint on the conduct of monetary policy. That is how Henry Simons (1936), following in the footsteps of Irving Fisher (see, e.g., 1920) used it. Or it can mean a systematic policy reaction function, employed by the monetary authorities to govern the adjustment of their chosen policy instrument – the function's dependent variable – in the light of the behaviour of the economic variables that appear on its right-hand side. That is how it is used when we speak of a Taylor rule. We often get confused between these two very different usages because Friedman's (1960) k per cent money growth rate proposal happened to be a rule in both senses. It specified a particular (albeit degenerate) feedback function for his chosen policy instrument, namely the money supply, which was also to be legally binding on the Fed.[5]

Though it would be possible in principle to enshrine a Taylor rule in an administrative decree or even in a central bank's governing legislation, the wisdom of so doing would be at the very least questionable, and I am unaware of any proposals anywhere to do so. Starting in the early 1990s with New Zealand, Canada, and the UK, however, an increasing number of countries have adopted rules in the Fisher–Simons sense for the goal of monetary policy, albeit rules requiring stability in the rate of change rather than the level of some price index. Furthermore, the central banks that are required to implement these rules have typically – I suspect universally – found some form of Taylor rule to guide the behaviour of the short-term interest rates under their direct control a helpful guide as they carry out their obligations. Also, it is implicit in the structures of the economies in which they are operating that, even where the sole prescribed goal of policy is an inflation rate, the behaviour of real variables intrude upon the policy scene. They do so in two interrelated ways, both stemming from the fact that output and employment variations are central to the mechanism through which monetary policy's effects are transmitted to prices in an economy where money wages and prices are less than perfectly flexible.

The first of these, sufficient by itself to open up space for real variables in a policy reaction-function, should cause no discomfort even to the most ardent exponent of the view that monetary policy should concern itself with the behaviour of the price level alone. Monetary policy takes time to have its effects on prices, so under such a rule, today's policies must make use of forecasts of future inflationary pressures. If, as seems likely, today's levels (and perhaps rates of change) of output and employment contain information about those future pressures, then current monetary policy should use that information. Precisely how, and to what extent, is a purely technical question, but if a Taylor rule systematically geared to real variables turns out to be a useful guide for those seeking to stabilize the inflation rate, then so be it.[6]

Real variables also intrude on inflation-targeting regimes in another way. As the Bank of Canada tells visitors to its website: 'Inflation control is not an end in itself... Low inflation... contributes to better economic growth over time and works to moderate cyclical fluctuations in income and employment.' Furthermore, an injunction to pursue 'low inflation' is not sufficient to define a policy rule in the Simons–Fisher sense. Choices must be made about: what price index to target; whether to set an upper bound for inflation, or to pursue symmetry around some central tendency; whether to prescribe a time path for the price level or merely for the inflation rate; over what time horizon errors should be corrected when they occur; and so on. Each of these choices (and no doubt others too), once implemented, will have implications for the behaviour of real variables, which will, therefore, be taken into account in designing any inflation-targeting regime. Moreover, as our knowledge of how inflation targeting works evolves over time, so will the way in which these problems are addressed. An inflation-targeting regime will (and should) be open to modification in the light of experience, including experience of its effects on real variables.

IV

Inflation-targeting regimes do not ignore real variables, that is to say. Like older-style regimes, they see monetary policy as a means of promoting a desirable performance on the part of the real economy, but they differ from them in the way they implement this vision by pursuing a purely nominal target within a framework designed to maximize policy's beneficial *indirect* impact upon that performance. But, in focusing *directly* only on a nominal goal, inflation targeting is nevertheless entirely within the spirit of Friedman's own longstanding prescriptions for monetary policy (and of those of Simons from whom Friedman drew much of his inspiration). If its conduct in some jurisdictions also generates an inverse correlation between the variability of inflation on the one hand, and of income and employment on the other, and even relies explicitly on a Taylor rule with real variables on its right-hand side, one should not be disturbed by this.

However, I suspect that when Milton thinks about the deployment of a Taylor rule to guide monetary policy, it is not in the context of a regime ruled by inflation targets, such as Canada's, but of the US regime, which currently lacks that important self-imposed constraint, and within which, therefore, a temptation to implement policies that seek to maximize a social utility function in which both inflation and real variables have equal status is clearly present. That temptation is, moreover, made all the stronger by two other characteristics of the US policy scene: namely that the Fed. is already widely regarded as being subject to a so-called dual mandate to pursue both price stability and high employment, and that memories are beginning to fade of the damage that such policies did the last time they were tried and failed.[7] Moreover, the relationship of the politics of US monetary policy to politics more generally seems to be such that, were the Fed. to seek a mandate to pursue an explicit inflation target as the sole goal of monetary policy, it would risk opening up a political process that it would have no ability to control. Milton's concerns about monetary policy in the US these days, and the role of the Taylor rule, therein, are thus well justified, and given the US dollar's role as the world's prime international currency, even those of us who live under local inflation-targeting regimes should share them.

Notes

I am indebted to John Taylor and Edward Nelson for assistance in connection with this chapter.

1. I have discussed this matter in detail in Laidler (1997, as reprinted 2004). For a statement of the prosecution case against Samuelson and Solow, however, see Robert Leeson (1997).
2. The US data presented by Samuelson and Solow (1960) are much less convincing in their support for the relationship's existence. That these authors' conjectures about the existence of a trade-off were taken so seriously on the basis of such flimsy empirical analysis is a minor mystery in the history of postwar empirical economics whose resolution probably does have a great deal to do with the political background to work on the Phillips curve discussed by Leeson (1997).
3. That is how I interpreted postwar British experience in my (1972) Lister Lecture.
4. That this was not understood until well into the 1970s is attested to by the frequent references in the literature of that time to the freedom that the adoption of a flexible exchange rate would confer on policymakers to exploit the Phillips curve. Michael Sumner (1976) was a pioneer in debunking this dangerous myth.
5. I here set aside the complications arising from the fact that the money supply was not under the direct control of the Fed., so that its manipulation required some kind of feedback rule linking a variable that was under direct control – the monetary base in Friedman's analysis – to its evolution.
6. They are precisely the same types of question that must be asked about the helpfulness to policymakers of the behaviour of monetary aggregates. In economies such as Canada, where inflation targeting has produced a decade and a half over which inflation has remained on target on average, while moving out of its assigned two-percentage-point range rather infrequently and seldom for long, it is becoming harder and harder to assess the information content of any variables for future inflation, money growth, and output and employment gaps alike. The very success of the policy regime has all but eliminated the degree variability in inflation needed to keep such assessments up to date.

7. It is nevertheless the case that the 1977 Humphrey-Hawkins Act that put the Fed.'s explicit dual mandate in place (and set several unworkable and now largely forgotten policy goals, too) has now lapsed, with only that Act's requirement that the chairman of the board of governors testify twice a year to Congress remaining in force. It is now embodied in the American Home Ownership and Economic Opportunity Act of 2000. On this, and the original Humphrey-Hawkins Act, see John Crow (2002, 40–41).

References

Crow, J. (2002). *Making Money: An Insider's Perspective on Finance, Politics and Canada's Central Bank*. Toronto: Wiley.

Fisher, I. (1920). *Stabilizing the Dollar.* New York: Macmillan.

Friedman, M. (1953). "The Methodology of Positive Economics." In *Essays in Positive Economics*. Chicago: University of Chicago Press, pp. 3–34.

Friedman, M. (1956). "The Quantity Theory of Money, a Restatement." In M. Friedman, ed., *Studies in the Quantity Theory of Money.* Chicago: University of Chicago Press, pp. 3–21.

Friedman, M. (1957). *A Theory of the Consumption Function.* Princeton: Princeton University Press for the NBER.

Friedman, M. (1960). *A Program for Monetary Stability.* New York: Fordham University Press.

Friedman, M. (1968). "The Role of Monetary Policy." *American Economic Review* 68 (March), 1–18.

Johnson, H. G. (1968). "Problems of Efficiency in Monetary Management." *Journal of Political Economy* 76 (September/October), 971–999.

Laidler, D. (1972). "The Current Inflation – Explanations and Policies," as reprinted (1999) in *Money and Macroeconomics, the Selected Essays of David Laidler.* Cheltenham: Edward Elgar, pp. 85–101.

Laidler, D. (1997). "The Emergence of the Phillips Curve as a Policy Menu," as reprinted (2004) with additions, in *Macroeconomics in Retrospect, The Selected Essays of David Laidler.* Cheltenham: Edward Elgar, pp. 354–371.

Leeson, R. (1997). "The Political Economy of the Inflation Unemployment Trade-Off". *History of Political Economy* 29 (spring), 117–156.

Lipsey, R. G. (1965). "Structural and Deficient Demand Unemployment Reconsidered." In A. M. Ross, ed., *Employment Policy and the Labour Market.* Berkeley and Los Angeles: University of California Press, pp. 191–209.

Phelps, E. S. (1967). "Phillips Curves, Expectations of Inflation, and Optimal Unemployment Over Time." *Economica NS* 34 (August), 254–281.

Phillips, A. W. (1958). "The Relationship between Unemployment and the Rate of Change of Money Wage Rates in the United Kingdom 1861–1957." *Economica NS* 25 (November), 283–299.

Reuber, G. L. (1962). "The Objectives of Monetary Policy." Working paper prepared for the Royal Commission on Banking and Finance (The Porter Commission), Ottawa.

Reuber, G. L. (1964). "The Objectives of Canadian Monetary Policy, 1949–1961: Empirical Trade-Offs and the Reaction Function of the Authorities." *Journal of Political Economy* 72 (February), 109–132.

Samuelson, P. A. and R. Solow (1960). "Analytic Aspects of Anti-inflation Policy." *American Economic Review* 60 (May, papers and proceedings), 177–194.

Simons, H. C. (1936). "Rule versus Authorities in Monetary Policy." *Journal of Political Economy* 44 (February), 1–30.

Sumner, M. (1976). "European Monetary Union and the Control of Europe's Inflation Rate." In J. M. Parkin and G. Zis, eds., *Inflation in the World Economy.* Manchester: Manchester University Press, pp. 97–112.

8

From Money Targeting to Inflation Targeting: The Change in the Role of Money in the Conduct of Monetary Policy

Charles Freedman

Introduction

From the day of his arrival in 1975, David Laidler has made important contributions to both monetary theory and monetary policy in Canada. Of course, even before he came to Canada, he was well known by reputation to Bank of Canada staff, particularly from the first edition of his textbook on the demand for money (Laidler, 1969) and his involvement in the debate on the causes of inflation in the United Kingdom (Laidler and Parkin, 1975). But we were looking forward to interacting with him in person and hoping that he would become involved in the monetary policy debates in Canada. On both counts, David's time in Canada has been a great success. And for me personally, it has been an enormous pleasure to discuss and debate issues of monetary theory and policy with David over the past 30 years, as well as to learn from him, and not infrequently to disagree with him. Initially, we met at academic meetings of various types, later at the C. D. Howe Institute, and subsequently during a very pleasant year when David was the first visiting Special Adviser at the Bank of Canada.

David's views on monetary theory and policy were always taken seriously at the Bank of Canada. In some cases, such as in his discussion of active money (Laidler, 1999*a*), he challenged the Bank's thinking, forcing it to justify its approach in more depth than perhaps had been the case.[1] In other cases, such as the issue of monetary union with the United States, his views (Laidler, 1999*b*) were very similar to those of the Bank of Canada, always a source of comfort to the Bank. His C. D. Howe study (Laidler, 1991) on the mandate and governance of the Bank of Canada, entitled 'How Shall We Govern the Governor? A Critique of the Governance of the Bank of Canada', helped persuade the Government of Canada to set up the Manley subcommittee to study the 'mandate and governance of the Bank of Canada' (Canada, 1992).[2] Moreover, his monographs and shorter papers on monetary policy for the C. D. Howe Institute have for many years been the most insightful academic commentary on the framework and conduct of policy by the Bank of Canada. As former governor John Crow (2002) put it in discussing the role of Canadian economists in policy debates about the Bank of Canada, 'David Laidler in particular provided a stream of lively and constructive analyses of the issues through his association with Canada's major economic and social policy think tank, the C. D. Howe Institute'.

The year that he spent at the Bank of Canada was very fruitful from the Bank's perspective, both in terms of the issues that he addressed at the Bank (such as active versus passive money, and the flexible exchange regime and Canada's monetary order) and the relationships that he developed with the staff of the Bank. David always took a very scholarly approach to whatever issue was being discussed, educating Bank staff about the 19th-century debates on British monetary theory or the 20th-century debates about the Austrian theory of capital accumulation, and so on. And, regardless of what was being discussed, David had well-thought-out views and could bring his scholarly background to bear on the subject in a way that delighted his interlocutors and added greatly to their understanding. Moreover, not surprisingly for someone who had been following monetary policy for so many years as an academic, he had strong views on policy issues and was not shy to express them around the table at meetings of the Monetary Policy Review Committee of the Bank. Indeed, on the issue of how the Bank should respond to exchange rate movements, the views put forward by David (along with some members of the staff) caused the Bank to reconsider its position as to whether an exchange rate movement, for which there was no evident explanation, should be considered initially as likely to be coming from a portfolio shock or a real shock. A final contribution that David made in his year at the Bank of Canada, which I will discuss in more detail later, is the assistance that he gave to the staff in developing the Blue Book, a document intended to pay more attention to money growth in forecasting future developments than was done in the main forecast process.

Ultimately, it has been David's ability to move comfortably between monetary theory and policy that has made him one of the most important and influential participants in the monetary debates in Canada. His involvement in the policy debates over the years has certainly been appreciated by the Bank of Canada, as well as by me personally.

In line with David's particular interest in money, I decided to discuss the role of money in the conduct of monetary policy over the past three decades. From the heyday of monetary targeting, through the period in which there was no nominal anchor, to the inflation-targeting period, David has consistently argued for an approach to policy that treated money seriously and, in particular, gave money as a causal variable a more prominent role than did most central banks. I want to begin with the monetary aggregate targeting period, briefly discuss the intermediate period in which there was no nominal anchor, and then examine in considerable detail the inflation-targeting period. While the monetary policy of the Bank of Canada will be treated in some depth, I will also examine the role of money in the making of policy at other central banks, particularly in the inflation-targeting period. My approach will be to look at the models typically used in the academic literature on inflation targeting as well as the principal models used by inflation-targeting central banks in developing their forecasts, and then to compare the general assertions that a number of central banks make about the role of money in their policy process with what they actually say in their press releases, minutes, and formal reports when they set interest rates. To foreshadow the principal conclusion, over time money appears to have become less and less relevant to the conduct of monetary policy. Indeed, in most analytic models in use both inside and outside central banks during the inflation-targeting period, money seems not to play any role at all. This raises the question of whether there is no room for money in a monetary policy based on inflation targeting, or whether there is still something to be learned from movements in the monetary aggregates.

Monetary Aggregate Targeting in Canada, 1975–1982[3]

Against the background of unprecedentedly high rates of inflation, many industrialised countries started to target monetary aggregates in the mid-1970s, with the objective of bringing down the rate of inflation from the high level that it had reached to the much lower level that was believed to be necessary for good economic performance. Thus, the announced goal for monetary policy was to gradually bring down the targeted rate of growth of some measure of money (narrow in some countries, broad in others) from a high starting point to a much lower level and thereby wring inflation out of the system, and then to maintain a low rate of growth of money.

In Canada, the Bank of Canada introduced monetary aggregate targeting in late 1975, aiming at achieving a decelerating rate of growth of the narrow aggregate M1 in the expectation that such a policy approach would bring down the rate of inflation from the double-digit level that it had reached to a much lower rate. While a great deal of academic research had been done on the relationship between the growth of monetary aggregates and the rate of inflation, a lot of internal analysis had to be done in the Bank on the demand for money relationship in Canada and on some of the mechanics of using a monetary aggregate as the target. George Freeman, then a deputy governor at the Bank of Canada, played a prominent role in advancing the view that money growth led the rate of inflation, and that containing and bringing down the growth in money would help bring down the rate of inflation.

Economists held different views of the mechanism at work that would link the deceleration of money growth to a decline in the rate of inflation. The more monetarist view focused on a direct causal link between money growth and the rate of inflation. Among the proponents of this view were the Federal Reserve Bank of St Louis and economists who were associated with the buffer stock money view (see Laidler, 1982, 1999*a*; Goodhart, 1984; Laidler and Robson, 1995). The more typical view in central banking circles was that the mechanism operated through traditional, structural relationships and was associated with the concept of endogenous passive money. Thus, too high a rate of inflation (that is, one that was higher than consistent with the targeted growth rate of money) would result in a rise in the rate of growth of money demanded above the target rate, leading the central bank to raise the policy interest rate. This would lead to an increase in short-term market interest rates, and, to a lesser extent, long-term interest rates, as well as to an appreciation of the exchange rate. These, in turn, would slow the growth of aggregate demand (relative to capacity) and bring about a lower rate of inflation.

Essential to the sequence of events in the latter approach were two preconditions. First was stability in the demand for money. This was necessary so that the appropriate signal would be forthcoming regarding the pace of growth of nominal spending and the needed change in interest rates. Second, the response of interest rates to the deviation between money and targeted money had to exert appropriate effects on demand and inflation.

While the Bank of Canada was successful in gradually reducing the rate of growth of M1, it was less successful in keeping down the rate of inflation after an initial slowing. This lack of success in reducing inflation in the context of a significant decline in M1 growth was due to the fact that the two preconditions needed for monetary aggregate targeting were not met.

The first and more important problem was the instability in the demand for money, especially in the early 1980s. Indeed, this type of instability in the money demand relationship turned out to be a problem in most countries. While economists initially attributed the instability to the deregulation of financial institutions and markets that was then going on in many countries, it occurred also in some countries that had deregulated much earlier. In those countries, and Canada was one of them, the instability seemed to be related to innovations initiated by financial institutions in which they changed the characteristics of the various financial instruments and services that they offered to the public (Courchene, 1983; Freedman, 1983). As experience in many countries has subsequently shown, these kinds of innovations have continued apace and have lessened the information content of the monetary aggregates to the extent that they cannot bear the weight of being a formal target for monetary policy. In the case of Canada, as the then Governor Gerald Bouey (1983) put it in a memorable phrase after the withdrawal of the targets in 1982, 'We did not abandon M1, M1 abandoned us'. By the mid-1980s, just ten years later, most countries had abandoned monetary targets or had significantly downgraded the role of the monetary aggregates.

The second factor behind the lack of success of the monetary aggregate targeting regime in Canada was that the interest rate elasticity of M1 turned out to be too high (and higher than had originally been thought).[4] As a consequence, the interest rate increase needed to bring M1 back to target in response to upward pressure on inflation and on the growth of M1 was relatively small and, indeed, was probably insufficient to counter the inflationary pressures over the short to medium run (Thiessen, 1983).

There were a number of interesting issues that were the subject of considerable debate at the time regarding the techniques used by the Bank of Canada in conducting policy with a monetary aggregates target.

Should the central bank target a narrow monetary aggregate or a broader monetary aggregate? In large part, the judgment on which monetary aggregate would perform best as the target for monetary policy was an empirical one and depended on the tightness of the relationship between the growth in different definitions of money and nominal spending growth (for those who took the active money view), or the tightness of the money demand relationship between different definitions of money and a scale variable and a market interest rate (for those who took the passive money view). In addition, the issue of controllability played a role, with some central banks (including the Bank of Canada) focusing on their ability to adjust interest rates to move along the demand for money curve. The need for controllability was a factor in leading some central banks to target a monetary aggregate with an appreciable interest rate elasticity of money demand. In fact, as just noted, M1 in Canada turned out to have an unexpectedly large interest rate elasticity of money demand, which led to problems in carrying out monetary policy over this period.

Should money growth targets be set to achieve a gradual deceleration of money growth or a more rapid decline? This was usually termed as the gradualism versus cold shower or cold turkey debate. It tended to hinge on two key factors – the size of the response of price and wage inflation to slack in the economy, and the speed of the adjustment of inflation expectations to actual movements of inflation and/or announced target growth rates in money. Thus, for example, if the mere announcement of a disinflationary monetary policy based on a specified rate of decline in the target for the growth rate of money led to a sharp reduction in inflation expectations, there would be little reason to have a lengthy disinflationary process. Central banks, including the Bank of Canada, typically did not expect such a credibility effect to play a major role in the process of disinflation and hence tended on the whole to aim for a gradual decline in inflation. The logic behind such gradualism was to avoid the unduly large effects on output that might have resulted from a much steeper decline in the rate of growth of M1 in the absence of credibility effects. The experience of the monetary aggregates targeting period and that of the inflation-targeting period are supportive of the conclusion that inflation expectations adjust only gradually, and with a lag, to declines in the actual rate of inflation, at least in countries where the rate of inflation is not extremely high.

Should central banks use an interest rate instrument or adjustments in the monetary base to control the monetary aggregate chosen as the target of policy? With a couple of possible exceptions, virtually all central banks used interest rate control and not base control as their mechanism for achieving the target growth of money. The possible exceptions were Switzerland, and the United States in the 1979 to 1982 period. An alternative interpretation of the apparent use by the Federal Reserve of non-borrowed reserves as the instrument of policy to target money growth in the 1979 to 1982 period is that it was a technique for raising interest rates in order to achieve the desired decline in inflation, without suffering the political fallout from being seen to explicitly set short-term interest rates. It is of interest to note that in the last few years, the academic literature has largely accepted the interest rate-setting approach of central banks, and most recent articles on the conduct of monetary policy have therefore treated the very short-term interest rate as the policy instrument.[5]

The Intermediate Period, 1982–1991

Following the withdrawal of the M1 targets in 1982, the Bank of Canada spent a great deal of time and energy searching for an alternative monetary aggregate that could be used as the basis for policy. What it was looking for was an aggregate that bore a stable relationship to output, prices, and the interest rate. In 1983 Bank staff actually found an aggregate that was slightly broader than M1, which was called M1A, and that appeared to be stable.[6] While there was pressure both from inside the Bank and from outside commentators to introduce a new money target, those involved in the analysis were more cautious. Although the demand for total M1A appeared stable, this stability was the outcome of large and offsetting errors in its two components, household deposits and business deposits. And, indeed, in the following year, the fortuitous offsetting of errors disappeared and aggregate M1A followed M1 into instability. Staff reservations about introducing M1A as the new monetary aggregate target were clearly vindicated.

The role of money in inflation targeting

Introduction

In early 1990, the Reserve Bank of New Zealand formally introduced a new framework for the conduct of monetary policy – inflation targeting (or, as some would prefer to call it, inflation forecast targeting). In the 16 years since that event, 23 other countries have chosen to use inflation targeting as the basis for their monetary policy. Of the 24 countries choosing to use inflation targeting, 10 were industrialised countries and 14 were emerging market countries. While two countries that used inflation targeting (Finland and Spain) later went on to join the EMU, so far no country has abandoned the framework because of inability to achieve the desired objectives of policy. Thus, the inflation-targeting approach has lasted longer than the monetary aggregates targeting framework and seems to be less vulnerable to shocks than the target exchange rate arrangements that preceded it in a number of countries.

While the first two countries that adopted this framework, New Zealand and Canada, chose without any external pressure to use it as a way of bringing down the rate of inflation and maintaining it at levels lower than they were able to achieve earlier, the next three countries (United Kingdom, Sweden, and Finland) decided upon inflation targeting as their monetary policy anchor after they were forced off the fixed exchange rate regime in 1992 by market forces. These countries were no longer able to use a fixed exchange rate as the basis of their policy, and they were unwilling to use a monetary aggregate as a policy target because of the instability that monetary aggregates had undergone in their countries. The relatively new inflation-targeting approach appeared to them to offer an alternative way of controlling inflation. As the initial group of inflation-targeting countries was seen to be increasingly successful at controlling inflation, a number of other central banks became interested in this approach to policy and gradually joined the ranks of inflation targeters. Moreover, the advantages of the new approach in contributing to low output volatility, at the same time as it allowed central banks to maintain low rates of inflation,[7] also added to the attractiveness of inflation targeting. Another attractive feature of the new approach that became apparent over time was that the increasing credibility of inflation-targeting central banks allowed them to cope with supply shocks more effectively than had been anticipated. As a result of the perceived benefits of inflation targeting, over time more and more emerging market economies have decided to use inflation targeting as their approach to the conduct of monetary policy. In some cases, the movement to inflation targeting resulted from the breakdown of fixed exchange rate arrangements; in others, it was a more gradual process in which countries that had previously been on a fixed exchange rate regime of some sort slowly reduced the role of the exchange rate target and increased the role of the announced inflation target as the centerpiece of policy.

What is the role of money in inflation targeting? While the situation differs somewhat across countries, it is fair to say that money has played a relatively minimal role in the conduct of policy in most inflation-targeting countries. This is not to say that central banks were happy to abandon money. Indeed, central bankers typically feel that they should be paying some attention to the behaviour of monetary aggregates. And, as we shall see, there is a view among some that money still has a role to play in the longer-term conduct of monetary policy. Nonetheless, over the short-term to medium-term horizon that is relevant for policy, I will argue that money no longer plays much of a role in most countries. And even those inflation-targeting countries that have made an effort to incorporate money into their policy framework have not found it easy to do so, and the results have not been particularly satisfactory.

IMF and central bank models

As I noted, inflation targeting can more appropriately be called inflation forecast targeting (Svensson, 1997). Thus, underlying the interest rate-setting process is a forecast for the rate of inflation (and for other key economic variables) over the next few quarters. While the inflation forecast can be, and typically is, based on a broader range of factors than just the macroeconomic model used by the staff of the central bank, this model is usually the key ingredient in the forecast. There are different kinds of models in use in central banks, ranging from relatively simple models with four or five structural equations, to more complex models containing a relatively large number of structural equations, to the more recently developed stochastic dynamic general equilibrium models based on microeconomic foundations. In most cases, these models have little or no role for money. If money is introduced at all in the forecast process, it is, typically, via a satellite model or by judgment external to the model.

Let me examine some of these models in a little more detail. In two recent working papers (Berg, Karam, and Laxton, 2006*a*, 2006*b*), IMF researchers have presented a relatively small model 'that blends the New Keynesian emphasis on nominal and real rigidities and a role of aggregate demand in output determination, with the real business cycle tradition methods of dynamic stochastic general equilibrium modeling with rational expectations'. The two working papers provide a model-based approach to forecasting and monetary policy analysis, as well as a set of tools that facilitates this approach. Effectively, the macroeconomic model has at its core four equations: (1) an aggregate demand curve relating output to expected and past output, the real interest rate, and the real exchange rate; (2) a price-setting equation or augmented Phillips curve relating inflation to past and expected inflation, the output gap, and the exchange rate; (3) an uncovered interest parity condition for the exchange rate, with some allowance for backward-looking expectations; and (4) a rule for setting the policy interest rate as a function of the output gap and expected inflation. In addition to these behavioural equations, there are a number of identities and equations specifying steady-state and equilibrium conditions. As is evident, money has absolutely no role to play in this model. Effectively, inflation is driven by the output gap, past and expected inflation, and the exchange rate, and money growth does not influence any of these variables. The authors recognise that the Monetary Policy Committee (MPC) of a central bank would also use other variables and information in determining the forecast rate of inflation on which policy is based. But money would be only one of many variables external to the model that the MPC would use in coming to a view on the forecast rate of inflation and the appropriate path for the policy rate of interest.

The IMF has also developed a much more sophisticated stochastic dynamic general equilibrium model that can be used for analysis and forecasting. This global economy model (or GEM) is an extension of the stylised models considered in the new open economy macroeconomics theoretical literature and is described in some detail in Laxton and Pesenti (2003). The version of the model used in this paper has 46 equations, and the structural equations are based on microeconomic foundations. In the model, the demand for money is based on a transaction motive, with shopping costs inversely related to households' holdings of real money balances. Over time, rapid money growth will be associated with high inflation, high nominal interest rates, a decline in the holdings of real money balances, an increase in shopping costs, and therefore a reduction in the level of consumption (net of shopping costs) that influences consumer welfare. While it would be possible to derive the optimal rate of inflation in the model, work with the model thus far has assumed that money is passive, and monetary policy has been modeled by a standard monetary policy reaction function in which the interest rate is adjusted to move inflation gradually back to a fixed inflation target. In future work with the model the authors plan to do formal welfare analysis to derive the optimal inflation rate that will trade off the increasing distortions associated with higher levels of inflation and the costs of deflation that arise from the zero interest rate floor.[8]

The previous Bank of Canada forecast model (QPM), which was used for many years, also does not provide for a role for money growth. Nor does the Bank of Canada's more recent model, TOTEM (or terms of trade economic model). And neither do the primary models used at the Riksbank and the Reserve Bank of New Zealand, which are similar to the models used at the Bank of Canada. The new

Bank of England Quarterly Model (Bank of England, 2004, 2005) includes money as one of a range of financial assets and, by including money in the household utility function, creates a demand for real money balances. Nonetheless, money does not appear to have a role of any importance in the working of the model, nor is it even discussed in the simulations of the model that are presented in the monograph describing the model (Bank of England, 2005). I should add, however, that although the principal forecasting model has no role for money, other models in the Bank of England's suite of forecasting models do take account of money growth and other financial developments (such as the financial accelerator).

The role of money growth in practice at selected central banks

The Bank of Canada

The main mechanism whereby money growth (and other financial variables) enters into the process for setting interest rates is through a document known in the Bank of Canada as the Blue Book. The origins and history of the Blue Book as part of the Bank of Canada's forecasting and interest rate-setting process are of interest from the perspective of the role that money growth can play in an inflation-targeting framework.

There were two key contributing factors to the development of the Blue Book. One element that played an important role at the origin of this initiative was the view on the part of the staff in the Special Studies section of the Department of Monetary and Financial Analysis in the Bank of Canada, which was responsible for longer-term research on money and financial matters, and which reported ultimately to me as deputy governor in charge of the department, that the research they had been doing on money was not having any influence on the interest rate-setting process. My response to them was that they should develop an analysis that reflected their research and insights, and which could be used as an input into the interest rate-setting process. What we were looking for was something equivalent to a US Shadow Open Market Committee analysis and recommendation, in which more weight could be put on the monetary aggregates than was done in the main staff projection.

I made two further suggestions to the staff at that time. First, while the staff had developed a number of equations relating output growth and inflation to developments in various money growth measures, they should use their judgment regarding the quality of the various equations to aggregate all the information into a single forecast for output and a single forecast for inflation, since they were the experts on the linkage between money, on the one hand, and output growth and inflation, on the other. Of course, there would be considerable uncertainty about the forecast, as is true of all forecasts, but the Bank's Governing Council was not interested in seeing a series of forecasts that suggested that equation 1 implied such and such an inflation outcome, equation 2 implied a different inflation outcome, equation 3 yet another, etc. Second, their forecast and their recommendation on the interest rate path needed to keep inflation at target or to bring it back to target did not have to be based solely on money growth. Rather, the intention was to incorporate developments in money as one of the factors influencing future inflation elements, but to give it a weight commensurate with their view that money is an important determinant of inflation.

The second factor that was important in the decision to develop the Blue Book as a way of enhancing the role of money growth in the decision-making process was the desire for a diversification strategy in which the Bank could use a diversified set of models from different paradigms to minimise the risk of policy error. The view of some staff in the Department of Monetary and Financial Analysis was that reliance on a single paradigm (the mainstream New Keynesian model described above, which had no role for money) was dangerous and could lead to serious policy errors from time to time because any model is by necessity incomplete. Models in which money growth played a role in determining the rate of inflation were seen as a natural alternative paradigm because of their long history in the academic and central banking community.[9]

With the assistance of David Laidler, who was the special adviser at the Bank during the year that the Blue Book was under development, the staff was able in fairly short order to create a document that became one of the inputs into the forecasting process. Macklem (2002) describes the process by which the Bank of Canada comes to a decision about the setting of its policy instrument (the target for the overnight rate of interest).

> About a week before the announcement, the Governing Council receives four additional important pieces of information:
>
> i) An analysis of the risks around the staff projection and the implications of alternative paths for interest rates;
> ii) The perspective from the regional offices, including a national forecast constructed from individual regional forecasts;
> iii) An analysis of the information coming from money and credit; and
> iv) Financial market expectations about policy actions.
>
> Each of these components is designed to complement the staff economic projection from a different perspective.

The third item in this list is the Blue Book.

Longworth (2003) described the use of the monetary aggregates in the policymaking process at the Bank of Canada as of the end of 2001, and concluded that monetary aggregates continued to play a role in monetary policy decision-making at the Bank at that time. It would appear, however, that the attention paid to monetary aggregates in decision-making has declined appreciably since then, as M1 has been undergoing another bout of financial innovation. The decline, over time, in the attention paid to money growth is reflected in the way that the Blue Book has changed in character over the years. Originally, its main focus was on the monetary aggregates and their possible contribution to forecasting inflation and output growth, and determining the appropriate interest rate path needed to maintain inflation at its target or to bring it back to target. However, on many occasions when money growth appeared on the surface to be signaling excessive or deficient monetary stimulus to the economy, the staff explained away the behaviour of the aggregates as a result of some specific development in the economy or in the financial system, and ended up recommending that the unusual developments in the growth of money be ignored in the context of the interest rate-setting process. As an extreme example, following the terrorist attacks of September 11, 2001, there was a sharp increase in M1 growth, which was the result of an increase in the demand for precautionary balances as a result of the rise in uncertainty generated by the attacks. In the circumstances, rapid M1 growth was certainly not signaling excessive monetary stimulus and the need to tighten policy, and was appropriately treated as a shift in money demand.

But it was not simply in such extreme circumstances that money growth turned out not to be useful as a signal to policymakers. On other occasions, the staff downplayed money growth movements that might have been interpreted as a signal to take action in one or the other direction. In effect, the noise to signal ratio in monetary aggregate growth was very high and the staff were unable to extract the signal with any degree of confidence. As a result, money growth did not provide much assistance in coming to a view on likely future developments in the rate of inflation. As well, the recommendation of the staff responsible for preparing the Blue Book was, typically, similar to or only marginally different from that of the main forecast. As a result of the apparent inability of money growth to give much assistance to the Governing Council in the interest rate-setting process, the Blue Book was generalised into a broader compendium of financial developments. Over time, it came to contain, among other things, a general description of financial developments in the household and business sectors, the credit conditions faced by borrowers at banks and in credit markets, an analysis of various measures of the stance of monetary policy (such as yield curves, term spreads, risky spreads, and monetary conditions[10]), the output of various monetary policy rules, an analysis of inflation expectations, forecasts of future growth in money aggregates, output, and inflation, a discussion of upside and downside risks to the inflation forecast, and recommendations for the path of the policy interest rate over the next few months, as well as for the interest rate setting at the upcoming meeting of the Governing Council. Thus, the emphasis has shifted away from money growth to a much more general assessment of the financial situation in Canada and its implications for future developments in output, inflation, and the path for the policy interest rate. In this way, the Blue Book is useful in helping to identify risks to the base-case forecast related to developments in the financial area that are not incorporated in the process that results in the base-case forecast.

Macklem (2002) summarised the role of the money and credit aggregates and other financial variables in the interest rate-setting process as follows:

> The economic model used in the staff projection focuses on the links from interest rates to spending by households and firms. Information on various holdings of money and credit provide yet another view of what consumers and firms are doing and planning to do. In order to spend, consumers and firms

need money or credit, so the evolution of the monetary and credit aggregates provides clues to spending plans. In practice, these aggregates are also affected by portfolio shifts and other purely financial developments, so, as with other high-frequency indicators, the challenge for the staff is to separate the genuine signals about economic activity and inflation from volatility related to other factors. Regular contact with financial institutions provides useful insight into the particular developments that appear to be affecting the growth of money and credit at the time. Information is also obtained on credit spreads in bond markets and on any changes in the conditions under which banks are lending to businesses and households as indicators of changes in credit quality and availability.

The staff in the Bank's Department of Monetary and Financial Analysis assemble this information to provide an overall view from the financial side of the economy on the outlook for output growth and inflation, as well as on the risks surrounding this outlook. Based on this analysis, they also make a recommendation to the Governing Council on the setting of the target overnight interest rate at the next fixed announcement date.

With forecasts coming from several different economic models and advice based on a wide variety of data, the Governing Council has to decide how to integrate all the information it receives. As the various forecasts and indicators often differ, the Governing Council has to decide how much weight to give to the various pieces of information. This will depend on the judgments of the members of Governing Council as to which factors are the most relevant in the current situation, the track records of the various models and indicators, and the lessons Council members have drawn from past experience. Thus, in the end, the decision reflects the Council's best judgment.

Although not a foolproof way of assessing the importance of monetary aggregates in the policy process, in practice an analysis of the documents on interest rate setting and monetary policy published by the Bank of Canada can give one some idea of the current role of money in policymaking. The Bank issues a short press release following each of the eight interest rate-setting meetings during the year, whether or not the policy interest rate has been changed. Over the past year (July 2005 through June 2006), none of the eight press releases contained any reference to money, monetary aggregate, M1, or M2. The principal publications explaining monetary policy in Canada are the Monetary Policy Report (issued twice a year in April and October) and the Monetary Policy Report Update (issued twice a year in January and July). The October 2005 Monetary Policy Report, a document of 31 pages, contained only one reference to money and one chart showing the growth of real GDP and the growth of M1+. The reference was as follows.

Data on narrow money are generally consistent with the Bank's current monitoring of growth in real GDP of about 3 per cent in the third quarter of 2005 and some slowing in the fourth quarter (Chart 5).

In the April 2006 Monetary Policy Report, there were short references to both M1 and M2 type variables.

> Since the October *Report*, growth in narrow money (M1+) has picked up, largely owing to stronger business deposits. This stronger growth suggests some pickup in real output growth in the first half of 2006 (Chart 16). Over the same period, growth of broad money (M2++) has also picked up slightly (Chart 17), which is consistent with a modest rise in core inflation through 2006.[11]

The two Monetary Policy Report Updates issued in July 2005 and January 2006 contained no references to money or monetary policy.

The Governor of the Bank of Canada, David Dodge, made 20 speeches and statements over the period July 2005 through June 2006, covering a multitude of subjects and issues. The only references to money or the money supply in those speeches and statements related to the sterilisation of foreign-exchange interventions on the domestic money supply and the rapid growth of the money supply when the domestic economy was already operating at capacity in the year 1950.

I would conclude that the Bank of Canada is currently paying little attention to money growth in its policymaking process.

The Riksbank

The Sveriges Riksbank, the central bank of Sweden, recently issued a memorandum (Sveriges Riksbank, 2006) providing a description of the goal and strategy of its monetary policy. While covering a number of areas, including the formulation of the target, the role of different measures of inflation, the targeting horizon and real stability, monetary policy and financial markets, the inflation forecast and interest rate decisions, and openness, clarity, and communication, there is no reference to money or monetary aggregates in the document except in the context of a brief discussion of the lack of success of a money supply target in preventing excessively high rates of inflation. In the Riksbank's most recent Inflation Report (2006, 2), the rapid growth of the money supply was cited as a cause of inflation in the section on the determinants of inflation but was not mentioned in the section on the inflation assessment. The previous Inflation Report (2006, 1) contained references in the inflation assessment section to the rapid growth of money, noting it as one factor in the assessment of risks to the inflation forecast. The minutes of the meetings of the executive board responsible for making interest rate decisions showed no references to money in the seven meetings in 2005, but there were references to the high rate of growth of broad money in two of the four meetings so far in 2006. And there were no references to money in the speeches made by the Governor and the Deputy Governors in the first half of 2006.

The Reserve Bank of New Zealand

The Reserve Bank of New Zealand pays even less attention to money growth. In the last four Monetary Policy Statements (two in the second half of 2005 and two in the first half of 2006), there is not a single reference to money. And the Governor's recent speeches on monetary policy do not feature any references to money growth in spite of the continuing concern about inflation in New Zealand.

The Bank of England

The Bank of England has been more explicit than the other inflation-targeting central banks that I have discussed in explaining the role that money growth plays within an inflation-targeting framework. The then deputy governor Mervyn King delivered a paper entitled 'No money, no inflation – the role of money in the economy' at the *Festchrift* in honor of Charles Goodhart (King, 2003). The summary of that paper in the Summer 2002 Bank of England Quarterly Bulletin is as follows:

> In this article, Mervyn King, Deputy Governor, examines the apparent contradiction that the acceptance of the idea inflation is a monetary phenomenon has been accompanied by the lack of references to money in the conduct of monetary policy during its most successful period. The disappearance of money from the models used by economists is, however, more apparent than real, with official interest rates playing the leading role as the instrument of policy, with money in the wings off-stage. Nevertheless, there are real dangers in relegating money to this behind-the-scenes role.

In addition to focusing on the long-run relationship between money and inflation, King argues that there are three dangers in downplaying the role of money in monetary policy and discussing monetary policy in terms of a conceptual model in which money plays only a hidden role. First, there is a tendency to neglect the parts of the transmission mechanism operating through the impact of quantities on risk and term premia of various kinds, a tendency that is magnified by the absence of financial yields other than the short-term interest rate in many models of the transmission mechanism. Second, King argues that there is a danger of misleading people into thinking that there is a permanent trade-off between inflation and output and employment if the role of money is ignored. And third, by discussing policy in terms of real variables rather than monetary variables, central banks can leave the impression that monetary policy can fine-tune short-run movements in output and employment, and can offset each and every shock to the economy.

There have also been a number of other articles on money and its role in inflation targeting published in the Bank of England Quarterly Bulletin. Most noteworthy were the articles by Hauser and Brigden (2002) and Benati (2005).

Hauser and Brigden (2002) argue that monetary variables can be helpful to policymakers in a number of ways. First, they can be used as short-run indicator variables. The Bank of England uses both economy-wide aggregates and sectoral data in this way. Second, data on money and credit can provide incremental information on the transmission of shocks to the economy, thereby reducing the probability of making policy mistakes. While this can be particularly useful at times of potential financial instability, the credit channel may be important more generally, as the recent financial accelerator literature stresses. Third, such data can provide incremental information on the tightness or looseness of policy over and above other measures.

Benati (2005) uses frequency domain analysis on money growth and inflation to illustrate that in the United Kingdom there has been 'remarkable stability across monetary regimes in the correlation [between inflation and the rates of growth of narrow and broad money] for longer-run trends in the data, but some instability in the short to medium term'. He provides additional evidence from the United States that confirms the overall stability of the correlation between money growth and inflation for the longer-run trends.

The basic thrust of all these papers is that there is a relationship between money growth and inflation over the longer run, but that the relationship is much less evident in the short to medium run. In the Bank of England's view, the principal policy roles of money growth (and for that matter of credit growth) seem to be as a crosscheck on the output from the Bank's macroeconometric model and on provisional outputs of the forecast process, and as a source of information on assessing the risks around the central projections for inflation and output, reflected in the fan charts published in the Inflation Report. Also, because the financial data are available more rapidly than most other economic data, they may provide early information on the near-term economic outlook.

How does this perspective show up in the way that monetary policy is conducted in the United Kingdom? The Bank issues a substantive news release at the time of the interest rate decision only if there is a change in the policy interest rate. On the last six occasions prior to the most recent meeting in which interest rates have been changed at the MPC meeting (from November 2003 through August 2005), there has been no mention of money in the news release and only once has there been a reference to credit. This occurred in the news release of November 6, 2003, following an increase in the policy interest rate, and referred to credit growth remaining strong. The press release following the most recent MPC meeting (August 3, 2006) did mention 'rapid growth of broad money and credit' as a factor behind the interest rate increase.

The minutes of the Bank of England MPC meetings are considered to be an important communications tool in explaining the factors that led the Bank to change the policy interest rate or to leave it unchanged. In the section entitled 'Money, credit, demand and output', there is often a paragraph describing money growth and its possible implications for output growth and inflation. In the section on 'immediate policy decision' in the minutes for the six meetings in the first half of 2006 (in all of which interest rates were held unchanged), the first four had no references to money growth, while there is mention of the strength in money growth in this section in the minutes for the May and June meetings. Since interest rates were held unchanged at these latter meetings, the strength in money growth was apparently not an important factor in the decision.

Turning to the minutes of the most recent meetings in which there were changes in interest rates, we find the following. In the meeting of November

6, 2003, in which interest rates were raised by 1/4 percent, the minutes indicate that 'The credit aggregates suggested greater strength. The annual growth rate of aggregate M4 lending to the non-bank private sector had been over 11% for several months. Total lending, secured and unsecured, to individuals had increased by 14% in the twelve months to September, and this rate had picked up during the year'. In the meeting of February 5, 2004 at which there was an increase of 1/4 percent, the minutes indicate that 'the monetary aggregates were consistent with continued resilience of consumption'. In the meeting of May 6, 2004, at which the MPC decided on an increase of 1/4 percent in the interest rate, there was virtually no discussion of money, although there was some reference to the rapid growth in credit card lending. The meeting of June 10, 2004 resulted in an increase in the interest rate of 1/4 percent. The financial data presented a mixed picture as 'aggregate broad money growth had eased a little in April, but lending growth continued to be very strong. The monetary data were consistent with steady growth in aggregate nominal demand'. In the meeting of August 5, 2004, at which interest rates were increased by 1/4 percent, the minutes suggest that money growth was a factor supporting 'some signs of a possible easing in the pace of growth', pointing in a direction that was inconsistent with the policy decision. In the August 4, 2005 meeting, at which interest rates were reduced by 1/4 percent, the minutes indicate that 'the money and credit data had not pointed to a marked further softening in activity; rather, they were consistent with a recovery in consumption and GDP growth in the second half of the year'. Thus, in this case, the financial aggregates were also pointing in a direction that did not support the policy decision. The minutes for the August 3, 2006 meeting noted that 'Supporting evidence of potential demand pressures in the medium term came from the rapid rates of broad money and credit growth. The implications of that for inflation would depend on the extent to which higher money balances would eventually be used to finance the purchases of either goods and services or financial and other assets, and some Committee members interpreted the money numbers as a possible indication of longer-term inflationary pressures'. Also, in the paragraph on the committee decision to raise interest rates, specific reference was made to 'rapid growth of broad money and credit' as one of the factors in the decision.

Thus, of the most recent seven meetings in which the Bank of England decided on a change in interest rates, only in the first meeting (November 6, 2003) and the most recent meeting (August 3, 2006) were the financial variables moving in such a way as to provide a strong indication of the need for the change in policy.

The Bank of England's quarterly Inflation Report typically contains considerable information about money and credit, and their possible implications for output growth and inflation. The first main section of the Report is entitled 'Money and asset prices', with a subsection on 'Money, credit and balance sheets'. In some Reports, there is a more detailed discussion of the relationships, at times presented in a box section. For example, in the May 2006 Report, there was a box that examined 'Estimates of excess broad money growth' and assessed their usefulness in identifying inflationary pressures. It concluded that:

> Since the beginning of the inflation-targeting era in 1992, estimates of excess money growth and official interest rates have been related, though by no means perfectly...That could indicate that policymakers have at times reacted to the information contained in that estimate, or to other information that correlates well with excess money growth. Whatever the reason, this leaves open the possibility that estimates of excess money growth may contain useful information about future inflationary pressure.

In contrast, in the last section of the Inflation Report, which discusses the prospects for inflation, the inflation projection, and the policy decision, there is, typically, little or no mention of money growth.

What do we conclude from all this? It appears to be the case that, while the Bank of England takes seriously the long-run relationship between money growth and inflation, in its short-run interest rate decision process, money and credit growth play a relatively minor role. This does not mean that they are ignored. Rather, it would probably take unusual and protracted changes in the growth rate of money and credit aggregates for them to become a more important factor influencing the monthly interest rate-setting decision.

The European Central Bank

Finally, I would like to turn to the case of the European Central Bank (ECB). Although the ECB is not a full-fledged inflation targeter, in many ways it behaves in very similar fashion to inflation-targeting central banks. It has an explicit target (of below, but close to, 2 percent over the medium term) and a medium-term orientation of policy in which it focuses on future inflation. Where it differs from inflation-targeting central banks, at least on the surface, is in the role of the two pillars in its monetary policy strategy. The first pillar is based on economic analysis and appears very similar to the approach taken by inflation-targeting central banks in their interest rate-setting process. The second pillar is based on monetary analysis. The volume entitled *The Monetary Policy of the ECB* (ECB, 2004) devoted a chapter to the ECB's monetary policy strategy. It is worth quoting from it at some length.

> The ECB's approach to organising, evaluating and cross-checking the information relevant for assessing the risks to price stability is based on two analytical perspectives, referred to as the two 'pillars'...
>
> In the ECB's strategy, monetary policy decisions are based on a comprehensive analysis of the risks to price stability. This analysis is organised on the basis of two complementary perspectives on the determination of price developments. The first perspective is aimed at assessing the short to medium-term determinants of price developments, with a focus on real activity and financial conditions in the economy. It takes account of the fact that price developments over

those horizons are influenced largely by the interplay of supply and demand in the goods, services and factor markets. The ECB refers to this as the 'economic analysis'. The second perspective, referred to as the 'monetary analysis', focuses on a longer-term horizon, exploiting the long-run link between money and prices. The monetary analysis mainly serves as a means of cross-checking, from a medium to long-term perspective, the short to medium-term indications for monetary policy coming from the economic analysis.

The two-pillar approach is designed to ensure that no relevant information is lost in the assessment of the risks to price stability and that appropriate attention is paid to different perspectives and the cross-checking of information in order to come to an overall judgement on the risks to price stability. It represents, and conveys to the public, the notion of diversified analysis and ensures robust decision-making based on different analytical perspectives.

****

The ECB singles out money from within the set of selected key indicators that it monitors and studies closely. This decision was made in recognition of the fact that monetary growth and inflation are closely related in the medium to long run [...] This widely accepted relationship provides monetary policy with a firm and reliable nominal anchor beyond the horizons conventionally adopted to construct inflation forecasts. Thus, assigning money a prominent role in the strategy is also a tool to underpin its medium-term orientation. Indeed, taking policy decisions and evaluating their consequences not only on the basis of the short-term indications stemming from the analysis of economic and financial conditions but also on the basis of money and liquidity considerations, allows a central bank to see beyond the transient impact of the various shocks and avoids the temptation of taking an overly activist course.

In order to signal its commitment to monetary analysis and to provide a benchmark for the assessment of monetary developments, the ECB announced a reference value for the broad monetary aggregate M3. This reference value refers to the rate of M3 growth that is deemed to be compatible with price stability over the medium term [...]

The reference value therefore represents a 'natural' benchmark for analysing the information content of monetary developments in the euro area. It constantly reminds the central bank of the fundamental principle that, while responding to economic developments, it must never lose sight of the fact that, over sufficiently extended horizons, the rate of money growth must be consistent with the price stability objective. Owing to the medium to long-term nature of the monetary perspective, however, there is no direct link between short-term monetary developments and monetary policy decisions. Monetary policy does not therefore react mechanically to deviations of M3 growth from the reference value.

What has been the experience of the ECB in the use of the two-pillar strategy? Let me begin by noting the change in May 2003 in the order of the presentation by the President of the ECB at the press conference following the interest rate decision. Previously, such presentations began with the monetary analysis as the first pillar of the monetary policy strategy and economic analysis as the second pillar. Since that time, as is reflected in the above quotation, the ECB has reversed the order in which it presents its two analytical perspectives, beginning with the economic analysis and then continuing with the monetary analysis. This seems to signal a change in the emphasis on the two pillars. However, this apparent change in focus may just be a reflection of the reality that has prevailed for several years.

From early 2001 until the present, the growth of M3 has consistently exceeded its reference value of 4 1/2 percent. Over that period, it has ranged from just over 4 1/2 percent to as much as 9 or 10 percent, depending on the measure used. Moreover, and more importantly, there appears to be virtually no relationship between the growth of M3 and the interest rate actions by the ECB. Thus, over the period between the beginning of 2001 and mid-2003, while M3 growth was accelerating from about 4% to over 8%, the ECB reduced its interest rates by 2 3/4 percentage points in seven steps. From mid-2003 to mid-2004, while money growth decelerated from over 8 percent to about 5 percent, interest rates remained unchanged. It was only in the most recent period, since mid-2004, that the movements in the growth rate of M3 (from 5 percent back up to 8 percent) were consistent with the change in interest rates (an increase of 75 basis points in three steps). I am not suggesting by this comparison of money growth and interest rate changes that the policy actions were wrong. Rather, over the last five years, monetary policy actions appear to have been taken without much regard for the growth rate of money. Of course, the ECB provided good explanations for the movements in money growth over the period – for example, portfolio shifts at times of uncertainty and the response of money growth to movements in nominal interest rates. Nonetheless, if over a period as long as half a decade, M3 growth does not provide much assistance to the policymaking process, it raises legitimate questions as to how seriously one should take the role of monetary analysis as the second pillar of the monetary policy strategy, or even as a crosscheck to the economic analysis.

The Monthly Bulletin of the ECB provides a very detailed analysis of monetary and financial developments in the euro area. It covers such areas as growth rates of the various monetary aggregates, analysis of their components and counterparts, credit expansion both at financial institutions and in markets, and developments in short-term and long-term interest rates. While providing a useful survey of financial developments, it does not appear to offer much support for any special role for money growth over and above that of all the other information in the financial area. Indeed, it may well be that credit growth offers more useful information with respect to future developments in aggregate demand and inflation.

A very different view of this issue from that just presented can be found in a recent speech by Otmar Issing (2005). The then chief economist of the ECB argued that the role of money growth remains an important element in the policy strategy of the ECB, and he emphasised the importance, in interpreting

M3 developments, of using the information in the components and counterparts of M3 growth.[12] He also noted that the ECB found an M3 measure adjusted for portfolio shifts very useful in interpreting price developments. He concluded his speech by asking, 'How can any central bank afford to ignore the information stemming from monetary analysis?' In my view, the issue is not so much one of ignoring the information stemming from monetary analysis, but the weight that should be put on it relative to other information about economic and inflation developments. This is an empirical question, not a theoretical one, and the answer depends on how much incremental information there is in money growth relative to other indicators of the economy and inflation. In most countries, in recent years, the answer appears to have been relatively little. And other financial indicators, such as credit and various interest rate measures (for example, various spreads) may well contain as much, or more, information than money growth.

Summary of central bank behaviour

To read the explanations by central banks of their policy process and of the way that they make interest rate decisions, there appears to be something of a continuum from the central banks that place little weight on the monetary aggregates (such as the Riksbank, the Reserve Bank of New Zealand, and the Bank of Canada), to those that place some weight on monetary aggregates as a crosscheck to the approach based on the balance between aggregate demand and aggregate supply (such as the Bank of England), to those that place even more weight on the monetary aggregates (such as the ECB).[13] In practice, however, the differences among the central banks in the weight that they put on money growth in setting interest rates seem considerably less than the differences in their rhetoric.

Some academic literature

Svensson (1999) argued that monetary aggregates can play no useful role, in the context of the mainstream paradigm of the transmission of monetary policy. In discussing forecasting in the Eurosystem, he reaches the following conclusion:

> The weights given to different indicators should be derived from their predictive power in the broadly based assessment of the outlook for future price development... There is no convincing case for giving money a primary role beyond that motivated by its weight in the broadly based assessment. Indeed, the deviation of money growth from the reference value is likely to be a redundant, or even misleading, indicator. The clarity and transparency of the Eurosystem monetary policy is likely to be best served by letting the reference value fade into oblivion, unless new surprising evidence to the contrary is found.

While Svensson (1997), in his seminal article on inflation forecast targeting, had a section on money growth targeting and the possible role that money growth might play in inflation targeting, his analysis is based on a money demand equation and consequently on the passive view of money. Ultimately, his conclusion is as follows:

> Inflation forecast targeting generally uses all relevant information for predicting future inflation. This information may include some measure of the money stock, but normally also other macro variables. In the (rare) special case when future inflation is best predicted by just the growth rate of some monetary aggregate, that is, money growth is a sufficient statistic for future inflation, inflation forecast targeting will be equivalent to money growth targeting...But normally money growth... [is] not [a] sufficient [statistic] for future inflation; that is, other information has additional predictive value.

The subject index of the widely quoted monograph on inflation targeting by Bernanke, Laubach, Mishkin, and Posen (1999) contains no items referring to the use of monetary aggregates in the context of inflation targeting. In their discussion of a proposal for inflation targeting in the European Monetary Union, the authors argue that the differences that exist between monetary aggregates targeting and inflation targeting, 'notably, the de-emphasis on money growth as an inflation forecaster under inflation targeting – favour the inflation-targeting approach'. The possible use of monetary aggregates as part of the process of forecasting within an inflation-targeting framework is not even raised in the discussion.

More generally, the type of three- or four-equation model described in the earlier discussion of the IMF working papers is frequently used in the literature on inflation targeting, and it is widely accepted in this literature (usually implicitly) that there is little or no role for money in the inflation-targeting framework.

Concluding remarks

Let me conclude this paper as I began it, with David Laidler's contribution to monetary thinking in Canada. In the paper that he presented at the *Festchrift* held at the Bank of Canada on the occasion of my retirement (Laidler, 2004), David made a strong case for not ignoring money in the conduct of monetary policy. The paper was entitled 'Monetary policy without money: *Hamlet* without the ghost' and provided a thoughtful overview of the importance of paying attention to money in thinking about monetary policy issues. As the above analysis of central bank statements has indicated, however, central banks are not in fact paying much attention to money growth in their policymaking over the two- to three-year policy horizon that is currently being used by most of them.

What conclusions would I draw from all this for the conduct of monetary policy going forward? I would argue that central banks should always keep one eye on monetary developments. Even though, more often than not, worrisome movements in money in recent years have been explained away by institutional changes or by behaviour that is not particularly relevant as an input to the ongoing policy process, there remains the possibility that this will not always be the case. Hence, I would find it worrisome when money growth was very high or very low and no obvious institutional explanation came to mind for its behaviour.

Nonetheless, while central banks should keep one eye on money growth, they should not pay overly much attention to it in policymaking, unless and until it proves to be a more reliable indicator of future spending and inflation than it has been in recent years. Central banks should also continue to do background research on the potential role of money, both as a leading indicator of future economic and inflation developments and as a potential element in the transmission mechanism. More generally, the possible roles of all financial variables – money, credit, interest rate spreads, etc. – as inputs into the monetary policy process, should continue to be the subject of serious study at central banks. Indeed, a very interesting area of academic research in recent years has been on the credit channel and how it may help explain economic developments, particularly at times of unusual pressure on banks or markets.

Although I do not anticipate any near-term change in the role of money in policymaking at inflation-targeting central banks, there is always the possibility that changes in economic relationships and/or new research will result in increased attention to money growth in the policymaking process. And I am sure that David's research in his so-called retirement will provide further support to those who believe that money continues to be important and should be taken seriously.

Notes

Scholar in Residence, Economics Department, Carleton University, Ottawa, Canada. The author was an official of the Bank of Canada for 30 years until his retirement in September 2003, serving as Deputy Governor for the last 15 years of his career at the Bank. He would like to thank Øyvind Eitrheim, David Longworth, and Jack Selody for helpful comments on an earlier draft of this paper. Any errors of interpretation remain those of the author.

1. Evidence supporting the active money view for the Canadian economy can also be found in Engert and Hendry (1998).
2. In the acknowledgment section of the report of the subcommittee, the chairman, John Manley, wrote that "Further stimulus was provided by the very important monograph written by Professor David Laidler and published by the C. D. Howe Institute in May 1991."
3. This section and the next section of this paper draw heavily on Freedman (2005).
4. Over the years, re-estimations of M1 demand equations showed increasingly large interest rate elasticities of money demand.
5. Technically, in many cases the true instrument is some form of base or reserves, but that instrument is used to achieve the desired level of the short-term interest rate and is not used to try to directly achieve money growth or a target rate of inflation. The assignment of the role of instrument to the short-term interest rate is thus a very good approximation to reality, even in such cases. In countries such as Canada, New Zealand, and Australia, where central banks use the corridor system to control the very short-term interest rate, the supply of base or clearing balances plays a very secondary role to the announcement of the target rate of interest and the bands of the corridor.
6. M1 is equal to the sum of currency and net demand deposits. M1A includes, in addition, daily interest chequable savings deposits and non-personal notice deposits.
7. See Svensson (1997) for a discussion of the flexible inflation-targeting approach, which aims at both achieving a target rate of inflation and moderating the amplitude of output fluctuations.

8. Private communication from one of the authors.
9. Arguments for paradigm diversification can be found in Engert and Selody (1998) and Selody (2001). Longworth (2003) also argues for attention to be paid to money growth when formulating and conducting monetary policy. He notes that "the mainstream paradigm, which gives no useful role to money, is unlikely to capture the full richness of the transmission mechanism. Moreover, on the face of it, the empirical evidence in Canada is inconsistent with the mainstream paradigm."
10. Early discussions of the use of the monetary conditions index by the Bank of Canada can be found in Freedman (1994, 1995), and an explanation of its reduced importance in the communication of monetary policy can be found in Freedman (2000).
11. Chart 16 compared the growth of real GDP with the growth of real M1+, and Chart 17 compared the rate of increase in core CPI with the growth of M2++.
12. In Issing and Gaspar (2005), he notes that while it is difficult to extract information on future price developments from short-run movements in money growth, there exists a trend relationship between money and prices, implying that money can play an important role as an indicator of future inflationary pressures at medium-term horizons.
13. But there has been considerable discussion among market participants and academics as to the weight that is really put on the monetary aggregates by the ECB Governing Council in arriving at monetary policy decisions.

References

Bank of England (2004). "The New Bank of England Quarterly Model." *Bank of England Quarterly Bulletin* Summer, 188–193.

Bank of England (2005). *The Bank of England Quarterly Model*. London, England: Bank of England.

Benati, L. (2005). "Long-run Evidence on Money Growth and Inflation." *Bank of England Quarterly Bulletin* Autumn, 349–355.

Berg, P., P. Karam, and D. Laxton (2006a). "A Practical Model-Based Approach to Monetary Policy Analysis – Overview." International Monetary Fund, Working Paper WP/06/80.

Berg, P., P. Karam, and D. Laxton (2006b). "Practical Model-Based Monetary Policy Analysis – a How-to Guide." International Monetary Fund, Working Paper WP/06/81.

Bernanke, B. S., T. Laubach, F. S. Mishkin, and A. Posen (1999). *Inflation Targeting: Lessons from the International Experience*. Princeton: Princeton University Press.

Bouey, G. K. (1983). *Minutes of Proceedings and Evidence*. Ottawa, Canada: House of Commons Standing Committee on Finance, Trade and Economic Affairs, No. 134, 28 March.

Canada (1992). Parliament, House of Commons, Standing Committee on Finance, The Mandate and Governance of the Bank of Canada, First Report of the Sub-committee on the Bank of Canada.

Courchene, T. J. (1983). *No Place to Stand? Abandoning Monetary Targets: An Evaluation*. Toronto, Canada: C. D. Howe Institute.

Crow, J. (2002). *Making Money: An Insider's Perspective on Finance, Politics, and Canada's Central Bank*. Etobicoke, Canada: Wiley.

Engert, W. and S. Hendry (1998). "Forecasting Inflation with the M1-VECM: Part Two." Bank of Canada Working Paper 98–6.

Engert, W. and J. Selody (1998). "Uncertainty and Multiple Paradigms of the Transmission Mechanism." Bank of Canada Working Paper 98–7.

European Central Bank (2004). *The Monetary Policy of the ECB*, 2nd ed. January. Ottawa, Canada: Bank of Canada.

Freedman, C. (1983). "Financial Innovation in Canada: Causes and Consequences." *American Economic Review* 73:2, 101–106.

Freedman, C. (1994). "The Use of Indicators and of the Monetary Conditions Index in Canada." In T. J. T. Balino and C. Cottarelli, eds., *Frameworks for Monetary Stability.* Washington: International Monetary Fund, pp. 458–476.
Freedman, C. (1995). "The Role of Monetary Conditions and the Monetary Conditions Index in the Conduct of Policy." *Bank of Canada Review* Autumn, 53–59.
Freedman, C. (2000). "Recent Developments in the Framework for the Conduct of Monetary Policy in Canada." *Canadian Business Economics* November, 3–6.
Freedman, C. (2005). "Reflections on the Bank of Canada's Monetary Policy Framework." In P. Arestis, M. Baddeley, and J. McCombie, eds., *The New Monetary Policy: Implications and Relevance.* Cheltenham, U.K. and Northampton, U.S.: Edward Elgar, pp. 172–191.
Goodhart, C. (1984). *Monetary Theory and Practice – the U.K. Experience.* London, England: Macmillan.
Hauser, A. and A. Brigden (2002). "Money and Credit in an Inflation-Targeting Regime." *Bank of England Quarterly Bulletin* Autumn, 299–307.
Issing, O. (2005). "The Monetary Pillar of the ECB." Speech to The ECB and Its Watchers Conference VII, June 3.
Issing, O. and V. Gaspar (2005). *Imperfect Knowledge and Monetary Policy.* Cambridge, UK: Cambridge University Press.
King, M. (2003). "No Money, No Inflation – the Role of Money in the Economy." In P. Mizen, ed., *Central Banking, Monetary Theory and Practice: Essays in Honour of Charles Goodhart,* Volume One. Cheltenham, U.K. and Northampton, U.S.: Edward Elgar, 62–89. Also in *Bank of England Quarterly Bulletin* Summer 2002, 162–177.
Laidler, D. (1969). *The Demand for Money – Theories and Evidence,* 1st ed. Scranton, PA: International Textbook Company.
Laidler, D. (1982). *Monetarist Perspectives.* Oxford, England: Philip Allan.
Laidler, D. (1991). *How Shall We Govern the Governor? A Critique of the Governance of the Bank of Canada.* Toronto, Canada: C. D. Howe Institute.
Laidler D. (1999a). "Passive Money, Active Money, and Monetary Policy." *Bank of Canada Review* Summer, 15–25.
Laidler, D. (1999b). "The Exchange Rate Regime and Canada's Monetary Order." Bank of Canada Working Paper 99–7.
Laidler, D. (2004). "Monetary Policy Without Money: *Hamlet* Without the Ghost." In C. Goodlet, D. Longworth and J. Murray, eds., *Macroeconomics, Monetary Policy, and Financial Stability: A Festschrift in Honour of Charles Freedman.* Ottawa, Canada: Bank of Canada, pp. 111–134.
Laidler, D. and M. Parkin (1975). "Inflation – a Survey." *Economic Journal* December, 741–809.
Laidler, D. and W. Robson (1995). "Endogenous Buffer-Stock Money." In *Credit, Interest Rate Spreads and the Monetary Policy Transmission Mechanism.* Ottawa, Canada: Bank of Canada, pp. 231–258.
Laxton, D. and P. Pesenti (2003). "Monetary Rules for Small, Open, Emerging Economies." *Journal of Monetary Economics* 50, 1109–1146.
Longworth, D. (2003). "Money in the Bank (of Canada)." Bank of Canada Technical Report 93.
Macklem, T. (2002). "Information and Analysis for Monetary Policy: Coming to a Decision." *Bank of Canada Review* Summer, 11–18.
Selody, J. (2001). "Uncertainty and Multiple Perspectives." In H-J. Klöckers and C. Willeke, eds., *Monetary Analysis: Tools and Applications.* European Central Bank, 31–45.
Svensson, L. (1997). "Inflation Forecast Targeting: Implementing and Monitoring Inflation Targets." *European Economic Review* 41:6, 1111–1146.
Svensson, L. (1999). "Monetary Policy Issues for the Eurosystem." *Carnegie-Rochester Conference Series on Public Policy* 51, 79–136.
Sveriges Riksbank (2006). Monetary Policy in Sweden, May 18.
Thiessen, G. G. (1983). "The Canadian Experience with Monetary Targeting." In Paul Meek, ed., *Central Bank Views on Monetary Targeting.* New York, US: Federal Reserve Bank of New York, pp. 100–104.

Discussion

Charles Goodhart

As usual, Chuck has written an excellent and clear paper on the recent changes in the role of money in the conduct of monetary policy.

Let me, perhaps, start by emphasising how much the recent shifts in the analysis and conduct of monetary policy, that is, the switch to inflation targets, with operationally independent central banks using interest rates to achieve such targets, have brought harmony and widespread agreement to a field of macro-analysis that was fractured by deep analytical divisions in the past. I recall a conference at Brown University, in about 1975, which featured a confrontation between James Tobin and the neo-Keynesians on the one hand, and Milton Friedman and the monetarists on the other. After that conference, it is reported apocryphally that a large band of monetarists were flying back to Rochester or Chicago, when one of them said, "What a disaster for monetary theory it would be if this plane was to crash." Anyhow, there happened to be a Keynesian on board at the same time, who immediately responded, "In my case, I think that the self-sacrifice would be worthwhile."

Be that as it may, the present system of inflation targetry, combined with the small core model of the economic system, has united a wide church, ranging all the way from most monetarists to most Keynesians, excluding only the Real Business Cycle zealots on the one hand, and some extreme post-Keynesians on the other. Personally I find this degree of commonality much more pleasant than the, often violent, disagreements in the '70s and early 1980s.

My only specific comment on Freedman's paper comes when he states that, "All central banks use interest rate control and not base controls." As it happens, I have just returned from visiting two countries where this is not so; these were Uruguay and Argentina. And it may, perhaps, be interesting to discuss briefly why this was so in their case. For Uruguay, the problem was that the vast majority of their financial system is dollarised. This includes the key bank lending rates; most lending is done in dollar format, and the relevant interest rate relates to the underlying US interest rate, with the addition of a risk premium. Essentially, the main monetary aggregate that remains in peso form is a consequence of the need for pesos to undertake current transactions; so the main peso aggregate is a narrow, M1, monetary aggregate; the Uruguay Central Bank tries to control the availability of narrow peso money by controlling the base, Uruguayan M0, by undertaking open market transactions in the peso–US dollar market in Montevideo.

The case of Argentina is somewhat more complicated. There, following the crisis in 2000–2001, the financial and banking systems have been forcibly shifted back to a completely local peso format. So they certainly could control interest rates, in principle. However, the Argentine Central Bank is extremely subservient. Interest rates, like so many other market prices in Argentina, are subject to strict political control. The Central Bank cannot control interest rates, at least by its own decisions, and, indeed, the attempt to keep inflation in check in that country is now being undertaken by prices and incomes policies, rather than by monetary means. So, in this context, the Central Bank is not really in any position to seek to control the inflation rate either. Under these circumstances, (missing) a monetary target is, perhaps, likely to generate fewer accusations of failure than an inflation target. Furthermore, I would guess that the Argentine economy is well on its way towards the use of direct credit controls, in addition to controls over prices in other parts of the economy as well. A monetary target, reinforced by such direct credit controls, is more in keeping with their system, than an inflation target achieved by adjusting the market mechanism of interest rates.

Let me return from this digression, however, to the main theme of Chuck Freedman's paper. Here, he notes the inherent tension between the dictum that "Inflation is everywhere and at all times a monetary phenomenon," which virtually all central bankers would adhere to as being true, and the stylised fact that, in changing interest rates, relatively little, or no, attention seems to be given by these same central banks to the course of the monetary aggregates. There is a real problem here, and several of the major central bankers in the world are both conscious of this and concerned about it; Mervyn King has made exactly this point in a couple of speeches.

So, what I want to do now is to try to develop somewhat further two salient issues raised in Chuck Freedman's paper, which are Active versus Passive money, and the connected topic of the role that monetary variables might play in the interest rate decision. For this purpose, I want to revert to the small set of equations that I used in my own presentation. These are shown below:

$$y_t = b_1 + (i_t - E\pi) + \varepsilon_t$$

$$\pi_t = b_2 + (y_{t-1}) + v_t$$

$$i_t = b_3 + (E\pi_{t+i} - \pi^*) + b_4\,(Ey_{t+i})$$

$$M_t = b_5 + (\pi, E, i) + \upsilon_t$$

The first three equations are rather short-hand versions of the standard three-equation model, which lies at the heart of the modern consensus. The first of these is the standard IS equation; the second is the standard supply, Phillips, equation; and the third is the standard-type Taylor reaction function equation. Normally these are the only equations that are shown. But there is, however, a fourth equation, a demand for money function, which is actually part of the system, as Ben McCallum has often shown. The reason that this fourth equation is generally left out of the system is that its main determinants on the right-hand side, interest rates, real output, and the inflation rate, are already determined in the top three equations of the system. So, if the demand for money is behaving normally, there is no information in the fourth equation that is not already contained in the first three; in that sense it is entirely superfluous.

Note, however, that the demand for money function does not always fit perfectly; there is an error term. When the money stock diverges from what one otherwise might have expected, then the question arises about whether this disequilibrium in the demand for money function will feed back into the other equations in the system; in other words, is the faster, or slower, rate of growth of money, than one might have expected from what else is going on in the economy, likely to be a significant factor in influencing the economy? The answer depends in some large part on what caused this disequilibrium in the first place. Sometimes this faster (or slower) rate of growth of the money stock may have economic significance; sometimes it may not. It depends on what caused that deviation, the context, and circumstances. The problem is that the authorities have to interpret the causes of the deviation of the monetary aggregates from what might otherwise have been expected; and this latter is a complicated and difficult issue, requiring attention to ancillary evidence such as the particular sectors in which the excess (or insufficient) monetary stocks may have accumulated, other factors affecting markets, such as shifts in volatility in asset prices and liquidity preference, etc.

Let me take an example from recent developments in the euro zone. I attach a figure from a recent paper that I have written on "The ECB and the Conduct of Monetary Policy (2006)."

As can be seen from Figure 8.1, from the beginning of the period when the euro was adopted at the start of 1999 until 2001, M3 (broad money) grew at a pace fairly close to its intended reference value of 4½ percent p.a. Then towards the middle of 2001, M3 rose very rapidly and remained much higher than its reference value until 2004. The ECB took no notice whatsoever of this overshoot, and during this period interest rates were cut. There were several reasons for this. First, this was a period of depression; the rate of growth of output was declining, and the rate of inflation was returning to its target value of close to, but below, 2 percent. Meanwhile, as can be seen from the figure, bank credit to the private

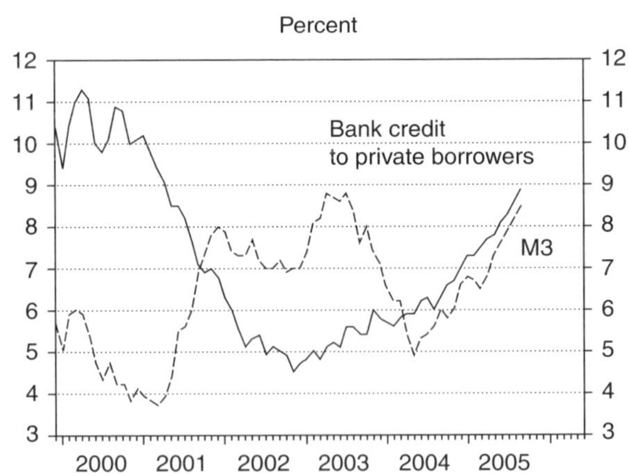

Figure 8.1 M3 and Bank Lending in the Euro Area
Source: Neumann (2005).

sector was declining very rapidly. This was a period when asset markets were declining quite sharply, following the NASDAQ and IT bubbles and busts. And volatility and uncertainty about developments in asset markets were rife. There was some research undertaken at this time (Greiber and Lemke, 2005) which suggested that the rise in money holdings was due to a shift in liquidity preference, owing to an increase in uncertainty about asset markets. Under these circumstances, the authorities reckoned that the deviation of money from its expected value was due to factors such as a shift in liquidity preference, which would not lead to any faster rate of growth of either output or inflation, relative to other factors, in either the medium or longer term. In this sense, they had assessed the explanations for the shift in the error term in the demand for money function, and had decided that there was no adverse likely effect on inflation arising as a consequence.

Monetary growth then subsided in 2004, but afterwards in 2005 and early 2006 the rate of growth of broad money (M3) accelerated again. Circumstances were now quite different. Markets had recovered, and there was relatively little volatility in them, so there was no reason to believe that there was another shift in liquidity preference. Moreover, bank lending to the private sector was accelerating at the same time. At this time the Euro-area real economy was beginning to recover reasonably strongly, with a rate of growth that may well have been near, or even above, the underlying sustainable rate of growth, though this latter is not observable. Again, the rate of inflation remained stubbornly somewhat above the desired level, and there were worries whether it might rise even further, if only perhaps because of the blip in energy prices. For all these reasons, the divergence of monetary growth from its reference level in 2005/2006 was, in this case, regarded as a potential indicator of future inflationary developments. Unlike the earlier years, the assessment of the cause of this deviation was perceived as having a bearing on medium- and longer-term inflationary trends. So in this case the analysis of the development of the monetary aggregates did play a significant role in the determination of monetary policies.

Moreover, almost exactly the same can be said of developments in the UK. During the summer of 2006 the prospects of the future development of real output in the UK did not appear to provide any strong justification for an increase in interest rates. But if you combined the historically fast rate of growth of the monetary aggregates with the tendency for inflation to start rising above target, there was, in August 2006, as Chuck Freedman recounts, an example of a case where assessment of the monetary data did play a significant role in the decision to vary interest rates.

Let me conclude. I have tried to demonstrate that it is the deviation of monetary growth, from what otherwise might have been expected from developments in interest rates, inflation, and output, that is relevant to the decision on whether it is a significant factor in the prospects for medium- and longer-term inflation. Quite often, since the reasons for such deviations, that is, the error term in the demand for money function, are many, various, and difficult to untangle, the answer will be that the authorities will take no notice of such deviations, for better or worse. But, on other occasions they will. And recent developments in the Euro-zone and in the UK have indicated just such occasions.

References

Goodhart, C. (2006). "The ECB and the Conduct of Monetary Policy: Goodhart's Law and Lessons from the Euro Area." *Journal of Common Market Studies* 44:4, 757–778.

Greiber, C. and Lemke, W. (2005). "Money Demand and Macroeconomic Uncertainty." Deutsche Bundesbank, Discussion Paper No. 26/2005.

Neumann, M. (2005). EMU Monitor Outlook, 25 November.

9

Monetary Institutions and Monetary Theory: Reflections on the History of Monetary Economics

Warren J. Samuels

Introduction

Monetary economics is part of the belief system of society. It is also part of the system of social control. And those institutions studied by monetary economists are part of the power structure of society.

The argument of this chapter is that monetary economists have practiced a narrow conception of their field. Let us assume that conventional monetary economics, the usual topics dealt with by monetary economists, is X and that these other topics are Y. Monetary economists have studied X and not Y. In so concentrating their studies, not only do monetary economists assume the existing belief, social control, and power systems of society, Y, in restricting their analysis to only X they avoid or finesse topics and issues raised by and in Y. Instead of dealing with the system as a whole – X plus Y – monetary economists have avoided questions that might place at risk their individual status and the prestige of their subdiscipline and of the larger economics.

A further argument is that in their failure to cope constructively with multiplicity, monetary economists have foregone a deeper and less superficial understanding of their field.

The reader should reflect on what he or she reads in this Introduction and wonder why these things are being said in an introduction to a chapter on monetary economics; surely monetary economics has nothing to do with these topics. The answer is very simple: the money and banking systems of society do involve these topics but monetary economics does not. The determination of interest rates and the price level are central problems for monetary economics. But those determinations are worked out, in part, through determining who has rights to create money, especially in the form of credit, and in part who has rights of access to the newly created credit – which are key aspects of the conflicts identified below. The objective of this chapter is to show that the claims made in this Introduction are correct.

The history of monetary economic thought is not presented in any detail as a whole. I have had to choose between concentrating on a detailed critique of the history of monetary economics, on the one hand, and showing that the proposed extended conception of monetary economics can be done and, through detailed references to unfamiliar literatures, providing examples of how it can be done, on the other. I am well aware that the resulting history of monetary economics is something of a caricature. The reader must appreciate, however, that my purpose is not to critique the content of the history of monetary economics but to suggest that the domain of the field be extended.

One aspect of the neglect of Y is found in the juxtaposition of manifest and latent function. Emile Durkheim argued that when people enter a church their religious training leads them to feel in the presence of God. That is manifest function. Latent function is that that feeling leads to the reinforcement of the existing society, its structure of power and institutions (except insofar as religion is an instrument of change, which also happens through latent function) (Durkheim 1964; Merton 1949). A related interpretive significance of latent/manifest function is given by Seaford (2004, 87; quoted in Tandy, 2005).

The deepest problem confronting the social scientist, including the monetary economist, is that of how to deal, as an object of study, with the ways in which every society maintains and protects the performance of latent function and thereby achieves some degree of continuity. And the deepest, and most ironical, aspect of that problem is reconciling continuity with change. If one assumes that society is always in a process of becoming, each state of being, with its performance of latent function, morphs into and is eclipsed by the next state so that *what constitutes continuity changes over time*. Two other deep aspects, also ironical, are relevant. First, what is actually at stake in the conflict between continuity and change is not principally the array of substantive structural and other arrangements of society with which people can identify and in whose terms the conflict is understood. What is at stake is *the conflict of mechanisms of change*. There will be mechanisms of change; the question is, which will be dominant in the future – the mechanism of religion, or of government (public government), or of private government, or the market, belief system, technology, or, inter alia, groups of change-seeking or change-avoiding individuals. These are all artifacts and not elements of the natural order of things. Emphasis on continuity or change becomes a contest between, say, old and new dominant mechanisms of change. Second, the conflict of continuity with change is itself one aspect of the problem of order. The other aspects are the conflict of freedom (or autonomy) and control (or the conflict of freedom to and freedom from), and the conflict of equality and inequality (the problem of order is still more complicated; see Samuels 1996 and sources given therein). Also involved, because freedom for some often means control over others, are the questions, whose freedom, whose control. Pervading all of these conflicts, therefore, is the conflict over power, namely, the problem of the structure of decision-making and the bases thereof, with the object of fundamental decision-making the control of all these conflicts. Because monetary economists are not silent on how these conflicts should work out, they insinuate themselves into the working out of these conflicts, implicitly taking positions on them. The importance and relevance of these conflicts are two reasons for monetary economists to deal directly, as disinterestedly as possible,[1] and explicitly with them; that monetary economists already position themselves with respect to them is a third reason, with a fourth being intellectual honesty, and a fifth, candor.

The history of monetary and banking theory has been a microcosm of general economic theory in its seeming lack of richness and inability to handle institutions and multiplicity. Monetary economists have learned much since John Locke and David Ricardo, to mention only two of the field's founders, but not enough, and what they have learned they have not effectively incorporated into their analysis. Monetary economics is richer, or could manifestly be richer, than it credits itself. Inasmuch as monetary economics, along with value and price theory, has been at the pinnacle of economic theory, and inasmuch as many leading economists have been monetary economists, the foregoing is a serious complaint.[2] Presumably 'everybody wants to know about money' (Cole, 1933) but it is rarely the case that one can be confident about what one knows and there is much more available to know.

I am not a specialist in monetary economics. It was one of my fields as a graduate student at Wisconsin (1954–57), under James S. Early and Walter A. Morton. I have more or less kept up with general developments in the field. Much work has been interesting and suggestive. Given the importance and salience of monetary and banking theory, this work has been hard to avoid; it has, in part due to Milton Friedman, often been at the center of public policy discussion. As a historian of economic thought, I have also studied the early history of monetary theory and policy. As a methodologist, I have perceived that major parts of monetary theory have been pure a priori assertion. These judgments are not based on a favoured interpretation of monetary theory and a conclusion that everyone but me is wrong. I have no specific monetary theory to advance. Nor do I reject monetary theory under the rule that the history of economic thought is the history of error (see Fiorito and Samuels, 2006). Several types of error may be found in monetary theory, but error per se is not the present issue.

This chapter focuses on the nature and role of monetary theory, monetary economics as comprising much more than the Quantity Theory, its inadequate treatment of institutions, especially the legal foundations of money and banking, and its inadequate treatment of multiplicity. In particular, monetary economists seem not to have learned the fact, importance, and principal implication of theoretical and institutional multiplicity at every turn and on every issue – a complaint also applicable to economics as a whole.

Part I, Monetary Institutions, identifies first the institutional context in which monetary theory has meaning; second, institutions in relation to economic theory and to money and banking theory; and third, the legal foundations of money and banking. Part II, Monetary Theory, examines, first, several shortcomings of monetary theory; second, a further shortcoming, multiplicity; and third, an approach with which to deepen our knowledge using multiplicity. The chapter concludes with further reflections.

Part I Monetary Institutions

The Context of Meaning of Monetary Theory

Although in some important respects I have come to appreciate certain flawed aspects of monetary theory, in these respects monetary theory is a microcosm of economics as a whole. In regard to neither economics as a whole nor monetary theory alone, do I intend to solely condemn past work. I do find that the field of monetary theory is an example of Adam Smith's theory of practice in his *History of Astronomy* (1980). There Smith argued that while truth is the premier desired objective, we very often have to be content merely with propositions that quiet the imagination or, as George Shackle expressed it, put minds at rest (Shackle, 1967; Smith, 1980; see also the use of the argument in Evensky, 2005, chapter 1. Smith made this point a chief element of his theory of intellectual history, but with relatively few, recent exceptions, it has been largely forgotten in that field). Ironically, Smith's theory itself can be given more than one reading. One is that given above: truth is the desired objective but we very often must settle for propositions that set minds at rest. Another reading is that truth is impossible and we are left with multiple interpretations.

Whichever interpretation of Smith is chosen, monetary economics can be considered a part of a larger system of thought and to derive its larger meaning from that context. One interpretation thereof is suggested here; others exist, hence further multiplicity, even at the meta-theory level. The elements of my suggested interpretation are the following.

System of belief

Throughout intellectual history various thinkers have emphasised that what is important is not what people should believe – because true – but what they do believe, because it is the belief, correct or incorrect, even meaningless, on which they act.[3] These thinkers include Adam Smith, John Stuart Mill, Karl Marx, George Herman Mead, Vilfredo Pareto, and Kenneth Boulding. People have a need to believe – to have their minds set at rest. Even people who aver that they have no system of belief hold that view on the basis of a system of belief. Their system of belief may be very different from that of most people but it is nonetheless a system of belief – possibly, but not necessarily, deeper or more 'correct' in some sense than others' belief systems (Harris, 1971; Kselman, 1991).

For present purposes it is useful to contemplate people's mental state as a combination of two positions, one of which is usually dominant. For many people a system of belief is attractive to the extent that it offers a sense of determinacy and closure. Their system of belief defines reality for them. Other people have a dominant system of belief which also provides a definition of reality but these people treat it as more problematic and pragmatic. (I believe that all systems are at bottom pragmatic, but that is another story.) These people are content with open-endedness and ambiguity.[4]

Particularly attractive to those who seek determinacy and closure is the possibility of having only one explanation or a uni-directional line of causation to believe. In such cases, however, there always tend to be significant multiple variations. Multiplicity renders nugatory all claims to determinacy and closure, yet even this is finessed by those who are willing to accept some one variation. It is no surprise, therefore, that constitutional law, theological doctrine, and economic theory exhibit similar problems of interpretation (Samuels, 2006).

Systems of belief are not, or not fully, scientific matters, even within a putative scientific discipline. Systems of belief define reality for people, who thereby are provided with principles of order and/or of authority.[5] A fundamental function of monetary economics is to provide, for its field, a definition of reality, with its principles of order and authority, not merely or solely principles of monetary and banking analysis and policy. As a system of belief, etc., monetary theory itself is an institution which defines and structures freedom, power, and opportunity. General economic theory does so likewise, but more broadly and perhaps more deeply.

A system of belief, such as one of those provided by monetary theory, provides a filter or sieve through which an individual processes and frames experience, statements of putative fact, etc. Different systems of belief enable different people to interpret what they read or hear differently.[6]

The use of 'code words' in political and other discourse, including economic discourse, enables interpretation at the unconscious level. The meaning of terms such as 'competition', 'freedom', 'property', 'money', 'bank', and so on, varies between individuals because of their respective belief systems (see Straub, 2006). Pareto is not the only scholar who combined belief system and non-cognitive and rational behaviuor and choice with the structure and struggle for power (Samuels, 1974; see, for example, Parsons (1949) and Moessinger (2000), who trace the stability of social structures – their concept of order – to non-deliberative conduct, somewhat in the manner of Hayek, in effect combining psychology and sociology).

From the 1620s to the present, Americans have exhibited predominantly two cultural belief systems. One is theological fundamentalism, which would have all people pursue a life of piety; the other is economic fundamentalism, which legitimises the world of business and trade. Each has its own goals, rules, concept of order, and so on, as well as varied ideational formulations (sects, schools of thought, etc.). The two often coexist quietly; at other times they clash, reinforcing (and perhaps changing) the distinctiveness of each as well as their contradictions – about God versus Mammon, democracy, work, capitalism, corporate capitalism, wealth, freedom, and so on, including the Money Power, robber barons, and the power elite (see Ellul, 1984; Cottrell and Moggridge, 1988; Means, 2001).[7] In the late 19th century the conflict was between Social Darwinism and the Social Gospel. In the half-century after World War II the conflict was between economic and social conservatism. The assignment of descriptive/interpretive terms is less important than the fact of their opposition (and the genesis of society in their conflict).

In the domain of general culture, an interactive, dialectical, or over-determined process seems to exist in which folk etymology and beliefs help form the society's (collective) definition of reality (Rundblad and Kronenfeld, 2003, who envision the operation of an invisible-hand process therein) in a process somewhat akin to Thomas Kuhn's notion of scientific revolution.[8] The folk belief system may then become an established, ingrained, and encrusted status-emulative mode of social control, which in turn becomes the object of scorn by new aspirants. Such may at first glance seem far removed from the domain of money but as Karl Rodbertus

(Gonner, 1899) and others understood, power exists in the form of rights to create new money (to control the level of money supply) and rights to have access to new money.

Typically, each side in a controversy offers its own putative factual support. The following is typical of those offerings. The facts offered by each side are selectively framed and incomplete and therefore inconclusive. The facts tending to be selectively formed also tend to be tautological with the theory on which the facts are constructed; the facts are theory-laden and the theory is a function of a particular reading of the facts. The putative facts lack the capacity conclusively to choose between sides. Pervading the foregoing is the system of belief, and it is the attractiveness of the system of belief, possibly more than anything else, that accounts for the power of the story so told.[9]

Language

A strong tendency has been observed for people to presume/believe that words correspond with and derive from reality: 'the whole point is that if we define the terms precisely and sort out the various possible scenarios, we can learn more about market clearing than if we remain vague' (Gani, 2005; see also Kendall, 1995 on the selective use of discourse in presidential campaigns). Ludwig Wittgenstein, however, repudiated his earlier holding of this belief on the ground that that was not how language operates. Words – our system of belief – do not derive their meaning from reality; rather, our definition of reality is derived from the words used in our system of belief.[10] To believe that words derive from and correspond with reality is to neglect both the social construction of language and the multiplicity of words/belief systems each of which defines reality for some people. This situation leads to numerous linguistic problems of specification and interpretation in economics and other fields (Jones, 1983; Chomsky, 1988; Samuels, 2001). More generally, in the sense not of less intensive but of greater ubiquity, money, language, and thought (perception and definition of monetary reality) critically interact (Shell, 1993; see also Binswanger, 1994 and Zelizer, 1994; on the recomposition of practices and ideas interacting with the recomposition of markets, see Kwon, 2004).

Belief systems are part of the system of social control

Taking the existing or current system of social control for granted is tantamount to accepting the felt hegemonic belief system as given. Inasmuch as the substance and objective of social control in any particular case exhibit multiplicity, excluding multiplicity is tantamount to finessing varying antecedent normative and other premises. Nonetheless, such has not kept many people from expressing belief in the omnipotence of words. The psychology of belief (religious (Kselman, 1991), or political, or economic) has revealed the ubiquitous practice of using words nominally to define reality but especially to control reality (Anthony Smith, 1980).

Accordingly, belief system is an object of control; society, as spelled out by Pareto (Samuels, 1974), is very much a process of mutual manipulation of belief systems and thereby of power and psychology. Democracy, insofar as it posits individual political judgment, thus becomes a process of mutual manipulation and the manufacture of consent or pseudo-consent. One dramatic and enlightening episode in US history was the contest between the gold standard and the free coinage of silver, or the struggle between creditors and debtors, in the late nineteenth century. One might have thought that the later success of paper currency might have been more dramatic, but it was not. Over a half-century after the adoption of the Federal Reserve System, when President Nixon drove the final nail in the coffin of the gold standard, the event elicited commentary but not controversy. Other contests have been over branch banking, the relative reliance upon currency and credit (bank balances), and the combination versus separation of commercial and investment banking, and of the underwriting and sale of corporate securities.

People hold on to belief systems for purposes of psychic balm (having their minds set at rest), and are induced to do so by institutions of social control (having their political propensities promote some meaning of 'order' or at least keep quiet). Secularists may debate using some linguistic formulation reducing to 'My belief system is truer than yours'. Non-secularists use language ultimately reducing to 'My invisible friend can beat up your invisible friend'.[11] During October 2005, the sports network ESPN[12] televised commercials on its own behalf, one line of which ran, 'Without sports, what would we hold on to?'

People are induced to adhere to a particular belief system, even when it is undergoing change. Pareto insisted that government social control consisted of force and fraud, the latter involving the manipulation of belief through the use of pseudo-knowledge. In the 1960s, the sports editor of the *Miami Herald* wrote that the principal argument for sports is that sports helps prevent communism.[13] Some observers of high school, college, and professional sports think of them as aphrodisiacal; the *Herald* editor seems to widen Karl Marx's thesis of religion as the opiate of the masses (to which Frank Knight added, and the sedative of the classes). The Cold War provided ample opportunity for various interests to promote their cause by investing it with the function of combating communism (or attributing the opposite to their opponents). The stockbroker Charles Merrill 'argued that nothing "would provide a stronger defense against the threat of Communism, than the wide ownership of stocks in the country"' (Wallace, 2005, 30; Wallace also quotes Franklin Roosevelt's statement of concern over the money power: 'we cannot allow our economic life to be controlled by that small group of men whose chief outlook upon the social welfare is tinctured by the fact that they can make huge profits from the lending of money and the marketing of securities' (Wallace, 2005, 30)). The conservative columnist, George Will, has condemned the business, financial, and accounting practices that led to the Enron collapse, insisting that 'It will remind everyone – some conservatives, painfully – that a mature capitalist economy is a government project. A properly functioning free market system does not spring spontaneously from society's soil as dandelions spring from suburban lawns. Rather, it is a complex creation of laws and mores ...' (Will, 2002, 3; quoted in Mercuro, 2005, 16).

Social control as social construction of reality

Social control is not simply a matter of controlling individual belief and behaviour. Social control is surely that, such that actions seen as coercion by some Alphas are seen as freedom-enhancing by some Betas (Samuels, 1984, 1995*b*, 1996, 1997). But more is involved than that. A further role of social control is to establish the legal and moral foundations of the economy, not economies in general but the actual economic regime in place. In so doing, social control – the sum of and interactions between agencies and institutions of social control – is engaged in the social construction of reality (Berger and Luckmann, 1966; Sederberg, 1984; Searle, 1995). Social control and the social construction of reality are themselves aspects of the problem of order (Samuels, 1996). One aspect thereof is the choice between continuity and change in particular cases but overall encompassing both continuity and change. The adjustment of continuity and change can be posed in terms of property and/or covenants (Taylor, 1966) but must encompass both continuity and change.

The legal–economic nexus (Samuels, 1989) is the domain in which public and private sectors interact and each is continually being reconstituted through that interaction, i.e., over-determination. The economy, for example, business, provides much of the input to and influences the result of the governmental process (legislature and courts), while government simultaneously influences the organization and operation of business. If the legal–economic nexus is narrowly and tightly held, conflict nonetheless exists within and among the ruling class(es). In regimes in which power is more widely diffused, tension still exists among those who seek to capture and control the state for pragmatic (e.g., money-making) purposes and among those who seek to dominate the social construction of reality, for example, markets, arguably for non-pragmatic short-term interests, and between the pragmatists and social constructionists. In all cases, the distinction between pragmatic and social control motivations is problematic. In all cases, too, the state will be/must/will tend to be in the hands of some group; the need to provide control or to influence the state is fundamental.

In all the foregoing, a key role is performed by expectations and change of expectations. If manipulation of the system of belief can achieve passive consent if not belief by those putatively, objectively, negatively affected that their predicament is due to the natural order of things, their predicament will less likely be perceived as a problem to which redress by government is relevant. What people expect and/or do not expect is not only one basis on which conflicting claims of right are worked out by courts, they can serve as a foundation of the basic jural postulates (in the sense of Roscoe Pound (1937) and Hans Kelsen (1945)). Much legal change ensues from changes in expectations per se or from the expectations which the courts are willing to recognise.

Struggle over power structure and the state

In every type of state/government, the question, 'Who decides?', inevitably arises. The state itself is an answer to that question. Thus arises the struggle over control of the institutions of social control, including those of the legal–economic nexus. As Pareto emphasised, much of this struggle takes place through mutual, if asymmetrical, manipulation of the system of belief and of language itself in order to control and mobilise the political psychology which is at the basis of policy (Pareto, 1963, Samuels, 1974; this includes the languages of class (Jones, 1983; Degré, 1985; Burke and Porter, 1987; Reddy, 1987; Corfield, 1991)). Much money is spent on lobbying and litigation to influence government policy – the interests the state will be used to promote and/or inhibit – not because government is unimportant, as some writers would have everyone believe, but because government (collective action) is in fact important. The gold standard did not eliminate the need for a law of money and banking; such law was nonetheless important, albeit its content varied, and at its core are the decisions as to whose interests are to count in instituting the gold standard, decisions largely made out of sight and for which saccharine explanations tend to be given. Nor did the gold standard prevent the money and banking elite, as part of the business elite, from having influence on government policy, with government an instrument of those who forged links with and controlled it.

I increasingly prefer to speak of the entirety of the system of governance, meaning by 'governance' the making of decisions which importantly affect other people. Normally there is a more or less ambiguous line of demarcation between public government and private government. The situation is illustrated by the Federal Reserve System which is 'privately owned' and an 'independent' government agency. It is also found in the Constitution's seemingly exclusive assignment of power to the Congress 'To coin Money, regulate the Value thereof, and of foreign coin' (Article I, Section 8) but which has precluded neither paper money, nor state involvements in matters of money and banking, nor the issuance by private banks of perhaps 90% of the money supply through credit creation, nor government bonds constituting satisfaction of private banks' required reserves. (James M. Buchanan and A. Allan Schmid have each proposed that the national debt can be financed through the issue of interest-free bonds (Buchanan and Flowers, 1975, 335; Schmid, 1982, 1984, 2004; see also Shultz and Harriss, 1965, 488). The demand by banks for such bonds would be generated by having them satisfy bank reserve requirements. The present system enables banks to charge government interest on the money it borrows because the government has enabled them to create money and to charge interest.) It also resonates in the enforcement of private contracts by the courts, including loan contracts of various types made by banks. Finally, commercial banks and the commercial banking system create, in the process of making loans, the money that they lend and on which they charge interest, and do so in a multiplicable expansionary or contractionary manner.

A millennium ago, the deep interpretive questions were whether the Church was operating in the name of and/or on the behalf of God, or in the interests of churchmen, or as an institution of secular social control (to which a large measure of absolutist legitimization had been added). More recently, the deep interpretive questions were whether government and other institutions, many of the latter operating under color of law, were serving God's will, or the will of their leaders, and/or a ruling elite, or the functions of social control. As monetary and banking institutions developed during the transition from feudal and post-feudal to capitalist market economies, comparable questions arose. Money, banking, and finance became key parts of the institutions by which a new and still changing ruling class stood astride both government and economy. In time it became increasingly difficult to distinguish whether the monetary and banking system – with its control over both currency and credit, with the latter becoming by far the more important – was a socially functional set of institutions or a vehicle of the ruling economic elite. Whether in some sense it was performing in one way or the other, or a bit of both, what came to count was what it was believed to be; thus, as with government as a whole, enormous efforts were made to manipulate the belief system of the great mass of people. Certainly no independent test was available; it was a matter of what people were induced to believe by the powerful who competed among themselves to control and use government, and who manufactured consent to that end. Thus one interpretation-application of the Constitution would dominate and exclude another not because it was *the law*, but it was the law because of whose/which interpretation served the interest of those whose interest counted for more than that of others'. The deepest problem may well have become balancing the need for order on almost any terms with the public discussion of the foregoing. Public discussion might mean that the former was threatened; quietude would tend to safeguard the status quo power structure.

One point that is fundamental to the argument presented in this chapter concerns laissez-faire. For several centuries some people have believed in laissez-faire and governmental non-intervention. Other people have believed, equally sincerely, in government intervention and rejected laissez-faire. These two systems of belief are solely that, systems of belief, and do not accurately describe the economic role of government. Government, like it or not, is important and ubiquitous not solely in the area of money and banking. These are fundamental economic institutions and, while some nominally private interests have great influence on, even control over, government, government has great influence on and control over them. Government protection of certain interests *ipso facto* means government non-protection of other interests in the same field of action. Regulation of Alpha means protection of Beta; deregulation of Alpha means government no longer protecting the conflicting interest of Beta. That some people treat them differently is a function of selective perception of government, a selective perception intimately connected by manufactured and non-manufactured belief systems.

One implication of the foregoing is that laissez-faire, which is not descriptively accurate with regard to the economy and economic policy, nonetheless serves the Paretian function of mobilizing political psychology and manipulating belief systems for many people. What is literally substantively impossible is functionally possible.

Another way of making the point is to say that while the dominant ideology is non-interventionist, the accurate, positivist description of actual legal–economic systems is the ubiquity and importance of government and governance (Samuels,

1995*b*) and thereby of politics – meaning by politics having to do with decision-making that affects others. The irony here is that arrangements that are political and socially constructed in nature are reified so as to be given the veneer of something given, transcendent, and grandiose. Monetary and banking institutions are legal and therefore political in nature, absolutist legitimization to the contrary notwithstanding; laissez-faire is a name for another political agenda. The political meaning of monetary and banking institutions is not unique in society. The reach of politics is ubiquitous (Feibleman, 1969); meaning is political (Sederberg, 1984; see also Straub, 2006). Like it or not, identity (Aronowitz, 1992), knowledge (Lagemann, 1989; Meja and Stehr, 1990), including framing paradigms and theories of social change (Janos, 1986), information (Anthony Smith, 1980), music (Buch, 2003), landscape (Turner, 1979) and religion (Tinder, 1989) are political in nature. Religion in particular has been deeply involved in the political/legal status of lending, banking, and interest (Jones, 1989). The topic of a theology of the corporation is highly suggestive of both the use of religion for economic purposes and the use of economics for religious purposes, and thereby the similar nexus between religion and government (Novak and Cooper, 1981*a*, 1981*b*; suggestive of the absolutist legitimization of business, including banking corporations, paralleling legitimization through absolutist ontological realism). Relevant here is not only what passes for science but also belief without substance (Robinson, 1921; Pareto, 1963;,Samuels, 1974). Knowledge, or what people accept as knowledge and act upon, is often a matter of imagery (Boulding, 1956; Bloor, 1991) and therefore of illusion (Skillen, 1978; Geuss, 2001) and myth (Bondi, 1967; Campbell, 1972; Barbour, 1974; Mishan, 1986; Samuel and Thompson, 1990; Fitzpatrick, 1992). Politics is a domain of symbols (Eaton, 1925; Arnold, 1935, 1937; Boorstin, 1958; Edelman, 1964) and figures of speech (Lakoff and Johnson, 1980; Ortony, 1993), a domain populated by entrepreneurs of myth (Nossiter, 1964) engaged in the defense and invention of tradition (Hobsbawn, 1962; Hobsbawn and Ranger, 1983), including demystification (Rex, 1974). Each of these topics (for which only a small sample of references is given) has been the subject of diverse, multiple explanations. For present purposes it is the general theme in each case that counts, not the differences of theoretical formulation (consider the variety of theories of value each of which tends to deal with something, vis-à-vis price, that is metaphysical), although the matrix analysis of multiplicity is applicable (see below). Further apropos of mystification (and demystification; see Chomsky, 1988), giving something a name seems for some or many people tantamount to establishing ontological status – a phenomenon by no means irrelevant to money and banking arrangements.

Silence (see Achino-Loeb, 2005 on the role of silence on power; on silence and the unseen in a general theory of ignorance, see Samuels et al. 2004–06) on the part of what I call below a-institutional economic theory/theorists means either that existing institutions are rendered unimportant or that they comport with or exemplify pure abstract theory, neither of which is necessarily true; indeed, it is widely recognised (though not practiced) that the pure theory of economics does not apply to existing institutions. Instead, theory obfuscates the processes of power through which institutions evolve, thereby facilitating the continuity of those processes and the applicability of what an earlier age called 'God-given institutions'. The world is made safe for economists and the institutions upon which they cast luster. Economists become members of the ruling elite, occasional criticisms of, for example, monetary and banking institutions being minuscule in importance compared with the legitimacy provided by economics and its theory(ies) of the optimality of (money) markets. Considerations such as the foregoing are far more important than the velocity of money, the functions of money, endogenous versus exogenous money, and so on; but on those questions hegemonic monetary theory is relatively silent. Economists tend also to be silent on the question of whether law is policy. Ending this silence would strongly tend to torpedo the laissez-faire and non-interventionist approach to government. If the legal foundations of the monetary and banking system, and indeed the entire economy, are important and ubiquitous, if legal and law-based institutions are inevitable, if nothing of the foregoing is given by nature but is a matter of the parallelogram of power that is both cause and consequence of the struggle to control and use government, then both conservative and liberal rationalizations of temporarily favoured policies are shown to be merely means of marshaling and manipulating political psychology. Politicians can get away with this because much of it is unseen, some has deniability, most non-politicians are emotionally inoculated against the machinations of all politicians and are, besides, more interested in what is closer (they feel, and are induced to feel) to their own lives, and, a sense that, like it or not, this is the nature of collective decision-making, i.e., politics is the way we govern ourselves, all the alternatives being less fine and more dangerous than 'democracy'.

Institutions and economic theory

Economists and others tend either to take institutions for granted as part of the natural order of things – to possess an independent and given ontological existence – or, as a methodological assumption that institutions exist, when, as a matter of fact, institutions are matters of human social construction, human belief systems, and the use of government. This propensity to reify existing institutions and render them sacred is never, however, strictly followed. Whenever a problem is perceived, recourse is made to policy in order to change the relevant covering body of law, thus giving effect to another observable propensity, that of interested parties to compete over the use of government to change the law in one direction or another. In these respects, institutions are pragmatic, problematic, and dialectical. They are pragmatic insofar as people value them for their consequences. They are problematic insofar as their existence depends on the competition among interested parties over potential changes in the policies and laws governing individual institutions. They are dialectical insofar as any policy/law has both opportunity benefits and opportunity costs reckoned in terms of opposite policies and contrary laws, and changes in policy and in law give effect to now one and now another set of beliefs – sets of belief which tend to become modified in the process. This situation is rendered even more complex by the heterogeneity as well as alterability of human arrangements, and even more confusing by the evident lack of internal coherence and reasonableness of each principle or set of beliefs.

Two modes of doing economics exist, with the first strongly tending to dominate the discipline. In the first, markets are treated as pure abstract a-institutional conceptual entities. A disjunction marks this form of economic theory. Analysis is conducted without reference to institutions, yet the results of analysis are more or less freely applied to policy – using implicit selective antecedent normative premises – in a manner thought consonant with a particular research protocol. This protocol stipulates that the researcher achieve unique determinate optimal equilibrium solutions. The disjunction derives in part from the fact that in actuality no such unique solutions exist, only solutions specific to and derived in part from the institutions which privilege and give effect to some interests and not others. In order to achieve ostensibly unique determinate results, everything that would otherwise interfere with the achievement of those results is ruled out of analytical bounds. An enormous irony arises in that such procedure is internally contradictory, for the following reason. Different analysts can rule different things out of bounds and each thereby can achieve ostensibly unique determinate results. But these are unique only with respect to what is excluded; and, with different sets of exclusions, multiple, different results can be achieved. Both the uniqueness and the determinacy are contrived. In the second mode of doing economics, markets are examined for the factors, forces, and agents – firms and governments – which together determine the nature and structure of actual markets and, to a point, whose interests count. George Shackle (1967, 294) has expressed the situation beautifully:

> There is the world of what we take to be 'real' objects, persons, institutions and events; on the axis of abstract-concrete this world is at the concrete pole. There is the logical or mathematical construct or machine, a piece of pure reasoning, almost of 'pure mathematics', able to exist in its own right of internal coherence, as a system of mere relations amongst undefined thought-entities; this world lies at the abstract pole. And between these two worlds there lies the world of names, linking the real-world elements with the undefined entities of the abstract machine.

Money and banking theory and institutions (I)

The foregoing is the context in which monetary theory has meaning and applies with especial force to the subjects of money and banking. The shortcomings of monetary (or monetary and banking) theory derive from (1) failures to adequately deal with the socially constructive nature and complexity of monetary and banking phenomena in actual economies, (2) acceptance of elements of the belief system that has been developed over the centuries and/or positions as to whose interest should count based on antecedent implicit normative assumptions, and, inter alia, (3) participation in the struggle for power, including the control of the state, indeed, not only the state but also custom and habit (Searle, 1995) as well as such 'private' institutions as corporations. The history of monetary and banking thought is actually an aspect of working out the belief system, power structure, and use of government in a developing capitalist market economy. By expressing myself in language such as that just italicised I do not wish to adopt a conspiracy explanation. Some of this was deliberative and some non-deliberative. Increasingly, it became a matter of doing what came 'naturally', given the increasingly historically distinctive system that was emerging (that is what societization is 'all' about).

Modern monetary and banking institutions and arrangements have several characteristics. One is the aura of mystique and mystery that has surrounded these arrangements.[14] This aura has to some extent developed on its own; it has also been deliberately cultivated by people in money and banking, in part to promote and take advantage of their status. A second characteristic has been the deep involvement of monetary and banking institutions in the structure of social power. The term 'money power' has been used, typically by critics, to refer to the combination of institutions actively engaged in creating and allocating new credit, and doing so, the critics contend, in nefarious ways. Of present importance, monetary and banking theorists have treated their chosen topics as if the industry were no different from other industries. By having their theory abstract from institutional details, yet by also making policy recommendations as to institutional details, they have given effect, selectively and to some extent non-cognitively, to the belief system and power structure of society in general and bankers in particular – arrangements which themselves are socially constructed and the object of the struggle for control. Some or much of this is obfuscated by the mystique surrounding money and banking in general, and certain arrangements in particular. Strikingly, money is one of the institutions identified by Searle (1995) as representing facts through human agreement, vis-à-vis brute reality, the former maintained by custom and habit as well as by law. This distinction, related to but not identical with Friedrich von Hayek's and Frank Knight's (1960) distinction between deliberative and non-deliberative decision-making, would be sufficient to warrant a broader monetary economics except for the propensity of many economists to reify monetary and banking institutions.

Differences in the treatment of institutional details by bankers (and other entrepreneurs), on the one hand, and by economists, on the other, help explain the disappointing record of monetary theorists. Bankers tend to adopt some theory of money and/or of banking depending on their belief system, their participation in the process of controlling government, and so on, but inevitably focus on the institutional details of banks and money markets. Given their judgments of which institutional changes will conduce to their greater incomes, status, and power, they seek change through litigation and lobbying as well as public relations. Economists, by taking no notice of the institutional (read: legal) foundations of banking and money markets, treat the elements of the equation of exchange/Quantity Theory of money as conceptual a-institutional entities. Insofar as their model has only a-institutional elements, they can propose changes in institutions only on some a priori basis.

The Banking and Currency Schools, for example, represented conflicting interests and conflicting systems of belief. They also constituted efforts to identity *the* one and only correct theory of money and of banking – in a world in which *both* principles may be found to operate simultaneously, perhaps in different institutions, perhaps in the same institution, and in which each principle is advanced and appealed to as if it and it alone were solely governing. The 'special force' alluded to just above refers to several characteristics of the field(s) of money and banking. For many people, the fields are ensconced in mystery and have an aura of magic; some people find it in their interest to allude to or invoke the mystery and the magic; most people are led so to believe (Binswanger, 1994). The fields are important in part because they govern access to new money and the potential for redistribution of opportunity and sacrifice represented by access to new money. The fields are therefore also important, in part, insofar as they are entwined with the class and power structure of society. All of this exhibits asymmetry, or inequality.

This latter point may easily be elaborated. In early 1958 I attended a conference of bankers held in Columbia, Missouri.[15] On almost every subject in the sessions I attended a striking difference of view emerged as to the social nature of banking. One group took as given and proper that banking be organised and conducted on a 'full service' basis. By full service the advocates meant not only the provision of a wide range of services or products but that every person or every family would, in principle, have a bank account, certainly a checking account, and possibly also a line of credit. Another group, however, had the very different and hierarchical view that only the well-to-do would have bank accounts. The banker in any small town or city is a member of the elite of the community; to expect them to interact and do business with just anyone was, in their view, a challenge to their social status and to the maintenance of the social system in which they had status. This situation is a microcosm of the structure of banking in the economy as a whole. The proposal for full-service banking was a challenge to their privileges.

Concern for who has access to credit was hardly new. In the 1830s and 1840s, Karl Rodbertus (Gonner, 1899), as part of his proposed 500-year transition to socialism, included an initial set of banking institutions making new credit available, especially to landowners – of which he was one. In the first three decades of the 20th century, the same concern led to the creation of land-and-agriculture-oriented banks focusing on long, intermediate, and short-term credit, respectively.

Writing generally, individuals who wrote as economists, including very eminent ones, took different positions on what qualified a study to be a candidate for acceptance and application by others. Taking a position, typically, involved assertion and little if any serious justification for their position in this case than in another held by either them or someone else. Epistemological justifications were, typically, superficial. In the 60 years since the end of World War II, they seem more sophisticated, what with mathematical and econometric tools becoming increasingly dominant. But the same and still other problems remained, typically buried under layers of pseudo-precision, and incomplete and presumptuous formulations. Notably in econometrics, fertile ground was tilled for new problems. But economists remained largely insensitive to the epistemological and substantive limitations of their work (see, for example, Sutton, 2000). The inferences of logic were too often taken to be correct as to either description or explanation. The results of empirical work similarly were overgeneralised. Logical or ideological priors, some version of the dominant paradigm, were held out as having been conclusively established. The work of economists increasingly became purely conceptual and in principle did not involve any but purely conceptual arrangements; whereas financial and other entrepreneurs, largely uninterested in a purely conceptual world, were pragmatic, letting their conclusions be driven by what seemed plausible, conceptually and profitably, and then translated into institutional change. Of course, some authorities, for example, Alan Greenspan, have learned how to use language with studied ambiguity.

Some or much of this analytical work was conducted by economists who were especially sensitive to the limits of their work, notably in the late twentieth century. Desirous of placing their work in the best light, they nonetheless paid attention to epistemological and substantive limits. Most of their work, however, took very important, but different, things for granted.

What constituted the money economy and what constituted macroeconomics (once it became recognised to be a meaningful category) still varied enormously, again with great heterogeneity within schools and groups.

Somewhat more narrowly, various forms which money arguably took were embraced by some people and rejected by others; what constituted 'real' money (not real balances) has been an issue in many controversies. 'Money' in some realist sense was often juxtaposed to money in the 'functional' sense, to the disadvantage of the latter and to the intended advantage of the former. The functionalist view, that money is whatever serves the functions of money, eventually came to dominate, perhaps because it was open-ended and permanently subject to revision. Recognition of the utility of money as a social construction was delayed by widespread continued belief that, whatever was customary, only customary money was *money*.

A similar but not identical distinction arose between the entrepreneur as a person and the entrepreneurial function performed by all economic actors. The non-functionalist view applauds the emulative status of those who already perform the function, implicitly seeking to repel those who do not or do not yet. A narrow notion of money and/or entrepreneur thus serves to legitimise a small group with power. Money can be issued beyond either the non-inflationary level or inflation at a certain level. Even a small number of people with the right to issue money can overissue the money supply. Wishful thinking reigns supreme here as elsewhere. To some people, there can be too many entrepreneurs. Efforts by business to use government to limit competition are the equivalent of efforts to limit the number and/or the effectiveness of entrepreneurs.

At stake, therefore, is the structure of power, given the socially emulative form of power in the particular society. One can imagine comparable arguments within a church over the range of admissibility of candidates for position who hold an array of views different from the existing body of religious.

Economists, like most people most of the time, seek solutions to problems that will be so attractive to others that the appearance of success and status will attach to them. Adam Smith, Thorstein Veblen, and George Shackle recognised that theory could set minds at rest. People settle for belief when truth was not available. More typically, they took belief to be truth. People in the lower social ranks come to admire the judgments and ideas of those in the higher social ranks. Truth ultimately connoted different solutions rooted in different epistemological positions, though it eventually became widely accepted that fact was a function of theory and theory a function of a particular reading of facts. In any objective analysis (of which there was precious little), the solutions may appear simplistic, congruent with and driven by ideology and/or dominant paradigm or certain salient of certain factors and forces, and purely instrumental. The solutions, typically, will manifest little if any sense of the multiple nature of the phenomena under study. Financial entrepreneurs' efforts (unanimous or not) to change institutions in their favour contrasted with economists' efforts to recommend institutional changes on selective theoretical grounds, albeit ignoring institutions and institutional change for analytical purposes.

The actual situation with regard to the law of money and banking has several characteristics. First, people, for all their often outspoken praise of 'laissez-faire', as I have stressed above, have been exceedingly and fundamentally pragmatic. They have resorted to government and to changing the law whenever they, as individuals and as subgroups, were concerned about what they deemed a problem, even in conflict with others within the same industry. Second, when government has responded in a manner they find suitable, the new activity or change of law has not, in some fundamental sense, been identified as 'government'. It may have been 'conceded' to be an exception to the 'rule' of laissez-faire but more likely it was seen as either a problem solution and/or a means of getting a fair shake. Third, money markets do not exist *de natura*, they are social creations. As such they are the result of actions by firms, governments, and the interactions among them (Samuels, 2004). The law of money and banking forms and operates through the institutions of money, banking, and money markets of various kinds. This body of law has emanated from both legislatures and courts. Fourth, every action by a court or legislature could have been decided to an opposite result. If Alpha and Beta are in the same field of action, government deciding in favour of one party amounts to deciding against the other party; for one to be granted a right means that the other has a no-right and exposure to the actions of the right-receiving party (Samuels, 1989).

Economists, therefore, could pay attention to only purely conceptual versions of money and banking, and of money and banking institutions, and by doing so be able properly to say nothing about institutional details. Theirs was theory without institutional details but with policy recommendations as to institutions somehow generated. Financial entrepreneurs could pay attention to what interested them – institutional change as a source of private profit – but not necessarily with a theory of monetary economics except insofar as some such theory – or propositions masquerading as a theory – was serviceable in manipulating the public's belief system and political psychology. The financial entrepreneur knew several things that the monetary economist either did not know or considered outside of/irrelevant to monetary and banking theory. One was that the business of money and banking required a set of legal foundations, a covering body of law, that different legal foundations would mean very different money markets and economic performance, and that the legal foundations of money and banking were neither given by nature nor in place once and for all time. The other was that, contrary to the dominant laissez-faire doctrine, one could expect entrepreneurs to seek (as somehow consistent with laissez-faire) frequent, indeed continuous, efforts to change the law as a means to greater profit. If economists believed that they could proceed as if all conflicts as to rights had already been worked out satisfactorily, the financial entrepreneurs knew that legal action to change rights and/or markets was an alternative to market action as a means to greater profit and that, therefore, it was wrong to assume that all conflicts as to rights had been already worked out (see Lerner, 1972, 259). In principle, the economists knew this – why else propose institutional change? – but not only was there no place for it in their pure theory, it conflicted with their a-institutional methodology and laissez-faire-oriented theory of economic policy. What the financial entrepreneur knew, took advantage of, and promoted – the creation, revision, and use of legal institutions – was substantially ignored by economists.

Money and banking theory and institutions (II): the legal foundations of money and banking

The history of economic thought is laden with ironical episodes. Two are among the most dramatic in general economics. First, Joseph Schumpeter (1950) noted that the task of European Socialist parties, when elected to power, was to preside over a bourgeois system. Second, Ronald Coase (1992) eventually insisted that the meaning of his work on social cost is the importance for resource allocation of the assignment of rights, i.e., institutions matter. This contradicted George Stigler's earlier identification of the so-called Coase Theorem as the allocative neutrality of rights' assignments (Stigler, 1966, 110–114). In monetary theory, we find the mathematical reducibility of the Quantity Theory expressed in terms of the equation of exchange (or Fisher's version) to the Cambridge version, and vice versa. Economically, V and K were very different. V tended strongly to elicit questions about the facility of the banking system in transferring balances, and K the strength of liquidity preference (length of holding period). Mathematically, they were the same: one could substitute $1/K$ for V, or $1/V$ for K. In monetary policy, Alan Greenspan, the long-serving head of the Federal Reserve System, was a disciple of Ayn Rand. The ostensible believer in individualism, free markets, and minimal government had become the monetary manager of the US economy. Of comparable irony is the use of the neo-Walrasian auctioneer as the necessary central planner to explain the workings of market economies. Of course, the auctioneer has, in principle, no politics, whereas Greenspan was acceptable to presidents of both parties because he was 'safe' and, accordingly, grand issues of macroeconomic and monetary policy could be avoided or finessed. His position was further whitewashed by his invocation of 'the market' and market forces, as if markets were transcendent to policy and not a product of policy.

It is, however, not such ironical episodes that are suggestive and/or important for our purposes, however numerous they may be. The failure of monetary theory to develop is due to day-to-day practices in the field and need not rely upon ironical situations for its explanation. Here we take up, first, aspects of the legal foundations of the money economy and, second, the practices of economists.

It is, of course, impossible to summarise in any kind of detail the legal histories of either money and/or banking, or the varieties of their interpretation. Nor, for the purposes of a reflective essay such as this, is it necessary to do so. The following discussions, generalizing from US and British experience, should suffice.

1. The money of which we have spoken in monetary economics is principally, almost exclusively, legal tender money, whether currency or credit. In one form or another, the state is involved in its legalization, provision, and control. That money without legal tender status has been provided by private companies illustrates how difficult it is to make a statement about money historically that is not in some respects, say, for particular places and periods, false in material respects. Especially insofar as the law of money arose from litigation over the legal status of particular instruments or particular organizational forms, the history is almost impossible to summarise – a condition pointing to the presumptuous nature of idealised conceptual economic models.
2. Money, in one form or another, has been supplied and regulated by monarchs, by legislatures, and by courts. I do not mean by 'regulated' only the control of something originating outside of government, though that is included. These institutions of government were interested in money and in banking for several reasons: (1) a more or less deep sense of their social importance and/or their importance for money markets, government finance, and of government providing the legal foundations thereof, (2) an often acute sense of their importance for the institution of government in question, (3) corrupt relationships between government institutions and banking institutions (not necessarily more corrupt than non-banking businesses and government), and (4) pressures on government institutions to do better, and so on.
3. The modern law of money, including the laws of bills and notes and other negotiable instruments, as well as contract law in general, originated, in large part, in business practice, and became the Law Merchant, which in time was adopted by Common Law courts. The law that originally had been worked out within the domain of business – including the piepowder courts of fairs which eventually partly replaced mediation and arbitration – became the relevant body of commercial law applicable to all people in their relations with business.
4. Subsequently, and to some extent simultaneously, with the institutionalization of legislative government and an 'independent' judiciary, the law of money was

increasingly generated by statute and through litigation, and less by monarchical actions. Only rarely, it would seem, would law be uninfluenced by business practice; for example, decisions through commercial law were influenced by private arbitration, and vice versa – justice, as it were, chasing its own tail. In this way, the law of business practice has been a source of the law of money, not surprising in a society increasingly a business, market, pecuniary, and middle-class society. Not only court decisions made law; for example, groups representing legislators, judges, the bar, and others worked out uniform codes, subsequently widely adopted. But the foregoing is but a thin slice of the relevant history and its meaning.

What has been true of the law of money has also been true of the law of banking. The law determined whether banks of any kind would exist, and, if so, the kind of banking companies that would be permitted. The law governed such phenomena as reserves (if any) and their organization and function, and the relative rights, duties, immunities, and exposures of owners, managers, depositors, borrowers, and bank as lender. The working out of law and of rights varied between governments of different types: monarchical, legislature-dominated, and independent or dependent courts.

5. The development of the law of money and of banking did not happen in a vacuum. The early history of the law of bills and notes, which was a source of Anglo-American commercial law, emerged from several centuries of conflict between a belief system in which capitalist values and practices were at least suspect and often severely controlled, if not restricted or made illegal, and a belief system in which those values and practices were built into and protected by the law. The Weberian question of whether belief preceded practice or vice versa was a grand one. More manageable is the particular question of the 16th- and 17th-century origins of contract law and the law of bills and notes in light of the controversies over exchange in general and over the scope of usury (whether the exchange of money for goods was included) (as stressed in Rogers, 1995, chapter 4). (In this and other connections, the economic significance of the historical jurisprudential distinction between private and public law qua law may be exaggerated; both are law.)

Money and banking issues have been tied up with the larger argument over the type of culture – one in which a more or less fundamentalist religion reigned or a trade-oriented one. Further, at some times/for some people religion and theology are passive and given lip-service; alternatively, they are politically aggressive and outspoken. During the second Iraq war, the Bush administration, relying on the fundamentalist Christian right for support, both opposed the fundamentalist Islamic right and promoted a culture of markets, production, and preoccupation with material well-being. The relations between government and religion as institutions of social control are obviously exceedingly complex and important as well as objects of manipulation. Both are, of course, institutions of social control: 'For

God and Country' is much more common than 'God versus Country' (Yee, 2005; see also Lelyveld, 2005). The place of monetary and banking institutions in either kind of Islamic society (nominal or fundamentalist) was hardly a public issue in the US. But the existence and treatment of usury separated fundamentalist and modernist Islamic economic and religious authorities. The separation was, however, porous; rationales for the payment of interest more or less easily arose in both fundamentalist and modernist regimes. Sharia law was as potentially elastic as the US Constitution and Canon Law. As for modern, mainstream monetary economics, its positions on interest, profits, markets, and similar topics, reflect the mindset and values of a particular type of culture. Its treatment of them as seemingly ontological entities is culturally based.

The earlier conflictual cultural forces at work were, in a sense, not merely those between a puritan fundamentalist religious regime and one founded upon and preaching trade. There was also, especially in England, the conflict between monarchy and legal system (apropos of 'in a sense', the Revolution of the late 17th century was in part monarchy versus legislature, in part monarchy versus 'independent' judiciary, and so on, as well as Puritan and other religious fundamentalism versus trade). Raffield (2004, 263–264) stresses 'the representation of the conflicting imperatives of rights and sovereignty, embodied respectively by an expansionist, politicised legal profession and a centralised, autocratic executive body'. The transformation of law was often caught up on these other conflicts as well as, eventually, party politics. The logics of schools of economic thought may have been latent but they were not central to the development of commercial law.

Apropos of the deployment of subjective individual interpretations of imagery, Raffield argues that 'the singular development... was the appeal to reason rather than metaphysics' (2004, 265). One page earlier, however, he writes that the legal profession 'successfully exploited the imaginary quality of the common law, constructing a political community that attempted to give form and shape to the invisible principles of justice' (264; apropos of the present-day use of absolutist justification, see Samuels, forthcoming). Invisibility has been an important category of human thought and rhetoric (absolutist formulation and justification). Reference to the invisible arose in both law and economics; *vide* Adam Smith's 'invisible hand'. The principal source of both was undoubtedly theology.

What is above called 'transformation' is designated 'reconceptualization and systemization' by Rogers (1995, 252 and *passim*). Apropos of the 'incorporation of the law merchant' into the common law, he writes that 'What the English judges "incorporated" into the common law was not commercial *law* but commercial *practice*; by doing so they composed commercial law' (252).

6. The fact and importance of the legal foundations of money and of banking are now manifest in two of the principal research tools available to scholars in the field of law and economics. In one, only central banking is treated (Backhaus, 1999); in the other, only the regulation of financial markets is included (Bouckaert and de Geest, 1992). Such is not surprising, given the

myopic approach and highly stylised mode of analysis typically used by mainstream practitioners in the field.

Much richer is work done in the Wisconsin legal history tradition. Yet the work and the major contributors in that tradition are absent from the two reference works noted just above. More surprising, the law of money and banking law are largely ignored in one of the tradition's seminal works (Auerbach et al., 1961), notwithstanding earlier work on those subjects. Still, the book amply examines law as process and the judge as policymaker rather than finder of law. A neat model of law and social change is that of Auerbach (1959) in which the author identifies two overriding functions of law in society, (1) the allocation of decision-making between private and public spheres, and (2) the adjustment of conflicting claims and the allocation of decision- making within the private sphere. Another preeminent theme is the use of law in preventing the consolidation of social life antagonistic to the advent and deepening of industrialization, the converse of which is that of Hurst (1964*a*) which examines how law has both promoted growth and helped determine the path that growth would take (see also Nelson, 1975, chapter 8). Hurst has produced a series of books on the legal foundations of the economic system (1964*a*, 1964*b*, 1970, 1977, 1982). His emphases on the relation of law to economic growth, markets, freedom, and social order, are amply evident in his study of the legal history of money in the US (Hurst, 1973).

In the preface to his *Legal History of Money*, Hurst emphasises that he is concerned with money as neither a 'shorthand for economic, social, or political power held through command of economic assets' nor 'with money in politics' and 'the influence that command of disposable economic assets has when men seek office or seek to influence officeholders'. Instead, writing about money as a more comprehensive phenomenon than contemplated by most economists, he indicates his concern with 'money as a distinct institutional instrument, employed primarily in allocating scarce economic resources, mainly through government and market processes' (Hurst, 1973, vii–viii). His first chapter, 'Functions of Law and Functions of Money', stresses the recursive relationships between law and money and concludes that:

> One way to sum up the record is to say that the existence of the system of money profoundly affected the law by helping shape attitudes – and limitations of perspective – which worked first to extend the influence of market processes at the expense of governmental processes in resource allocation, and later to delay public policy responses to the increasing imperfections of market processes themselves. (Hurst, 1973, 101–103)

The economics and the law of money, for both Hurst and me, represent a conception of the economy, the market, the legal–economic nexus, and monetary economics that is far richer than a concentration on the Quantity Theory. His second chapter deals with 'Allocations of Control over the System of Money' and demonstrates the pragmatic, political nature of what actually transpired but in a more objective, less conceptually or ideologically biased way than one typically finds in economists' work bearing on the topic. Hurst's approach to legal–economic history helps demonstrate the close affinity of the Wisconsin school of legal history and the Wisconsin school of institutional economics and its approach to the legal foundations of the economy. Indeed, no institutional economist has done for our knowledge of monetary economics and the nature of the pecuniary economy what Hurst has done – and done very much along the lines proposed by Wesley Mitchell.

7. The literature on legal history generally stresses, and not just in passing, the transformational character of the law. The law itself has changed. The law has helped change the economy. Economic change has brought pressures to bear on law and wrought changes in law. And so on. The discussions of money and of banking in most of the general histories are spread over such topics as property, competition, contract, negotiability, usury, and commercial law in general (Nelson, 1975; Horwitz, 1977; Tigar and Levy, 1977; Friedman, 1985).

Some specialists in legal history are content with reporting and interpreting the development of one or more fields of law. Other writers of legal history seek to develop interpretive and explanatory theories, such as the interrelationship between legal and economic processes, some emphasizing the economic impact of the law and others the impact on the law itself of economic pressures and ambitions. The categories are general, and the actions of individuals are subordinated to general causal forces. A few authors seek to model and/or explain the mutual impact of the two fields of action. Chicago law and economics tends to denigrate other such ventures, for example, for not being grounded in economic theory (meaning Chicago economics). Yet much theory has been developed, but not presented with the élan, panache, sense of grandiosity, and so on that have been the hallmark of the highly self-promoting, and effective, Chicago school. Writers such as Hurst and Auerbach have been more modest and less pretentious in their claims; indeed, well before Chicago turned to its brand of law and economics, several dozen articles were published that attempted to make sense, including theorise about, law and economics (Samuels, 1998).

Given the foregoing, surely it is clear that neither the institution of 'money' nor the mechanics and mores of a money society, nor the provisioning of money will mean the same thing in different situations. Not all nations will provide for 'money' to be supplied by the respective logics of the Currency and Banking Schools in the same way or in the same proportion. Conflict between the Currency and Banking Schools relates to conflicts over the mode and level of money issue, conflicts between political parties or factions within government, conflict between levels of government, conflicts among nominally private banking institutions, and between government and private institutions, as well as conflicts over central banks' organization, functions, and limits. However one characterises the relation of the Law Merchant to the Common Law, as Rogers makes clear in his own way, the categories and logic of the legal system were not those of commercial transactions, nor, by extension, were they those of Currency versus Banking Schools.

In every society, imagery of some idealised system notwithstanding, banking and politics are intertwined, the combination being a key component of the legal–economic nexus. Various economists have had more or less different idealised systems in mind. If ever a field of economics was laden *ab initio* with a vision of a self-adopted idealised domain, it has been monetary economics with its idealised monetary and banking systems. But, one could say, every idealised system amounted to a Platonic construction, each thinker deriving in a (non-pejorative) utopian manner his or her idealised monetary system from existing institutional arrangements cum imagination. Yet all the while government – legislatures, courts, and kings, presidents, and prime ministers – was a more or less decent, more or less corrupt, more or less legitimate process of working out the institutions, forms, mechanics, and quantities of money. Economists may look upon that process as chaotic and inefficient but legal minds surely looked upon what many economists had to say as no less chaotic, as holding some idealised system to be efficient only on some narrow institutional base, and as neglecting the actual legal institutions of money and banking, and the mode of their adoption. A pragmatist might look kindly upon both the legal and the private entrepreneurial processes as being engaged in working things out, and upon economists, statesmen, judges, and legislators as making their individual incremental contributions to a process of composite choice (in the sense of Hayek, Robert A. Solo, and others), even though they tend to overly ignore each other.

It is undoubtedly both impossible and unnecessary for monetary economists to incorporate explicitly the details, even the broad outlines, of legal and legal–economic history. At the very minimum, however, monetary economists can and should abstain from presenting their a-institutional pure conceptualizations as if they constituted some transcendent economic reality, especially implying not only their direct relevance to existing arrangements but the unequivocal efficacy of the policy recommendations accompanying the pure theory. It would be helpful if these abstentions were accompanied by eliminating the pretense of achieving unique determinate solutions, when these result from assuming away all the factors and forces which otherwise would prevent such solutions. If the legal foundations of money cannot be incorporated in detail, then they should be incorporated by reference, with some elaboration based on history and not paradigm-driven conjecture, however much it is true that history enables multiple stories. This would both caution the reader and help escape from the absolutist formulation of unique determinate solutions. Similarly, monetary economists should desist from projecting one policy analysis as if it and it alone were the 'correct', 'efficient', or otherwise beneficent approach. These points have been unwelcome among the hard core of mainstream economists, most monetary economists included, even the heterodox ones. The principal substantive arguments have been over the definition of economic reality and the desirable values, for example, inflation control versus unemployment control. As we shall now see, monetary economists within the mainstream of monetary economics have disagreed so much and so deeply that they have talked past each other and avoided the pursuit of more subtle and sophisticated approaches to meaning.

8. The legal history of money and banking merges ever so subtly with the economic history and legal history of the same period. Pressnell (1956) has shown something of the details that comprise the story of the combined histories. Like other authors, when he focuses on the law, he focuses on note issues, the law of partnership, and various Acts of Parliament. He emphasises the foundational role of law but does not make anything special out of it. The law is everywhere present but its very ubiquity (like the forest relative to the trees) leads us to take law for granted. A dangerous situation.

Part II Monetary Theory

The Shortcomings of Monetary Theory (I)

Cyclical and repetitive nature of monetary theory

Perhaps the most conspicuous characteristic of monetary theory and a principal basis for its lack of progress has been the cyclical and repetitive nature of discussions in the field and the concomitant failure to develop its body of theory. Echoing throughout the subsequent history of the field have been the positions arrayed against each other on the Bullion Report and the controversy between Banking and Currency Schools. A further characteristic has been the importance given to inflation/deflation and the inadequate attention to unemployment.

In a recent paper, Dimand (2005) surveys central post-1945 developments in macroeconomics in their relations to interwar monetary and business cycle theory. He concludes that certain approaches, problems, and debates have recurred in ways such that 'theoretical innovation' occurs within a background of earlier contributions and attendant controversy that often replicates earlier debates (often in different terms). He found that postwar developments in monetary and macroeconomics were the consequence of new empirical evidence, policy experience, and advances in formal technique, and the discipline's prior evolution. Repetition derived from path dependence coupled with negligible substantive development.

Most monetary and macroeconomists have a limited and superficial grasp of what their forebears did and did not accomplish. Coupled with multiplicity of views on every topic, the result has been that people do not appreciate what they are doing. I say that with considerable temerity, inasmuch as most intellectual work is conducted similarly.

'Faddism'

The history of the work of monetary economists has been by no means solely a matter of cyclicality and repetition. Indirect evidence of lack of growth has taken the form of faddism – attention to a series of topics, whose salience in the journals suggests depth of importance yet each becomes passé in seemingly a matter of months, a relative few with somewhat longer staying power in the journals and general textbooks. Among the topics which had very short half-lives in the postwar period were disintermediation, asymmetrical information, efficiency–wage theory, efficient markets theory, insider–outsider theory, menu theory, the effect of industrial concentration on the effectiveness of monetary policy, debt finance, liquidity trap, adjustment costs, exchange rates, contract theory, bank policy, and so on. Among the topics with greater durability were those of Federal Reserve monetary targets, rules versus discretion, natural rate of unemployment, rational expectations, inflation as primarily a monetary phenomenon or not, the Phillips curve, IS-LM, equilibrium analysis per se, price inflexibility or stickiness, and so on. The term 'faddism' may be prejudicial.[16] On the one hand, short-term efforts along new pathways are to be expected in a serious discipline. On the other hand, in some or many cases the expectation that the new topic would lead to a major revision of monetary/macroeconomic theory suggests intemperate and anxious scholars rather than serious ones, a feeling reinforced by the assertive character of the introduction of a new topic and by the tendency to evaluate new developments on the basis of an ideological or other position (see below). Too much should not be made of the distinction between the two groups based on durability just suggested. The important points involve differential lifespan and, possibly, the relevance and impact of Thomas S. Kuhn's criteria for the existence of normal science.

A view alternative to that of faddism is that with which Robert Clower began his famous essay, 'The Anatomy of Monetary Theory': 'Modern discussions of monetary theory have fairly well demolished its traditional foundations without so far putting anything definite in their place' (Clower, 1977, 206).

Monetary theory as pure assertion

Much work involves pure assertion laden with varying degrees of exaggeration and omission. The history of monetary theory is replete with the use of the equation of exchange, itself an identity, and with various formulations of P, M, V, and T and their applications.

Especially important, in light of the problem of multiplicity discussed below, is the variety of formulations of the Quantity Theory, the elements of the Quantity Theory, the nature and role of money, what drives the elements of the Quantity Theory, the source of money, and so on. The career of Irving Fisher manifests whole series of assumptions as pure assertions on every aspect of monetary theory and policy. Fisher was not alone, however, in seeking the holy grail of monetary theory; the content of the grail changed from economist to economist but its status as pure assertion unencumbered by serious foundational development cannot be gainsaid. In each case, typically, much was omitted, with negligible if any justification. The meanings of the many variants of 'gold standard', for example, were pure social constructions, asserted on the basis of what was possible and perceived (Cassel, 1932, chapter I).

Monetary theory is not the only field in which pure assertion reigns. Because of what I have to say below about law and social control, I call attention to the widespread invocation of law and other pertinent concepts. My points are principally that positions on them are typically taken, and largely only asserted, on narrow, superficial, and question-begging grounds; that the critical issue often tends to be that of continuity versus change – whether a received position is to be replaced by another, on what basis, and by whom; and the fundamental ambiguity and multiplicity that attends each. I have in mind what constitutes the category and the substance of law, morals, justice, freedom, custom, coercion, etcetera (see Lloyd, 1964). For example, in Adam Smith's understanding, the moral sentiments evolve, as do moral rules; but we now more fully understand that if a given set of moral rules is replaced by another, each set likely will be seen by its opponent as not worthy of the designation 'moral'. Similarly with law. As between law and morals, each receives input from the other, some of which is rejected. In the process, law, the history of law, custom, and the history of custom are socially constructed – invented, redefined, and so on, accomplished by those who have power, that is, those in control of the state or who identify with them (Commons, 1924; Friedman, 1972; Ackerman, 1983; Starr and Collier, 1989, parts III and IV). Also, such notions as justice, freedom, coercion, etcetera, are sufficiently multidimensional as to render most discussions either empty or presumptuous, matters of pure assertion; terms such as these also change with use, subtly and incrementally. Such language does not constitute analysis and seems to be used principally for purposes of mobilizing political psychology. The theory is attractive because of its congruence with particular political and/or ideological positions. Consider, for example, the claim that inflation/deflation is unjust. Positions thereon will largely, but not completely, be influenced by social and economic position as well as training in economics. Arguments will tend to exhibit circular reasoning and infinite regress. But the determination of whose interests and customs will count, that is, be given government protection, proceeds apace. And the values recognised in and promoted by the field of law and economics, as with monetary economics, will vary and change (Malloy, 2000). For some, money is power; for others, money conveys liberty (Reddy, 1987; Ferguson, 2001).

An incisive example is provided by David Laidler. Laidler emailed me that 'I think maybe that I've been a bit too sympathetic to Austrian "spontaneous order" ideas about the evolution of monetary institutions which does tend to lead to a "what exists is all that could possibly exist" view of the world that is pretty hard to justify when thought about – which in turn tends to discourage thinking' (Laidler to Samuels, February 5, 2006). A particular argument was taken as conclusive and served to set his mind at rest. The proposition constituting the argument was itself only an assertion.

Monetary theory as a vehicle for the expression and application of ideas from outside the field

Any monetary and macroeconomic theory must have some place and some significance for the supply of money and the other variables expressed in the equation of exchange/Quantity Theory of money and their underlying determination. But monetary theory, in one or another (conservative) formulation, has been a vehicle for the expression and application of ideas from outside the field. This specifically includes reformulations of theory intended to give effect to and provide sanction for political preferences and to reflect changed conditions.

The Quantity Theory of money and Say's Law were themes of Classical economics that became extraordinarily useful to those (conservatives) who were concerned, as they saw it, to minimise the economic role of government and inflation, and who, typically, ruled unemployment out of theoretical and policy bounds. This continuing attraction and its associated rhetorical role have been a principal source of the longevity of both theories.

Some years ago, I was present at a meeting of a small group at the annual meeting of the American Economic Association. Friedrich von Hayek was present, the center of attention and conversation. Hayek insisted on one point: that the reason for such leading conservative positions as opposition to inflation and support of the gold standard, balanced budgets, and the Quantity Theory of money was their ideological service in limiting the economic role of government.[17]

The rhetorical role of traditional monetary theory has been important. Preoccupation with such use of the Quantity Theory both channeled and limited the development of the Quantity Theory. Joan Robinson (1962) argued that ideology has been a source of theoretical development; perhaps more likely ideology has influenced the path rather than the substantive content of the field and has also had a constraining role. Moreover, monetary theory is not the only field in economics in which one finds such a driving force. Historically, conflict over theories of the distributions of income, wealth, power, and opportunity has been a premier source of innovation in such fields as distribution theory, capital theory, wage theory, public finance and value, and price theory as a whole. Such conflict is the basis in economic theory for conflict over the economic role of government itself, attesting to the inexorable importance of government in such matters. Conservative economic theory, or the conservative use of economic theory, has influenced the history of traditional monetary theory.

Conservatives believe that their policies constitute laissez-faire. From my point of view, their policies, no less than any other, constitute one set of uses of government.

Status emulation

Positions on monetary theory taken by economists have been driven not only by positions on policy and by ideology, but the quest for professional status and safety, that is, identification with certain groups in society, themselves seeking to attain and defend professional and social status. Economists are like other people. They like to be thought well of, at least by those they recognise as their peers. They recognise, admire, and seek to emulate people of rank above them. They seek to be successful. In short, they practice the status emulation examined by Adam Smith and Thorstein Veblen. This is driven in part by the twin quests for disciplinary and personal status; by a desire to have something to say about government policy; and by a felt need to create an environment safe for economics and economists.

The foregoing leads to several ironies. One irony involves a discipline which generally supports laissez-faire yet is deeply embroiled in promulgating and taking positions on policy. Another is the conflict between advocacy and objectivity. Still another permits individual economists to criticise particular institutions while being involved in institutional policy. I have in mind, for example, the Federal Reserve System, the World Bank, and the International Monetary Fund. (Similar points could be made, for example, about national and state regulatory institutions, including public utility commissions.) Policies with professional status often are not perceived to violate the general rule prohibiting government activism.

It seems to be the rare economist who can maintain independence and conduct arm's- length research and policy analysis, and still derive status from his or her relations with well-known, important, and status-dispensing institutions – not least those within the domain of monetary economics. At the very least, economists seek implicit status from their relationships with those institutions. They especially also want access to people with power, current data, the inner workings of policymaking, and so on. Invitations to have lunch or dinner in the highest-level institutional dining facility will impress the invitees and outsiders to whom the invitation becomes known. Inter alia, the games being played are cooptation versus resistance, and acquisition and defense of status.

The foregoing is based largely on my observation of relevant phenomena in the United States during some 50 years. I have no serious insight into conditions in Canada. I specifically neither believe nor intend to be understood as implying that David Laidler is at fault in regard to the problems noted. On the contrary, from what I know and have heard, he is particularly sensitive to the problem of crossing the line with regard to cooptation, etc. I have similar views with regard to any efforts by leading governmental–central bank figures in seeking cooptation, etc. If anything, where this occurs, it arises from the nature of the situation perhaps more so than individual or institutional intentions. The situation in the United States is generally different in the field of economic consultancy and forensic economics in corporate business.

I further note that some economists are so enamored of particular policy goals and outcomes that they are willing to compromise or sacrifice democratic structure and pluralistic principles – namely, an open process of working things out – in order to achieve their desired results. Identification with a particular power elite in order to better assure control of inflation and thereby serve a public interest, is a case in point. The danger here resides in failure to perceive that a power elite is likely more interested in maintaining its status and achieving goals especially rewarding it, than in combating inflation per se. As my vignette regarding Hayek suggests, anti-inflation may have an ideological use value. To the dismay of certain Republicans in the US, 'fiscal responsibility' with regard to deficit spending has seemed to have been a readily abandoned value during the Reagan–Bush–Bush administrations when tax and spending policies yielded enormous increases in the national debt. Another example is the relationships of 'Chicago' economists with the Pinochet regime. A potentially modifying effect is wrought by the claim that the individuals involved would have given the same advice to, for example, Communist China (also *vide* the language of Keynes in the Preface to the German edition of his *General Theory* (Keynes, 1973)).

The Shortcomings of Monetary Theory (II)

Multiplicity

Every aspect of human existence and use of mind has been shown to have elicited diverse, hence multiple, responses, interpretations, or criteria. It is only by omitting all other responses, interpretations, and criteria that one of them can become the paramount principle or frame of reference, the beginning of a line of logical analysis (Krausz, 2002).

An intellectual discipline moves slowly, in pieces or steps. Monetary theory manifests such incrementalism. But there is precious little progress, principally only repetition and incompleteness. Studies of substance, as many are, largely only apply new techniques to old issues, which remain inconclusive. And, again, positions are taken that are often premised on mere assertion.

Consider the term 'cost'. The term has several definitions, each definition predicated on a particular theory of cost. Among the theories are real cost, opportunity cost, money costs, and rights. No one theory tells us everything we might want to know about cost, yet different economists tend to insist on one or another as *the* theory of cost. The idea of multiplicity is alien to such minds, which seem to feel deeply that if one definition and one theory are correct, then all others must be wrong. The idea that the combination of all definitions and the respective theories of cost to which they give effect may have heuristic value is not recognised by them; or, if seen, is rejected as a threat to their pet theory.

Consider Malthus's law of population (Malthus, 1798). He argued that population growth tends to exceed the capacity to produce food. That may or may not be the case; it is an empirical question. Here we have a model in which two variables play off each other. Ricardo introduced differential cost of production, so the capacity to produce food is itself a function of cost of production and technology (both possibly in part a function of population). Malthus also introduced institutions in the form of preventive and positive checks. Now we have a model in which the strength of the sexual drive plus the strength of the urge to reproduce plus institutions promoting preventive and positive checks govern population growth, and cost of production and technology govern the capacity to produce food. Even so generally and loosely stated, the upshot of nineteenth century population theory was, in effect, such a multi-variable model. In actuality, however, different economists gave greater weight to different variables. Controversy centered, not surprisingly, on a narrow construction, with much wishful thinking and much subjective use of data (such as it was). An empirical question was transformed, or reduced to, a logical question.

Compare how the general theory of price has been handled. Here we have price as a function of demand and supply. Demand is a function of a host of variables operating on the demand side; supply, another host of variables. At various times different topics have been stressed, for example, demand as in part a function of supplier marketing activity, supply as a function of cost of production, technology, and R&D, the nature of competition, rationality, and so on. Different authors stress different variables vis-à-vis other variables, and different specifications of variables vis-à-vis other specifications, such as the derivation of the demand curve and the nature of the conceptual periods. Most of the controversies are short-lived; they tend to end up, with different weights, in the textbooks.

In each case all the subsidiary variables and the question of their weights, from time to time and from place to place, are legitimate considerations. This legitimacy tends to be obfuscated by the practice of economists to make and invoke assumptions, especially assumptions that permit unique determinate optimal equilibrium results, by economists seeking to promote a particular theory, etc.

Turning to monetary economics,[18] two preliminary points are warranted. First, the Quantity Theory in any form is no substitute for either a comprehensive monetary theory or a comprehensive macroeconomics. There is more to the history of the Quantity Theory than the price level as a function of either the supply of money or the demand for money. There are several different 'monetary theories of production'. There is less to the Quantity Theory than many of its devotees often would have us believe, inasmuch as they exaggerate that which they prefer to promote; yet there is more, inasmuch as they tend to omit a great deal. The Quantity Theory is not alone in deriving its attractiveness from its utility for mobilizing political psychology. Second, the problem of multiplicity extends to what is 'absolute truth' in monetary economics, whether such existed, and, if it did, what it was; over the relative weight to be given to inflation and unemployment as policy goals; over what is 'sound' or 'proper' monetary policy; and the evaluation of current policies and current events. Faith in monetary orthodoxy eventually became a badge of non-crackpot respectability.[19]

Everywhere one turns in monetary theory, even the Quantity Theory, there has been multiplicity. Quantity Theory formulations could vary among theorists and each was nested in a larger and variegated model of the money economy. Sophisticated versions of the Quantity Theory were possible but because of the vast number of possible complications, advocates were often interested in simple versions easily discussed and taught. Singular explanations of macroeconomic phenomena, such as real balance effects and/or sticky or inflexible prices, were prevalent. The problem was, in part, that economists tend to adopt the simplest and most highly stylised versions of their theories, often caricatures of the sophisticated versions held by at least some leading theorists. Advocates were either unaware of the magnitude of possible complications or had their perception thereof narrowed and/or finessed by ideologically driven a priori beliefs, and so on.

The Quantity Theory was ubiquitous but given highly variegated content. One formulation or another constituted the core of what most economists considered monetary theory. While the Quantity Theory was its most conspicuous component, monetary theory included more than the Quantity Theory. Disagreements centered in part on different versions of the Quantity Theory using different elements of monetary theory and on what else was to be included.

Every aspect of monetary theory has been given multiple formulations (Samuels, 1995*a*). The Fisher approach was formulated in different ways by Fisher himself. The Fisher equation contrasts with the Cambridge equation. Each of those formulations leads to emphasis on different things: the Fisher equation, by focusing on velocity, leads to emphasis on the facility of the banking system in clearing checks; the Cambridge equation leads to attention on the reasons for holding money. Yet Fisher's V is reducible mathematically to the Cambridge K by substituting 1/K for V: less desire to hold money means higher velocity. The devotees of each equation recognise multiplicity largely only insofar as they consider multiplicity objectionable: There can be only one correct, true, formulation. Theoretical pluralism seems beyond the pale. Monetary and other economists tend to be uncomfortable with the fact of multiplicity and largely do not deal with it in the open, preferring to assert some *one* definition of reality and corresponding policy – whether belief in one correct position is a matter of belief alone, pretense, or a peculiar concept of science. Yet, at different times and places, M can influence V, V can influence M, liquidity preference can influence T, and T can influence liquidity preference, a change in C can influence change in I, and change in I can influence change in C, and similarly with interest rates and investment and consumer durables… the point is obvious. In a market economy, relationships among variables, and the variables themselves, need not be stable.

The development, or at least the history, of monetary theory and of macroeconomic theory has consisted, in part, of efforts to place enormous interpretive and analytical weight on a few topics, typically one at a time, that are asserted to control or characterise the putatively self-adjusting economy. These include the real balance or Pigou effect, liquidity trap, flexible prices, rate of interest, and so on. Also present are topics that some economists and some schools have emphasised and others have tried to finesse. The chief of these is uncertainty, especially in the form of radical indeterminacy or of rational expectations. Others include exclusive attention to quantities defined in real terms while ignoring changes in the price level, the coercive nature of involuntary unemployment, the role of finance, the meaning of equilibrium, problems of aggregation and of causality, the significance of fiscal policy, the interest elasticity of investment, the existence and ontological status of business cycles, the relevant microfoundations, and so on. That at one point in time the functional significance of a topic or variable may be greater and at another point, lesser, that in actuality the economy has several if not many adjusting or stabilizing mechanisms, and that stability need not be attained by any of them, was typically incongruous with the quest for unique determinate solutions, i.e., one adjustment mechanism.

One problem is that money is treated as a given phenomenon, with negligible serious and objective attention to the different ways in which money is institutionalised, and why, and to the roles of institutionalised money and banking, which are also variable, that is, multiple. It is the unusually astute monetary economist who insists that to know the behaviour of 'money' one has to know the behaviour of 'banks' and 'central banks', and who also insists on recognizing the limits imposed by mathematical and other techniques on the behaviour of monetary aggregates.

In the concluding paragraph of Edmund S. Phelps' survey of seven schools of macroeconomics, he says of one approach that it 'has also the defect of its virtues. It is perhaps too easy a game to explain a single episode in a maximally pleasing way without the constraint that the method, enriched with a full menu of shocks, be able to fit booms and other depressions as well. Unfortunately, to look for the same compact explanation of other depressions will prove a vain quest if, as I suppose possible – like Tolstoy's unhappy families – each is depressed in its own way' (Phelps, 1990, 105). The predicament of monetary and macroeconomic specialists is that the phenomena that they study are not identical over time. Each cycle, or each comparable phase of the cycle, has characteristics in common (perhaps only with a high probability), but each also has characteristics that vary more or less importantly from cycle to cycle. It seems to this economist that the sensible procedure is to keep all possible explanations on a shelf near at hand. Sometime in the 1970s, when I was editor of the *Journal of Economic Issues*, a manuscript was submitted applying IS-LM to a problem. I thought that *JEI* was an inappropriate outlet. But, nonetheless wondering whether that judgment was incorrect and the paper might have something of substance, I sent it to four readers. The result was each reader disagreed with the author and each had their own way of applying IS-LM to the problem. I was left with five versions of application. I sent the reports to the author, saying that he needed to revise in accordance with the four reports. No resubmission was received. It was clear to me that the paper was generated by several things: the problem, the structure of IS-LM, and the implicit premises on which the IS-LM model was applied to the problem. The different applications derived from the different implicit premises. This was a paradigmatic example of both multiplicity and inability to make something of it, in part because the author and the four readers each thought that only one application was correct.[20]

Consider the theory that lowering the rate of interest will induce more investment. If one takes the interest rate to be the relevant cost of investment, then the responsiveness of investment to a lowering of the interest rate will depend, *ceteris paribus*, on the expected rate of profit. Other ways of expressing the point are, first, the interest elasticity of investment and, second, that the rate of interest be higher enough than the marginal efficiency of capital. Several points here: (1) No single relationship exists between the interest rate and investment. The responsiveness of investment to a change in interest rate depends on interest elasticity of investment, and it, in part, on expectations, and it can change. (2) The implicit *ceteris paribus* clause recognises other factors but then isolates them in Marshall's pound. Multiplicity is thus finessed – and forgotten. (3) An engineered fall in the interest rate can elicit increased investment spending but it need not. The fact of the engineered cut can elicit a fall in the expected rate of profit (marginal efficiency of capital) and thus a reduction, not an increase, in investment. The crux of the matter is the mental state of businesspeople. Not only is multiplicity finessed but changes in the variables and in the direction of causation can also be rendered obscure and thus forgotten. Different economists have made different assumptions about these matters (at the same point in time) even when they did not know that that was what they were doing. Some differences were due to wishful thinking, some sincere, and some to counter other assumptions and positions.

Consider the definition of money in terms of its stipulated functions: unit of account, medium of exchange, standard of deferred payments, and store of value. Monetary theories may focus on one of them to the exclusion, or effective exclusion, of the others. A monetary theory that includes all four will be more complicated but more complete than a theory covering only one.

Economists were not much ahead of the general public in matters such as what constitutes money, the role of reserves, the nature and role of a central bank, and so on.

The money economy could be examined in pure abstract terms, independent of monetary, banking, and other financial institutions, or with an emphasis on the actual institutions that helped form and operated through the money economy. Significant disagreements exist as to the nature and substance of fundamental monetary and other macroeconomic processes, the nature and origin of actual monetary and macroeconomic problems, and the solutions to those problems. Considerable confusion results from some economists' claims that their agenda for government monetary/macroeconomic policy constitutes non-interventionism – because the 'correct' policies were being pursued – whereas all other agendas are interventionist.

Major controversies were waged over what is money, the monetary standard, the role of reserves, what commercial banks do, the nature and role of a central bank; fractional reserves and the money multiplier; the role of the interest rate, the Cambridge cash-balance approach, Wicksell's monetary theory, the relation of money to capital, that is, definitions of money in relation to definitions of capital, and so on.

Some work postulated the economy to be fundamentally stable (e.g., through great weight given to Say's Law); others postulated particular combinations of quantity-theory and business-cycle models. Changes in M could be deemed to affect only changes in P and nominal Y (i.e., T). Changes in Y (or T) could be seen as leading to changes in M and thence in P; or changes in Y (or T) could be seen as leading to changes in P and thence in M. Different supplementary assumptions might lead to changes in the direction of flows of causation or influence. Especially critical was whether an increase in Y (or T) was possible: whereas an increase in M and thence P could lead to an increase in Y (or T) at less than full employment, at full employment an engineered increase in M could not lead to an increase in real Y (or real T).

Much work seemed directly or indirectly influenced by monetary and banking arrangements existing within some form of gold standard. A monetary system predicated upon gold meant that changes in either gold or money led to a change in the other and in the price level. Currency and credit could be treated differently (as was done by Fisher, for example), influenced by differences in view of specie, paper, and bank balances. Among other differences were the relation of reserves to M, the money multiplier, the reasons for holding money or spending on consumer and/or capital goods, the respective roles of commercial banks and central bank (including targets), the relation of interest rates to the Quantity Theory variables, neutral versus non-neutral money, and so on.

A popular form of monetarism held that the private sector is stable, or would be stable in the absence of monetary and fiscal policy; that changes in the supply of money, vis-à-vis a stable demand for money (expectable in a stable economy), lead to changes in the interest rate and, especially, the price level; that changes in the supply of money generate changes in spending; that prices are generally flexible; and that vis-à-vis all other factors only money matters or money matters most (hard versus soft monetarism). The Keynesian fiscalist alternative held that the private sector is unstable, and that government can reinforce this instability, introduce its own instability, or counter instability; that changes in spending are governed by more than developments in the supply of money; that changes in the supply of money are the consequence, not the cause, of changes in spending – in part, the supply of money is a function of the demand for money; prices are generally inflexible; inflation is largely or typically a function of aggregate demand increasing beyond the full employment level; that increases in the supply of money can generate inflation but changes in the supply of money are not the critical factor governing changes in spending; that price-level instability is not the only monetary/macroeconomic problem, because full employment is not guaranteed and the supply of money is key to neither the price level nor the level of real income. Whether the foregoing be considered monetary theory or macroeconomic theory, multiplicity is present at every turn.

In sum, words such as 'monetary', 'monetarist', and 'fiscalist' are primitive terms which have no specific meaning. They cover a multitude of variations. When they are used, different readers or auditors attribute their own individual, subjectively chosen meanings.

Individual words are not alone given multiple specification. The two schools – monetarism and fiscalism – identify different transmission processes applicable to changes in the supply of money leading to increased spending. The fiscalist argues that increases in the supply of money are endogenous, resulting from increases in the demand for money by borrowers seeking to spend more, and that increases in the supply of money limit increases in interest rates (generated by the increased demand for money) and thereby increase investment and income. The monetarist argues that increases in the supply of money are exogenous (generated by the central bank), leading to excess money balances, which leads to greater spending in order to return monetary balances to desired levels. The differences turn on whether the increases in the supply of money are endogenous or exogenous, whether the increased supply of money is felt through the lowering of the interest rate or the creation of excess balances, and whether a stable economy and a stable demand for money is a suitable or a utopian premise.

Modeling the demand for money is also no simple matter; no singular model has resulted. Even putting aside (and there is no conclusive reason to do so) the fiscalist–Keynesian model of transaction, speculative and precautionary motives, the monetarist demand for money has been modeled differently by different monetary theorists. The demand for money generally is said to be a function of permanent income, wealth, price level, expected rate of inflation, and liquidity preference; more narrowly, it is a function of permanent income, wealth, and price level, all felt by Friedman and others, but by no means all monetary economists, to be relatively stable in the short run (i.e., if the economy is left to run well on its own), plus the interest rate.

Anyone not permanently wedded to either monetarism or fiscalism likely might consider a much more complex interplay of monetary and spending variables and relationships, including structural and expectational factors. Keynesian fiscalism is likely more capable of encompassing a wider range of variables than is the Quantity Theory but that generalization is subjective. A major point, however, is that there are a multitude of possible complex interplays of all such variables, relationships, and factors – permitting a variety of specifications. Another important general point is that all of the foregoing constitutes the social construction of economic/monetary theory. The argument over monetarism and general monetary theory is part of that process. Only in part is the argument a controversy about the actual economy. It has been primarily, albeit not solely, a quest for a theory with which successfully to challenge Keynesian fiscalist economics and policies. The argument is about the control of government policy and the discipline of economics. The quest for power and control over policy drives economic theory.

The question arises as to whether the Quantity Theory – in whatever form – is itself (1) a definition of economic reality, (2) a tool of analysis with which to investigate economic reality, or (3) an instrument of rhetoric with which to mobilise and manipulate political psychology. Economists of my generation will recall how Samuelson and Friedman, in their televised debates in the 1960s, each invoked aggregate demand and the supply of money; but Samuelson had changes in aggregate spending drive changes in the supply of money, whereas Friedman had changes in the supply of money drive changes in aggregate spending. More is at stake than a conflict about direction of causal flow, just as when advocates of both under-consumption and over-investment theories of the business cycle pointed to the same data to prove their case: unsold goods.

Perusal of several standard reference works confirms the foregoing argument that the Quantity Theory is not something given but a matter of social construction, a work in progress, and characterised by multiple specifications and interpretations. The entry in the *Elgar Companion to Classical Economics* indeed opens with the caution:

> One of the conclusions drawn by Hugo Hegeland...from his thoroughgoing study of the historical development and interpretation of the Quantity Theory of money was that 'the interpretation of the Quantity Theory shows almost as many variations as the number of its interpreters'. This assertion is hardly an

> exaggeration and even after half a century of further intensive research in this field it is probably as valid now as then.... the theory is like a chameleon. From the outset writers on the subject have understood [the] Quantity Theory of money to mean sometimes very different things' (Rieter, 1998, 230)

Actual monetary and banking systems tend not to be systematically thought out in advance, nor need they be. Their origins and reorganizations result from various combinations of business interests, legislative and executive policy and politics, and court decisions. In the 19th and 20th centuries, the major force behind changes in monetary and banking law has been private bankers and other private business interests. Those successful in convincing state legislatures and the Congress have been able to change the structure of relative rights (without compensation: no one has a property right in particular government policies), the nature and structure of money markets, and so on. Economists have had some input into the process but they have not been a major force, nor should they necessarily be one. For the most part, economists have been interested in the more abstract issues of monetary theory; most economists, until relatively recently, have been unaware or neglectful of the impact of incremental legal changes on the actual world of their theoretical terms.

The US economy, or for that matter any economy, would not be what it is without a history of changing law. Largely, but not only, driven by business practice in a society that has been increasingly ruled by businessmen – the middle class, so-called – the legal system has changed from that of a rural and agricultural, typically tradition-bound economy to that of an urban and industrial economy that invariably evidences Schumpeterian creative destruction driven by technology, strategic decisions by businessmen, and efforts to control the formation and structure of markets and to capture income. (Some administrations are more transparent than others in regard to the fact of their aiding business.) For various reasons, which need not be examined further here, economists have held out a model of fully defined, stable rights – than which nothing could be further from the truth. Some writers, such as Bruno Leoni and James Buchanan, go so far as to define legal change (change of law) as contra-freedom and socialist. If such were the case, the owners and managers of business would be the leading socialists. Schumpeter tended to identify the growing corporate system as comporting with his definition of socialism, but that is, or may be, another matter. Ironically, part of the economy that is the world of money and banking, a world whose defining institutions were imposed not by an alien and exogenous government but a Lockean system of middle-class dominated legislatures and courts.

The argument of this chapter, concerning the development of a richer monetary economics, is completely independent of such considerations as to whether one likes the existing or some other system of banking and of money. The irony is that notwithstanding the non-interventionist mindset of economists, they have been more than willing to offer and promote suggestions for changing institutions. Not least attractive as candidates for legal change have been the institutions of money and of banking; and not least interested in producing such proposals have been ostensibly 'conservative' economists. These economists, not unlike socialists, measure the status quo against their ideal system(s), find it wanting, and seek to change it. Like it or not, this is the nature of the economic-policy game played by economists (and others) with all sorts of ideologies and all sorts of idealised images. I cannot say that the policy game would be better if its component ideology game were somehow muted. But all of us would have a better idea of what we were doing – which may well be the reason why transparency has not come about: it is in the interests of the powerful and the would-be powerful to obfuscate what is actually going on. Even if we could abstract from the ideology game, problems of freedom versus control, continuity versus change, and egalitarianism versus inequality are sufficiently complex and open-ended, that politics – the legal–economic nexus – is every bit as messy as they appear to be, not least in the domain of money and banking.

The matrix approach

Two complementary solutions present themselves to avoid the predicament indicated above. One is so obvious that it needs neither a name nor extended discussion. In fact, it is a proscription rather than a prescription (as is the second). The point of the first solution is to avoid exclusivism. In a complex world, the price of omission is too high to reduce definition, theory, and causation to one definition, one theory, and one-way causation.

The second solution is what I have called the matrix approach, originally formulated in regard to schools of thought but clearly applicable to multiplicity of definitions and theories. Assume that five schools of economic thought exist (one of which can be the hegemonic, orthodox school), A, B, C, D, E. Each school presumably has a certain meaning, in part in relation to the other schools but each meaning can be defined differently. Thus A consists of A^1, A^2, and A^3. What, then, is the meaning of each school? That of A as given, say, by A^1, A^2, and A^3? Or, of A by B, or by B^1, B^2, or B^3? It is not clear that devotees of A, or one subgroup thereof, are the best or most conclusive interpreters of A; some of those within B, C, D, or E may have insights of great value. It seems to me that one can form a matrix of the array of meanings of each school, and of all schools, from both within and without. The matrix can provide a putatively higher level of insight than can any particular view of A. It can also avoid the loss of knowledge and/or insight resulting from a more or less cavalier dismissal of any reading.

The meaning of the different positions on the Bullion Report, Currency versus Banking Schools, endogenous versus exogenous money, etc. need not be restricted to the position someone prefers over all other positions. Call the totality of the different positions X. The meaning of X derives from some (there likely will be more than one) such totality, now enabling and helping form a higher-level matrix.

The matrix analysis can be applied to the array of interpretations of a theory or school. It can also be applied to the array of interpretations of any initial array of interpretations. Taking examples from other fields, a cross-cultural generic concept of 'law' can be attempted by one analyst; the same with 'religion'. Numerous analysts could attempt the same thing for each term. Each would help clarify some issues but the analyses likely would differ. A matrix analysis could be undertaken by a number of scholars working independently, each producing a matrix analysis, each likely different in some material or conceptual regard, of the different conceptualizations. Then a matrix analysis of those different matrices could then be conducted, et seq.

One important and useful benefit will be to reduce the intrusion of implicit antecedent normative premises or values. Those for whom the Quantity Theory is attractive precisely because it supports some prior ideological or other position, will find it more difficult to do so. This is as true of the variety of Keynesian premises as of the variety of Quantity Theory premises, etc. Values should be used in description or explanation only if they are a part of description or explanation, and not as a driving force or premise. They are, however, necessary in evaluating alternative policies and alternative social constructions of reality. The further point is to make them explicit.

The matrix analysis is more consonant, but not exclusively so, with a *verstehen* approach to inquiry, one providing at best understanding rather than Truth.

The scope of monetary economics

The foregoing is wide ranging. But monetary economics, like the larger economics of which it is a part, is not, or not as much as it could and should be. The core of monetary theory is the Quantity Theory. But monetary economics is more than MV = PT or P = MV/T. It is more than the interest rate equilibrating the demand and supply of money (or loanable funds), or the tension between IS and LM. It is more than the interactions between the monetary policies of central bank and commercial banks, or between liquidity preference and expectations. And so on. Economists of the typical monetary persuasion self-define their field and themselves in those terms. The problem with the Quantity Theory and with quantity theorists, therefore, is that the theory has been used to obfuscate and rule out of monetary economics most other important aspects of a money economy. The reason is simple and straightforward: monetary economists largely accept the market economy, its mindset, and its system of money and banking. They strongly tend to treat the existing monetary and banking regime as part of the natural order of things, as something to study in a scientific manner as if it were not a matter of politics and policy, and to do so in a way that envelops two motivations long held by economists: one, to serve as the cheerleaders for the market economic system and its institutional integuments and two, to study the economy and its institutions in such a way as not to invite feedback challenging the safe existence of economics in general and monetary economics in particular. The fact that criticism of various practices and structures is voiced by economists shows only exceptions and does not negate the conclusion.

Conventional practice strongly tends to omit the monetary and banking system within which the typical monetary economists' work is conducted. Monetary journals, treatises, and textbooks rarely even touch on the politics of money and banking and its financing, or on the nature and consequences of a pecuniary economy, or...(the classic work in economics is Mitchell, 1937; in sociology, Simmel, 1990; see also Poggi, 1993; Zelizer, 1994).

But monetary economists, like economists in general, are averse to admitting/placing within their theories that the monetary system, like the economic system, has its legal foundations, that interests in the private sector attempt to control and use government for their own purposes in both establishing and changing those foundations to suit their needs and desires, and that government is ubiquitous and important as well as a means of control and of change. They treat the monetary and banking system as if it were given and transcendent and not a matter of human social construction – all this in spite of the fact, obvious to anyone looking with an open mind, that these same people are actively engaged in policy promotion of one kind or another. Absolutist justification is combined with pragmatic revision. They portray the system as magical and mysterious – which only they have mastered. The cumulative effect is that laissez-faire is descriptively and normatively meaningless, largely a sentimental state of mind, and a belief that is selectively used to mobilise and manipulate political psychology. For all the putative errors of commission by monetary economists, the errors of omission seem vastly more important. To omit something from a field is to render it nugatory. One wonders if such is intentional or habitual, or both. It is social control by one's friends.

Conclusion

I conclude with the questions, what do people want to know about money and banking, and what do and can they know? Contrast the two epigraphs in John H. Wood's history of central banking (2005, viii). One is from Hansard's account of a House of Commons speech (June 12, 1822) by David Ricardo. Ricardo admonished his colleagues about those who 'possessed the power of regulating the quantity of money...but who, nevertheless...did not acknowledge the true principles of the currency, and who, in fact, in his opinion, did not know anything about it'. The other is from a speech by Carter Glass to the House of Representatives (September 10, 1913). Glass assured his colleagues that '[N]o semblance of acquisitiveness prompts [the Federal Reserve Board's] operations, no banking interest is behind, and no financial interest can pervert or control it. It is an altruistic institution, a part of the Government itself, representing the American people, with powers such as no man would dare misuse'.

I have concentrated here on monetary economics, only touching on macroeconomics, largely because the latter is too vast to deal with in one article. A complete macroeconomics would encompass monetary economics as business cycle theory. But a complete macroeconomics would likely still have the problems identified above. Perhaps the analytically most important difficulty involves ruling out of bounds certain factors in such a way as to limit the possible performance paths of actual economies. Some examples include the following: (1) the idea that one can have a glut and therefore unemployment in a few fields of production but not in all fields, neglects the usual situation that there only needs enough unemployment to be a problem. The predicament cannot be eliminated by assuming that money is a commodity, so holding money precludes there being a glut of all commodities. The problem, of course, is that assuming money to be a commodity underlies the situation that liquidity preference (holding money) means a shift from real to portfolio investment, less spending, income, and employment. Should the defective story be believed, however, it might lead to an increase in the marginal efficiency of capital, consequent to an improvement in expectations, and hence an increase in investment spending, income, and employment. Should, however, the defective story not be believed, the marginal efficiency of capital likely would fall, with further negative, not positive, consequences. The total story just told turns in part on unemployment increasing sufficiently to become a problem. The problems now become centered on full employment. Unless one defines full employment as 100% of the labor forces employed but minus frictional unemployment, then one assumes that any level of spending = income is the full employment level. This raises the question of how it becomes a problem, and a problem in what sense, when there is 'enough' unemployment. This is a matter of expectations, and it is one social function of macroeconomic and monetary economics to influence expectations and thereby economic performance. Economics thus becomes, willy-nilly, one of the factors in the subject it studies – because the results of its studies can affect expectations. (2) Expectations can change, therefore, due to the content of the economics story being believed, becoming part of the social belief system. What if, in a recession, government were to increase its spending and cut taxes in order to generate an expansionary deficit? If the story underlying that account is believed, expectations will improve and spending on capital goods will increase et seq. But if people are led to believe that anything government does is ineffective (and other pejorative terms), then expectations will worsen further and capital goods spending will fall (further). In macroeconomic models the likely path will depend upon the assumptions built into the models. In actual economies the likely path will depend upon the assumptions built into economic actors' expectations. While in principle, economists can change their assumptions, it is more likely, I think, in a world of a hegemonic school, that economic actors are more likely to do so – but what that means depends upon their belief system, which is, in part, a matter of economists.

Consider the following propositions:

> The whole is more than the sum of its alternative formulations.
>
> The phenomena of money and banking – and of economics generally – do not warrant singular, simple and unequivocal specification.
>
> No one definition/theory can answer all the questions we have; no one definition/theory can encompass the relevant phenomena in their entirety.
>
> The legal foundations of money and banking are at least as important as conventional economic categories.
>
> Multiplicity is a source of theoretical strength; reducing or finessing diversity and complexity by adopting one from an array of definitions/theories

amounts to limiting analysis to one dimension and eliminating or rendering heterodox possible analysis along other dimensions.

The proposals suggested above – doing away with exclusivism, adopting the matrix approach, expanding the scope of monetary economics – will not satisfy those who seek determinacy, closure, simplistic formalism, and promotion of their favourite theory, definition, and policy. But the price of those latter goals is great. The price is nothing other and nothing less than the continued impoverishment of monetary economics. History has shown that.

Monetary economists, like other economists, have been substantially unwilling to accept (1) the legal foundations of money and banking and its implications, (2) the existence of families of causal sequences, reversals, and changes in overdetermination of the variables, their structures, and their direction, and (3) the existence and importance of questions deeper than the questions actually dealt with and which, by their silence, they render harmless and thereby participate in social control. The problem is not that they take the system for granted – the system is what they should be studying – but that they have an unduly narrow conception of it.

Inter alia, monetary economics has been principally of the pure conceptual type and relatively negligibly of the type studying objectively the institutional foundations of the existing monetary and banking system, though there has been much biased talk about them. Monetary economists of both types readily jump from relatively positivist analysis to normative analysis, with negligible serious, deep attention to the normative premises involved, typically making assertions. The function of the Quantity Theory, like that of the gold standard, has been as an instrument of control of the monetary and banking system, though rarely so perceived. In any event, the Quantity Theory is but a narrow slice of what monetary economics can be (for example, Zelizer, 1994). The problem of multiple definitions and interpretations is typically avoided (except to reject unfavoured alternatives); instead, the use of primitive terms is ubiquitous, with meaning unspecified by speaker or author and left to each auditor and reader to identify (differently) themselves.

D. H. Robertson divided his little book, *Money* (1929) into eight chapters averaging some 25 pages. The chapters cover (I) the merits and drawbacks of money, (II) the value of money, (III) the quantity of money, (IV) the gold standard, (V) money and saving, (VI) money in the great muddle, that is, monetary collapse and restoration, (VII) the question of the standard, and (VIII) the question of the cycle. The 1957 edition added (IX) money in the second great muddle, and (X) problems of words, thought and action. Had he agreed with this chapter, Robertson would have added several additional chapters. These would have covered the ontology and epistemology of monetary theory; institutions and monetary theory, especially the legal foundations of money and banking; money and banking institutions in the light of belief system and the social structure of power; money and banking theory as social control and the social construction of a money economy; the nature and consequences of a pecuniary economic system; the practices of monetary theorists; multiplicity, and the matrix approach. Monetary theory would never have been the same.

John Maynard Keynes might more readily than Robertson have appreciated the expanded coverage and its arguments. If so, his Introduction to the Cambridge Economic Handbook series, of which series Robertson's was one volume, likely would have changed. Instead of talking of economic theory as 'an apparatus of the mind' helping 'its possessor to draw correct conclusions', he would have stressed that 'correctness', or 'soundness', was an inappropriate or question-begging concept. Instead of countering the picture of there being 'not yet a complete unanimity of opinion amongst professional students of the subject' on 'matters of principle', with the vision of an economics cleared up of controversy, he would have stressed the multitude of possible legal foundations of money and banking, and the multiplicity of answers to all of the relevant questions comprising the field (Robertson, 1929, v–vi). But Keynes was the student of Alfred Marshall. For all his celebrated heterodoxy, Keynes sought the status of professional scientist for economists, sought to bring economics to bear on questions of government policy, and to promote a certain view of science (providing unique determinate solutions) underlying the involvement of economists in policy. His celebrated activism, opposition to laissez-faire, and belief in monetary management were, at bottom, not much if at all different from the effective belief system of other economists, whose agendas for government were less conspicuous. What was different was his refusal to adopt the venerable myths prescribing 'correct' or 'sound' policy unless a substantive and ultimately pragmatic case could be made for them. Much of the difficulty in interpreting Keynes may well stem from his treating, or seeming to treat, certain policies in a non-pragmatic way, that is, substituting his own myths for the received ones.

David Laidler, among others, has shown that one can do the history of monetary economics within the terms understood by the monetary economists who did the work on which he was reporting and interpreting, and do that job very well indeed (Laidler, 1991, 1999). I hope to have shown that monetary economics did in fact encompass more than its previous practitioners recognised. It could have been, it could be in the future, richer than it was in the way it then was practiced.

It is not an exaggeration to argue that the end result of centuries of monetary economics is an underlining of the importance of radical indeterminacy, that is, of uncertainty, and therefore of expectations. It is expectations with which every monetary and macroeconomic theorist has had to come to grips and somehow handle, and they have done so in different ways (Samuels and Spiegel, 1984), some of them almost laughable. The inevitable result of the argument of this chapter is to further emphasise uncertainty and expectations. Take, for example, Jean-Michel Grandmont's elegant, open-minded, and candid *Money and Value* (1983). He concludes, in part, that:

> whenever the traders' learning processes involve short-run rigidities of their expected real interest rates – which is the case in traditional neoclassical macroeconomic models – a short-run Walrasian equilibrium in which money has

> positive value may not exist. Real balance effects are then the essential regulating mechanism of the economy, but they may be too weak to equilibrate the markets.... [I]n order to guarantee the existence of a short-run monetary equilibrium, one has to appeal to... the intertemporal substitution effects that are induced by a variation of the traders' expected real interest rates.... [T]his required basically that some or all traders' expectations about future prices and interest rates are to a large extent insensitive to the variations of current prices and rates of interest. The fact that such restrictions on anticipations are rather implausible show that the existence of a short-run Walrasian monetary equilibrium raises more problems than neoclassical theorists like to believe. (Grandmont, 1983, 150)

If one truly pays attention to the full complexity of actual economies, how much more implausible is any story that ignores, for example, the legal foundations of the monetary and banking system? One conclusion of a century of work by institutional economists is that economic actors resort to government policy to enhance their opportunity sets and to help solve perceived problems. Such legal–institutional changes are an adjustment mechanism functionally no different from, and arguably no more necessarily effective than, interest rates, real balance effects, and the like. Such is the real world of actual economies, not some mystical laissez-faire – like it or not.

Grandmont supports the Keynesian view that 'full price flexibility may not lead to market clearing after all, for the quite simple reason that there may not exist a set of prices and interest rates that would equate Walrasian demands and supplies' (1983, 150). Substitute expectations and legal changes for prices and interest rates, and the enormity of the difficulties of monetary and macroeconomic theory increases exponentially.

A further conclusion reached by Grandmont concerns 'the possibility for monetary authorities to manipulate interest rates or the money supply through their credit or open-market operations.... [T]he main finding was that such a control could well be problematic if the traders' expected real interest rates were to some extent rigid in the short run' (1983, 150–151).

'These conclusions', Grandmont cautions, 'have been reached by studying models deliberately kept simple' (1983, 151). How much greater are the problems of uncertainty and expectations, if one no longer simplifies by omitting the legal foundations, including the processes of legal change.

As for the neutrality of money, Grandmont found that:

> Changes of the money stock or of the nominal rate of interest were found to be neutral in the long run... As for the short run... [traditional monetary policy] was neutral indeed if all agents believed this policy move to be neutral. (1983, 151)

Grandmont also casts 'serious doubts' upon any claim of 'the neutrality of perfectly anticipated, deterministic changes of the money supply' (1983, 151).

Grandmont further concludes that 'the traders' learning processes are among the important characteristics of an economy, and... must be carefully studied, both from a theoretical and an empirical viewpoint'. Thus does a monetary and macroeconomic theorist conclude that belief system, and the attendant process of learning, is important, even for comparatively narrow conceptions of uncertainty and expectations. In a broader context, such as is suggested here, one can even more readily appreciate the importance of efforts to manipulate political–economic psychology and thereby the belief system insofar as it affects economic performance. The actual economy is full of examples of business demands for regulation motivated by desires, for example, to create situations in which it is clear whose interest counts (and, of course, not only clarity is involved but also a structure of rights favourable to them) (Crawford, 1990). Such efforts to change the law comport with and illustrate John Kenneth Galbraith's notion of stability planning in the 'new industrial state' (Galbraith, 1967). The crux of Grandmont's analysis, in any event, is that:

> Postulating rational expectations... is an elegant way to avoid the issue rather than to face it. (1983, 152)

It would be a great irony if physics (Laughlin, 2005), after which many economists think they have been modeling economics as a science, can reinvent itself in terms of parts and wholes, and economics cannot. Clearly, the material lies at hand: there is more to monetary economics than demand and supply, real balance effects, liquidity preference, reserve balances, and the like. From this point of view, it is both important and possible to have more complete understandings of how the economy works than to finesse and obfuscate what it is all about and to have mathematically elegant and ostensibly uniquely determinate results. Uniquely determinate results seem to require conditions that do not exist, and for reasons that underscore and go beyond classical, neoclassical, Keynesian, and post-Keynesian monetary and macroeconomics.

Monetary economics is not fixed in stone. It has long been driven by analytical and ideological motives. No ontologically given monetary economics exists; monetary economics is what monetary economists make it and believe it to be. Its discourse, its definition of scope, its epistemology, can change. Because of the capture of the Quantity Theory by ideological and analytical motives, those who would do monetary theory differently have been marginalised. They need not be. Indeed, it is in the interest of a richer monetary economics that the field expand and change.

Notes

The author is indebted to Robert Babe for many helpful suggestions for revising an earlier version of this chapter.

1. One is almost tempted to say 'objectively' but given the inexorability of multiple viewpoints and interpretations, 'objectively' falsely implies that there is one truth to be

discovered and available for all people. This does not deny the importance of the quest for truth; it does, however, emphasise the interpretation of Adam Smith's argument in his *History of Astronomy* given in the text.

2. The author is aware – indeed, emphasises – that even at the level of abstraction pursued in this paper, a useful objection(s) could be made to every sentence. Some things are, however, well stated, such as 'The IS-LM Model: Its Rise, Fall, and Strange Persistence' (De Vroey and Hoover, 2004) and 'The IS-LM Enigma' (Young, 1987). I also refrain from becoming too specific, for three reasons: I have no personal agenda to advance, I do not predict the future, and I do not want to become involved, any more than is necessary here, in internecine conflicts.
3. A colleague once met a former student on the street. The student remarked that something which he had learned in the professor's course was of enormous value to him. The professor asked what that something was. He later told me that the former student's reply made no sense and that, if he had taught such a doctrine, it was not only wrong and meaningless, he should have been fired.
4. The statements in this paragraph may appear startling, especially if one interprets it as adopting a psychology-inspired, methodological individualist theory of knowledge, untempered by social construction, persuasion, indoctrination, education, money, quest for prestige, etc. As subsequent discussion will show, the political–economy aspects are central, inasmuch as they help determine which of the unidimensional theories will be accepted.
5. This is true also of so-called hard-science scientific communities, not just the softer social sciences; e.g., the Kuhnian and post-Kuhnian reassessment of science.
6. Of course, one could also say the reverse, that different interpretations of what they read or hear enable people to have different systems of belief. Meaning is a site of struggle or tension between different readings, whatever the direction of the flow of causation. There are different systems of belief in complex relationships with different lived positions within the socio-politico-economy (race, class, gender, living conditions).
7. The most recent account of these conflicts is Fraser 2005. See also, for examples, Chesterton, 1978; Gatell, 1967; Means, 2001; Aronson, 1977. For money power as economic nationalism, see Hont, 2005.
8. I do not intend to say that Kuhn has an invisible-hand process in his theory of scientific revolution; only that there is a literature that finds such a process at work in science.
9. The term 'attractiveness' may seem ambiguous here, even perhaps tautological. I intend it to signify that belief-holders might fit in with a group, and as a member of a group receive differential support in accordance with how they align with established power.
10. Postmodernist positions on signs circulating independently of material reality are contradicted but not negated – hence limited – (1) Popperian conjectures, predictions, and refutations, (2) evolutionary language as an adaptive strategy, and (3) the political economy of signs.
11. Believers in a flat earth and in phlogiston give non-secularism a bad name. I emphasise the quest for truth, the improbability of achieving conclusive truth, the fact of the deliberative manufacture of untruth, and that metaphysics (inclusive of theology) with regard to material reality is dubious.
12. 'The Entertainment and Sports Programming Network' (1979–85), ESPN thereafter.
13. Unable to determine date or exact words.
14. Karl Menger wrote of the 'procedure' through which money evolved as 'so opposed to the ordinary course of things [as to seem] downright "mysterious"' (Menger, 1892, 1). Clower, who quoted Menger, writes that 'organized markets arise from the working of natural economic forces; there is no mystery here' (Clower, 1977, 209). Invocation of 'natural economic forces' begs the question of the meaning of 'natural'.
15. Unable to identify name and date of conference.

16. Brunner and Meltzer (1993, 45) identify three stages of the anti-Keynesian critique and counter-revolution, lauding real business cycle theory ('a triumph of ingenuity and technical virtuosity over observation') and saying that 'Rational expectations models of the business cycle began with a particular way of expressing the problem of information'. Their three-stage model is a serious approach, though they build in such obvious minimalism. See also Leeson, 2000.
17. Hayek was clearly deliberative in his presentation; acting as high priest, he performed Durkheim's manifest function. Not all advocates of the policies he identified are, by any means, self-consciously ideological; for them the function served is latent. See also Hayek, 1999a and 1999b. Unable to identify date and name of session.
18. The ensuing discussion follows parts.
19. For centuries economists have been alert to the possibility that admitting to multiplicity might open the door to crackpot views.
20. Unable to identify author, title, or any subsequent publication of the manuscript. (*JEI* files destroyed.)

Discussion

Roger Sandilands

This chapter offers an unusually broad approach to the nature of contemporary monetary theory. It considers monetary theory and policy from a sociological, philosophical, and methodological standpoint that forces us to think of the values or value judgments that lie behind the kind of work we do, or the topics we choose. He forces us to ask whether our work is motivated by a search for esteem from the power elite – whether in society or in academe – or from 'purer' motives.

There might be no conflict if the power elite – what we might call the conventional wisdom – was where Truth and Justice reside. Naturally, Warren rejects that as naive and tries to force us to think of vested interests and what beliefs 'put our mind to rest' and why.

My view is that Warren rather caricatures monetary theory. Or, rather, my impression on reading his paper is that it is largely motivated by his impatience with a narrow version of the quantity theory of money as an abstraction, but also as a core element of a conservative political agenda: viz, money is important; money is power. But the quantity theory can also be read as telling us that if we leave the control of money to the power elite they can use it to keep inflation under control, stabilise the economy, and so serve the *public* interest, too. Having achieved that, conservative adherents to the theory may go further and imply that there would then be no need to worry too much about the need to intervene in other areas of the economy: that can be left to the market, to laissez-faire. This seems to be one of Warren's complaints.

This view perhaps caricatures Warren's position but, despite his early disclaimers, I do sense that a prime underlying motive is to attack a popular view of the Chicago School approach to monetary theory and policy, and their related world view. Be that as it may, his is a plea for eclecticism and a recognition of not only the diversity of schools of economic thought, but also of what other social disciplines can offer. Also, he sees a disjoint between our theorizing – abstract, unrealistic, devoid of historical and institutional context – and our eagerness to be policy advisers or practitioners in the real world of power politics. Cynically, and not so cynically, he sees this as evidence on the one hand of our seeking the prestige and academic advancement that come from clever theorizing, while at the same time seeking the money and power that come from engaging in the dirty business of policymaking.

It is not a pretty picture, and I am naive enough to believe there are many more economists who do not deserve Warren's scorn than he is prepared to admit. In other words, I think he protests o'er much.

Be that as it may, I found this chapter extremely stimulating, and as I read it I thought of a multitude of examples that both supported and denied his thesis. Permit me to refer to one example drawn from my own contribution to the Laidler conference in which I detailed the case of Lauchlin Currie as an example of an economist who has combined intelligent theoretical analysis of a problem in monetary economics with the intelligent *application* of that analysis to policy-making, the law, and institution-building.

In my chapter I mention his diagnosis of the theoretical belief system of the Fed. in 1928–29 as being that what mattered was close monitoring of productive credit rather than control of the money supply. This showed (as least in the eyes of Currie and, later, of Friedman and Schwartz, and Allan Meltzer) the damage that the real-bills doctrine could cause. The opposing 'monetary' diagnosis was not just an abstraction. It was a matter of empirical analysis of how the money supply and its velocity moved with the business cycle (though Warren's paper does warn us that every business cycle 'is depressed in its own way'). Currie's pioneering estimates of the income velocity of money showed it to move pro-cyclically. This, in turn, led to a study of the banking structure and how differing reserve requirements and degrees of indebtedness among different classes of bank affected movements of money during the cycle. This led on to the question of the beneficence or otherwise of branch banking and investment banking (as also mentioned by Warren in his paper), and also to how to increase or strengthen the instruments available to the central bank to control money more effectively, and in the public interest.

This was the point of the ensuing 1935 Banking Act. This resulted from the collaboration of Currie with the new governor of the Fed., Marriner Eccles, who was appointed by President Roosevelt only after Eccles had sought an assurance that the president would support the conditions of an eight-point plan drawn up by Currie. The conditions were entirely in line with a restructuring of the Fed. and its powers over reserves, eligible assets, etc. that would better enable it to control the money supply and avert another Great Contraction. These conditions flowed from theory – they involved institutional and legal arrangements that conformed with the theory, plus an awareness of how to cultivate and influence the people who could better implement policy within the reformed institutions.

I can give a second example more directly familiar to me in my work with Currie in Colombia over 25 years. There, Currie diagnosed a propensity to chronic inflation – and the immense damage this did – as residing in the composition of the Junta Monetaria – the monetary board of the central bank. This was dominated by the spending ministers and it served both as a Central Bank and as a Development Bank. Multiple objectives make for great confusion (as Milton Friedman reminded us in his conference presentation). Preserving stability for the value of money *was* a noble objective. It ultimately served the interests not only of the power elite – and our mission must be to make them aware of that – but also of the general public, not least the poorest and weakest.

In particular, inflation had severe non-neutral effects on the allocation of resources. It especially discriminated against the capture of savings for housing finance. The indexation of the assets and liabilities of new specialist housing finance institutions was a plan that encountered extreme hostility from vested interests, especially bankers and those who had already bought houses with conventional fixed-interest mortgages. By invoking an obscure clause in the Constitution that vested in the president personal power to intervene in the field of personal savings, just three people were able to push through highly controversial legislation against all that opposition: the president, Currie, and the head of the national planning department, Roberto Arenas, whom Currie cultivated, advised, and educated as assiduously as he had done with Marriner Eccles in the 1930s.

Again, though, it was a case of *conformity* of theory with the general interest above the vested interests; indeed, of the possibility that the money interest may be made to *coincide* with the public interest – to give a twist to the title of the book by Perry Mehrling (*The Money Interest and the Public Interest: American Monetary Thought 1920–1970*, Harvard University Press, 1997) that Warren has cited. Mehrling has shown that in the hands of some of our best monetary theorists – and his book treats of Allyn Young, Alvin Hansen, and Ed Shaw – Warren's indictment of our profession is both too overblown but also very salutary.

References

Achino-Loeb, Maria-Luisa (2005). *Silence: The Currency of Power*. New York: Berghahn.

Ackerman, Bruce A. (1983). *Reconstructing American Law*. Cambridge, MA: Harvard University Press.

Arnold, Thurman (1935). *The Symbols of Government*. New Haven, CT: Yale University Press.

Arnold, Thurman (1937). *The Folklore of Capitalism*. New Haven, CT: Yale University Press.

Aronowitz, Stanley (1992). *The Politics of Identity: Class, Culture, Social Movements*. New York: Routledge.

Aronson, Jonathan David. (1977). *Money and Power: Banks and the World Monetary System*. Beverly Hills, CA: Sage.

Auerbach, Carl A. (1959). "Law and Social Change in the United States." *UCLA Law Review* 6, 516–532.

Auerbach, Carl A., Lloyd K. Garrison, Willard Hurst, and Samuel Mermin, eds. (1961). *The Legal Process*. San Francisco, CA: Chandler.

Backhaus, Jürgen G., ed. (1999). *The Elgar Companion to Law and Economics*. Northampton, MA: Edward Elgar.

Barbour, Ian G. (1974). *Myths, Models and Paradigms*. New York: Harper & Row.
Berger, Peter L. and Thomas Luckmann (1966). *The Social Construction of Reality*. Garden City, NY: Doubleday.
Binswanger, Hans Christoph (1994). *Money and Magic: A Critique of the Modern Economy in the Light of Goethe's Faust*. Chicago, IL: University of Chicago Press.
Bloor, David (1991). *Knowledge and Social Imagery*, 2nd ed. Chicago, IL: University of Chicago Press.
Bondi, H. (1967). *Assumption and Myth in Physical Theory*. New York: Cambridge University Press.
Boorstin, Daniel J. (1958). *The Mysterious Science of the Law*. Boston, MA: Beacon.
Bouckaert, Boudewijn and Gerrit de Geest, eds. (1992). *Bibliography of Law and Economics*. Boston, MA: Kluwer Academic Publishers.
Boulding, Kenneth E. (1956). *The Image*. Ann Arbor, MI: University of Michigan Press.
Brunner, Karl and Allan H. Meltzer (1993). *Money and the Economy: Issues in Monetary Analysis*. New York: Cambridge University Press.
Buch, Esteban (2003). *Beethoven's Ninth: A Political History*. Chicago, IL: University of Chicago Press.
Buchanan, James M. and Marilyn R. Flowers (1975). *The Public Finances, An Introductory Textbook*. Homewood, IL: Richard Irwin.
Burke, Peter and Roy Porter, eds. (1987). *The Social History of Language*. New York: Cambridge University Press.
Campbell, Joseph (1972). *Myths to Live By*. New York: Bantam.
Cassel, Gustav (1932). *The Crisis in the World's Monetary System*, 2nd ed. London: Oxford University Press.
Chesterton, A. K. (1978). *The Menace of the Money-Power: An Analysis of World Government by Finance*. Metairie, LA: Sons of Liberty.
Chomsky, Noam (1988). *Language and Politics*. C. P. Otero, ed. New York: Black Rose Books.
Clower, Robert W. (1977). "The Anatomy of Monetary Theory." *American Economic Review, Papers and Proceedings* 67:1 (February), 206–212.
Coase, Ronald H. (1992). "The Institutional Structure of Production." *American Economic Review* 82:4 (September), 713–719.
Cole, G. D. H., ed. (1933). *What Everybody Wants to Know About Money*. London: Victor Gollancz.
Commons, John R. (1924). *Legal Foundations of Capitalism*. New York: Macmillan.
Corfield, Penelope J., ed. (1991). *Language, History and Class*. Cambridge, MA: Basil Blackwell.
Cottrell, P. L. and D. E. Moggridge, eds. (1988). *Money and Power: Essays in Honour of L. S. Pressnell*. Basingstoke: Macmillan.
Crawford, Mark (1990). "Biotech Companies Lobby for Federal Regulation." *Science* 248 (May 4), 546–547.
Degré, Geerard (1985). *The Social Compulsion of Ideas*. New Brunswick, NJ: Transaction Books.
De Vroey, Michel and Kevin D. Hoover, eds. (2004). *The IS-LM Model: Its Rise, Fall, and Strange Persistence*. Durham, NC: Duke University Press.
Dimand, Robert W. (2005). "The Roots of the Present are in the Past: The Relation of Postwar Developments in Macroeconomics to Interwar Business Cycle Business Cycle and Monetary Theory." Manuscript.
Durkheim, Emile (1964). *Rules of Sociological Method*. New York: Free Press.
Eaton, Ralph Monroe (1925). *Symbolism and Truth*. Cambridge, MA: Harvard University Press. Reprinted by Dover, New York: 1964.
Edelman, Murray (1964). *The Symbolic Uses of Politics*. Urbana, IL: University of Illinois Press.
Ellul, Jacques (1984). *Money and Power*. Downers Grove, IL: Inter-Varsity Press.
Evensky, Jerry (2005). *Adam Smith's Moral Philosophy*. New York: Cambridge University Press.

Feibleman, James K. (1969). *The Reach of Politics: A New Look at Government*. New York: Horizon.
Ferguson, Niall (2001). *The Cash Nexus: Money and Power in the Modern World, 1700–2000*. New York: Basic Books.
Fiorito, Luca and Warren J. Samuels (2006). "Robert Hoxie's Introductory Lecture on the Nature of the History of Political Economy: The Problem of the Teaching the History of Error." *Research in the History of Economic Thought and Methodology* 24-C, 40–97.
Fitzpatrick, Peter (1992). *The Mythology of Modern Law*. New York: Routledge.
Fraser, Steve (2005). *Every Man a Speculator: A History of Wall Street in American Life*. New York: HarperCollins.
Friedman, Lawrence M. (1985). *A History of American Law*, 2nd ed. New York: Simon & Schuster.
Friedman, Wolfgang (1972). *Law in a Changing Society*, 2nd ed. Baltimore, MD: Penguin.
Galbraith, John Kenneth (1967). *The New Industrial State*. Boston, MA: Houghton Mifflin.
Gani, Mohammad (2005). "Why Teach the History of Error?" *EH.Net* (June 21), 8:19 AM.
Gatell, Frank Otto (1967). *The Jacksonians and the Money Power, 1829–1840*. Chicago, IL: Rand McNally.
Geuss, Raymond (2001). *History and Illusion in Politics*. New York: Cambridge University Press.
Gonner, E. C. K. (1899). *The Social Philosophy of Rodbertus*. New York: Macmillan.
Grandmont, Jean-Michel (1983). *Money and Value: A Reconsideration of Classical and Neoclassical Monetary Theories*. New York: Cambridge University Press.
Harris, Nigel (1971). *Beliefs in Society*. Baltimore, MD: Penguin.
Hayek, Friedrich A. von (1999a). *Good Money, Part I: The New World*. Stephen Kresge, ed. Chicago, IL: University of Chicago Press.
Hayek, Friedrich A. von (1999b). *Good Money, Part II: The Standard*. Stephen Kresge, ed. Chicago, IL: University of Chicago Press.
Hobsbawn, E. J. (1962). *The Age of Revolution, 1789–1848*. Cleveland, OH: World.
Hobsbawn, E. J. and Terence Ranger, eds. (1983). *The Invention of Tradition*. New York: Cambridge University Press.
Hont, Istvan (2005). *Jealousy of Trade: International Competition and the Nation-State in Historical Perspective*. Cambridge, MA: Harvard University Press.
Horwitz, Morton J. (1977). *The Transformation of American Law, 1780–1860*. Cambridge, MA: Harvard University Press.
Hurst, James Willard (1982). *Law and Markets in United States History*. Madison, WI: University of Wisconsin Press.
Hurst, James Willard. (1977). *Law and Social Order in the United States*. Ithaca, NY: Cornell University Press.
Hurst, James Willard (1973). *A Legal History of Money in the United States, 1774–1970*. Lincoln, NE: University of Nebraska Press.
Hurst, James Willard (1970). *The Legitimacy of the Business Corporation in the Law of the United States, 1780–1970*. Charlottesville, VA: University Press of Virginia.
Hurst, James Willard (1964a). *Law and the Conditions of Freedom in the Nineteenth-Century United States*. Madison, WI: University of Wisconsin Press.
Hurst, James Willard (1964b). *Law and Economic Growth*. Cambridge, MA: Harvard University Press.
Janos, Andrew C. (1986). *Politics and Paradigms: Changing Theories of Change in Social Science*. Palo Alto, CA: Stanford University Press.
Jones, Gareth Stedman (1983). *Languages of Class: Studies in English Working Class History, 1832–1982*. New York: Cambridge University Press.
Jones, Norman (1989). *God and the Money Lenders*. Boston, MA: Basil Blackwell.
Kelsen, Hans (1945). *General Theory of Law and State*. Cambridge, MA: Harvard University Press.

Kendall, Kathleen E. (1995). *Presidential Campaign Discourse: Strategic Communication Problems*. Albany, NY: SUNY Press.
Keynes, John Maynard (1973). *The General Theory of Employment, Interest and Money*, ed., Donald Moggridge, London: Macmillan, volume 7 of *Collected Writings of John Maynard Keynes*.
Knight, Frank H. (1960). *Intelligence and Democratic Action*. Cambridge, MA: Harvard University Press.
Krausz, Michael, ed. (2002). *Is There a Single Right Interpretation?* University Park, PA: Penn State University Press.
Kselman, Thomas, ed. (1991). *Belief in History*. Notre Dame, IN: University of Notre Dame Press.
Kwon, Hyeong-Ki (2004). *Fairness and Division of Labor in Market Societies*. New York: Berghahn.
Lagemann, Ellen Condliffe (1989). *The Politics of Knowledge: The Carnegie Corporation, Philanthropy, and Public Policy*. Chicago, IL: University of Chicago Press.
Laidler, David (1999). *Fabricating the Keynesian Revolution*. New York: Cambridge University Press.
Laidler, David (1991). *The Golden Age of the Quantity Theory*. Princeton, NJ: Princeton University Press.
Lakoff, George and Mark Johnson (1980). *Metaphors We Live By*. Chicago, IL: University of Chicago Press.
Laughlin, Robert B. (2005). *A Different Universe: Reinventing Physics from the Bottom Down*. New York: Basic Books.
Leeson, Robert (2000). *The Eclipse of Keynesianism: The Political Economy of the Chicago Counter-Revolution*. New York: Palgrave.
Lelyveld, Joseph (2005). "The Strange Case of Chaplain Yee." *New York Review of Books* (December 15), 8–14.
Lerner, Abba (1972). "The Economics and Politics of Consumer Sovereignty." *American Economic Review* 62:2 (May), 258–266.
Lloyd, Dennis (1964). *The Idea of Law*. Baltimore, MD: Penguin.
Malloy, Robin Paul (2000). *Law and Market Economy. Reinterpreting the Values of Law and Economics*. New York: Cambridge University Press.
Malthus, Thomas Robert (1798). *An Essay on the Principle of Population*. London: J. Johnson.
Means, Howard B. (2001). *Money and Power: The History of Business*. New York: Wiley.
Mehrling, Perry G. (1997). *The Money Interest and the Public Interest: American Monetary Thought, 1920–1970*. Cambridge, MA: Harvard University Press.
Meja, Vollker and Nico Stehr, eds. (1990). *Knowledge and Politics: The Sociology of Knowledge Dispute*. New York: Routledge.
Menger, Karl (1892). "On the Origin of Money." *Economic Journal* 2 (June), 239–255.
Mercuro, Nicholas (2005). "Government's Touch Pervades Technology." *Fedtech* 2:3 (August), 16–17.
Merton, Robert K. (1949). *Social Theory and Social Structure*. Glencoe, IL: Free Press.
Mishan, Ezra J. (1986). *Economic Myths and the Mythology of Economics*. Atlantic Highlands, NJ: Humanities Press.
Mitchell, Wesley C. (1937). *The Backward Art of Spending Money, and Other Essays*. New York: McGraw-Hill.
Moessinger, Pierre (2000). *The Paradox of Social Order*. New Brunswick, NJ: Transaction.
Nelson, William E. (1975). *Americanization of the Common Law*. Cambridge, MA: Harvard University Press.
Nossiter, Bernard D. (1964). *The Mythmakers: An Essay on Power and Wealth*. Boston, MA: Houghton Mifflin.
Novak, Michael and John W. Cooper, eds. (1981a). *The Corporation: A Theological Inquiry*. Washington, D.C.: American Enterprise Institute for Public Policy Research.

Novak, Michael and John W. Cooper, eds. (1981b). *Toward a Theology of the Corporation.* Washington, D.C.: American Enterprise Institute for Public Policy Research.

Ortony, Andrew, ed. (1993). *Metaphor and Thought*, 2nd ed. New York: Cambridge University Press.

Pareto, Vilfredo (1963). *The Mind and Society.* New York: Dover.

Parsons, Talcott (1949). *The Structure of Social Action.* Glencoe, IL: Free Press.

Phelps, Edmund S. (1990). *Seven Schools of Macroeconomic Thought.* London: Oxford University Press.

Poggi, Gianfranco (1993). *Money and the Modern Mind: Georg Simmel's Philosophy of Money.* Los Angeles, CA: University of California Press.

Pound, Roscoe (1937). *An Introduction to the Philosophy of Law.* New York: Oxford University Press.

Pressnell, L. S. (1956). *Country Banking in the Industrial Revolution.* London: Oxford University Press.

Raffield, Paul (2004). *Images and Cultures of Law in Early Modern England: Justice and Political Power, 1558–1660.* New York: Cambridge University Press.

Reddy, William M. (1987). *Money and Liberty in Modern Europe.* New York: Cambridge University Press.

Rex, John (1974). *Sociology and the Demystification of the Modern World.* Boston: Routledge & Kegan Paul.

Rieter, H. (1998). "Quantity Theory of Money." In Heinz D. Kurz and Neri Salvadori, eds., *The Elgar Companion to Classical Economics*, Vol. 2. Cheltenham: Edward Elgar, pp. 239–248.

Robertson, D. H. (1929). *Money.* New edition revised. New York: Harcourt, Brace.

Robertson, D. H. (1957). *Money.* Chicago, IL: University of Chicago Press.

Robinson, James Harvey (1921). *The Mind in the Making.* New York: Harper.

Robinson, Joan (1962). *Economic Philosophy.* London: Watts.

Rogers, James Steven (1995). *The Early History of the Law of Bills and Notes: A Study of the Origins of Anglo-American Commercial Law.* New York: Cambridge University Press.

Rundblad, Gabriella and David B. Kronenfeld (2003). "The Inevitability of Folk Etymology: A Case of Collective Reality and Invisible Hands." *Journal of Pragmatics* 35, 119–138.

Samuel, Raphael and Paul Thompson (1990). *The Myths We Live By.* New York: Routledge.

Samuels, Warren J. (Forthcoming). "Poletown and Hathcock: An Essay on Some Problems in the Language of the Law." In Warren J. Samuels, ed., *The Legal-Economic Nexus.* New York: Routledge, pp. 175–252.

Samuels, Warren J. (2006). "Interpreting the Bible, the U.S. Constitution, and the History of Economic Thought." *Research in the History of Economic Thought and Methodology* 24-A, 79–98.

Samuels, Warren J. (2004). "Markets and Their Social Construction." *Social Research* 71:2 (Summer), 357–370

Samuels, Warren J. (2001). "Some Problems in the Use of Language in Economics." *Review of Political Economy* 13:1, 91–100.

Samuels, Warren J., ed. (1998). *Law and Economics*, 2 vols. London: Pickering & Chatto.

Samuels, Warren J. (1997). "The Concept of 'Coercion' in Economics." In Warren J. Samuels, Steven G. Medema and A. Allan Schmid, eds., *The Economy as a Process of Valuation.* Lyme, NH: Edward Elgar, pp. 129–207.

Samuels, Warren J. (1996). "Joseph J. Spengler's Concept of the 'Problem of Order': A Reconsideration and Extension." In Philip Arestis, ed., *Employment, Economic Growth and the Tyranny of the Market.* Brookfield, VT: Edward Elgar, pp. 185–199.

Samuels, Warren J. (1995a). "Some Thoughts on Multiplicity." *Journal of Economic Methodology* 2 (December), 287–291.

Samuels, Warren J. (1995b). "Society is a Process of Mutual Coercion and Governance Selectively Perceived." *Critical Review* 9:3 (Summer), 437–443.

Samuels, Warren J. (1989). "The Legal-Economic Nexus." *George Washington Law Review* 57 (August), 1556–1578.
Samuels, Warren J. (1984). "On the Nature and Existence of Economic Coercion: The Correspondence of Robert Lee Hale and Thomas Nixon Carver." *Journal of Economic Issues* 18 (December), 1027–1048.
Samuels, Warren J. (1974). *Pareto on Policy*. Cleveland, OH: World.
Samuels, Warren J., Marianne Johnson and Kirk Johnson (2004–6). "The Duke of Argyll and Edwin L. Godkin as Precursors to Hayek on the Relation of Ignorance to Policy." Part I. *Storia del Pensiero Economico* 1:1, 5–32. Part II, *Storia del Pensiero Economico* 1:2 (2004), 37–67. Part III, *Storia del Pensiero Economico* 2:1 (2005), 35–71. Part IV, *Storia del Pensiero Economico* 2.
Samuels, Warren J. and Henry W. Spiegel, eds. (1984). *Contemporary Economists in Perspective*, 2 vols. Greenwich: JAI Press.
Schmid, A. Allan (1982). "Symbolic Barriers to Full Employment: The Role of Public Debt." *Journal of Economic Issues* XVI:1 (March), 281–294.
Schmid, A. Allan (1984). "Broadening Capital Ownership." In Guy Alperovitz and Roger Skurski, eds., *New Directions in Economic Policy*. Notre Dame, IN: University of Notre Dame Press, pp. 117–137.
Schmid, A. Allan (2004). *Conflict and Cooperation: Institutional and Behavioral Economics*. Oxford: Blackwell, pp. 187–190.
Schumpeter, Joseph A. (1950). *Capitalism, Socialism, and Democracy*. Cambridge, MA: Harvard University Press.
Seaford, Richard (2004). *Money and the Early Greek Mind*. New York: Cambridge University Press.
Searle, John R. (1995). *The Construction of Social Reality*. New York: Free Press.
Sederberg, Peter C. (1984). *The Politics of Meaning: Power and Explanation in the Construction of Social Reality*. Tucson, AZ: University of Arizona Press.
Shackle, George L. S. (1967). *The Years of High Theory: Invention and Tradition in Economic Thought, 1926–1939*. New York: Cambridge University Press.
Shell, Marc (1993). *Money, Language, and Thought*. Baltimore, MD: Johns Hopkins University Press.
William J. Shultz and C. Lowell Harriss (1965). *American Public Finance*. Englewood Cliffs NJ: Prentice-Hall.
Simmel, Georg (1990). *The Philosophy of Money*. David Frisby, ed. 2nd ed. New York: Routledge.
Skillen, Anthony (1978). *Ruling Illusions: Philosophy and the Social Order*. Atlantic Highlands, NJ: Humanities Press.
Smith, Adam (1980). "The History of Astronomy." In *Essays on Philosophical Subjects*. New York: Oxford University Press, pp. 33–105.
Smith, Anthony (1980). *The Geopolitics of Information*. New York: Oxford University Press.
Starr, June and Jane F. Collier, eds. (1989). *History and Power in the Study of Law*. Ithaca, NY: Cornell University Press.
Stigler, George J. (1966). *The Theory of Price*, 3rd ed. New York: Macmillan.
Straub, Jürgen (2006). *Narration, Identity, and Historical Consciousness*. New York: Berghahn.
Sutton, John (2000). *Marshall's Tendencies: What Can Economists Know*. Cambridge, MA: MIT Press.
Tandy, David (2005). "Book Review." *EH.Net* (March 9, 10:42).
Taylor, John F. A. (1966). *The Masks of Society*. New York: Appleton-Century-Crofts.
Tigar, Michael E. and Madeleine R. Levy (1977). *Law and the Rise of Capitalism*. New York: Monthly Review Press.
Tinder, Glenn (1989). *The Political Meaning of Christianity: An Interpretation*. Baton Rouge, LA: LSU Press.
Turner, James (1979). *The Politics of Landscape*. Cambridge, MA: Harvard University Press.

Wallace, Mike (2005). "All the World is Green." *The Nation* April 18, 25–32.

Will, George (2002). "It's Time Bush Showed Anger Over Enron." *Jewish World Review* (January 16), 3.

Wittgenstein, Ludwig (1953). *Philosophical Investigations*. Oxford: Basil Blackwell.

Wood, John H. (2005). *A History of Central Banking in Great Britain and the United States*. New York: Cambridge University Press.

Yee, James (2005). *For God and Country: Faith and Patriotism Under Fire*. New York: Public Affairs.

Young, Warren (1987). *Interpreting Mr Keynes: The IS-LM Enigma*. Boulder, CO: Westview.

Zelizer, Viviana A. (1994). *The Social Meaning of Money*. New York: Basic Books.

10
Monetary Policy Implementation: A Microstructure Approach

Perry Mehrling

In classic central banking theory, the 'discount house' played a central role (Bagehot, 1873, Sayers, 1976).[1] As holders of short-term commercial bills, the discount houses financed the holding of goods on their way from producers to consumers, and, in turn, financed themselves primarily by borrowing from banks. Just so, an expansion of trade went hand in hand with an expansion of both the assets and liabilities of the discount houses, and also an expansion of both the assets and liabilities of the banking system. Looking through the balance sheet relationships, it was clear to observers that the expansion of trade was financed by an expansion of bank money, meaning the deposit liabilities of the banking system.

It was further clear to observers that the key to potential control of such a system was the regular exposure – not to say the systematic vulnerability – of the discount houses. In their search for profit, the discount houses regularly sought to expand their balance sheets to the maximum on a given capitalization base, while at the same time holding essentially no cash reserve. For their daily cash needs, they relied instead on inflows from maturing bills in their possession, on access to bank credit, and ultimately on a discount facility at the Bank of England.

The institutional importance of this discount facility is the fundamental reason for the central role in classic central banking theory of so-called Bank Rate, which was the rate charged by the Bank of England for the discount. Whenever the discount houses ran short of cash, they turned to the Bank of England as their lender of last resort and paid the posted price. This was so, whether the shortage arose from some imbalance in the flow of their own discounts that banks were unwilling to accommodate, or because of imbalances elsewhere in the economy that caused banks to reduce their outstanding exposure to the discount houses.

It is important to emphasize here that normally Bank Rate was set somewhat above the prevailing market rate of discount. It was supposed to be a penal rate in order to discourage regular use, and also to permit the Bank of England to control its own balance sheet (and hence the central reserve) rather than to accept passively any and all requests for rediscount. When the Bank engaged in the market on its own initiative, buying or selling bills for its own account, it did so not at Bank Rate but rather at the prevailing market rate. Such open market operations, as we would now call them, had the effect of expanding or contracting the deposit liabilities of the Bank of England, and hence ultimately the cash reserves of the banking system.

What leverage the Bank enjoyed over the market rate of interest derived from its ability to make cash sufficiently scarce that banks would call in loans to the discount houses, which, in turn, would borrow from the Bank at Bank Rate. Seemingly, if it was prepared to apply enough pressure, the Bank could force market rate to equal Bank Rate. Hence, by application of somewhat less force, the Bank could presumably move market rate closer to or farther from Bank Rate. That was the theory anyway. In practice, banks could, and sometimes did, frustrate the intentions of the Bank by allowing their reserve ratios rather than their call loans to absorb open market operations.[2] (Even in classic central banking theory, the 'velocity' of money was by no means a constant, neither in theory nor in practice.) Over time the problem of 'making Bank Rate effective' became all the more challenging as the size and sophistication of money and capital markets increased relative to the Bank's own balance sheet.

The underlying context for all this balance sheet activity was of course the working of the international gold standard, according to which net payment flows into and out of the country caused the gold reserve at the central bank to fluctuate. Every gold flow posed a policy choice for the Bank, whether to allow cash outstanding to fluctuate with gold holdings, or instead to allow the gold reserve ratio to fluctuate, or some policy in between. Phrased in terms of prices rather than quantities, the choice was whether to allow fluctuation of international reserves fully to affect the market rate of interest, or not at all, or something in between. This choice, it will be perceived, was analogous to the choice that individual banks faced when subject to fluctuation of their own reserve, and in line with that analogy central bank discretion proved to be an additional locus of potential elasticity in the velocity of money.

For various reasons, this classic mode of analysis fell into disfavor in the decades after World War II. One reason was the shift of the center of the world monetary system from London to New York, where the commercial bill had never played such a central role. Another reason was war finance, which flooded the world with government paper, much of it in the form of long-term bonds rather than the traditional short-term Treasury Bills. And yet a third reason was the shift at Bretton Woods from a gold standard to a dollar standard. These institutional

Banking System		**Discount Houses**		**Bank of England**	
Assets	**Liabilities**	**Assets**	**Liabilities**	**Assets**	**Liabilities**
Cash Loans	Deposits	Bills	Bank loans	Gold Bills	Cash

Figure 10.1 Simplified balance sheet relationships

changes called for adjustment of the classic theory, and some such adjustments were forthcoming (Sayers, 1957, 1960, chapter 10), but they failed to carry the day. Instead, a new style of analysis, that elsewhere I have called Monetary Walrasianism (Mehrling, 1997), took the forefront, exemplified by the work of Patinkin, Modigliani, and above all James Tobin (1969).

Under the new theory, attention shifted from Bank Rate to the market rate, and to some extent from the short rate to the long rate, as attention shifted also from financing trade to financing capital investment. Now the central bank was supposed to derive its leverage over market rates from its ability to alter the relative supply of various financial assets outstanding, using its own balance sheet. In this way of thinking, open market operations were nothing more than the purchase of one asset and the simultaneous sale of another, and they produced their effect on the structure of asset prices depending on the relative demand elasticities of the final asset-holders. The discount facility of the Federal Reserve System fell into disuse, and so, too, did the classic theory of central banking with its emphasis on Bank Rate.[3]

The new theory was perhaps well suited to the relatively rigid and highly regulated structure of banking and finance in the immediate decades after World War II. That was, after all, the institutional setting for which it was developed. (The new theory was also well suited to the new styles of academic discourse, but that is another story.) Subsequent decades, however, saw fundamental change in the institutional setting, including the revival of flexible private capital markets and the deregulation of banking. For this new institutional setting, Monetary Walrasianism had a big problem. The balance sheet of the central bank was simply dwarfed by the size of the markets in which it dealt. The idea that open market operations on any reasonable scale could have a significant effect on relative asset supplies was called into question (Friedman, 2000). And the idea that changes in relative asset supplies could have significant effects on asset prices was further called into question by the rise of modern finance theory, with its implication that the demand for any particular financial asset should be highly elastic (Black, 1970).

Given this state of affairs, it may be time to reconsider classic banking theory, albeit in suitably updated form. To recapitulate, the classic theory emphasized not the direct effects of open market operations, but rather the indirect effects on the balance sheets of financial intermediaries. Given institutional change, it seems clear that an updated version of the classic theory should emphasize security dealers rather than discount houses. Financing their long bond positions largely with repurchase agreements, and their short bond positions largely with reverse repurchase agreements, modern security dealers operate simultaneously in both capital and money markets, playing a key role in each but most importantly providing the key link between the two markets. From the point of view of classic central banking theory it is here, if anywhere, that the modern central bank must acquire its leverage over the asset prices that influence spending decisions.

Indeed, from the classic point of view, it is surprising how little attention has been paid in the modern literature to the money market in general, and to the repo market in particular. On the one hand, the tradition of Monetary Walrasianism has offered well-developed theories of the demand and supply of money proper, but that has meant mainly bank deposits and almost nothing on money markets more broadly (Tobin, 1969; Modigliani, Rasche, and Cooper, 1970). On the other hand, the newer financial economics has offered well-developed theories of the microstructure of capital markets, but that has meant mainly stocks and bonds, and again almost nothing on money markets (Harris, 2003). The repo market has largely fallen between these two intellectual stools.

Recent bridge-building between the two intellectual traditions of monetary and financial economics has begun to remedy this gap. From the monetary side, we have seen the growth of a literature on monetary policy implementation, a literature that takes seriously the operations of the financial markets in which the central bank intervenes (Bindseil, 2004). From the finance side, we have seen the growth of a literature on the microstructure of foreign exchange markets, a literature that expands the concerns of finance from capital markets to currency markets (Lyons, 2001; Evans, 2005). The present chapter uses the microstructure approach of the latter as a theoretical entrypoint for the practical problems addressed by the former.[4]

The repo market

In both the US and Europe, repo markets have grown enormously over the postwar period.[5] One survey reports US outstanding volume of repo and reverse repo (both DVP and tri-party) as $5.2 trillion (Bond Market Association, 2005).[6] (By comparison, the most recent measure of the M1 money supply is about $1.4 trillion, which includes $621 billion checkable deposits against $43 billion aggregate reserves, much of which is held in the form of vault cash. Depository institution reserves held at the Fed are only $21 billion.[7]) Within the enormous repo market, dealer-to-dealer transactions account for more than half of the volume, but the range of other counterparties includes essentially all types of financial institutions, both public and private, as well as non-financial corporations. Of particular interest for this chapter, the Federal Reserve Bank is identified as the counterparty in only 1.2% of non-dealer DVP transactions.[8]

Given the scale of the market, it is fair to say that the overnight repo rate is the best general measure of the cost of funds in the money market, but there are two other more specialized interbank rates that tend to receive more attention. The Eurodollar rate, more often today called US LIBOR to distinguish it from Euro LIBOR, is the rate banks charge both bank and non-bank clients for their own overnight interbank deposits. Even more specialized, the Fed Funds rate is the rate banks charge other banks for overnight deposits at the Federal Reserve.[9] In general, the three money markets are closely integrated and all three rates move together (Demiralp, Preslopsky, and Whitesell, 2004; Bartolini, Hilton, and Prati, 2005). However, on average (though not always) the repo rate has been lower than the Fed Funds rate, and the Eurodollar rate slightly higher than the Fed Funds rate.[10]

As an illustration, the chart below shows a year of variation of the overnight repo rate and the overnight Eurodollar rate around the Fed Funds target. Except for days immediately preceding a target hike, when market rates typically rise above the current target in anticipation, the repo rate was consistently below the target. Indeed, the dates of target hikes stand out by contrast: August 9, September 20, November 1, and December 13 in 2005, and January 31, March 28, May 10, and June 29 in 2006.

The reason for this rate pattern is, in my view, an open question. Credit risk is the standard answer since repo is secured credit while Fed Funds are unsecured, but this answer is not convincing. No one lends $10MM overnight if there is even the slightest perceived risk of default, nor has there been historical experience of default in the Fed Funds market; default risk is handled by strict controls on credit lines, not by price.[11] To anticipate the argument below, I suggest alternatively that the Fed Funds rate should be viewed as analogous to the classic Bank Rate, a penal rate that lies normally above the repo rate which is analogous to the classic market rate (Figure 10.2).

The Fed Funds rate is the rate targeted by the Federal Reserve, but the operational implementation of that rate involves almost daily trading in the much larger repo market at the repo rate of interest. In 2005, the Fed undertook 256 separate short-term temporary operations in the repo market, with an average size of $6.54 billion (Federal Reserve Bank of New York, 2006). By design, the Fed is typically a lender in the market, and it increases its repo assets by increasing its deposit liabilities, so increasing system reserves.[12] The size of these daily interventions is tiny in comparison with the size of the repo market, but huge

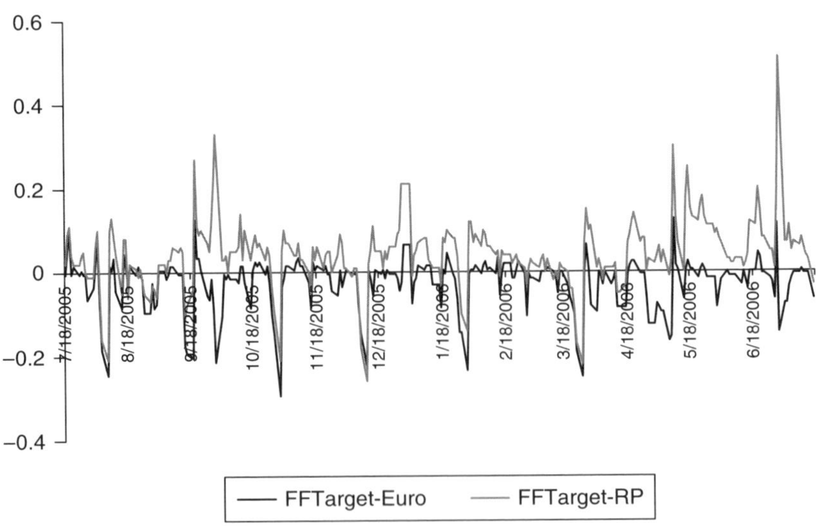

Figure 10.2 A year of bank rate

in comparison with the stock of reserves.[13] (Recall that total depository institution reserves held at the Fed are only $21 billion.) The perceived importance of the Fed Funds market for monetary policy has stimulated an extensive empirical literature to understand how it works.[14] By comparison, repo markets are almost entirely unstudied; the Fed does not even publish a repo rate series among its extensive statistical coverage of interest rates.

What we know about the repo market comes mainly from balance sheet data for the subset of so-called primary security dealers who commit to bid at Treasury debt sales. As dealers, they stand ready at all times to buy and sell securities at posted bid and ask prices, and hence operate as suppliers of liquidity to the bond market.[15] But their net positions in the market as of March 15, 2006 show more than that (see Table 10.1). As arbitrageurs, buying in one market and selling in another closely related market, dealers operate also as 'porters' of liquidity from

Table 10.1 Primary dealer positions in U.S. Government, Federal Agency, Government Sponsored Enterprise, Mortgage-backed, and Corporate Securities, as-of close of trading March 15, 2006, in millions of dollars

Type of Security	Net Outright Position
U.S. Government Securities	
Treasury Bills	23,556
Coupon Securities	
due in 3 years or less	–48,088
due in 3–6 years	–46,342
due in 6–11 years	–36,638
due in more than 11 years	–13,505
Treasury Inflation Index Securities (TIIS)	655
Total	–120,362
Federal Agency and Government Sponsored Enterprise Securities	
Discount Notes	45,283
Coupon Securities	
due in 3 years or less	41,022
due in 3–6 years	15,837
due in 6–11 years	–58
due in more than 11 years	5,826
Total	107,910
Mortgage-backed Securities	14,148
Corporate Securities	
due in 1 year or less	46,027
due in more than 1 year	131,895
Total	177,922

Source: Federal Reserve Bank of New York.

one market to another. With long positions in agency and corporate securities, and short positions in Treasuries, dealers are long the credit spread. Similarly, with long positions in Treasury bills and short positions in Treasury bonds, they are short the Treasury term spread. For our purposes, however, the most important arbitrage implicit in the dealers' balance sheet is the net long outright position of $179,618 million. This position represents a speculation on the direction of rates of course,[16] but more important it represents a positive inventory that must be financed, either by the dealers' own capital (which is relatively small), or by borrowing. The dealers are thus net long bonds, but short money. If we think of them as net suppliers of liquidity in the bond market, they must also be net takers of liquidity in the money market.

Table 10.2 speaks to the way that dealers finance their gross bond holdings, and reveals the overwhelming importance of the repo market for that purpose. 'Securities in' includes all the multitudinous ways that a security might come to be delivered to a dealer, including reverse repurchase agreements. 'Securities out' includes all the multitudinous ways that a security might come to be delivered out from a dealer, including repurchase agreements. The net financing need of the dealers is the difference between securities out and securities in, which is $309,818 million in this case.[17] Of that amount, the net financing provided by the repo market (repurchase agreements minus reverse repurchase agreements) was $1,132,565 million. Dealers raise a lot more funds in this market than they require for the financing needs of their security portfolio.

Table 10.2 Primary dealer financing. Amount outstanding as of March 15, 2006, in millions of dollars

Type of Financing	Overnight & Continuing	Term	Total
Securities In			
U.S. Treasury Securities	1,185,692	1,277,214	2,462,906
Federal Agency and Government Sponsored Enterprise Securities	154,650	247,641	402,291
Mortgage-backed Securities	93,198	392,368	485,566
Corporate Securities	111,338	92,913	204,251
Securities Out			
U.S. Treasury Securities	1,168,625	1,108,254	2,276,879
Federal Agency and Government Sponsored Enterprise Securities	304,618	169,951	474,569
Mortgage-backed Securities	553,068	241,313	794,381
Corporate Securities	261,687	57,316	319,003
Memorandum			
Reverse Repurchase Agreements	736,926	1,630,826	2,367,752
Repurchase Agreements	2,011,693	1,488,624	3,500,317

Source: Federal Reserve Bank of New York.

The point to emphasize here is that there are two sides to the operations of the primary security dealers. On the one hand, as dealers in securities, they hold inventories of securities that they finance by borrowing in the money market. On the other hand, they are also *dealers* in money; they are not simply takers of liquidity in the money market, but also providers of liquidity. To see this, rearrange the numbers in Table 10.2 as in below (Table 10.3), treating repo (borrowing money) as a liability and reverse repo (lending money) as an asset.

These numbers reveal, furthermore, that the money market operations of security dealers are about more than simple liquidity provision. The dealers are apparently porters of liquidity in the money market as well. They are net long in term repo (reverse holdings are greater than repo), and net short in overnight and continuing repo. In other words, the security dealers are long the money market term spread. From the standpoint of liquidity provision, this arbitrage represents the transport of liquidity from one market to another. From a money point of view, the dealers are borrowing short (overnight) and lending long (term). They are acting, in fact, like banks.[18]

They are acting like banks, but with essentially no cash reserve. For their daily cash needs, they rely instead on the daily cash flow from their money market operations, and ultimately on access to bank credit. (Unlike the classic discount houses, they have no guaranteed access to the discount facility at the central bank.) The balance sheets of US commercial banks quite typically contain well over $100 billion of security credit to brokers and dealers, both RP credit and outright loans, so commercial banks provide a significant fraction of the finance needed to operate a dealer operation.[19] For our purposes, however, the important relationship is largely off-balance-sheet, through the lines of credit that function as the dealers' lender of last resort. If dealers require cash, their banks stand ready to provide it. Significantly, these dealer loans typically key off the Federal Funds rate, with a spread of 25–50 basis points.

Why does the dealer loan rate key off of Fed Funds? Because the Fed Funds rate is the marginal cost of funds for the banking system as a whole. Indeed, just as the banking system is the lender of last resort for the security dealers, so too the Fed is the lender of last resort for the banking system. The important point to emphasize is that, under current institutional arrangements, it is the Fed Funds rate and not the discount rate that is the relevant cost of this lender of last resort facility. The discount rate (now called the primary credit facility) stands at 100 b.p. over the Fed Funds target, and it is available as a backup for individual banks that might get into trouble. But the marginal source of funds for the market

Table 10.3 Security dealers as money dealers

Assets	Liabilities
736 Overnight reverse RP	2,011 Overnight RP
1,630 Term reverse RP	1,488 Term RP
1,132 Net financing	

Table 10.4 Daily open market operations as a discount facility

Central Bank		Dealer		Clearing Bank		Needy Bank	
Assets	Liabilities	Assets	Liabilities	Assets	Liabilities	Assets	Liabilities
+RP	+reserves		+RP -dealer loan	+FF loan -dealer loan		+reserves	+FF loan

as a whole is the Fed's daily intervention in the market, an intervention that is designed to stabilize the Fed Funds rate around the target (Taylor, 2001). So long as individual banks have access to the Fed Funds market, the Fed's lending to the market might as well be a discount facility available to each individual bank (albeit with one day lag).

Indeed, although individual banks rarely make use of the loan facility offered at the discount window, the banking system as a whole *always* makes considerable use of the closely analogous loan facility offered at the daily repo auction. When the Fed lends to the market using repo, the consequence is an increase in some primary dealer's net position with its clearing bank, and an increase in that bank's reserve position at the Fed, which position the clearing bank can then lend on to whatever bank needs it at the Fed Funds rate. Looking through the balance sheets, it is clear that the Fed provides the funds that the needy bank borrows, just like the classic discount window albeit more indirectly. The Fed lends at the repo rate, while the needy bank borrows at the Fed Funds rate (Table 10.4).

Classic central banking theory revolved around the difference between the market rate of interest and Bank Rate. In modern banking, the closest analogue to market rate is apparently the repo rate, and the closest analogue to Bank Rate is apparently the Fed Funds rate. As in the classic theory, the Fed Funds rate tends to be a penal rate above the repo rate. The modern version of the classic question how to make Bank Rate effective must be about the effect of Fed operations not on the Fed Funds rate but on repo rate. Why can the Fed affect repo rate, despite its negligible importance in the repo market? I suggest it is because the Fed can affect the Fed Funds rate which affects the dealer loan rate, which then affects the repo rate that dealers are willing to offer to finance their operations. Before developing that suggestion further, it will be helpful to review the current state of professional discussion which has focused instead almost exclusively on determination of the Fed Funds rate.

Monetary Policy Implementation

The monetary policy implementation literature has focused narrowly on the problem of a central bank trying to achieve a target market rate of interest i_M by manipulating the variables under its control, namely the standing facility lending rate R, the standing facility deposit rate r, and the net monetary injection M.[20] In the US context, the target is the Fed Funds rate set by policymakers, around which the actual Fed Funds rate fluctuates depending on the forces of supply and demand. Considerations of arbitrage lead to the idea that the market rate of interest is a weighted average of the two standing rates,

$$i_M = \pi_B R + \pi_L r,$$

where the probabilities are determined by the projected stochastic fluctuation of the net demand for reserves at the end of the reserve maintenance period. Further considerations of arbitrage over time during the reserve maintenance period lead to the idea that the current-day market rate of interest is just the expectation of the last-day market rate of interest,

$$i_{MT\text{-}n} = E(i_{MT}).$$

The whole point of the exercise is to inform the operational practice of central bank intervention (see Figure 10.3). Considerations of symmetry lead to the idea that the right operational goal for the managers of open market operations is to set the standing rates equidistant on either side of the interest rate target, and then to inject sufficient reserves to equalize the probabilities that the system will end the period short (hence borrowing at rate R) and long (hence lending at rate r). In this way of thinking about the implementation problem, open market operations set the supply of reserves equal to the expected demand. The practice of lagged reserve accounting means that in any reserve maintenance

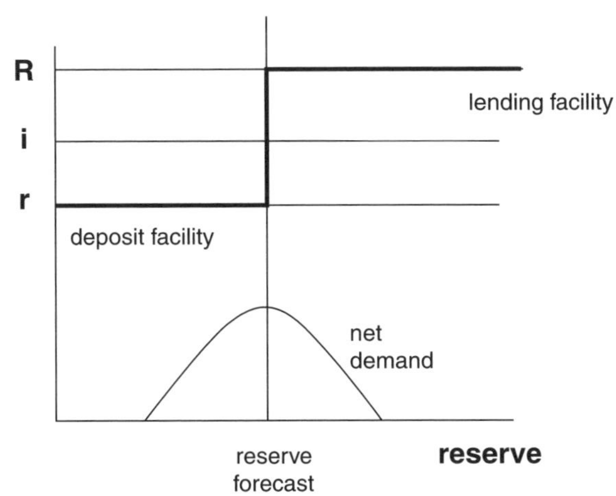

Figure 10.3 Monetary policy implementation

period, central bankers already know the quantity of required reserves, so they focus their attention on forecasting the autonomous factors. If they do a good job, then the expected market rate of interest should be equal to the target rate of interest, although, of course, stochastic fluctuation will cause some deviation from day to day.

The European practice has been fairly close to this stylized model, with a 100 basis point spread on either side of the target, reduced to 25 basis points on the last day of the two-week maintenance period, and with intervention focused on the start of each maintenance period. In European experience, banks find themselves using the standing facilities relatively often, to the extent of 300 million euro outstanding on average (Bindseil, 2004, 74).[21] In such a context, it makes sense that changes in the standing facility rates would translate immediately into changes in the market rate of interest, as the model suggests.

In the US, by contrast, the Fed currently sets the primary credit facility at 100 basis points over the target, and sets the rate on Fed deposits at zero, but intervenes almost daily to maintain the Fed Funds rate close to the target. As a consequence, the standing facilities are hardly used. In 2005, there were only 7 business days when the Fed arranged no short-term RPs, and there were only 15 days when borrowing at the primary credit facility was $100 million or more (FRBNY, 2006, 13, 23). It is therefore hard to believe that the standing facility rates have much to do with the determination of the Fed Funds rate. If the Fed were to reduce the rate on the primary credit facility by 50 basis points, the model suggests that the Fed Funds rate should fall, *ceteris paribus*. But if the probability of having to resort to that facility is near zero, as it appears to be, such a change should have no effect on the market rate. In the US context, it is the daily intervention, and the market's expectation of future daily intervention, that keeps the Fed Funds rate tracking the target.

The difference between Europe and the US on the details of monetary policy implementation reflects further difference in broader financial development within the two systems. The depth and breadth of the market in Europe is, even now, no match for the US. It is the imperfection of money markets that accounts for the continuing importance of standing facilities in Europe. And it is the perfection of money markets that accounts for their insignificance in the US. The entire US payments system is able to function smoothly on deposit reserves at the Fed of $21 billion only because of the significant netting of payments that occurs elsewhere in the system before final settlement on Fedwire. It is precisely this efficiency of the netting system outside the Fed that has raised concerns about a possible decoupling of the Fed from the larger financial system it is supposed to be controlling. Such concerns are clearly not allayed by arguments about how standing facilities work in economies that are less financially developed than that of the US.

To explore these concerns further, it seems reasonable to start with the idea that, in the US case, daily intervention more or less absorbs all fluctuation in net reserve demand. The question, however, remains whether fluctuation in individual reserve demand might provide some leverage. To answer that question requires more detailed consideration of the various channels for netting payments that allow individual payers to avoid reserve flows. To fix ideas, focus on a stylized example of fluctuation in the individual demand for reserves that stems from an end-of-day imbalance in the payments system.

Consider the position of two among many economic agents, both of whom start the day with zero transactions balances. Over the course of the day they make and receive payments of all kinds, perhaps running daylight overdrafts and surpluses for the purpose, but always with the goal of ending the day back at zero. By the end of the day they are almost back, but A is ahead by $10 and B is behind by $10. In this scenario, B is overdrawn, so let us consider the variety of ways that this untenable situation can be corrected.

Note first that if B has some asset worth $10 that A is willing to purchase, they could both make this final transaction and achieve their goal. More relevantly, B could use the asset as collateral for an overnight loan, and A could invest its excess transaction balance in the resulting fully secured instrument. The opportunity cost to B of ending the day overdrawn, and the opportunity cost to A of ending the day in surplus, provide bounds for the negotiation of a satisfactory overnight interest rate. The wide gap between these bounds presumably leaves room for a dealer spread, so we may imagine the payment imbalance being resolved on the balance sheet of a repo dealer (see Table 10.5). In this case the last two transactions of the day would be a payment from A to the dealer, and a payment from the dealer to B, allowing everyone to end the day with zero transaction balances. Note that in this case, there is zero demand for central bank reserves and so the central bank hits its reserve target exactly.

Table 10.5 Payment system imbalance

Case 1: Repo Dealer Intermediation

Agent B		**Repo Dealer**		**Agent A**	
Assets	**Liabilities**	**Assets**	**Liabilities**	**Assets**	**Liabilities**
	+10 repo	+10 reverse	+10 repo	+10 reverse	

Case 2: Eurodollar Intermediation

Agent B		**Bank β**		**Bank α**		**Agent A**	
Assets	**Liabilities**	**Assets**	**Liabilities**	**Assets**	**Liabilities**	**Assets**	**Liabilities**
	+10 bank loan	+10 loan	+10 Euro borrowing from α	+10 Euro lending to β	+10 deposit	+10 bank deposit	

Case 3: Central Bank Standing Facilities Intermediation

Bank β		**Central Bank**		**Bank α**	
Assets	**Liabilities**	**Assets**	**Liabilities**	**Assets**	**Liabilities**
	+10 lombard loan	+10 lombard loan	+10 deposit	+10 deposit	

But suppose that B does not have collateral, and so cannot use the repo market, and consider instead how the banking system can help. Suppose A holds its transaction account at Bank α, and B at Bank β, so the payment imbalance between A and B shows up as a payment imbalance between α and β. The two banks can resolve their own imbalance by an overnight loan from α to β, which then enables each bank to resolve the imbalance of their respective clients. Bank α funds the interbank loan with A's transaction balance, and passes along some of the interest received on the loan to make it worthwhile to A. Bank β raises the money to pay the overnight interest on the interbank loan by on-lending the money to its overdrawn client B at a somewhat higher rate of interest. In this second case there are two dealer spreads rather than one (actually three if we include a commission on the interbank loan) but it remains the case that there is still zero excess demand for reserves, so the central bank can hit its target. The difference is that there has been an expansion of bank deposits (to Agent A) which may possibly result in additional required reserves in the next reserve maintenance period.

Now suppose that α and β cannot arrange a loan between themselves to offset the payment from B to A. In this case the payment imbalance remains at the end of the day in the two banks' transactions balances at the central bank. Here, finally, is where the standing facilities come into play with an overnight loan to β at rate R and an overnight deposit by α at rate r. (For simplicity, the table does not show agents A and B, who are the ultimate recipients of the deposit and loan respectively.) Only in this third case is the payments imbalance resolved by a one-for-one expansion of reserves in line with the increase in demand.

This series of three examples has been designed to suggest a story about the relationship between three money markets: the repo market, the Eurodollar market, and the Fed Funds market. They offer, it is clear, alternative ways to resolve a payment imbalance at the end of the day, but the central bank is not indifferent between them. From the point of view of control over its own balance sheet, the central bank would like to ensure that as much of the imbalance as possible gets resolved elsewhere, meaning in the repo market or the banking system. The banking system is the lender of last resort in the event that the repo market solution fails, and the central bank is the lender of last resort in the event that the banking system solution fails. The objective of the central bank is to establish a system in which these failures are few and far between, and in fact recourse to the central bank balance sheet is rare in the US.

In practice, the daily operation of the payments system typically involves *sequential* use of these three mechanisms.[22] Repo markets are most active in the (New York) morning when dealers arrange financing for continuing balance sheet positions and settle security trades made the previous day (or two). The Eurodollar market is then most active during the day, and the Fed Funds market is most active at the end of the day. Just as the Fed tries every morning to forecast the autonomous factors that may hit its balance sheet during the day, so too does everybody else, and the repo market is available to everyone to make the anticipated adjustments. After that, the interbank Eurodollar market picks up the slack, and unanticipated imbalances show up as swings in the Eurodollar rate which naturally pulls the effective Fed Funds rate with it. Only at the end of the day do the standing facilities come into play.

Why does the central bank care whose balance sheet resolves a payment imbalance? One reason, as I have stated, is the desire to retain control over its own balance sheet. A second reason is the enforcement of payments discipline in the market as a whole. During the day, elasticity is the objective, and daylight overdrafts at all levels of the system are permitted in order to facilitate payments. But overnight, discipline is the objective and that means that credit expansion is ideally kept off the books of the banking system, and certainly off the books of the central bank. The point is to provide an ongoing incentive for economic agents to settle their debts, and not simply to roll them over to the next day. That incentive is the price of overnight money. In practice, the way the central bank imposes payments discipline is by setting the bid–ask spread for overnight money on its own balance sheet ($R - r$) sufficiently wide to encourage the development of credit arrangements at a narrower bid–ask spread on the balance sheet of the banking system, and an even narrower bid–ask spread on the balance sheet of repo dealers.

The important point to emerge from this discussion is that the more successful the central bank is in its institutional objective to push the resolution of payment imbalance off of its own balance sheet, the less likely it is that the central bank's standing facilities will be needed. But if the standing facilities are not needed, then the story of how the market rate of interest is determined by the probability weighted average of those facility rates loses some of its appeal. Clearly the repo rate and the Eurodollar rate will lie inside the wide bounds set by any standing facilities, but payments imbalances provide scant reason for expecting such rates to track a target set somewhere in the middle of these bounds. This is the specter of decoupling.

But the specter of decoupling arises only because we have been adopting a narrowly payments-oriented view of the money markets. After all, in a closed economy payments *always* net to zero, so the more perfect is the credit system, the less need for cash reserve. In what follows, we sketch an alternative theory of monetary policy implementation that focuses not on the Fed's role in the payments system, but rather its role as a lender of last resort to the dealers and banks who act as market makers in the money market.

A Model of Microstructure

Return therefore to the earlier focus on the primary security dealer. He posts bid and ask prices for each security in which he deals, and in doing so in effect offers liquidity to the security market. The bid–ask spread compensates him for the risk involved in offering liquidity, which is partly inventory risk (the risk that the value of his security holding will change), and partly adverse selection risk (the risk that the counterparty who takes the offered liquidity has better information than the dealer himself about the true value of the security).[23] In the case of fixed income securities, the former source of risk is probably relatively more important

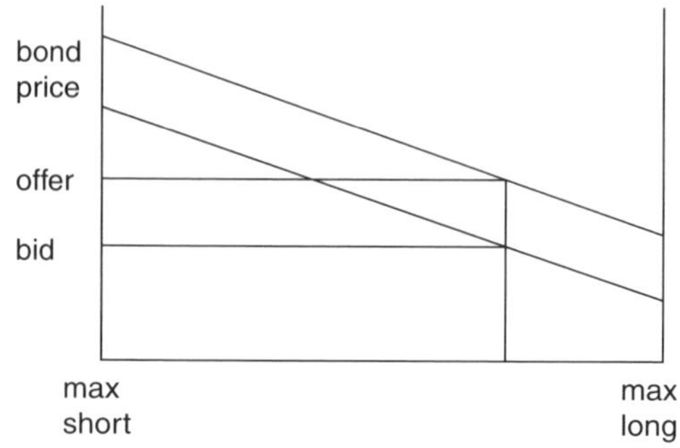

Figure 10.4 Economics of the security dealer

than the latter, for the simple reason that bond prices depend mostly on relatively unforecastable macroeconomic factors, so that inside information is less important. Indeed, it might be argued that dealers themselves are likely to be more informed than non-dealers about the value of fixed income securities because of their ability to observe order flow.[24] In any event, the fact is that bid–ask spreads in the most actively traded fixed income markets are considerably tighter than in equity markets.

Figure 10.4 shows one stylized model of the economics of the dealer function (Treynor, 1987).[25] Imbalances in order flow, whether intentional or not, have the effect of moving dealer inventories in one direction or another, and the resulting exposure to inventory risk causes dealers to change the level of prices they quote. If dealers have been building up a long position, they lower price to compensate for the added inventory risk; if they have been building up a short position, they raise price in order to compensate for the added inventory risk. The important point is that the dealer quote curve is downward sloping; for simplicity, and without loss of generality for what follows, we take it to be linear.

Now, if the order flow imbalance continues, notwithstanding successive price changes, then eventually the dealer will run up against his position limit, a limit imposed by his ability and/or willingness to finance the burgeoning inventory, which is to say by the risk aversion of his bank or himself. At that point, he must find someone willing to take his excess inventory. For simplicity, and without loss of generality for what follows, we take that position limit to be a single point, and the price at which the dealer can unload his position to be a single price.

When the dealer hits his position limit, the job of providing liquidity passes over to the value trader, who trades only when price deviates significantly from what he considers to be true value, but who is willing to step up in size when the price is right. Value traders are thus 'liquidity suppliers of last resort' (Harris, 2003, 227). Dealers provide immediacy, but value traders supply depth. (Indeed, it is because value traders supply depth that dealers are able to supply immediacy; they know that if their positions get too far out of balance, they can rely on value traders for support.) For concreteness, take these value traders to be institutional investors such as pension funds and insurance companies whose naturally vast capitalization enables them to take advantage of an opportunity to pick up a bargain, on either side of the market. This is more or less the standard model, familiar from the standard market microstructure literature in finance.

Now we know, from section 'The repo market', that dealer operations are quite a bit more involved than this. If dealers decide to take a long position in the credit spread, for example, they accomplish this by raising the bid on corporate and agency securities, and lowering the ask on Treasuries. Similarly, if dealers decide to take a short position in the Treasury term spread, they accomplish this by raising the bid on bills and lowering the ask on notes and long bonds. In both cases, the object is to use order flow to establish a desired portfolio position. The point to emphasize is the relationship between the spreads and the size of the dealers' position. Dealers will be willing to take a large position only if they are compensated by an apparently large spread. In this way the dealer model of Figure 10.4 extends naturally.

For our purposes, it is useful to focus attention on one particular spread, that between the actual repo rate and the so-called implied repo rate. Dealers pick up this spread by means of the so-called 'cash-and-carry' arbitrage, which works as follows (Stigum, 1990, 748–749). Consider a trade with three elements: purchasing a six-month Treasury bill, financing that bill with three-month term repo, and hedging the tail risk by selling Treasury bill futures. The bill and futures positions taken separately amount to a three-month investment with a return called the implied repo rate. The overall trade is profitable when the actual term repo rate is less than the implied repo rate, and the opposite trade is profitable when the reverse is the case. Note that a cash-and-carry trade like this would show up in the weekly dealer reports to the Fed as an increase in outright bill holding and a simultaneous increase in repo financing (a pattern that matches the current data).

For our purposes the importance of the cash-and-carry trade is that it links up the bill rate with the repo rate, and so also the capital market with the money market. Such an arbitrage opportunity can persist only if there is some risk involved that limits the willingness of dealers to exploit it. However, it can't be inventory risk in the case of the cash-and-carry trade because that risk is perfectly hedged with the futures contract. Instead, I suggest that the key is liquidity risk, a kind of risk that does not appear in the usual accounts of market microstructure.

To see the presence of liquidity risk, suppose that there is a liquidity premium in the term structure so that long rates are higher than the sequence of future expected short rates. Then the futures price of short bills will be below the expected spot price. But at maturity the futures price must equal the spot price, so the futures price must be expected to increase over the life of the trade. It follows that daily mark-to-market of a short futures hedge must be expected to require cash outflow over the life of the trade. A dealer who is long the cash-and-carry trade must be prepared to meet that likely cash flow consequence, and moreover to meet it at any moment during the life of the trade, since the convergence to spot need not be smooth. This is liquidity risk, and the relevant cost of that risk is the rate of interest on the dealers' line of credit with his clearing bank. It is this

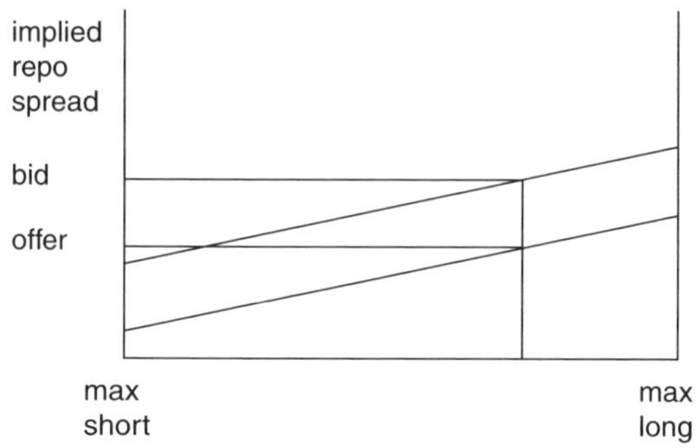

Figure 10.5 Economics of the repo dealer

liquidity risk that prevents dealers from extending their positions far enough to eliminate the implied repo spread. And it is this liquidity risk that links up the Fed Funds rate with the repo rate.

To see this link more clearly, Figure 10.5 extends the dealer model to the case of cash-and-carry arbitrage. The dealer quote curve is now upward sloping because the vertical axis is a yield (spread) rather than a price. Using the diagram, now consider the effect of contractionary open market operations on the dealer's desired position. Whether we think of such operations as a reduction in the quantity of dealer reserves, or an increase in the Fed Funds rate that drives the price of such reserves, the effect on the dealer will be to contract his desired position limits. He will be willing to hold his current position only if the implied repo spread increases, so he will change his bid and ask in order to increase that spread. As a consequence, other things equal, his position in the cash-and-carry trade can be expected to shrink as order flow responds to the new quoted spread.[26] In this way, the immediate effect of contractionary open market operations is a contraction of the balance sheet of the dealers. This is a channel of monetary transmission that does not depend on any imperfection in the payments system, but rather only on the dealer's problem of managing the liquidity risk involved in making markets.

Notes

The author would like to thank Larry Glosten, Suresh Sundaresan, Spence Hilton at the Federal Reserve Bank of New York, Ulrich Bindseil at the European Central Bank, and Goetz von Peter at the Bank for International Settlements, as well as seminar participants at Columbia University and Brandeis University for helpful comments on early versions of this chapter.

1. The desperately brief summary that follows does justice to the sophistication neither of theory nor of practice. Most egregious probably is my single-minded focus on discount rate policy, to the exclusion of all other channels through which central banks attempted to influence market conditions. See Bloomfield (1959) and the extensive references therein for a more complete treatment.

2. For example, Sayers (1936, 46) remarks that banks distinguished between "artificial" reserve contractions at the discretion of the Bank, and reserve contractions produced by international gold flows, being more inclined to frustrate the former and adjust to the latter.
3. The various submissions to the 3-volume collection, *Reappraisal of the Federal Reserve Discount Mechanism* (Board of Governors 1971–1972) mark the decisive confrontation of the new view with the old view.
4. The closest predecessor of the present chapter is probably Bank for International Settlements (1999), but that paper is mainly empirical.
5. An early and prescient account is Minsky (1957). The best sources on how this market now works have been written for practitioners: Stigum (1990, chapter 13), Taylor (1995), Choudhry (2002). Garbade (2006) provides a useful account of the maturation of repo contracting conventions.
6. The official data on repo outstanding can be found in Table L.207 "Federal Funds and Security Repurchase Agreements" published by the Federal Reserve Board as part of the Flow of Funds accounts. These numbers, however, report only *net* issue of repo by commercial banks ($1131.3 billion) and by brokers and dealers ($817.8 billion), and so neglect the very large interbank and interdealer market. Further, the statistical discrepancy of $481.2 billion between the measure of total repo held and the measure of total repo issued suggests that much of the activity in this market escapes the statistical net entirely. The most recent flow discrepancy of $278.0 billion (Table F.207) is by far the largest instrument discrepancy in the entire set of accounts (Table F.12).
7. Table L.108 "Monetary Authority."
8. For comparison, another survey reports European outstanding volume as EUR 5.9 trillion (International Capital Market Association, 2006), but this number is not strictly comparable to the US number because the European survey explicitly excludes all repo transactions with the central bank. The reason is not that such transactions are unimportant, but rather the reverse. Repurchase agreements (mainly against the public debts of the various member governments) are the dominant form of domestic credit held by the European Central Bank. As a consequence of its balance sheet, the ECB is thus a much bigger part of the repo market than is the Fed, and there is no question of its losing contact. See Bindseil (2004, chapter 2).
9. Henckel et al. (1999) have coined the evocative terminology of "Treasury money," "clearinghouse money," and "central bank money" to describe the instrument traded in each of these three markets.
10. The repo market is heterogeneous and the rate charged depends on the underlying collateral. The phrase "the repo rate" should be understood therefore as shorthand for "the repo rate on general Treasury collateral" which tends to be higher than the repo rate on any specific Treasury security, but still below the Fed Funds rate.
11. Another reason sometimes offered is the fact that corporate lenders can invest in repo but not Fed Funds. That could possibly explain why repo can be below Fed Funds, if it were not for the fact that corporate lenders can invest in Eurodollars which are also persistently above repo.
12. If the stock of reserves were higher, then on days when the Fed currently injects minimal short-term reserves, it would have to withdraw reserves through reverse repo, or securities lending, in order to achieve the same total reserves target. As a matter of policy, apparently the Fed has decided to devote its securities lending facility to a different task, that of providing specific securities that happen to be temporarily in short supply.
13. The Fed itself prefers to think of its interventions as soaking up fluctuations in so-called "autonomous factors" that influence the demand for reserves. These daily fluctuations are large relative to the outstanding supply of depository reserves, but not large relative to the size of the Fed's entire balance sheet.

14. Hamilton (1996, 1997); Furfine (1999, 2000); Bartolini et al. (2005); Hilton (2005); McAndrews (2005); Carpenter and Demiralp (2006).
15. Here I follow the terminology of the microstructure literature in finance, where liquidity means the ability to make a trade, quickly, in size, and at low cost. The mechanics of payment are thus pushed to the background, and instead attention focuses on the mechanics of trading and the institutions of exchange (O'Hara, 1995; Harris, 2003). Since limit orders to buy or sell at stated prices provide the opportunity for other people to trade if they want to, such orders are considered to *offer* or supply liquidity. By contrast, market orders to buy or sell take advantage of the opportunity offered by limit orders, and such orders are considered therefore to *take* or demand liquidity.
16. It is important to add the caveat that the table does not capture the entire balance sheet, nor the entire risk exposure. The most important omission is exposure in futures and options markets, no longer reported since 2001.
17. The difference between the net position in Table 10.1 and the net financing in Table 10.2 is apparently largely an artifact of institutional peculiarities of the mortgage-backed securities market which trades with significantly delayed settlement. See Adrian and Fleming (2005) for details.
18. "In providing that service, the dealer takes in securities on one side at one rate and hangs them out on the other side at a slightly more favorable (lower) rate; or to put it the other way, the dealer borrows money from his repo customers at one rate and lends it to his reverse customers as a slightly higher rate. In doing so, the dealer is operating like a bank, and dealers know this well" (Stigum 1990, 446).
19. Table L.224 "Security Credit" in the Flow of Funds accounts reports $257.1 billion security credit from commercial banks to broker dealers, of which $101.8 billion is direct and $155.3 is channeled through foreign banking offices in the U.S.
20. I take Bindseil (2004) to be an exemplary contribution, but the literature is much larger. The approach has been eagerly embraced in central banking circles (Woodford, 2001; Whitesell, 2003; Bernanke, 2005; Clews, 2005) and has already made it into the textbooks (Mishkin, 2004; Cecchetti, 2005). For the European context, which is Bindseil's experience, the market rate of interest to which the theory refers is taken to be the repo rate, because of the much larger presence of the ECB in that market.
21. That number has come down in recent years but still averages over 100 million euro daily, according to ECB Annual Report 2005.
22. I thank Spence Hilton for repeatedly insisting on this feature of the system, but without implicating him in my interpretation of its importance.
23. Biais, Glosten, and Spatt (2005) provide a synthetic model that encompasses most of the existing theoretical literature. They emphasize market power as a third potential source of the bid–ask spread, but this seems likely to be more important in equity markets than fixed income. I thank Larry Glosten for stimulating criticism of an earlier draft in this regard, but without implicating him in my current position.
24. Here I take my cue from Lyons (2001) who finds that order flow provides a much better forecast of exchange rate fluctuations than macroeconomic variables.
25. The vast academic literature reviewed by Biais, Glosten, and Spatt (2005) does not, typically, cite Treynor's paper, but that paper's focus on the economics of the dealer function makes it arguably the more relevant for the concerns of the present analysis. Treynor was a very early contributor to this literature, writing under the pseudonym Walter Bagehot (1971), republished as Treynor (1995). His subsequent writings are well known in practitioner circles, especially his chapter in the reader *Managing Investment Portfolios* (Maginn and Tuttle, 1983).
26. Other things may not of course be equal. Most important, the dealer's position depends on how his customers respond to the new spread and that depends, in part, on their own balance sheet positions as well as expectations about the future.

References

Adrian, Tobias and Michael J. Fleming (2005). "What Financing Data Reveal about Dealer Leverage." Federal Reserve Bank of New York *Current Issues in Economics and Finance* 11:3.

Bagehot, Walter (1873). *Lombard Street: A Description of the Money Market*. London: Henry King.

Bagehot, Walter (pseud.) (1971). "The Only Game in Town." *Financial Analysts Journal* 27:2 (March/April), 12–14, 22. Reprinted as Treynor (1995).

Biais, Bruno, Larry Glosten, and Chester Spatt (2005). "Market Microstructure: A Survey of Microfoundations, Empirical Results, and Policy Implications." *Journal of Financial Markets* 8, 217–264.

Bank for International Settlements (1999). "Implications of Repo Markets for Central Banks." Report of Committee on the Global Financial System, No. 10.

Bartolini, Leonardo, Spence Hilton, and Allesandro Prati (2005). "Money Market Integration." Federal Reserve Bank of New York, *Staff Report* No. 227.

Bartolini, Leonardo, Svenja Gudell, Spence Hilton, and Krista Schwarz (2005). "Intraday Trading in the Overnight Federal Funds Market." Federal Reserve Bank of New York, *Current Issues in Economics and Finance* 11:11.

Bernanke, Ben S. (2005). *Implementing Monetary Policy*. Washington, DC: Federal Reserve Board.

Bindseil, Ulrich (2004). *Monetary Policy Implementation: Theory, Past, and Present*. New York: Oxford University Press.

Black, Fischer (1970). "Banking and Interest Rates in a World without Money: The Effects of Uncontrolled Banking." *Journal of Bank Research* 1, 8–20.

Bloomfield, Arthur I. (1959). *Monetary Policy under the International Gold Standard: 1880–1914*. New York: Federal Reserve Bank of New York.

Board of Governors of the Federal Reserve System (1971–1972). *Reappraisal of the Federal Reserve Discount Mechanism*, 3 vols. Washington, DC: Board of Governors of the Federal Reserve System.

Bond Market Association (2005). "Repo and Securities Lending Survey of U.S. Markets." *Research* (January).

Carpenter, Seth and Selva Demiralp (2006). "The Liquidity Effect in the Federal Funds Market: Evidence from Daily Open Market Operations." *Journal of Money, Credit, and Banking* 38:4 (June), 901–920.

Cecchetti, Stephen (2005). *Money, Banking, and Financial Markets*. New York: McGraw Hill.

Choudhry, Moorad (2002). *The Repo Handbook*. Boston: Butterworth-Heinemann.

Clews, Roger (2005). "Implementing Monetary Policy: Reforms to the Bank of England's Operations in the Money Market." Bank of England, *Quarterly Bulletin* (Summer), 211–220.

Demiralp, Selva, Brian Preslopsky, and William Whitesell (2004). "Overnight Interbank Loan Markets." Unpublished mimeo. Washington, DC: Board of Governors of the Federal Reserve System.

Evans, Martin (2005). "Foreign Exchange Market Microstructure." Mimeo, Georgetown University, Washington, DC.

Federal Reserve Bank of New York (2006). *Domestic Open Market Operations during 2005*. New York: FRBNY.

Friedman, Benjamin M. (2000). "Decoupling at the Margin: The Threat to Monetary Policy from the Electronic Revolution in Banking." NBER Working Paper No. 7955. Cambridge, MA: National Bureau of Economic Research.

Furfine, Craig H. (1999). "The Microstructure of the Federal Funds Market." *Financial Markets, Institutions and Instruments* 8:5 (November), 24–44.

Furfine, Craig H. (2000). "Interbank Payments and the Daily Federal Funds Rate." *Journal of Monetary Economics* 46, 535–553.

Garbade, Kenneth D. (2006). "The Evolution of Repo Contracting Conventions." Federal Reserve Bank of New York, *Economic Policy Review* 12:1 (May), 27–42.
Hamilton, James D. (1996). "The Daily Market for Federal Funds." *Journal of Political Economy* 104:1 (February), 26–56.
Hamilton, James D. (1997). "Measuring the Liquidity Effect." *American Economic Review* 87:1 (March), 80–97.
Harris, Larry (2003). *Trading and Exchanges: Market Microstructure for Practitioners*. New York: Oxford University Press.
Henckel, Timo, Alain Ize, and Arto Kovanen (1999). "Central Banking without Central Bank Money." Working Paper WP/99/92 of the International Monetary Fund. Washington, DC: IMF.
Hilton, Spence (2005). "Trends in Federal Funds Rate Volatility." Federal Reserve Bank of New York, *Current Issues in Economics and Finance* 11:7.
International Capital Market Association (2006). *European Repo Market Survey No. 10*. Zurich: ICMA.
Lyons, Richard K. (2001). *The Microstructure Approach to Exchange Rates*. Cambridge, MA: MIT University Press.
Maginn, John L. and Donald L. Tuttle (1983). *Managing Investment Portfolios: A Dynamic Process*. Sponsored by the Institute of Chartered Financial Analysts. Boston: Warren, Gorham and Lamont.
McAndrews, James (2005). "The Microstructure of Money." Unpublished mimeo. Federal Reserve Bank of New York.
Mehrling, Perry (1997). *The Money Interest and the Public Interest, American Monetary Thought 1920–1970*. Cambridge, MA: Harvard University Press.
Minsky, Hyman P. (1957). "Central Banking and Money Market Changes." *Quarterly Journal of Economics* 71:2 (May), 171–187.
Mishkin, Frederic S. (2004). *The Economics of Money, Banking, and Financial Markets*, 7th ed. Boston: Addison-Wesley.
Modigliani, Franco, Robert Rasche, and J. Phillip Cooper (1970). "Central Bank Policy, the Money Supply, and the Short Term Rate of Interest." *Journal of Money, Credit, and Banking* 2:2 (May), 166–218.
O'Hara, Maureen (1995). *Market Microstructure Theory*. Malden, MA: Blackwell Publishers.
Sayers, Richard S. (1936). *Bank of England Operations, 1890–1914*. London: P.S. King and Son.
Sayers, Richard S. (1957). *Central Banking after Bagehot*. London: Oxford University Press.
Sayers, Richard S. (1960). *Modern Banking*, 5th ed. London: Oxford University Press.
Sayers, Richard S. (1976). *The Bank of England 1891–1944*, 3 vols. Cambridge: Cambridge University Press.
Stigum, Marcia (1990). *The Money Market*, 3rd ed. Burr Ridge, IL: Irwin Professional Publishing.
Taylor, Ellen. (1995). *Trader's Guide to the Repo Market*. Greenwich, CT: Asset International.
Taylor, John B. (2001). "Expectations, Open Market Operations, and Changes in the Federal Funds Rate." *Federal Reserve Bank of St. Louis Review* 83:4, 33–47.
Tobin, James (1969). "A General Equilibrium Approach to Monetary Theory." *Journal of Money, Credit, and Banking* 1:1 (February), 15–29.
Treynor, Jack (1987). "The Economics of the Dealer Function." *Financial Analysts Journal* 43:6 (November–December), 27–34.
Treynor, Jack (1995). "The Only Game in Town." *Financial Analysts Journal* 51:1 (January/February), 81–83.
Whitesell, William (2003). "Tunnels and Reserves in Monetary Policy Implementation." Working Paper. Washington, DC: Board of Governors.
Woodford, Michael (2001). "Monetary Policy in the Information Economy." Unpublished mimeo, Princeton University.

Discussion

Neil T. Skaggs

In this highly informative chapter Perry Mehrling seeks to provide a microeconomic answer to the question, 'How does the Federal Reserve implement monetary policy?' I found his answer quite informative and quite sensible, and I have no real criticisms of his effort.

My major substantive thought regarding the chapter is, 'What goes around, comes around'. I am specifically juxtaposing the latest thinking on monetary policy implementation with the earliest, Henry Thornton's *Enquiry into the Nature and Effects of the Paper Credit of Great Britain*, published in 1802. Mehrling refers to Walter Bagehot and the mid-19th-century procedures of the Bank of England, which is an apt starting point for a discussion of the appropriate conduct of monetary policy. However, it's nearly a half-century too late to include what was – perhaps excluding *Lombard Street* – the best discussion of how a central bank should operate within the constraints of a sophisticated credit system available for nearly a century.

Thornton begins his discussion not by arguing that gold is the solid foundation upon which Britain's economy operates, nor by referring to money at all. He begins with a discussion of commercial credit, which, he argues, is the source of paper credit. Paper credit includes all sorts of promissory notes, bills, and bonds, having a wide range of maturities and liquidities. Thornton treats gold as a *measure* of value, rather than the source of value, which inheres in claims to valuable goods and services.

In the first section of *The Paper Credit* Thornton mounts a strong defense of the need to protect the economy's credit. In a wartime economy, forced off the gold standard and forced into huge increases in government military spending, inflationary pressures were evident. The pressure on prices led many important Englishmen to criticize the Bank of England and to call for deflation. Thornton resisted such pleas, arguing that preserving the nation's credit was the first priority of the Bank of England.

In his discussion of the British financial system, Thornton made much of the conditions under which one asset substitutes for another. He argued that the market was capable of providing more or less liquidity in response to the demand for it, more bills of exchange being drawn into circulation when needed and excluded from circulation when not needed. And he wrote at length about the importance of protecting the liquidity of the London bill market, through which most of the final payments of the entire kingdom were made. Like Mehrling, Thornton saw the British monetary system as intricately intertwined with the British securities system, including government bills and bonds of various types.

This 'integrated view' of money and finance was transmitted down to Bagehot's time by such worthies as John Stuart Mill, Thomas Tooke, John Fullarton, and J. E. Cairnes. Though their theoretical systems differed in various respects, these Banking School writers maintained the integrated view of money and finance that Thornton originated and Mehrling explicates. Against this view was arrayed the Currency School, the heirs of David Ricardo, who were ready to place rigid quantitative restrictions on the monetary system, if that was what was necessary to curb the inflationary expansions of credit and inevitable collapses that punctuated the period from 1825 to 1844. In the event, the Ricardians succeeded in quantitatively restricting the Bank of England note issue, as well as limiting the elasticity of the country-bank note issue. The results of the Bank Act of 1844 were almost exactly as predicted by John Fullarton. Only the suspension of the Act saved the British financial system from collapse on two occasions.

Of course, considered in Mehrling's framework, this makes good sense. The financial system is constantly on the stretch, one dealer depending upon other dealers and his banker for liquidity, the whole lot of them ultimately depending upon the Bank of England. If the Bank is forcibly withdrawn from the game, illiquidity spreads from one trader to another, bringing the system to its knees.

Fullarton's advice on amending the system in the 1840s appears to me to be the best offered. He argued that the Bank of England should, on average, hold a larger gold reserve than historically it had held and that once the reserve had dwindled beyond a still-healthy point, the Bank should begin raising Bank Rate systematically until the drain of gold subsided. He noted that a large hoard could be accumulated merely by setting Bank Rate above the market discount rate, thereby inducing bill holders to repay their debts to the Bank of England and to seek liquidity in the market. As the Bank's bill portfolio shrank, its gold reserve would rise. The similarities with Mehrling's story are obvious.

I'll end this discourse with two quick thoughts. First, the 'monetarist interlude' in US monetary policy, from late 1979 to late 1982, is widely viewed more as political subterfuge than monetarism à la Friedman. Exceedingly high interest rates were made politically palatable by dressing them up in monetarist clothing. Though nominal rates topped 20 percent, the markets retained liquidity.

Second, the currently dominant analysis of monetary policy, Michael Woodford's *Interest and Prices*, draws explicitly on Knut Wicksell's model of a credit economy. It seems worth noting, that Wicksell credited Thomas Tooke with shaping his views and that Tooke's system bears crucial similarities to Thornton's. Financial markets keep driving perceptive theorists away from a quantitative approach toward a market-price approach to monetary policy.

References

Fullarton, John (1969 [1845]). *On the Regulation of Currencies*. New York: A.M. Kelley.

Thornton, Henry (1978]1802]). *An Enquiry into the Nature and Effects of the Paper Credit of Great Britain*. Edited by F.A. Hayek. Fairfield, NJ: A.M. Kelley.

Woodford, Michael (2003). *Interest and Prices: Foundations of a Theory of Monetary Policy*. Princeton, NJ: Princeton University Press.

11

Monetarism and Market Clearing

Michel De Vroey

Introduction

The 1970s and the 1980s were marked by fierce controversies between Keynesian and monetarist economists.[1] A quarter of a century later, the macroeconomics scene has changed dramatically with the dethroning of Keynesian macroeconomics and its replacement by new classical macroeconomics and real business-cycle models. This evolution can be encapsulated as the rising of Walrasian macroeconomics.[2] A reshuffling of standpoints has ensued. In the face of this new way of practising macroeconomics, the old foes of Keynesianism and monetarism have discovered that they have more in common than they previously believed, in particular that they share the same Marshallian affiliation.

My paper explores the relationship between Keynesianism and monetarism but only in an indirect way. Its main purpose is narrower as my aim is to investigate the position taken by eminent monetarist authors on the matter of market clearing and flexibility – in particular, market clearing in the labour market – and their opposites. Do all monetarist authors take the same stance on these topics? I will claim that the answer is 'No'. There is a tension between authors, who, to all intents and purposes, anticipate the Lucasian postulate of market clearing, and others, who come closer to the Keynesian vision by claiming that prices and wage are sluggish, and that market non-clearing is an important trait of existing market economies. I will claim that Milton Friedman belongs to the first group, while Karl Brunner, Alan Meltzer, and David Laidler belong to the second.

In section 'Friedman, Brunner and Meltzer, and Laidler on market clearing, flexibility, and unemployment', I discuss these authors' views on market clearing, flexibility, and unemployment. Since they all claim a Marshallian allegiance, it is worth returning to Marshall and examining whether market clearing and flexibility are central components of the Marshallian model. This is the task undertaken in section 'Is market clearing always realised in Marshallian theory?'. The usual view to the contrary notwithstanding, I shall claim that, with one caveat, market clearing is an ever-present outcome of Marshallian theory. In section 'From Marshall's *Principles* to Friedman's Phillips curve model', I ponder upon the Phillips curve model. First, I present a few comments on Lipsey's work. Second, addressing Friedman's expectations-augmented Phillips curve model, I claim that, after Friedman's rhetorical or meta-model comments are disposed of, his model witnesses to the strictest Marshallian orthodoxy by incorporating market clearing and flexibility. The irony is that while this model has been credited with having introduced the notion of the natural rate of unemployment, the truth is that it comprises no unemployment at all! In the last section, returning to Brunner and Meltzer, and Laidler, I engage in a methodological discussion of their claim that sluggishness can cause market non-clearing.

Three claims will be made. The first, already mentioned, is that monetarist authors hold different views about the need for, and usefulness of, assuming price and wage flexibility and market clearing. The second is that market clearing is not a new classical invention. It was already present in Marshallian theory (and of course also in Walrasian theory). The third is that the standard account of the Phillips curve initiated by Lipsey and widely taken up, in particular by Friedman, comprises an unnoticed flaw: the summing of incompatible forms of unemployment.

My chapter is written from the point of view of the history of economics. While its aim is to bring out overlooked differences within the community of monetarist authors, I do not see it as my role to take a stance about them, to give good or bad marks to the views expounded.

Friedman, Brunner and Meltzer, and Laidler on market clearing, flexibility, and unemployment

Friedman[3]

Market clearing and flexibility in general

Does Friedman adhere to the Lucasian principle that market clearing should be adopted as a matter of principle? No direct answer can be given to this question for the simple reason that he does not address it, at least not directly. As far as I am aware of, the market clearing terminology is absent from Friedman's writings. Yet, the fact that the term is absent does not preclude the presence of the thing that it designates. This absence may be due to the fact that market clearing is a Walrasian notion. We must then ask ourselves what its Marshallian equivalent is and ponder upon the presence of such an equivalent. In section 'Is market clearing always realised in Marshallian theory?', I shall show that the equality of market supply and demand (a notion distinct from that of the equality of normal supply and demand) is this equivalent.[4]

Every discussion of equilibrium must address two questions: can an equilibrium position exist logically? And if so, how can it be arrived at? What I find striking when looking at Friedman's (1976) *Price Theory* book is how little attention he devotes to the subject of interactive equilibrium as opposed to individual equilibrium, to borrow Hayek's terminology ([1937] 1947). No more than a few paragraphs are addressed to it, and not a word is to be found about how equilibrium is arrived at.

> In a free market, the point of intersection of the supply and demand schedules is of particular significance. At this particular price, and only at this price, will the desires of demanders and suppliers be simultaneously satisfied. At any other price, either demanders will want to buy more than suppliers want to sell (a 'shortage') or suppliers will want to sell more than demanders want to buy (a 'surplus'). At point A [in the accompanying graph], the underlying forces of demand and supply, not demand and supply themselves, have established a price that equates the quantity supplied and the quantity demanded. (Friedman, 1976, 17)
>
> The concept of an equilibrium price has been employed in the above analysis, and perhaps some elaboration of this concept of equilibrium is in order. An equilibrium position is one that, if attained, will be maintained. (Friedman, 1976, 19)

As to flexibility, Friedman's opinion can only be deducted in a roundabout way from noting his rejection of the opposite assumption (rigidity), which he views as the hallmark of the Keynesian approach.[5]

Friedman endorses Leijonhufvud's characterisation of the Marshallian approach in terms of differences in the speed of adjustment between prices and quantities, with the prices adjusting quasi-instantaneously, while quantities need more time to do so.

> Alfred Marshall's distinction among market equilibrium, short-period equilibrium, and long-period equilibrium was a device for analyzing the dynamic adjustment in a particular market to a change in demand or supply. This device has two key characteristics.... The second is the assumption that prices adjust more rapidly than quantities, indeed, so rapidly that *the price adjustment can be regarded as instantaneous*. An increase in demand (a shift to the right of the long-run demand curve) will produce a new market equilibrium involving a higher price but the same quantity. The higher price will, in the short run, encourage existing producers to produce more with their existing plants, thus raising quantity and bringing prices back down toward their original level, and, in the long run, attract new producers and encourage existing producers to expand their plants, still further raising quantities and lowering prices. Throughout the process, it takes time for output to adjust but no time for prices to do so. (Friedman, 1974*a*, 16–17; my emphasis)

However, Friedman parts company from Leijonhufvud when Leijonhufvud claims that Marshall's ordering of the speeds of adjustment ought to be reversed, which leads him to suggest that prices are changing more slowly than quantities. To Friedman, no rationale for this view exists.

> The rigid price assumption of Keynes is, in this sense, much more arbitrary. It is entirely a *deus ex machina* with no underpinning in economic theory. (Friedman,1974*a*, 44)[6]

To Friedman, flexibility versus rigidity is the bone of contention between Keynesians and non-Keynesians:

> Yet, Keynes's assumption about the relative speed of adjustment of price and quantity is still a key to the difference in approach and analysis between those economists who regard themselves as Keynesians and those who do not. Whatever the first group may say in their asides and qualifications, they treat the price level as an institutional datum in their formal theoretical analysis. (Friedman, 1974*a*, 20)

So, beyond doubt, the conclusion to be drawn is that Friedman is a defender of the flexible price assumption. While he provides little positive justification for this standpoint, I guess that any vindication he might give would be an 'as if' argument. In effect, as far as observation is concerned, Friedman recognises in his interview with Snowdon and Vane that wage rigidities are a fact of life (Snowdon and Vane, 1997, 205).

Unemployment

One of Friedman's most praised contributions to economics is his presidential address to the American Economic Association (Friedman, 1968) introducing his expectations-augmented Phillips curve model. This initiated the radical overhaul of macroeconomics led by new classical and real business-cycle theorists.

To all outward appearances, this is a paper about unemployment since it introduces the notion of the natural rate of unemployment. Yet, there are good reasons for suggesting that nothing would be lost by considering the paper's real object of analysis to be the variations in the level of activity rather than employment *strictu sensu* (more on this below).

In the Snowdon and Vane interview, Friedman defines the natural rate of unemployment: as 'that rate at which demand and supply are equal so there is no excess supply or demand and in which people's expectations are satisfied' (1997, 199). This definition abides by the standard Marshallian conception of equilibrium. Note that it has two components. In effect, it does not suffice that (market) supply and demand match. It is also necessary that agents lack any incentive to change their behaviour. In other words, market equilibrium, the matching of supply and demand on a given market day, is a necessary but not a sufficient condition for equilibrium. If there is such a matching, but incentives to act differently are also present, this counts as disequilibrium.

Two observations are in order. First, in this light, it is obvious that the expectations-augmented Phillips curve model is about disequilibrium states. Yet what remains unclear is whether it features permanent market clearing. Friedman's text is sufficiently ambiguous that some readers find it obvious that it deals with market non-clearing, while others, viewing the notion of disequilibrium and market non-clearing as synonymous, are of the opposite opinion. This ambiguity will be resolved in section 'From Marshall's *Principles* to Friedman's Phillips curve model'.

Second, as far as markets in general are concerned, it is usually taken for granted that market clearing and market rationing are two opposite traits. When the discussion bears on markets in general, it is scarcely ever stated that market clearing coexists with some sellers being unable to sell the quantity they wish at the ongoing price. However, this is no longer true when it comes to the labour market. In fact, it is frequently asserted that market clearing can coexist with unemployment. This standpoint follows from the implicit assumption that different types of unemployment can be encompassed by the same theory. It amounts to declaring that unemployment of the market non-clearing type is absent (Keynes's involuntary unemployment), while unemployment of the frictional type is present. Again, the assessment of this point of view is postponed until section 'From Marshall's *Principles* to Friedman's Phillips curve model'.

Brunner and Meltzer[7]

Market clearing and flexibility in general

Unlike in Friedman's work, market clearing is a notion that crops up regularly in Brunner and Meltzer's writing. They make it clear from the outset that they are against it on the grounds that the market structure inducing market clearing is hardly ever present in reality. Hence the basic irrelevance for them of Walrasian theory – market clearing and the Walrasian approach being (rightly) viewed as part and parcel of each other – and their criticism of new classical and real business-cycle economists for having adopted it.

> The auction market, the choice of new classical macroeconomists, requires several conditions for its functioning. Market participants must be, more or less, uniformly informed. Each must acquire the specialized knowledge and skill to assess the qualities of the goods traded in the market. Major informational asymmetries are ruled out by this assumption. Market participants must also involve a sufficiently large number of potential buyers and sellers who assemble and trade simultaneously. Each of these conditions is more frequently violated than satisfied. (Brunner and Meltzer, 1993, 135)

To Brunner and Meltzer, the most salient real-world feature that a theory of the market must encompass pertains to information and the cost of acquiring it. While they hail Lucas for having broached this dimension in his 1972 'Neutrality of money' article, they regret that this line has been abandoned since then.

> Recognition of the failure of the Phelps-Lucas model of local-global confusion confronted macroeconomists with a choice. They could retreat to an assumption of full information, or they could recognize that the problem of incomplete information is a central problem. The new classical macroeconomists chose the first course. This choice was probably strongly influenced by their reluctance to abandon the assumption of full market clearing (up to the current realization of the shock) and fully flexible prices. (Brunner and Meltzer, 1993, 64)

A better depiction of the functioning of markets, they claim, consists of viewing them as 'bazaars' where 'Simultaneous assembly is replaced by arrangements whereby one market side, buyer or seller, stands ready to serve at irregular arrival times. The bazaar or a system of posted prices emerges' (Brunner and Meltzer, 1993, 136).

Brunner and Meltzer's rejection of market clearing is accompanied by a rejection of flexibility. 'Observations show that real and nominal wages are inflexible – slow to adjust to changes' (1993, 139). If sluggishness is a fact of life, it ought to be embodied in the theoretical discourse. They blame both new classical and Keynesian economists for their failure to take this fact on board. The former are criticised for sticking to a flawed paradigm resting on the flexibility assumption while common observation runs counter to it, the latter for taking sluggishness as evidence in support of a disequilibrium analysis and activist policy. For their part, Brunner and Meltzer see no reason to associate sluggishness with disequilibrium.

> Decisions are entirely rational. People use all available information, but they misinterpret the nature of the shock. Once they perceive that the shock is permanent, prices and output fully reflect the information. (Brunner and Meltzer, 1993, 143)[8]

Nor do Brunner and Meltzer see any reason why sluggishness should support activist policy. No market failure is involved.

> It is a market failure only if we measure it against an ideal world without information and transaction costs. Failure to consider these costs and their implications neglects the central problem – why prices are not fully flexible. (1993, 141)

Unemployment

In Brunner and Meltzer's view, unemployment becomes a recurrent event whenever the cost of acquiring information and sluggishness are taken into account. It arises because the economy undergoes shocks, of different kinds, shifting output and employment from their normal positions. Although economic agents use all available information, they often misinterpret the nature of the shock, for example, whether it is permanent or not. This is a standpoint that fits the Marshallian conception of equilibrium perfectly.

Brunner and Meltzer have no qualms about resorting to the antiquated typology of frictional, cyclical, and structural forms of unemployment. In their 1993 essay, they focus on structural unemployment, which, they claim, has afflicted Europe since the 1970s. However, they disagree with the Keynesian demand deficiency view. Instead, they argue that the cause lies in the fact that 'heightened institutional restrictions on the labour market raised the effective wage – the relevant total cost of employment per output unit – and reduced both aggregate supply and the expansion of employment' (Brunner and Meltzer, 1993, 147). They end up endorsing Blanchard and Summers' (1986) model combining an insider–outsider approach with a hysteresis perspective. Such an endorsement may look odd, since Blanchard and Summers used this approach to support a Keynesian claim. Be that as it may, when it comes to policy conclusion, the monetarist standpoint regains the upper hand. While Brunner and Meltzer admit that the status quo state of European unemployment, although a state of equilibrium, may fail to be optimal, they claim that the remedy should be sought elsewhere than in fiscal or monetary expansion (1993, 152).

Laidler[9]

Market clearing and flexibility in general

Laidler challenges the view that it is a legitimate practice to act 'as if' markets always clear. He argues that this approach is admissible for specialised markets but should not be extended to many components of final output, and certainly not to the labour market (1981, 12). The latter ought to be assigned to the Hicksian category of 'fixprice markets'. For these markets, false trading and slow reaction to shocks are observable realities.

Another of Laidler's observations worth mentioning is his highlighting (in his 1991 Thornton Lecture) of the idea that price and wage stickiness has a long standing in the economic literature while, in contrast, flexibility is a new idea.

> Throughout the history of macroeconomics until the early 1970s, debates were always between advocates of greater or lesser stickiness. Until the 1970s, no one used phrases such as ' wage and price flexibility' to characterise continually clearing markets such as are found in so called, as we can now see, misleadingly, New classical models, for the simple reason that no school of macroeconomic thought entertained the possibility that markets always cleared. (Laidler [1991] 2004, 284)

Laidler's views are close to Brunner and Meltzer's. However, in his case the Keynesian connection is stronger. Laidler does not share Brunner and Meltzer's reluctance to adopt the disequilibrium approach. In his 1981 paper, he makes it clear that he stands on Hicks's side when separating 'flexprice' and 'fixprice' markets (Laidler, 1981, 145). In another paper, he goes as far as accepting the rejection of Say's Law ([1991] 2004, 269). In particular, he endorses the view of disequilibrium theorists, such as Patinkin, Leijonhufvud, and Clower, that trade takes place at false prices and that 'quantity signals, perhaps amplified by multipliers effects, become an integral part of the mechanism whereby monetary changes are transmitted to the behaviour of the price level' (1981, 13). Laidler's empathy for these authors rests on their insistence on duration, on the idea that adjustment forces, although present, only exert their effects slowly.

Unemployment

Taken in isolation, Laidler's passages on unemployment could come from a Keynesian author, as the following quotation illustrates:

> If adjustment in the level (or rate of change) of money wages and prices to aggregate demand shocks are anything other than instantaneous, then markets fail to clear, trade takes place at false prices, and quantity signals, perhaps amplified by multiplier effects, become an integral part of the mechanism whereby monetary changes are transmitted to the behaviour of the price level. This line of analysis is as 'Keynesian' in spirit as the clearing market approach is 'Austrian', and its existence permits one to subscribe to the expectations augmented Phillips curve without also being committed to a clearing market rational expectations approach to the analysis of economic fluctuations. Moreover, the approach in question does *not* differ from the clearing market view in denying that individuals perceive and then engage in all available mutually beneficial trades. It simply denies that they do so infinitely rapidly. (Laidler, 1981, 13)

Laidler has also repeatedly commented on Friedman's expectations-augmented Phillips curve model, pointing out that Friedman's paper can be interpreted in two different manners. The first follows Phillips and Lipsey 'in treating variations in measured unemployment as a proxy measure of the state of excess demand or supply in the labour market' (2005, 20). Here it is assumed that agents face an effective state of disequilibrium or labour market non-clearing, and hence react to a quantity signal. In short, the Phillips curve is treated as a 'manifestation of market adjusting to disequilibrium' (Laidler, 2005). In contrast, the second interpretative stream is different since it views the Phillips curve as 'a consequence of remaining in equilibrium under conditions of less than perfect information' (Laidler, 2005). Whenever this last approach is taken, the expectations-augmented Phillips curve must be viewed as an aggregate supply curve. 'Fluctuations in output and employment in response to price level variations represent the voluntary choices of individuals operating in markets which are continually clearing' (Laidler, 1981, 142).

Laidler greatly prefers the first explanation, despite the fact that when Friedman returned to the topic in his *Price Theory* book (Friedman, 1976), he supported the second approach. Laidler regrets this choice, which, in his opinion, amounts to abandoning the Marshallian vision of how monetary factors impinge upon economic life.[10]

For all his agreement with disequilibrium Keynesians as to the theoretical basis of price–output relations, Laidler parts company with them when it comes to macroeconomic policy. Here he stands firmly on the monetarist side:

> One can rest the monetarist case against activist policy on the proposition that markets always clear and that expectations are rational, but one can also rest it on the much more down-to-earth proposition that we are too ignorant of the

> structure of the economies we live in and of the manner in which that structure is changing to be able safely to implement activist stabilisation policy in the present environment, or in the foreseeable future. (Laidler, 1981, 19)
>
> There is more to practical monetarism than scepticism about fiscal fine-tuning and opposition to wage and price controls. Its key positive tenet is that monetary weapons should be assigned to the attainment and maintenance of long-run stability, and hence that the same monetary weapons not be used for fine-tuning purposes. (Laidler, 1981, 21)

* * *

My examination of the views of Friedman, Brunner and Meltzer, and Laidler has shown that, for all their common background – their belonging to the Marshallian tradition and their common rejection of fiscal and monetary activism – these authors hold different views of market clearing, flexibility, and unemployment. If a divide is to be established between them, Friedman should be put on one side and Brunner and Meltzer and Laidler on the other.

Is market clearing always realised in Marshallian theory?

Friedman, Brunner and Meltzer, and Laidler have in common that they are all anti-Walras and pro-Marshall. Therefore, it may be interesting to return to the writings of the Cambridge economist to examine what he had to say on the themes studied in the previous section. This is the task pursued in this section. A preliminary clarification bears on the differentiation between the economics of Marshall and Marshallian economics, to paraphrase the distinction that Leijonhufvud (1968) made about Keynes.

The economics of Marshall versus Marshallian economics

Marshall's intention in writing his *Principles of Economics* (1920) was to build an intellectual engine allowing practical issues pertaining to the working of market economies to be resolved. The distinctive feature of his book is that it combines a wealth of subtle insights on different economic subjects with a value-theoretical core aimed at constructing an equilibrium theory of the market. One way of contrasting it with Walras's *Elements of Pure Economics* (1954; English translation), published in the same period, is to compare the doses of strict model and meta-model in these two studies. Of course, no precise quantitative assessment can be made, but it is obvious that in the *Elements* the model part is by far greater than the meta-modelled part, while the opposite is true for the *Principles*. To many admirers of Marshall, his book achieved a perfect blend between the two components, while Walras's book is of little relevance for understanding reality because of its opposite approach. Be that as it may, the model or value-theoretical component of Marshall's theory was bound to become autonomous from its author's broader vision. My investigation as to whether market clearing is a central element of Marshallian theory bears on this autonomous outgrowth, as recast in the works of authors such as, e.g., Frisch (1950), Viner ([1931] 1953), and Newman (1965). In other words, by Marshallian theory I mean the ideas put forward by Marshall in Book V of the *Principles*.

Equilibrium in Marshallian theory

The term market clearing does not appear in Marshall's writings. According to Laidler, the same is true for the notion of flexibility. As to unemployment, Marshall touches on it, yet it is hardly a central theme. As a result, my inquiry must take a roundabout route. I shall start by briefly discussing Marshall's conception of equilibrium.[11]

Marshall held three distinct concepts of equilibrium: market equilibrium, normal short-run equilibrium, and normal long-run equilibrium. According to Hicks, this classification allows each of these concepts to be taken as a separate object of analysis. Hicks saw Keynes's and his own role in the evolution of economics as having led to a long-needed shift in interest from the long run to the short run (Hicks, 1967). Hicks's view that Marshall's equilibrium and time categories can be disconnected has been widely adopted. In my opinion, this is unfortunate for it has the drawback of leaving the links between the time periods in the dark, of not even trying to piece them together. An alternative interpretation, my preferred one (which, by the way, is also Friedman's) consists of putting Marshall more firmly in the lineage of the classical standstill–gravitational conception of equilibrium by reducing these three categories to two: market equilibrium and normal equilibrium.[12] These two equilibrium concepts stand in a relationship of hierarchy, with normal equilibrium being the higher or more fundamental concept and market equilibrium the lower or less fundamental one. That is, market equilibrium will gravitate around normal equilibrium and the market will come to a standstill only when the market equilibrium values coincide with the normal equilibrium values.

Normal equilibrium exists whenever the market outcome in a given branch is such that firms lack any incentive to change their behaviour, any previous decision to change behaviour having been finalised (Marshall's attention focused more on firms than on households). Market equilibrium indicates that agents' plans have been made compatible, the quantity produced being given. As soon as market equilibrium values fail to coincide with normal equilibrium values, disequilibrium can be said to prevail. Disequilibrium should hardly be considered an odd occurrence in the Marshallian framework. On the contrary, it is the permanent achievement of equilibrium that is considered exceptional.[13]

This duality of equilibrium concepts translates into a duality of adjustment processes. Adjustment towards normal equilibrium occurs across market days, while adjustment towards market equilibrium occurs within a given market day. As to supply and demand functions, normal equilibrium pertains to the matching between *normal* supply and demand, market equilibrium to the matching between *market* supply and demand.

The issue of what the equivalent of the Walrasian notion of market clearing is in the Marshallian universe then boils down to the question of which of the two Marshallian equilibrium concepts should be associated with market clearing. The spontaneous answer is 'normal equilibrium', in which case the question of the permanent achievement of market clearing in Marshallian theory can be answered at once, in the negative. Yet there is no logical reason for such an association, which is very demanding. The very existence of two equilibrium concepts allows market clearing to be given a narrower scope of relevance. A given trade round can have two outcomes, either the matching of supply and demand or the lack thereof. Market clearing then designates the occurrence of the first of these, no assessment being made as to whether this outcome qualifies as a normal equilibrium.[14]

If this point of view is adopted, market clearing is present in the Marshallian approach whenever market supply and demand end up matching in a particular market on a given market day – in other words, whenever the quantity and price observed at the end of the market day coincide with what Marshall called the 'true equilibrium' (he should have called it the 'true market equilibrium'), i.e., the equilibrium values calculated by the outside economist. But what needs to be assessed is whether market clearing is always realised in Marshallian theory (as it is in Walrasian theory). This task is attempted in the next section.

The presence of market clearing in Marshallian theory[15]

To assess whether market clearing is an always-present outcome in Marshallian theory, we must turn to Marshall's corn market model (Book V Chapter II of the *Principles*) and his barter appendix (Marshall, 1920, 791–93). Again, I suppose that the reader is well acquainted with Marshall's reasoning.

One preliminary observation is worth making. Marshall's suggestion to the contrary notwithstanding, his object of discussion is not an ongoing market of Brunner and Meltzer's bazaar type. Trade takes place within well-delineated boundaries pertaining to time, space, product, and participants. In this sense, the Marshallian market can be characterised as centralised. The time delineation is particularly important. Instead of being an ongoing process, trade is confined within the bounds of periods of exchange.

The issue I am interested in is how market equilibrium is arrived at. Most commentators on the corn model insist that Marshall was able to demonstrate a convergence towards true equilibrium coexisting with false price trading. Thereby, Marshall's account acquires a real 'haggling and bargaining' flavour. The underlying condition for it is the assumption of a constant marginal utility of income, itself the consequence of the assumption that agents' expenditure in the market under study is small relative to their total expenditure. As a result, the path dependency that would normally ensue from false trading is eliminated.

Strictly speaking, the outcome of this false trading process does not correspond to market clearing although it comes close to it. The quantity of corn traded coincides with the true equilibrium quantity. The same is true for the price of the last transaction. However, trade takes place at different prices, and the distribution of money across agents is different from what it would have been without false trading.

Unfortunately, the assumption of a constant marginal utility of income is ad hoc and cannot be generalised. Yet Marshall had a second iron in the fire, the assumption that agents have the ability to reconstruct the market supply and demand functions mentally, and to conjecture market equilibrium outcomes. As soon as this is the case, the only transactions that are effective are the equilibrium transactions.

At first sight, the perfect information assumption does not look too worrying. If markets are small and agents specialised, the total amount of information agents, which have to master, is manageable. However, upon closer scrutiny a less sanguine conclusion emerges. The perfect information assumption, it turns out, has the flaw of running counter to a basic trait of a decentralised economy, namely that it is a private economy, the term 'private' applying not only to ownership but also to information. Market supply and demand functions are underpinned by private factors. Considering them as common knowledge is a betrayal of the nature of a decentralised system. So, first impressions to the contrary notwithstanding, the perfect information assumption is as much a deus ex machina as the auctioneer. Both assumptions play the same role, namely to dodge an intractable issue – for no other scenario explaining how the true market equilibrium can be arrived at is available.

The perfect information assumption has one important implication. The notion of a market day, lasting for example from 8 a.m. to 4 p.m., conveys an element of duration. This element cannot be discarded when the possibility of false trading is admitted because transactions need to be dated. In contrast, when the omniscient agent's assumption is made, there is no need to consider duration. Using Occam's razor, equilibrium can as well be considered as taking place instantaneously or in logical time, in the same way as the time needed to conclude an auction sale is irrelevant to its outcome. As a result, the claim dear to authors such as Hicks and Laidler, that the time span considered could be too short to allow market clearing, becomes groundless.[16]

I am now able to answer the question raised at the beginning of this section – is market clearing always present in Marshall's theory? As seen above, whenever the constant marginal utility of money is deemed to be relevant, the answer has to be ambiguous. I would prefer to speak of the ever presence of quasi-market clearing. In contrast, whenever, the constant marginal utility of money is deemed to be inapplicable, a straightforward positive answer can be given. In as far as it is admitted that the constant marginal utility of money has limited relevance, the conclusion that market clearing is always realised ought to be reached.[17]

Unemployment

Of all possible markets, there is one for which the claim of the permanent realization of market clearing seems particularly inappropriate, and that is the labour market. Should this be an exception to my conclusion above?

It cannot be claimed that unemployment is absent from Marshall's writings. Yet Marshall hardly broached this subject in the value theory part of his work.

When discussing unemployment, he related it to low human capital, sectoral shifts in employment, and the business cycle. As noted by Matthews (1990),

> Cyclical unemployment was *par excellence* a 'Vol. II' subject, along with business cycles generally. It does get some treatment in the *Principles*, but to a large extent Marshall's views have to be pieced together from his various writings. Those are often fragmentary or aphoristic. (Matthews, 1990, 35)

Several explanations for this relative neglect can be given. Mine is as follows. I view Marshall as subscribing to a methodological practice that held sway until recently. It consists of dividing economics into two broad subfields: value theory, dominated by equilibrium principles, where market clearing always obtains, and business-cycle theory, where monetary disturbances are supposed to play a central role, and which is divorced from those principles. The notions of equilibrium and disequilibrium may still be evoked, but their use is non-analytical. While no room existed for market rationing in his value theory, this was deemed of little consequence because unemployment had full right of abode in business-cycle theory. The latter was, as it were, an annexe of value theory – things which could not be generated in value theory, such as unemployment, would find a place in business-cycle theory. I am not claiming that this was Marshall's explicit conception but in practice this is what it amounted to.

In this light, it may be presumed that Marshall's inability to write volume II of *The Principles* was less due to external circumstances than to the intrinsic difficulty of integrating value theory and business-cycle theory, a task that was too daunting for any economist of the time.[18]

This consideration explains how two outwardly contradictory statements (that the category of unemployment is present in Marshall's theoretical work, and that the standard Marshallian model of the labour market features market clearing in the same way as the corn or the fish market, and thus has no place for unemployment) can both be valid.[19] Of course, this proved to be an awkward position for the first generation of Marshallian economists (e.g., Pigou) to hold. A few ways out were considered – the exogenous wage floor hypothesis, sluggish wages, market imperfections – yet to little avail. While the mandatory wage idea was too trivial a solution, the other two lacked a theoretical foundation. No clear indication as to how they could occur within the basic Marshallian exchange model was provided. With hindsight, this is not surprising, not because the idea of friction makes no sense but rather because (as modern search models make clear) its theorisation requires a framework different from the standard Marshallian trade organisation.

From Marshall's *Principles* to Friedman's Phillips curve model

Lipsey on the Phillips curve

Lipsey has played an important role in providing theoretical micro-underpinnings for the empirical Phillips curve (Lipsey, 1960, 1974, 1978).[20] The gist of his contribution can be summarised in three points.

First, he grafted the category of frictional unemployment onto a standard Marshallian account of the labour market.

> When demand is equal to supply (wage rate Ow_e in Fig.4) [reproduced below as Figure 11.1, upper panel], there will be jobs available for all those who wish to work at the going wage rate. This is not equivalent to saying that there will be no one unemployed but rather that the number of unemployed will be matched by an equal number of unfilled vacancies. Given that workers change jobs for any reason whatever, and that a finite time is taken to change, zero excess demand must be accompanied by some positive amount of *frictional unemployment*. From this it follows that, when the wage rate is stable (at Ow_e in Fig.4) [here Figure 11.1, upper panel], there will be some quantity of unemployment (*Oa* in Fig. 6) [here Figure 11.1, lower panel], the exact quantity being determined by the amount of movement and the time taken to move. (Lipsey, 1960, 14)

Figure 11.1 reproduces Lipsey's two graphs. Frictional unemployment being always present, three situations are conceivable: (a) market clearing (i.e., the absence of involuntary unemployment) accompanied with frictional unemployment;

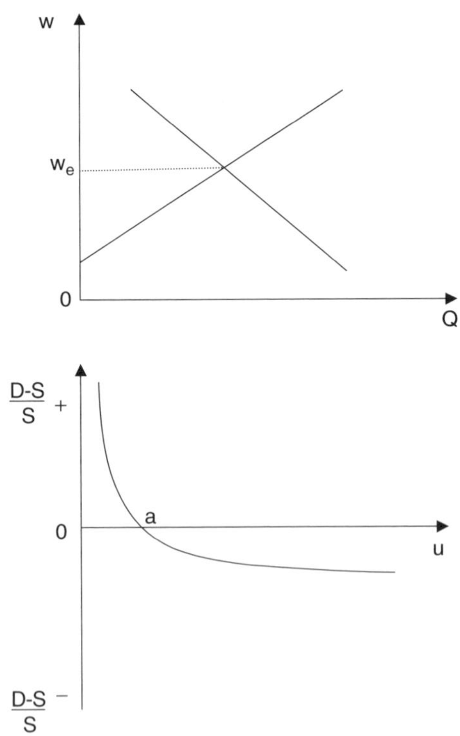

Figure 11.1 Lipsey on unemployment

(b) excess supply of labour (involuntary unemployment) accompanied with frictional unemployment; (c) excess demand for labour accompanied with frictional unemployment. In (a) only one type of unemployment exists, in (b) total employment results from the addition of involuntary and frictional unemployment, in (c), as in (a), only one form of unemployment, frictional unemployment, is present, although to a lesser extent than in (a).

Snowdon and Vane (2005, 43) offer a single graph conveying the same idea, where 'the schedule SL shows how many people are prepared to accept job offers at each real wage and the schedule LT indicates the total number of people who wish to be in the labour force at each real wage rate' (2005, 44).

Lipsey's second contribution (Figure 11.2) was to show that the Phillips curve is underpinned by labour markets that are in a state of disequilibrium (case (b) of the taxonomy above), which in turn trigger changes in wages. It is central to his view that these adjustments do not operate instantaneously. In other words, Lipsey adheres to the Patinkinian interpretation of Keynes according to which what Keynes called an involuntary unemployment equilibrium is actually a state of disequilibrium, due to slow adjustment (1978, 55).

> the whole spirit of Phillips's dynamics [is that] transactions occur out of equilibrium because prices do not adjust instantaneously. (Lipsey, 1974, 69)

Third, Lipsey does not join the crowd in positing that outcome reached at the closure of the labour market pertains to the formation of a quantity of hours worked/real wage mix. To him, the magnitude to be placed on the vertical axis of the labour market graph is the nominal wage.

> Shortly after I published my first Phillips curve article, Milton Friedman visited me at the London School of Economics. He argued that I was perpetrating money illusion by putting a nominal wage variable on the vertical axis of my figures rather than using some variant of the rate of change of real wages.

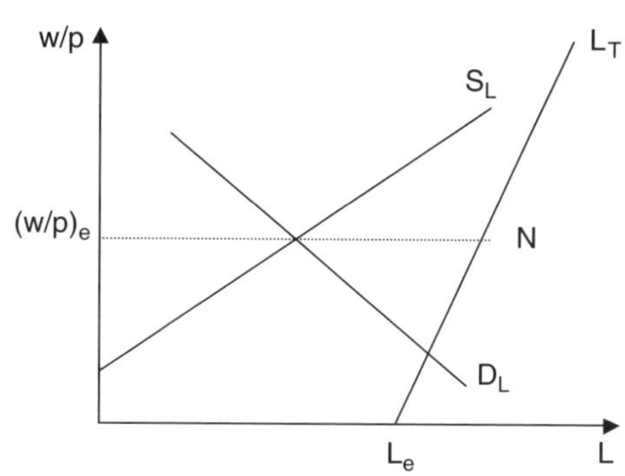

Figure 11.2 Snowdon and Vane on unemployment

> My answer to him then was the same as my response now. The variable that workers bargain over is the nominal not the real wage (with rare exceptions). If workers care about the real wage, then their expectation of how the nominal rate and the real wage may differ should enter the wage formation equation as an independent variable. But the dependent variable should be the true behavioural variable, the nominal wage change. (Lipsey, 2000, 70)

Let me comment on these three points in reverse order. To begin with, I fully agree with Lipsey's last point.[21] It constitutes another example of the confusion between the Walrasian and the Marshallian approaches. In the former, only the real wage (i.e., the *numéraire* wage) matters. But this observation should not be transposed to a Marshallian world. The irony here is that we have anti-Walrasian authors such as Friedman, unnecessarily incorporating a Walrasian trait into their Marshallian language.

As to Lipsey's second point, for which he gives hardly any justification, it falls prey to the criticism I made above. There is no way to account for the claim that slow adjustment can cause market non-clearing, while sticking to the canonical Marshallian model of the functioning of markets.

I now come to Lipsey's first and most important point. Lipsey's account combines two types of unemployment, involuntary unemployment, expressing a mismatch between supply and demand of labour, and frictional or search unemployment.

This combination or adding-up procedure has been widely adopted.[22] Yet, to me, it has no foundations. Let me start my indictment by observing that Lipsey treads in Keynes's footsteps. Remember what Keynes wrote in chapter 2 of the *General Theory*:

> This state of affairs [absence of involuntary unemployment] we shall describe as 'full' employment, both 'frictional' and 'voluntary' employment being consistent with 'full' employment so defined. (Keynes, 1936, 15–16)

Keynes was reasoning against the background of the Great Depression and felt that, if unemployment had developed to such an extent, this meant that a new cause was at work leading to the emergence of a distinct type of unemployment. The implicit assumption was that only other forms of unemployment were present in rosier times. A good Marshallian, Keynes did not bother to draw a clear distinction between two levels of discourse or two types of statements: those which are valid only within the fictional theoretical world, and those which purport to be descriptively correct. When looking at the *General Theory* in the light of this distinction, it is clear that frictional unemployment is only evoked as a real-world category. The book's core argument, the theory of effective demand, deals exclusively with involuntary unemployment, without attempting to integrate the two types of unemployment. To me, this is the correct standpoint to adopt: a model of unemployment must rest on a single concept of unemployment.

But this is not what Lipsey does. To show this, let me return to the graphs presented above (Figure 11.2). Take Snowdon and Vane's graph. Does it make sense to represent in a single graph both the supply of labour and the decision to participate in the labour market? I do not think so. The same criticism applies to Lipsey's two graphs (Figure 11.1). To see why, we must reflect on the institutional set-up or trade technology underpinning the Marshallian account of the labour market. Individual supply of and demand for labour schedules express the quantity of hours traded that each agent finds optimal. Hence the notion of a job has no place in this framework. Nor has the distinction between belonging to the labour force and being employed. The underlying trade technology is centralised. As already stated, the market must be a well-delineated entity. The rise of a single equilibrium price–quantity mix ensues from this centralised trade technology. Frictions have no place in this model (whatever their possible evocation in the meta-model comments). If any labour rationing is introduced into it, it will result from the wage being fixed for some reason at a market non-clearing magnitude, and this has nothing to do with the existence of frictions.[23]

To conclude, Lipsey's reconstruction is flawed. The Phillips curve ought to be viewed as underpinned either by an account of the working of the labour market, where the only conceivable form of unemployment is involuntary unemployment (which does not imply that this form is effectively present), or by an account allowing exclusively for the existence of search or frictional unemployment. Strictly speaking – and the widely held implicit view to the contrary notwithstanding – it cannot be underpinned by a mix of these two forms of unemployment.

Friedman's expectations-augmented Phillips curve model

Let me now return to Friedman's Phillips curve model using his 1976 recasting of it rather than the original presentation.[24] My aim is to settle the matter of the automatic realization of market clearing as well as to shed more light on the relationship of Friedman's model to the canonical Marshallian model.

Before beginning this task, a general remark is worth making. The IS-LM model resulted from the special interpretation of Marshall's tripartite classification of equilibrium and time concepts put forward by Hicks, according to which each of these concepts could safely be studied separately from the others. That is, the IS-LM model is a study of the short period, which remains disconnected from the long period. As a result, any gravitational process is excluded from the theoretical picture. I view Friedman's contribution as having broken away from this Hicksian isolation precept, reintroducing the gravitational link between the short period and the long period (or in my preferred terminology, the Marshallian market equilibrium/normal equilibrium divide). In this way the Marshallian notion of disequilibrium and its associate re-equilibrating process props back to the forefront. In others words, Friedman put his finger on a central flaw of the Keynesian model: 'there is no direct link between the short-run model and the long-run model, no way of connecting the one to the other' (Friedman, 1974*a*, 44).

We have seen that the canonical Marshallian model has no place for unemployment. Yet Friedman's paper became famous for having introduced the notion of a natural rate of unemployment. This discrepancy can be interpreted in two ways: either Friedman's model turns out to be an amendment of the canonical

Marshallian model, the result of which is that the excluded concept becomes acceptable; or Friedman fell prey to the not-so-unusual flaw of pasting a non-Marshallian narrative onto a Marshallian model. I shall argue that this second possibility is in fact the case. Figure 11.3 reproduces the central graph of Friedman's argumentation.

Whenever inflation is absent, Friedman's reasoning runs, everything proceeds smoothly. Before entering the market, all participants know its equilibrium values, the coordinates of 0 in the graph. The market outcome (E0) corresponds to the natural rate of unemployment (an appellation that I will declare misplaced below). However, whenever inflation enters the picture as the result of monetary expansion, a different outcome emerges.[25] Consider the first trading round at which the impact of a monetary expansion becomes visible in the labour market. Employees develop a false conjecture about the prices of goods, the result of their adaptive expectations. Failing to anticipate that a rise in price is going to occur in the consumer goods markets, they expect that a higher real wage will be associated with a higher nominal wage. On the basis of this conjecture, they mentally construe the new market equilibrium as the intersection (Aw) of the new perceived demand curve and the unchanged supply curve. They are ready to trade at a higher employment/nominal wage mix.[26] As to firms, they are aware of the workers' misperception. They realise that it is tantamount in its effect to a change in workers' preferences. Hence they are ready to move down their demand curve to the point of intersection with the shifted supply curve, Ae.[27] Endowed with their respective conjectures about the market equilibrium values, workers and firms come to the market with an exchange proposal that happens to involve the same increased quantity of labour traded (Ef) and the same nominal wage (not on the graph). Exchange on this basis is possible and will take place.

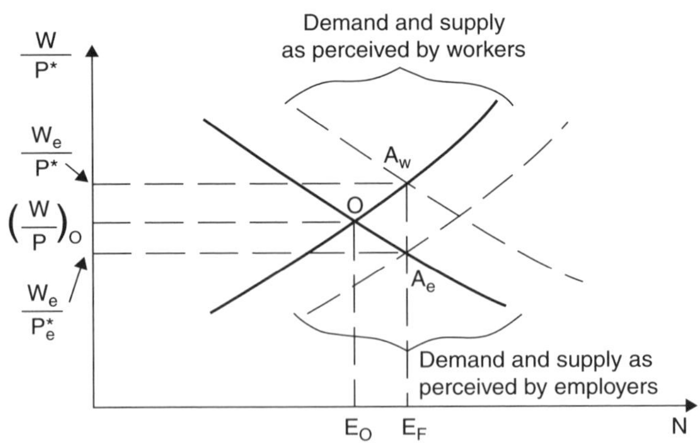

Figure 11.3 Friedman's labour market with workers' misperceptions

This is Friedman's model of the labour market. Two comments are in order. First, looking at Friedman's graph, we can observe that his model features market clearing: market-day supply and demand for labour are equal and amount to E_F.

At this juncture, Friedman treads in Lipsey footsteps by resorting to frictional unemployment:

> At the point of intersection 0, the market is in equilibrium at the wage rate W_0, with the amount of labour employed E_0, equal to the amount of labour demanded. Unemployment is zero – which is to say, as measured, equal to 'frictional' or 'transitional' unemployment, or to use the terminology I adopted some years ago from Wicksell, at its 'natural' rate. (1976, 217)

Unlike Lipsey, Friedman does not add a certain quantity of frictional unemployment to another quantity of involuntary unemployment. The latter is absent since, as just seen, he assumes market clearing. So, all Friedman's unemployment is frictional. Still, Lipsey's mistake of grafting a search perspective into a standard Marshallian account of the working of the labour market is reproduced. As soon as a distinction is drawn between the theory itself (i.e., the model), and the meta-theoretical comments made about it, it becomes crystal clear that frictional unemployment, though present in the meta-model, is absent from the model itself.[28]

As a result, Friedman's introduction of the natural rate of unemployment notion must be questioned.[29] What he calls the natural rate of unemployment is nothing other than the quantity component of Marshallian normal equilibrium. The result described in Figure 11.3 can be viewed as a standard case of Marshallian disequilibrium, featuring a deviation of the market-day equilibrium values (Ef, We) from their normal equilibrium values (Eo, Wo).[30] What is intriguing, however, is the evocation of the unemployment notion for a model from which unemployment is absent. Departures from the natural rate of *employment* – leading either to over-employment (as here) or under-employment – rather than from the natural rate of *unemployment* are the real object of Friedman's model.

My claim is not that all natural rate of unemployment models are misnamed but that this is the case for Friedman's model. Moreover, this observation does Friedman little disservice. In his book *Models of Business Cycles*, Lucas (1987) remarked that equilibrium models of the business cycle evolve without resorting to the unemployment category.[31] The same must be said about Friedman's Phillips curve model. It abides by the equilibrium discipline, featuring both optimizing behaviour and market clearing.[32]

Such a conclusion confirms Laidler's point that the Phillips curve has become a supply of labour function. I also agree with Laidler's diagnosis that Friedman 'perhaps inadvertently, set in motion the demise of the Marshallian tradition in macroeconomic theory of which both he and Keynes were such distinguished exponents' (Laidler, 2005, 26–27). Nonetheless, we differ on two points. First, unlike Laidler, I see nothing un-Marshallian in interpreting the Phillips curve as a supply of labour function. Second, I go one step further than Laidler by criticising the adding-up methodology and claiming that unemployment is absent from Friedman's model.

My second comment pertains to the way in which equilibrium is arrived at in Friedman's model. In his reasoning, the formation of labour market equilibrium involves workers and firms striving to assess the market demand and supply schedules – and hence their intersection – on their own. This confirms my claim above that agents' ability to mentally reconstruct market supply and demand functions is the key factor in explaining the formation of market equilibrium, whenever the assumption of a constant marginal utility of money cannot be made. 'To the workers, it will appear as if the demand for labour has shifted to the right.' 'For employers as a whole, it will appear as if the supply curve had shifted to the right.' These sentences, drawn from Friedman's comment (see notes 27 and 28), make sense only if the formation of equilibrium results from agents' ability to assess market supply and demand functions. Although Friedman does not stress it – and might not even have realised it – his reasoning rests on the premise that the agents in the model are as knowledgeable about these functions as the economist, except for the element of misinformation (workers' misperceptions), which is integral to the model.

Methodological issues

My analysis above leads me to set up an opposition between Friedman, on the one hand, and Brunner and Meltzer and Laidler, on the other, with respect to their relationship to the canonical Marshallian model. Once his misleading meta-model comments are put aside, Friedman's views turn out to be perfectly congruent with the Marshallian approach while those of Brunner and Meltzer and Laidler are less so. The aim of this section of the paper is to reflect on these last authors' methodological position.

It can be objected that my account of Marshallian theory betrays Marshall's intentions. This I admit, but I want to reiterate the point made earlier – texts get a life of their own. Subsequent authors may develop the insights of the founder of a new line of research in a way that this founder would have found uncongenial. Marshall would probably not have liked his corn model to be taken as seriously as I have taken it.

I am also ready to admit that Brunner and Meltzer and Laidler are right when they stress that real-world markets are closer to a bazaar than to an auction, and that prices, and in particular wages, are slow to adjust after a shock.[33] Such statements definitely have a ring of truth to them. The problem is their methodological status. As long as they are not integrated into a fully fledged theoretical framework, they remain, as it were, hanging in the air. The problem, in other words, is how to translate a statement that may be considered a fair description of what goes in reality into a statement that is congruent with the premises of the theoretical language. The authority of reality is not a sufficient condition for giving theoretical legitimacy to a fact of life.

The notion of sluggishness or slow adjustment is central to Brunner and Meltzer and Laidler's argument. For my part, I am amazed by the discrepancy between the central role they attribute to it and the lack of serious reflection on its meaning, or on the possible obstacle that its incorporation into established equilibrium theory will face. Let me try to fill this gap.

We must start with the notions of rigidity and flexibility. The first interpretation of them that comes to mind runs as follows. Rigidity exists whenever a price or a wage that should change does not do so, as the result of some externally imposed impediment to the formation of equilibrium. In turn, flexibility is said to prevail when no such impediment is present.

Keeping to this definition, the main distinction made about rigidity, especially with reference to wages, is between nominal and real rigidity. The problem presents itself differently in a Marshallian and a Walrasian framework. In the Marshallian model, if we accept, as I think we should, Lipsey's observation that the nominal wage is the *operandum* factor in the formation of market equilibrium, any rigidity affecting the market must be nominal. The obvious yet trivial candidate is a mandatory wage floor. Other more interesting factors are staggered contracts or menu costs.[34] All these can indeed cause market non-clearing. In a Walrasian framework, real rigidity comes to the forefront. Any blocking of the price vector, expressed in a non-monetary *numéraire*, will obviously impede the formation of equilibrium (unless by chance it is blocked at the equilibrium value). However, such an impediment runs counter to the auctioneer assumption, as aptly argued by Lucas (1987, 52–53). So, flexibility and Walrasian theory can be considered part and parcel of each other.

The matter would remain simple if left at this stage. The compounding factor is that another understanding of the notion of real rigidity, relevant for non-Walrasian models, is to be found in the literature. According to this, real rigidity characterises any model that features an equilibrium result departing from the perfect competition (or Walrasian) outcome.[35] On the basis of this definition, efficiency wage models, to take an example, are called real rigidity models in spite of the fact that in such models wage are perfectly flexible in the sense of the first definition. The same is true for most of the imperfectly competitive models that have been proposed recently. Depending on the model considered, such real rigidity will generate either involuntary unemployment (i.e., market non-clearing) or under-employment (i.e., a sub-optimal state of market clearing).[36]

Yet Brunner and Meltzer and Laidler have something different in mind, sluggishness. This refers to the situation in which it takes time for equilibrium to be reached: duration is of the essence. Several authors have claimed that rigidity is an extreme case of sluggishness, so that any model explaining rigidity would by the same token also explain sluggishness.[37] I, for one, doubt this argument. Models incorporating nominal or real rigidities are based on the assumption that equilibrium is arrived at instantaneously. In no way is their rigidity an extreme case of sluggishness. Therefore, the view that rigidity can explain market non-clearing should not be extended to sluggishness.

The reason I have dismissed the Brunner–Meltzer–Laidler claim is that it runs counter to the centralised account of markets that characterises Marshallian theory. But why should such an account be accepted? After all, real-world markets look more like bazaars than like auctions. They are decentralised. Their operation is not confined within strict time and space boundaries. Likewise, their boundaries, in terms of goods and services traded and in terms of participants, are difficult to trace. Neither sellers nor purchasers are gathered together or connected within a unique network. Sellers are dispersed and post prices whereas buyers have to visit them sequentially. In this framework there is no reason to assume that, during a given period, all transactions take place at the same price. Likewise, the existence of queuing and rationing is hardly surprising as soon as the principle that trade may go on a 'first come, first served' principle is accepted.

Nonetheless, most economic models are based on the assumption that markets function in a centralised way, search models being the important exception. The reason why is easy to fathom. Constructing the theory of a bazaar economy is a daunting task, especially if the equilibrium notion is deemed to play a central role in it. Brunner and Meltzer's work testifies to this difficulty. They may well evoke the bazaar notion yet they are unable to make much out of it. When it comes to explaining unemployment, they fall back on an existing model that has nothing to do with the bazaar. In contrast, more or less unwittingly, standard Marshallian economists have opted to avoid this difficulty. They take the short cut of postulating that markets do work, which allows them to go on to study other topics, in particular the formation of normal equilibrium.

Brunner, Meltzer, Laidler, and I might all agree that, as soon as a market is decentralised, market clearing will not occur. At first sight, such a statement looks acceptable. Still, I would refrain from endorsing it. In effect, I think that as soon as a market is decentralised, it is hardly worthwhile raising the question of whether it features market clearing. In other words, the notion of market clearing makes sense only with reference to a centralised market structure.

Concluding remarks

Friedman and Brunner and Meltzer have in common their Marshallian affiliation and their dismissal of fiscal and monetary activism. Yet, they differ on the topic of whether theory should be based on the assumptions of price and wage flexibility and market clearing. When Friedman's position is properly reconstructed, it turns out that his theory is based on these assumptions. In contrast, Brunner and Meltzer and Laidler reject them on the grounds that sluggishness and market non-reality are obvious facts of life. My paper has shown that Friedman's position is more congruent with the Marshallian canonical model. While Marshallian theory, broadly understood, has developed in such a way as to incorporate rigidity results, the same is not true for sluggishness. A methodological explanation of this state of affairs has been attempted in the final section of the paper.

Notes

1. See, e.g., Friedman (1974*a,* 1974*b*), Laidler (1981), Tobin (1981), Brunner (1983).
2. Cf. De Vroey (2005).
3. As Friedman's writings are too numerous to be fully considered, I will focus on the following pieces: his 1967 *AEA* Presidential Address (Friedman, 1968) – introducing the expectations-augmented Phillips curve model – his 1976 *Price Theory* textbook, his Monetary Framework essay (1974*a*), a later piece on Keynes (Friedman [1989] 1997), and, finally, his interview with Snowdon and Vane (Snowdon and Vane, 1997).
4. I refer to the market equilibrium/normal equilibrium dyad rather than to the short-/long-run distinction because of the ambiguities in the latter. In doing so, I am returning to Marshall's own terminology.
5. Unlike new classical economists, Friedman has always praised Keynes's work. His affinity with Keynes follows from the fact that the finds him 'a true Marshallian in method' (1974, 18). While Friedman ends up claiming that the Keynesian project failed, this is not because Keynes constructed the wrong kind of theory but rather because his theory failed to be confirmed by experience (1974, 134).
6. The same point is made in his article on Keynes (Friedman, [1989] 1997, 8).
7. My examination of Brunner and Meltzer's position is mainly based on their 1993 book, *Money and the Economy: Issues in Monetary Analysis*.
8. The difference is that to Brunner and Meltzer market non-clearing, the result of sluggishness, is still accompanied with individual equilibrium while to Keynesians market non-clearing involves individual disequilibrium.
9. Laidler has written extensively on the themes of my inquiry. For this essay, I have examined the following pieces: Laidler (1981), ([1986] 2001), ([1991] 2004), (1999), (2005), (2006).
10. I agree with Laidler that the presence of two distinct theoretical approaches can be detected in Friedman's presidential address. However, I am of the opinion that the first was present almost inadvertently, so that the second approach should be viewed as having had the upper hand from the outset.
11. Cf. De Vroey (2006).
12. The distinction between the short and the long period is still present but each of these is now considered as a subcase of normal equilibrium. At present, the market equilibrium/normal equilibrium terminology has been replaced by the short-period/long-period terminology, which is confusing. As far as possible, I shall stick to the original designation.
13. As noted by Viner, 'the ordinary economic situation is one of disequilibrium moving in the direction of equilibrium rather than of realised equilibrium' ([1931] 1953, 206).
14. We touch here on a frequent confusion. In the Walrasian approach, market clearing and equilibrium are part and parcel of each other. This is not true for the Marshallian approach, where market clearing can be separated from equilibrium. The belief that market non-clearing is a normal outcome in the Marshallian approach rests on the mistaken importation of the Walrasian notion of disequilibrium into Marshallian theory.
15. This section is based on De Vroey (2007).
16. This conclusion does not amount to expelling duration from Marshallian theory for it may still play a role in the formation of *normal* equilibrium.
17. It is worth noticing that subsequent Marshallian authors have scarcely taken up the constant marginal utility of money assumption.
18. Readers may or may not like new classical and real business-cycle theory but it must be acknowledged that it has been able to achieve this integration, thereby bridging the divide that previously existed.

19. My claim that unemployment has no place in the standard Marshallian labour market does not exclude labour market disequilibrium. The latter will simply take the form of over- or under-employment, a departure from the level of employment associated with normal equilibrium.
20. For a comparison between Phillips's own view of his construct and that of subsequent economists, see Leeson (2000).
21. As a result, Keynes's well-known second observation in chapter 2 of the *General Theory* collapses (cf. De Vroey, 2004, 63).
22. For example, it is to be found in Santomero and Seater's *Journal of Economic Literature* survey: 'Because of market frictions and structural changes, unemployment always is positive. By implication, then, there will be unemployment even when the economy is in general equilibrium, defined as the absence of excess demand in each market' (Santomero and Seater, 1978, 515). Another example is Hall and Taylor's (1991) *Macroeconomics* textbook. They define the natural rate of unemployment as 'the amount of unemployment when the labour market is in equilibrium' (1991, 71), while they define equilibrium employment as 'the volume of employment at the intersection of supply and demand' (1991, 85).
23. The fact that frictional unemployment requires a different trade technology is witnessed in the works of authors like Mortensen (1986) and Pissarides (1990). To mention just one element, in a search model the market functions in a more decentralized way since workers have to visit firms and to get informed about the prices that are posted. Also, the so-called law of a single price is no longer being respected. On this see, Batyra and De Vroey (2009).
24. As a result, the ambiguity brought out by Laidler disappears.
25. Here, an element of difference in speed of adjustment is needed, since it must be assumed that the speed of adjustment for final goods is higher than that for inputs.
26. 'As yet they have no reason to suppose a change in the price level, hence they have no reason to change their supply function. It will remain the solid supply curve on Figure 12.6 [Figure 11.3], if we interpret P^* as the price level *perceived* or *anticipated* by workers. To them, it will appear as if the demand for labour had shifted to the right, to the dashed demand curve. At each nominal wage rate (also real wage as perceived by them), employers are seeking to hire more workers' (Friedman, 1976, 224; his emphasis).
27. 'Employers faced with an increased nominal demand for their products will count on being able to get a higher price or the equivalent. The same nominal wage means a lower real wage in terms of that higher price of his product. For employers as a whole, it will appear as if the supply curve had shifted to the right to the dashed supply curve' (Friedman, 1976, 224).
28. A few authors have pointed out Friedman's flaw. For example, Hahn (1995, 52) writes: 'Traditional search theory finds no *formal* representation of the economy in macro theories of the natural rate. It is referred to, or better appealed to, but it is not connected with the theory proposed'. See also Rogerson (1997) who confronts Friedman's categories with the search approach and makes it clear that his model is far from being a search model. Later on, models of the natural rate of unemployment based on a search-theoretical perspective were developed which were not based on the canonical Marshallian model of the market.
29. Some interpreters have taken in earnest Friedman's reference to Walrasian theory in his definition of the natural rate of unemployment. Leeson is amongst them (Leeson, 2000). To me, this reference is an ecumenical gesture, which is deprived of any theoretical content.
30. Friedman's unease in this respect is illustrated by his awkward use of the expression 'overfull employment' (1976, 223).
31. 'In most such models [of the business cycle] unemployment as a distinct activity plays no role whatever. For many other economists, explaining the business cycle is taken to *mean* accounting for recurrent episodes of widespread unemployment. From this

alternative viewpoint, a model with cleared markets seems necessarily to miss the main point, however successful it may be in accounting for other phenomena, and the work of "equilibrium" macroeconomists is often criticized as though it were a failed attempt to explain unemployment (which it surely does fail to do) instead of as an attempt to explain something else' (Lucas, 1987, 48).

32. If it departs from Lucas's model, it is on another point, namely in exhibiting a coexistence between market clearing and disequilibrium, the result of the Marshallian character of Friedman's model.
33. This point was documented by Bewley (1999).
34. Another possible candidate, the inverse L supply of labour considered by Modigliani in his influential 1944 paper, must be discounted. Here, agents have special preferences – they are indifferent between leisure and work at the nominal wage corresponding to the horizontal section of the supply curve – yet no impediment to the formation of market equilibrium is present. Put differently, in order to cause market non-clearing, rigidity must be a feature of the market rather than a trait characterizing participants in the market.
35. In Lucas's words: 'Certainly, the term rigidity does *not* refer to some characteristic of nominal price or wage series by themselves, but rather to the behaviour of these series relative to the way they would have been predicted to behave under a particular class of models' (Lucas, 1987, 89).
36. Cf. De Vroey (2004).
37. Cf. Tobin ([1993] 2001, 145).

References

Batyra, A. and M. De Vroey (2009). "From One to Many Islands: The Emergence of Search and Matching Models," University of Louvain, Department of Economics, Discussion paper N°200905, http://sites.uclouvain.be/econ/DP/IRES/2009005.pdf.

Bewley, T. (1999). *Why Wages Don't Fall during a Recession*. Cambridge: Cambridge University Press.

Blanchard, O. and L. Summers (1986). "Hysteresis and Unemployment." *NBER Macroeconomics Annual*.

Brunner, K. (1983). "Has Monetarism Failed?" *Cato Journal* 3:1, 23–62.

Brunner, K. and A. Meltzer (1993). *Money and the Economy: Issues in Monetary Analysis*. Raffaele Mattioli Foundation lectures, Cambridge: Cambridge University press.

De Vroey, M. (2004). *Involuntary Unemployment: The Elusive Quest for a Theory*. London: Routledge.

De Vroey, M. (2005). "The History of Macroeconomics Viewed Against the Background of the Marshall-Walras Divide." In M. De Vroey and K. Hoover, eds., *The IS-LM Model. Its Rise, Fall and Strange Persistence*, Annual Supplement to Volume 36, *History of Political Economy*. Durham and London: Duke University Press, 2004, pp. 57–91.

De Vroey, M. (2006). "Marshall versus Walras on Equilibrium." In G. Becattini, M. Dardi, and T. Raffaeli, eds., *The Elgar Companion to Marshall*. Cheltenham: Edward Elgar, pp. 237–248.

De Vroey, M. (2007). "Did the Market-clearing Postulate Pre-exist New Classical Economics? The Case of Marshallian Theory." *The Manchester School 75*, 3–38.

Friedman, M. (1968). "The Role of Monetary Policy." *American Economic Review* 58, 1–17.

Friedman, M. (1974*a*). "A Theoretical Framework for Monetary Analysis." In R. J. Gordon, ed., *Milton Friedman's Monetary Framework*. Chicago: Chicago University Press, pp. 1–62.

Friedman, M. (1974b). "Comments on the Critics." In R. J. Gordon, ed., *Milton Friedman's Monetary Framework*. Chicago: Chicago University Press, pp. 132–177.

Friedman, M. (1976). *Price Theory*. Chicago: Aldine Publishing Company.

Friedman, M. ([1989] 1997). "John Maynard Keynes." Federal Reserve Bank of Richmond, *Economic Quarterly* 83 (2), 1–23.
Frisch, R. (1950). "Alfred Marshall's Theory of Value." *The Quarterly Journal of Economics* 64, 495–524.
Hahn, F. (1995). "Theoretical Reflections on the 'Natural Rate of Unemployment'." In R. Cross, ed., *The Natural Rate of Unemployment. Reflections on 25 Years of the Hypothesis.* Cambridge: Cambridge University Press, pp. 43–56.
Hall, R. and J. Taylor (1991). *Macroeconomics. Theory, Performance, and Policy.* New York: Norton.
Hayek, von F. A. ([1937] 1948). "Economics and Knowledge." In F. A. von Hayek, ed., *Individualism and Economic Order.* Chicago: The University of Chicago Press, pp.33–55.
Hicks, J. R. (1967). "Monetary Theory and History – an Attempt at Perspective." In *Critical Essays in Monetary Theory.* Oxford: Clarendon Press, pp. 155–173.
Laidler, D. (1981). "Monetarism: An Interpretation and an Assessment." *Economic Journal* 91, 1–28.
Laidler, D. ([1986] 2001). "The New-Classical Contribution to Macroeconomics." In Snowdon and Vane, eds., *A Macroeconomic Reader.* London: Routledge, pp. 334–358.
Laidler, D. ([1991] 2004). "Wage and Price Stickiness in Macroeconomics: An Historical Perspective." The Thirteenth Henry Thornton Lecture, in *Macroeconomics in Retrospect. The Selected Essays of David Laidler.* Cheltenham: Edward Elgar.
Laidler, D. (1999). *Fabricating the Keynesian Revolution. Studies of the Inter-war Literature on Money, the Cycle, and Unemployment.* Cambridge: Cambridge University Press.
Laidler, D. (2005). "Milton Friedman and the Evolution of Macroeconomics." *EPRI Working papers Series,* Department of Economics, University of Western Ontario, No. 2005–11.
Laidler, D. (2006). "Keynes and the Birth of Modern Macroeconomics." In B. Bateman and R. Backhouse, eds., *The Cambridge Companion to Keynes.* Cambridge: Cambridge University Press, pp. 39–57.
Leijonhufvud, A. (1968). *On Keynesian Economics and the Economics of Keynes.* Oxford: Oxford University Press.
Leeson, R. (2000). *The Eclipse of Keynesianism. The Political Economy of the Chicago Counter-Revolution.* Basingstoke: Palgrave.
Lipsey, R. (1960). "The Relationship between Unemployment and the Rate of Change of Money Wage Rates in the United Kingdom, 1862–1957: A Further Analysis." *Economica* February, 1–31.
Lipsey, R. (1974). "The Micro Theory of the Phillips Curve Reconsidered: A Reply to Holmes and Smyth." *Economica* 41, 62–70.
Lipsey, R. (1978). "The Place of the Phillips Curve in Macroeconomic Models." In A. Bergstrom, A. Catt, M. Peston and B. Silverstone, eds. *Stability and Inflation, A Volume of Essays to Honour the Memory of A.W.H. Phillips.* Chichester: Wiley, pp.49–75.
Lipsey, R. (2000). "IS-LM, Keynesianism, and the New Classicism." In Backhouse, R. and A. Salanti, eds., *Macroeconomics and the Real World, vol. 2 Keynesian Economics, Unemployment and Policy.* Oxford: Oxford University Press, pp. 57–82.
Lucas, R. E. Jr. ([1972] 1981). "Expectations and the Neutrality of Money." In *Studies in Business Cycle Theory.* Cambridge, MA: The M.I.T. Press, pp. 65–89.
Lucas, R. E. Jr. (1987). *Models of Business Cycle.* Oxford: Basil Blackwell.
Marshall, A. (1920). *Principles of Economics,* 8th ed. London: Macmillan.
Matthews, R. (1990). "Marshall and the Labour Market." In J. Whitaker, ed., *Centenary Essays on Alfred Marshall.* Cambridge: Cambridge University Press, pp. 14–43.
Modigliani, F. (1944). "Liquidity Preference and the Theory of Interest and Money." *Econometrica* 12, 44–88.
Mortensen, D. (1986). "Job Search and Labour Market Analysis." In Ashenfelter, O. and R. Layard, eds., *Handbook of Labour Economics.* Amsterdam: North-Holland, pp. 849–919.

Newman, P. (1965). *The Theory of Exchange*. Englewood Cliffs: Prentice-Hall.
Pissarides, C. (1990). *Equilibrium Unemployment Theory*. Oxford: Basil Blackwell.
Rogerson, R. (1997). "Theory Ahead of Language in the Economics of Unemployment." *Journal of Economic Perspectives* 11, 73–92.
Santomero, A. and J. Seater (1978). "The Inflation-Unemployment Trade-off: A Critique of the Literature." *Journal of Economic Literature* 16, 499–544.
Snowdon, B. and H. Vane (1997). "Modern Macroeconomics and Its Evolution from a Monetarist Perspective: An Interview with Professor Milton Friedman." *Journal of Economic Studies* 24:4, 192–222.
Snowdon, B. and H. Vane (2005). *Modern Macroeconomics. Its Origin, Development and Current State*. Cheltenham: Edward Elgar.
Tobin, J. (1981). "The Monetarist Counter-Revolution Today. An Appraisal." *Economic Journal* 91 (March), 29–42.
Tobin, J. ([1993] 2001). "Price Flexibility and Output Stability. An Old Keynesian View." In Snowdon, B. and H. Vane, eds., *A Macroeconomic Reader*. London: Routledge, pp. 135–155.
Viner, J. ([1931] 1953). "Cost Curves and Supply Curves." In Stigler, G. and K. Boulding, eds., *Readings in Price Theory*. London: Allen and Unwin, pp. 198–232.
Walras, L. (1954). *Elements of Pure Economics*, translated by W. Jaffé. London: Allen and Unwin.

Discussion

Hans-Michael Trautwein

My quick summary of the main arguments in Michel De Vroey's complex chapter is this:

1. There are fundamental differences between monetarist authors concerning their use of assumptions about market clearing and price flexibility, with Milton Friedman in one camp, and Karl Brunner, Allan Meltzer and David Laidler in the other.
2. With respect to Friedman, the Walras-Marshall divide between the Lucasian principles of continuous market clearing and flexible prices on the one hand, and monetarist macroeconomics on the other is smaller than it is generally claimed to be.
3. The divide is smaller, because both Marshall's and Friedman's models of markets differ from their rhetorics about market adjustment.
4. Even so, Marshall's and Friedman's views on market clearing and price flexibility are more thoroughly grounded in theory than those of Brunner, Meltzer and Laidler.

Thus, the chapter seems to lead to the conclusion that Marshall and Friedman are half-baked Walrasians, whereas Brunner, Meltzer and Laidler are just realists without proper theory. At least that is my 'reconstruction' of De Vroey's reconstructions. His distinction between different monetarist approaches is certainly warranted, to some degree; and I agree that it is useful to check in how far the models, in which authors attempt to fix their ideas, really correspond to those ideas. In the following passages, I will argue, however, that (some of) De Vroey's definitions of what constitutes proper theorising about market adjustment are overly rigid, that his account of the connections between Marshall, Friedman and Laidler is crucially incomplete, and that a different overall conclusion emerges, if money – the key word in 'monetarism' – is taken seriously.

First to Marshall: De Vroey argues that Marshall's corn market model can be interpreted to imply continuous market clearing, even though false (price) trading is possible. As noted by De Vroey, Marshall makes a number of restrictive assumptions to minimise the likeliness and consequences of disequilibrium transactions. Most importantly, he defines his country-town corn market as a quasi-centralised set-up, narrowly limited in space, time and the number of participants. Marshall postulates that the agents have more or less perfect information about the market supply and demand functions, and hence about the equilibrium outcomes. Just in case some transactions happen to be made at false prices, they are assumed to have no income effects. Do all these restrictions warrant De Vroey's conclusion that in Marshall's theory 'market clearing is always realized'? (p. 246) I don't think so. The care with which Marshall guards his Walras-like results in a framework that could (unlike Walras's framework) lead to rather different outcomes indicates that Marshall's approach is, in principle, more open than De Vroey wants to make us believe.

Marshall's assumption of 'market equilibrium' (in De Vroey's terms) may simply have served to allow Marshall to deal with price and output adjustments with the limited tools of formal modelling available to him. The convergence of transactions within the 'market day' to a market-clearing *price* provides the base for *output* adjustments (within given capacity constraints) between the market days, and hence for new price postings on the side of the suppliers. The iterative process of price adjustment *within* and output adjustment *between* the trading periods is assumed to converge on a short-period equilibrium, in which output is constant. If production capacities change, different laws of motion may come into play, as economies of scale and other factors change firm behaviour and market structures (cf. Leijonhufvud, 2006). Hence I would not subscribe to De Vroey's suppression of Marshall's short-/long-period distinction. If Marshall's assumption of intra-day price-adjustment was a tribute to the limits of modelling techniques in his time, rather than a deep conviction about the nature of market processes in general, it should not be interpreted as an anticipation of Lucasian macroeconomics (as suggested by De Vroey, p. 236).

Moreover, what is missing from De Vroey's account of Marshall's corn market model is the fact that Marshall focuses on a classical good which can be stocked up for both consumption and investment purposes. He includes, among the different groups of agents, merchants who act as intermediaries. Thus, in the words of Hicks (1989, 9–10), Marshall's model 'allows his merchants to carry over surplus stocks at the end of the day; and if at the end, why not at the beginning? What then is the significance of the "end of the day"? A market in which carry-over is permitted is a continuing market; it does not "finish up"'. The presence of middlemen and carry-over is not easily reconcilable with De Vroey's interpretation of Marshall's model as a centralised market with limited duration that, as such, would imply quasi-instantaneous price adjustments to clearly defined excess demands (positive or negative). The implicit problems of making clear distinctions between price and quantity effects have actually led to the famous reconstruction of Marshall's model in terms of a market for a perishable good, the fish market (ascribed by Hicks, 1989, 10 fn. 6, to Dennis Robertson; see also Leijonhufvud, 2006). The pressure on suppliers of a perishable good, like fresh fish, to come to (price) terms within a market day may affect their production to an extent that casts doubts, not only on the general applicability of Marshall's exclusion of income effects but also on De Vroey's definition of the 'normal equilibrium' position of price and quantity as an independent attractor for the quasi-continuous 'market equilibria'. Since De Vroey compares Marshall's market model with Friedman's discussion of the labour market, it should be noted that labour markets are like fish markets (without refrigeration) in the sense that the sellers of labour cannot create stocks of their supplies. One can hardly ignore the income effects that false wage trading has for the spending decisions of wage earners in other markets and for the investment decisions (including capacity changes) of employers. So it is difficult to draw a straight line from Marshall's corn market model to the labour market. Some elements are clearly missing from De Vroey's account.

Next to Friedman: If Friedman's 'deeper' understanding of the natural rate of unemployment as a market-clearing phenomenon is supposed to run parallel to Marshall's corn market, what are we to make of the key role of imperfect information in his model? De Vroey's distinction between Marshallian market equilibrium and normal equilibrium may fit with Friedman's story about workers' misperceptions, as illustrated in Figure 11.3. However, Friedman's acceleration hypothesis also contains the possibility of substantial rationing on the way back from inflationary 'under-unemployment equilibrium' to the 'natural rate of (un)employment'. There are two alternatives on that way: either workers realise that the nominal wage that they can negotiate in the face of inflation implies a real wage that is lower than their desired real wage at the (politically targeted) 'under-unemployment' position of the system. In this case, they cut back their labour supply, and reach DeVroeyian 'normal equilibrium', sooner or later, or workers are able to compensate themselves for earlier and expected losses from inflation by pressing up nominal wages. In that case, they are likely to be rationed in their supply of labour. As the short-side rule applies, market clearing is ruled out. This may be considered a temporary phenomenon, even though it did take a while, in the 1970s and 1980s, until workers and trade unions had acquired sufficient information (about the behaviour of central banks and the rest of the world) to take these consequences into account. If rationing is done on an unequal basis (some persons work full time, others become fully unemployed), and if, for example, there are substantial turnover costs (due to the existence of job-specific human capital, etc.), insider–outsider divisions may emerge, and unemployment may become persistent to the degree that it becomes unclear whether it is beyond the 'natural rate' or whether that rate has shifted. De Vroey himself draws the attention to the fact that Brunner and Meltzer have discussed such processes with respect to European unemployment. Friedman himself may not have paid much attention to labour supply rationing, but the possibility of temporary disequilibrium is present in the general framework of his acceleration hypothesis. And it provides a counterargument to De Vroey's claim that price (or wage) sluggishness cannot explain non-clearing (p.251).

Finally to Laidler: The addressee of this *Festschrift* gets rather little attention in De Vroey's chapter, which may explain why the key points in the Marshall connection of monetarism are missing from it. David Laidler, for one, has emphasised Marshall's pioneering role in the development of theories of the stock demand for money (see, for example, Laidler, 1991, ch. 3). The Cambridge equation – or M = KPY, as Laidler's license plate has it – is the backbone of monetarism. In the 'buffer stock' extensions that Laidler has been working on, it has also led to some interesting challenges to the neo-Walrasian modes of thinking (or refusing to think) about price stickiness and economising on information. It is amazing that De Vroey finds himself 'amazed by the discrepancy between the central role [Brunner, Meltzer and Laidler] attribute to [the sluggishness of prices] and the lack of serious reflection on its meaning, or on the possible obstacle that its incorporation into established equilibrium theory will face' (p.225). Those who have read Laidler's 'Taking Money Seriously' (1990) will hardly complain about a lack of serious reflection. Take, for example, Laidler's argument that '[i]f individual agents find it costly to vary money wages and prices, and to gather the information upon which to base such changes, then the availability of a buffer stock of money which softens for them the consequences of making errors about these matters will itself be a source of wage and price stickiness. The agent will trade off the cost of holding money against the costs of obtaining information and of changing prices' (Laidler, 1990, 30). De Vroey may be right about the 'possible obstacle' that the incorporation of price sluggishness into 'established equilibrium theory' will face, if the latter is equated with neo-Walrasian macroeconomics à la Lucas. But that is only too bad for this kind of establishment! It was, after all, Lucas himself who – at a conference at which De Vroey, Laidler and the writer of these lines were present – stated that 'the theories embedded in general equilibrium dynamics of the sort that we know how to use pretty well now... don't let us think about... the real effects of monetary instability' (Lucas, 2004, 24). The shortcomings in Marshall's own corn market model notwithstanding, the Marshallian approach seems far better suited for the exploration of the interaction between possible failures of markets to clear continuously, money holdings and the stickiness of prices.

References

Hicks, J. (1989). *A Market Theory of Money*. Oxford: Oxford University Press.
Laidler, D. (1990). *Taking Money Seriously, and Other Essays*. New York: Phillip Allan.
Laidler, D. (1991). *The Golden Age of the Quantity Theory*. New York: Phillip Allan.

Leijonhufvud, A. (2006). "Market Adjustment Processes." In Tiziano Raffaelli, Giacomo Beccatini, and Marco Dardi, eds., *The Elgar Companion to Marshall*. Cheltenham: Edward Elgar, pp. 226–235.

Lucas, R. (2004). "My Keynesian Education." In Michel De Vroey and Kevin Hoover, eds., *The IS-LM Model: Its Rise, Fall, and Strange Persistence*. Durham: Duke University Press, pp. 12–24.

12
Less Than an Ideal Type: Varieties of Real Bills Doctrines

Neil T. Skaggs

Conventional histories of monetary policy often focus on three episodes that allegedly illustrate the battle between proponents of the quantity theory of money and proponents of the real bills doctrine. As defined by Lloyd Mints (1945, 9), the real bills doctrine is the assertion that 'if only "real" bills are discounted, the expansion of bank money will be in proportion to any extension in trade that may take place, or to the "needs of trade."' The doctrine maintains that money created by this process provides liquidity to the monetary system without generating inflationary pressures. The three frequently cited episodes are the Bullionist Controversy in Great Britain during the Napoleonic wars, when the convertibility of the pound sterling into gold was severed; the Currency School–Banking School Controversy of the 1840s (and after), which centered on the Bank Act of 1844, during a period when the pound was convertible into gold; and the origins of the Federal Reserve System and its behavior from the early 1920s through 1932, when monetary policy was blamed to lesser or greater degree for the onset of the Great Depression. That the three episodes differ in crucial ways is widely understood. However, the two approaches have been treated as 'ideal types' reflective of the major elements of the competing approaches.

In this chapter I argue that this common view misconstrues the evidence, largely by failing to understand the dramatically different nature of the 'real bills doctrine' supposedly applied in these three instances. The directors of the Bank of England and their 'anti-bullionist' supporters sought to cover themselves with the mantle of Adam Smith by using the real bills doctrine to defend their policies (though their definition of the doctrine differed in important ways from Smith's).[1] The major concerns of the Banking School – the purported heirs of the anti-bullionists[2] – were quite different. The pound sterling was fully convertible in the 1830s and '40s when the debate heated up, and the question at issue was how best to avoid – or, at least, to weather – the financial panics that had periodically threatened the convertibility of the pound beginning in 1825. Despite some statements that can be interpreted (or *misinterpreted*) as advocacy of the classic real bills doctrine, a strong case can be made that none of the major writers in the Banking School tradition made use of the doctrine in their arguments. Finally, though the creators of the Federal Reserve System sought to create *de novo* a monetary system and monetary-policy apparatus based squarely on the real-bills approach, they pursued a strategy that violated some of the basic principles of the Banking School writers, including, in the late 1920s, making implementation of the real bills doctrine their primary goal, at the expense of conforming to the rules of the classical gold standard. My ultimate conclusion is thus quite easy to foresee: Treating these three episodes as *sui generis* is less than ideal.

The Bullionist controversy

> Though the Bank directors of that day at last fell into errors, yet on the whole they acted with singular judgment and moderation. But when, in 1810, they came to be examined as to their reasons, they gave answers that have become almost classical by their nonsense.
>
> Walter Bagehot, *Lombard Street* (1873)

In the latter half of the eighteenth century the British currency consisted of full-bodied gold coin, issued in denominations of £1 and higher, a fractional, and heavily worn, silver coinage, and bank notes issued by a large number of 'country banks', as well as by the Bank of England. The country banks were, by law, partnerships of no more than six individuals, ensuring that nearly all were small and relatively poorly capitalised. The Bank of England, a private corporation chartered by the British government, was by this time the sole issuer of notes within a 65-mile radius of London. All notes, both of the Bank of England and the country banks, were convertible into gold at a rate of £3 17*s*. 10½ *d*. per ounce.

Although a privately owned institution, the Bank of England was closely tied to the British government, and it served, even in 1797, as Britain's de facto central bank. Of course, the Bank's shareholders and directors denied this, and few people, even in the London financial district, clearly understood the fact. But insiders in the banking sector recognised that, almost literally, the Bank of England held the entire gold reserve for the banking system, as the crisis of 1793 had demonstrated. On 1 February that year, France declared war on Great Britain, placing further stress on what was, according to Thomas Tooke (1838, 176–179), a significantly overextended credit system.[3] The onset of war, and the necessity of extensive government borrowing, drove interest rates sharply higher, thereby reducing the value of financial assets held by many financial and trading firms. The war itself disrupted trade with Europe. The effects on the overextended credit system were profound. Even solvent commercial firms found it difficult to obtain the credit needed to sustain their businesses, as banks and bill dealers became more conservative in their lending. Rather than stepping into the breach, the Bank of England also tightened credit, throwing many creditworthy borrowers into a panic. A general collapse of credit was averted when, in April 1793, Parliament passed an Act permitting the loan of Exchequer bills, not to exceed 50 percent of the value of collateral posted by the recipients, to traders in need of liquid, transferable, assets. The government's action brought the crisis to a quick end.

In parliamentary hearings held in the wake of the panic, London banker Henry Thornton entered the public record for the first time, arguing that the Bank directors should have increased their lending, rather than restricting it, since what the trading community needed wasn't more loans per se but more high-quality, transferable assets, which the Bank could have provided. That is, Thornton argued that the Bank should act as the nation's lender of last resort.[4]

In early 1797, as hostilities between Great Britain and Napoleonic France intensified, rumors of a purported French landing in the northwest of England set off a run on the country banks. Country bankers were quickly deluged with their own notes, returned in demand for coin. They, in turn, began converting their London assets into gold as fast as possible, greatly intensifying the ongoing decline in the Bank of England's gold reserve. On 26 February the Government of William Pitt ordered the Bank to restrict cash payments. The Act required country banks to continue converting their notes into Bank of England notes on demand but severed the connection of Bank notes to gold. This ostensibly temporary measure was renewed periodically for more than two decades, as Great Britain fought, and ultimately defeated, France and then readjusted its economy to a peacetime setting.

While its notes were convertible, the Bank had adjusted its note issue in response to the size of its gold reserve, which, in general, depended upon the state of the balance of trade. With its notes no longer convertible on demand, the Bank directors were forced to consider anew the principles by which they would control the Bank's lending and note issue. Certainly, the suspension of convertibility did not free the Bank from behaving in a manner supportive of the British economy. Nor did it free the Bank from the necessity of supporting the war effort against France; quite the contrary, the Bank became a major source of finance throughout the war. By what principle would the Bank be guided?

One possible answer was suggested by any number of men in the financial and commercial sectors: the Bank should seek to maintain the exchange rate at its par level, and it should attempt to maintain a market price of gold bullion equal to its mint price. Conventional wisdom maintained that, were the pound to fall below its par value on the foreign exchanges, the Bank should raise its discount rate and discount fewer bills, allowing the quantity of Bank notes in circulation to fall. Higher prices should be met by the same procedure. And, to a large extent over the next few years, the Bank actually behaved in this manner.

Despite the Bank's cautious policies from 1797 through 1801, agricultural prices rose sharply and the exchange rate fell below par. Walter Boyd, who had personal and political axes to grind with the Bank, lodged the first serious public attack on the Bank, arguing that 'the suspension of specie payments had permitted the Bank to issue more notes than would have been possible under convertibility, and this was responsible for the rise of the price of commodities and of foreign exchange' (Fetter, 1969 [1978]). Because Boyd overstepped his case – he treated the large increase in crop prices and the modest decline in sterling exchange as equivalent confirmations of malpractice by the Bank – his pamphlet embarrassed the Bank but had little lasting impact. Sir Francis Baring soon pounced on Boyd's inconsistency, arguing that the rise in agricultural prices was caused by consecutive years of bad weather and the increased difficulty of importing grain from Europe, not by excessive Bank issues.

Ironically, a second, much better known, defense of the Bank, published early in 1802, provided the theoretical framework for a devastating critique of later Bank policy pronouncements. In *An Enquiry into the Nature and Effects of the Paper Credit of Great Britain*, Henry Thornton defended the Bank directors from charges of excess issuance of notes during the period 1797 through 1801. Thornton was satisfied that the unfavorable exchange rate and the rise in agricultural prices were sufficiently explained by the substantial foreign payments to prosecute the war on the continent and 'two seasons in succession of extraordinary dearth', to use Thomas Tooke's (1838, 228) felicitous phrase. But Thornton's *Paper Credit* was more a monograph on monetary theory than a pamphlet on current events, and it provided a well-rounded (if not well-written) discussion of both monetary theory and policy.

Lower commodity prices combined with a higher exchange rate to minimise criticism of the Bank for several years thereafter, although monetary issues continued to be examined closely.[5] However, in 1808 and 1809 significant increases in prices and a sharp decline in the exchange rate generated a flood of criticism of the Bank, forcing its directors and their supporters to defend the Bank's policies. The Bank's directors and their allies followed the lead of the officials of the Bank of Ireland, who, in 1804, based their defense on the real bills doctrine.

Any number of illustrations of anti-bullionist logic might be adduced, including Charles Bosanquet's *Practical Observations on the Report of the Bullion-Committee* (1810), which drew David Ricardo's famous *Reply* (1811 [1951], 156–256) and the speeches in Parliament by Nicholas Vansittart (1811 [1994]). Here I will confine myself to the argument made by Robert Torrens, who was known for his sharp logic (and who later aligned himself with the Currency School). In *An Essay on Money and Paper Currency,* Torrens stated that:

> it will be found that limiting the issues of bank paper, to the discounting of solid mercantile bills, payable at a fixed and moderate date, is an effectual means of returning all superfluous paper upon the bank that issued it, and of bringing the supply of circulating medium within the measure of the demand. When the bank discounts a real mercantile bill, it does not throw its paper gratuitously into the channel of circulation; it exchanges its notes for a just equivalent – it supplies a real demand: for the merchant, whose bill was discounted, was desirous of possessing the bank paper, and able to pay for it. Desire to possess, and ability to pay, are all that is necessary to constitute effectual demand. The increased issue of currency, therefore, occasioned by the discounting of the mercantile bill, could not, in this first stage, overstock the market, and produce depreciation. (1812 [1994], 179–80)

No finer statement of the classic real bills doctrine exists. Torrens defends it while admitting that banknotes put into circulation via the discounting of real bills are likely to be spent multiple times and may, in the short run, have some effect on prices. But this is only a temporary matter, since the notes will be used by manufacturers to purchase material inputs and labor which will be used to expand the supply of goods in the market. Once the supply expands, prices will return to their former level (Torrens, 1812 [1994], 188–190). So long as 'the bank paper, issued in discounting mercantile bills, [is] payable at a short date, [it] would not, even if employed, in the first instance, in the trade of consumption, remain long enough in the market, to enhance the money price of commodities, and to be itself absorbed into the mass of currency' (Torrens, 1812 [1994], 193).

Torrens goes even further in defending lending of inconvertible paper notes against real bills:

> Thus we see, that every issue of bank paper, made on good mercantile bills, payable at a short date, produces a two-fold effect upon the currency; in the first place, it encourages industry, and increases the quantity of commodities to be circulated; and, in the next place, in consequence of the deduction of the legal interest, diminishes the medium by which commodities are circulated. Instead, therefore, of producing an excess and depreciation of the currency, the issues of the bank, when regulated by just principles, have a perpetual tendency, both by increasing the demand, and diminishing the supply, to raise the value of the circulating medium. This increased demand and diminished supply, consequent to each well-regulated issue of bank paper, are met by succeeding issues; the interest perpetually becoming due, and paid in upon these; securing the public against an excess of currency, and constituting the banker's profit. (1812 [1994], 200–201)

That someone of Torrens' intellectual stature could make such an argument a decade after Henry Thornton had lodged his devastating critique of just this version of the real bills doctrine is rather remarkable. In *The Paper Credit of Great Britain* Thornton had leveled a three-pronged argument against the real bills doctrine: (1) mercantile bills do not represent any real goods, since the same goods may be used to obtain multiple discounts as the goods move through the supply chain (1802 [1978], 86); (2) bills discounted for longer periods can effect more payments than shorter-dated bills (1802 [1978], 86); (3) an increase of notes that raises prices provides the means by which merchants are able to obtain even larger loans on discount.[6] Furthermore, if the discount rate is below the 'rate of mercantile profit', the demand for discounts would know no limit (Thornton, 1802 [1978], 253–254). What was required to hold prices in check was quantitative restriction of the Bank's note issue – something Thornton argued that the Bank had achieved from 1797 through 1801.

The fact that the governors of the Bank of England actually applied some quantitative restrictions to the note issue indicates that they recognised the necessity of directly limiting the quantity of Bank notes put into circulation. That the directors used the real bills doctrine to shield themselves from criticism, by enabling them to call upon the authority of Adam Smith and to deny that quantitative control of the currency was theoretically justified, is almost certain (though Thornton had argued cogently in *The Paper Credit* that such quantitative control was exactly what was required if an inconvertible currency were to work well). Yet it cannot be denied that some anti-bullionists found Thornton's argument wanting, and argued their case from a sincere belief that lending only on real bills would indeed prevent an inconvertible currency from depreciating (cf. Mints, 1945, 45–50).

The currency–banking controversy

> [T]he recommendations of Thomas Tooke, the leading member of the Banking School, were based on greater insight into the manner in which the monetary system worked prior to 1844, and were very much what a modern economist might suggest within the constraint of the policy goals ruling in the nineteenth century.
>
> David Laidler, 'Thomas Tooke on Monetary Reform' (1972).

In 1821, the Bank of England resumed convertibility of its notes into gold at the pre-war par. Rather than ending Britain's monetary problems, the return to convertibility altered the nature of the problems encountered. With the pound sterling tied to gold, the general level of prices could not long vary from the level determined by the international value of the precious metal before setting underway the process of correction. However, the economy was rocked by a series of monetary panics that threatened the convertibility of Bank notes. In the wake of the panic of 1825, a host of voices raised the cry that the country banks, aided and abetted by the Bank of England, had, by the issuance of too many notes, incited the speculation in commodity markets that nearly led to the suspension of cash payments by the Bank.

In the wake of the panic, an array of writers produced a flurry of pamphlets and articles on the subject. Of particular note, Thomas Tooke – author of the recently published, and widely acclaimed, *Thoughts and Details on the High and Low Prices of the Last Thirty Years* (1823) – contributed a small book entitled *Considerations on the State of the Currency* (1826). Tooke followed the path taken by other writers of bullionist persuasion in criticising both the country banks and the Bank of England for the roles they allegedly played in fostering the crisis. In subsequent years, Tooke was joined by writers of such caliber as George Warde Norman, Samuel Jones Loyd (Lord Overstone), and Robert Torrens, now recast as the very antithesis of the anti-bullionist he once was. Between 1826 and 1844 these men, and others, developed a body of thought known as Currency School doctrine. They adopted the framework developed by David Hume and David Ricardo, adhering to a more-or-less rigid version of the quantity theory/price-specie-flow mechanism of international adjustment. Like Tooke in 1826, they argued that the source of the problem in 1825 and of similar problems in the 1830s was the failure of the note issue to fluctuate as a fully metallic currency would. They believed that, when Britain began to run an international trade deficit and gold began to flow abroad from the Bank, the total note issue should shrink at the same rate as gold flowed abroad. Ultimately, they succeeded in passing the Bank Act of 1844 which, in operational terms, required the Bank of England to reduce its note issue pound for pound when Bank notes began flowing into the Bank in demand for gold. This, the Currency School writers argued, would restrain the lending of country banks by reducing their reserves, and would thereby promptly set in motion the contraction of banking credit and note issues needed to slow demand for commodities and begin the reduction of prices needed to re-establish international equilibrium.[7]

Some months after Tooke's entry to the debate, John Stuart Mill rose to the defense of both the country banks and the Bank of England. Utilising the data assembled by Tooke for empirical support, Mill argued that the received wisdom on the relationship between the note issues of banks and periods of speculative frenzy was simply wrong. Neither the notes issued by the country banks nor the note issues of the Bank of England played any appreciable role in the run-up of commodity prices. Moreover, artificially restricting the issuance of notes by the banks would prove ineffective in staunching episodes of 'rash' speculation in the future.

The proximate cause of speculation, said Mill, was the 'anticipated deficiency of supply' of particular commodities (1826 [1967], 73). Using Tooke's *High and Low Prices* to substantiate his argument, Mill noted that real shortages in the stocks of selected commodities gave rise to speculative purchases in those markets, driving up prices. Other merchants, caught up in the possibility of earning large profits, began speculating in markets in which shortages were less evident, driving up prices in those markets as well. The excitement of rising commodity prices spilled over into markets in which the expectation of higher prices and large profits was less justified or completely unjustified. Some measure of dishonesty was involved, as some speculators apparently drove up prices in well-stocked markets, held stocks briefly, then sold at a profit before the prices inevitably returned to normal levels. In short, justified speculation in particular markets became unjustified speculation across a wide range of markets. Mill's assessment of the situation is succinct: the cause of the evil was 'the universal propensity of mankind to over-estimate the chances in their own favor' (1826 [1967], 77).

But surely such widespread speculation would not have been possible without the easy credit provided by country banks and the Bank of England through the medium of their notes? Parliamentary investigations immediately focused on the currency. But Mill argued, on the basis of both logic and Tooke's empirical evidence, that currency – that is, banknotes – played little if any role in the bubble. The bullionist/nascent Currency School argument rested on three contentions:

> 1. That even in non-speculative periods, a paper currency, although convertible into specie, by law, at the option of the holder, is yet liable to *over-issue*.
> 2. That in speculative periods there is always an over-issue, which, by producing a general tendency of prices upwards, heightens and prolongs the spirit of *speculation*: That, when at length the revulsion arrives, the destruction of the

> extra paper which has been called into existence by the speculation, renders the recoil of the prices more violent, and for this reason, more destructive: And that these circumstances have actually taken place during the last three years.
>
> 3. That when the paper currency is suddenly increased, (at least if it be a paper currency issued, as ours is, chiefly through the medium of loans), a fall takes place in the *rate of interest*, which, by diminishing the incomes of the owners of small capitals, induces them to engage in hazardous speculations: and that this also actually happened during the last three years. (Mill, 1826 [1967], 81)

Mill proceeds to argue that none of these processes was operative during the period of speculation and collapse. In brief, Mill follows Adam Smith in arguing that an increase in the issue of banknotes will, at first, displace gold (1826 [1967], 82). To those who object that this requires time and that prices must generally rise before the price-specie-flow mechanism is set in motion, Mill replies that commodity arbitrage begins immediately, turning the exchange against Britain with the shortest of lags. Once the exchange hits the lower gold point, an outflow of gold begins, offsetting the increase in banknotes (1826 [1967], 83–85). Nor is this only a theory: Mill draws on Tooke's data to show that the exchanges turned against Britain nearly at the same time that the speculation commenced, noting that Tooke's evidence 'may be regarded as an admission, since it makes against his theory' (1826 [1967], 86).

Mill's denial that bank currency caused the speculative bubble does *not* amount to the argument that credit played no role in the rising commodity prices. Far from it: speculative behavior was driven by credit in the form of bills of exchange. The 'circulating medium' did indeed increase significantly, and it underpinned the higher prices, which made the ultimate collapse all the more catastrophic. But since banknotes weren't the problem, suppressing the country bank issues wouldn't have prevented the speculation or the succeeding collapse.[8]

In Mill's 1826 essay we see all the essential elements of the Banking School view: the endogeneity of credit, the demand-determined nature of particular forms of credit, the substitutability of one type of credit instrument for another, the importance of maintaining convertibility. What we *don't* see is *any* reference to lending on real bills as adequate security against over issue. Indeed, Mill argues that the speculation was driven by mercantile bills – the very opposite of the real bills doctrine. But then, Mill had read Thornton's *Paper Credit* (see p. 91) and understood Thornton's logic full well (Mill, 1826 [1967], 91). The first contribution to Banking School thought makes no reference to the real bills doctrine in any form.

The same can be said of the final contribution to the Banking School cause. Written in 1854 by John E. Cairnes, who correctly anticipated the impending commercial collapse and accompanying challenge to the convertibility of Bank notes that would come in 1857, *An Examination into the Principles of Currency Involved in the Bank Charter Act of 1844* (1854 [1966]) draws heavily on Thornton's *Paper Credit* in making its case against the rigidities built into the Bank Act. Cairnes argues that a monetary system appropriate to the complex British economy must be flexible enough to adjust to a variety of different shocks. Like Mill, Cairnes sees the roots of financial crises in speculation and overtrading supported by credit. Any increase in banknotes is a consequence of the higher prices, rather than the cause. Ironically, by separating the Banking Department from the Issue Department of the Bank of England, the Bank Act had freed the Banking Department from the responsibility of refraining from entering into speculative lending. Not surprisingly, the Bank had responded to profit incentives by expanding its loans inappropriately during periods of speculation (Cairnes, 1854 [1966], 20).[9]

The major theme of Cairnes' tract is that the Ricardian doctrine followed by the Currency School is overly simplistic. Any number of factors can cause a nation's balance of trade to fluctuate, and not all of them call for the rigid decrease or increase of currency necessitated by the Bank Act. Crop failures, foreign wars, and internal drains of coin require different responses than do trade deficits caused by an overheated domestic economy. The authors of the Bullion Report had understood this:

> The mere numerical return of the amount of bank notes in circulation, cannot be considered as at all deciding the question whether such paper is or is not excessive.... The effective currency of the country depends on the quickness of circulation and the number of exchanges performed in a given time, as well as upon its numerical amount; and all the circumstances which have a tendency to quicken or retard the rate of circulation, render the same amount of circulation more or less adequate to the wants of trade (quoted on pp. 40–41 of Cairnes (1854 [1969])).

Whatever effect the Bank Act may have had on the length and severity of periods of speculation came at a high price. Cairnes harks back to the crisis of 1847, when finance and commerce were paralyzed by 'universal distrust' (1854 [1966], 50). 'There was capital in the country, there was currency in the country; but neither could be got to perform its functions' (1854 [1966], 50). Country bankers were in possession of large quantities of Bank notes, but they would not part with the scarce, inelastic, currency for fear of not being able to obtain their usual accommodations from the Bank, were they to run short of ready cash. But when the Government drafted a letter suspending the Bank Act, the credit crisis passed – without necessitating any expansion of the note issue by the Bank of England. The 'precautionary demand' for money, to use a Keynesian term, fell immediately, and normal credit relations resumed.

Cairnes followed Tooke and Fullarton in his policy proposals, seconding Tooke's proposal for a large bullion reserve and adjustment of the discount rate as a superior approach to managing the currency. Other than the extent to which he drew directly on Henry Thornton's ideas, there is nothing novel in Cairnes's views. But for the purposes at hand, Cairnes's pamphlet is, like Mill's, instructive: One can defend Banking School views without so much as mentioning the real bills doctrine.

Tooke and Fullarton developed their views far more fully than did Mill or Cairnes. For at least the first 15 years of his career as an author Tooke might be labeled, without injustice, a moderate bullionist, after the manner of Henry

Thornton. As I have shown in a previous paper (Skaggs, 2003, 188–189), the similarities between Thornton and the 'early Tooke' are extensive:

- They both 'envisioned the monetary system as a network of loose linkages among institutions and markets' in which a variety of negotiable credit instruments served, when needed, as 'circulating media'.
- They both focused on broad measures of money, rather than the narrow measures used by Ricardo and the Currency School.
- They both believed that international adjustment worked through income and wealth effects, as well as price movements, and they both rejected the idea that prices should always be pushed down to restore international equilibrium.
- They both argued that the Bank of England should hold a large bullion reserve to absorb shocks to the economy and provide additional time to adjust to international disequilibrium.
- They both rejected rigid quantitative control of the note issue and emphasised the use of Bank rate as the key tool of monetary policy.

Sometime after the release of volumes I and II of his *History of Prices* in 1838 Tooke altered his approach to monetary *theory* quite dramatically. As I have discussed briefly (Skaggs, 2003) and Matthew Smith (2001, 2002) has documented extensively, Tooke abandoned his moderate-bullionist approach in favor of a dual-circulation model on the order of Adam Smith's approach in the *Wealth of Nations*. Tooke unveiled his new theoretical approach in parliamentary hearings in 1840. In his famous *Inquiry into the Currency Principle* (1844), Tooke's new theoretical approach is on full display.[10]

As radical as Tooke's new 'Banking School' model appeared to his contemporaries (and to generations of twentieth-century economists [Skaggs, 1999]), Tooke's new *theoretical* approach affected his *policy* recommendations very little. One of the theoretical innovations that has caused the most consternation among modern economists is the 'law of reflux', which plays an important role in Tooke's *Inquiry into the Currency Principle* and an even more prominent role in John Fullarton's *On the Regulation of Currencies* (1845 [1969]. Both Tooke and Fullarton used the law of reflux to argue that banks cannot issue their notes to excess, that is, that banks cannot force their notes into circulation. Any notes not desired by the public will be returned to the issuing banks in repayment of bills, or deposited into interest-bearing accounts, or in exchange for coin. Many commentators have seen the law of reflux as nothing more than a thinly veiled reworking of the real bills doctrine, but David Laidler (1972) argued that, as used by Tooke, the law of reflux was something quite different:

> If we interpret the 'law of reflux' as operating with the level of economic activity given, determined in part by the volume of bank lending, it becomes part of a theory analogous to the modern analysis of the public's demand for currency relative to other assets, rather than a component of some erroneous doctrine of the effect of bank credit. (Laidler, 1972, 174)

Laidler recognised in Tooke's discussion of the law of reflux something previous commentators knew but had consistently overlooked in their criticism of Tooke: that the debate in 1844 was, quite specifically, over the wisdom of controlling the *note issues* of country banks and of the Bank of England. Tooke did *not* argue that banks were incapable of extending their loans to an inflationary level; he argued that the quantity of *bank notes* was determined endogenously. That Tooke apparently went too far when he applied this argument to the 'circulating medium' as a whole (which Laidler mentions) and to the note issue of the Bank of England itself (which he fails to mention) doesn't turn the law of reflux into a naive version of the real bills doctrine.

In *On the Regulation of Currencies* (1st ed., 1844; 2nd ed., 1845), John Fullarton came to largely the same conclusions as had Tooke, utilising a theoretical framework that differed dramatically from Tooke's. Fullarton's approach baffled twentieth-century students of his work until the 1970s, when Earl Thompson wrote 'The Theory of Money and Income Consistent with Orthodox Value Theory' (Thompson, 1974). This paper provided an answer to a conundrum raised by Lloyd Metzler. Thompson's student David Glasner (1985, 1989) was quick to apply Thompson's model in reassessing the works of British classical writers. Following Thompson's and Glasner's lead, I demonstrated (Skaggs, 1991) that Fullarton's model could be well categorised as a combination of a competitive theory of money supply combined with a monetary approach to the balance of payments.

Like Tooke, Fullarton argued that the quantity of banknotes in circulation was endogenously determined by the demand for notes. Any excess of notes in circulation would be returned to the issuing banks on deposit, to repay debts, or in exchange for coin (though he downplayed the exchange for coin, arguing that unless prices were rising, no one would want to hold more coin).[11] However, unlike Tooke, who argued that the reflux automatically applied to the Bank of England, Fullarton demonstrated that the reflux of Bank notes depended upon Bank rate. If, during periods of a low market interest and speculative activity, the Bank were to hold Bank rate above market rate, the reflux of Bank notes would prevent the Bank from adding to any excessive lending. However, were the Bank to join in the competition for loans, it would drive the market rate down and cut off the reflux. In short, lending only on good bills was *not* a guarantee that the Bank of England's note issue would not become excessive. The Bank had to exhibit restraint in its discount business, making sure that its lending did not drive the market rate below the desired level of Bank rate. Furthermore, the Bank must not reduce Bank rate to attract a larger share of business when the economy is already operating at a high level of activity.

The overriding concern of Mill in 1826, Tooke and Fullarton in 1844, and Cairnes in 1854 was the same: The Bank of England should pursue a policy of protecting the credit system from large shocks, while taking care not to contribute to excessive lending that would lead to inflation and an inevitable recoil of prices. The way to do this was not by assuming tight linkages between one particular portion of the 'circulating medium' and applying a mechanical rule to it. Rather, the Bank of England should hold a much larger bullion reserve than it had held historically, and it should adjust Bank rate and its own lending policies to avoid adding to speculative increases in credit. These policies are in line with those advocated by Henry Thornton, whose dissection of the real bills doctrine set a standard yet to be surpassed.

The creation and early performance of the Federal Reserve System

> Too strong an attempt has been made to identify Federal Reserve thinking and practice closely with the nineteenth-century banking principle.
>
> Elmus Wicker, Federal Reserve Monetary Policy, 1917–1933 (1966)

Though certainly not alone, both David Laidler and I (Skaggs, 1995, 3) have noted that the driving force behind the creation of the Federal Reserve System, J. Laurence Laughlin and his followers, were 'exponents of a version of the nineteenth-century Banking School needs-of-trade doctrine' (Laidler, 1999, 18). But one need not delve very deeply into the doctrines advanced by the Banking School to discover that the act promoted by their American heirs – Laughlin, H. Parker Willis, Benjamin M. Anderson, and their fellow travellers – differed in economically significant ways from Banking School doctrine. Thus, Thomas Humphrey is simply wrong when he says, 'Written into the [Federal Reserve] act was the prototypal version of the doctrine inherited from 19th-century Banking School economists' (2001, 296).[12] The point is that the 'version...of the needs-of-trade doctrine' promoted by the Banking School writers focused on preserving the liquidity of the banking system operating on an international gold standard. As I argued in the preceding section, the Banking School had little to say about lending on real bills, other than approving of their short maturities. The creators and early leaders of the Federal Reserve System, on the other hand, had much to say in support of the real bills doctrine.

The English banking system grew up around the Bank of England, which was established before the goldsmiths turned to banking or the country banks began to form. Commercial bills of exchange were the primary instrument through which credit was extended in England and were a popular, though by no means so dominant, manner of borrowing in Scotland as well. Over a period of more than a century, the Bank of England evolved into a central bank and of necessity adapted its approach to the institutional realities of the British system. The Bank of England discounted bills of exchange as a de facto central bank because it had discounted bills of exchange for decades as a commercial bank. Furthermore, by transacting with bill brokers rather than other commercial banks – for the Bank of England itself was a privately owned commercial bank – the Bank erected a buffer between itself and its competitors.[13] It also had purchased large quantities of government debt, the very reason for which the Bank was chartered. While, in the eighteenth and nineteenth centuries, the Bank did not, in the ordinary course of events, engage in 'open-market operations' as a means of influencing the economy, its holdings of government debt were widely recognised to have provided a large share of the reserve base upon which the British monetary system operated.

That was exactly the point of the 'fiduciary issue' of £14 million of Bank notes secured by government debt held by the Bank of England and written into the Bank Act of 1844. So far as I am aware, no Banking School writer ever criticised the existence of the fiduciary issue.

The situation was far different in the United States, where a number of commercial banks existed before the first Bank of the United States was created. After the demise of the second Bank of the United States in 1838, nothing resembling a central bank existed in the United States until the Federal Reserve System began operations in 1914. In the latter decades of the nineteenth century, the US Treasury acted as a surrogate central bank on multiple occasions, helping to overcome some of the rigidities built into the National Banking System, under which the supply of banknotes was limited by rigid reserve and bond-backing requirements that constrained the elasticity of the currency in essentially the same manner as the Currency Principle limited the elasticity of Bank of England notes. Despite the efforts of Treasury officials and major clearinghouse associations, recurrent liquidity crises disrupted the US banking system every decade or so, from the 1870s through 1907. These crises led to widespread efforts to reform the currency, with heavy emphasis on increasing its elasticity.

An elastic currency can be created in more than one way.[14] However, the designers of the Federal Reserve System sought to create a convertible paper currency narrowly modeled after the English system, and thus they focused on the issuance of banknotes on the security of good commercial bills of exchange. But instituting such a system proved problematic, because in the United States most US commercial lending did *not* involve the discounting of bills of exchange. To follow the English example, the Federal Reserve would have to *create* a national bill market, something that proved difficult to do.[15] This made the real-bills advocates the innovators in the financial system, seeking – as had the Currency School before them – to devise a banking system that would enable them to employ their previously selected policy approach successfully.

The process of creating a Federal Reserve System based on real-bills theory was immediately disrupted by the United States' entry into World War I. Though the dollar remained tied to gold and the quantity of Federal Reserve notes was restricted by a minimum gold-to-note ratio, the war effectively terminated the international gold standard. Furthermore, the Federal Reserve supported the war effort through massive open-market purchases of government bonds. When the war ended, the Fed. could not institute the legislated system, because the international gold standard was not re-established until 1925 (and then in name more than in fact). But, as Friedman and Schwartz (1963, 191) note, 'the gold standard ruled supreme when the act was passed, and its continued supremacy was taken for granted'. Lacking an operative international gold standard, Federal Reserve officials found themselves in a completely different economic environment than had been anticipated when the Federal Reserve was created.

Federal Reserve officials were divided over how to proceed.[16] Some wished to move toward a real-bills system immediately, while others – in particular Benjamin

Strong, governor of the Federal Reserve Bank of New York – argued for taking a more quantity-theoretic approach, focused on stabilisation of the price level. So long as Strong was alive, the Federal Reserve used quantitative rules as one component of Federal Reserve policy. Beginning in 1922, the Fed. used open-market purchases of government bonds to acquire earning assets, to enable District Banks to make dividend payments to their stockholders. The Fed.'s *Tenth Annual Report*, issued in 1923, clearly recognised the importance of open-market operations for general credit policy and their effects on member banks' levels of rediscounting of commercial bills (see Friedman and Schwartz, 1963, 251). Internal battles over the extent to which the Federal Reserve should purchase government securities to offset declines in rediscounts outstanding raged throughout the mid-1920s (see Wicker, 1966, chapters 6–8). Only after Governor Strong's death in 1928 did the qualitative approach of the real-bills advocates attain dominance.[17]

What happened thereafter is the true measure of the real-bills policy in the United States.[18] The Federal Reserve soon began following the lead of Board member Adolph C. Miller (who had helped write the Federal Reserve Act). In the Stabilisation Hearings held from 1926 to 1928 (see Hetzel, 1985), Miller had stated that, 'The total volume of money in circulation is determined by the community. The Federal reserve system has no appreciable control over that and no disposition to interfere with it' (quoted in Timberlake, 2005, 214). Consequently, the Fed. shifted to a passive real-bills policy during a period when the gold standard was 'nothing but formal window dressing waiting for an opportune time to reappear' (Hetzel, 1985, 15).

In 1929 and 1930, the Fed. pursued a dedicated policy of 'accommodating business' by rediscounting real bills, while paying no attention to the price level. However well this policy may have accorded with the real bills doctrine, it flew in the face of the rules of an international gold standard. As economic activity fell off from late 1929, the demand for rediscounts at Federal Reserve Banks fell. At the same time, the Fed.'s gold reserves grew dramatically. By the rules of the gold standard, Fed. policy was deflationary when it should have been inflationary (Timberlake, 2005, 216–218). Even in 1931, when Federal Reserve officials engaged in open-market purchases to increase the money supply, they brought the monetary expansion to a halt, with gold bullion exceeding reserve requirements by more than a billion dollars still in their possession. Had they chosen to suspend the gold reserve requirements – which they could have done under the Federal Reserve Act – Fed. officials could have pumped several billion dollars more into the economy. That they chose not to do so says much about their priorities.

Conclusions

Careful study of the Currency School–Banking School controversy has convinced me that the lynchpin of the Banking School system was not the real bills doctrine but the international gold standard. Had Banking School writers truly believed that, by following the real bills doctrine, the Bank of England could have managed the British credit system better, they would have said so. John

Table 12.1 Summary of the three alleged real bills regimes

	Situation	Actual Policy	Justification of Policy
Restriction Period 1797–1821	Inconvertible paper currency issued by private banks; usury law limited Bank rate	Loans on real bills; Bank of England quantitatively restricted lending during some periods	Real Bills Doctrine
Banking/Currency Controversy 1826–1857	Full-bodied coin plus paper currency convertible into gold at par value; international gold standard in effect	Bank of England should hold large gold reserve; raise and lower Bank rate to smooth adjustments	Supply of banknotes is endogenous (Law of Reflux); total money supply is influenced by Bank lending
Early Federal Reserve System 1914–1932	Convertible notes without an international gold standard until 1925; very limited international gold standard thereafter	Financed war effort through government bond purchases; used some quantity controls through 1928; real-bills approach, ignoring rules of gold standard, 1929–1931	Necessity; Real Bills Doctrine – lending on anything other than commercial bills is inflationary

Fullarton acknowledged that a paper currency would work fine, 'provided only the quantity of its issues be kept under due limitation' (1845 [1969], 21). But, he continued, '*we have no regulating principle by which that quantity can be kept in exact proportion to the transactions which the currency has to perform*' (1845 [1969], 22, my italics). If this does not amount to an out-and-out rejection of the real bills doctrine, I have no clue what it means. The real connection between the Banking School and the Federal Reserve in the late 1920s lies in their joint rejection of direct quantitative control of the currency, not in their joint acceptance of the real bills doctrine. But as Timberlake (2005) makes clear, proper operation of the international gold standard precludes discretionary quantitative control of the money supply.

A convenient way to summarise my argument is to place three pieces of information from each of the three periods into a 3 × 3 matrix.

Boiled down to the basics, the real bills doctrine is a policy prescription for creating the correct quantity of 'money'. If constrained by convertibility into gold or silver, the doctrine will have no lasting effect on prices, though it enhances procyclical movements in economic activity. The anti-bullionists professed the belief that lending only against good-quality real bills was sufficient to prevent inflation. Most of these writers undoubtedly believed this. But Bank of England officials, by their willingness to place quantitative limits on their discounting of bills, indicated that they understood that something more than the real bills doctrine was needed to prevent inflation from arising.

The Banking School specifically applied the law of reflux to a convertible currency. They focused solely on the note issue, which was held to be endogenously determined by the demands of note holders. All major Banking School writers recognised that lending on commercial bills could be carried to speculative levels, and that the total 'circulating medium' – and thus prices – could be affected. However, if the Bank of England would only hold a large enough gold reserve on average, nearly all deflationary phases could be ridden through with relatively few commercial failures.

The founders of the Federal Reserve System specifically built the real bills doctrine into the Federal Reserve Act. Although events constrained them from fully implementing a policy based strictly on the doctrine for some 14 years, a policy of lending only against good quality commercial paper was put into effect in 1929. Federal Reserve officials effectively abandoned the international gold standard in their effort to follow the real bills doctrine.

The differences between Currency School–Banking School debates and the other two episodes are, I would argue, clear and compelling. The Banking School writers were engaged in a different program than were the anti-bullionists or the Federal Reserve Board of Governors. To label all three groups as supporters of the real bills doctrine on the basis that 'real bills doctrine' is an 'ideal type' appears to obfuscate, rather than clarify, the positions taken in these historical episodes.

Notes

Charles Goodhart, David Laidler, Perry Mehrling, and, especially, Michael Bordo made helpful comments on a previous draft of this paper.

1. Perlman (1989) convincingly argues that Smith intended the doctrine to serve as a rule for individual bankers who wished to avoid costly shortages of gold reserves. Smith's doctrine clearly assumes that bank notes are convertible into gold.
2. But the real heirs of Henry Thornton, a 'moderate bullionist', as I have argued (Skaggs, 1995).
3. Fetter (1969 [1978], 12) comments that 'the evidence seems to bear him out'.
4. Ironically, Thornton's brother Samuel, a director of the Bank of England, was the person who proposed that the Government should issue the Exchequer bills. See Fetter (1969 [1978], 15).
5. The dramatic fall of the Irish exchange against Great Britain contributed to the continued examination of monetary issues. In 1804 Parliament appointed a committee to examine the causes of the collapse of the Irish pound, on which Henry Thornton played a major role. See Fetter, 1955.
6. '[T]he bank [of England] itself, if we suppose a progressive enlargement of notes, must be assumed to furnish perpetually increasing means of effecting payments, and thus to render punctuality in fulfilling even the most extravagant engagements convenient and easy to the merchants' (Thornton, 1802 [1978], 253).
7. The Bank Act of 1844 partitioned the Bank of England into two separate departments. The Issue Department was permitted a 'fiduciary issue' of £14 million backed by government securities. Beyond that, it could issue notes only upon the receipt of gold – a 100 percent marginal reserve requirement. The Banking Department would carry on the Bank's commercial lending business by crediting borrowers' deposit accounts at

the Bank or by providing them with Bank notes obtained from the Issue Department in exchange for gold. Country banks were prohibited from extending their note issues beyond the average amount of notes in circulation during the three months preceding the implementation of the Act.

8. Mill also exonerated the Bank of England from the charge of having driven down the rate of interest, thereby causing investors to take on more risk to obtain a higher return.
9. '[W]hatever may be thought upon this point, it is at least certain that the facilities supplied by the Bank of England to imprudent speculation have been greater since the passing of the Bank Charter Act, than were ever afforded previous to its enactment' (Cairnes, 1854 [1966], 20).
10. M. Smith (2001) provides the best detailed explanation of Tooke's new theory, of which I am aware. Santiago-Valiente (1988) provides a brief, but quite helpful, overview of Tooke's theory.
11. Glasner (1989, 217) has noted that Fullarton's version of the law of reflux was incompletely developed. He failed to note that the actual mechanism checking the over-issue of notes was the cost of paying interest on notes placed on deposit in the issuing banks. A profit-maximizing bank will issue notes on loan only to the point at which the marginal revenue earned on loans equals the marginal cost of maintaining that quantity of notes in circulation. Fullarton recognized that the quantity of notes in circulation was demand-determined, but the marginal revenue–marginal cost logic that causes it to hold was beyond him.
12. Meltzer (2003, 43) asserts that the 'so-called banking school...wanted the bank to discount only real bills, and they claimed that a real bills policy would prevent over- and underissue of money and credit'. He provides no references to any Banking School writings that might back his assertion. On the other hand, Wood's (2005) brief discussion doesn't link the Banking School to the real bills doctrine.
13. As Charles Goodhart pointed out to me.
14. For example, the Scottish cash accounts system described by Adam Smith in *The Wealth of Nations* (1776 [1976], II.ii., 44–47) added elasticity to the Scottish note system. Open-market operations can be a policy-directed source of elasticity.
15. 'The main practical problem in applying [the Bank of England's approach, as elaborated by Ralph] Hawtrey to the U.S. case was the failure of an active national bill market to develop even in the face of privileged discount treatment' (Mehrling, 2002, 214).
16. Friedman and Schwartz (1963), Wicker (1966), and Meltzer (2003), among others, discuss the debates within the Fed. Timberlake (2005) provides a useful brief survey of the period.
17. 'With the exception of the New York Fed, most of [the district Federal Reserve Banks] embraced the real bills doctrine – as the Federal Reserve Act suggested was their duty' (Timberlake, 2005, 213).
18. What follows draws heavily on Timberlake's (2005) excellent summary of this period.

References

Bagehot, Walter (1873 [1999]). *Lombard Street: A Description of the Money Market.* New York: John Wiley and Sons.

Bosanquet, Charles (1810). *Practical Observations on the Report of the Bullion-Committee.* London: Richardson.

Cairnes, John E. (1854 [1966]). *An Examination into the Principles of Currency Involved in the Bank Charter Act of 1844.* New York: A.M. Kelley.

Fetter, Frank Whitson (1955). *The Irish Pound.* Evanston, IL: Northwestern University Press.

Fetter, Frank Whitson (1969 [1978]). *Development of British Monetary Orthodoxy, 1797–1875*. Fairfield, NJ: Augustus M. Kelley.
Friedman, Milton and Anna Jacobson Schwartz (1963). *A Monetary History of the United States, 1867–1960*. Princeton: Princeton University Press.
Fullarton, John (1845 [1969]). *On the Regulation of Currencies*. London: John Murray, 1855. Reprinted: New York: A.M. Kelly, 1969.
Glasner, David (1985). "A Reinterpretation of Classical Monetary Theory." *Southern Economic Journal* 52:1, 46–67.
Glasner, David (1989). "On Some Classical Monetary Controversies." *History of Political Economy* 21 (Summer), 201–229.
Hetzel, Robert (1985). "The Rules versus Discretion Debate over Monetary Policy in the 1920s." Federal Reserve Bank of Richmond. *Economic Review* November–December, 3–14.
Humphrey, Thomas M. (2001). "The Choice of a Monetary Policy Framework: Lessons from the 1920s." *Cato Journal* 21 (Fall), 285–313.
Laidler, David (1972). "Thomas Tooke on Monetary Reform." In Maurice Peston and Bernard Corry, eds., *Essays in Honour of Lord Robbins*. London: Weidenfeld and Nicolson, pp. 168–186.
Laidler, David (1999). *Fabricating the Keynesian Revolution*. Cambridge, U.K. and New York: Cambridge University Press.
Mehrling, Perry (2002). "Economists and the Fed: Beginnings." *Journal of Economic Perspectives* 16 (Fall), 207–218.
Meltzer, Allan H. (2003). *A History of the Federal Reserve*, Volume I: *1913–1951*. Chicago: University of Chicago Press.
Mill, John Stuart (1826 [1967]). "Paper Currency and Commercial Distress." *Parliamentary Review*. Reprinted in *Collected Works of John Stuart Mill*, edited by J.M. Robson, Vol. 4, pp. 71–123. Toronto: University of Toronto Press.
Mints, Lloyd W. (1945). *A History of Banking Theory in Great Britain and the United States*. Chicago and London: University of Chicago Press.
Perlman, M. (1989). "Adam Smith and the Paternity of the Real Bills Doctrine." *History of Political Economy* 21 (Spring), 77–90.
Ricardo, David (1811 [1951]). "Reply to Mr. Bosanquet's *Practical Observations on the Report of the Bullion Committee*. Reprinted in *The Works and Correspondence of David Ricardo*, Vol. III, edited by Piero Sraffa with M.H. Dobb. Cambridge: Cambridge University Press, 1951.
Santiago-Valiente, Wilfredo (1988). "Historical Background of the Classical Monetary Theory and the 'Real-Bills' Banking Tradition." *History of Political Economy* 20 (Spring), 44–63.
Skaggs, Neil T. (1991). "John Fullarton's Law of Reflux and Central Bank Policy." *History of Political Economy* 23 (Fall), 457–480.
Skaggs, Neil T. (1995). "The Methodological Roots of J. Laurence Laughlin's Anti-Quantity Theory of Money and Prices." *Journal of the History of Economic Thought* 17 (Spring), 1–20.
Skaggs, Neil T. (1995). "Henry Thornton and the Development of Classical Monetary Economics." *Canadian Journal of Economics* 28:4b, 1212–1227.
Skaggs, Neil T. (1999). "Changing Views: Twentieth-Century Opinion on the Banking School-Currency-School Controversy." *History of Political Economy* 31 (Spring), 363–391.
Skaggs, Neil T. (2003). "Thomas Tooke, Henry Thornton, and the Development of British Monetary Orthodoxy." *Journal of the History of Economic Thought* 25 (June), 177–197.
Smith, Adam (1776 [1976]). *An Inquiry into the Nature and Causes of the Wealth of Nations*. Glasgow Edition. Indianapolis, IN: Liberty Press.
Smith, Matthew (2001). "Endogenous Money, Interest and Prices: Tooke's Monetary Thought Revisited." *Contributions to Political Economy* 2001, 31–55.
Smith, Matthew (2002). "Tooke's Approach to Explaining Prices." *European Journal of the History of Economic Thought* 9 (Autumn): 333–358.

Thompson, Earl A. (1974). "The Theory of Money and Income Consistent with Orthodox Value Theory." In George Horwich and Paul A. Samuelson, eds., *Trade, Stability, and Macroeconomics*. New York: Academic Press, pp. 427–453.

Thornton, Henry (1802 [1978]). *An Inquiry into the Nature and Effects of the Paper Credit of Great Britain*, with an introduction by F.A. Hayek. Fairfield, NJ: A.M. Kelley.

Timberlake, Richard H. (2005). "Gold Standards and the Real Bills Doctrine in U.S. Monetary Policy." *Econ Journal Watch* 2 (August), 196–233.

Tooke, Thomas (1823 [1824]). *Thoughts and Details on the High and Low Prices of the Thirty Years from 1793 to 1822*, 2d ed. London: John Murray.

Tooke, Thomas (1826). *Considerations on the Wood States of the Currency*, 2d ed. London: John Murray.

Tooke, Thomas (1838). *A History of Prices*, Vol. I. London: Longman, Orme, Brown, Green, and Longmans.

Tooke, Thomas (1844). *An Inquiry into the Currency Principle*. London: Longman, Orme, Brown, Green, and Longmans.

Torrens, Robert (1812 [1994]). *An Essay on Money and Paper Currency*. Selected passages reprinted in *Foundations of Monetary Economics*, Volume III: *The Anti-Bullionists*, edited by D.P. O'Brien. London: William Pickering, 1994.

Vansittart, Nicholas (1811 [1994]). Substance of Two Speeches made…in the House of Commons to which the Report of the Bullion Committee was referred. pp. 22–25 reprinted in Foundations of Monetary Economics, Vol. III: The Anti-Bullionists, edited by D.P. O'Brien. London: William Pickering.

Wicker, Elmus R. (1966). *Federal Reserve Monetary Policy, 1917–1933*. New York: Random House.

Wood, John H. (2005). *A History of Central Banking in Great Britain and the United State*. Cambridge, U.K. and New York: Cambridge University Press.

13

Hans Neisser's Views on Money and Structural Change, and Modern 'Quantity Theory' Implications

Hans-Michael Trautwein

Introduction

David Laidler's *Fabricating the Keynesian Revolution* (1999) is an outstanding collection of studies of the interwar literature on money, the cycle, and unemployment. It provides a rich picture of various developments in macroeconomic thinking that preceded, anticipated, and criticized much of what came to be marketed as 'the Keynesian Revolution' – a paradigm shift that allegedly put those developments out of date. Roughly 120 economists and policymakers of that era figure in David's histodrama, and Hans Neisser is *not* missing from the list.[1] He is mentioned in a footnote on underconsumption theories (Laidler, 1999, 169, n. 16).

As I will argue in this chapter, Neisser deserves more than that footnote, as he made important contributions to the interwar literature on money, the cycle, and unemployment. He published in leading journals and other well-known sources, and he was cited as an authority by many contemporaneous economists, including John Maynard Keynes. By pushing Neisser further towards the foreground of the scene, I do *not* intend to criticize David's script for the play. On the contrary, I take his book as stimulation to add further evidence to his argument.[2] Moreover, I think that Neisser is not only of interest in a cross-sectional perspective, as an interwar economist. In a longitudinal perspective, from the pre-war (World War I) past to the present, Neisser's views on money and structural change have a connection with various aspects of David's writings on *The Golden Age of the Quantity Theory* (Laidler, 1991*a*), on the perennial controversiality of that theory (e.g., Laidler, 1991*b*), and on its current disrepute in academia and empirical work (e.g., Laidler, 2005).

In order to connect the cross-sectional with the longitudinal perspective (and to raise the level of attention) I should first point out that Neisser was an odd bird in many respects, by the standards of his time and by those of our time. He was one of the very few economists in the Weimar Republic who used and defended the quantity theory when that theory 'was something of a minority taste' in German monetary thought (cf. Laidler, 1991*b*, 294, n. 9). He was ranked among the Wicksellians, but unlike the Austrians, the Stockholm School and the Keynes of the *Treatise on*

Money (1930) he did not endeavour to extend Wicksell's interest-rate gap theory into an explanation of the cycle. Neisser rather related both cycles and growth to irregular technical progress,[3] whose interaction with capital accumulation was his central theme. He exposed flaws in the Walras–Cassel system, rejected Say's law and discussed persistent equilibrium underemployment before Keynes (1936), without taking recourse to liquidity preference or other such motives. In all this, Neisser made use of a classical version of the quantity theory that set the focus on the flow of money (and credit) in the circulation of capital, not on the holding of assets as in the Cambridge approach and, more so, in modern quantity theory.

Even though Neisser's quantity theory may look outdated by modern standards, it may help, a tiny bit, to explain why *modern* quantity theory is now largely considered to be out of date as foundations for monetary policy. On the purely theoretical side, the reasons for this turning away are surely not to be found in any of Neisser's writings, but rather in the idiosyncrasies of inter-temporal general-equilibrium modelling that, in its core, has no essential role for money to play and hence creates a bias towards minimizing the role of 'monetary frictions' (cf. Laidler, 2005, 2006). Yet, on the empirical side, a look back on Neisser may be useful, since his approach was focused on aspects of structural change that have most likely contributed to the problems encountered in the use of money demand functions as a guide for setting monetary targets. With an eye to that aspect, the focus of this chapter is set on Neisser's theory of the value and circulation of money. His (likewise noteworthy) contributions to the literature on business cycles and unemployment will be dealt with rather briefly in the sketch of Neisser's life and works that follows in the next section.[4] Section 'The Value and Circulation of Money' presents Neisser's approach to the quantity theory, especially his views on the circulation of money in the business sphere. Section 'Neisser's Approach, Modern Quantity Theory and Monetary Policy' explores the modern quantity-theory implications of Neisser's approach. The final section concludes.

Neisser's Life and Views on Structural Change

Hans Philipp Neisser was born in Breslau, Silesia (then Germany), in 1895 and died in Berkeley, California, in 1975.[5] He worked as economic adviser to various governments in the Weimar Republic, then as research director of the Kiel Institute of World Economics from 1927 until 1933. Together with Adolf Löwe (later Adolph Lowe) he formed the 'Kiel School', a distinctive group of economists at the institute that included, among others, Wassily Leontief and Jacob Marschak (cf. Hagemann, 1994). The core project of the Kiel School was to extend the classical analysis of the circular flow to models of cyclical growth. In this context Neisser set the focus on the determination of the price level in changing structures of production and transactions. Two publications stand out. The first is his habilitation thesis on the exchange value of money, *Der Tauschwert des Geldes* (1928). The second is a long essay on the circulation of money, 'Der Kreislauf des Geldes' (1931*a*). Both attracted much attention because of their thorough treatment of the circulation of money.[6] Some of the central passages on credit expansion and other references in Hayek's *Monetary Theory and the Trade Cycle* (1933) show that Hayek had strongly profited from Neisser (1928). Keynes, in his *Treatise on Money* (1930, vol. I, 178 n.), even remarked in an unusually humble tone: 'I find Dr. Neisser's general attitude to monetary problems particularly sympathetic, and am hopeful that he may feel the same about my work.'[7] Neisser's early writings on money will be discussed in the section on 'The Value and Circulation of Money'.

Persistent involuntary unemployment was the central theme of Neisser's writings in the 1930s. Unlike Keynes (1936), Neisser attempted to embed its explanation in a dynamic theory of capital accumulation and technical progress. In the following, I describe his approach in an *ex post* logical rather than strictly chronological order. The starting point is Neisser's essay on the wage rate and employment in market equilibrium (1932). Here he first showed that the Walras–Cassel system of the equations that determine general equilibrium, is not necessarily economically meaningful, as 'the prices which solve the.. system of equations may well be negative' (1932, 1990, 146).[8] He then refuted the assertion that full competition always eliminates involuntary unemployment by wage adjustments, demonstrating that the employment effects of wage changes are narrowly limited by the economies of scale associated with the given stock of real capital. Neisser argued that the displacement of labour through advances in technology is not automatically compensated by the absorption of labour through capital accumulation, not even in the long run. The use of new techniques normally requires an increase in capital intensity, 'capital intensification' in his words. Net of intensification, the rate of accumulation is likely to fall short of the rate of extensive growth required for the full absorption of the labour force, if that grows at its normal rate. Wage reductions (or rises in interest rates) cannot reverse the secular increase in capital intensity because the return to labour-intensive techniques is normally unprofitable, due to the economies of scale that come with technical progress. Wages would then have to be negative to make full absorption profitable. The ratchet effect of technical progress may thus lead to persistent unemployment, even if wages are squeezed to the minimum level of subsistence. Neisser (1990 [1932], 162) concluded that '[t]he common opinion that in equilibrium there will always be full employment of the labour force, provided wages are sufficiently low, has been shown to be incorrect'.

Ten years later, Neisser (1942) argued in a similar paper in the *American Economic Review* that persistent technological unemployment can develop because, as stated by John Stuart Mill (and quoted in the subtitle of the article), 'demand for commodities is not demand for labour'. When Neisser (1942) criticized various fallacies in the extension of Say's law to labour markets, he had already questioned the validity of Say's law in its original domain, the commodity markets, in an essay on 'General Overproduction', published in the *Journal of the Political Economy* (1934), and in the book *Some International Aspects of the Business Cycle* (1936*a*). He had pointed out that certain combinations of capital intensification and technical progress have the potential to produce contractions of credit that lead to a general glut of markets.

The causal connections that Neisser (1934, 1936*a*) made between growth, credit cycles and unemployment were all related to the effects of advances in technology on productivity, capital intensity, and output: technical progress has a tendency to raise them all. Yet if the composition of additional net output is not exactly in accordance with the spending schedule of additional income, receipts may fall short of costs. Whether such discrepancies between the structures of production and demand develop into general overproduction, depends partly upon where they arise. If there is overproduction in the producers' goods industries, it tends to remain partial. Since it may lead to a fall in prices, consumers' goods industries might even profit from lowered costs of inputs. Due to their increased demand, profit expectations in producers' goods industries should recover sooner or later. Say's law holds. If there is overproduction in the consumers' goods industries, it tends to become general, as demand for producers' goods falls as well. Profit expectations are negatively affected in all sectors. However, as Neisser (1934, 444–445) pointed out in critique of 'the underconsumption school', this would not be sufficient to refute Say's law, because nominal purchasing power in the system would be unchanged. Neisser actually invoked the quantity theory of money with a dose of Schumpeter (plus an early version of the Clower constraint) to show why Say's law does not hold in modern economies:

> Purchasing power can be destroyed only by monetary processes like hoarding, discharging of bank debt, etc.: it does not disappear simply because production and sale of goods has undergone some structural changes, for goods have not the purchasing power required to buy them tied around their necks (Neisser, 1934, 444).

In modern economies, the volume of money can be quickly reduced by the discharge of debts at the banks. If expectations of losses make this happen on a larger scale, partial overproduction – even if starting only in the producers' goods sector – sets off a vicious circle of reductions in purchasing power and deflation.[9] In this case, receipts fall short of costs throughout, and Say's law no longer holds. Yet, Neisser argued, the system has a tendency of self-stabilization – though possibly at a higher level of unemployment. The 'working of the credit mechanism explains, also, why the crisis...must terminate sooner or later': The repayment of bank loans (plus hoarding) 'leads eventually to a condition of liquidity that almost forces the granting of new credit to those industries which have readjusted their cost or show profit for other reasons' (Neisser, 1934, 446).

Small wonder that Neisser (1936*b*, 473), in his review of Keynes's *General Theory* (1936), considered the liquidity preference theory to be the weakest part of that book, pointing out that 'liquidity preference is in fact a function not only of the interest rate but also of profit expectation'. His explanation of equilibrium underemployment differed essentially from Keynes's story of effective demand failures. For Neisser it was *the lending* during and at the end of a crisis that, in its focus on cost-cutting techniques, would contribute to turning cyclical unemployment into structural unemployment by way of labour-saving technical progress.[10]

In the end, such permanent unemployment could even be perceived as a sort of capital-shortage unemployment that could be characterized as an equilibrium in capital and goods markets: '[O]wing to the harmony between the structure of expenditure and the structure of production, capital, but not labor, would be utilized optimally' (1936*b*, 63)

Neisser's views on cyclical growth and structural unemployment were conditioned by the waves of 'rationalization' in German industries in the late 1920s, more than by the Great Depression in the early 1930s. In public debate with Marschak (Neisser, 1930, 1931*c*) as well as in secret consultations at the Reichsbank and in open critique of Richard Kahn's multiplier formula (Neisser, 1933, 1936*c*), Neisser took a cautious middle-of-the-road position.[11] He criticized proposals to stimulate demand by way of wage increases, and was sceptical of multiplier reasoning because of crowding-out effects and formal inconsistencies. But he also attacked fervently the orthodox belief that wage cuts and 'sound credit' restrictions would cure the depression, arguing that the crisis had broken the sequence which normally leads from wage cuts to increases in profits and employment. In the deep crisis of the early 1930s wage cuts contributed to a cumulative process of capacity underutilization, debt deflation and contractions of demand. Neisser (1931*c*, 1933) therefore advocated credit-financed public works that would stimulate demand, but not induce inflation as long as capacities are not fully utilized. This also explains, why Neisser later came to be ranked as a 'proto-Keynesian' (Klausinger, 1999) – though, as David's *Fabricating the Keynesian Revolution* reminds us, advocacy of public works in the face of the Great Depression was not at all as uncommon among economists as Keynesian legends would have it.

Neisser's productivity and the continuity in his works on unemployment, growth and cycles in the 1930s is remarkable in view of his personal situation. Neisser was an active Social Democrat and he had Jewish ancestors. In April 1933, shortly after Hitler came to power, Neisser was brutally evicted from the Kiel Institute by SA troops. A few weeks later, he emigrated to the United States where he was appointed professor of monetary theory at the Wharton School of Finance and Commerce, University of Pennsylvania. During the war Neisser served as Principal Economist in the Research Division of the US Office of Price Administration. In 1943 he was apparently offered positions at the National Bureau of Economic Research and at the New School for Social Research in New York (Krohn, 1987, 200). Some of his former colleagues from Kiel and other German universities were at the 'University in Exile', and this may be part of the explanation why he chose the New School, where he remained until retirement in 1965.

In his postwar contributions to economic literature, Neisser explored new fields. The wartime activities in the Office of Price Administration had rekindled his interest in industrial economics, elements of which were present in his early monetary writings and in the Kiel School's attention to monopolistic overpricing as a cause of unemployment. In 'Oligopoly as a Non-Zero-Sum Game' (1957) Neisser extended the game-theoretical approach of John von Neumann and Oscar Morgenstern to the strategic behaviour of oligopolistic players. Macroeconometric modelling was another field in which Neisser excelled by combining experiences from his Kiel years with new research methods. Together with Franco Modigliani he wrote *National Income and International Trade* (1953), a much-quoted empirical study of the world economy in the interwar period. Last but not least, there was Neisser the critic. His reviews (1934*b*, 1936*b*, 1941) of Hayek, Keynes, and Myrdal are particularly noteworthy for their precision, originality, and the attention that they received in the contemporaneous literature. The reviews, as well as his other writings, reveal an openmindedness that makes it difficult to stick any of the common school labels on Neisser's 'general attitude to monetary problems'.

The Value and Circulation of Money

Given the attention that Neisser's early monetary works received in the contemporaneous literature, a first look at his treatise on the exchange value of money (1928) and his essay on the circulation of money (1931*a*) may produce some disappointment. Both works are hard and hardly exciting reading, not only because they were written in German.[12] They consist of painstaking dissections of the components and determinants of the circulation of money, in which the few details often make it difficult to see the grand design. The following description of (some parts of) both works is selective, with a view to the implications of Neisser's approach for present-day issues (see the section on 'Neisser's Approach, Modern Quantity Theory and Monetary Policy').[13]

In *Tauschwert des Geldes*, Neisser (1928) examined the determinants of the value of money, defined as the inverted price level. With reference to Irving Fisher's *Purchasing Power of Money* (1911), a book with a similar title, he started from a 'deposits and income' version of the equation of exchange:[14]

$$MV + M'V' = PY \tag{13.1}$$

where M is the volume of cash, V the velocity of cash, M' the volume of checkable bank deposits, V' the velocity of deposits, P the 'average price level' and Y the 'net social product' (1928, 1–3). Neisser (1928, pp. 10–11) stressed that the equation of exchange does not per se prove the propositions of the 'naïve quantity theory' that P is exclusively and proportionally dependent on M. He rejected the common assumptions that M/M' is constant, that V, V' are independent of M, M' and constant in the short run, and that Y is independent of monetary factors in the long run. The purpose of his treatise was to show how the value of money is determined by the interaction of all these factors in the circulation of goods. He discussed at great length: the determinants of the velocities (Chapter II), the relationship between cash and deposits (Chapters III–IV), price levels and exchange rates (Chapter V), the effects of deflation and inflation on the social product, the fallacies of needs-of-trade (or real bills) doctrines, and the authorities' control of loans and deposits via interest-rate policy (all Chapter VI).

To make a long story short: the results, at which Neisser arrived, did not differ substantially from the causality proposition of the 'naïve quantity theory'. Since the volume of money ($M + M'$) tends to change more rapidly and frequently than the velocities and the social product, changes in the price level should primarily be considered as reactions to changes in the volume of money (1928, 156). Neisser (1928, chapters VI and VII) pointed out that V, V' and Y could nevertheless have an influence on the price level – and in this respect he deemed the proportionality proposition ($\Delta P = \Delta M + \Delta M'$) of the 'naïve quantity theory' invalid. But he stressed that the elasticity of the money supply, due to reactions of M′ to changes in interest rates, could easily compensate such influences. If the central bank follows a policy of price-level stabilization, it has the power, with its discount rate, to neutralize the real effects of (potential) changes in the price level that are caused by changes in real income or the velocities of cash and deposits. Neutrality of money was, for Neisser, a normative concept that meant guaranteeing a stable price level or, in his words, a constant value of money.[15]

Neisser's approach differed strongly from the metaphysical tracts on money that dominated the German literature in the 1920s.[16] It was not entirely new, though, since Wicksell (1898), Schumpeter (1917–18) and Marschak (1924) had re-examined the quantity theory under the aspect of expenditure flows in a credit economy. And in most parts, it did not essentially differ from the well-known contributions of Fisher, the Cambridge School and Hawtrey – all well described by David (Laidler, 1991*a*).[17] However, Neisser's analysis of the structural determinants of the circulation of money (the left-hand side of the equation of exchange), which started in chapter II of his 1928 treatise and culminated in the 1931 essay, contained some innovations.

Neisser developed his theory of the circulation of money in two steps. In the first step (1928, chapter II) he distinguished between two types of money holdings in the economy: balance reserves and operating funds. Reserves represent the precautionary demand for money. From an individual point of view they are hoarded to meet contingencies, but that does not imply, in view of the monetary system, that they are completely out of circulation. Reserves that are held in demand deposits provide a base for bank lending, which affects the size and composition of the monetary aggregate ($M + M'$). The velocity of reserves is normally close to zero, but rises and affects the average total of velocity in times of high inflation, when there is a flight into real assets, or in severe crises, when current income falls short of expenditures (1928, 18). Total velocity (the average of $V + V'$) is thus determined by the ratio of balance reserves to the operating funds which represent the transactions demand for money, and by the velocity of the operating funds which varies inversely with the length of the average period between the payments of income.

In the second step, Neisser (1931*a*) set the focus on the operating funds, which he now described as 'active money', since these funds are spent in the circular flow of goods at more or less regular intervals.[18] This shift of emphasis required a change in the underlying concept of the equation of exchange. Neisser (1931*a*) dropped the distinction between cash and deposits, and related the circulation of the monetary aggregate to the total volume of transactions, *T*, instead of the net social product, *Y*, only. The relevant equation can thus be written as a consolidated version of the original equation in Fisher (1911):

$$MV = PT \tag{13.2}$$

In order to be able to discuss the relationship between *T* and *Y*, Neisser (1931*a*, 369–384) introduced a distinction of active money in terms of 'income money' (*Einkommensgeld*) and 'business money' (*Geschäftsgeld*) – a classical concept that he traced back to Adam Smith's *Wealth of Nations,* while mentioning that it was now used in a similar fashion by Keynes (1930).[19] Neisser argued that the total of payments for goods cannot be completely dissolved into factor incomes, as there are circular flows of capital goods in the production of both consumer *and* capital goods. He referred to Karl Marx's distinction between constant capital (*c*), the fund for the purchases of machinery, auxiliary goods and raw materials that are required to reproduce the (physical) capital stock, and variable capital (*v*), the fund for payments of labour and other income required to keep production going and to increase the capital stock. In the empirical observation of the circulation of active money, it is difficult to draw strict dividing lines between business money (the '*c*-fund') and income money (the '*v*-fund'). The distinction is merely hypothetical insofar as the same units of money are transferred through both spheres.[20] It has nevertheless important implications for the *income* velocity of money (its circulation in the *v*-sphere): It is not only determined by the length of the average period between payments in both spheres, but also affected by changes in capital intensity. If capital intensity increases, while neither the average payment periods nor the volume of money change, income velocity falls because the given volume of money mediates more transactions in the business sphere (Neisser, 1931*a*, 403–408).

As described in section 'Neisser's Life and Views on Structural Change', Neisser considered a long-run trend of increasing capital intensity to be a stylized fact. In his view, it is another stylized fact that the technical and institutional determinants of velocity (both income and transactions velocity) change at a slower pace than capital intensity (Neisser, 1931*a*, 370–378). This leads to an increased demand for (business) money in the *c*-sphere, and if the supply is not forthcoming, structural change will create downward pressure on the price level:

> If we have a genuine increase in capital intensity, which is connected with an increase in the efficiency of the productive capacities and hence an increase in the volume of production at every stage, the social product will rise and hence the amount of goods that need to be payed from the *v*-fund. If the volume of money remains constant, we have a *twofold* tendency towards deflation, firstly due to the growth of the social product, secondly because each *unit* of the social product has, so to speak, passed intermediate stages of greater volumes, due to capital intensification. The price level falls by more than the social product will increase. (Neisser, 1931*a*, 378 – emphasis his, translation mine.)

This passage provides the base for the 'dynamics' of the interaction of the circulation of money with technical progress and growth that Neisser analyses in a later section (1931*a*, 391–397). The twofold tendency towards deflation may indicate 'needs for money' (*Geldbedarf*), if the aim of monetary policy is a constant value of money or, at least, a constant nominal income. However, it need not pose a real problem. A smooth transition to an equilibrium with higher output and lower prices is possible, if the following conditions are fulfilled:

(a) capital intensification is supported by savings of money that are channelled from the income sphere to the business sphere at a lower interest rate;[21]
(b) capital intensification comes with technical progress that increases productivity and lowers costs to the extent that profits are not negatively affected by deflation.

These conditions for *equilibrium deflation* allow Neisser to provide a systematic discussion of cases in which the dynamic equilibrium of the economy is disturbed. These are cases in which the 'needs for money' in the business sphere must be met by increases in the volume of money, in order to avoid that receipts fall short of costs. In Figure 13.1, I refer to these cases as *deflationary gaps*, though Neisser (1931*a*) did not use that term (which came into use only after Keynes, 1940):

- The first case is *spurious capital intensification*, which is confined to changes in the degree of vertical integration. In this case, there would not be any addition of intermediate stages of production, but simply a disintegration into a larger number of firms. The volume of transactions is increased without affecting the material structure of production. If velocity does not adjust, the 'needs for money' can be satisfied only by increases in the volume of money (1931*a*, 381).
- The second case is *extensive growth* which implies an increase in the inputs of capital and labour without a rise in productivity growth that would lower unit costs (1931*a*, 393–394). The income and transaction velocities of money and the proportions of the *v*- and *c*-funds remain unchanged. If the supply of money is constant, equilibrium may be disturbed by contractual rigidities of nominal wages and interest.[22]
- The third case is *bank-dependent capital intensification*. Intensive growth implies that the increase in the social product is achieved by an increase in the ratio of capital to labour. Even so, condition (*b*) must be fulfilled to keep the economy in equilibrium. If technical progress is not sufficient, increases in capital intensity will only happen if banks lower their lending rates of interest.

To sum up, Neisser's (1931) essay draws attention to the fact that growth, technical progress and other structural change lead to increases in the volume of transactions, *T*, that are not fully reflected in changes in income, *Y*. As there is no mechanism that makes technical progress, increases in capital intensity and

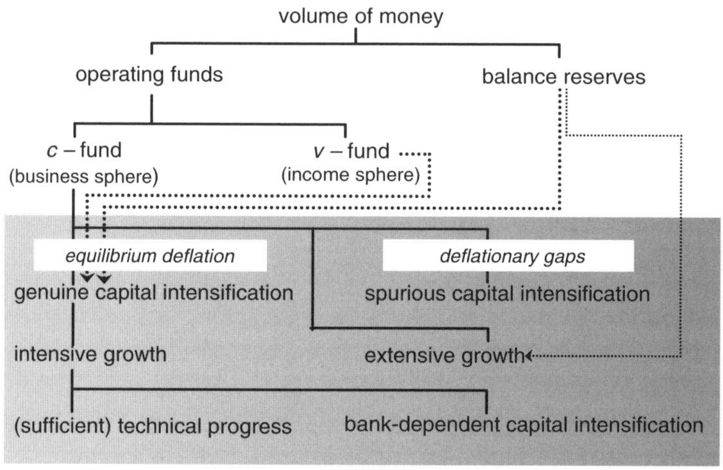

Figure 13.1 Deflation tendencies in Neisser's circulation of money

the transactions velocity of circulation of money automatically move in step, additional demands for money (*Geldbedarf*) emerge in the business sphere. If these demands are not met by releases from balance reserves or by increases in the total volume of money, the pressure is on the price level. If technical progress is not sufficient to lower costs to the extent that profits remain intact, deflation leads to disturbances in the economy. With his 1931 essay, Neisser laid some of the ground for his views on cyclical growth and structural unemployment that have been described above, in section 'Neisser's Life and Views on Structural Change'.

Neisser's Approach, Modern Quantity Theory and Monetary Policy

It is obvious that Neisser's approach to the quantity theory of money differs substantially from the monetarist approach, if not from most of modern monetary theory. To put it in Robertsonian terms, monetarism is based on a theory of demand for 'money to hold', whereas Neisser's theory is about the demand for 'money to spend'. Monetarism sets the focus on stocks of money (in varying measures) relative to other assets in the income sphere, whereas Neisser dealt primarily with flows of money in the business sphere. Monetarism is generally associated with warnings of an inflation bias in institutional environments, in which the government's power to print money is not clearly restricted. Neisser, on the other hand, claimed that the interaction of capital accumulation, technical progress, and other structural change creates a deflation bias which monetary policy might have to counteract.

By the standards of the interwar years, Neisser's writings on money could hardly be considered as extraordinary novelties, despite the praise that they received. They were firmly rooted in the classical tradition of transactions approaches to the quantity theory that Fisher (1911, 25, n. 2) traced back to David Ricardo and John Stuart Mill. Neisser's choice of specific theme – the effects of capital accumulation on the circulation of money – had a close connection with part three of volume II of Marx's *Kapital* (1885), on 'the reproduction and circulation of the aggregate social capital'. The Marxian reproduction schemes were a pivotal point in the Kiel School's works on cycles, growth, and unemployment.[23] Neisser's 1931 essay – especially the *c*- and *v*-fund terminology and the diagrams – can be read as an attempt to explore the monetary implications of the chapter on 'accumulation and reproduction on an expanded scale' (Marx, 1885, chapter 21), though Neisser does not refer to it.[24] In a general fashion, these implications had already been formulated by Fisher (1911, 76):

> The greater and the more productive the stock or capital in any community, the more goods it can put into the currents of trade... Since increase in trade tends to decrease the general level of prices, anything which tends to increase trade likewise tends to decrease the general level of prices. We conclude, therefore, that among the causes tending to decrease prices are increasing geographical or personal specialization, improved productive technique, and the accumulation of capital.

In his *Golden Age of the Quantity Theory* (Laidler, 1991*a*, chapter 3), David emphasizes that Fisher's quantity theory, even though 'sometimes termed mechanical', is closely connected to the choice-theoretical approach of the Cambridge School, which in turn has much in common with monetarism.[25] It is obvious though – and described in detail by David (Laidler, 1991*a*, 68–76) – that Fisher's *Purchasing Power of Money* (1911) revolves around the volume of transactions and transactions velocity, two concepts that are wider than those used in most (if not all) monetarist models of the demand for money. There is a number of reasons for turning away from the transactions/flow approach to the income/stock approach to quantity theory. I recollect having heard the following from David over the years[26]:

- to provide a choice-theoretical base for the demand for money that overcomes the dichotomy between the theories of relative and absolute prices;
- to take account of the second-round effects of changes in the volume of money in terms of decisions to hold and spend;
- to be able to build small, empirically testable models that economize on data and ad hoc parametrization;
- to avoid data problems in the measurement of the volume of transactions, the construction of relevant price indices and the relationship between current and capital transactions – in Neisser's terms: the relationship between the business and income spheres and the financial circulation.

Neisser's approach obviously runs counter to all of this. Setting the focus on the difference between T and Y, it seems to epitomize the difference between

Fisher's transactions approach and the common ground of Fisher and monetarism. Moreover, with hindsight on the heated Latin American controversies of 'monetarism' vs. 'structuralism', Neisser's structural approach to the quantity theory may elicit defensive reflexes; and Marxian themes – such as the reproduction schemes – have hardly ever been high on the monetarist agenda.

Nevertheless, I think that Neisser's approach helps to explain one of the problems that monetarism has encountered in recent decades. That problem is the widespread failure of demand-for-money functions to provide reliable guidance for monetary policy. Regardless of the wonders that one can do with cointegration techniques (cf. Laidler, 1993, chapter 9), the instability of money demand – at least over the time horizons that are relevant for most policymakers – has become a stylized fact. This has contributed to the 'benign neglect' of monetary aggregates, both in the central banks' communication of their strategies[27] and in the mainstream 'foundations of a theory of monetary policy', most impressively displayed in Michael Woodford's *Interest and Prices* (2003).[28] Much of the breakdown in the predictive power of money demand functions is attributed to financial innovation and other institutional change in the income sphere. Goodhart's law, that famous combination of the Lucas critique and Murphy's law, has achieved the status of an iron law.[29] I would nevertheless add that neglect of structural change in the business sphere (of industrial and commercial corporations) is a further reason why conventional money demand functions failed, and that Neisser's framework might be suitable to get that change back into sight.

Let me put it slightly differently, in terms of the dynamic version of the equation of exchange that, for example, the German Bundesbank used for a long time:

$$m = p + y - v \tag{13.3}$$

where m is the growth rate of the relevant monetary aggregate, p inflation, y the rate of change in potential output, and v the rate of change in income velocity. It has been observed frequently over recent decades, not only in the euro area, that monetary aggregates grow at a considerably faster pace than potential output, without generating the inflation rates that one would expect (cf., e.g., De Grauwe and Polan, 2005). In equation (13.3), income velocity would have to make up for the difference; it should have dropped significantly. Empirical studies of recent changes in income velocity are rather rare, and studies of changes in transactions velocity or the volume of transactions are even rarer.[30] However, *if* there has in fact been a significant decrease in income velocity, or a significant increase in the volume of transactions, capital intensification à la Neisser should provide part of the explanation (see section 'The Value and Circulation of Money'). There is plenty of evidence in World Bank data that world trade has grown much faster than world GDP since the 1980s. Much of the difference is caused by vertical disintegration, or 'slicing up the value chain' by way of offshoring and cross-border outsourcing. Similarly, outsourcing has taken place at domestic levels. Some of that may be entirely 'spurious capital intensification', some of it represents certainly 'genuine' increases in capital intensity. Concomitant productivity growth may have slowed down inflation, and some of the money required to mediate the greater volume of transactions may have been released from the income sphere, by way of cutting wage costs. Increases in capital intensity have, on the other hand, been accommodated by finance from banks, directly and indirectly through increasingly globalized financial markets. Neisser's framework might help to explain why money growth rates do not always and everywhere translate into proportional inflation.

Conclusion

My conjecture that the relatively low inflation of recent years can (partly) be explained by the type of structural change that Neisser analysed in his theory of the circulation of money is admittedly rather loose. However, it can hardly be argued to the contrary, since there is little statistical evidence of what is going on in terms of changes in the volumes of transactions. I am not convinced that this is entirely in the nature of the data, or rather: that there is a divisive difference in the quality of income and transactions data. In the days of Fisher and Neisser, national accounting was in its infancy; by the mid-1930s, Colin Clark, Simon Kuznets, Erik Lindahl and Jan Tinbergen, among others, had only just provided important concepts and pilot studies (cf. Vanoli, 2005, chapter 1). In those days, time series on transactions data were more readily available than income-related data.[31] The standard system of national accounts (SNA) was developed only after World War II, partly based on wartime efforts and partly due to the interest in indicative and other state planning of economic activities in those times. However, the SNA data on national income are derived from transactions data, and most of the estimates of potential output that are used for purposes of monetary policy are generated by more or less sophisticated extrapolation of trends – even when based on aggregate production functions and/or NAIRU estimates (cf., e.g., Cotis, Elmeskov and Mourougane, 2005).

There might be a number of conceptual problems with transactions data, but it is not clear to me why these should be much bigger than those we have with income data. Since the persistent overshooting of monetary aggregates over their reference values tends to impair the credibility of monetary targetry, political pressure might generate greater attention to transactions data (though only if and when the strategies of inflation targeting have run into empirical problems as well). At the end of the day, the real challenge is probably on the side of theory: to find a 'general quantity theory' that can accommodate both the stock/income- and the flow/transactions perspectives in an operational way. Attempts to develop such a theory will probably be 'always and everywhere controversial'. But for a theory that – according to J. C. R. Dow, cited by David (Laidler, 1991*b*, 289) – 'seems, like a cat with nine times ninety lives, however many times discredited, never to die', this should be taken as a sign of vitality.

Notes

Fak. II – VWL, Carl von Ossietzky Universität Oldenburg, 26111 Oldenburg, Germany (michael.trautwein@uni-oldenburg.de). This paper has been presented at the David Laidler Festschrift conference at the University of Western Ontario, London, Ontario, 18–20 August 2006. Thanks for comments go to Angela Redish and other conference participants.

1. In my quick count I took 'interwar' to mean, with some lead and lag in terms of war, to comprise publications and activities in the period from 1914 until 1945.
2. I am sure that David would hate that old metaphor of 'standing on the giant's shoulder', so I refrain from using it.
3. Neisser was thus closer to Wicksell's own approach to business cycle theory; cf. Wicksell (1907), Laidler (1991*a,* 143–146) and Boianovsky and Trautwein (2001).
4. For longer and more integrated treatments of Neisser's writings on money, the cycle and unemployment see Trautwein (2003) and (2010).
5. A more detailed biography is provided by Hagemann (1999).
6. Neisser is among the most-quoted authors in Ellis (1934) and Marget (1938), and he is frequently cited in Haberler (1937) and Lundberg (1937), two rather different attempts at creating a synthesis of business cycle theories.
7. Neisser actually wrote a long review of Keynes's *Treatise*, but stated dryly that, despite all the complexities in Keynes's treatment of the circulation of money and credit, 'certain basic ideas of the quantity theory are confirmed, again and again' (1931*b*, 2).
8. Neisser's (1932) critique of the insufficiency of deducing the existence of a general equilibrium from the numerical equality of the unknowns and the equations inspired Abraham Wald to develop a more general proof of the existence of a general equilibrium in a stationary economy (in 1935/36), and John von Neumann to repeat the exercise (in 1937) for a growing economy (cf. Hagemann 1990, 134 n.2).
9. Even though Neisser referred generously to Irving Fisher in other contexts, he did not refer to Fisher's debt-deflation theory here; he mentions only, and critically, Schumpeter's theory of '"self-deflation" by repayment of loans' (Neisser, 1934*a*, 446, n.31).
10. As Neisser (1936*a*, 63–64) explained, the implicit increase in productivity has two aspects: investment in new machinery and the scrapping of obsolete machinery. He concluded pessimistically that 'successive waves of displacement, capital destruction, etc., might for a very long period, if not forever, hinder the absorption of all unemployed'.
11. The minutes of the secret Reichsbank conference are documented in Borchardt and Schötz (1991); for a thorough discussion of Neisser's position see also Klausinger (1999).
12. Right before Keynes' humble praise for Neisser, cited in Section 2, we find that well-known reservation: '[I]n German I can only clearly understand what I know already! – so that new ideas are apt to be veiled from me by the difficulties of language' (Keynes, 1930, 178).
13. For more complete discussion of both works see Trautwein (2003) and (2010).
14. In Fisher (1911) – as well as in the second edition of 1913, from which Neisser cited in German translation – the equation of exchange is not related to income *(Y)*, but to the volume of transactions *(T)* only.
15. He added nevertheless agnostically: 'This does not, of course, imply that price-level stabilization is the one and only desirable policy' (1928, 156).
16. Ellis (1934) provides a comprehensive survey. Neisser (1936*c,* 109) deplored the 'long seclusion' of German monetary thought and its 'invincible antipathy to any kind of the quantity theory, however modernized'.
17. Other notable contributions from outside the German language-area were, for example, the Wicksell–Fisher synthesis of Fanno (1912) and the velocity analysis of Holtrop (1928).

18. Neisser considered the circulation of 'inactive money' (reserves) to be irregular in the sense that it is 'completely dependent upon the arbitrary decision of the holder' (1931*a*, 368). In contrast with Holtrop (1928) and Keynes (1930) he did not attempt to provide a systematic discussion of stock transactions in the 'financial circulation', but treated those partly as inactive money in the sense of exchanges of reserves, and partly as leaks and buffers for the circulation of money in the spheres of industry and the public sector.
19. See Ellis (1934, 170–171) for a detailed discussion of the differences between the approaches of Neisser and Keynes (1930, chapter3).
20. In several diagrams Neisser (1931*a*, 373, 376, 377) illustrates how the *c*- and *v*-funds in the economy circulate through different stages of production and spheres of expenditure. The transactions velocity of the circulation of money is far higher than the income velocity, which Neisser (1931*a*, 404) estimates to be 'slightly higher than 4'.
21. Neisser (1931*a*, 397–398) included the possibility that inactive money (balance reserves) is released into circulation in the business sphere. The dotted lines in the diagram refer to both sources of additional money for the *c*-fund.
22. It is unlikely that the economy embarks onto a path of extensive growth, unless expectations of rising profits induce a credit expansion at the going rate of interest. In that case, a change in the supply of money (deposits) is presupposed. Another possible source of finance is the release of balance reserves, as indicated by a dotted line in the diagram. Similar arguments may be made for the first and third case, but are not followed up here.
23. For example, much of Leontief's input-output analysis has a background in the Kiel School. Note that, in the early 1930s (some years before Lundberg, Harrod, Domar and Solow), the Marxian reproduction schemes provided a benchmark model for systematic analysis of growth – including its structural requirements. Austrian capital theory was one of the few alternatives, briefly discussed in Laidler (1999, 34–35).
24. Neisser (1928) was in all his references (traceable by the index) deeply critical of Marx as a monetary theorist.
25. See also Laidler (1991*b*, 291). It should be noted that another connection between Fisher and the income/stock approach of monetarism can be made through Fisher's capital theory.
26. These arguments can also be found in, for example, Friedman (1987) and Laidler (1991*b*, 1993).
27. See Freedman's contribution to this Festschrift (Chapter 8).
28. See, however, David's critique of Woodford in Laidler (2005) and (2006).
29. 'Any observed statistical regularity will tend to collapse once pressure is placed upon it for control purposes'; cf. Goodhart (1989, 95–103).
30. For the nowadays 'classical' approach to studying the long-run behaviour of income velocity see Bordo and Jonung (1987). One of the most thorough recent studies is Brand, Gerdesmeier and Roffia (2002), who show that there is a strong downward trend of income velocity in the current euro area since the 1980s. However, they also demonstrate that different methods yield strongly differing estimates and that the time series, if controlled for structural breaks, indicate a reduction in the decline of income velocity in the 1990s. Despite investing some effort, I have not found any studies of transactions velocity, nor much material on changes in the volume of transactions – apart from evidence in Howells and Hussein (1997) that the ratio of real total transactions to real GDP in the UK rose from about 15 in 1970 to about 50 in the late 1980s, remaining around 40 in 1994.
31. A brief look at the NBER Macrohistory Database should confirm that impression.

References

Boianovsky, Mauro and Hans-Michael Trautwein (2001). "Wicksell's Lecture Notes on Economic Crises (1902/05)." *Structural Change and Economic Dynamics* 12, 343–365.

Borchardt, Knut and Hans Otto Schötz, eds. (1991). *Wirtschaftspolitik in der Krise. Die (Geheim-) Konferenz der Friedrich-List-Gesellschaft im September 1931 über Möglichkeiten und Folgen einer Kreditausweitung.* Baden-Baden: Nomos.

Bordo, Michael and Lars Jonung (1987). *The Long-Run Behaviour of the Velocity of Circulation. The International Evidence.* New York: Cambridge University Press.

Brand, Claus, Dieter Gerdesmeier and Barbara Roffia (2002). "Estimating the Trend of M3 Income Velocity Underlying the Reference Value for Monetary Growth." *European Central Bank Occasional Paper* No. 3. Frankfurt.

Cotis, Jean-Philippe, Jørgen Elmeskov and Annabelle Mourougane (2005). "Estimates of Potential Output: Benefits and Pitfalls from a Policy Perspective." Forthcoming in *Euro area business cycle: Stylized facts and measurement issues,* ed. by Lucrezia Reichlin. London: Centre of Economic Policy Research.

De Grauwe, Paul and Magdalena Polan (2005). "Is Inflation Always and Everywhere a Monetary Phenomenon?" *Scandinavian Journal of Economics* 107, 239–259.

Ellis, Howard (1934). *German Monetary Theory, 1905–1933.* Cambridge, MA: Harvard University Press.

Fanno, Marco (1912). *Le Banche e il mercato monetario* (translation of part II: *The Money Market,* forewords by Augusto Graziani and Michio Morishima. London: Macmillan, 1995).

Fisher, Irving (1911). *The Purchasing Power of Money. Its Determination and Relation to Credit, Interest and Prices,* 2nd ed., 1913. New York: Macmillan.

Friedman, Milton (1987). "The Quantity Theory of Money." In John Eatwell, Murray Milgate and Peter Newman, eds., *The New Palgrave: A Dictionary of Economics.* Basingstoke: Macmillan, pp. 3–20.

Goodhart, Charles (1989). *Money, Information and Uncertainty,* 2nd ed. Basingstoke: Macmillan.

Haberler, Gottfried (1937). *Prosperity and Depression. A Theoretical Analysis of Cyclical Movements.* Geneva: League of Nations.

Hagemann, Harald (1990). "Neisser's ‚The Wage Rate and Employment in Market Equilibrium': An Introduction." *Structural Change and Economic Dynamics* 1, 133–139.

Hagemann, Harald (1994). "Hayek and the Kiel School: Some Reflections on the German Debate on Business Cycles in the Late 1920s and Early 1930s." In Marina Colonna and Harald Hagemann, eds., *Money and Business Cycles. The Economics of F.A.Hayek,* Vol.I. Aldershot: Edward Elgar, pp. 101–120.

Hagemann, Harald (1999). "Hans Philipp Neisser." In Harald Hagemann and Claus-Dieter Krohn, eds., *Handbuch der Emigration deutschsprachiger Wirtschaftswissenschaftler nach 1933,* Vol. 2. Munich: K.G. Saur, pp. 488–495.

Hayek, Friedrich August (1933). *Monetary Theory and the Trade Cycle.* London: Jonathan Cape.

Holtrop, Marius (1928). *De Omloopssnelheid van het Geld.* Amsterdam (German translation in *Beiträge zur Geldtheorie,* ed. by Friedrich A. Hayek. Vienna: Julius Springer, 1932, pp. 115–209).

Howells, Peter and Khaled Hussein (1997). "The Demand for Money: Total Transactions as the Scale Variable." *Economics Letters* 55, 371–377.

Keynes, John Maynard (1930). *A Treatise on Money,* Vol.I: *The Pure Theory of Money* (Collected Writings of John Maynard Keynes, Vol. 5, 1971). Basingstoke: Macmillan.

Keynes, John Maynard (1936). *The General Theory of Employment, Interest and Money.* Basingstoke: Macmillan.

Keynes, John Maynard (1940). *How to Pay for the War. A Radical Plan for the Chancellor of the Exchequer.* London: Macmillan.

Klausinger, Hansjörg (1999). "German Anticipations of the Keynesian Revolution? The Case of Lautenbach, Neisser and Röpke." *European Journal of the History of Economic Thought* 6, 378–403.

Krohn, Claus-Dieter (1987). *Wissenschaft im Exil. Deusche Sozial- und Wirtschaftswissenschaftler in den USA und die New School for Social Research.* New York: Frankfurt.

Laidler, David (1991*a*). *The Golden Age of the Quantity Theory.* Hemel Hempstead: Philip Allan.

Laidler, David (1991*b*). "The Quantity Theory is Always and Everywhere Controversial – Why?" *Economic Record* 67, 289–306.
Laidler, David (1993). *The Demand for Money. Theories, Evidence, Problems*, 4th ed. New York: Harper Collins.
Laidler, David (1999). *Fabricating the Keynesian Revolution. Studies in the Inter-war Literature on Money, the Cycle and Unemployment.* Cambridge (UK), New York: Cambridge University Press.
Laidler, David (2005). Theoretical Foundations for Monetary Policy. Paper given at 2005 SUERF – Bank of Finland Conference on 'Open Market Operations and the Financial Markets' Helsinki, 22–23 September 2005.
Laidler, David (2006). "Woodford and Wicksell on *Interest and Prices:* The Place of the Pure Credit Economy in the Theory of Monetary Policy." *Journal of the History of Economic Thought* 28, 151–160.
Lundberg, Erik (1937). *Studies in the Theory of Economic Expansion*. London: P.S. King.
Marget, Arthur (1938). *The Theory of Prices. A Re-Examination of the Central Problems of Monetary Theory*, Vol.I. New York: Prentice Hall.
Marschak, Jakob (1924). "Die Verkehrsgleichung." *Archiv für Sozialwissenschaften und Sozialpolitik* 52, 344–384.
Marx, Karl (1885). *Das Kapital. Kritik der politischen Oekonomie*. 2. Bd.: Der Cirkulationsprocess des Kapitals. Hamburg: Otto Meissner.
Neisser, Hans (1928). *Der Tauschwert des Geldes*. Jena: Gustar Fischer.
Neisser, Hans (1930). "Lohnsenkung als Heilmittel gegen Arbeitslosigkeit?" *Magazin der Wirtschaft*, 1301–1306, 1447–1448.
Neisser, Hans (1931*a*). "Der Kreislauf des Geldes." *Weltwirtschaftliches Archiv* 33, 365–408.
Neisser, Hans (1931*b*). "Kredit und Konjunktur nach J.M. Keynes." *Weltwirtschaftliches Archiv* 34, 1*–15*.
Neisser, Hans (1931*c*). "Ankurbelung oder Inflation? Eine Entgegnung." *Der Deutsche Volkswirt* 6, 80–85.
Neisser, Hans (1932). "Lohnhöhe und Beschäftigungsgrad im Marktgleichgewicht." *Weltwirtschaftliches Archiv* 36, 414–455 (translation: The Wage Rate and Employment in Market Equilibrium, *Structural Change and Economic Dynamics* 1 (1990), 141–163).
Neisser, Hans (1933). "Öffentliche Kapitalanlagen in ihrer Wirkung auf den Beschäftigungsgrad. Ein Beitrag zur Theorie der Arbeitsbeschaffung." In *Economic Essays in Honour of Gustav Cassel*. London: George Allen & Unwin, pp. 459–470.
Neisser, Hans (1934*a*). "General Overproduction. A Study of Say's Law of Markets." *Journal of Political Economy* 42, 433–465.
Neisser, Hans (1934*b*). "Monetary Expansion and the Structure of Production." *Social Research* 1, 434–457.
Neisser, Hans (1936*a*). *Some International Aspects of the Business Cycle*. Philadelphia: University of Pennsylvania Press.
Neisser, Hans (1936*b*). "Commentary on Keynes." *Social Research* 3, 459–487.
Neisser, Hans (1936*c*). "Secondary Employment: Some Comments on R.F. Kahn's Formula." *Review of Economic Statistics* 18, 24–30, 147–148 (Rejoinder).
Neisser, Hans (1936*d*). "German Literature on Money and Credit." *Social Research* 3, 109–112.
Neisser, Hans (1942). "'Permanent' Technological Unemployment. 'Demand for Commodities Is Not Demand for Labour'." *American Economic Review* 32, 50–71.
Neisser, Hans (1957). "Oligopoly as a Non-Zero-Sum Game." *Review of Economic Studies* 25, 1–20.
Neisser, Hans and Franco Modigliani (1953). *National Income and International Trade. A Quantitative Analysis*. Urbana: University of Illinois Press.
Schumpeter, Joseph Alois (1917–18). "Das Sozialprodukt und die Rechenpfennige. Glossen und Beiträge zur Geldtheorie von heute." *Archiv für Sozialwissenschaft und Statistik* 44, 627–715 (translation: Money and the Social Product, *International Economic Papers* 6 (1956), 148–211).

Trautwein, Hans-Michael (2003). "Neisser's Unorthodox Quantity Theory of Money." In Edward J. Nell und Matthew Forstater, eds., *Reinventing Functional Finance. Transformational Growth and Full Employment*. Cheltenham, Northampton: Edward Elgar, pp. 66–82.
Trautwein, Hans-Michael (2010). "On 'Dr. Neisser's General Attitude to Monetary Problems'." In Riccardo Bellofiore, ed., *German Monetary Theory Revisited*. London: Macmillan, Forthcoming.
Vanoli, André (2005). *A History of National Accounting*. Amsterdam: IOS Press.
Wicksell, Knut (1898). *Geldzins und Güterpreise. Eine Untersuchung über die den Tauschwert des Geldes bestimmenden Ursachen*. Jena: Gustar Fischer.
Wicksell, Knut (1907). "Krisernas gåta." *Statsøkonomisk Tidskrift* 21, 255–284 (translation: 'The Enigma of Business Cycles' in *Interest and Prices*, reprint, New York, 1965, pp. 223–239).
Woodford, Michael (2003). *Interest and Prices – Foundations of a Theory of Monetary Policy*. Princeton: Princeton University Press.

Discussion

Angela Redish

This chapter introduces us to an economist of the 1930s who was in many ways remarkably modern. Hans Neisser worried about the interaction between growth and business cycles, and the impact of going extending the quantity theory of money by acknowledging the different types of money aggregated in 'M'. Michael Trautwein argues that Neisser's work has not been given its due, and that it helps to explain economic theory during the interwar period, and the evolution of theory throughout the twentieth century. Not being a historian of economic thought I will focus my remarks on how I see Neisser's work in the context of macroeconomics today.

As Michael shows, Neisser's theory of growth and cycles evolved over time. I saw two separate approaches, first, an emphasis on how the capital intensity of new technology inherently led to reduced employment (I wasn't clear whether this was equivalent to structural unemployment) and second, a more elaborate chain of causation that emphasized how over time the banking system and inside money would reduce employment and transform cyclical unemployment into structural unemployment. In both cases the models focus on equilibrium unemployment and deflation reflected the characteristics of the German economy in the 1930s.

Following World War II the study of economic growth and of business cycles were essentially divorced. Business cycles were the primary focus of macroeconomic interest with Keynesian and Monetarist theories that were virtually devoid of dynamics (at least at the theoretical level; empirical analysis was dynamic in that estimated equations included lagged variables, albeit without a structural motivation). The empirical vapidity of this approach combined with modelling innovations gradually led to the construction of dynamic models that integrated business cycles and economic growth, first in the context of real business cycle models and then in more sophisticated models. Examples of these latter include models where expectations of the payoff to technological innovations, perhaps unrealized, drive (over)investment generating subsequent periods of underinvestment. Other models have emphasized the industrial organization of R and D, noting that the complementarities between innovations may lead to bursts of innovative activity followed by relatively dry spells.

Thus I see Neisser's macroeconomics, as presented in this chapter, as very modern in its understanding that growth and cycles should not be dichotomized, and I would encourage Michael Trautwein to pursue the linkages between Neisser's work and that of the current generation of macroeconomists.

Neisser's monetary theory focused on transactions rather than income, a natural approach in the days before the SNA when data on transactions (such as debits and cheques cleared) were far more available than data on GDP. Neisser argued that economic growth driven by technical progress and rising capital intensity would raise the number of transactions relative to income and, if the money stock was constant, this would cause secular deflation. Michael suggests that this phenomenon provides part of the explanation for the instability of the money demand function over the last quarter of the twentieth century, and the low inflation rates of the last 15 years. He then suggests that policymakers might usefully learn from Neisser's approach and that we should consider collecting and using transactions data in the conduct of monetary policy.

I am sympathetic to the idea that the volatility of the money demand function may reflect the changing number of transactions per unit of GDP, but I am not convinced that this has been a key driver of low inflation. The world in which Neisser was writing was at least notionally connected to a gold standard, and the supply of high-powered money was consequently not seen as a policy instrument. As presented by Michael, Neisser saw deflation arising from the interaction of inside money (bank created), money demand and the 'volume of money'. Yet while the first two factors are carefully analysed, the volume of money is treated as essentially exogenous. From the perspective of the history of thought, I would have been interested to learn more about how Neisser viewed the supply of money. But I am not sure that his views are useful as a theory of current price level behaviour. Specifically, today the leading central banks have either explicitly or implicitly adopted inflation targeting and consequently adjust the stock of money to achieve that target.

In summary, I appreciated Michael Trautwein's elaboration of Neisser's views on money and macroeconomics, which reminds – at least this non-historian of economic thought – of the richness of the economic analysis that occurred in the interwar period.

14

Harry Johnson, Keynes, and Keynesian Economics

D. E. Moggridge

David Laidler arrived in Chicago from the University of Syracuse in 1960. At Chicago he learned his monetary economics from Harry Johnson's 1960–61 lecture course and, after a year teaching at the LSE, in the 1962–63 Money Workshop at Chicago (both of which Harry had taken over because Milton Friedman was on leave). David was involved with Harry in the founding of the British Money Study Group in 1969 and found Harry's advice invaluable when moving to Manchester in 1969 and Western Ontario in 1975 (Laidler, 2000). He also surveyed Harry's contributions to macroeconomics in 1984 and had Harry playing an important role in the development of the Phillips curve as a policy menu in a 1997 paper. In these circumstances, it seems more than appropriate to honour David with a paper on Harry Johnson.

Introduction

On 19 January 1943, in a University of Toronto course on money and banking taught by Roger Anderson, a recently hired Harvard Hansenian, Harry Johnson received his first introduction to 'savings-investment analysis' (Box 43, Economics 3d, Money and Banking). The discussion continued for another six lectures before the instructor turned to international finance, although at the end of the course, on 8 April, there was a discussion of monetary and fiscal policy, which, according to Johnson, finished up 'with an innocuous dose of Keynesian interest theory' (1974 Memoir I, 27). His reading notes for the course show that he read Dennis Robertson's *Money* (1928), Keynes's *General Theory* (1936, chapters 8, 10, 11–13, 15 and 22), two chapters of Gottfried Haberler's *Prosperity and Depression* (1939, part II, chapters 9 and 10), and Alvin Hansen's *Fiscal Policy and Business Cycles* (1941). With the exception of one fourth-year class on Oscar Lange's 'The Rate of Interest and the optimum Propensity to Consume' (1938) which also had a cross reference to Mabel Timlin's *Keynesian Economics* (1941), neither of which he appears to have read at the time, this was Johnson's only exposure to Keynesian economics as a University of Toronto undergraduate.[1]

Thus began Harry Johnson's dealings with Keynesian economics. Over the next 34 years, he would reflect on Keynes, his economics and his influence on many occasions, with his last publications completed before his February 1977 stroke being *The Shadow of Keynes: Understanding Keynes, Cambridge and Keynesian Economics* (with Elizabeth Johnson) (1978*b*) and 'Monetarism: A Historic-Theoretic Perspective' (with A. R. Nobay) (1977).

The purpose of this chapter is to trace Johnson's evolving understanding of and attitude towards Keynes and his economics in both his published and unpublished papers.

From Toronto to Harvard

After graduating from Toronto, Johnson, aged 20, spent the 1943–44 academic year (on Harold Innis's recommendation) as Professor of Economics at St Francis Xavier University in Antigonish, Nova Scotia. He was in fact the entire economics department there, teaching both introductory and advanced economics. For the latter he took his students through Edward Chamberlin's *Theory of Monopolistic Competition* (1933) as well as business cycles and Keynes, for which he used exactly the same books that he had been exposed to at Toronto in 1943. In the macroeconomic section of the course, his lecture notes, which are very extensive, showed that he stayed close to Hansen and emphasized the simple theory of income determination and the determination of investment and said little about Keynes's theory of the rate of interest (Box 44, Economic Theory – Advanced).

Johnson's next contact with economics came in Cambridge during 1945–46, when, before his repatriation to Canada after military service in England, he took Part II of the Economics Tripos, earning the top First. His memoirs of that year and his subsequent years as a Cambridge don are heavily coloured by what came later, particularly as regards the seemingly endless debate over liquidity preference versus loanable funds as the appropriate theory of the rate of interest – a debate for which his later guide for students would provide him with an influential 1952 article (below, pp. 304–305) (Johnson 1978*b*, 130–131).

From his lecture and reading notes for the year one can trace his exposure to monetary economics. It was in that year, at his first meeting of the Political Economy Club, recently revived by Dennis Robertson, that he heard Keynes himself talk on his posthumously published article 'The Balance of Payments of the United States', as well as being unlucky enough to be Keynes's first discussant on that occasion (1978*b*, 131–134). As far as formal lectures were concerned, two sets are relevant: Joan Robinson's on 'Money' in the Michaelmas term of 1945 and Dennis Robertson's on 'The Theory of Money and Economic Fluctuations' in the Easter term of 1946 (Box 44). The Robinson lectures had a very minimal discussion of the determination of the rate of interest, which was done in the course of the lecture for 9 November, where to judge from Harry's notes loanable funds was only touched on in passing. Indeed, the lectures were less about monetary theory than a discussion of employment theory and policy. The Robertson lectures, the first set of which he gave in 1946, were eventually published as volume 3 of his *Lectures on Economic Principles* (1959). There, of course, Robertson criticised Keynes's theory of the rate of interest. However, as far as undergraduate teaching was concerned, the dispute between Keynes's disciples and Robertson did not break out until the next year, when, of course, the Cambridge Keynesians believed that they had to 'inoculate' students against Robertson's Easter Term lectures.

Confirmation of this comes from Johnson's surviving supervision essays for Maurice Dobb, where the issue was not discussed (Box 34, Writings 1975 part 3); and also from the Tripos papers themselves, where there was no place, even in the 'money' paper, for a student to demonstrate his skill or position on the liquidity preference/loanable funds issue. It also comes from the memory of Aubrey Silberston, another undergraduate economist at Jesus who had returned to Cambridge after learning economics as a prisoner of war.[2]

> I soon discovered that Harry already knew a lot of economics.... He hadn't, however, done much Keynesian economics, which was very much a Cambridge specialty.... I vividly remember walking around the College playing fields with Harry for an hour or more, trying to sort out the Keynesian theory of liquidity preference. There was little attempt at critical appraisal. We were simply trying to understand what was then a novel and difficult theory.... We did not become fully aware of Dennis Robertson's criticisms of Keynes' theory until later in the year because Robertson discussed these issues only in the final term. (1978, 2)

The level of Johnson's interest in 1946 is best indicated by the fact that he did not buy Robertson's *Essays in Monetary Theory* until he was in Cambridge in 1947, after his year in Toronto (copy in the author's possession).

After his year in Cambridge, despite an invitation to put in for an assistant lectureship at the LSE and an offer of further support for postgraduate studies in Cambridge, Johnson returned to the University of Toronto to do the MA in economics that he had intended to do in 1943 before the call to St F.X. As well as being a graduate student, he was also an instructor in economics with responsibility for a large section of the second-year course in microeconomics. At the time there was no compulsory course in economic theory for MA students. For his degree he took four courses: economic history, an economic history seminar (both under Innis), a seminar in human relations in industry, and a seminar of the theory of employment and international trade. This last seminar was organised by William Hood, a graduate of Mount Allison University in New Brunswick who after two years' teaching at the University of Saskatchewan had returned to Toronto to do a PhD and to teach. After a post-doctoral year at the Cowles Commission at the University of Chicago (1949–50), Hood would return to Toronto where he remained until he moved to the federal Department of Finance in 1968. Johnson reported to Hood in 1974 after 'recently working over some memories' that 'your ... seminar ... was probably what got me into the field' of international economics (Box 52, Correspondence 1971–77, H- J, to W.C. Hood, 22 February 1974).

For this course (Box 44) we have typed lecture notes for 26 September to 24 October 1946 on 'The Keynesian Theory of Employment' and summary notes for 15 March to 3 April 1947, plus Johnson's reading notes for these lectures, as well for Keynes and Pigou compared, international trade theory, and Haberler's 'International Aspects of Business Cycles' (part II, chapter 12 of *Prosperity and Depression*). There are also a series of typed 'reports' on 'Employment and International Trade: the Harrod Approach', 'Machlup's Contribution to the Theory of International Capital Movements', 'Metzler's Contribution to the Theory of Trade and Employment', 'The Meaning and Measurement of International Economic Equilibrium', 'International Aspects of Full Employment', 'Oscar Lange, Price Flexibility and Employment' and 'Monopolistic Competition in International Trade and its Relation to Domestic Employment'. There is also a paper by Johnson on Machlup's *International Trade and the National Income Multiplier* (1943). In a separate file elsewhere in his papers (Box 55) there are reading notes and a paper by him on Lange's book which takes account of reviews by J. R. Hicks (1945), Mabel Timlin (1946) and Milton Friedman (1946). Hood's course saw Johnson working for the first time on what were materials at a frontier of his field, carefully and critically. Given that Hood's dissertation was 'Some Aspects of the Theory of Employment and International Trade' (Mills and Dombra, 1968, 48), the coverage of the course was understandable.

After his year in Toronto, Johnson went on to Harvard where he did his 'generals' in November 1948 before taking up an assistant lectureship in Cambridge from January 1949. The 15 months in the other Cambridge put their stamp on Johnson. Aubrey Silberston, who had put him up for several weeks during a visit to London and Cambridge in the summer of 1947, remembered the post-Harvard Johnson:

> I noticed quite a change in Harry. Personally he was not very different: a little more assured and mature perhaps, but as nice as ever. However, as an economist he had altered dramatically. He *knew* so much. He had apparently read everything and remembered everything. He was in a different league.... [I]t seemed to have been Harvard that had made the big difference. (Silberston, 1978, 6)

Judging from the surviving materials (course outlines, lecture notes, reading notes and essays), his most influential teachers at Harvard were Gottfried Haberler, Alvin Hansen, Joseph Schumpeter, and John Henry Williams. Schumpeter's history of economic analysis course and his encouragement gave Johnson his first two professional journal publications, 'An Error in Ricardo's Exposition of His Theory of Rent' (1948) and 'Demand for Commodities is not Demand for Labour' (1949).[3] Haberler's very thorough international trade lectures covered the monetary aspects of the subject before turning to the pure theory of trade and policy issues involving trade and payments (Box 54). Williams's half of money and banking covered not only the employment policy discussions in both Britain and the United States but also contemporary international economic issues – the

Anglo-American Loan Agreement of December 1945 and its subsequent unravelling, as well as the postwar international monetary plans and their realisation in the International Monetary Fund (Box 44). Johnson used Williams's 39-page reading list for his fall 1948 International Monetary Organization and Policy (which included trade theory) as a check-list for books and articles he had read and noted (Box 44). He used the reading notes from this course as the core to which he added others once he left Harvard. As a result, the notes contain reports on, among others, Lloyd Metzler's 'Tariffs, the Terms of Trade and the Distribution of Income' (1949) and Sidney S. Alexander's 'Effect of a Devaluation on a Trade Balance' (1952). Hansen's half of money and banking had him reading about the nuts and bolts of American monetary institutions and management, the classics of monetary theory – Marshall, Wicksell, Hayek, Hawtrey, Robertson, and Keynes – and the moderns – Lerner, Modigliani, Tobin, and, of course, Hansen himself (Box 43). Johnson was becoming very well read in economics – something that would remain his trademark as an author and teacher.

The Cambridge Don

When Johnson arrived in Cambridge in January 1949, his teaching responsibilities were for money and banking, a course that was very institutionally oriented, and the advanced theory of international trade. In 1952–53 he added a series of classes with the Phillips Machine, a hydraulic model of the British economy in which the circular flow of income and expenditure is represented by coloured water flowing in clear plastic tubes, and from 1953 he added a series of classes in monetary theory with Joan Robinson and Richard Kahn. Finally, from 1953 he also began to teach what he came to call international monetary theory, which was also the subject of a course of lectures he gave at the LSE in 1954–55 and 1955–56.

At the time Harry arrived in Cambridge, he had a position on Keynes and Keynesian economics. To judge from his preparation, its origins were less Cambridge than Hood and Harvard. The best sources for his position are two 1949 lectures on 'The Significance of Lord Keynes' for a Ministry of Education course in commerce and related subjects,[4] and his discussion with Dennis Robertson 'Some Cambridge Controversies in Monetary Theory' (1951–52).

In his first lecture, Johnson began

> I might describe myself as a third-generation Keynesian – Keynesian, in that I am convinced, as many economists are not, of the usefulness of the approach originated by Lord Keynes, and the importance of the problems with which it deals; third-generation, in both the time I came to the study of the theory and my attitude towards it. I have neither the passionate conviction of revealed truth of the first generation, with its tendency towards bibliolatry, hero-worship, and intolerance towards critical points of view; nor the pioneering enthusiasm of the second generation, acknowledging the limitations of Keynes' book but not of his analysis, and assuming that the 'General Theory' is the starting point of economic wisdom. I regard Keynes' 'General Theory'

> as an extension rather than a replacement of previously existing knowledge, a book which omits not only some of the answers but also some of the questions; and I believe that further progress required a further synthesis of the Keynesian analysis with the general corpus economic theory. (Box 54, 'The Significance of Lord Keynes', Lecture 1, 3)

The introduction may have sounded eclectic and conciliatory but the lecture that followed was an orthodox presentation of both simple 45° Keynesianism and the more sophisticated IS-LM version to which Johnson had added aggregate supply and employment functions. The more sophisticated model, he claimed, demonstrated the possibility of unemployment equilibrium – one which did not depend on the assumption of rigid money wages. He ran through what he regarded as the standard criticisms, making most of the limitation of the theory as a theory of prices, of its inappropriateness for the study of cycles and growth and the static over-simplification of Keynes's treatment of consumption. The Keynesian emphasis on full employment had, he argued, 'serious, even dangerous limitations', not so much because full employment as a fact involves various economic wastes but because full employment as a policy goal involved 'a mistaken diagnosis of the British economic problem' – ignoring the change in Britain's world trade position with the rise of the United States and Germany and the industrialisation of formerly agricultural economies – a theme he would return to in *The Overloaded Economy* (1952*a*) (Box 54, 'The Significance of Lord Keynes', Lecture 2, 15 and 16).

After the event, Harry showed his lectures to Dennis Robertson. Robertson, who had 'extreme admiration for their compactness and lucidity of exposition', but naturally disagreed with some of their conclusions:

> Of course *it does* seem to me that what you say on II, 12–13 about the unsuitability of the apparatus for the analysis of cyclical changes and the evanescence of the various functions makes a bigger hole than you admit in the value of 'unemployment equilibrium' (I, 18), in the value of the alleged 'exact and quantitative formulation' of the forces at work (II, 17) and above all in the claim that the rigidity of wage-rates is not vital to the whole caboodle (I, 4; II, 3–4). I think that your whole-hearted backing of this last claim is the real surprise of the paper – my own view (as you know from the QJE article)[5] having hardened considerably in the other direction. (Box 54, 'The Significance of Lord Keynes', 23 May 1950)

Robertson's note to Johnson also had another purpose, which illustrates his peculiar position in Cambridge at the time despite his being a Fellow of King's College and a member of the Keynesian 'secret seminar':

> I wonder if you would have time to ready during the summer my 12 summer term lectures – over which I took some trouble last vacation?[6] They are all pretty fully written out (jokes and all) and (for me) pretty legible.

It is not surprising that Johnson would later provide Robertson with technical support in a mathematical appendix for a 1955 paper. Nor is it surprising that Robert Clower would still later report to him from Cambridge: 'Have had long conversations with Dennis Robertson – he misses you. ...' (Box 31, Correspondence to 1963, A-C, 12 December 1962).

Robertson's willingness to discuss their differences bore fruit in the Michaelmas term of 1950 when, in an attempt to elucidate the issues in the liquidity preference versus loanable funds debate for students, Johnson wrote an extended commentary on Robertson's 'Mr Keynes and the Rate of Interest'(Robertson, 1940, chapter 1). Once he had a draft, he gave copies to Joan Robinson, Kenneth Berrill, and Robertson – sending Robertson a substantial revision in the light of Joan Robinson's comments. Robertson replied with a letter and a 13-page note. Discussions with Robertson, and some revision of their original pieces, continued the next term – it was agreed by Robertson that meeting to take stock of where they had got to 'might be a suitable religious exercise for Good Friday!' (Box 33, Notes on DHR, 17 March 1951). Eventually they agreed that the interchange with a suitable editorial introduction would appear in the *Review of Economic Studies* for February 1952 under the title 'Some Cambridge Controversies in Monetary Theory'.

Johnson gave an early version of his part of the exchange to the Economics Club of the University of Birmingham on 21 February 1951. His introduction to the paper sheds some light on his view of the Cambridge controversy.

> In giving this paper the title 'Current Controversies in Cambridge Interest Theories' I may perhaps have been a trifle misleading. Such a title might suggest that Cambridge is bursting with new ideas on the subject, new ideas which are being hotly debated and which will eventually lead to progress being made in the theory of interest. This, unfortunately, is not the case: instead, Cambridge is still debating the old issues of the 1930s, the controversy over liquidity preference versus loanable funds. ...
>
> Outside Cambridge, I think it is fair to say, there issues have largely lost their heat: in large part the two approaches have been reconciled in a more general approach to the theory of interest, with matters of controversy being reduced to differences in technique, emphasis or factual assumption. Inside Cambridge, however, the debate goes on in its old form.
>
> Just why this should be so is an extremely interesting question .... Fundamentally it is a matter of the personalities involved. The contrast between the personalities involved in the original debate, Keynes and Robertson, both Cambridge men and close personal friends for a long time, was itself sufficient to ensure that the controversy on the theoretical plane would be charged with personal feeling. ...
>
> The personal nature of the controversy of the thirties has been carried on into the forties and fifties, past the death of Keynes himself, by Keynes's disciples – people who were the younger generation of the thirties, and who have added to the controversy the iconoclasm of youth and the perpetual

> war between the generations, sometimes forgetting in the delight of the debate that as time passes they themselves are becoming the older generation. Robertson also has his supporters; but they are either members of the unconvinced older generation, too senior to carry the debate into fresh fields, or applied economists, not particularly interested in monetary theory, but hostile to the personalities or politics of the Keynesians themselves; none of them are in the class, in monetary theory, with the Keynesians or with Robertson himself. The preservation of old controversies is also facilitated by the peculiar nature of Cambridge academic life, with its intimate society and the College system which cuts sharp across Faculties; loyalty to College is as important as loyalty to Faculty, and to some extent the theoretical controversy can be interpreted as internecine war between King's and Trinity, John's and Caius.[7]
>
> The perpetuation of this kind of controversy, however stultifying it may be for the progress of economics, is always fun for the participants.... But it is not fun for the student who has to find his way through the tactical manoeuvres of controversy to the economic truth either as an undergraduate at Cambridge or as a reader of the writings of Cambridge economists. He is apt to find, not merely that the issues and arguments are wrapped up in *ad hominem* arguments and debating tricks of phrase, but there several logically distinct issues have become amalgamated in the controversy over liquidity preference versus loanable funds. The result is a great waste of student man hours.... (Box 33, Writing 1951)

Johnson's 1970s memoirs of Cambridge after 1949 were, to judge by his own papers and writings in that period, consistent with the facts.

In his *Review of Economic Studies* paper, Johnson was concerned solely with the logic of an economic model. At the time he wrote the paper, as he revealed at greater length in his review of James Meade's *The Balance of Payments* (1951*c*), Johnson saw the job of economic theory as being to elucidate the implications of different factual assumptions – and no more. He did not refer to the model in question: instead he noted that 'the reader familiar with the literature will realise that the writer has drawn heavily on the work of Professors Fellner, Hansen, Hicks, Klein, Modigliani, Somers, and Tobin, to name but a few' (1951–52, 90, n.1.). Nonetheless, the model he was working with was that developed by Modigliani in 1944.

During a 1952 visit to Toronto, Johnson provided the first article in a series 'Shapers of the Modern Outlook' for *The Canadian Forum*, a journal of progressive opinion then edited by his friend Stefan Stykolt. His subject was 'Lord Keynes and Modern Economic Thought'. He claimed that 'no economist since Ricardo has had an influence on the thought of his time comparable to that of John Maynard Keynes; not even Ricardo's influence grew so quickly or spread so widely.' He then set out the central doctrine of the *General Theory* 'that there was no natural tendency of the economic system to generate full employment of labour' and sketched the accompanying analytical apparatus. The propagation of Keynes's ideas was attributable to the context in which the book appeared, as well as the boldness of Keynes's own presentation of his claims. Johnson admitted that the claim for generality was misleading but argued that the book had re-invigorated 'all branches of the subject'. He noted the success of the apparatus when adapted for wartime use and 'the culmination of the influence of Keynes' analysis ... in the commitment of governments to the maintenance of full employment in the post-war world'(1952*b*, 176). The post-war period itself had brought a synthesis of Keynesian and pre-Keynesian analysis. It had also highlighted the rigidities and inflationary problems created by full employment policies, and the experience cast doubt on the doctrine of the tendency of the capitalist system towards chronic mass unemployment. Nonetheless, the 'agreement on the broad lines of both theory and policy [among contemporary economists] is the true measure of Keynes' influence on modern economic thought' (1952*b*, 177).

During the rest of his period in Cambridge, Johnson's contributions to macroeconomics centred largely around discussions of the revival monetary policy in Britain after November 1951 and its subsequent conduct, although there were by-products of his never-completed Harvard thesis on changes in British banking between 1930 and 1950.[8] These papers had an existence that was seemingly independent from his monetary theory. The only exception came in 'Some General Aspects of Monetary Policy', a paper delivered to the Association of University Teachers of Economics on 4 January 1954 (Box 33, Writing 1953).

From a longer-term perspective, the most interesting section of the AUTE paper was the second where he started with the premise that 'the post-War experience which has led to the revival of monetary policy emphasises certain shortcomings of the Keynesian analysis' (8) which was worth examining even though 'there can be no possibility of dismissing Keynesian theory as a temporary aberration of the 1930s' (9). He also made what he regarded as 'the obvious point'

> that the Keynesian prejudice against monetary policy ... is less the work of Keynes himself ... than of some of his critics, and even more of those of his followers who did not share his expressed desire to save free enterprise from itself. (9)

As he summarized his argument

> [T]he Keynesian theory tends to understate the scope for monetary policy, by imparting a spurious impression of precision and stability to the determination of the level of income in the short run; while the theory of liquidity preference – which incidentally illustrates many of the disadvantages of the two-dimensional Marshallian tradition – is too narrowly conceived to provide an adequate approach to the theory of how monetary policy works. (12)

No wonder Dennis Robertson could say that he read the paper 'with interest, and a great deal of agreement, especially (as you would expect) with the middle section' (Box 33, Writing 1953, 21 January 1954).

A 1956 paper, 'Some Reflections on the Revival of Monetary Policy in Great Britain', introduced a new theme to his writing: 'the major long-term problem of the British economy, the tendency for British wages and prices to increase more rapidly than those of Britain's international competitors' (1956*b*, 19). Although he recognised long-term inflation as a monetary problem, he did not see monetary policy as playing an important role in its solution:

> experience suggests that substantial unemployment would be required to prevent wages from increasing at an inflationary rate. Given the narrow limits set by current opinion as to what constitutes a tolerable margin of unemployment, this means that neither monetary policy nor alternative methods of controlling aggregate demand offer much prospect of a solution. (1956*b*, 19)

But he thought that none of the other possible solutions would work, given 'such methods attempt to solve the economic problem by ignoring the economic forces that produce it' (1956*b*, 20). The only solution seemed to be 'to stagger on as we have been doing', hoping that in the absence of a need to devote large resources to defence and to meet an adverse shift in the terms of trade would allow rising productivity to raise real incomes, allowing for 'the necessary condition for a workable "national wages-policy" – the possibility of substantial non-inflationary wage increases'(1956*b*, 20).

The vague hope for a national wage policy as the ultimate solution was not linked to what David Laidler (1984, 596) called 'a rather ill-defined cost-push explanation of inflation based on the failure of real incomes to rise'. As Johnson set out the argument in an article 'On British Crises' for *Granta* in April 1956.

> [T]he source of chronic inflation is to be found in a chronic tendency towards placing excessive demands on the capacity of the economy. Why has this been the case with the British economy since the war? The answer lies in the coincidence of the victory of what may be broadly described as socialist ideas on domestic and foreign economic policy with a relative decline in the ability of the British economy to give effect to these ideas and the survival of other ideas with which they have been uneasily combined. (1956*a*)

Parts of the argument echoed *The Overloaded Economy* (1952*a*), his 1952 public lectures at the University of Toronto. The adoption of the welfare state, the commitment to full employment, the commitment to assist in the economic development of backward countries, the desire to maintain Britain's political and economic position in the world (including a commitment to heavy defence expenditure and the re-establishment of Britain's position in trade and finance) all implied a reduction in the proportion of output available to individual consumption. Unless the public was reconciled to this by acceptance of the social philosophy underlying the policies or there was a substantial rise in the output available to allow for these policies, inflation was inevitable. Neither the reconciliation nor the rise in output came to pass: Britain retained 'the philosophy of personal capitalism and of capitalist incentives, particularly collective bargaining' and economic developments (the effects of the war itself and the postwar deterioration of the terms of trade) meant that additional capacity was not available to meet the additional demands. This explanation was socio-political – the sort Johnson would decry later in life – rather than cost-push, although one might concede that the implications of 'frustrated desires for higher living standards' for trade-union behaviour would look like cost push.

This sort of explanation of inflation did not sit well with another aspect of Johnson's later Cambridge thinking. In September 1954 he delivered the paper, 'The Determinants of the General Level of Wage Rates', although it was not published until 1957. That paper, as well as being extremely critical of Keynesian theory, stated flatly

> the conclusion which emerges from the argument is the rather obvious one that the level of money wages is a proper subject for economic analysis, unless we are to reject the assumption that wage-earners (and other economic units) are in some sense rational and that the level of money wages will be governed by the quantity of money, though not in the simple way postulated by classical monetary theory in its unsophisticated form. (1957, 35)

In 1954, he thought that the practical applicability of the conclusion was limited by the absence of a theory of the rate at which wages change and the traditional belief that the quantity of money was an autonomous variable – in the modern economy the money supply was a matter of government policy and it and the wage/price-level were jointly determined by government policy.

Johnson also discussed Keynesian economics in critical terms in one of a series of lectures he delivered in Karachi in July 1956 – three months after he had moved from Cambridge to Manchester – 'Monetary Theory and Keynesian Economics'. The lecture was not published until 1958 and was not widely available until he republished it in *Money, Trade and Economic Growth* (1962). The notes for this lecture survive (Box 43, Karachi and Singapore Lectures 1956) and they have the very strong criticisms of Keynesian doctrine whose distinctive features were noted by David Laidler (1984, 597–598) although Laidler was using the slightly revised 1962 version – the point that Keynesian economics was a special case of neoclassical economics and the weakness of Keynesian economics as a theory of prices. Johnson made reference to the trend towards reconsidering the quantity theory with the work of A. J. Brown, whose *The Great Inflation* he had reviewed in the *Economic Journal* for March 1956 (1962, 121–123) and explicitly to Milton Friedman, whose *Studies in the Quantity Theory of Money* with its 'The Quantity Theory of Money a Restatement' appeared in 1956 but whose ideas could have been known to Johnson when he was at Northwestern on leave in the spring of 1955, if not earlier. Thus it is likely that 'Harry Johnson's first large step away from orthodox Cambridge Keynesianism' was taken not in Manchester, as David Laidler claimed (1984, 598) but in Cambridge. However, one might argue that, given the nature of his training, he had never been an 'orthodox' Cambridge Keynesian.

The Manchester years were, in terms of evidence on Johnson's views on Keynesian economics, relatively barren. He taught an advanced undergraduate course in monetary theory, but, surprisingly, neither his lecture notes nor his course outlines survive. The only development one might note was a moderation of his views on inflation in a June 1958 symposium on wage policy and inflation. His paper 'Two Schools of Thought on Wage Inflation' (1958) largely concerned the views of others, but he also clearly set out his own views. He saw British inflation as predominantly a reflection of excess demand. However, he did not believe that inflation of the postwar British variety had done any serious damage. Rather

> the argument against inflation in Britain is ... that the gradual erosion of the value of money entails a host of unfairness – some cumulative and some temporary, but all irritating – between different members of the community, and makes more complicated and frustrating the task economic calculation for all concerned including the government itself.
>
> How much weight should be attached to this argument is a difficult problem in the making of value judgements to which neither the convenience of a decent salaried existence nor the habit of thinking of the working class in RSPCA terms is a fair guide.[9] But it is at least arguable that neither the desperate need for more employment nor the need in the 1940s for more production is the appropriate standard for the present situation, and that the country can probably now afford to trade some loss of output and employment for greater stability of prices. (1958, 151)

He was uncertain about the costs of restraint, but thought that 3 per cent was probably an optimistic view of the level of unemployment necessary to stop wage inflation. He thought that the machinery of collective bargaining needed some improvement, but that this might come more easily in an environment of restrained demand (1958, 153). These views differed from those of 1954 but the source of the change was unclear. One suspects that it was probably less the effects of Manchester than the slow change in opinion outside some Labour circles and Keynesian Cambridge that had come to accept that more unemployment might be a price paying for price stability.

Chicago

Johnson's next forays into Keynesian economics came soon after he arrived in Chicago in September 1959 as the successor to Lloyd Metzler. On 29 January 1960, Paul Samuelson, the President-elect of the American Economic Association, wrote to him:

> I should like to invite you to give a substantial paper [at the A.E.A. meetings] if you have some suitable topic in mind. ... No particular topics occur to me beyond the one I mentioned earlier.[10] A provocative discussion of monetary

> policies here and there might be suitable. The issues connected with a low and high pressure economy might suggest themselves. Or perhaps you have some unified research that you would like to report on. (Box 31, Correspondence to 1963, S–Z)

In a 1969 'Autobiographical Note' and a 1974 'Self-Assessment', Harry reported that Samuelson had suggested the topic on which he eventually spoke in St Louis, 'The *General Theory* after Twenty-five Years', but if he did so no other record survives. Just over a month later, on 3 March 1960, B. F. Haley, the editor of the *American Economic Review*, invited Harry to prepare one of the Surveys of Economic Theory jointly sponsored by the American Economic Association and the Royal Economic Society (Box 25, AEA Survey). Harry briefly hesitated, but, once he knew that he would be teaching money and banking in Chicago in the 1960–61 academic year while Milton Friedman was on leave and that he could do the bulk of the work in the summer of 1961, he accepted (5 April 1960).[11]

The St Louis lecture, when eventually reprinted in *Money, Trade and Economic Growth*, brought a new term into the economic literature – bastard Keynesian. Reviewing the book in the *Economic Journal* for September 1962, Joan Robinson accused him of not knowing what he was talking about.

> Unluckily he was just the wrong age to make such an appraisal. A younger man would have felt obliged to do some research to find out the orthodox theory that Keynes was attacking; an older man would himself have once been submitted to it. Professor Johnson, who grew up amid the controversies around the *General Theory*, thinks he knows what it was all about, but actually he does not discuss the changes which Keynes' theory made in economic thought; he is confronting it with its own bastard progeny. (1965, 100)

The review went on to discuss the bastard Keynesian criticisms of Keynes.

Johnson's lecture had a number of features.[12] It continued his practice, but more sharply this time, of distinguishing between 'the economics of Keynes' and 'Keynesian economics' – a distinction he highlighted in his discussion of the policy implications of the *General Theory*. The distinction also came out in his discussion of liquidity preference *versus* loanable funds, where he made the comment that 'the prolonged defence in the English literature of the proposition that an increase in the propensity to save lowers the rate of interest by reducing the level of income is a credit to ... ingenuity rather than ... scientific spirit' (1962, 134). He saw several weaknesses in the *General Theory*. 'Keynes drastically over-generalized a particularly bad depression which was made worse by errors of economic policy' (1962, 143). The 'consumption function is nowhere as simple as Keynes made it out to be and unemployment equilibrium is a special case of dynamic disequilibrium and anyway not the chronic problem of modern capitalism' (1962, 143–144). 'Keynes made the analysis of the demand for money explicitly a branch of capital theory, whereas the role of money as a form of wealth-holding had been left implicit in the neo-classical analysis', but 'his theory of the demand for money ... is misleadingly presented, very confused and, as a theory of the demand for money in capital theory terms, seriously incomplete' (1962, 135). He concluded, however,

> The contribution of the *General Theory* to modern economics is certainly not Keynes's specific model of income determination. ... Rather the contribution lies in the general nature of Keynes's approach to the problem of income and employment. In the first place, he concentrated attention on the expenditure-income and income-expenditure relationships which was much easier to understand and apply than the quantity theory relationships and which provides, in the multiplier analysis, a key dynamic process of change. In the second place, he provided a useful macro-economic general equilibrium model for the analysis of the monetary economy. ... Finally, what is most important for scientific economics ... he set out his theory in a model in which the important variables and relationships are specified in a form suitable for statistical testing. The stimulation given by the *General Theory* to the construction and testing of aggregative models may well prove to be Keynes's chief contribution to economics in the longer perspective of historical judgment, since the application of capital rather than income concepts to monetary theory may well produce better and more reliable results, and the present predominance of the income-expenditure approach prove to be a transitional phase in the analysis of economic behaviour. (1962, 144)

Johnson's criticism of the Keynesians took two main tacks. First, they turned 'a theory in which money is important ... into the theory that money is unimportant'. Part of the explanation was a hardening of certain of Keynes's conclusions into rigid dogmas in the hands of his disciples, but another part arose from the fact that 'Keynesians have tended to be politically left of centre, a position associated with a distrust of central bankers – particularly in England' (1962, 145). As a result, the Keynesians ran in problems in dealing with 'the dominant post-war policy problem of inflation' where 'the Keynesian approach has tended to degenerate into a confused and often obstructive eclecticism' which 'virtually assumes away the possibility of controlling inflation by monetary means' (1962, 145–146).

Johnson's 1962 Survey article, instead of being organised around the issues raised by Keynes concentrated on current topics of research. In his discussions with B. F. Haley on writing his 1962 survey, Johnson remarked that he had 'resisted a lot of pressure of various kinds to make the survey a statement of the current position of the Chicago School' (Box 25, AEA Survey, 7 March 1962). Even if he successfully resisted the pressure, he still he had to deal with the School. If he regarded Keynes's great weakness as his 'neglect of the influence of capital on behaviour' (1962, 147).

> Friedman's application to monetary theory of the basic principles of capital theory – that income is the yield of capital and capital the present value of income – is probably the most important development in monetary theory since Keynes (1967, 33).

Naturally, he praised the postwar consumption-function literature associated with Friedman, Modigliani, and others for the same reason. Similarly, he praised 'the approach to monetary dynamics that has been emerging in the past few years, from both "Keynesian" and "quantity" theorists, as an outgrowth of the formulation of monetary theory as a part of the general theory of asset holding', citing Friedman in the company of Tobin, Cagan, and Brunner from the last of whom he drew a lengthy quotation (1967, 50). Nonetheless, although Friedman started his discussion of the demand for money 'from the fundamentals of capital theory', Johnson thought that 'in its final form Friedman's demand for money function is hard to distinguish from a modern Keynesian formulation' and he put Friedman in a theoretical tradition that started with Keynes (1967, 32). Johnson would maintain this position in a 1963 lecture in Argentina and in his 1965 review of Friedman and Schwartz's *A Monetary History of the United States, 1867–1960* (1965, 395–396).

Johnson's views on inflation, not dealt with in his 1962 survey, continued to develop in the 1960s. In 1963, as well as lecturing on 'Recent Developments in Monetary Theory' he provided his Argentinian audience with 'A Survey of Theories of Inflation'. In this survey, he discussed Keynesian and monetarist theories of inflation as well as recent work on the Phillips curve which related the rate of inflation to the rate of unemployment. He was uncomfortable with several aspects of the Keynesian theory, most notably the absence of a theory of wage determination in Keynes's own work and the tendency of his followers and successors to make arbitrary assumptions about wage and price behaviour and to ignore the fact that this behaviour would depend on expectations of the future once an inflationary process got under way, as well as assuming that their models were independent of the monetary environment. This meant that they implicitly assumed a permissive monetary policy would continue and avoided the need to consider how spending would be financed and how rising money incomes would affect the demand for money. In contrast, the quantity theory assumed

> that in an inflation the economy becomes accustomed to the expectations of a continuation of inflation, so that the processes of determining wages and prices are fundamentally real processes and not arbitrary processes determined exogenously. (1967, 122)

In this scheme of things there was a stable demand for money and the rate of inflation represented the cost of holding real balances and affected the demand for them. However, he saw the evidence as ambiguous.

> So far as substantial inflations are concerned, the evidence seems to favour the quantity theory over the Keynesian approach. For the mild type of inflation typical of the United States and other advanced countries, the approach has not proved nearly so useful. The theory implies the existence of a stable demand function for money in which the expected rate of inflation appears as an argument, but while many researchers have established the existence of satisfactorily stable demand functions, the expected rate of inflation

> has not appeared as a significant determinant of the quantity demanded. (1967, 126)

As for the Phillips curve, he found it 'new and very interesting'. It substituted 'an empirical relationship ... for ... vague literary and judgmental arguments'. But he acknowledged 'serious doubts' as to its applicability to policy. It was a statistical description resting on a simple model with little traditional theory behind it, and he doubted whether it would retain its shape 'if an attempt were made by economic policy to pin the economy down to a point on it' (1967, 132–133). He was attracted, however, by the possibility of a trade-off between inflation and unemployment and cited the work by Grant Reuber for the Canadian Royal Commission on Banking and Finance which he would publish in the *Journal of Political Economy* (Reuber, 1964; Laidler, 1997). In a June 1964 paper at McGill, 'Employment Theory and Public Policy in the North American context', he called Reuber's paper 'a major step forward' (Box 53, Green Box, 7).

In February 1965 Johnson gave a lecture to social science undergraduates at Chicago on 'Keynes and Modern Economic Thought'(Box 27, Manuscripts – HGJ). He saw Keynes as 'one of the four great thinkers who have shaped twentieth-century thinking about man and society' – the others being Darwin, Marx and Freud. As previously, Keynes's contribution was 'the notion that a capitalist or a monetary society ... does not automatically produce full employment' with all that implied for government's role in the economy.

He provided a sketch of the circumstances in which the *General Theory* appeared, paying attention to the 'empirical experiments' of governments dealing with the problem of depression, popular views on the appropriate economic policy and the position of contemporary economic theory on the issues.

Keynes's *General Theory* attacked these ideas – both popular notions and the ideas of classical economists – as being derived from the economics of a barter economy and being untrue for the money economy that actually existed (4).

The key principle that Keynes deployed in his attack was the theory of effective demand which Johnson developed at some length.

Beside the basic point for economic theory that a monetary economy was crucially different from a barter economy, Johnson argued that Keynes's theory 'challenged the prevailing ethics of capitalism' (10) by showing that thrift was not necessarily a virtue and that unemployment was 'not necessarily the result of individual shiftlessness and incompetence, or of the greediness and graspingness of trade unions' (11). The theory also had revolutionary implications for the role of government.

Johnson explained the attractiveness of Keynes's theory to economists, especially to those just entering the profession: its relevance as a positive response to real problems; its challenge to the dominant orthodoxy of Marshall and his followers; and the complementarity of the new theory with the growing use of mathematics in economics and the growth of national income accounting. The experience of the World War II gave a fillip to these other developments.

Johnson went on to discuss the fortunes of Keynes in the postwar world – the synthesis that made unemployment equilibrium the special case (albeit perhaps the relevant one); the improvement of Keynes's theories of the consumption function and the demand for money; and the extension of Keynes by his followers to consider economic growth and a more complex mix of policy goals. He also mentioned 'something of a counter revolution, which emphasised the relevance of the older style of monetary theory and the necessity of following a proper monetary policy' but noted that this was aimed at the excesses of some Keynesians rather than Keynes himself (18).[13]

And the LSE

From 1966 to 1974 Johnson held a joint appointment at the LSE and Chicago. This shifted the focus of his work. As he later recalled

> My own scientific work, so far as the English end of it was concerned, lay in the field of monetary economics. My interests at Chicago had been in international trade theory, but the L.S.E. was well stocked body-wise if not brain-wise with teachers in that area, whereas no-one in Britain seemed aware of the 'monetarist counter-revolution' that had been going on in the United States and in the scientifically active academic world generally and it seemed important to me that our own students should be instructed in post-*General Theory* developments and controversies. (1974 Memoir IV, 31)

In establishment economic circles at the time Johnson returned to England, Keynesianism was still in the ascendency – a Keynesianism that emphasised money's unimportance and denied the evidence of a stable demand function for money. In such a context Johnson looked monetarist and was usually so regarded. Moreover, his attempts to revive and foster the academic study of theoretical monetary economics and the empirical testing of such theory in Britain, particularly through the Money Study Group, set him in opposition to much of the economics establishment – as did his efforts to publicise the views of people such as Friedman. The Cambridge dominance of the economics establishment also heightened Johnson's anti-Cambridge biases. Yet at the same time his intellectual curiosity led him to explore how such establishment ideas could take root and flourish – which took him back to Keynes.

There was a further complication to the story after 1966: Johnson's own thinking was in transition. The results of the transition would become clearer in 1972 and 1973 with the publication of the first papers on the monetary approach to the balance of payments and the October 1971 de Vries Lectures *Inflation and the Monetarist Controversy*. But during the period there was, as he admitted in his preface to his LSE lectures in *Macroeconomics and Monetary Theory* (1971), a certain schizophrenia in his writings as he considered and reconsidered the changing face of economic theory and his own place in it (1971, iii).

In the same paragraph of the preface Johnson referred to Axel Leijonhufvud's *On Keynesian Economics and the Economics of Keynes: A Study in Monetary Theory* which had appeared in 1968. In the book, Leijonhufvud argued that Keynesian economics, particularly as developed by Keynes's American followers and by the econometricians and forecasters was actually quite different from Keynes's own macroeconomics which was 'deeply rooted in the preceding quantity theory tradition' (1971, 4).

Johnson was taken with the book. It went onto the 1968–69 reading list for his LSE lectures before publication as 'a critical analysis of modern trends in macroeconomics' and a 'stimulating complement' to more orthodox approaches. He invited Leijonhufvud to give two lectures on 'Keynes and the Classics' at the LSE in March 1969 which were subsequently published by the Institute of Economic Affairs (1969).[14] He also reviewed Leijonhufvud's book in *Encounter* (1970).

Although he had some doubts as to 'how far Leijonhufvud's re-reading of Keynes is snatching at straws in order to prevent the breaking of the camel's back and to retain the beast as a working member of the caravan of progress' (1972*a*, 72), he accepted Leijonhufvud's basic misinterpretation hypothesis. He repeated it in his 1970 Ely Lecture, 'The Keynesian Revolution and the Monetarist Counter-Revolution' (1978*b*, 190), his preface to his LSE lecture notes (1971, iv), his de Vries lectures (1972*b*, 2) and many of his post-1971 papers where he rethought the evolution of monetary theory and Keynes's place in it, culminating in his 1976 Innis Lecture 'Keynes's *General Theory*: Revolution or War of Independence', where he also noted 'that English Keynesianism, at the popular and policy level is a creation of Oxford and not of Cambridge'– an echo of Leijonhufvud (1978*b*, 242; Leijonhufvud 1968, 405).

Johnson's thinking on inflation reflected the transition. He returned to the subject in his May 1969 introduction to the second edition of *Essays in Monetary Economics*, in a survey paper for a November 1969 conference at Hove in Sussex marking the tenth anniversary of the publication of the Radcliffe *Report* on the working of the British monetary system and in his 1969–70 LSE macroeconomics lectures. By then Edmund Phelps (1967) and Milton Friedman (1968) had both attacked the Phillips curve for ignoring the role of expectations in the wage-setting process. If inflation was fully anticipated in wage and price fixing there was no trade-off between employment and inflation. If the coefficient of the expected rate of inflation on wages was unity the trade-off vanished and only one rate of unemployment, the 'natural rate', was consistent with a constant rate of inflation. At the same time, there had been further doubts about the concept of the curve as 'an arbitrary and illegitimate linkage of the behaviour of the labour market under conditions of approximately full employment and mass unemployment.' (1972*a*, 46) In his 1969 introduction he argued that the empirical evidence suggested that there were sufficiently long lags in the adjustment of expectations to experience for contemporary policymakers to disregard them (1967, 2nd ed., x). In the Hove paper, he reported results from 'a rather obscure source' where empirical work by Robert Solow 'strongly supported' and other work by Phillip Cagan that 'did not refute' a coefficient for expected inflation well below unity (1972*a*, 47). Thus the trade-off still appeared to be alive, if less favourable. His 1969–1970 lectures followed the Hove paper with more supporting evidence. In general the discussion was more Keynesian or Phillipsian. He developed the Solow model where people were rational and adjusted to inflation but were subject to an element of money illusion that implied the existence of a long-run Phillips curve with some trade-off. He added a model by Albert Rees where there was a range of unemployment rates given the transactions costs of adjusting real wages under inflationary conditions. In this situation one also got a long-run Phillips curve with a trade-off (1971, 159–161). He remained attached to that model in his de Vries lectures (1972*b*, 65–66) and in his 'Comments on Inflation Theory' in a November 1972 conference organised by Robert Mundell at the University of Waterloo (1975, 149–151) where he concluded

> The general conclusion to be drawn from all this is that ... economists would be better advised to invest more economics in what was originally and remains a very crude model of the inflation-unemployment problem. (1975, 151)

In 1970 and 1971 Johnson wrote little on inflation. He was more preoccupied with the international monetary system and its disintegration and, incidentally, with the early stages of developing the monetary approach to the balance of payments which would carry his thinking about inflation in a new direction. He was also, perhaps because of the monetary approach and its potential importance, concerned with the nature of revolutions and counter-revolutions in macroeconomics, devoting his December 1970 Ely Lecture to the American Economic Association to the subject.[15] In particular he was concerned with 'the social and intellectual conditions that make a revolution of counter-revolution possible' (1972*a*, 66) and with the rate of diffusion of Keynesian and monetarist ideas.

In doing so he found it useful

> to adopt the 'as if' approach of positive economics as expressed by the chief protagonist of the monetarist counter-revolution, Milton Friedman, and to ask: suppose I wanted to start a counter-revolution against the Keynesian revolution in monetary theory, how would I go about it – and specifically, what could I learn about the technique from the revolution itself? To pose the question this way is, of course, to fly in the face of currently accepted professional ethics, according to which purely scientific considerations and not political considerations are presumed to motivate scientific work. (1972*a*, 52–53)

He then proceeded to set out what was needed in terms of the social situation in which the theory was first proposed and of the desirable characteristics of the new theory. First one needed an established orthodoxy which was inconsistent with contemporary reality yet still sufficiently confident of its own explanatory power to try and explain that reality thus exposing its own difficulties. To displace orthodoxy the new theory would have to offer its own convincing explanation of the difficulties and to provide a set of policy prescriptions based on that explanation. But to win intellectual acceptance the new approach would require five characteristics. First, it would have to attack a central proposition of the old theory. In the Keynesian case the central proposition of orthodoxy had been the automatic tendency of the economy to full employment which with the concept of unemployment equilibrium and the output-equilibrating mechanism of the consumption function and the multiplier Keynes had provided an alternative. Second, although it had to appear new, it had to absorb as much as possible of the non-disputed aspects of the old theory. This Keynes did by giving old concepts new names such as transforming the money/income ratio of the Cambridge quantity theory into an aspect of the theory of liquidity preference and emphasise as crucial analytical steps that were previously regarded as unhelpful such as the *ex post* equivalence of savings and investment. Third, the

> new theory had to be so difficult to understand that senior academic colleagues would find it neither easy nor worthwhile to study, so that they would waste their efforts on peripheral issues, and so offer themselves as easy marks for criticism by their younger and hungrier colleagues. At the same time, the new theory had to appear intellectually difficult to challenge the intellectual interest of younger colleagues, but actually easy enough for them to master adequately with a sufficient investment of intellectual endeavour. (1972*a*, 55)

In Keynes's case it put established scholars like Pigou and Robertson on the sidelines, allowed some middle-aged and younger scholars such as Alvin Hansen,[16] John Hicks, and Joan Robinson 'to jump on and run the bandwagon' and permitted the young to ignore the wisdom of the past and demolish the pretensions of their seniors. Fourth, it had to develop a methodology which was more appealing than that currently available. In this Keynesian economics was able to take advantage of the recent spread of general equilibrium and mathematical skills and work in terms of the aggregative general equilibrium models such as IS-LM. Finally, it had to offer important economic relationships for empirical testing, where Keynesian economics was able to take advantage of the emergence of national income provided the raw material for estimating consumption functions and other relationships.

In turn, by the mid-1950s Keynesianism had become an orthodoxy as ripe for attack as 'classical' economics had been in the 1930s. The new problem was inflation, where the Keynesians had over-reached themselves as they tired to deal with in by Keynesian means. Monetarism was aided by the professionalisaton of economics which made it 'increasingly possible for an issue to be deemed scientifically interesting and worthy of investigation even if the general public displays no visible interest in it' (1972*a*, 60). The other pillars of the counter-revolution were the proposition that money did matter; stating the quantity theory as a generalisation of the theory of liquidity preference on a more sophisticated basis; invoking the methodology of positive economics and emphasising 'the crucial relationships that permit one to predict something large from something small regardless of the intervening chain of causation... [offering] liberation to the small-scale intellectual'; and providing in the demand for money 'an empirical relationship for determined estimation by the budding econometrician' (1972*a*, 62) But the counter-revolution went one step further to establish an intellectual continuity with the past which had been disrupted by the original revolution. In part this involved 'the invention of a University of Chicago oral tradition that was alleged to have preserved understanding of the fundamental truth among a small band of the initiated during the dark years of the Keynesian despotism' (1972*a*, 64). But, he continued, citing the work of Don Patinkin

> There was no lonely light constantly burning in a secret shrine on the Midway, encouraging the faithful to assemble in waiting for the day when the truth could be safely revealed to the masses; that candle was made, and not merely lit, only when its light had a chance of penetrating far and wide and attracting new converts to the old-time religion. (1972*a*, 65)

Subsequent discussion has favoured Friedman over Johnson on this point (see Leeson, 2003).

With his monetary approach to the balance of payments, Johnson would follow his own Ely Lecture prescriptions to the letter, even including the necessary history. At the same time, in his de Vries Lectures of October 1971, he signalled a change in his general position. In his first lecture he announced that the monetarist position

> that the real economy is inherently fairly stable, but can be destabilised by monetary developments, which therefore need to be controlled as far as possible by intelligent monetary policy ... seems to me the only alternative consistent with the facts (as distinct from the myths of historical experience). (1972*b*, 7)

He reported that he had

> arrived at this judgement, not by dogmatic conviction, but out of growing dissatisfaction with the explanatory power of the theories and the empirical results in which I was instructed during my youth at the two centres of the [Keynesian] revolution. (1972*b*, 7)

He spent much of the remainder of the first lecture making the argument that recent work on the costs of inflation and the role of money in growth models had resulted 'in a strong case for stability in the trend of prices ... but a very weak case ... for the pursuit of a zero price trend (price stability) as a major goal of economic policy.' (1972*b*, 35–36)

In his second lecture, he turned to the theory of inflation, noting that the accepted theory of inflation and of anti-inflationary policy up until the Keynesian revolution was firmly based on the quantity theory of money. The Keynesian revolution ... destroyed the intellectual credentials of that approach – which has only painfully and slowly been restored to academic respectability in the past fifteen years and especially in the last five – and created an intellectual vacuum. ... (1972*b*, 51)

But since the early post-war period, Keynesian theory 'produced only one significant contribution to monetary analysis – the Phillips curve' (1972*b*, 58) but that empirical rather than theoretical relationship had become increasingly suspect for three reasons. First, it was a statistical artefact linking incompatible periods of full employment and depression. Second, the theory behind the Phillips curve was 'about the crudest and least sophisticated possible exploration of the dynamics of economic models' where price adjustment was determined by excess demand and supply in one market, the labour market, irrespective of developments in other markets, and that a single theory tried comprehend real and relative price adjustments which were assumed identical. Finally, the relationship seemed 'to have broken down completely in the face of the inflationary facts of the last two years or so' (1972*b*, 59). Then, after mentioning the postwar revival of the quantity-theory approach through the work of Friedman and his students, with the recent supporting leadership of Allan Meltzer and Karl Brunner, he described the rise of monetarism; its 'staged' empirical victories over Keynesianism; and Friedman's use of his 1967 presidential address to the American Economic Association to restate the essence of his critique: monetary policy can control monetary magnitudes but not real magnitudes which are determined by the real forces in the economy. But he thought that monetarism would be triumphant only briefly. Monetarists exaggerated the power of monetary restraint, in terms of the amount and duration of unemployment, as a means of stopping inflation. It was not that it was wrong but that the political process attached a low cost to inflation and a high cost to unemployment. The result had been theoretical and empirical counter-attacks. But although monetarism was important,

> the particular formulation embodied in the past works of Milton Friedman is not in fact tolerably consistent with the empirical evidence.... Moreover, at the level of abstract theory, Friedman has recently attempted to fill the gap in the empirical applicability of the quantity theory by his restatement of that theory as a theory of the demand for money, with no implications as to the relative magnitudes of the effects of monetary impulses on money prices and real quantities of output, with results that in my judgment cone very close to returning monetary theory to the position reached in Franco Modigliani's classic article of 1944. (1972*b*, 66–67)

In other words, 'This was where I came in'.[17]

On 29 April 1973 Johnson sat down to write a paper for a volume of *Essays on John Maynard Keynes* that Keynes's nephew Milo Keynes was preparing for Cambridge University Press (1975). 'Keynes and British Economics' accepted that Keynes was an important figure in economics but Johnson's take was different from before.

Had the policymakers of the 1930s really understood what was occurring in the international monetary system and their own part in it, or had the economists of the time understood it (as they could have done by developing available monetary theory) and explained it effectively, the Great Depression of the 1930s would have been nipped in the bud and *The General Theory* either not written, or perceived as one eccentric English economist's rationalization of his local problems (1978*b*, 207).

But monetary economists, including the Keynes of the *Treatise on Money*, although concerned with the shorter-term problem of the 'conditions of monetary equilibrium', maintained the traditional assumption of full employment that they had used in discussing the longer term – the assumption successfully challenged in the *General Theory*, whose

> importance from the long-range point of view of the development of economics…lies not in its refutation of a classical 'orthodoxy' but in its application of capital theory to the theory of the demand for money and the stimulus it provided to study the dynamics of price and quantity adjustments to changes in aggregate demand. (1978*b*, 212)

Less than three weeks later, Johnson was back at Keynes – this time considering the question 'Is Keynes Dead?' for a banker's newsletter that appeared in August.[18] In the short article, Harry saw Keynes's two legacies as the theory of employment and the Bretton Woods system; so it might, he thought, seem easy to answer the question, given the coexistence of high inflation and high unemployment in a context of wage and price controls, and the collapse of Bretton Woods and increased restrictions on international trade and payments. But, he argued, this was not the case. Internationally the world had retreated from 'the Victorian cosmopolitanism that motivated… [Keynes's] thinking on international monetary problems' (6). As for employment policy, Keynes's complex definition of full employment was turned by 'subsequent theorists and amateur theorists, beginning with Beveridge and his stable of left-wing economists' into a statistic,[19] while politicians competed by promising even lower rates and changing circumstances made inflationary wage and price increases possible long before full employment had come to pass (6). Added to this was the embedding of inflationary expectations into the collective bargaining process. Despite these problems, he concluded

> By convincing the public and its politicians that mass unemployment is a political crime and not a just punishment meted out by the invisible hand of God, Keynesian teaching has probably insured us for the foreseeable future from a recurrence of ... [the disaster of the 1930s]. And though the world will be a less liberal and more mean-spirited place than his plans envisioned it to become, it is still likely to progress economically at quite an acceptable rate. So in this sense Keynes is not dead; he just smells of tired and cranky old age. (7)

Johnson's de Vries Lectures marked the end of his contributions to traditional macroeconomics, as he devoted more of his time to the monetary approach to the balance of payments. He did, however, write a substantial paper with A.R. Nobay (1977) where he expanded some of his comments in his de Vries lectures and his contribution to Milo Keynes's volume. What he was trying to do was to get some perspective on contemporary theoretical discussions and his own theoretical position, and to situate both in terms of an inter-war discussion which had included Robertson, Hayek, the Swedes and the Keynes of *A Treatise on Money* before the publication of the *General Theory* had sent discussions off in another direction. This was not the first time he had brought a historical perspective to his surveys – that had always been one of their strengths – but the attempt here was more provocative and inclusive in its documentation. There was a similar attempt at perspective in his June 1976 Innis Lecture at the Canadian Economics Association, 'Keynes's *General Theory*: Revolution or War of Independence?', which had the added twist of looking at the evolution of 'Keynesian economics' over the previous 40 years. The conclusion of the lecture, not surprisingly given his 1973 paper in Milo Keynes's collection, was that Keynes's change had been a war of independence rather than simply a revolutionary change of personnel at the top.

'[I]n the long perspective of the development of monetary theory ... the so-called Keynesian Revolution has to be viewed as the third stage of the evolution of the theory of a monetary (and capitalist) economy' (1978*b*, 236). In the first stage, the classical economists elucidated 'the nature of the economic system as a coherent, interdependent system that tended towards an equilibrium solution of price and quantity variables' (1978*b*, 236–237). In that system the chief function of monetary theory was to demonstrate the neutrality of money – the purpose of the quantity theory. In the second stage monetary economists 'shifted from demonstrating the neutrality of money to investigating the conditions under which money would be neutral ... the conditions of monetary equilibrium' (1978*b*, 237). This line of thinking was stopped by the Keynesian successes and only began to be revived in the late 1960s. Keynes's contribution in the *General Theory* then became the replacement of a price-adjustment mechanism with a quantity-adjustment system, a narrower contribution than the one he had outlined in 1973. However, Keynes's removal from professional action by a heart condition in 1937 left the way open for a different enterprise which obliterated Keynes's alternative 'war of independence'. In this endeavour money came not to matter and the original Keynesian model became crystallised in the IS-LM formulation of Hicks and Hansen. This stage culminated in the 'Keynesian synthesis' which accepted full employment as a policy objective as well as the Keynesian model, but admitted that the notion of 'unemployment equilibrium' rested on either an approximation of wage rigidity or some other 'peculiar and not seriously empirically defensible behavioral assumptions' (1978*b*, 243). Over the ensuing decades, the work of Tobin, Patinkin and Friedman consolidated and extended 'the new theoretical approaches and insights provided by Keynes the monetary theorist' (1978*b*, 243). This consolidation and synthesis with the insights of Keynes's predecessors had been succeeded by a period of questioning of the usefulness of both Keynesian and monetarist economics. This had produced a number of responses, one of which was that

> the spirit of revolution ... needs to be revived by a denunciation of the bastards and a return to the pure principles and noble spirit of the original revolution (as remembered, reconstructed or invented by the saved survivors and elect descendants of the disciples). (1978*b*, 247)

Obviously Johnson did not support this approach of the Cambridge Keynesians. He thought that the *General Theory*

> involved a process of looking past the models and the problems of pure theory to the real world to which theory claimed to be a scientific guide, recognizing a glaring gap between the assumption and hypothetical economy of the models and the actual behaviour of the real world, and attempting to remedy the deficiency by redesigning the machinery of theory while thriftily cannibalizing those component parts that remained useful. (1978*b*, 248)

The present discontents of monetary economics required more such attempts to define problems as they really were and then trying to solve them.

In September 1974, Johnson discussed the causes of the perpetual crisis that seemed to affect British economic policy. What is surprising is that his explanation was not that different from the one which he offered in his 1952 University of Toronto lectures *The Overloaded Economy* (above pp. 307–308).

> To put the matter briefly, British policy has been struggling ever since the World War II with the conflicting claims of an imperial world role and a society socially just according to a mixture of trade union and patrician criteria; both required additional resources, which can only be created by appealing to the patriotism of businessmen who are ranked morally and intellectually third-class citizens – neither working-class nor culturally or intellectually distinguished nor official or unofficial servants of the public good – who are denied more than a fraction of the fruits of their labour by a tax system carefully designed to appear to aim at the beneficiaries of 'unearned' wealth but in fact to stamp out the earnings of hard labour while safeguarding the positions of those who have inherited property or possess jobs or who are 'lucky' at gambling on the pools; trends in teenage tastes (the young single adults are the only significantly large group of people in England with large amounts of what the ad-men used to call 'discretionary income' to spend), the stock market, or urban property. It is no wonder, therefore, that the country is in continual economic crisis, since the extra resources to satisfy current demands can only be secured temporarily from foreigners by running balance-of-payments deficits; and no wonder either that there is a frantic search for gimmicks that will provide secure painless rapid economic growth in a society in which nobody wants it except the politicians – and they only want the resources produced, not the economic dynamics of growth (1974, Memoir IV, 1–2).

Conclusion

Harry Johnson was educated at the two centres of the Keynesian revolution, Cambridge and Harvard. He emerged, as he put it, 'a third generation Keynesian' regarding Keynes's work as an extension of previous work and looking for a further synthesis of Keynes's insights with the rest of economic theory. That point of view put him somewhat outside Cambridge Keynesianism of Richard Kahn, Joan Robinson and Nicholas Kaldor. During his Cambridge years, he began to make the clear distinction between Keynes and his Keynesian followers, to find increasing difficulties in Keynes's original formulation of his ideas, finding them a special case of neo-classical economics and inadequate as a theory of prices. He also became 'dissatisfied with Cambridge – my colleagues ... stuck in dead monetary controversies, or immersed in growth models with little relevance to the real world' (1978*b*, 150), with being 'unwillingly forced to take sides' (Box 44, Correspondence 1949–1956, from Robin Marris, 20 June 1955) and with the intellectual isolation – 'I often didn't see colleagues for weeks or months on end'(Box 31, Correspondence to 1963, H-L, to R.G. Lipsey, 17 February 1960). This dissatisfaction combined with few prospects of preferment in Cambridge[20] to take him first to Manchester and then as the Keynesian replacement for Lloyd Metzler at Chicago, where as he put it in a 1961 speech

> A Keynesian ... is a weak and spineless creature, who blindly follows the master along the path of error, refusing to modify or develop the system of thought Keynes started, or to test it in any way, or to consider the allegedly conclusive evidence thrust before his nose by Chicago economists. (Box 25, Writing 1960, 'A Keynesian's Impressions of Chicago', 28 October 1960)

From Chicago, firmly labelled as a 'bastard Keynesian' by Joan Robinson, he developed his reputation as a monetary economist with his thoughtful evaluation of the *General Theory* after 25 years and his survey of monetary theory and policy. In both, he maintained his own brand of consensus Keynesianism where Keynes's contribution lay in his general approach to the problem of income and employment which provided 'a useful macro-economic general equilibrium model for the analysis of the monetary economy' and stimulated the construction and testing of aggregative economic models (1962, 144). He noted, however, that Keynes's introduction of capital theory into the demand for money might in the end lead to the end of the predominance of the income-expenditure approach. He was not, however, at first, or ever, enamoured with Milton Friedman's brand of monetarism and consistently put Friedman in the theoretical tradition started by Keynes.

In the course of the later 1960s and early 1970s his position became somewhat schizophrenic. The greater concern with inflation as a policy problem meant that he put greater emphasis on monetary matters than before. At the same time, he moved away from the view that unemployment was the normal capitalist state of affairs and in his 1971 de Vries lectures embraced the view that full employment was more often than not the norm in capitalist economies. But he did not align himself with the monetarists, noting that 'All monetary theorists agree that money influences only monetary variables and not real variables in the long run' (1978*a*, 4). He also allowed a significant role for expectations in wage an price setting. He was also sceptical on theoretical grounds of the existence of the Phillips curve and thought it discredited by its breakdown in the early 1970s. Yet he continued to hold to the view that the empirical evidence favoured the view that there still was a trade-off between inflation and unemployment even though the finding was 'not very satisfactory, either theoretically or empirically' and called for 'broadening the microeconomic foundations of the relationship' (1972*b*, 66). His monetary approach to the balance of payments showed some of the same schizophrenia – his first models were characterised by extreme assumptions (one world price level, full employment, one world interest rate) yet he hoped in the end that one might

> marry the monetarist and the Keynesian analysis in a way relevant to the short-run context ... with which policy-makers are concerned, and which is characterised both by variations in production and employment as well as money prices. (1972*a*, 14)

His ambivalence naturally affected his appreciation of Keynes. A further complicating factor was his love-hate relationship with British economics and Keynes's followers and successors – which grew particularly acute in 1974–75 when it all came together in a dispute over the editorship of the *Economic Journal* and the publications policy of the Royal Economic Society, then engaged in producing *The Collected Writings of John Maynard Keynes*. It was encapsulated in the fall of 1975 as 'Keynes was an exceptional economist when he lived but has become a malevolent myth since he died' (1978*b*, 226).

Notes

I should like to thank Susan Howson, David Laidler, Robert Leeson, Dan Hammond and participants at the 2005 History of Economics Society Meeting at Tacoma, as well as those attending the 2005 British History of Economic Thought Conference at Exeter for comments on earlier drafts.

In the text that follows, all references to Harry Johnson's own papers in the Regenstein Library at the University of Chicago are by box number and file title. The Memoirs mentioned are in the possession of his widow Elizabeth Simpson. Where possible, references to Johnson's publication are to the volume in which they were first collected.

1. He would not have been exposed to it in his introductory course taught by V. W. Bladen. The textbook that Bladen produced a year after Johnson took the course, *An Introduction to Political Economy* (1941), was innocent of Keynes's work after 'The Question of High Wages' (1930), even in its 3rd edition of 1956.
2. Silberston's supervisor was Joan Robinson.
3. His first professional publication was a pamphlet, *The Antigonish Movement* (1944).
4. The first dealt with 'The Keynesian Theory'; the second was 'An Evaluation of the Keynesian Approach'.
5. 'A Revolutionist's Handbook' (1950).
6. These were the lectures that Johnson had attended in 1946.
7. Trinity was Robertson's College. The Johnians were Jan Graaff and Robin Matthews; those at Gonville and Caius Stanley Dennison, Robertson's political lieutenant, and Peter Bauer.
8. 1951*a* and 1951*b*. Johnson had initially planned to do a thesis on Hugh Dalton's attempt to introduce cheaper money and reduce the long-term rate of interest to 2½ per cent in 1946–47. He changed topics when at his first meeting of the Association of University Teachers of Economics he found that 'three others were already engaged in studies of cheap money, one of whom was in the process of submitting a completed thesis

to a Midlands university' (Houghton Library, Harvard University, HUG(FP 3.11 A.H., Hansen Correspondence 1926–59, File 1951, HGJ to Hansen, 24 May 1951). Instead of completing his thesis on the revised topic, he eventually took advantage of a change in the Harvard degree regulations that allowed the submission of previously published work – in his case *International Trade and Economic Growth* (1958).

9. RSPCA – Royal Society for the Prevention of Cruelty to Animals.
10. 'A slashing and well-thought-out attack on what passes for the current theory of economic development'.
11. Not surprisingly, his lectures followed his survey article closely (Laidler, 2000, 330).
12. Robert Dimand (2001, 676–677) correctly notes that there are differences between the version published in the *American Economic Review* in May 1961 and the version published in *Money, Trade and Economic Growth* (but not in *On Economics and Society*). In addition to providing full bibliographical references, Harry also added to the text on pages 2 (2 changes), 6 and 8 and made a correction on page 15. However, in the cases Dimand cites the revised paper, the text is identical to that originally printed in the *American Economic Review*. This is important because the impression created by Dimand's citation procedure is that *Money, Trade and Economic Growth* version was more critical of Harry's former senior Cambridge colleagues than the original.
13. As he put it to Milton Friedman on 2 February 1965 (Box 56, Correspondence 1964–66).

    I would be inclined to lay more blame on the followers of Keynes, who transformed a fairly subtle and judgmental analysis into a simplified mathematical model with particularly specified functions, than on Keynes, who never lost his historical sense.

14. The fee for the Institute's Occasional Paper, arranged by Johnson, was sufficient to cover Leijonhufvud's airfare and living expenses (Hoover Institution. Institute of Economic Affairs Papers, Box 99, Folder OP 30 'Keynes and the Classics', Johnson to Ralph Harris, 27 November 1968; Johnson to M. Mann, 15 January 1969).
15. He gave a dry run of his lecture under the title 'The Monetarist Revolution' to the AUTE conference in Belfast on 7 April (Leeson, 2000, 747).
16. Johnson forgot that Hansen (born 1887) was older than Robertson (born 1890).
17. Milton Friedman (1970, 15) used the same phrase but in a rather different context. I am indebted to Robert Leeson for the reference.
18. Box 28, Manuscripts 1972–73, written version 19 May, published version in Morris Wigram Limited *Newsletter*, (August 1973), 5–7. The other contributors were Roy Harrod, Patrick Hutber and C. Gordon Tether.
19. The reference is to Sir William Beveridge's *Full Employment in a Free Society* (1944) with its definition of full employment as 3 per cent unemployment on the basis of Nicholas Kaldor's Appendix C, 'Quantitative Aspects of the Full Employment Problem in Great Britain'.
20. The last Reader appointed was Nicholas Kaldor who had obtained the post aged 44; Joan Robinson had been a few months younger when she was promoted in 1947. If Johnson was to be as high a flier as they were, it would be 1967 before he would find preferment and there were indications that he was regarded as very good technically but not as original as Kaldor or Robinson.

References

Alexander, Sidney S. (1952). "Effects of a Devaluation on a Trade Balance." *IMF Staff Papers* 2 (April 1952), 263–278.

Beveridge, Sir William (1944). *Full Employment in a Free Society: A Report*. London: Allen and Unwin.

Bladen, Vincent (1941). *An Introduction to Political Economy*. Toronto: University of Toronto Press.

Brown, A. J. (1955). *The Great Inflation, 1939–1951*. London: Oxford University Press.
Dimand, Robert (2001). "Harry Johnson as Chronicler of the Keynesian Revolution: His Search for a Non-Revolutionary Account." *American Journal of Economics and Sociology* 60 (July), 667–691.
Friedman, Milton (1946). "Lange on Price Flexibility and Employment." *American Economic Review* 36 (September), 613–631.
Friedman, Milton (1968). "The Role of Monetary Policy." *American Economic Review* 58 (March), 1–17.
Friedman, Milton (1970). *The Counter-Revolution in Monetary Theory*. London: Institute of Economic Affairs, Occasional Paper 33.
Friedman, Milton, ed. (1956). *Studies in the Quantity Theory of Money*. Chicago: University of Chicago Press.
Friedman, Milton and Anna J. Schwartz (1963). *A Monetary History of the United States, 1867–1960*. Princeton: Princeton University Press.
Haberler, Gottfried (1939). *Prosperity and Depression*, 2nd ed. Geneva: League of Nations.
Hansen, Alvin H. (1941). *Fiscal Policy and Business Cycles*. New York: McGraw Hill.
Hicks, J. R. (1945). "Recent Contributions to General Equilibrium Economics." *Economica* 17 (November), 235–242.
Johnson, Elizabeth S. and Harry G. Johnson (1978). *The Shadow of Keynes: Understanding Keynes, Cambridge and Keynesian Economics*. Chicago: University of Chicago Press.
Johnson, Harry G. (1944). *The Antigonish Movement: A Lecture to the Students of Acadia University*. Antigonish Nova Scotia, St. Francis Xavier University.
Johnson, Harry G. (1948). "An Error in Ricardo's Exposition of His Theory of Rent." *Quarterly Journal of Economics* 62 (November), 792–793.
Johnson, Harry G. (1949). "Demand for Commodities is not Demand for Labour." *Economic Journal* 59 (December), 531–536.
Johnson, Harry G. (1951*a*). "Some Implications of Secular Changes in Bank Assets and Liabilities in Great Britain." *Economic Journal* 61 (September), 544–561.
Johnson, Harry G. (1951*b*). "Clearing Bank Holdings of Public Debt, 1931–1950." *London and Cambridge Economic Service Bulletin* 29 (November), 102–109.
Johnson, Harry G. (1951*c*). "The Taxonomic Approach to Economic Policy." *Economic Journal* 61 (December), 812–832.
Johnson, Harry G. (1951–52). "Some Cambridge Controversies in Monetary Theory." *Review of Economic Studies* 19 (February), 90–104.
Johnson, Harry G. (1952*a*), *The Overloaded Economy*. Toronto: University of Toronto Press.
Johnson, Harry G. (1952*b*). "Lord Keynes and Modern Economic Thought." *Canadian Forum* 32 (November), 176–177.
Johnson, Harry G. (1955). "Keynes and Supply Functions: A Mathematical Appendix (to an article by D.H. Robertson)." *Economic Journal* 65 (September), 457–458.
Johnson, Harry G. (1956*a*). "On British Crises." *Granta* 59 (April), 5–6.
Johnson, Harry G. (1956*b*). "Some Reflections on the Revival of Monetary Policy in Great Britain." *Three Banks Review* (June), 3–20.
Johnson, Harry G. (1957). "The Determinants of the General Level of Wage Rates." In John T. Dunlop, ed., *The Theory of Wage Determination*. London: Macmillan.
Johnson, Harry G. (1958). "Two Schools of Thought on Wage Inflation." *Scottish Journal of Political Economy* 5 (June), 149–153.
Johnson, Harry G. (1959). "British Monetary Statistics." *Economica* 26 (February), 1–17.
Johnson, Harry G. (1962). *Money, Trade and Economic Growth*. London: George Allen and Unwin.
Johnson, Harry G. (1965), "A Quantity Theorist's Monetary History of the United States." *Economic Journal* 75 (June), 388–396.
Johnson, Harry G. (1967). *Essays in Monetary Economics*, 2nd ed., 1969. London: George Allen and Unwin.

Johnson, Harry G. (1970). "Keynes and the Keynesians: Some Intellectual Legends." *Encounter* 34 (January), 70–73 (reprinted in 1972*a*).

Johnson, Harry G. (1971). *Macroeconomics and Monetary Theory*. London: Gray-Mills.

Johnson, Harry G. (1972*a*). *Further Essays in Monetary Economics*. London: George Allen and Unwin.

Johnson, Harry G. (1972*b*). *Inflation and the Monetarist Controversy*. Amsterdam: North Holland.

Johnson, Harry G. (1973). "Is Keynes Dead?" Morris Wigram Limited, *Newsletter* (August), 5–7.

Johnson, Harry G. (1975) "Comments on Inflation Theory." In R. A. Mundell and B. E. van Snellenberg, eds., *Policy Formation in an Open Economy, I*. Waterloo: University of Waterloo Press.

Johnson, Harry G. and A. R. Nobay (1977). "Monetarism: A Historic-Theoretic Perspective." *Journal of Economic Literature* 15 (June), 470–485.

Johnson, Harry G. (1978*a*). *Selected Essays in Monetary Economics*. London: Allen and Unwin.

Johnson, Harry G., with Elizabeth Johnson (1978*b*). *The Shadow of Keynes: Understanding Keynes*. Cambridge and Keynesian Economics.

Keynes, John Maynard (1930). "The Question of High Wages." *Political Quarterly* 1 (January), 110–124.

Keynes, John Maynard (1936). *The General Theory of Employment, Interest and Money*. London: Macmillan.

Keynes, Milo, ed. (1975). *Essays on John Maynard Keynes*. Cambridge: Cambridge University Press.

Laidler, David (1984). "Harry Johnson as a Macroeconomist." *Journal of Political Economy* 92 (August), 592–615.

Laidler, David (1990). *Taking Money Seriously*. London: Philip Allen.

Laidler, David (1997). "The Emergence of the Phillips Curve as a Policy Menu." In B. C. Eaton and R. G. Harris, eds., *Trade, Technology and Economics: Essays in Honour of Richard G. Lipsey*. Cheltenham: Edward Elgar.

Laidler, David (2000). "David Laidler." In R. Backhouse and R. Middleton, eds., *Exemplary Economists I: North America*. Cheltenham: Edward Elgar.

Lange, Oscar (1938). "The Rate of Interest and the Optimum Propensity to Consume." *Economica* 5 (February), 12–22.

Lange, Oscar (1944). *Price Flexibility and Employment*. Bloomington IN: Principia Press.

Leeson, Robert (2000). "Patinkin, Johnson and the Shadow of Friedman." *History of Political Economy* 32 (Winter), 733–764.

Leeson, Robert, ed. (2003). *Keynes, Chicago and Friedman*. London: Pickering and Chatto.

Leijonhufvud, Axel (1968). *On Keynesian Economics and the Economics of Keynes: A Study in Monetary Theory*. London: Oxford University Press.

Leijonhufvud, Axel (1969). *Keynes and the Classics: Two Lectures*. London: Institute of Economic Affairs, Occasional Paper 30.

Machlup, F. (1943). *International Trade and the National Income Multiplier*. Philadelphia: Blakiston.

Metzler, Lloyd (1949). "Tariffs, the Terms of Trade and the Distribution of Income." *Journal of Political Economy* 57 (February), 1–29.

Mills, Judy and Irene Dombra (1968). *University of Toronto Doctoral Theses, 1897–1967*. Toronto: University of Toronto Press.

Modigliani, Franco (1944). "Liquidity Preference and the Theory of Interest and Money." *Econometrica* 12 (January), 45–88.

Phelps, E. S. (1967). "Phillips Curves, Expectations of Inflation and Optimal Unemployment Over Time." *Economica* 34 (August), 254–281.

Reuber, G. L. (1964). "The Objectives of Canadian Monetary Policy, 1949–1961: Empirical Trade-offs and the Reaction Function of the Authorities." *Journal of Political Economy* 72 (May), 109–132.

Robertson, D. H. (1928). *Money*. London: Nisbet.
Robertson, D. H. (1940). *Essays in Monetary Theory*. London: P.S. King.
Robertson, D. H. (1950). "A Revolutionist's Handbook." *Quarterly Journal of Economics* 64 (February), 1–14.
Robertson, D. H. (1959). *Lectures on Economic Principles, III*. London: Staples.
Robinson, Joan (1962). "Review of Money, Trade and Economic Growth." *Economic Journal* 72 (September), 690–692.
Robinson, Joan (1965). *Collected Economic Papers, III*. Oxford: Blackwell.
Silberston, Z. A. (1978). *Harry Johnson as a Young Man*. London: Imperial College.
Timlin, Mabel (1941). *Keynesian Economics*. Toronto: University of Toronto Press.
Timlin, Mabel (1946). "Review of Oscar Lange's *Price Flexibility and Full Employment*." *Canadian Journal of Economics and Political Science* 12 (May 1946), 204–213.

15

Hawtreyan 'Credit Deadlock' or Keynesian 'Liquidity Trap'? Lessons for Japan from the Great Depression

Roger J. Sandilands

In this chapter, much inspired by David Laidler's work in the field of monetary theory and policy, I shall compare the mistakes of monetary policy before and during the Great Depression in the United States in the 1930s with the conduct of monetary policy in Japan since the late 1980s.

For the United States, my analysis will draw heavily on the contemporary 1930s writings of Lauchlin Currie (1902–93) whose biography I completed in 1990 (Sandilands, 1990) which led to a fruitful correspondence with Laidler on Currie's monetary economics. This stemmed initially from his review article on Karl Brunner (Laidler, 1991). David was surprised to learn of Brunner's close connection with Currie and that he had written an introduction to the reissue of *The Supply and Control of Money in the United States* (Currie, 1934*a* [1968]). It was this and several related papers, notably 'The Failure of Monetary Policy to Prevent the Depression of 1929–32' (Currie, 1934*b* [1962]),[1] that induced Jacob Viner, then a special adviser at the US Treasury, to invite Currie to join a young Treasury group known as the 'Freshman Brain Trust' for the summer of 1934. Currie's remit was to develop the proposal for a 100 per cent reserve banking system that he had made in his recent book, and devise what would be, in the absence of any political obstacle to its implementation, 'the most perfect banking system for the United States'.

100% money, as this scheme became known, was indeed a political non-starter, but its main logic – the need to gain firm control over bank reserves for effective control of the supply of money, hence the business cycle – was the inspiration for the 1935 Banking Act that was to establish a true central bank for the United States and shift the power base of the Federal Reserve System from New York to Washington. For at the Treasury Currie met Marriner Eccles, who was soon to be the new governor of the Fed, taking Currie with him.

Currie's views on monetary and fiscal policy as the way out of depression had found little favour among the senior professors at Harvard, and when he applied for a further leave of absence at the Treasury (initially to be Viner's assistant) this was denied. So, somewhat embittered, he resigned from Harvard and his three month stint in Washington would extend to 11 years – at the Treasury, the Fed, and, from 1939 to 1945, as President Roosevelt's administrative assistant for economic affairs in the White House. He moved with Eccles to the Fed in November 1934 and they immediately drafted what was to become the 1935 Banking Act.

On Currie's contributions to monetary theory and policy in the depression years, Karl Brunner wrote:

> [He] was among the pioneers in our field in assembling and assessing data on the money stock. He fully appreciated that meaningful analysis cannot proceed in the absence of reliable data. This pioneering work eventually forced the Federal Reserve Authorities to develop suitable monetary data on a broader scale, and particularly collect and publish data bearing on the nation's money stock. (Brunner, 1968, ix–x)

He added:

> Currie's systematic discussion of policy issues considers also some notions often repeated by the Federal Reserve authorities... Many believed that the Federal Reserve had tried to stem the deflationary tide of the preceding years by means of an expansionary policy. The experience was interpreted as a demonstration that monetary policy was useless... Currie shows that this belief is a myth... The examination reveals not inability to exert influence but a persistent inactivity and drift. Open market policy and acceptance policy were not used to raise the monetary base. His analysis shows that the Federal Reserve authorities could have effectively prevented the collapse in the monetary stock during the Great Depression. (Brunner, xxiv)

In this chapter I explore some intriguing parallels between Currie's analysis of Fed policy in the turbulent years after the 1929 Wall Street crash and recent debates on Bank of Japan policy during the protracted 'growth stagnation' period that followed Japan's asset market crashes of 1990–91. In particular, controversy focuses on (i) how far central bank policy should be influenced by asset price inflation; (ii) the appropriate role of the central bank as lender of last resort to the commercial banking system in the face of mass liquidation of debts and non-performing assets; (iii) the criteria for judging whether monetary policy has been active or acquiescent; (iv) the alleged impotence of monetary policy and whether there exists a Keynesian 'liquidity trap' or whether the problem has been more like a Hawtreyan 'credit deadlock'; (v) the relationship between monetary and fiscal policy in recovery from severe deflation; and (vi) the significance of a build-up of excess bank reserves.

I turn first to Currie's diagnosis of the causes of the Great Depression, drawing partly on Sandilands (2004).

Federal Reserve Policy, 1927–41, and Hawtrey's concept of 'credit deadlock' in a monetary theory of the cycle

As Thomas Humphrey (1971), Laidler (1993, 1999), and Frank Steindl (1995) have explained, Currie's publications in the early 1930s presented a diagnosis of the

1929–32 collapse in the United States economy that was substantially the same as that advanced by Friedman and Schwartz (1963), as Friedman has since acknowledged (see his *mea culpa* in Laidler, 1993, 1077, n. 12).

In his 'restatement' of the quantity theory of money, Friedman (1956) had contended that there was a unique Chicago oral tradition that made Chicago relatively immune to the Keynesian 'virus', and that his own restatement was in that Chicago tradition. This sparked heated debate on the nature of that tradition: whether it was unique, and whether Friedman's restatement was closer to that tradition or to the 'Cambridge' tradition of Marshall, Pigou and Keynes (especially the pre-*General Theory* Keynes), as Patinkin (1969, 1981) maintained.

Evidence relevant to this was later found in a January 1932 Harvard memorandum on anti-depression policy written by Currie, Paul Theodore Ellsworth and Harry Dexter White (2002 [1932]). On seeing this document Friedman again retreated (in a letter reproduced in Laidler and Sandilands, 2002, 518) from his earlier position on the supposed uniqueness of the Chicago tradition; see also Robert Leeson (2003) and John Smithin (2004). The 1932 memorandum indicted recent monetary, fiscal, tariff and reparations policies for causing the 1929–32 collapse, and called for a drastic reversal of these policies, including substantial open market bond purchases together with so-called 'fiscal inflationism' – a deliberate increase in the fiscal deficit financed by monetary expansion. This was seen as a necessary feature of a reactivation programme if crowding-out effects from public expenditures were to be avoided and *aggregate* monetary expenditures increased.

In this the memorandum was close to the position taken at that time by Hawtrey (1929, 1931), whose assistant Currie had been during Hawtrey's year at Harvard in 1928–29, and close also to the position said by Friedman to be characteristic of a unique Chicago tradition. For example, the memorandum stated: 'Our banking policy has not exerted any effective influence to check the decline in the means of payment. Instead of offsetting the decline in the demand for goods caused by the decreased rate of spending, our policy has intensified it by permitting a contraction of the volume of the means of payment.' By 1931 the deflationary forces had gone too far to be reversed through purely monetary actions:

> With confidence as badly shaken as it is at present, and with prices continuing to fall, there is little in the current outlook to make it attractive to business men to borrow in amounts sufficient to stimulate recovery... Since the initiation of a voluntary program of expansion by independent, scattered producers must wait upon the appearance of the prospect of profits, and since the Federal Government is the sole agency in a central position and strong enough to undertake drastic remedial action, it is strongly recommended that the government immediately commence a program of public construction on a nationwide scale... This program should be financed, not by taxation, which serves principally to divert expenditures from one channel to another, but by an issue of bonds... eligible for rediscount at the Federal Reserve Banks, and

also as collateral for the issue of Federal Reserve notes. (Currie, Ellsworth and White 2002 [1932], 540)

The publication of this document in 2002, together with several of Currie's hitherto unpublished memoranda on recovery policy published in Sandilands (2004), shone new light on the pre-1936 intellectual antecedents to Keynes's *General Theory* that had already been ably discussed in Laidler's *Fabricating the Keynesian Revolution* (1999), with its apposite *double entendre*. And as Laidler wrote to me in August 2003: 'Until the profession gets it straight that the post-war macroeconomic policy consensus had as many (more?) roots in the original work of the New Dealers as it did in JMK's efforts, its understanding of its own history will be defective.'

Currie's unpublished Harvard PhD thesis on bank assets and banking theory (January 1931) was a clear antecedent both to the January 1932 memorandum on anti-depression policies, and to his later recommendations on reform of the United States banking system.[2] In the opening chapter he outlined the history of the Banking and Currency Schools debate to show the importance of the composition and control of bank assets. It reveals that if the central bank automatically accommodates 'self-liquidating', short-term commercial loans ('real bills') then this could be dangerously pro-cyclical.[3] Furthermore, commercial loans were not the most liquid or marketable, and if banks are forced to hold too large a portion of their assets in this form they may end up with excess reserves (that is, they would not be fully loaned up).

He later explained why excess reserves can frustrate the central bank's ability to control the nation's money supply, hence the business cycle. Adherence to the real-bills doctrine had, in his view, led the Federal Reserve Board in 1929 to be excessively preoccupied with banks' security loans and stock market inflation, hence to a tightening policy at the very moment when the real economy was moving into recession. Currie referred to this doctrine as the 'commercial loan' or 'needs of trade' theory of central bank policy, in which banks' short-term 'productive' loans were prudent and non-inflationary while long-term security loans were speculative, imprudent and a recipe for boom and bust in stock markets and the real economy. He blamed this theory for inducing the Fed to raise interest rates in early August 1929, and for then conducting an essentially passive monetary policy during the 1929–32 period of mass liquidations and economic contraction (see especially Currie, 1934*a*, 146–148, 1934*b*, 194–198). In other words, for its failure to use fully its lender-of-last-resort responsibilities at a time of crisis.

A popular view is that a 'speculative orgy' on Wall Street was the prime cause of the Great Depression. According to the commercial loan theory, security loans diverted credit from more productive uses, thereby denying the 'legitimate needs of industry'. Currie disputed this claim. First, he found that interest rates were only weakly related to stock market activity but strongly related to restrictive Fed policies, and in 1929 these were more severe than any since 1921, made worse for being applied when recession was already under way. Second, banks' security loans were only a small proportion of all security loans. The majority were effected via brokers in the stock market clearing house, thus requiring little *net* use of bank deposits. And an examination of individual stock prices revealed a considerable degree of rational selectivity (rather than 'irrational exuberance') based on the differing earnings record and potentials.[4]

In his 1931 thesis, and in line with his criticism of the commercial loan theory, Currie endorsed, with qualifications, Hawtrey's monetary theory of the business cycle. Hawtrey stressed the 'inherent instability of credit',[5] due to the sensitivity of wholesalers and merchants (more than manufacturers) to changes in the short-term rate of interest. The rate naturally falls in a depression when demand for commercial loans is low, and vice versa in the upswing. With a fall in demand for loans there is a fall in output, incomes and expenditures (effective demand) until declining interest rates arrest and then reverse the fall in loan demand. In the upswing, rising incomes increase the public's demand for cash. This squeezes the banks' reserves and interest rates rise. Eventually this arrests and then reverses the upswing – in the absence of astute counter-cyclical policy by the central bank.

Currie offered several criticisms of Hawtrey's monetary theory but stressed that none was fatal. In particular, he argued that banks are able and willing to expand and contract their holdings of (relatively marketable, hence liquid) securities, stocks and bonds to compensate for opposite movements in the demand for (relatively illiquid) short-term commercial loans. Furthermore, this ability to vary their asset holdings (hence their deposit liabilities) is a more important counter-cyclical influence than variations in the short-term interest rate. For the demand for commercial loans is lowest when demand for goods is lowest, and in those circumstances a lowering of short-term rates will not compensate. Earlier in his thesis, Currie wrote:

> If business men were as sensitive to short-term interest rate changes as Mr. Hawtrey seems to believe, commercial loans could be easily expanded by a fall in rates and contracted by a rise. A contrary view, however, which corresponds more closely to reality, is that the cost of short-term borrowing is not an important consideration in the calculation of borrowers. Of much more importance is the actual and anticipated demand for goods. If business conditions are receding, a fall in the short-term interest rates will not induce manufacturers and traders voluntarily to accumulate inventory. It is precisely at such a time that they are most eager to reduce inventories. This is one of the reasons why the movement of interest rates and commercial borrowings have a direct rather than an inverse relation to one another. (Currie, 1931, 86)[6]

By taking the initiative in buying and selling a wide range of assets the banks could better maintain the money supply and so exert a stabilizing influence on business.[7] Elsewhere, Hawtrey did acknowledge this. In *Trade Depression and the Way Out* (1931, 44), he wrote that 'the acquisition of *any* asset by *banks* [as opposed to non-banks] involves the creation of new bank credit [the key variable in his cycle theory]. Investment securities provide a very convenient vehicle for the creation of credit, because they can readily serve as collateral for bank advances'.

In an earlier passage entitled 'Deadlock in the Money Market', Hawtrey (1931, 30–33) examined the role of open market operations by the central bank to supplement variations in its bank rate. In a normal, moderate depression low rates would suffice to revive business. On the other hand, if conditions are allowed to deteriorate, a 'credit deadlock' could emerge in which lenders are too afraid to lend and borrowers too afraid to borrow – a case of an unusually inelastic demand for and supply of loans with respect to the short-term rate of interest.[8] In Hawtrey's explanation there is even a hint of what, in the recent Japanese context, has come to be called 'the zero lower bound problem' in which no practical reduction in short rates could, by itself, effect recovery:

> [I]f the depression is very severe, enterprise will be killed. It is possible that no rate of interest, however low, will tempt dealers to buy goods. Even lending money without interest would not help if the borrower anticipated a loss on every conceivable use that he could make of the money. In that case the purchase of securities by the Central Bank, which is otherwise no more than a useful reinforcement of the low Bank rate, hastening the progress of revival, becomes an essential condition of the revival beginning at all. By buying securities the Central Bank creates money, which appears in the form of deposits credited to the banks whose customers have sold the securities. The banks can thus be flooded with idle money, and given a new and powerful inducement to find additional borrowers. (Hawtrey, 1931, 30–31)

Elsewhere, Hawtrey goes further and – consistent with Currie, Ellsworth, and White (1932 [2002]) above – argues that fiscal deficits arising from public works can be an effective supplementary measure to revive a deeply depressed economy, *but only if the deficit is financed by money creation*, for otherwise private sector spending would usually be crowded out (the famous 1929 'Treasury View' that originated with Hawtrey). When deficits were financed by money creation, it was this money, and not any direct expenditure associated with fiscal policy, that would do the work (Laidler and Sandilands, 2002, 524). Later, we shall return to this argument in the context of recent Japanese macroeconomic policy.

Here is Hawtrey on the 'credit deadlock' in *Currency and Credit* (1950 edition, 75):[9]

> When the vicious circle of depression takes hold, and traders find their efforts to keep down their stocks defeated by too rapid decline in sales, the relaxation of credit may find them so burdened with unsold goods that no facility of borrowing can induce them to add to their stocks. A deadlock results, productive activity failing to respond to cheap money...
>
> If the banks fail to stimulate short-term borrowing, they can create credit by themselves buying securities in the investment market. The market will seek to use the resources thus placed in it, and it will become more favourable to new flotations and sales of securities. But even so an expansion of the flow of money is not ensured. If the money created is to move and to swell

> the consumers' income, the favourable market must evoke additional capital outlay. That is likely to take time and conceivably capital outlay may fail to respond. A deficiency of demand for consumable goods reacts on capital outlay, for when the existing capacity of industries is underemployed, there is little demand for capital outlay to extend capacity...
>
> The deadlock then is complete, and, unless it is to continue unbroken till some fortuitous circumstance restarts activity, recourse must be had to directly inflationary expedients, such as government expenditure far in excess of revenue, or a deliberate depreciation of the foreign exchange value of the money unit.

Currie's (1931) related argument was that even when banks are limited by inadequate demand by business for long-term loans, they may, by quoting sufficiently high prices, induce holders of old issues to part with their holdings.[10] By driving down the long-term interest rate, this may induce issue of new securities; and 'loans for fixed capital purposes is the very best way in which credit can be created in times of depression. What is needed is that consumers' incomes should be increased with no corresponding immediate increase in finished consumer goods' (218). Likewise, if banks promote a strong bond market this might not only improve business sentiment but 'would at least furnish those public authorities who are in favor of an expansion of public works with an additional argument. In so far as the policy of expanding public works in times of depression is adopted, and banks purchase bonds of public authorities, the additional bank credit will be spent directly and will not involve any decrease in the spending ability of private individuals' (236).

However, the supply of high-grade bonds (including those issued by public authorities and foreign borrowers) may be inadequate (in the absence of substantial bond-financed public works) to meet the requirement of banks; and if their purchases of old bonds 'do not stimulate new issues the long-term interest rate may decline to a point at which banks may, perhaps, prefer to maintain excess reserves rather than risk a future loss from depreciation when interest rates rise' (Currie, 1931, 216). This was probably written in 1930 before a credit deadlock had fully taken hold, and he noted then that while this consideration does not seem to have deterred banks in the past – hence 'the objection to the monetary theory of the business cycle which rests on the inability of the banking system to take the initiative in expanding credit, is by no means conclusive' (218) – it may conceivably do so in the future.

Actually Currie found that the figures

> do not bear out the common belief that excess reserves mount rapidly in times of depression. It is of particular interest that throughout 1930 and much of 1932, when the depression was probably worse than had ever before been experienced, excess reserves were but little larger than in 1929...The rapid increase in excess reserves in 1932 and again in 1933 occurred at highly abnormal times and should not be used as a basis for generalizations as to what

> might be expected to happen in the type of depression we had experienced up to that time. (Currie, 1934*a*, 115)

He concluded:

> [T]he demand for loans does not impose a very serious limitation on the volume of deposits. Unless the depression is abnormally severe banks can offset the decline in their commercial loans by increasing their investment portfolios, and our greatest hope in promoting business stability through monetary means lies in action taken before a depression becomes a disaster. (124)

Thus both the magnitude and the timing of monetary measures were crucial. Later Currie wrote:

> After the upturn in business in early 1930 proved abortive, I despaired of the efficacy of monetary measures in the conditions of the times and started both in my classes and in discussions advocating deficit spending. But this had to be done almost surreptitiously. Even so, the heresy became known and I fell from grace and was reprimanded by the Chairman of the Department. (Currie, 1978 [1935], 541)

Effectively Currie had decided by the middle of 1930 that this was no ordinary depression. Even though excess reserves did not build up significantly until 1932 (indicating insufficient lending opportunities relative to reserves at that time), mass liquidations had earlier forced bank closures and surviving banks had been losing reserves to uncompensated cash drains. Thus both deposits and income velocity had been falling, with disastrous effects on income and demand for loans – a classic credit deadlock. In these circumstances open market operations were unlikely by themselves to revive lending and spending. If there is great excess capacity and a slump in the demand for loans, open-market purchases of bonds would initially increase the supply of money, but if that money is then put into liquid savings deposits (in banks or non-banks) it would merely end up as idle, excess bank reserves, with no increase in the money supply as such.

The later Keynesian concept of a highly elastic 'speculative' motive for holding idle money balances when the long-term interest rate had fallen to an abnormally low level was given as the reason for the ineffectiveness of open market purchases of bonds in a depression. A 'liquidity trap' (a term coined by a sceptical D. H. Robertson in 1940; see Laidler [1999, 286], and Laidler [2004*a*, 336–339]) would render monetary policy useless.

Currie criticised the Keynesian concept because the private non-bank sector could always avoid capital-value risk by placing savings in short-term interest-bearing bank and non-bank time deposits.[11] If the proceeds from central bank purchases of securities go into time rather than demand deposits, the money supply would only increase if the banks were then able and willing to increase their lending instead of accumulating reserves. In an acute depression this may not be possible for lack of available high-grade alternatives. In other words, a Hawtreyan type of credit deadlock required an expansion of the money supply that, as depression deepens, may only be possible via unconventional fiscal means. By contrast, a Keynesian liquidity trap supposedly meant that monetary policy was useless, while a pure fiscal policy, financed via sale of bonds, could work even with no new money.[12]

Hawtrey (1931, 31) noted at the time that the Fed resorted freely to open market purchases up to June 1930 but made no further considerable purchases until June 1931 and 'the holding of Government securities was not raised beyond the point at which it had provided the member banks with the means of reducing their rediscounts to a minimum'. Bank loans and the money supply declined.

Large-scale withdrawals of gold from the United States around the time that Britain left the gold standard in September 1931 forced member banks into debt again.[13] Currie (1934*b*, 108) noted how the banks responded by selling bonds and calling loans. Bond prices fell drastically, followed by bank failures, increased hoarding of notes, more liquidation, more failures, more hoarding, and a severe contraction of money.

On the importance of timing, Currie wrote:

> If action is taken before the upswing in business has reached its peak a comparatively mild easing policy will be sufficient to stimulate investment [in the subsequent downswing]. If, on the other hand, action is delayed until business has acquired a considerable momentum on the downswing a drastic expansion of money is called for. If the depression has become so severe as to entail a widespread loss of confidence in the solvency of both corporations and banks it may be impossible to bring about immediate utilization of any excess reserves given to member banks.
>
> For the sake of straight thinking on the subject of control it is essential to interpret it in terms of the changing industrial situation. Many writers, unfortunately, fall into the error of applying conclusions true of banking control at one particular time to other occasions quite different. The existence of excess reserves in the latter part of 1932 and again in 1933 have given force to the oft repeated assertion that the central bank cannot bring about expansion of money in a period of depression. But the phrase 'period of depression' is obviously not a precise one. There was, for example, less difference in industrial activity between the 'depression' of 1930 and the 'prosperity' of 1929 than there was between the former and the 'depression' of 1932. It is, therefore, illegitimate to assume that a certain banking policy would be as effective in 1932 as in 1930, or, to put it differently, to assume that because reserves were not immediately and fully utilized in 1932 they would not have been utilized in 1930. (Currie, 1934*a*, 146)

He continued:

> Much of the current belief in the powerlessness of the reserve banks appears to arise from a complete misreading of the monetary history of 1929–32. It

> is generally held that the reserve administration strove energetically to bring about expansion throughout the depression but that contraction continued despite its efforts. Actually the reserve administration's policy was one of almost complete passivity and quiescence. (Currie, 1934*a*, 147)

On the excess reserves question, Hawtrey (1950, 84) also wrote that 'much depends on the *magnitude* of the idle balances. If they are too considerable to be offset by increased advances to traders, the banks may create credit by purchase of securities. But they must buy at prices which investors are beginning to find unattractive, and by buying will force prices higher still'. At this point he alluded to Keynes's *General Theory* in which, by thus driving down the long-term rate of interest, 'an *increased* absorption of cash will then result' from the risk of capital depreciation when the long rate has reached its conventional minimum. Hawtrey acknowledged:

> When this minimum is reached, the market's stimulus is exhausted. Even the banks will require a minimum yield; they are no more ready than others to tie up their money without any compensation.
>
> But a state of things in which the investment market cannot *by any means* elicit sufficient active accumulation to use up current savings is not to be remedied by merely monetary means... If the desire to save encounters an insurmountable deficiency of forms of wealth capable of accumulation, there is a deep-seated breakdown of the economic system.
>
> Then indeed recourse may be had to deficit finance, not necessarily public works...but any excess of public expenditure over revenue, to be covered by securities (yielding a minimum of interest) in which those addicted to saving can accumulate titles to wealth. (Hawtrey, 1950, 85)

What mattered then was the size of the compensatory direct injection of spending into the system by the government. This was totally inadequate during President Herbert Hoover's watch to arrest the decline in business activity and, in Currie's view, still inadequate after Roosevelt came to office in March 1933.

Currie's second (but still not fatal) criticism of Hawtrey's cycle theory was that he placed too much stress on the supply of demand deposits (or 'credit' as defined by Hawtrey) and too little on movements into and out of cash, as well as on short-term variations in the 'circuit velocity' of deposits and cash (purchasing power).[14] Nonetheless, fluctuations in the supply of purchasing power, and also in its secular trend, do exercise a profound influence on the business cycle. And if this be true then 'it follows that the mechanism by which the volume of credit is expanded and contracted is also of significance' (Currie, 1931, 222).

Currie goes on to state that 'the study of credit movements in the business cycle involves an explanation of two problems: first, the forces affecting the reserves of member and non-member banks, second, the means by which banks are enabled to adjust their deposits to their reserves' (Currie, 1931, 222). The latter problem is the focus of Currie's PhD thesis on the links between the business cycle and the supply and control of various classes of bank asset. The former was more the focus of his 1934 book on the control of the supply of money. There he examined the different reserves (legally required and otherwise) held by different classes of bank and different type of deposit during the various stages of the business cycle, and the often perverse or pro-cyclical elasticity of the money supply that had resulted from that bank structure.

In the concluding chapter of his 1931 thesis Currie referred to conditions in 1930 and complained that '[a]s long as the demand for commercial loans continues to decline the Board apparently sees no necessity of permitting the expansion of credit to take place' (Currie, 1931, 243–244). This was a recipe for pro-cyclical monetary policy that was to deepen the on-going depression. The Fed was too preoccupied with the composition and perceived relative productivity of bank assets, to the neglect of its primary function, that of controlling the overall volume of bank deposits:

> It is evident that the commercial loan theory of banking is incompatible with the view that the chief function of the banking system is to supply purchasing power, and that a central bank should control this supply in the interests not only of commercial borrowers, but of the community in general. (Currie, 1931, 242)

Finally, he advanced a number of recommendations for amending the Federal Reserve Act, especially in respect of the question of bank assets eligible for rediscount (Currie, 1931, 248), and of the need to relax the gold reserve requirement against notes. After he had teamed up with Marriner Eccles in 1934, he was to effect some of these measures, designed to convert a 'perversely elastic' banking system into an effective 'maladjustment-compensating factor'.

Allan Meltzer highlights Currie's influence on Federal Reserve policy after 1934 but was puzzled by the contrast between his focus on monetary policy failures in his publications to 1934 and his focus on fiscal policy in his work with Eccles. He wrote:

> Eccles differed from his predecessors in his belief that government had to take responsibility for the economy. He devoted much of his time to advocating fiscal measures, especially increased spending on investment financed by government borrowing to expand demand. Currie seems to have shared this view. Although he analysed the Federal Reserve's failure to expand as a consequence of adherence to the real bills doctrine and neglect of the falling money stock, he does not seem to have pursued this view at the Federal Reserve. He devoted much of his research after 1935 to developing measures of fiscal thrust and the case for unbalanced budgets... Later, he described his 1934 book as 'partly obsolete when it was published'... The reason he gave was that money (deposits) depend on member bank borrowing, and there was no borrowing. This is an odd conclusion. (Meltzer, 2003, 478–479)

The puzzle is resolved by recognising the key conditions that make for effectiveness of monetary policy in the different phases of slump and recovery. To effect recovery from a slump, the Fed must first get member banks out of debt. This the Fed had failed to accomplish adequately in 1929–32. The policy of passive acquiescence to banks' loss of deposits resulted in mass liquidations and a downward spiral into depression. An acute Hawtreyan credit deadlock then meant that banks could not find enough credit-worthy customers when eventually they were able to lend again, and so they accumulated substantial excess reserves. In such conditions monetary policy alone is, in the famous words of Marriner Eccles, like pushing on a string.

Currie believed that the deadlock required not only vigorous open market operations but also an active fiscal policy to spend new and old money into circulation, just as he, Ellsworth and White emphasised in their January 1932 Harvard memorandum.

Hawtrey was more lukewarm than Currie on the need for government expenditure and fiscal deficits as a way out of depression, though he did not deny their potential effectiveness. As noted above, Hawtrey (1925, in 1928, 110–111) had argued that in exceptional circumstances, where businesses were accumulating idle balances that could not find profitable outlets, the issue of bonds to finance government spending could increase the velocity of circulation and, even in the absence of new bank lending (creating new money), this could give additional employment. But 'the case is completely transformed' in the case 'where the government finances its operations by the creation of bank credits', and would then definitely give additional employment, without crowding out. Nonetheless, 'the same reasoning shows that a creation of credit unaccompanied by any expenditure on public works would be equally effective in giving employment' (Hawtrey, 1925 in 1928, 112). And it is only when a low bank rate, reinforced by the purchase of securities on the part of the central bank in the open market 'has been tried and has failed, [is] there any case for recourse to Government borrowing. Personally, I have no doubt that by the former method it is possible to find an escape from depression, *however severe*' (113, italics added).[15]

By contrast, as depression deepened in 1930, Currie argued that fiscal deficits had become essential to break the deadlock. From 1934 he pioneered (with Martin Krost) a 'net Federal income-creating expenditure' series that indicated how different types of fiscal deficit could contribute to an expansion of the circular flow of money. In 1933–37 this was through (i) the ways in which deficit financing helped the banks to make use of the reserves that accumulated as gold flowed in from abroad (their excess reserves may have been increased even more in the absence of these deficit financing opportunities); and (ii) the way deficit spending stimulated the private sector to make use of their idle balances to expand production.

Hawtrey probably did not contemplate, in the 1920s, just how severe a depression could be. In his retrospective assessment of the 1930s Hawtrey, wrote:

> Conditions in the United States offered an exceptionally suitable opportunity for the application of this theory [that public works could give employment by creating credit and/or 'may set stagnant cash balances in motion'].

> The American banking system was becoming clogged with idle money. The New York rediscount rate had been reduced to 1½ per cent. in January, 1934, and remained unchanged till it was reduced to 1 per cent. in 1937. The excess reserves of the member banks...rose to $3000 millions. With this gigantic reserve of lending power, the banks still could not induce their customers to borrow. (Hawtrey, 1950, 410–411)

However, while 'the banks created credit by taking a considerable part of the securities issued by the Government to meet the deficit', he noted that the growth of money national income was slower than the growth of bank deposits. Thus the policy of 'lavish public expenditure [that] came to be called 'priming the pump'' had disappointing results, and 'when the banking system has to be unceasingly inundated year after year, the analogy wears rather thin' (Hawtrey, 1950, 411).[16] Hawtrey accepted that 'we cannot suppose that the Government borrowings of $3000 millions a year...from 1933 to 1937 were wholly without effect. But recovery was extremely slow.' Though unemployment fell from about 13 millions in March 1933 to 6 millions in 1937, this was still greatly in excess of the 1.5 millions in 1929. Hawtrey placed part of the blame on wage increases after 1933, and especially those in 1937 by which time:

> the measures making for expansion were being deliberately slowed down. The budget deficit for 1937–38 was reduced to $1377 millions. The statutory reserve requirements of the banks were raised in 1936 so as to reduce excess reserves from the $3,105 millions that they had reached by August 1936...
>
> A recession followed, and in 1938 unemployment was once again up to the level of July, 1933. Expenditure of $20,000 millions of borrowed money by the Government had been incurred in vain. (Hawtrey, 1950, 412)

Hawtrey noted that revival in Britain was achieved with no recourse to public works or budget deficits as an expedient for inducing a monetary expansion until 1937 when borrowing for rearmament started (just at the time of the unhelpful US recession). He seemed to hint that the United States should have been able to achieve the same results without the government expenditures that 'had been incurred in vain'.

Fiscal deficits, excess reserves and the recession of 1937–38

This was not how Currie saw it. For him, Roosevelt's budget deficits were the major – and essential – ingredient in recovery after 1933, and thus were not in vain. The raising of reserve requirements in 1936–37, while unhelpful was not the main source of trouble. Recovery could have been maintained, and the recession of 1937–38 avoided, if the government's net contribution had been maintained. His own estimate of the degree of fiscal contraction in 1937 was even greater than Hawtrey's figures, based as it was on how individual components of the government budget added to or subtracted from the expenditure flow. He estimated the 'net federal contribution' at over $4 billions in 1936 and less than $1 billion in 1937.[17] Expenditures had been inflated in 1936 by a one-off accelerated payment of veterans' bonuses, passed over the president's veto, and deflated in 1937 by large payments into a national pension fund mandated by the 1937 Social Security Act.

By mid-1936 it appeared that excess reserves posed a threat to effective control of a potentially inflationary recovery in the future. Open market bond sales would not reduce the money supply if purchased out of excess reserves. Effective deflation requires that the banks be forced to borrow, and then for their repugnance to indebtedness to induce them to curtail their lending.

As loan demand picked up, excess reserves would allow banks to accommodate the demand without restraint. This would permit a multiple expansion of deposits which, together with a reversion to the historically higher average velocity of circulation, could cause monetary expenditures (MV) to expand greatly in excess of any feasible increase in real national production. The expansion in the money value of national income (Py) would then mainly be via a rise in prices (P) than in real output (y). For this reason Currie advised Eccles to raise reserve requirements in late 1936 and early 1937, but only as a precautionary measure. There was no deflationary intent. In fact, because of the continuing inflow of gold from Europe, the doubling of reserve requirements during this period still left the banks with substantial excess reserves at the end of the process, in the spring of 1937.

However, from the beginning of June 1937 recovery turned rapidly into an alarming recession. Real GDP would fall by 18 per cent over the next 13 months (Meltzer, 2003, 522). The unemployment rate rose from its best 1937 figure of 12.5 per cent to about 22.5 per cent in the spring of 1938, including as unemployed those on emergency relief employment (Black, 2003, 430). At the time few people blamed the monetary measures, though there was a slight increase in bond yields, from an all-time low of 2.46 per cent in early March to 2.8 per cent in early April (after which they declined again). This had angered Treasury Secretary Henry Morgenthau Jr., though it was a Treasury decision to sterilize gold inflows from December. He was worried that a rise in interest rates would increase the financial cost of the deficit, and he kept pressing Roosevelt to trim government spending and balance the budget. Eccles agreed that higher interest rates were undesirable and supported the Federal Open Market Committee's decision in April to engage in compensatory open market purchases.

There is no evidence that banks were suddenly denying requests for loans by business or government, or imposing stricter conditions as a result of the increased reserve requirements. Thus the modern focus on a supposedly inept monetary policy as the cause of the downturn in 1937 (see, e.g., Steindl, 1995, 2004, in support of Friedman and Schwartz's 1963 view) may be misplaced. Meltzer (2003, 521–522) and Christina and David Romer (1989, 131–132) emphasized at least two non-monetary forces acting to decrease output in 1937: the fiscal downturn, and the way the Wagner Act led to large inventory accumulations in anticipation of the labour market strife that did occur in 1937, coinciding with an end to inventory accumulations. They also note that the behaviour of reserve holdings ran counter to Friedman and Schwartz's interpretation in that there was no discernible change in reserves as a fraction of deposits until December 1937, 17 months after the first increase in reserve requirements was announced and after the declines in money and industrial production were largely complete.

Currie admitted that probably the reserve requirements would not have been raised if the recession of 1937 had been accurately forecast.[18] But he wrote that 'this is a different matter than holding the raising responsible for the recession. For that the very sharp, even drastic, reduction in the fiscal cash deficit is the more convincing explanation of the sharp decline in the rate of growth in sales and the consequent piling up of inventories.' He also noted that 'few theorists would expect an immediate impact on incomes and sales to result from the small decline in deposits that took place, especially as there is such an other more convincing explanation of the causation of the fall in aggregate demand'.

In his 'Public Spending as a Means to Recovery' (August 1936) and 'Stabilization of Purchasing Power through the Use of Public Credit' (December 1936), both in Sandilands (2004), Currie believed that the 1933–36 recovery would be sustained even if the then relatively substantial fiscal deficit should decline somewhat over the coming year. He did not anticipate the extent of the fiscal contraction that was to occur, nor the effects of the Wagner Act on labour costs, expectations, and inventory accumulations. However, these memoranda are important for showing Currie's understanding of the essential relationship, in time of depression, between fiscal deficit and banks' ability to lend, thereby ensuring continued increase of monetary incomes and expenditures until recovery could be self-sustaining – with declining and eventually negative fiscal deficits.

Currie's August 1936 memorandum, 'Public Spending as a Means to Recovery' (in Sandilands, 2004), noted the importance of fiscal deficits for the maintenance of bank lending up to that point:

> The volume of checking accounts in all banks, plus the demand deposits of the Government in commercial banks, expanded by $8 to $9 billion between June 1933 and June 1936. Part of this increase was attributable to an increase in the banks' holdings of Government guaranteed bonds, part to the deposit of incoming gold, and the major part to the increase in banks' holdings of the public debt. The increase in the member bank holdings of $4.8 billion amounts to 43 percent of the increase in the gross public debt in this period.

Lester G. Telser (2003) has emphasised the importance of the veterans' bonus payments (mostly in 1936) on the buoyancy of recovery in that year, even though it was financed by borrowing from the public so that it did not change the money supply (240). He states that the fiscal deficit in June 1937 was less than a quarter of its June 1936 level (238), with a correspondingly smaller impact on the economy in 1937. On Currie's measure of the 'net federal contribution', the fall was even greater ($101 million in June 1937 compared with $543 million in June 1936). This may be partly explained by the differing spending propensity of the veterans compared to those who financed their bonuses.

In 'The Decline in the Federal Contribution to the Growth in Community Expenditures' (October 1937, in Sandilands 2004), he showed that in the three years 1934–36 the net contribution had been $3.2, $3.1 and $4.0 billion. These were sizable fractions of the growth of national income in those years: respectively $7.8, $5.4 and $8.8 billion. In the eight months from February to September 1937, the Currie–Krost series showed that the net contribution had fallen to only $573 million ($68 million a month and still falling – it was estimated at only $37 million in September) compared with $2,789 million ($348 million a month) in the same period of 1936. He warned that the government's contribution to buying power, already insufficient to offset the slowdown in private expenditures, may well turn negative in the near future.

On a Keynesian interpretation of the downturn in 1937–38, this fiscal reversal was a crucial causal factor. By comparison, variations in the degree of excess liquidity in the banks were of secondary importance. By cutting the federal deficit there was a fall in the supply of safe earning assets that the banks had previously relied on. They could not easily or quickly replace them with a corresponding increase in private sector lending, for the decline in government spending and the increase in tax and social security receipts were themselves depressing demand for private sector output. This naturally restrained private loan demand. These factors, rather than the raising of reserve requirements, may account for the diminution of demand deposits from mid-1937 and the continued high level of excess reserves.

Telser (2001) also disputes Friedman and Schwartz's (1963) view that the 1937–38 recession was caused by the raising of reserve requirements. He shows that there was no decline in bank lending to the private sector until the end of the first quarter of 1938, hence higher reserve requirements could not explain the decline of business. The decline in banks' earning assets was entirely in their holdings of government bonds. The changed composition of bank assets (as well as their decline) differed radically from the experience of the previous recessions of 1920–22 and 1929–33. But if this meant that the private sector was not starved of loans, the question remains: what did cause the 1937–38 recession in private business?

Telser does not explicitly address this. Currie's explanation, however, was that fiscal tightening of 1937 led to a much smaller supply of new and relatively riskless bonds for banks to purchase. Thus, even without an increase in reserve requirements they would have been liquidating maturing bonds. Also, they were inclined to sell bonds anyway because of profit-taking at the apparent end of a three-year bull run for bond prices that occurred in January 1936 even before the announcement of the rise in reserve requirements. In his May 1938 speech to the Illinois Banking Association he concluded:

> It seems reasonable to assume that the desire to take profits was the major motivating factor in bank sales of Government bonds, particularly since sales were engaged in by so many banks that possessed more than adequate reserves to meet the new requirements. Moreover, had the purpose been merely to obtain

> reserves, banks could have reduced their holdings of short-term Government paper instead of liquidating long-term bonds. (Sandilands, 2004, 352)

If banks had continued to buy bonds on secondary markets this would have increased the riskiness of their asset portfolio by further depressing interest rates. If they had maintained their assets by making more fresh loans to the private sector in place of loans to government, this would also have increased their risk, in the absence of a strong increase in loan demand by credit-worthy customers. In other words, the economy still had not broken out of a state of credit deadlock, or self-sustaining growth, and was still dependent on direct injections of monetary expenditures by the public sector. There was some increase in private sector loans throughout 1937 but insufficient to compensate for the public sector's decreased demand, especially as private profit prospects were dented by the decline in the government's 'net contribution'. Thus if the Fed had not raised reserve requirements there would probably have been further accumulations of excess reserves.

Nonetheless, the increased reserve requirements under these conditions could not have helped matters, and must partly explain why banks sold bonds to maintain their liquidity. Again, however, Currie gave greater weight, in his May 1938 Illinois address, to banks' desire to avoid capital-value losses at the end of the bond market's bull run, with the decline 'initiated by municipal and Federal bonds in January [1937] before action with reference to excess reserves was announced'.[19] He insisted that action on reserves would not have worsened the recession whose causes lay elsewhere – in the smaller deficit plus other non-monetary factors, notably the exceptional inventory accumulations in late1936 that would be worked off a few months later.

Steindl (2004, 66) has written that in his analysis of recovery Currie had abandoned the quantity-theoretic analysis that he had applied to the contraction of 1929–33: 'He therefore did not see the recovery as the product of an increasing stock of money. For him, the quantity of money was now an endogenous variable, subject to the needs of business as it sought to borrow, thereby affecting deposits, money, and excess reserves.' The quantity theory's identity ($MV = Py$) states that if velocity is constant then the value of national income (Py) will increase in line with M. But in the unusual conditions of the mid-1930s Currie feared that both velocity and money would be excessively pro-cyclical as and when a firm recovery was assured, since business and consumers would then be able and willing to draw down their substantial idle balances.[20] Steindl's belief that he showed little interest in the money supply after 1934, is not borne out by his Federal Reserve Board memoranda, though it is certainly true that he continued to believe that monetary policy had then become relatively powerless as a recovery measure except in conjunction with a vigorously expansionary fiscal stance. Its role would remain a subsidiary or complementary one until full recovery had been firmly established.

On 8 November 1937, WPA administrator Harry Hopkins arranged for his economic adviser Leon Henderson, together with Currie and Isador Lubin, Commissioner of Labour Statistics, to meet with President Roosevelt for an interview that lasted an unprecedented four hours (see Lash, 1988, 317–327). *The New York Post* reported the next day that 'the four advisers minced no words in giving Roosevelt a hard-boiled review of economic conditions and with equal bluntness and vigor they told him that a disastrous recession can only be averted by a resumption of big-scale Government spending'. The group laid a report before the president that showed that 'in August, for the first time since 1931, the government took more out of the income stream than it poured back in...If the Government takes taxes away from workers or corporations and uses these in bookkeeping items, such as old age reserve accounts, gold purchases, debt retirement, etc., and the amount exceeds what is paid for men and materials, then there is a deficit. That is what is happening now.'

In a speech to Congress a few days after his 'Keynesian' seminar, Roosevelt asked: 'What does the country ultimately gain if we encourage businessmen to enlarge the capacity of American industry to produce unless we see to it that the income of our working population actually expands sufficiently to create markets to absorb the increased production.' But in practice Roosevelt initially sided with Secretary Morgenthau's call for a balanced budget 'to restore confidence'. Disaster followed. Not until 14 April 1938, after the worst period of his long tenure in the White House and after a strong letter from Keynes in February, did Roosevelt at last ask Congress (over the continuing objections of the Secretary of the Treasury) for more than $3 billion of spending or lending in the immediate future for relief, public works, housing, and assistance to state and local governments (see Barber, 1996, 114; also Black, 2003, 428–436). Economic recovery resumed.

The lasting legacy of the theoretical, empirical, and practical experience of the depression and war years was the February 1946 Employment Act. Its passage through Congress was stormy, and the original bill was much watered down. Nevertheless, a statute that affirmed governmental responsibility for 'maximum employment, production and purchasing power' was a significant advance over the more limited mandate for government that, for example, was preferred by Irving Fisher and the Chicago School with their rules-based price stability goal for monetary policy and with fiscal policy aimed at low-level balanced budgets. The war itself accustomed people to higher and more progressive rates of taxation and government spending, and these were only partially retrenched in peacetime. This introduced a much greater degree of built-in stability by effectively increasing the marginal savings rate at the full employment level of income and expenditure.

Postwar prosperity and the Japanese experience

To the extent that these automatic stabilizers mitigate the business cycle and make credit deadlocks rarer, they may also have made monetary policy normally the most effective discretionary instrument for macroeconomic stabilization. And indeed, for the more developed countries, including Japan, there has been no repeat of depression on the scale and duration of the 1930s. Following recovery from the World War II, Japan was labelled an economic 'miracle'. Its average annual growth rate in the 1950s was an impressive 9.1 per cent, and this rose further to 10.7 per cent in the 1960s. It grew at a creditable average of 5.2 per cent in the 1970s despite the worldwide OPEC crisis years. In the early 1980s, while the world was painfully unwinding inflation, her growth slowed to 3 per cent (1980–84); but from 1985 to 1990 it increased to 4.6 per cent, about double the OECD average.[21]

It was from late 1991 that Japan entered its long period of 'growth stagnation' and abnormally high unemployment, from which only recently (2006) did it appear to emerge. While this poor record does not compare with the Great Depression in its intensity, it does in terms of its duration and abnormality. The annual average growth rate, 1992–2004, was a mere 0.7 per cent (or 1.2 per cent if the recovery years 2003–05 are included), with four years in which growth was negative (see Table 15.1). This significantly underperformed both its previous postwar record and, for the first time, that of the rest of the OECD. During this period inflation averaged 0.2 per cent, with a negative rate in seven of the years since 1995.

There is also an interesting parallel between Japan in the years immediately preceding its Great Stagnation and the United States in the years before its Great Depression. In the United States from 1922 to 1929, annual average growth was buoyant but not necessarily unsustainable at around 4.7 per cent. Population growth was 1.8 per cent a year, wages grew by only 1.5 per cent a year, and inflation was virtually zero. In the recovery from post-war depression, stock prices naturally rose strongly but were not obviously out of line with fundamentals. During the 5-year bull run from mid-1924 to the crash in October 1929 the Dow Jones index rose by about 250 per cent, accelerating in 1928 and 1929. On the first day of the crash, 28 October 1929, the index plunged by over 12 per cent, by nearly 30 per cent over the next six days, and by mid-1932 it had lost another 80 per cent. It did not regain its 1925 level until 1938. The rise and initial plunge in the market in the 1920s were very similar to the 5-year 'Reagan' bull run of mid-1982 to late 1987. On Black Monday, 19 October 1987, the Dow fell by a record 22.6 per cent. But the response of the Fed in 1987 was very different from the response in 1929–33, the stock market soon recovered, and the crash had no more than a very temporary adverse effect on US growth.[22]

In Japan from 1985 to 1991, average annual growth was, as we have seen, running at a not unusual rate of 4.6 per cent. The consumer price index had been rising by only 1.7 per cent a year. This was a period of recovery from the slower growth of the early 1980s and it sparked a 6-year bull run on the stock market. The Nikkei index rose by nearly 300 per cent: from 9,927 in January 1984 to a peak of 38,951 in January 1990. It then fell by nearly 40 per cent over the year to January 1991 and by a further 30 per cent over the next two years, to 16,875 in January 1993. It continued to slide for another 10 years to its trough of 7,804 on 1 May 2003, before recovering to a local high of 17,498 on 7 April 2006 (similar to where it stood in 1986).

Along with the stock market bull run, and outrunning it by a year, was a property boom. Rising land values helped fuel the stock market in that bank loans for

Table 15.1 Key Japanese statistics, 1985–2005

Year	Real GDP growth rate, %	M1 % change (1)	M2 + CDs, % change (2)	M1 as % of M2 + CDs (3)	Average Interest rate on time deposits* (4)	Interest rate on ordinary postal savings (5)	Inflation rate consumer price index (6)
1985	5.0	4.5	9.2	28.5		2.88	1.9
1986	2.6	8.4	8.1	28.6	5.15	1.68	0.0
1987	4.1	6.9	11.4	27.4	4.35	1.68	0.5
1988	6.2	10.2	10.7	27.4	4.58	1.68	0.8
1989	4.8	−2.0	10.6	24.2	5.34	1.92	2.9
1990	5.1	6.1	8.5	23.7	7.54	3.48	3.3
1991	3.8	8.8	2.0	25.3	7.06	2.88	2.8
1992	0.9	1.9	−0.4	25.9	4.12	1.80	1.6
1993	0.4	3.4	1.3	26.4	2.77	1.32	1.2
1994	1.0	4.9	2.9	26.9	2.02	1.35	0.4
1995	2.5	12.8	3.2	29.5	1.11	0.25	−0.1
1996	3.6	10.0	2.9	31.5	0.48	0.25	0.4
1997	0.6	8.9	3.8	33.0	0.47	0.25	2.0
1998	−0.9	5.7	3.5	33.6	0.53	0.15	0.2
1999	0.6	11.7	2.6	36.6	0.22	0.08	−0.5
2000	2.5	4.2	2.0	37.4	0.18	0.12	−0.5
2001	−1.1	13.6	3.3	41.1	0.09	0.02	−1.0
2002	0.8	25.1	2.2	50.3	0.04	0.005	−0.6
2003	2.0	4.1	1.5	51.6	0.04	0.005	−0.2
2004	1.9	4.1	2.0	52.7	0.06	0.005	−0.1
2005	2.6	3.0	1.9	54.5	0.09	0.005	−0.1

Notes: *For 1986–93 the interest rate refers only to the rate on large deposits over 10 million yen. These are usually about 1 per cent above the rate for smaller deposits, but after 1993 there was almost no difference in the rates for different size of deposit.
Sources: Bank of Japan websites:
http://www.boj.or.jp/en/index.htm; http://www.boj.or.jp/en/type/stat/dlong/fin_stat/money/index.htm; http:// www.boj.or.jp/en/type/stat/dlong/fin_stat/money/cdab0020.csv; Bank of Japan (2005), pp. 19–20; United Nations *Yearbooks*.

stocks were largely collateralized by them. The urban land price index for the six largest cities (base 1990 = 100) tripled from approximately 33 in January 1985 to a peak of 107 in January 1991 before falling by 15.5 per cent in 1991, 19.4 per cent in 1992, and then sliding by around 10 per cent a year for the next 10 years. A slight recovery was registered for the first time only in mid-2005 when the index stood at around 20.[23]

A major difference between the behaviour of the late 1980s asset price boom in Japan and that of the United States in the late 1920s was the way in which the Bank of Japan (BoJ) put extreme pressure on commercial banks to meet high credit targets. Werner (2005, chapter 20) provides compelling evidence that the secretive BoJ continued 'window guidance' (a type of credit control) during the whole of the 1980s despite official pronouncements that credit controls were abolished in 1982. The 'guidance' involved the BoJ insisting that commercial banks adhere strictly to specified sectoral as well as quantitative targets in their allocation of credit, and were heavily penalised for under-shooting targets that, in the 1980s were set quite high. Furthermore, the BoJ maintained the same size structure of banks and this made for a poor, non-competitive allocation of credit. From 1982 to 1991 banks scrambled to meet loose credit targets by dropping their own preferred standards of credit-worthiness.

Werner concludes that the BoJ bears responsibility for encouraging banks to lend recklessly on speculative property ventures, or to non-bank financial intermediaries who would then also channel funds to property speculators. He deemed most of these 'unproductive', with more than a hint of the real bills doctrine underlying his critique of central bank policy (Werner, 2005, 230). He favoured selective credit controls, but ones directed to 'productive' investment activities, believing these to be the only credits that promote real, non-inflationary growth. However, in this case there is strong evidence that the window guidance did indeed distort the allocation of funds and caused inflated asset prices to deviate from fundamentals to a far greater degree than was true of the United States in the 1920s or 1980s.[24] Although the BoJ was not granted formal independence from the Ministry of Finance until 1998, Werner (2005, 293) emphasised that, acting secretively through its Banking Department, the BoJ possessed a high degree of de facto independence over credit creation:

> The problem was not that bank lending was out of control. To the contrary, it was controlled almost perfectly by the Bank of Japan's window guidance. Instead, the problem was the policy taken by the Bank of Japan in setting loan growth quotas. Since the Bank of Japan chose far larger quotas than banks thought necessary, compliance with window guidance meant that banks were forced to peddle their loans to real estate speculators... thus pushing up real estate prices. (Werner, 2005, 292)

Property values were then used as collateral for further loans, which meant further purchases and sales, with sellers re-depositing the proceeds. These would then be recycled as yet more new loans. Werner (2005, 184) notes that there was 'a remarkable surge in financial and real estate transactions during the second half of the 1980s'. Thus the money supply did not have to increase rapidly for asset prices to soar while consumer prices were quite steady. The transactions velocity of money (sometimes referred to as money's 'financial circuit velocity') is notoriously volatile. In the late 1980s it was obviously spiralling while the more important and economically meaningful income velocity (demand for money as a proportion of GDP) remained fairly stable. Thus, just as Currie claimed for the United States in the 1920s there is no strong evidence that stock market and real estate transactions were diverting money or credit from the circular flow of current GDP in Japan. From 1985 to 1991, Table 1 shows that the BoJ's preferred definition of money (M2 + CDs, which includes relatively low-turnover time deposits) rose by an average annual rate of 8.6 per cent. On the M1 definition (currency plus demand deposits) the average growth was just 6.1 per cent, consistent with a low inflation rate of 1.7 per cent and real GDP growth of 4.6 per cent, hence a constant and broadly satisfied demand for money.

Nevertheless, unlike US asset inflation in the 1920s and 1980s, Japanese asset prices may have been very little justified by underlying fundamentals. As indicated above, Werner blames unwise, aggressive window guidance, and concludes:

> Responsibility for the creation of the bubble of the 1980s, thus also for the bad debts of the banking system of the 1990s, and indeed the long economic slump that began in 1992, lies squarely with the Bank of Japan. This strengthens the case that any policies to deal with the bad debts and stimulate an economic recovery should also be paid for by the Bank of Japan. Thus the central bank could have purchased all bad debts of the banks at face value, thus eliminating them at no cost to society, as well as monetise fiscal stimulation or the recapitalisation of banks. (Werner, 2005, 294)

The director of the Banking Department of the BoJ from 1986 to 1989 was Toshihiko Fukui, who rose to be the BoJ's deputy governor in 1994 and governor in 2003. He and his mentor, Yasushi Mieno, deputy governor of the BoJ from 1989 to 1994 and governor from 1994 to 1998, have both placed blame for the creation of the asset market bubble on the private sector and Fukui has demanded that private sector bank leaders take responsibility for the bad debt problem (Werner, 2005, 294).

In any event, good times not bad would be the appropriate time to fix problems of poor debt management and inefficient banking structure – which may have been endemic for a long period, in good times and bad, hence not obviously the main cause of recession. As it was, shortly after the asset bubbles burst, growth declined – to 1.0 per cent in 1992 and 0.3 per cent in 1993. The economy continued to stagnate for the next 12 years. The bursting of the bubbles was a major shock to business and consumer confidence, which naturally led to determined attempts to restore battered wealth holdings and provision for pensions.

Interest rates and the money supply

What were the macroeconomic (monetary and fiscal) policy responses? Table 1 reveals the monetary response. In the critical year of 1992, the money supply (M1) grew by just 1.9 per cent. The broader measure (M2 + CDs) actually fell by 0.4 per cent. At the same time, interest rates on time and savings deposits were falling sharply. The fall in these deposit rates may well reflect not loose monetary policy but rather the way the wealth shock would have induced corporations and individuals both to try to replenish their wealth and to reduce their demand for loanable funds for investment in a depressed economy.[25] No doubt reflecting an excess supply of savings (loanable funds) relative to investment, short and long lending rates were also falling sharply. The excess savings were also reflected in a strong balance of payments on current account and rapid accumulation of foreign exchange reserves.[26] Presumably, much of this reserve accumulation was being sterilised, for it is not reflected in the money supply figures.

Over the next few years interest rates were to fall further. The rate on the more liquid savings deposits fell to a mere 0.25 per cent by 1994 and then to close to zero, below which they cannot fall unless some sort of 'Gesell tax' on money balances were imposed to overcome the 'zero lower bound' problem (as suggested by Mitsuhiro Fukao, 2004). This appears to have had a very strong effect on the composition of money and 'quasi-money' balances. Currency plus demand deposits (M1) rose by an average of 7.6 per cent a year over the whole period 1992–2005 while the broader (M2 plus CDs) series rose by only 2.2 per cent. With the return on savings deposits falling to almost the same as on demand deposits, the percentage of the latter to the former more than doubled – from 25.9 per cent in 1992 to 54.5 per cent in 2005 (see Table 15.1).

The shifting of low-turnover savings deposits into demand deposits has meant that the growth of M1 is misleading. The broader (M2 + CDs) series, with its much slower growth, better reflects the tight monetary conditions that prevailed from 1992 until recently.[27] The velocity of M1 declined over the period by about 7 per cent a year – as measured by the difference between growth of M1 and growth of nominal GDP. By contrast, the decline in the velocity of the broader (M2 + CDs) series was more modest at about 2 per cent a year.

In view of the rise in the demand for money as nominal interest rates declined, it would appear that the BoJ's response to asset price deflation and economic recession in late 1991 and into 1992 and beyond should have been more vigorously to offset the deflationary effect of a rise in the demand for money *to hold* and the related fall in the demand for money *to spend* (that is, demand for loans). Instead, it presided over a sharp fall in the growth of money that was partly the result of a fall in the demand for loanable funds which in turn inhibits expansion of money via new bank credits.

Recall that the characteristic of a Hawtreyan credit deadlock is that it prevents money being created, whereas a Keynesian liquidity trap suggests that even if money is created this would do no good by itself. But with interest rates falling to very low levels, many observers have concluded that the economy had fallen into a liquidity trap. For example, Paul Krugman (1999, 2) argued that if, as was happening in Japan, 'the interest rate is zero, bonds and money become in effect equivalent assets; so conventional monetary policy, in which money is swapped for bonds via open-market operation, changes nothing'; and 'once it became clear that the Bank of Japan really did consider itself unable to increase demand in an economy that badly needed it, it also became clear...that the theory of the liquidity trap needed a fresh, hard look'. He stressed that this trap 'is in a fundamental sense an expectational issue. Monetary expansion is irrelevant [to effective demand] because the private sector does not expect it to be sustained.'[28] His solution: influence inflationary expectations through an unconventional and credible commitment that the BoJ would uncompromisingly pursue a 15-year inflation target of 4 per cent in order to reduce the expected real interest rate to below zero (the postulated 'natural' rate if prices were perfectly flexible) to stimulate investment and escape the liquidity trap.

Kazuo Ueda (2005) suggests that Krugman's focus on the need to manipulate inflationary expectations was consistent with the BoJ's explicit commitment to an effectively zero (short-term) interest rate policy from early 1999 until such time as signs of inflation should appear, even when the Taylor rule might indicate the need to raise it. But when the economy did show signs of recovery (though with prices still falling) the overnight call rate was raised to 0.25 per cent in August 2000. The recovery was short-lived and in early 2001 the policy rate was brought back down and a 'quantitative easing policy' (QEP) initiated that flooded the market with liquidity through aggressive purchases of Japanese Government Bonds (JGBs). This generated a huge increase in the monetary base over the period 2001–2005. A modest but sustained real economic recovery was recorded at last, though consumer prices continued to fall until 2006.

Charles Goodhart (personal communication) has suggested that this ultra-loose monetary policy was inefficiently implemented in that the BoJ mainly bought JGBs from the banks rather than the non-bank private sector. If so, this could explain why the banks accumulated such a huge volume of excess reserves: economic conditions prevented them from finding lending opportunities for these reserves – a view again more consistent with a credit deadlock than a liquidity trap. If instead the BoJ had bought JGBs directly from the non-bank private sector, this sector, awash with liquidity, may have had a higher propensity to spend than if they first had to borrow spending money from the banks. What is required is not a massive infusion of base money but rather a moderate expansion of the supply of money in the hands of the public, at least sufficient to satisfy the modest increase in the demand for money to hold (decline in velocity) that has been registered during the deflationary period since 1998 – though one would expect this decline in velocity to be reversed as and when deflation is conquered.

As Laidler (2004*a*, 339) has argued, the Keynesian liquidity trap involved the demand for money becoming infinitely elastic with respect to the long not the short rate of interest. And in Japan (as the chart in Werner, 2005, 46 shows), the long-term government bond yield continued to decline, from around 5 per cent in 1992 to 2 per cent in 1998 and only since then has it been flat, at around 1.5 per cent. Thus for much of the 'growth stagnation' period it would appear that an expansion of money by purchase of bonds could have effected a fall in the long rate of interest to stimulate spending rather than it all being absorbed in idle balances. However, whether in fact the decline in the long rate (or, for that matter, in the short rate) can be attributed to a loose but ineffective monetary policy (as many aver) cannot be judged by looking only at the interest rate (the current preoccupation of policymakers and theory alike, as lamented by Laidler, 2006).

For just as Hawtrey and Currie found for the United States, so too it appears that the rate of interest is positively and endogenously correlated with the business cycle: as business declines so too does the interest rate even if – or, indeed especially if – monetary policy is tight, as revealed not by the (lower) interest rate but by the money aggregates. A tight monetary policy exacerbates a downturn in business and can turn a recession into a self-reinforcing deflation. Thus, as revealed by the slowdown of nominal monetary growth at the time of the bursting of the asset price bubbles there was no quantitative easing at all (though at least the BoJ did not preside over an actual contraction of the money supply, unlike the Fed in 1929–33). Thus the subsequent interest rate declines can be entirely explained by a rise in the saving rate and fall in the *demand for loanable funds*. At the same time, the observed fall in the velocity of circulation of money indicates that while the *demand for money* was rising as a proportion of the depressed GDP, it could not have been increasing in absolute terms relative to the slow growth of the money supply.

The question then arises: could the banks have increased the demand for loanable funds (hence investment and/or consumption spending) by further lowering the rate of interest on loans if the rate was falling precisely because macroeconomic conditions had been depressing that demand?[29] With slower growth of money partly the result of a decline in demand for loanable funds relative to banks' reserves, a reversal requires offsetting action by the central bank. A lowered discount rate in such circumstances may be an inadequate stimulus relative to the potential efficacy of open-market operations, as noted by Allyn Young and Lauchlin Currie in their critique of Hawtrey.[30] Nevertheless Hawtrey too was confident that so long as a normal downturn of a business cycle is not allowed to develop into an abnormally severe depression, flooding the market with new money via open-market bond purchases would usually do the trick.

However, we also saw that Young, Currie, Viner and others were more inclined than Hawtrey to call for the aid of fiscal deficits. Though Hawtrey did not rule out public spending to combat depression, he did insist that it would normally only work if financed with new money. Turning then to the role of fiscal policy in Japan's 'growth stagnation' since 1992, what has been the record?

Lack of fiscal and monetary coordination, 1992–2005

If there has been a liquidity trap at any time since 1992, conventional Keynesian theory suggests that fiscal deficits would boost the economy and, especially if sustained and large enough, could fairly quickly return the economy to full employment. Bank of Japan (2005, 67–68) shows that the fiscal deficit rose to 3.3 per cent of GDP in the first year of recession, 1992, and to 4.3 per cent in 1993 when economic growth was a mere 0.2 per cent. The deficit rose further, to 4.6 per cent and 4.8 per cent in 1994 and 1995, while the economy continued to stagnate. Between 1996 and 2005 the deficit averaged an astonishing 6.9 per cent of GDP, and the ratio of the national debt to GDP rose from 49.4 per cent in 1991 to 160 per cent in 2005, the highest in the developed world. Despite these unprecedented fiscal injections the economy remained mired in stagnation and deflation throughout.

It seems safe to conclude that much of the fiscal effort was ineffective – even wasted: the quality of a large part of the public works has been criticised as little better than leaf-raking or pyramid-building (in contrast to the productivity of US infrastructure projects in the 1930s, as highlighted by Alexander Field (2003)). For Keynes, useless pyramids were better than nothing for they could revive the economy through their indirect multiplier effects. But absent an expansion of money the multiplier effect would have to come entirely through an increase in the velocity of circulation. In the case of Japan we have, on the contrary, seen velocity declining.

The deficit increased each year since 1992 by an average of about 6 per cent of GDP. Since this was much greater than the average increase in the money supply, it is clear that the bulk of the deficits was financed not through the printing press (borrowing from the central bank), but by selling bonds to commercial banks and, mainly, to the non-bank private sector, especially major institutions such as large insurance companies, pension funds, and Japan Post.[31] In this way the government was absorbing a very large portion of the increase in savings over the period. To the extent that the propensity to save was increasing faster than the private sector was willing to borrow or the banks to lend, the increase in relatively risk-free government bills or bonds can at least be credited with having prevented a Great Depression of 1930s proportions. But because the deficits apparently did no more than that and/or actually crowded out some bank lending to the private sector (either because the banks had too few excess reserves or because they may have lowered their risk threshold had there been fewer opportunities to lend to the government), they failed to prevent a Great Stagnation. Some deficit spending (but much less than its actual extent) may have been a necessary condition for recovery, but evidently not a sufficient condition.

Werner (2005, chapter 18) argues that fiscal policy is ineffective if it is not monetised. There was a notorious absence of cooperation between the Ministry of Finance and the Bank of Japan in the 1990s so that very little of the deficit was financed with new money created by the BoJ. But Werner also claims the government could have done more to finance the deficit through commercial bank credit creation rather than bond market sales to non-bank financial institutions whose liabilities are not money and whose loans merely transfer savings without creating new money. Reliance on commercial banks, however, also assumes they always had sufficient spare reserves with which to make loans to government without diverting funds from the private sector. It is true that during the recent period of 'quantitative easing' the BoJ had been flooding the banking system with excess reserves, but this was signally not the case in the 1990s.[32] In this respect conditions were less propitious for stimulating the economy via fiscal deficits than in the United States after 1933 when the banks had significant excess reserves. And in any case it does not explain why Japanese banks were not more active in bidding for the bonds that were offered on the markets.

Without fully addressing this question, Werner (2005, 255) nevertheless insists that 'the institutional reality of banking systems [including credit rationing] allows banks to create purchasing power without withdrawing existing purchasing power from other parts of the economy'; and 'fiscal expenditure by borrowing from banks would increase credit creation and hence the total amount of purchasing power in the economy'. He continues:

> By shifting government funding away from bond finance and replacing it with borrowing from the commercial banks via simple loan contracts, credit creation will be stimulated. Unlike bond markets, banks create new purchasing power when they lend. This means that overall economic activity can be boosted (via fiscal policy), without any quantity crowding-out that rendered fiscal policy ineffective during the 1990s. Banks, though risk-averse due to their bad debts, would not mind lending to the government – a zero-risk borrower.

Werner claims (2005, 364) that if the banks had run up against a reserve constraint, the BoJ 'would be forced to inject any necessary amount of liquidity in order to maintain its targeted call rate'. But it is not at all clear that the BoJ did have a target call rate in the 1990s, except insofar as it was in continuous decline. That, in essence, appears to have been the problem: the BoJ was unwilling to monetise the deficit by providing the finance itself, but nor did it provide the commercial banks with the reserves they would have needed for that purpose. However, the latter, indirect method of monetising the deficit would need to have been at the initiative of the banks; and their potential bond purchases would have faced stiff competition from the non-bank financial intermediaries whose huge savings deposit liabilities were already sufficient for them to finance fiscal deficits in a non-inflationary – hence non-stimulatory – way. Ben Bernanke (2003) argues that greater cooperation between the BoJ and the Treasury, with greater BoJ purchases of government debt, could also mitigate the effect of deficits on the debt burden and future interest payments perceived by households, and so reduce any 'Ricardian equivalence' effect on their propensity to save. Another option would have been for the BoJ more comprehensively to have bought up the banks' non-performing loans. As noted above, Werner persuasively argues that these were created at least as much because of incompetent BoJ policy as because of irresponsible commercial banking policy. He thus dismisses 'moral hazard' arguments against central bank purchases of bad debts, and instead urges this as an effective way to increase the money supply.

Conclusion

In conclusion, our brief survey of economic conditions in Japan after the bursting of asset bubbles in the early 1990s indicates that Japan's Great Stagnation could probably have been avoided if a much more active monetary policy had been pursued after 1991. A very active fiscal policy was tried and found wanting. This suggests that Japan's problem was not that she was in a conventional Keynesian liquidity trap that could be escaped via the activation of idle balances with little increase in the money supply. But compared with the Great Depression of the 1930s, the authorities at least ensured that there was no contraction of the money supply, hence no actual collapse of the economy into another Great Depression; and fiscal policy may have helped.

In any case, the last word (in fact, many words) should go to David Laidler, who pointed out that when at last the BoJ engaged in a dramatically different, ultra-loose quantitative easing policy, instead of relying solely on a near-zero discount rate as a criterion of 'easing', prices and output at last began to show signs of recovery. He suggests that a model that puts the interaction of the supply and demand for money at the centre of things is much more informative about monetary policy's transmission mechanism than a focus on the interest rate alone:

> Consider, for example, the currently conventional wisdom about…the *zero lower bound* problem. It might happen, and indeed in the case of contemporary Japan, which has much in common with the United States in 1930–33, it has happened, that the economy still requires monetary stimulus in a situation in which the nominal interest rates under the authorities' direct control have reached zero. If all there was to monetary policy was shifting these rates about, then…it would be easy to be concluded that monetary policy had reached the limits of its powers. Some economists would agree with this conclusion, but most would argue, to the contrary, that 'unconventional' methods such as open-market purchase of long term securities or equities might be worth trying…The express purpose of such methods would, of course, be to increase the quantity of money, in the hope of generating an excess supply thereof, and hence extra expenditure. (Laidler, 2003*b*, 130)

And he writes that our prevailing theory of monetary policy's focus on interest rates (especially when zero *short-term* rates are taken to indicate a liquidity trap) has had some odd consequences:

> To begin with, a 'liquidity trap' is a state of affairs in which the demand for money becomes perfectly elastic with respect to a long rate of interest at some low positive rate of the latter. Until the policy of 'quantitative easing' was begun in 2001, the ratio of the Japanese money stock to national income…rose slowly at best and it was short, not long, rates of interest that were essentially zero. Given these facts it is hard to see what the empirical basis for the diagnosis of a liquidity trap could have been. On the other hand, and again before 2001, the empirical evidence gave no reason to reject the hypothesis that a quite separate and distinct phenomenon was at work, namely a Hawtreyan 'credit deadlock'. Here the problem is not a high elasticity of the economy's demand for money with respect to the long rate of interest, but a low elasticity of its demand for bank credit with respect to the short rate, which is a necessary prerequisite for money creation. The solution to a credit deadlock, as Hawtey pointed out, is vigorous open market operations to bring about increases in the money base and therefore the supply of checkable deposits, that mere manipulation of short term interest rates is usually sufficient to accomplish in less depressed times.

Now the conditions for a liquidity trap might indeed have existed in Japan in the 1990s. Until the credit deadlock affecting its monetary system was broken by quantitative easing in 2001 ... it was impossible to know this. As it has happened, however, the subsequent up-turn of the Japanese economy that began in 2002 and is still proceeding is beginning to suggest that there was no liquidity trap at work in that economy. If further evidence bears out this conclusion, a serious policy error was made in the 1990s ... based on a theory of monetary policy that treats the short interest rate as the central bank's only tool and characterizes the transmission mechanism as working solely through the influence of interest rates on aggregate demand.

That theory provided no means for Japanese policy makers to distinguish between a liquidity trap, which is a possible feature of a demand for money function, and a credit deadlock, which is a characteristic of the money supply process, or for them to entertain the possibility that variations in the money supply might affect aggregate demand by channels over and above any effect on market rates of interest. It was therefore a dangerously defective guide to the conduct of monetary policy in Japan, as it is in any depressed economy. (Laidler, 2006, 157–158)

It is hoped that the present chapter has offered some useful qualitative and quantitative evidence germane to David's succinct statement of an important but relatively little researched angle on the causes of long-lasting depression and stagnation in two of the world's largest economies.

Notes

Much of the research for this paper was undertaken while I was visiting professor at Sophia University, Tokyo, March–October 2005.

1. Selected by Harry Johnson for a volume of 24 'landmark' articles from the *Journal of Political Economy* (*JPE*) (Hamilton et al., 1962) and by Laidler for inclusion in *Foundations of Monetary Economics* (Laidler, ed., 1999). It was reported to Currie (as told to me by him) that Johnson chose this paper for the *Landmarks* volume because of the neglect of his work by Milton Friedman and Anna Schwartz in their forthcoming *Monetary History of the United States* (1963) whose diagnosis of 1929–33 was largely anticipated by Currie. Similar criticism of Friedman's neglect, and distortion of the historical record, came later from Don Patinkin (1969). Laidler extended this discussion in his 'Hawtrey, Harvard and the Origins of the Chicago School' that appeared in the *JPE* in December 1993, the same month as Currie's death. The current paper attempts to demonstrate the continuing relevance of Currie's and Ralph G Hawtrey's insights into the essentially monetary nature of the business cycle.
2. A revised version of the thesis was submitted for the Wells prize in October 1932. It initially tied with H. D. White's thesis on the French balance of payments, but Currie's supervisor, John H. Williams, told him that when they were given for adjudication to Gottfried Haberler, then a visitor to Harvard, Currie's was rejected because he was known in other contexts to have 'unsound' views on unbalanced budgets. His views contrasted sharply with what Laidler (1999, 47) termed the 'policy pessimism verging on nihilism' of the Austrian School.
3. A critique of the influence of the real bills doctrine on Fed policy in the 1920s and early 1930s runs through Allan Meltzer's (2003) recent history of the Federal Reserve, as highlighted by Laidler's (2003*c*) review.

4. Currie's views on stock prices in 1929 find confirmation in Santoni (1987). For further discussion of his views on the (relatively minor) impact of stock market prices on the circular flow of income via the wealth effect on savings, see Sandilands (1990, 35–37).
5. Hawtrey defined 'credit' as demand deposits. In the 1932 version of his PhD thesis, Currie deleted almost all reference to this word on the grounds that the term was too ambiguous. Currie's chapter IV, 'Credit in Contemporary Monetary Theory' (also Currie, 1933), explains the problem. Banks can extend 'credit' (loans and investments) on the basis of both demand and savings deposit liabilities, and from borrowings from reserve banks when the public's demand for currency increases. And in 1928–29 the Federal Reserve Board included security loans made by non-banks, as would be logical if by credit is understood loans and investments and if this is the control target (Currie, 1934*a*, 49). This 'credit' series can increase at very different rates than the supply of money (currency plus demand deposits). Regarding 1927–29, he wrote: 'The belief that "credit" was expanding rapidly was based on figures for loans and investments. The index of the entire money supply...indicates that the rate of expansion was less than that of production and the rate of expansion was declining steadily from June, 1925.' (Currie, 1934*b*, 167–68).

   For unknown reasons much of Currie's discussion of Hawtrey's cycle theory was deleted from the 1932 version of his thesis in favour of further allusions to Keynes's 1930 *Treatise on Money*. See also Laidler (1999, chapters 5 and 9) on Hawtrey's links with Allyn Young, Currie and the Chicago School.
6. Cf. Allyn Young in a 1928 LSE lecture (published in Mehrling and Sandilands, 1999, 387):

   > During the depression reserves accumulate in the bank so that interest rates fall. Now do not these falls in interest rates attract industrial enterprise until industry expands again? (cf. Keynes, Cassel, Hawtrey.) But actual industrialists (and bankers) deny that variations in the rate of interest influence the extent of their operations, providing their competitors pay the same. It is the 'market' on which they count.

   Likewise, cf. Currie (1931, 214) on Hawtrey: 'It has not been difficult for his critics to show that traders are more influenced by the state of the market than by interest rates.'
7. This is one reason why Currie favoured nationwide branch banking and opposed the provision in the Glass-Steagall Act of 1933 that prohibited commercial banks from dealing in corporate securities.
8. Not to be confused with a Keynesian 'liquidity trap', discussed below, in which the demand for money is supposed to be highly elastic with respect to the long-term rate of interest.
9. Laidler (2004*b*, 12) noted that by 1932 Hawtrey could not fail to see that a lowering of the short-term interest rate would need to be supplemented by open market bond purchases. Hawtrey (1932, 173) wrote that these should be on whatever scale was necessary to break a credit deadlock and the vicious circle of deflation, for 'there must ultimately be a limit to the amount of money that sellers would hold idle'. It is noteworthy that even at this late date Hawtrey did not stress fiscal deficits as an essential policy ingredient for expanding the monetary circulation (unlike Currie, Ellsworth and White, 1932). He seems to have regarded fiscal deficits as useful but inessential in breaking a deadlock. Patrick Deutscher (1990, 67) noted that Hawtrey 'never renounced the position that eventually profitable opportunities would be found and exploited by capitalists as long as credit remained accommodating'. He also (1990, 68) quotes Hawtrey as writing that 'People do not have an *unlimited* desire to hold idle balances. Because they already hold more than usual, it does not follow that they are willing to hold still more.' Further expansion of money 'is bound ultimately to reach a point at which demand responds'. However, Hawtrey did not stress that this may take much longer than if the money is spent directly into circulation by government.
10. Currie notes elsewhere (1931, p. 235) that 'if banks took over security loans by quoting very low rates, the former lenders might, of course, be content to allow the deposits

they received by the cancellation of their loans, to remain inactive'. He believed he was more conscious than Hawtrey that the public's demand for inactive balances (or circuit velocity) varies pro-cyclically, and that this justifies further offsetting action by the central bank.

11. These latter were not part of Currie's (nor Hawtrey's) definition of money, though any reserve requirements against them – which Currie opposed – would indirectly affect the supply of demand deposits and be deflationary for that reason.

    There could be a speculative demand for time deposits (this would be a *demand for liquidity* that interacts with the supply of interest-bearing assets to determine the rate of interest) but not for non-interest-bearing cash or demand deposits. It is the conventional *demand for money* (not liquidity) that interacts with the supply of money to determine prices and income. The demand for money (as a proportion of income), rises in a depression not for the Keynesian speculative motive but because the opportunity cost of money is low when interest rates are low. However, if income is falling the absolute demand for money will also fall, and this helps to keep interest rates depressed, so far as they can be depressed. So, paradoxically, if monetary policy is tight the interest rate can fall, while if the effect of a vigorous expansion of the money supply is to revive spending, the interest rate may rise.

    Mauro Boianovsky (2004, 97) also alludes to John Hicks's criticism of the Keynesian liquidity trap 'with its simplified two-asset structure comprising 'money' (representing short-term assets) and 'non-money assets'. Laidler (1999, 285) also cites Viner on the wide range of assets available to satisfy liquidity preference, so 'Keynes assigns to the desire for cash for hoarding purposes a grossly exaggerated importance'.
12. As Laidler (2003*a*, 10) expressed it: a credit deadlock prevents money being created, whereas in a liquidity trap money lies idle after it has been created. See also Laidler (1999, 286).
13. Laidler (1999, 236) noted that Currie implicitly denied there was a liquidity trap, in the sense of the powerlessness of monetary policy per se, even up to 1932. The reserve banks did buy an unprecedented amount of bonds, but not enough to get banks out of debt and to offset gold outflows; and because reserves did not increase he characterised the reserve administration's policy as 'one of almost complete passivity and acquiescence'. (A fuller quotation is given below.)
14. However, Hawtrey (1925), reprinted in Hawtrey (1928) to which Currie's 1931 thesis refers, acknowledged that government spending may, in a depression, be financed by borrowing from balances that lie idle, and that this could increase 'the ratio of consumers' income to the unspent margin' (i.e., money). This is another way of saying that the velocity of circulation must increase if public works are to increase employment in the absence of extra money.
15. He stressed that if government spending was to be invoked, then the impact on the necessary creation of credit would be far greater if it borrowed from the central bank rather than 'ordinary banks'.
16. See Sandilands (1990, 68–74) on Currie's various descriptions of the government's contribution to spending. He early abandoned the pump-priming analogy because it suggested that one short dose of government spending would be sufficient to revive the economic machine without further help. Depending on how private-sector offsets to saving were moving, he recognized that the government might have to keep pumping for some time. Sweezy (1972, 118) described Currie's 'net Federal income-creating expenditure' label as 'a semantic triumph of the first magnitude. It brought out the common element in all the government's fiscal operations. No one used to thinking in terms of the net contribution could advocate promoting recovery by increasing public works spending while at the same time cutting government salaries and raising tax rates'. See also Currie's early 1935 memorandum, 'Comments on pump priming', published in Currie (1978).
17. See his 1937 memorandum, 'The decline in the Federal contribution to the growth in community expenditures', in Sandilands (2004, 330).

18. Letter to author, 2 August 1988. His views on this were spelled out in a May 1938 speech to the Illinois Banking Association ('Some Aspects of Business and Banking Developments in 1936 and 1937', in Sandilands, 2004).
19. This part of his Illinois speech was taken from a memorandum, 'Causes of the Recession', 1 April 1938, later published in Currie (1980 [1938], 327). There he denied that monetary policy in 1936 or the rise in reserve requirements in January 1937 could 'be held responsible either as an initiating or contributory factor in the recession. As events turned out it would have been perfectly safe to have postponed the rise in reserve requirements that occurred in March and May of 1937. This however, was not evident in January of 1937 and is an entirely different matter' (Currie, 1980 [1938], 328–329).
20. Friedman and Schwartz (1963, 774) show that velocity averaged 2.3 between 1933–36, against 3.2 in 1925–29. In 'Stabilization of Purchasing Power through the Use of Public Credit' (December 1936) and 'Would a Further Expansion of Money be "Injurious"?' (January 1937), Currie showed velocity fairly steady during this period at just above 2. He thought that in the event of full recovery it would revert to a value close to, but a little below, its 1920s average of about 3. In fact velocity did not recover its 1920s values until the 1950s.
21. Figures in this paragraph were calculated from Maddison (2001, 206).
22. In the United Kingdom, a strong monetary response also averted recession but at the cost of an acceleration of inflation (the 'Lawson boom').
23. Data from Japan Real Estate Institute (2006), and Bank of Japan (2005), p. 66.
24. Friedman (2005) compares monetary policy in the stock market boom and post-boom periods in (i) the United States in the 1920s–30s, (ii) Japan in the 1980s–90s, and (iii) the United States in the 1990s–2000s. He shows that in the 1980s boom, Japan's monetary growth was faster than in either of the two US booms. And after the stock market's peak, 'money fell sharply in the first episode and so did nominal GDP; money growth stagnated in the second episode [Japan] and so did GDP; money grew at a rapid rate in the third episode and, after a brief lag... so did GDP' (147–148).
25. Laidler (e.g., 2004*a*, 2006) has lamented the modern focus on short-term interest rates as the central bank's most potent policy weapon and as the criterion of monetary looseness or tightness, to the relative neglect of the traditional focus on monetary aggregates.
26. Bank of Japan (2005, 69–70). The foreign reserves rose by 2.7 per cent in 1992, to $70 billion, but thereafter they climbed rapidly – to $101 billion in 1993 and then to $844 billion by mid-2005.
27. M2 exclusive of CDs grew slightly less fast than the (M2 + CDs) series since CDs, with their higher interest rate, naturally increased more than time deposits.
28. Mauro Boianovsky's (2004) review of the history of the liquidity trap concept lucidly explains John Hicks's emphasis on expectations, and the parallels with Krugman's view: the long rate of interest, and the term structure of rates, is determined by expectations about the future course of short-term rates. The current short rate, meanwhile, depends on the current supply and demand for money. But if the current rate cannot fall below zero, then it may be impossible to reduce the long rate, and it is the long rate that has the bigger influence on investment decisions, hence aggregate demand.
29. Ronald McKinnon (2006) alludes to his well-known views on the way that an alleged 'ever-rising yen syndrome' and international capital mobility drove Japanese interest rates to zero in order to satisfy the interest-parity condition when US rates were falling to around 3 per cent in the early 1990s. When after 1995 the yen ceased its secular tendency to appreciate, he argues that zero interest rates must now reflect a negative risk premium on Japan's vast holdings of dollar assets. He does not consider whether Japan's strong currency was a reflection of its tight monetary policy.
30. Not 'sound money and plenty of it' (which Laidler [2004*a*, 334] referred to as the 'Purvis principle' in the context of inflation control), but 'cheap money and plenty of it' perhaps better reflects their advice for countering recession, or even 'dear money

but plenty of it', if the consequence of vigorous monetary expansion would have been to avoid recession and thereby prevent the nominal interest rate from falling procyclically. See also footnote 12 above.

31. Life insurance companies, for example, increased their holdings of government bonds from ¥8.8 trillion in 1992 to ¥39.2 trillion in 2004; Japan's Postal Life Insurance holdings increased from ¥0.65 trillion to ¥55.6 trillion (Bank of Japan, 2005, 25). Together, these insurance company holdings of government bonds was almost the same size as holdings by the BoJ (Bank of Japan, 2005, 9). The increase of commercial bank holdings of government bonds was relatively small: from ¥2.7 trillion in 1992 to ¥10.2 trillion in 2004 (Bank of Japan, 2005, 23).
32. BoJ data show that excess reserves were minimal throughout the 1990s, only beginning to be significant from early 1999 and then extremely large after the policy of 'quantitative easing' (ending in 2006), was initiated in earnest in 2001.

References

Bank of Japan (2005). *Financial and Economic Statistics Monthly*. Tokyo: Research and Statistics Department, Bank of Japan (July).

Barber, William J. (1996). *Designs within Disorder: Franklin D. Roosevelt, the Economists, and the Shaping of American Economic Policy, 1933–1945*. Cambridge: Cambridge University Press.

Bernanke, Ben S. (2003). "Some Thoughts on Monetary Policy in Japan." Speech to the Japan Society of Monetary Economics, Tokyo, May 31. (http://www.federalreserve.gov/BoardDocs/speeches/2003/20030531/default.htm).

Black, Conrad (2003). *Franklin Delano Roosevelt: Champion of Freedom*. London: Weidenfeld & Nicholson.

Boianovsky, Mauro (2004). "The IS-LM Model and the Liquidity Trap Concept: From Hicks to Krugman." *History of Political Economy*, Annual Supplement to Volume 36, 92–126.

Brunner, Karl (1968). "On Lauchlin Currie's Contribution to Monetary Theory." In Lauchlin Currie, *The Supply and Control of Money in the United States*. New York: Russell & Russell, pp. x–xxxv.

Currie, Lauchlin (1931). *Bank Assets and Banking Theory*. Cambridge, MA: Harvard University PhD thesis.

Currie, Lauchlin (1933). "The Treatment of Credit in Contemporary Monetary Theory." *Journal of Political Economy* 41:1 (February), 509–525.

Currie, Lauchlin (1934*a*). *The Supply and Control of Money in the United States*. Cambridge, MA: Harvard University Press. Reprinted in 1968 by Russell & Russell, New York.

Currie, Lauchlin (1934*b*). "The Failure of Monetary Policy to Prevent the Depression of 1929–32." *Journal of Political Economy* 42:2, 145–177. Reprinted in Hamilton et al. (1962), 168–198.

Currie, Lauchlin (1978 [1935]). "Comments and Observations on 'Federal Income-Increasing Expenditures, 1933–35'." *History of Political Economy* 10:4, 507–548.

Currie, Lauchlin (1980 [1938]). "Causes of the Recession." *History of Political Economy* 12:3, 303–335.

Currie, Lauchlin, Paul Theodore Ellsworth and Harry Dexter White (2002 [1932]). "Memorandum on Anti-depression Policy." *History of Political Economy* 34:3, 533–552. Reprinted in Robert Leeson (ed.) (2003), Volume 2: 271–290.

Deutscher, Patrick (1990). *R. G. Hawtrey and the Development of Macroeconomics*. London: Macmillan.

Field, Alexander (2003). "The Most Technologically Progressive Decade of the Century." *American Economic Review* 93 (September), 1399–1414.

Friedman, M. (1956). "The Quantity Theory of Money – a Restatement." In M. Friedman, ed., *Studies in the Quantity Theory of Money*. Chicago: University of Chicago Press, pp. 3–21.

Friedman, M. (2005). "A Natural Experiment in Monetary Policy Covering Three Episodes of Growth and Decline in the Economy and the Stock Market.' *Journal of Economic Perspectives* 19:4 (Fall), 145–150.
Friedman, M. and Anna Jacobson Schwartz (1963). *A Monetary History of the United States, 1867–1960*. Princeton: Princeton University Press.
Fukao, Mitsuhiro (2004). "The Effects of 'Gesell' (Currency) Taxes in Promoting Japan's Economic Recovery." *International Economics and Economic Policy* 2:2, 173–188.
Hamilton, Earl, Harry G. Johnson and Albert Rees, eds. (1962). *Landmarks in Political Economy*. Chicago: Chicago University Press.
Hawtrey, R. G. (1925). "Public Expenditure and the Demand for Labour." *Economica* 5 (March), 38–48.
Hawtrey, R. G. (1928). *Trade and Credit*. London: Longman Group.
Hawtrey, R. G. (1929). "The Monetary Theory of the Trade Cycle." *The Economic Journal* 39 (December), 636–642.
Hawtrey, R. G. (1931). *Trade Depression and the Way Out*. London: Longman Group.
Hawtrey, R. G. (1932). *The Art of Central Banking*. London: Longman Group. Reprinted 1962 by Frank Cass, London.
Hawtrey, R. G. (1950). *Currency and Credit*, 4th ed. London: Longman Group.
Humphrey, Thomas (1971). "The Role of Non-Chicago Economists in the Evolution of the Quantity Theory in America, 1930–50." *Southern Economic Journal* 38 (July), 12–18.
Japan Real Estate Institute (2006). *Economic and Real Estate Trends*. Tokyo: Japan Real Estate Institute.
Krugman, Paul (1999). "Thinking about the Liquidity Trap." http://www.pkarchive.org/
Laidler, David (1991). "Karl Brunner's Monetary Economics: An Appreciation." *Journal of Money, Credit and Banking* 23:4, 633–658.
Laidler, David (1993). "Hawtrey, Harvard and the Origins of the Chicago Tradition." *Journal of Political Economy* 101 (December), 1068–1103.
Laidler, David (1999). *Fabricating the Keynesian Revolution: Studies of the Inter-war Literature on Money, the Cycle, and Unemployment*. Cambridge: Cambridge University Press.
Laidler, David, ed. (1999). *The Foundations of Monetary Economics*. Cheltenham, UK: Edward Elgar.
Laidler, David (2003*a*). "Price Level, Relative Prices, and Economic Stability: Aspects of the Inter-war Debate." Bank for International Settlements working paper 136.
Laidler, David (2003*b*). "Monetary Policy without Money: *Hamlet* without the Ghost." In *Bank of Canada, Macroeconomics, Monetary Policy and Financial Stability: A festschrift in honour of Charles Freedman*. Ottawa: Bank of Canada, pp. 111–134.
Laidler, David (2003*c*). "Meltzer's History of the Federal Reserve." *Journal of Economic Literature* 41:4, 1256–1271.
Laidler, David (2004*a*). "Monetary Policy after Bubbles Burst: The Zero Lower Bound, the Liquidity Trap and the Credit Deadlock." *Canadian Public Policy* 30:3, 330–340.
Laidler, David (2004*b*). "Central Banks as Lenders of Last Resort: Trendy or Passé?" University of Western Ontario: Working Paper # 2004–8.
Laidler, David (2006). "Woodford and Wicksell on *Interest and Prices*: The Place of the Pure Credit Economy in the Theory of Monetary Policy." *Journal of the History of Economic Thought* 28:2, 151–159.
Laidler, David and Roger J. Sandilands (2002). "An Early Harvard Memorandum on Anti-Depression Policies: An Introductory Note." *History of Political Economy* 34:3, 515–532.
Lash, Joseph P. (1988). *Dealers and Dreamers*. New York: Doubleday.
Leeson, Robert, ed. (2003). *Keynes, Chicago and Friedman*. London: Pickering & Chatto, 2 volumes.
Maddison, Angus (2001). *The World Economy: A Millennial Perspective*. Paris: OECD.
McKinnon, Ronald (2006). "China's Exchange Rate Trap: Japan Redux?" *American Economic Review, Papers and Proceedings* 96:2 (May), 427–431.

Meltzer, Allan H. (2003). *A History of the Federal Reserve. Volume 1, 1913–51*. Chicago: University of Chicago Press.
Mehrling, P. G. and R. J. Sandilands (1999). *Money and Growth: Selected Papers of Allyn Abbott Young*. London and New York: Routledge.
Patinkin, Don (1969). "The Chicago Tradition, the Quantity Theory and Friedman." *Journal of Money, Credit, and Banking* 1:1, 46–70.
Patinkin, Don (1981). "Keynes and Chicago." In Don Patinkin, ed., *Essays on and in the Chicago Tradition*. Durham, NC and London: Duke University Press, pp. 289–308.
Romer, Christina D. and David H. Romer (1989). "Does Monetary Policy Matter?" *Macroeconomics Annual, National Bureau of Economic Research* 4, 121–170.
Sandilands, Roger J. (1990). *The Life and Political Economy of Lauchlin Currie: New Dealer, Presidential Adviser, and Development Economist*. Durham, NC and London: Duke University Press.
Sandilands, Roger J., ed. (2004). "New Light on Lauchlin Currie's Monetary Economics in the New Deal and Beyond." *Journal of Economic Studies* 31:3/4, 169–403.
Santoni, G. J. (1987). "The Great Bull Markets 1924–29 and 1982–87: Speculative Bubbles or Economic Fundamentals?" *Federal Reserve Bank of St Louis Review* 69:9, 16–29.
Smithin, John (2004). "Keynes, Chicago and Friedman: A Review Essay." *Journal of Economic Studies* 31:1, 76–88.
Steindl, Frank G. (1995). *Monetary Interpretations of the Great Depression*. Ann Arbor, MI: University of Michigan Press.
Steindl, Frank G. (2004). *Understanding Economic Recovery in the 1930s: Endogenous Propagation in the Great Depression*. Ann Arbor: University of Michigan Press.
Sweezy, Alan (1972). "The Keynesians and Government Policy, 1933–1939." *American Economic Review* LXII (May), 116–123.
Telser, Lester G. (2001). "Higher Member Bank Reserve Ratios in 1936 and 1937 Did Not Cause the Relapse into Depression." *Journal of Post-Keynesian Economics* 24:2, 205–216.
Telser, Lester G. (2003). "The Veterans' Bonus of 1936." *Journal of Post-Keynesian Economics* 26:2, 227–243.
Ueda, Kazuo (2005). "The Bank of Japan's Struggle with the Zero Lower Bound on Nominal Interest Rates: Exercises in Expectations Management." Tokyo: CIRJE discussion paper F-375, at www.e.u-tokyo.ac.jp/cirje/research/03research02dp.html.
Werner, Richard A (2005). *New Paradigm in Economics: Solving the Riddle of Japanese Macroeconomic Performance*. Houndmills, Basingstoke UK: Palgrave Macmillan.

Discussion

Michel De Vroey

Professor Sandilands has written a rich and stimulating chapter, which I enjoyed reading. I learned a lot from it. Its main aim is to explore the possible parallels between Lauchlin Currie's analysis of the Fed policy during the Great Depression and recent debates about the Bank of Japan's monetary policy in the 1990s. But in fact, Sandilands's paper covers a wider territory, making incursions into several side topics. As a result, the reader is both fascinated by the breadth of knowledge displayed by the author and somewhat at a loss when faced with such a richness of ideas and themes.

In this commentary I shall limit myself to three critical observations. The first pertains to the issue that supplies the title for Sandilands's paper, the confrontation between the notions of credit deadlock and liquidity trap. Sandilands has devoted a large part of his intellectual career to rehabilitating Currie's contribution to economic theory, in particular monetary policy, and he has done a fine job in this respect. He returns to the subject in this chapter with a long section on Currie's dissertation (written in the middle of the Great Depression). In this work, Currie endorses Hawtrey's credit deadlock theory of the business cycle. A credit deadlock arises when traders are so burdened with stocks that they refuse to take advantage of easy borrowing conditions. In other words, cheap money does not result in an increase in productive activity. An alternative explanation of depressions is the liquidity trap. This was put forward by Hicks in his seminal 'Mr. Keynes and the classics' paper, which aimed at capturing the central message of Keynes's *General Theory*. While the credit deadlock is tantamount to an impediment to the creation of money, in the liquidity trap monetary expansion has no effects. Money is created but it remains idle.

In view of the fact that the contrast between these two notions forms the title of the chapter, I expected it to be the central issue of the paper. But this is not the case. In fact, the notion of preference for liquidity enters the scene only at the end of the chapter when the Japanese situation is being discussed. Until then, Sandilands's attention is focused on credit deadlocks, the liquidity trap being mentioned only in passing. I would have preferred Sandilands to begin his paper with a systematic comparison of the two notions but he only makes scattered remarks. For example, borrowing from Laidler's observations, he notes on p. 356, that the liquidity trap is a case of high elasticity of the economy's demand for money with respect to the long-term rate of interest while, in contrast, credit deadlock is characterised by a low elasticity of the economy's demand for bank credit with respect to the short rate.

I understand, following Krugman (1999) on Japan, that there can be a controversy as to whether the explanation of stagnation should proceed along the credit deadlock or the liquidity preference line. Yet, when looking at these concepts in a more general way, I wonder whether they can be put on the same footing as far as their theoretical ambition is concerned. The concept of credit deadlock aims at explaining a phase of the cycle, the recession, which in some circumstances (such as the Great Depression) can become dramatic. It involves a chain of actors and reactions. The concept of liquidity preference – not the term but the idea – was created by Hicks in his attempt to make sense of Keynes's *General Theory*. In one sentence in his article, Hicks mentioned that liquidity preference pertained to depression. But this hardly makes it a theory of depressions. At best, it can only be one element in a broader picture. I wonder whether Hicks (or Keynes for that matter) would have claimed that preference for liquidity on its own could be viewed as the decisive cause of a phenomenon such as the Great Depression or as a valid explanation of its protracted character.

My second observation concerns Sandilands's comparison of Currie's and Friedman and Schwartz's studies of the Great Depression. I find it a perfectly honourable point to make that Currie anticipated Friedman and Schwart's conclusions on the inactive attitude of the Fed. What is more perplexing is that authors who share the same diagnosis can diverge so much when it comes to policy. Does this mean that in Currie's case the link between analysis and policy prescription was thin? Or is it, as suggested by Meltzer, that Currie's views changed over time? This is a topic that I would have liked to have seen dealt with in a more detailed way.

My third and final comment concerns Sandilands's analysis of the Japanese crisis. I regret that he provides little vindication for his claim that fiscal policy did not succeed in preventing the Japanese depression. The justification of this view is too succinct. According to Sandilands, the Japanese stagnation boils down to a lack of cooperation between the Ministry of Finance and the Bank of Japan. This is of course possible, but there must be more at work than that. Otherwise, there is a disproportion between the cause of the phenomenon, which is anecdotal, and its huge effects. And why then is there any need to resort to the theoretical apparatus developed in the earlier parts of the paper?

Index